THE
OXFORD-DUDEN
PICTORIAL
CHINESE & ENGLISH
DICTIONARY

THE OXFORD-DUDEN
PICTORIAL
CHINESE & ENGLISH
DICTIONARY

OXFORD UNIVERSITY PRESS

1998

Oxford University Press

Oxford New York
Athens Auckland Bangkok Bogotá Buenos Aires
Calcutta Cape Town Chennai Dar es Salaam
Delhi Florence Hong Kong Istanbul Karachi
Kuala Lumpur Madrid Melbourne Mexico City
Mumbai Nairobi Paris São Paulo Singapore
Taipei Tokyo Toronto Warsaw

and associated companies in
Berlin Ibadan

Oxford is a registered trade mark of Oxford University Press

Duden is a trade mark of the Bibliographisches Institut for books of any kind

English text originally published as *The Oxford-Duden Pictorial English Dictionary* by
Oxford University Press 1981, 1995, 1998

Illustrations © Bibliographisches Institut & F.A. Brockhaus
AG, Mannheim 1977, 1981, 1995, 1998

English text © Oxford University Press 1979, 1981, 1995, 1998

This English-Chinese edition first published 1988
This impression (lowest digit)
5 7 9 10 8 6

ISBN 0 19 582785 6

Printed in Hong Kong
Published by Oxford University Press (China) Ltd
18/F Warwick House East, Taikoo Place, 979 King's Road, Quarry Bay, Hong Kong

Foreword

This English & Chinese pictorial dictionary is based on the third, completely revised edition of the German *Bildwörterbuch* published as Volume 3 of the ten-volume *Duden* series of monolingual German dictionaries. The Chinese text was jointly produced by Oxford University Press and Tung Hua Book Company Limited while the Chinese index was jointly prepared by Assistant Professor Bu Chun-ying of Hohai University Press and Assistant Professor Li Yu-cai of Nanjing Architecture & Civil Engineering Institute. The English text was produced by the Oxford University Press Dictionary Department, with the assistance of numerous British companies, institutions and technical experts.

There are certain kinds of information which can be conveyed more readily and clearly by pictures than by descriptions and explanations, and an illustration will support the simple translation by helping the reader to visualize the object denoted by a given word. This applies both to technical vocabulary sought by the layman and to everyday objects foreign to the general user.

Each double page contains a plate illustrating the vocabulary of a whole subject, together with the exact Chinese names and their correct English equivalents. The arrangement of the text and the presence of a radical index in Chinese and an alphabetical index in English allow the dictionary to be used either way: as a Chinese-English or an English-Chinese dictionary. This, together with the wide range of vocabulary, which includes a large proportion of specialized words and technical terms, makes the Oxford-Duden Pictorial Dictionary an indispensable supplement to any Chinese-English or English-Chinese dictionary.

序　言

本词典是根据经彻底修订的德文图解词典 Bildwörterbuch 第三版编写（该词典是共有十册的杜登德文词典中的第三册）。中文部分由牛津大学出版社和东华书局共同编译，英文部分由牛津大学出版社词典编辑部编译，并得到许多英国公司、机构和书业技术人员的协助。至于按中文部首编排的索引则由河海大学出版社副教授卜纯英及南京建筑工程学院副教授李育才协助编纂。

用图示来解释某些词汇，往往较文字的描述更简便和清晰。图示绘出词目所指涉的实物，使读者一目了然。对一般读者来说，本词典尤其适用于翻查专门术语和认识较陌生的日常用品。

本词典所收录的词目均以所属范畴分类，以说明同页或邻页的插图。为方便读者翻检，词典附有英文词目索引及中文词目索引。英文词目索引以字母先后排列，中文词目索引则以部首笔划排列，故本词典兼具英汉及汉英词典的双重功能。此外，因词目大部分为学术词汇及专门术语，故牛津—杜登英汉图解词典实能补充一般词典的不足，为专业人士案头必备的参考书籍。

Abbreviations used in the text

Am.	American usage	美国用法
c.	castrated (animal)	阉割了的（指动物）
coll.	colloquial	口语
f.	female (animal)	雌的（指动物）
form.	formerly	从前
zoc.	zocular	诙谐语
m.	male (animal)	雄的（指动物）
poet.	poetic	诗中用语
sg.	singular	单数
sim.	similar	类似的
y.	young (animal)	幼小的（指动物）

Contents

The arabic numerals are the numbers of the pictures

目 录

（图示的编号用阿拉伯数字表示）

Contents

Trades, Crafts, and Industry

目录

商业、工艺和工业

Contents

目录

Contents

目录

Contents

目 录

Contents

目 录

Contents

目 录

Contents

目 录

1-8 atom models
原子模型

1 model of the hydrogen (H) atom
氢原子模型

2 atomic nucleus, a proton
原子核，质子

3 election
电子

4 electron shell
电子自旋

5 model of the helium (He) atom
氦原子模型

6 electron shell
电子壳层

7 Pauli exclusion principle (exclusion principle, Pauli principle)
泡利不相容原理（泡利定理）

8 complete electron shell of the Na atom (sodium atom)
钠原子的（满）电子壳层

9-14 molecular structures (lattice structures)
分子结构（晶格结构）

9 crystal of sodium chloride (of common salt)
氯化钠（食盐）晶体

10 chlorine ion
氯离子

11 sodium ion
钠离子

12 crystal of cristobalite
白矽石（方石英）晶体

13 oxygen atom
氧原子

14 silicon atom
硅原子

15 energy levels (possible quantum jumps) of the hydrogen atom
氢原子的能阶（可能的量子迁跃）

16 atomic nucleus (proton)
原子核（质子）

17 electron
电子

18 ground state level
基态能阶

19 excited state
受激状态

20-25 quantum jumps (quantum transitions)
量子跃迁（量子转移）

20 Lyman series
赖曼系

21 Balmer series
巴耳麦系

22 Paschen series
帕申系

23 Brackett series
布喇开系

24 Pfund series
普芬德系

25 free electron
自由电子

26 Bohr-Sommerfeld model of the H atom
氢原子的波耳 - 索末菲模型

27 energy levels of the electron
电子的能阶

28 spontaneous decay of radioactive material
辐射（放射物）性质的自发衰变

29 atomic nucleus
原子核

30-31 alpha particle (α, alpha radiation, helium nucleus)
α粒子（α，α辐射，氦原子核）

30 neutron
中子

31 proton
质子

32 beta particle (β, beta radiation, electron)
β粒子（β，β辐射，电子）

33 gamma radiation (γ, a hard X-radiation)
γ辐射（γ，强辐射）

34 nuclear fission
核分裂

35 heavy atomic nucleus
重原子核

36 neutron bombardment
中子撞击

37-38 fission fragments
分裂碎片

39 released neutron
放出的中子

40 gamma radiation (γ)
γ辐射

41 chain reaction
（连锁反应）链式反应

42 incident neutron
入射中子

43 nucleus prior to fisson
分裂前的原子核

44 fission fragment
分裂碎片

45 released neutron
放出的中子

46 repeated fission
重复分裂

47 fission fragment
分裂碎片

48 controlled chain reaction in a nuclear reactor
核反应器内受控制的链式反应

49 atomic nucleus of a fissionable element
可分裂元素的原子核

50 neutron bombardment
中子撞击

51 fission fragment (new atomic nucleus)
分裂碎片（新原子核）

52 released neutron
放出的中子

53 absorbed neutrons
吸收的中子

54 moderator, a retarding layer of graphite
缓和剂，石墨缓和剂

55 extraction of heat (production of energy)
热的萃取（能量的产生）

56 X-radiation
X辐射

57 concrete and lead shield
混凝土和铅屏蔽

58 bubble chamber for showing the tracks of high-energy ionizing particles
显示高能游离粒子径迹的气泡计数室

59 light source
光源

60 camera
摄影机

61 expansion line
膨胀线，扩展线

62 path of light rays
光射线路径

63 magnet
磁盘

64 beam entry point
射束（光束）进入点

65 reflector
反射器

66 chamber
气泡室

1-23 radiation detectors
(radiation meters)
辐射探测器（辐射计）
1 radiation monitor
辐射监测器
2 ionization chamber (ion chamber)
游离室（离子室）
3 central electrode
中心电极
4 measurement range selector
（测量）量程选择器
5 instrument housing
仪器外壳（箱）
6 meter
读数盘，表头
7 zero adjustment
零点调整（装置），归零（装置）
8-23 dosimeter (dosemeter)
剂量计
8 film dosimeter
软片剂量计
9 filter
射线过滤片
10 film
软片
11 film-ring dosimeter
环型软片剂量计
12 filter
射线过滤片
13 film
胶卷
14 cover with filter
射线过滤片套
15 pocket meter (pen meter, pocket chamber)
小型剂量计（笔型剂量计，小型游离室）
16 window
（电离室）窥孔
17 ionization chamber (ion chamber)
游离室（离子室）
18 clip (pen clip)
夹子，笔夹
19 Geiger counter (Geiger-Mùller counter)
盖革计数管（盖革－米勒计数管）
20 counter tube casing
计数管套
21 counter tube
计数管
22 instrument housing
仪器壳（箱）
23 measurement range selector
（测量）量程选择器
24 Wilson cloud chamber (Wilson chamber)
威尔逊云室（威尔逊室）
25 compression plate
压（缩）板
26 cloud chamber photograph
云雾室照片
27 cloud chamber track of an alpha particle
α 粒子的雾室轨迹（雾迹）
28 telecobalt unit (*coll.* cobalt bomb)
钴照射设备（亦称：钴弹）
29 pillar stand
立柱
30 support cables
支撑钢索
31 radiation shield (radiation shielding)
辐射屏蔽（层）

32 sliding shield
滑动屏蔽
33 bladed diaphragm
叶状膜片
34 light-beam positioning device
光束定位装置
35 pendulum device (pendulum)
摆动装置（摆）
36 irradiation table
照射台
37 rail (track)
轨道
38 manipulator with sphere unit (manipulator)
带球关节装置的机械手
39 handle
手柄，把手
40 safety catch (locking lever)
安全把手（锁杆）
41 wrist joint
腕关节
42 master arm
主动臂
43 clamping device (clamp)
夹紧装置（夹钳）
44 tongs
（机械手的）抓手（夹子）
45 slotted board
有槽板
46 radiation shield (protective shield, protective shielding), a lead shielding wall [section]
辐射屏蔽（防护屏蔽层），一种铅屏蔽墙 [剖面]
47 grasping arm of a pair of manipulators (of a master/slave manipulator)
一双机械手（主动／被动机械手）的抓臂
48 dust shield
防尘护套
49 cyclotron
回旋加速器
50 danger zone
危险地带（区）
51 magnet
磁体
52 pumps for emptying the vacuum chamber
真空室抽气用的泵

1-35 star map of the northern sky (northern hemisphere)
北天（北半球）星图
1-8 divisions of the sky
天区
1 celestial pole with the Pole Star (Polaris, the North Star)
天极和北极星
2 ecliptic (apparent annual path of the sun)
黄道（太阳的视周年轨迹，轨迹）
3 celestial equator (equinoctial line)
天球赤道（天球平分线）
4 tropic of Cancer
北回归线
5 circle enclosing circumpolar stars
拱极星的界圈
6-7 equinoctial points (equinoxes)
二分点（春分和秋分）
6 vernal equinoctial point (first point of Aries)
春分点（白羊座的原点）
7 autumnal equinoctial point
秋分点
8 summer solstice (solstice)
夏至
9-48 constellations (grouping of fixed stars into figures) **and names of stars**
星座（恒星聚集而成的图形）和星名
9 Aquila (the Eagle) with Altair the principal star (the brightest star)
天鹰座及其主星河鼓二（牛郎星）（最亮的星）
10 Pegasus (the Winged Horse)
飞马座
11 Cetus (the Whale) with Mira, a variable star
鲸鱼座及其变星 — 蒭藁增二
12 Eridanus (the Celestial River)
波江座（天河）
13 Orion (the Hunter) with Rigel, Betelgeuse and Bellatrix
猎户座和参宿七，参宿四和参宿五
14 Canis Major (the Great Dog, the Greater Dog) with Sirius (the Dog Star), a star of the first magnitude
大犬座和天狼星（一颗一等星）
15 Canis Minor (the Little Dog, the Lesser Dog) with Procyon
小犬座和南河三
16 Hydra (the Water Snake, the Sea Serpent)
长蛇座
17 Leo(the Lion)
狮子座
18 Virgo (the Virgin) with Spica
室女座和角宿一
19 Libra (the Balance, the Scales)
天秤座
20 Serpens (the Serpent)
巨蛇座
21 Hercules
武仙座
22 Lyra (the Lyre) with Vega
天琴座和织女星
23 Cygnus (the Swan, the Northern Cross) with Deneb
天鹅座（北十字星）和天津四（天鹅座之α）
24 Andromeda
仙女座

25 Taurus (the Bull) with Aldebaran
金牛座和毕宿五
26 The Pleiades (Pleiads, the Seven Sisters), an open cluster of stars
昴星团（七姊妹星团，一个疏散星团）
27 Auriga (the Wagoner, the Charioteer) with Capella
御夫座和五车二（御夫座之α）
28 Gemini (the Twins) with Castor and Pollux
双子座和北河二（双子座之β）北河三
29 Ursa Major (the Great Bear, the Greater Bear, the Plough, Charles's Wain, *Am.* the Big Dipper) with the double star (binary star) Mizar and Alcor
大熊座和其目视双星开阳和辅星
30 Bootes (the Herdsman)
牧夫座
31 Corona Borealis (the Northern Crown)
北冕座
32 Draco (the Dragon)
天龙座
33 Cassiopeia
仙后座
34 Ursa Minor (the Little Bear, Lesser Bear, *Am.* Little Dipper) with the Pole Star (Polaris, the North Star)
小熊座和北极星
35 the Milky Way (the Galaxy)
银河

36-48 the southern sky
南天（星空）
36 Capricorn (the Goat, the Sea Goat)
摩羯座
37 Sagittarius (the Archer)
人马座
38 Scorpio (the Scorpion)
天蝎座
39 Centaurus (the Centaur)
半人马座
40 Triangulum Australe (the Southern Triangle)
南三角座
41 Pavo (the Peacock)
孔雀座
42 Grus (the Crane)
天鹤座
43 Octans (the Octant)
南极座
44 Crux (the Southern Cross, the Cross)
南十字座
45 Argo (the Celestial Ship)
南船座
46 Carina (the Keel)
船底座
47 Pictor (the Painter)
绘架座
48 Reticulum (the Net)
网罟座

1-9 the moon
月亮，月球

1 moon's path (moon's orbit round the earth)
月球轨道（月球绕地球运行的轨道），
白道

2-7 lunar phases (moon's phases, lunation)
月相（月的盈亏，变化）

2 new moon
新月

3 crescent (crescent moon, waxing moon)
蛾眉月

4 half-moon (first quarter)
半月（上弦月）

5 full moon
满月

6 half-moon (last quarter, third quarter)
半月（下弦月）

7 crescent (crescent moon, waning moon)
残月

8 the earth (terrestrial globe)
地球

9 direction of the sun's rays
太阳光线的方向

10-21 apparent path of the sun at the beginning of the seasons
各季节开始时太阳的视轨道

10 celestial axis
天球轴，天轴

11 zenith
天顶

12 horizontal plane
地平面

13 nadir
天底

14 east point
东点

15 west point
西点

16 north point
北点

17 south point
南点

18 apparent path of the sun on 21 December
12 月 21 日太阳的视轨道（冬至）

19 apparent path of the sun on 21 March and 23 September
3 月 21 日（春分）和 9 月 23 日（秋分）太阳的视轨道

20 apparent path of the sun on 21 June
6 月 21 日（夏至）太阳的视轨道

21 border of the twilight area
曙暮光区域的界限

22-28 rotary motions of the earth's axis
地轴的旋转运动

22 axis of the ecliptic
黄（道）轴

23 celestial sphere
天球

24 path of the celestial pole (precession and nutation)
天极的轨道（岁差和章动）

25 instantaneous axis of rotation
瞬间自转轴

26 celestial pole
天极

27 mean axis of rotation
平均自转轴

28 polhode
地极移动轨迹

29-35 solar and lunar eclipse [not to scale]
日蚀和月蚀 [未按比例绘制]

29 the sun
太阳

30 the earth
地球

31 the moon
月球，月亮

32 solar eclipse
日蚀

33 area of the earth in which the eclipse appears total
地球上的全蚀带

34-35 lunar eclipse
月蚀

34 penumbra (partial shadow)
半影

35 umbra (total shadow)
本影

36-41 the sun
太阳

36 solar disc (disk) (solar globe, solar sphere)
太阳面（太阳球）

37 sunspots
太阳黑子

38 cyclones in the area of sunspots
太阳黑子附近的气旋

39 corona (solar corona), observable during total solar eclipse or by means of special instruments
当日全蚀时或藉特殊仪器可观察到的日冕

40 prominences (solar prominences)
日珥

41 moon's limb during a total solar eclipse
日全蚀时的月球边缘

42-52 planets (planetary system, solar system) [not to scale] **and planet symbols**
行星（行星系，太阳系）[未按比例绘制] 和行星符号

42 the sun
太阳

43 Mercury
水星

44 Venus
金星

45 Earth, with the moon, a satellite
地球和卫星月球

46 Mars, with two moons (satellites)
火星，带两个卫星

47 asteroids (minor planets)
小行星群

48 Jupiter, with 14 moons (satellites)
木星，带14个卫星

49 Saturn, with 10 moons (satellites)
土星及其10个卫星

50 Uranus, with five moons (satellites)
天王星及其5个卫星

51 Neptune, with two moons (satellites)
海王星及其两个卫星

52 Pluto, with one moon
冥王星，带一个卫星

53-64 signs of the zodiac (zodiacal signs)
黄道十二宫的符号

53 Aries (the Ram)
白羊座

54 Taurus (the Bull)
金牛座

55 Gemini (the Twins)
双子座

56 Cancer (the Crab)
巨蟹座

57 Leo (the Lion)
狮子座

58 Virgo (the Virgin)
室女座

59 Libra (the Balance, the Scales)
天秤座

60 Scorpio (the Scorpion)
天蝎座

61 Sagittarius (the Archer)
人马座

62 Capricorn (the Goat, the Sea Goat)
摩羯座

63 Aquarius (the Water Carrier, the Water Bearer)
宝瓶座

64 Pisces (the Fish)
双鱼座

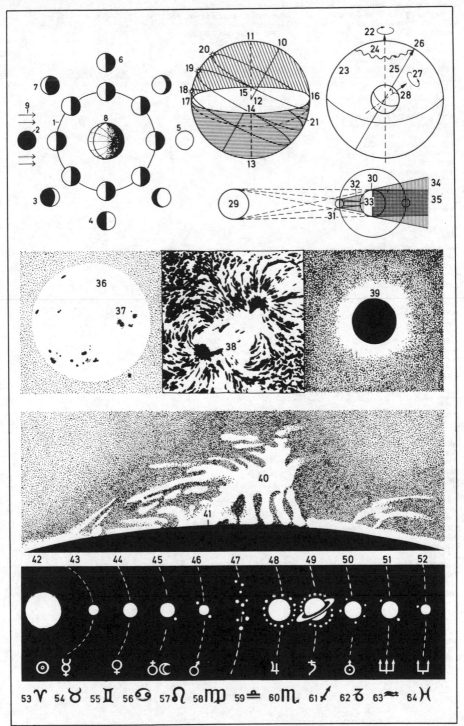

1-16 the European Southern Observatory (ESO) on *Cerro la Silla, Chile*, an observatory [section]
（位于智利塞罗拉西拉的）欧洲南方天文台（ESO），望远镜圆顶室 [剖面]

1 primary mirror (main mirror) with a diameter of 3.6m (144 inches)
口径 3.6 米（144 英寸）的主镜

2 prime focus cage with mounting for seconday mirrors
主聚焦笼和副镜架（固定副镜的装置）

3 flat mirror for the coude ray path
库德式（折轴）光路的平面镜

4 Cassegran cage
卡士格笼架

5 grating spectrograph
光栅摄谱仪

6 spectrographic camera
光谱摄影机

7 hour axis drive
时轴驱动装置

8 hour axis
时轴

9 horseshoe mounting
马蹄形镜架装置

10 hydrostatic bearing
静压轴承

11 primary and secondary focusing devices
主、副聚焦装置

12 observatory dome (revolving dome)
天文台圆顶（回转圆顶）

13 observation opening
观测窗

14 vertically movable dome shutter
上下活动的圆顶窗板

15 wind screen
风罩

16 siderostat
定星镜

17-28 the *Stuttgart* Planetarium [section]
斯图卡特天文馆 [断面图]

17 administration, workshop, and store area
管理处，工作室，储藏室

18 steel scaffold
钢骨支架

19 glass pyramid
金字塔型的玻璃夹层

20 revolving arched ladder
回转弧型梯子

21 projection dome
投影圆顶

22 light stop
挡光板

23 planetarium projector
星象投影器（星象仪，天象仪）

24 well
星象仪竖井

25 foyer
休息厅

26 theatre (*Am.* theater)
放映厅

27 projection booth
放映室

28 foundation pile
基（础）桩

29-33 the *Kitt Peak* solar observatory near *Tucson, Ariz.* [section]
（位于美国亚利桑纳州图克森附近的）基特峰太阳观象台 [剖面]

29 heliostat
定日镜

30 sunken observation shaft
倾斜式观测通道

31 water-cooled windshield
水冷式隔热板

32 concave mirror
凹面镜

33 observation room housing the spectrograph
安置摄谱仪的观测室

1 Apollo spacecraft 阿波罗太空船	**19** sunglass pocket [with sunglasses for use on board] 太阳眼镜袋 [于太空船中使用的太阳眼镜]
2 service module (SM) 辅助舱，服务舱	**20** life support system (life support pack), a backpack unit 生命供养系统（包），一种背包装置
3 nozzle of the main rocket engine 火箭主发动机的喷嘴	**21** access flap 存取物品盖
4 directional antenna 定向天线	**22** space suit helmet with sun filters 带日光滤色器的太空头盔
5 manoeuvring (*Am.* maneuvering) rockets 机动性火箭	**23** control box of the life support pack 生命供养包的控制盒
6 oxygen and hydrogen tanks for the spacecraft's energy system 太空船能量系统的氢氧贮槽（箱）	**24** penlight pocket 钢笔手电筒袋
7 fuel tank 燃料槽（箱）	**25** access flap for the purge valve 清洗阀用的存取口盖
8 radiators of the spacecraft's energy system 太空船能量系统的散热器	**26** tube and cable connections for the radio, ventilation, and water-cooling systems 与无线电，通风（气）装置和水冷系统连接的管线
9 command module (Apollo space capsule) 指挥舱（阿波罗太空船的太空舱）	**27** pocket for pens, tools, etc. 装钢笔，工具等等的袋子
10 entry hatch of the space capsule 太空船的进人舱门	**28-36 descent stage** 降落级
11 astronaut 航天 [字航] 员	**28** connector 连接器
12 lunar module (LM) 登月舱	**29** fuel tank 燃料箱
13 moon's surface (lunar surface) a dust-covered surface 覆盖尘埃的月球表面	**30** engine 发动机
14 lunar dust 月球尘埃	**31** mechanism for unfolding the legs 伸开支架用的机械装置
15 piece of rock 岩石块	**32** main shock absorber 主减震器
16 meteorite crater 陨石坑	**33** landing pad 降落垫
17 the earth 地球	**34** ingress/egress platform (hatch platform) 进出口台架（舱口台架）
18-27 space suit (extra-vehicular suit) 太空衣	
18 emergency oxygen apparatus 应急供氧装置	

35 ladder to platform and hatch 到舱门与台架的梯子
36 cardan mount for engine （引擎）发动机的十字（万向）接头装置
37-47 ascent stage 上升装置
37 fuel tank 燃料箱
38 ingress/egress hatch (entry/exit hatch) 进出舱口
39 LM manoeuvring (*Am.* maneuvering) rockets 登月舱机动火箭
40 window 窗
41 crew compartment 驾驶 [机务] 员舱
42 rendezvous radar antenna （轨道）会合雷达天线
43 inertial measurement unit 惯性测量装置
44 directional antenna for ground control 地面控制定向性天线
45 upper hatch (docking hatch) 上舱口（连接舱口）
46 inflight antenna 飞行天线
47 docking target recess 接合点凹槽

1 the troposphere
对流层

2 thunderclouds
雷雨云

3 the highest mountain, *Mount Everest* [8,882m]
埃佛勒斯峰（即珠穆朗玛峰），世界最高峰，高 8,882 公尺

4 rainbow
虹（霓）

5 jet stream level
喷射气流带

6 zero level (inversion of vertical air movement)
大气层温度递减的上限（指空气垂直运动的上限）

7 ground layer (surface boundary layer)
地面层（地面界层）

8 the stratosphere
平流层

9 tropopause
对流层顶

10 separating layer (layer of weaker air movement)
分离层（空气流动较弱层）

11 atomic explosion
原子弹爆炸高度

12 hydrogen bomb explosion
氢弹爆炸高度

13 ozone layer
臭氧层

14 range of sound wave propagation
声波传播范围

15 stratosphere aircraft
平流层飞机飞行高度

16 manned balloon
载人气球到达高度

17 sounding balloon
探空气球到达高度

18 meteor
流星体

19 upper limit of ozone layer
臭氧层上限

20 zero level
零层

21 eruption of Krakatoa
克拉卡托火山爆发到达高度

22 luminous clouds (noctilucent clouds)
夜光云

23 the ionosphere
游离层

24 range of research rockets
研究用火箭范围

25 shooting star
流星（指虽然看到光辉，但只在大气层中消失的）

26 short wave (high frequency)
短波（高频）反射高度

27 E-layer (Heaviside-Kennelly Layer)
E 层（海维赛—肯涅利层）

28 F_1-layer
F_1 层

29 F_2-layer
F_2 层

30 aurora (polar light)
极光

31 the exosphere
外气层

32 atom layer
原子层

33 range of satellite sounding
卫星探测范围

34 fringe region
（大气）边缘区

35 altitude scale
高度标尺

36 temperature scale (thermometric scale)
温度标尺

37 temperature graph
温度随高度变化曲线

1-19 clouds and weather
云和天气
1-4 clouds found in homogeneous air masses
均匀气团所见到的云
1　cumulus (woolpack cloud, cumulus humilis, fair-weather cumulus), a heap cloud (flat-based heap cloud)
积云（絮状积云，淡积云，晴天积云），一种堆积的云（平底积云）
2　cumulus congestus, a heap cloud with more marked vertical development
浓积云，一种垂直发展更明显堆积的云
3　stratocumulus, a layer cloud (sheet cloud) arranged in heavy masses
层积云，一种排列成大云块的层状云
4　stratus (high fog), a thick, uniform layer cloud (sheet cloud)
层云（浓雾）一种厚而均匀的层状云
5-12 clouds found at warm fronts
暖锋上见到的云
5　warm front
暖锋
6　cirrus, an ice-crystal cloud, thin and assuming a wide variety of forms, with height over 6,000 m
卷云，一种高度超过 6,000 公尺的冰晶云，薄且呈多种形状
7　cirrostratus, an ice-crystal cloud veil
卷层云，一种冰晶云�
卷层云，一种冰晶云幔
8　altostratus, a layer cloud (sheet cloud) of medium height
高层云，一种中等高度的层状云
9　altostratus praecipitans, a layer cloud (sheet cloud) with precipitation in its upper parts
降水性高层云，一种在其上端有降水的层状云
10　nimbostratus, a rain cloud, a layer cloud (sheet cloud) of very large vertical extent which produces precipitation (rain or snow)
雨层云，一种降雨层状云，一种垂直发展强，产生降水（雨或雪）的层云
11　fractostratus, a ragged cloud occurring beneath nimbostratus
碎层云，一种出现在雨层云下方的碎云
12　fractocumulus, a ragged cloud like 11 but with billowing shapes
碎积云，和碎层云相似，但呈波浪状
13-17 clouds at cold fronts
冷锋上的云
13　cold front
冷锋
14　cirrocumulus, thin fleecy cloud in the form of globular masses; *covering the sky*: mackerel sky
卷积云，呈球形云块的薄白云；覆盖天空成鱼鳞天
15　altocumulus, a cloud in the form of large globular masses
高积云，呈大型球状云块的云
16　altocumulus castellanus and altocumulus floccus, species of 15
堡状高积云和絮状高积云（15 项的一种）

17　cumulonimbus, a heap cloud of very large vertical extent, to be classified under 1-4 in the case of tropical storms
积雨云，一种垂直范围很广的堆积云，在热带暴风雨的情形下分在第 1-4 项下
18-19 types of precipitation
降水（的）类型
18　steady rain or snow covering a large area, precipitation of uniform intensity
大区域的稳定降雨或降雪，强度均的降水
19　shower, scattered precipitation
阵雨，分散降水
black arrow = cold air
黑箭头 = 冷空气
white arrow = warm air
白箭头 = 暖空气

1-39 weather chart (weather map, surface chart, surface synoptic chart)
天气图（地面天气图，地面综观天气图）
1 isobar (line of equal or constant atmospheric or barometric pressure at sea level)
等压线（海平面上，气压相等或恒定的线）
2 pleiobar (isobar of over 1,000mb)
高压等值线（高于1,000毫巴的等压线）
3 meiobar (isobar of under 1,000mb)
低压等值线（等压线低于1,000毫巴）
4 atmospheric (barometric) pressure given in millibars
以毫巴表示的气压值
5 low-pressure area (low, cyclone, depression)
低压区（低气压，气旋，低压区）
6 high-pressure area (high, anticyclone)
高压区（高气压，反气旋）
7 observatory (meteorological watch office, weather station) or ocean station vessel (weather ship)
气象台（气象观测所，气象站）或海洋气象观测船
8 temperature
温度
9-19 means of representing wind direction (wind-direction symbols)
表示方向的方法（风向符号）
9 wind-direction shaft (wind arrow)
风向箭杆
10 wind-speed barb (wind-speed feather) indicating wind speed
指示风速的风速羽
11 calm
无风（0级风）
12 1-2 knots (1 knot = 1.852 kph)
1-2 节（1 节=1 海里/小时 = 1.852 公里/小时）
13 3-7 knots
3-7 节
14 8-12 knots
8-12 节
15 13-17 knots
13-17 节
16 18-22 knots
18-22 节
17 23-27 knots
23-27 节
18 28-32 knots
28-32 节
19 58-62 knots
58-62 节
20-24 state of the sky (distribution of the cloud cover)
天空的状态（云量的分布）
20 clear (cloudless)
碧（空），晴（无云）
21 fair
晴，好天
22 partly cloudy
少云
23 cloudy
多云
24 overcast (sky mostly or completely covered)
密（云），阴天（天空大部或全部被云遮盖）

25-29 fronts and air currents
锋和气流
25 occlusion (occluded front)
囚锢（囚锢锋）
26 warm front
暖锋
27 cold front
冷锋
28 warm airstream (warm current)
暖气流
29 cold airstream (cold current)
冷气流
30-39 meteorological phenomena
气象现象
30 precipitation area
降水区
31 fog
雾
32 rain
雨
33 drizzle
毛（毛雨）
34 snow
雪
35 ice pellets (graupel, soft hail)
冰珠（霰，软雹）
36 hail
冰雹
37 shower
阵雨
38 thunderstorm
雷暴
39 lightning
闪电
40-58 climatic map
气候图
40 isotherm (line connecting points having equal mean temperature)
等温线（相同平均温度各点的连线）
41 0°C (zero) isotherm (line connecting points having a mean annual temperature of 0°C)
零度等温线（年平均温度为0°C各点的连线）
42 isocheim (line connecting points having equal mean winter temperature)
等冬温线（冬天平均温度相等各点的连线）
43 isothere (line connecting points having equal mean summer temperature)
等夏温线（夏天平均温度相等各点的连线）
44 isohel (line connecting points having equal duration of sunshine)
等日照线（日照持续时间相等各点的连线）
45 isohyet (line connecting points having equal amounts of precipitation)
等雨量线（降雨量相等各点的连线）
46-52 atmospheric circulation (wind systems)
大气环流（风系）
46-47 calm belt
无风带
46 equatorial trough (equatorial calms, doldrums)
赤道槽（赤道无风带）
47 subtropical high-pressure belts (horse latitudes)
副热带高压带（马纬度无风带）

48 north-east trade winds (north-east trades, tropical easterlies)
东北信风（热带东风带）
49 south-east trade winds (south-east trades, tropical easterlies)
东南信风（热带东风带）
50 zones of the variable westerlies
不定西风带
51 polar wind zones
极地风带
52 summer monsoon
夏季季风
53-58 earth's climates
地球的气候
53 equatorial climate: tropical zone (tropical rain zone)
赤道气候：热带（热带雨区）
54 the two arid zones (equatorial dry zones): desert and steppe zones
两个干燥带（赤道干燥带）：沙漠和草原带
55 the two temperate rain zones
两个温带多雨带
56 boreal climate (snow forest climate)
极北气候（雪林气候）
57-58 polar climates
极地气候
57 tundra climate
苔原气候
58 perpetual frost climate
永冻气候

1 mercury barometer, a siphon
   barometer, a liquid-column
   barometer
   水银气压表，一种虹吸式气压表，液柱
   气压表
2 mercury column
   水银柱
3 millibar scale (millimetre, *Am.*
   millimeter, scale)
   毫巴标尺（毫米标尺）
4 barograph, a self-registering
   aneroid barometer
   气压计，一种自记空盒气压表
5 drum (recording drum)
   记录筒
6 bank of aneroid capsules
   (aneroid boxes)
   感压盒组
7 recording arm
   记录杆
8 hygrograph
   湿度计
9 hygrometer element (hair
   element)
   湿度表元件（毛发元件）
10 reading adjustment
   读数调整
11 amplitude adjustment
   振幅调整
12 recording arm
   记录杆
13 recording pen
   记录笔
14 change gears for the clock work
   drive
   钟表驱动用的变换齿轮装置
15 off switch for the recording arm
   记录杆的停止开关
16 drum (recording drum)
   记录筒
17 time scale
   时间标尺
18 case (housing)
   外壳
19 thermograph
   自记温度计
20 drum (recording drum)
   记录筒
21 recording arm
   记录杆
22 sensing element
   感应元件
23 silver-disc (silver-disk)
   pyrheliometer, an instrument for
   measuring the sun's radiant
   energy
   银盘日射强度表，一种测量太阳辐射能
   的仪器
24 silver disc (disk)
   银盘
25 thermometer
   温度计
26 wooden insulating casing
   木制绝缘套
27 tube with diaphragm
   (diaphragmed tube)
   膜片管
28 wind gauge (*Am.* gage)
   风速器
29 wind-speed indicator (wind-
   speed meter)
   风速指示器（风速表）
30 cross arms with hemispherical
   cups
   半球形风杯的横杆

31 wind-direction indicator
   风向指示器
32 wind vane
   风向标
33 aspiration psychrometer
   通风式干湿球温度表
34 dry bulb thermometer
   干球温度表
35 wet bulb thermometer
   湿球温度表
36 solar radiation shielding
   太阳辐射防护罩
37 suction tube
   吸管
38 recording rain gauge (*Am.* gage)
   雨量计
39 protective housing (protective
   casing)
   防护外罩（防护外壳）
40 collecting vessel
   集水器
41 rain cover
   防雨罩
42 recording mechanism
   记录机械装置
43 siphon tube
   虹吸管
44 precipitation gauge (*Am.* gage)
   降水计（雨量计）
45 collecting vessel
   收集器
46 storage vessel
   储存器
47 measuring glass
   量杯
48 insert for measuring snowfall
   量雪尺
49 thermometer screen
   (thermometer shelter)
   百叶箱
50 hygrograph
   湿度计
51 thermograph
   温度计
52 psychrometer (wet and dry bulb
   thermometer)
   干湿表（干湿球温度表）
53-54 thermometers for measuring
   extremes of temperature
   测量温度极值的温度表
53 maximum thermometer
   最高温度表
54 minimum thermometer
   最低温度表
55 radiosonde assembly
   无线电探空装置
56 hydrogen balloon
   氢气球
57 parachute
   降落伞
58 radar reflector with spacing lines
   带距离线的雷达反射器
59 instrument housing with
   radiosonde (a short-wave
   transmitter) and antenna
   装有无线电探空装置（短波发射机）
   （发射）和天线的仪器箱
60 transmissometer, an instrument
   for measuring visibility
   （一种测量能见度的）透射仪
61 recording instrument (recorder)
   记录仪（记录器）
62 transmitter
   发射机
63 receiver
   接收机

64 weather satellite (ITOS satellite)
   气象卫星（艾托斯卫星）
65 temperature regulation flaps
   温度调节板
66 solar panel
   太阳电池板
67 television camera
   电视摄影机
68 antenna
   天线
69 solar sensor (sun sensor)
   太阳感应器
70 telemetry antenna
   遥测天线
71 radiometer
   辐射仪

1-5 layered structure of the earth
地球的层状构造

1 earth's crust (outer crust of the earth, lithosphere, oxysphere)
地壳（地球外壳，岩石圈，含氧圈）

2 hydrosphere
水界，水圈

3 mantle
地幔

4 sima (intermediate layer)
硅镁层（中间层）

5 core (earth core, centrosphere, barysphere)
地核（地核、核圈、重圈）

6-12 hypsographic curve of the earth's surface
地球表面陆高海深曲线

6 peak
山顶，峰

7 continental mass
大陆块

8 continental shelf (cotinental platform, shelf)
大陆棚（大陆台地，陆棚）

9 continental slope
大陆（斜）坡

10 deep-sea floor (abyssal plain)
深海底（深海平原）

11 sea level
海平面

12 deep-sea trench
深海沟

13-28 volcanism (volcanicity)
火山现象，火山作用，火山活动（火山性）

13 shield volcano
盾状火山

14 lava plateau
熔岩高原

15 active volcano, a stratovolcano (composite volcano)
活火山，成层火山（复合火山）

16 volcanic crater (crater)
火山口

17 volcanic vent
火山道

18 lava stream
熔岩流

19 tuff (framented volcanic material)
凝灰岩（成碎块的火山物质）

20 subterranean volcano
地下火山

21 geyser
间歇泉

22 jet of hot water and steam
热水和蒸汽的喷射

23 sinter terraces (siliceous sinter terraces, fiorite terraces, pearl sinter terraces)
泉华阶地（硅华阶地，珍珠硅华阶地）

24 cone
火山锥，锥状地形

25 maar (extinct volcano)
低平火山口（死火山）

26 tuff deposit
凝灰岩沉积

27 breccia
角砾石

28 vent of extinct volcano
死火山道

29-31 plutonic magmatism
深成岩浆活动

29 batholite (massive protrusion)
岩基，岩盘（块状（岩）隆凸）

30 lacolith, an intrusion
岩盖（侵入作用造成的岩体）

31 sill, an ore deposit
岩床，矿床

32-38 earthquake (*kinds:* tectonic quake, volanic quake) **and seismology**
地震（种类：造构地震，火山地震）和地震学

32 earthquake focus (seismic focus, hypocentrem *Am.* hypocenter)
地震震源（地震源，震源）

33 epicentre (*Am.* epicenter), point on the earth's surface directly above the focus
震央（从震源垂直引申到地面上的一点）

34 depth of focus
震源深度

35 shock wave
震波

36 surface waves (seismic waves)
表面波（地震波）

37 isoeismal (line connecting points of equal intensity of earthquake shock)
等震线（地震程度相等各点的连线）

38 epicentral area (area of macroseismic vibration)
震央区（强震区）

39 horizontal seismograph (seismometer)
水平地震仪

40 electromagnetic damper
电磁阻尼器

41 adjustment knob for the period of free oscillation of the pendulum
摆体自由振荡周期的调整钮

42 spring attachment for the suspension of the pendulum
摇摆体的弹簧装置

43 mass
重锤，摆体

44 induction coils for recording the voltage of the galvanometer
记录电表电压用的感应线圈

45-54 effects of earthquakes
地震效应

45 waterfall (cataract, falls)
瀑布（大瀑布）

46 landslide (rockslide, landslip, *Am.* rock slip)
山崩（岩滑，塌方，滑坡）

47 talus (rubble, scree)
岩屑堆（碎石，碎石坡）

48 scar (scaur, scaw)
巉岩，陡岩坡

49 sink (sinkhole, swallowhole)
落水洞（灰岩坑）

50 dislocation (displacement)
断层（位移、变位）

51 solifluction lobe (solifluction tongue)
土石缓舌（瓣）状地形（土溜舌）

52 fissure
裂缝，裂隙

53 tsunami (seismic sea wave) produced by seaquake (submarine earthquake)
海啸（地震海浪）（海底地震所产生的）

54 raised beach
隆起滩，上升滩

1-33 geology
地质学

1 stratification of sedimentary rock
沉积岩的层理

2 strike
走向

3 dip (angle of dip, true dip)
倾角（倾角，真倾斜）

4-20 orogeny (orogenesis, tectogenesis, deformation of rocks by folding and faulting)
造山运动（造山运动，造构运动，摺曲作用和断层作用所引起的岩石变形）

4-11 fault-block mountains (block mountains)
断块山

4 fault
断层

5 fault line (fault trace)
断层线（断层迹）

6 fault throw
断层落差

7 normal fault (gravity fault, normal slip fault, slump fault)
正断层（动断层，正滑动断层，塌陷断层）

8-11 complex faults
复断层

8 step fault (distributive fault, multiple fault)
阶状断层（分枝断层，复叠断层）

9 tilt block
倾斜地块

10 horst
地垒

11 graben
地堑

12-20 range of fold mountains (folded mountains)
摺曲山脉的范围

12 symmetrical fold (normal fold)
对称褶皱（正褶皱）

13 asymmetrical fold
非对称褶皱

14 overfold
倒转摺曲

15 recumbent fold (reclined fold)
伏卧摺曲（横卧摺曲）

16 saddle (anticline)
鞍状构造（背斜）

17 anticlinal axis
背斜轴

18 trough (syncline)
槽谷（向斜）

19 trough surface (trough plane, synclinal axis)
向斜槽面（向斜面，向斜轴）

20 anticlinorium
复背斜

21 groundwater under pressure (artesian water)
受压地下水（自流水）

22 water-bearing stratum (aquifer, aquafer)
含水层（蓄水层）

23 impervious rock (impermeable rock)
不透水岩

24 drainage basin (catchment area)
流域（集水区，集水面积）

25 artesian well
自流井

26 rising water, an artesian spring
上升水，一种自流泉

27 petroleum reservoir in an anticline
背斜层的储油层

28 impervious stratum (impermeable stratum)
不透水层

29 porous stratum acting as reservoir rock
多孔储油岩层

30 natural gas, a gas cap
天然气，一种气帽

31 petroleum (crude oil)
石油（原油）

32 underlying water
下伏水

33 derrick
（油井的）铁架塔，钻油塔

34 mountainous area
山岳地区，山区

35 rounded mountain top
圆形山顶

36 mountain ridge (ridge)
山脊

37 mountain slope
山坡

38 hillside spring
山腰泉

39-47 high-mountain region
高山地带

39 mountain range, a massif
山脉，山岭，古地块的一种

40 summit (peak, top of the mountain)
山顶（山峰，山的顶点）

41 shoulder
山肩

42 saddle
山鞍

43 rock face (steep face)
岩壁（绝壁）

44 gully
冲沟

45 talus (scree, detritus)
岩屑堆（碎石堆，碎屑）

46 bridle path
马道，小路

47 pass (col)
隘（口），逩（口），鞍（部）

48-56 glacial ice
冰川冰，流动冰

48 firn field (firn basin, nevé)
雪冰原（雪冰原，雪冰）

49 valley glacier
谷冰河

50 crevasse
冰隙

51 glacier snout
冰河鼻

52 subglacial stream
冰下河流

53 lateral moraine
侧碛

54 medial moraine
中碛

55 end moraine
终碛，尾碛

56 glacier table
盖石冰桌

1-13 fluvial topography
河流地形学

1 river mouth, a delta
河口，河流的三角洲

2 distributary (distributary
channel), a river branch (river
arm)
汊河（支流），江河的支流

3 lake
湖

4 bank
岸

5 peninsula (spit)
半岛（沙嘴）

6 island
岛

7 bay (cove)
（海）湾（小湾，澳）

8 stream (brook, rivulet, creek)
河、江、川（溪流，小河，溪）

9 levee
天然堤

10 alluvial plain
冲积平原

11 meander (river bend)
曲流（河湾）

12 meander core (rock island)
离堆丘（岩石岛）

13 meadow
草原，草地

14-24 bog (marsh)
沼泽（沼泽、湿地）

14 low-moor bog
低位沼泽

15 layers of decayed vegetable
matter
腐蚀植物层

16 entrapped water
截流水

17 fen peat [consisting of rush and
sedge]
沼泥炭［由灯心属植物和管茅构成］

18 alder-swamp peat
赤杨沼泽泥炭

19 high-moor bog
高位沼泽

20 layer of recent sphagnum
mosses
现代苔藓泥沼层

21 boundary between layers
(horizons)
层的分界（层位）

22 layer of older sphagnum mosses
古苔藓泥沼层

23 bog pool
沼泽水坑

24 swamp
沼泽地

25-31 cliffline (cliffs)
悬崖线

25 rock
岩石

26 sea (ocean)
海（洋）

27 surf
矶波，拍岸浪

28 cliff (cliff face, steep rock face)
悬崖（绝壁，断崖面）

29 scree
碎石堆

30 [wave-cut] notch
［波蚀］凹壁

31 abrasion platform (wave-cut
platform)
海（浪）蚀台地（波蚀平台）

32 atoll (ring-shaped coral reef), a
coral reef
环礁（环状珊瑚礁），一种珊瑚礁

33 lagoon
潟湖

34 breach (hole)
裂口（洞）

35-44 beach
海滩

35 high-water line (high-water mark,
tidemark)
高潮线（高潮标，潮标）

36 waves breaking on the shore
拍岸海浪

37 groyne (*Am.* groin)
防波堤

38 groyne (*Am.* groin) head
防波堤头

39 wandering dune (migratory dune,
travelling, *Am.* traveling, dune), a
dune
移动的沙丘，沙丘的一种

40 barchan (barchane, barkhan,
crescentic dune)
新月丘

41 ripple marks
涟痕

42 hummock
圆丘

43 wind cripple
风损，风残

44 coastal lake
滨海湖

45 canyon (cañon, coulee)
峡谷（深冲沟）

46 plateau (tableland)
高原（高地）

47 rock terrace
岩石阶地

48 sedimentary rock (stratified
rock)
沉积岩（成层岩）

49 river terrace (bed)
河流阶地（河床）

50 joint
节理

51 canyon river
峡谷河川

52-56 types of valley [cross section]
谷地类型［剖面图］

52 gorge (ravine)
峡（谷），（沟壑）

53 V-shaped valley (V-valley)
V型谷

54 widened V-shaped valley
宽V型谷

55 U-shaped valley (U-valley,
trough valley)
U型谷（U字谷，沟谷）

56 synclinal valley
向斜谷

57-70 river valley
河谷

57 scarp (escarpment)
悬崖（崖）

58 slip-off slope
滑走坡

59 mesa
方山

60 ridge
山岭，山脊

61 river
河，川

62 flood plain
泛滥平原

63 river terrace
河流阶地

64 terracette
小阶

65 pediment
山足面，山前侵蚀平原（麓原）

66 hill
丘陵

67 valley floor (valley bottom)
谷底

68 riverbed
河床

69 sediment
沉积物

70 bedrock
基岩

71-83 karst formation in limestone
石灰岩层的喀斯特地形

71 dolina, a sink (sinkhole,
swallowhole)
石灰坑，一种陷坑（渗穴，吞口）

72 polje
灰岩盆地

73 percolation of a river
河流渗漏（透）

74 karst spring
喀斯特泉

75 dry valley
干谷

76 system of caverns (system of
caves)
洞穴系统

77 water level (water table) in a
karst formation
喀斯特形的水位（地下水面）

78 impervious rock (impermeable
rock)
不透水岩石

79 limestone cave (dripstone cave)
灰岩洞（滴石洞）

80-81 speleothems (cave formations)
洞穴灰华（洞穴形成）

80 stalactite (dripstone)
钟乳石（滴水石）

81 stalagmite
石笋

82 linked-up stalagmite and
stalactite
石笋和钟乳石的连接部分

83 subterranean river
地下河，伏流

1-7 graticule of the earth
(network of meridians and
parallels on the earth's surface)
地球的地理格网（地球表面的经纬线网）
1 equator
赤道
2 line of latitude (parallel of
latitude, parallel)
纬线
3 pole (North Pole or South Pole)
a terrestrial pole (geographical
pole)
极（北极或南极），地极（地理学的
极）
4 line of longitude (meridian of
longitude, meridian, terrestrial
meridian)
经线（子午线，地理经度线）
5 Standard meridian (Prime
meridian, Greenwich meridian,
meridian of Greenwich)
标准子午线（本初子午线，格林威治子
午线）
6 latitude
纬度
7 longitude
经度
8-9 map projections
地图投影法
8 conical (conic) projection
圆锥投影法
9 cylindrical projection (Mercator
projection, Mercator's projection)
圆柱投影（墨卡托投影）
10-45 map of the world
世界地图
10 tropics
回归线，热带
11 polar circles
极圈
12-18 continents
大陆，大洲
12-13 America
美洲
12 North America
北美洲
13 South America
南美洲
14 Africa
非洲
15-16 Europe and Asia
欧洲和亚洲
15 Europe
欧洲
16 Asia
亚洲
17 Australia
澳洲（澳大利亚）
18 Antarctica (Antarctic
Continent)
南极洲（南极大陆）
19-26 ocean (sea)
洋（海）
19 Pacific ocean
太平洋
20 Atlantic Ocean
大西洋
21 Arctic Ocean
北极海（北冰洋）
22 Antarctic Ocean (Southern
Ocean)
南极海（南冰洋）
23 Indian Ocean
印度洋

24 Strait of Gibraltar, a sea strait
直布罗陀海峡
25 Mediterranean (Mediterranean
Sea, European Mediterranean)
地中海（欧洲的地中海）
26 North Sea, a marginal sea
(epeiric sea, epicontinental sea)
北海（缘海，陆缘海）
**27-29 key (explanation of map
symbols)**
图例（地图符号的解释）
27 cold ocean current
寒洋流
28 warm ocean current
暖洋流
29 scale
缩尺（比例尺）
30-45 ocean (oceanic) currents
(ocean drifts)
洋流（漂流）
30 Gulf Stream (North Atlantic
Drift)
墨西哥湾流（北大西洋漂流）
31 Kuroshio (Kuro Siwo, Japan
Current)
黑潮（日本海流）
32 North Equatorial Current
北赤道洋流
33 Equatorial Countercurrent
赤道逆流
34 South Equatorial Current
南赤道洋流
35 Brazil Current
巴西洋流
36 Somali Current
索马里洋流
37 Agulhas Current
阿古拉斯洋流
38 East Australian Current
东澳大利亚洋流
39 California Current
加里佛尼亚洋流
40 Labrador Current
拉布拉多洋流
41 Canary Current
加那利洋流
42 Peru Current
秘鲁洋流
43 Benguela (Benguella) Current
本吉拉洋流
44 West Wind Drift (Antarctic
Circumpolar Drift)
西风漂流（南极环极洋流）
45 West Australian Current
西澳大利亚洋流
46-62 surveying (land surveying,
geodetic surveying, geodesy)
测量（土地测量，大地测量，大地测
量学）
46 levelling (*Am.* leveling)
(geometrical measurement of
height)
水准测量（几何高度测量）
47 graduated measuring rod
(levelling, *Am.* leveling, staff)
标尺（水准标尺）
48 level (surveying level, surveyor's
level), a surveyor's telescope
水准仪，测量用的望远镜
49 triangulation station
(triangulation point)
三角点
50 supporting scaffold
支撑架
51 signal tower (signal mast)
测标（信号塔，信号柱）

**52-62 theodolite, an instrument for
measuring angles**
经纬仪，测量角度用的仪器
52 micrometer head
测微计钮
53 micrometer eyepiece
测微目镜
54 vertical tangent screw
高低微动螺旋
55 vertical clamp
高低（垂直）制动钮
56 tangent screw
微动螺旋
57 horizontal clamp
水平制动钮
58 adjustment for the illuminating
mirror
照明反光镜的调整装置
59 illuminating mirror
反光镜
60 telescope
望远镜
61 spirit level
气泡水准仪
62 circular adjustment
圆形调整钮
63-66 photogrammetry
(phototopography)
摄影测量（航空摄影测量）
63 air survey camera for producing
overlapping series of pictures
产生图像连续重叠的航测仪（摄影机）
64 stereoscope
立体镜
65 pantograph
缩放仪
66 stereoplanigraph
立体平面绘（测）图仪

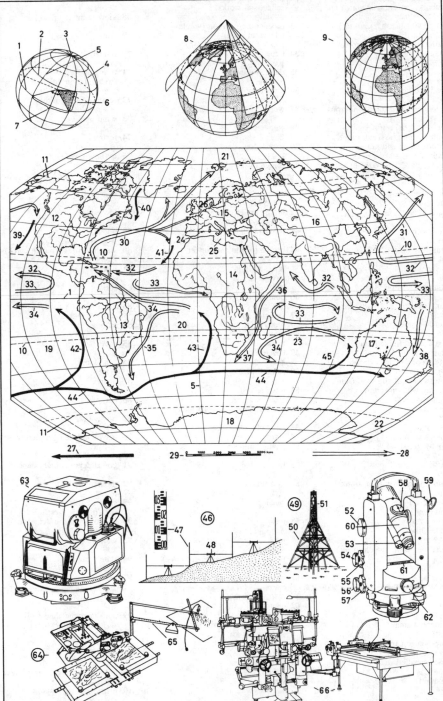

1-114 map signs (map symbols, conventional signs) on a 1:25000 map
（在1：25000 地图上用的）地图记号
（地图符号，习用地图记号）

1 coniferous wood (coniferous trees)
针叶树林

2 clearing
空地

3 forestry office
林务局

4 deciduous wood (non-coniferous trees)
落叶树林（非针叶树林）

5 heath (rough grassland, rough pasture, heath and moor, bracken)
灌丛；丛生的荒野（杂草丛生的草地，杂草丛生的牧地，灌丛和沼泽，羊齿蕨）

6 sand (sand hills)
沙地（沙丘）

7 beach grass
海（河）滩草地

8 lighthouse
灯塔

9 mean low water
平均干潮，平均低水位

10 beacon
航标

11 submarine contours
海底等高线

12 train ferry
火车轮渡

13 lightship
灯船

14 mixed wood (mixed trees)
混和树林

15 brushwood
低树林，灌木林

16 motorway with slip road (Am. freeway with on-ramp)
带岔道的高速公路

17 trunk road
干道

18 grassland
牧场，草地，草原

19 marshy grassland
沼泽草地

20 marsh
沼泽

21 main line railway (Am. trunk line)
铁路主线

22 road over railway
上跨道（铁路在下）

23 branch line
铁路支线

24 signal box (Am. switch tower)
信号箱

25 local line
地方路线

26 level crossing
平交道

27 halt
招呼站

28 residential area
住宅区

29 water gauge (Am. gage)
水位标尺

30 good, metalled road
好的碎石路

31 windmill
风车

32 thorn house (graduation house, salina, salt-works)
制盐场

33 broadcasting station (wireless or television mast)
广播台（无线电或电视天线柱）

34 mine
矿山

35 disused mine
废弃矿山

36 secondary road (B road)
二级公路（乙级公路）

37 works
工场

38 chimney
烟囱

39 wire fence
铁栅栏

40 bridge over railway
上跨桥

41 railway station (Am. railroad station)
火车站

42 bridge under railway
（铁路下的）下跨桥

43 footpath
人行道

44 bridge for footpath under railway
铁路下人行路桥

45 navigable rive
通航河流

46 pontoon bridge
浮桥

47 vehicle ferry
车辆渡船

48 mole
防波堤

49 beacon
航标

50 stone bridge
石桥

51 town (city)
城镇，市镇

52 market place (market square)
市场

53 large church
大教堂

54 public building
公共建筑物

55 road bridge
公路桥

56 iron bridge
铁桥

57 canal
运河

58 lock
水门，闸门

59 jetty
突堤码头

60 foot ferry (foot passenger ferry)
人的摆渡

61 chapel (church) without tower or spire
没有尖顶的小教堂

62 contours
等高线

63 monastery (convent)
修道院（女修道院）

64 church landmark
教堂标志

65 vineyard
葡萄园

66 weir
堰

67 aerial ropeway
空中缆索

68 view point
瞭望台

69 dam
堰

70 tunnel
隧道

71 triangulation station (triangulation point)
三角点

72 remains of a building
建筑物的遗迹

73 wind pump
风泵

74 fortress
要塞（城堡）

75 ox-bow lake
牛轭湖

76 river
河流

77 watermill
水磨

78 footbridge
人行桥

79 pond
池塘，水塘

80 stream (brook, rivulet, creek)
小河，溪流

81 water tower
水塔

82 spring
泉

83 main road (A road)
公路干线（甲级公路）

84 cutting
路堑

85 cave
岩洞

86 lime kiln
石灰窑

87 quarry
采石场

88 clay pit
黏土坑

89 brickworks
砖厂

90 narrow-gauge (Am. narrow gage) railway
窄规（轨）铁路

91 goods depot (freight depot)
货运站

92 monument
纪念碑

93 site of battle
战场遗迹

94 country estate, a demesne
乡间宅地，庄园

95 wall
城墙

96 stately home
华贵住宅

97 park
公园，私人花园

98 hedge
篱墙

99 poor or unmetalled road
难行之路或尚未铺沙石之路

100 well
井

101 farm
农场

102 unfenced path (unfenced track)
林间小路

103 district boundary
行政区域分界限

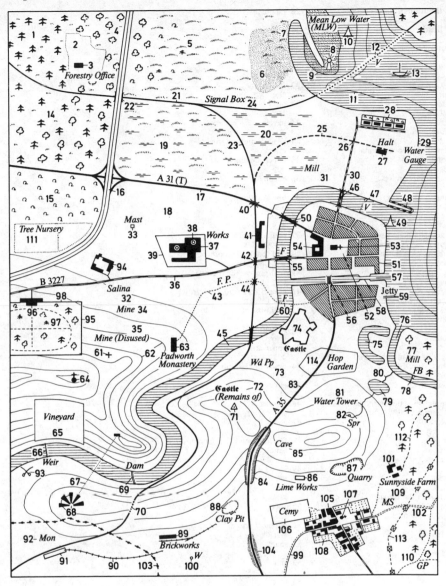

104 embankment
路基
105 village
村庄
106 cemetery
墓园
107 church (chapel) with spire
有尖顶的教堂（小教堂）
108 orchard
果树园
109 milestone
里程碑
110 guide post
路标

111 tree nursery
苗圃
112 ride (ride (aisle, lane, section line)
小路
113 electricity transmission line
输电线
114 hop garden
忽布子园，啤酒花种植园

1-54 the human body
人体

1-18 head
头

1 vertex (crown of the head, top of the head)
头顶（头的顶部）

2 occiput (back of the head)
后头，枕骨部

3 hair
头发

4-17 face
脸部

4-5 forehead
前额（头）

4 frontal eminence (frontal protuberance)
额结节

5 superciliary arch
眉弓

6 temple
太阳穴

7 eye
眼睛

8 zygomatic bone (malar bone, jugal bone, cheekbone)
颧骨（颧骨，轭骨，颊骨）

9 cheek
颊

10 nose
鼻

11 nasolabial fold
鼻唇沟（褶）

12 philtrum
人中

13 mouth
嘴

14 angle of the mouth (labial commissure)
嘴角（唇的接合处）

15 chin
颏，下巴

16 dimple (fossette) in the chin
下巴上的酒窝（小窝）

17 jaw
颚，颔骨

18 ear
耳朵

19-21 neck
颈

19 throat
颈前部

20 hollow of the throat
颈窝，前颈凹陷处

21 nape of the neck
后颈

22-41 trunk
干，躯干

22-25 back
背

22 shoulder
肩

23 shoulderblade (scapula)
肩胛骨

24 loins
腰，腰部

25 small of the back
腰背部

26 armpit
腋窝

27 armpit hair
腋毛

28-30 thorax (chest)
胸廓（胸部）

28-29 breasts (breast, mamma)
乳房

28 nipple
乳头

29 areola
乳晕

30 bosom
胸脯（胸骨前部）

31 waist
腰，腰部

32 flank (side)
腰窝，侧腹

33 hip
髋部

34 navel
脐

35-37 abdomen (stomach)
腹部

35 upper abdomen
上腹

36 abdomen
腹

37 lower abdomen
下腹

38 groin
腹股沟

39 pudenda (vulva)
外生殖器（阴门；女阴）

40 seat (backside, *coll.* bottom)
臀部（臀，屁股）

41 anal groove (anal cleft)
臀裂（肛隙）

42 gluteal fold (gluteal furrow)
臀褶（臀沟）

43-54 limbs
四肢

43-48 arm
臂

43 upper arm
上臂（肩与肘之间的部分）

44 crook of the arm
前臂弯曲处，臂弯

45 elbow
肘

46 forearm
前臂（肘至腕之间之部分）

47 hand
手

48 fist (clenched fist, clenched hand)
拳（握拳）

49-54 leg
腿

49 thigh
大腿

50 knee
膝

51 popliteal space
腘窝（后膝处）

52 shank
胫，小腿

53 calf
腓肠，小腿肚

54 foot
足，脚

1-29 skeleton (bones)
骨骼
1 skull
头骨，颅骨
2 - 5 vertebral column (spinal column, spine, backbone)
脊柱[脊柱，脊柱，脊骨（柱）]
2 cervical vertebra
颈椎
3 dorsal vertebra (thoracic vertebra)
背椎（胸椎）
4 lumbar vertebra
腰椎
5 coccyx (coccygeal vertebra)
尾骨（尾椎）
6 - 7 shoulder girdle
肩胛带，胸带
6 collarbone (clavicle)
锁骨（锁骨）
7 shoulderblade (scapula)
肩胛骨，膊骨（肩胛骨）
8-11 thorax (chest)
胸（胸廓）
8 breastbone (sternum)
胸骨
9 true ribs
真骨肋（连于胸骨的肋骨）
10 false ribs
假骨肋（两侧下五对肋骨，不直接与胸骨相接）
11 costal cartilage
软肋
12-14 arm
臂
12 humerus
肱骨
13 radius
桡骨
14 ulna
尺骨
15-17 hand
手
15 carpus
腕骨
16 metacarpal bone (metacarpal)
掌骨
17 phalanx (phalange)
指骨
18-21 pelvis
骨盆
18 ilium (hip bone)
肠骨，胯骨（臀骨）
19 ischium
坐骨
20 pubis
耻骨
21 sacrum
荐骨
22-25 leg
腿
22 femur (thigh bone, thigh)
股骨，腿节
23 patella (kneecap)
膑骨，膝盖骨
24 fibula (splint bone)
腓骨（赘骨）
25 tibia (shinbone)
胫骨（胫骨）
26-29 foot
足
26 tarsal bones (tarsus)
跗骨
27 calcaneum (heelbone)
跟骨（肿股）

28 metatarsus
跖骨
29 phalanges
趾骨
30-41 skull
头骨，颅骨
30 frontal bone
额骨
31 left parietal bone
左（颅）顶骨
32 occipital bone
枕骨
33 temporal bone
颞骨
34 external auditory canal
外耳道
35 lower jawbone (lower jaw, mandible)
下颌骨（下颚骨，大颚）
36 upper jawbone (upper jaw, maxilla)
上颌骨（上颚骨，小颚）
37 zygomatic bone (cheekbone)
颧骨（颊骨）
38 sphenoid bone (sphenoid)
蝶骨
39 ethmoid bone (ethmoid)
筛骨
40 lachrimal (lacrimal) bone
泪骨
41 nasal bone
鼻骨
42-55 head [section]
头-[剖面图]
42 cerebrum (great brain)
大脑
43 pituitary gland (pituitary body, hypophysis cerebri)
脑垂腺（脑垂体，脑下腺）
44 corpus callosum
胼胝体
45 cerebellum (little brain)
小脑
46 pons (pons cerebri, pons cerebelli)
桥脑
47 medulla oblongata (brain-stem)
延脑（脑干）
48 spinal cord
脊髓
49 oesophagus (esophagus, gullet)
食管，食道
50 trachea (windpipe)
气管，导管
51 epiglottis
会咽，会咽软骨
52 tongue
舌
53 nasal cavity
鼻腔
54 sphenoidal sinus
蝶窦
55 frontal sinus
额窦
56-65 organ of equilibrium and hearing
平衡和听觉器官
56-58 external ear
外耳
56 auricle
耳廓
57 ear lobe
耳垂
58 external auditory canal
外耳道

59-61 middle ear
中耳
59 tympanic membrane
鼓膜
60 tympanic cavity
鼓腔
61 auditory ossicles: hammer, anvil, and stirrup (malleus, incus, and stapes)
听骨：槌骨，砧骨和镫骨（槌骨，砧骨和镫骨）
62-64 inner ear (internal ear)
内耳
62 labyrinth
迷路
63 cochlea
耳蜗
64 auditory nerve
听觉神经
65 eustachian tube
耳咽管

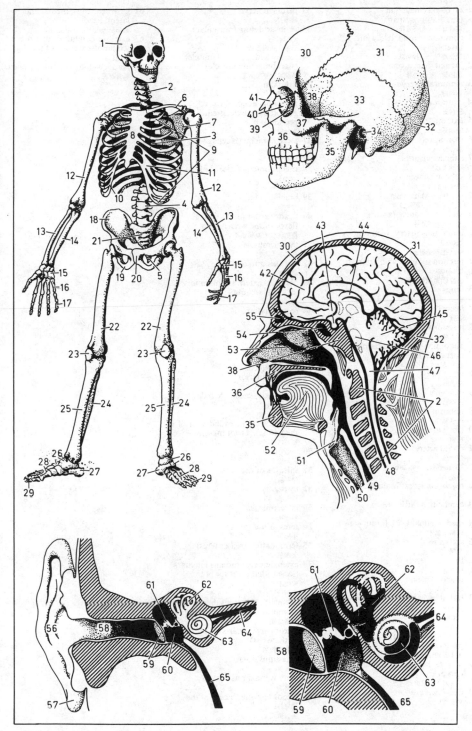

1-21 blood circulation
(circulatory system)
血液循环（循环系统）
1 common carotid artery, an
artery
颈总动脉，一种动脉
2 jugular vein, a vein
颈静脉，一种静脉
3 temporal artery
颞动脉
4 temporal vein
颞静脉
5 frontal artery
额动脉
6 frontal vein
额静脉
7 subclavian artery
锁骨下动脉
8 subclavian vein
锁骨下静脉
9 superior vena cava
上大静脉，上腔静脉
10 arch of the aorta (aorta)
（主）大动脉弓
11 pulmonary artery 'with venous
blood'
肺动脉[带静脉血]
12 pulmonary vein 'with arterial
blood'
肺静脉[带动脉血]
13 lungs
肺
14 heart
心脏
15 inferior vena cava
下大静脉，下腔静脉
16 abdominal aorta (descending
portion of the aorta)
腹大动脉（下行大动脉）
17 iliac artery
胯动脉
18 iliac vein
胯静脉
19 femoral artery
股动脉
20 tibial artery
胫前动脉
21 radial artery
桡动脉

22-33 nervous system
神经系统
22 cerebrum (great brain)
大脑
23 cerebellum (little brain)
小脑
24 medulla oblongata (brain-stem)
延脑（脑干）
25 spinal cord
脊髓
26 thoracic nerves
胸神经
27 brachial plexus
臂神经丛
28 radial nerve
桡神经
29 ulnar nerve
尺骨神经
30 great sciatic nerve 'lying
posteriorly'
大坐骨神经[大腿后部中间]
31 femoral nerve (anterior crural
nerve)
股神经（前股神经）
32 tibial nerve
胫前神经

33 peroneal nerve
腓神经

34-64 musculature (muscular
system)
肌系（肌肉系统）
34 sternocleidomastoid muscle
(sternomastoid muscle)
胸锁乳突肌（胸乳肌）
35 deltoid muscle
三角肌
36 pectoralis major (greater
pectoralis muscle, greater
pectoralis)
大胸肌
37 biceps brachii (biceps of the
arm)
肱肌二头
38 triceps brachii (triceps of the
arm)
肱肌三头
39 brachioradialis
肱桡肌
40 flexor carpi radialis (radial
flexor of the wrist)
桡侧屈肌（腕屈肌）
41 thenar muscle
拇指肌
42 serratus anterior
前锯肌
43 obliquus externus abdominis
(external oblique)
腹外斜肌
44 rectus abdominis
腹直肌
45 sartorius
缝匠肌
46 vastus lateralis and vastus
medialis
外股肌和内股肌
47 tibialis anterior
胫骨前肌
48 tendo calcanaeus (Achilles'
tendon)
跟腱
49 abductor hallucis (abductor of
the hallux), a foot muscle
外展拇肌，一种足肌
50 occipitalis
后头肌（枕肌）
51 splenius of the neck
颈夹肌
52 trapezius
斜方肌
53 infraspinatus
棘下肌
54 teres minor (lesser teres)
小圆肌
55 teres major (greater teres)
大圆肌
56 extensor carpi radialis longus
(long radial extensor of the
wrist)
桡侧伸腕长肌
57 extensor communis digitorum
(common extensor of the digits)
伸指总肌
58 flexor carpi ulnaris (ulnar flexor
of the wrist)
尺侧屈腕肌
59 latissimus dorsi
背阔肌
60 gluteus maximus
大臀肌
61 biceps femoris (biceps of the
thigh)
股二头肌

62 gastrocnemius, medial and
lateral heads
腓肠肌，内侧和外侧头
63 extensor communis digitorum
(common extensor of the digits)
伸趾总肌
64 peroneus longus (long peroneus)
腓骨长肌

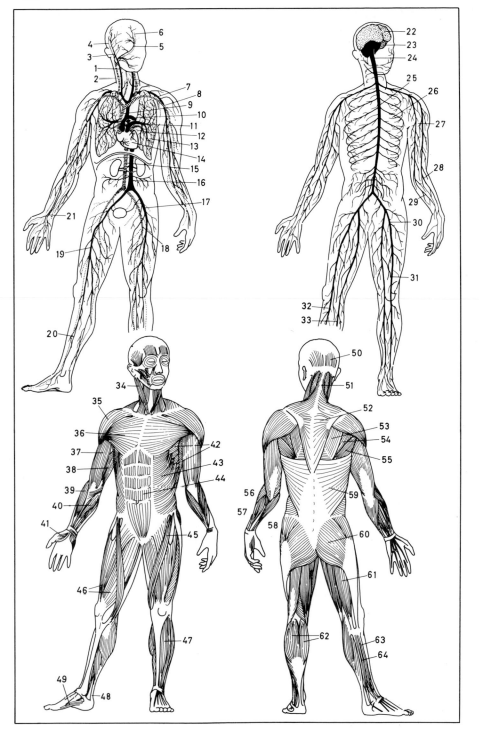

1-13 head and neck
头和颈
1 sternocleidomastoid muscle
胸锁乳突肌
2 occipitalis
后头肌（枕肌）
3 temporalis (temporal, temporal muscle)
颞肌
4 occipito frontalis (frontalis)
额肌
5 orbicularis oculi
眼轮匝肌
6 muscles of facial expression
面部表情肌
7 masseter
嚼肌
8 orbicularis oris
口轮匝肌
9 parotid gland
腮腺（耳下腺）
10 lymph node (submandibular lymph gland)
淋巴结[颌（颚）下淋巴腺]
11 submandibular gland (submaxillary gland)
（颚）颌下腺（颌下腺）
12 muscles of the neck
颈部肌肉
13 Adam's apple (laryngeal prominence) 'in men only'
喉结[唯男人有]

14-37 mouth and throat
口腔和咽喉
14 upper lip
上唇
15 gum
齿龈
16-18 teeth (set of teeth)
齿（牙组）
16 incisors
门齿
17 canine tooth (canine)
犬齿
18 premolar (bicuspid) and molar teeth (premolars and molars)
前白齿（二尖齿）和白齿
19 angle of the mouth (labial commissure)
咀角（咀唇接合处）
20 hard palate
硬颚
21 soft palate (velum palati, velum)
软颚
22 uvula
小舌
23 palatine tonsil (tonsil)
扁桃体，扁桃腺
24 pharyngeal opening (pharynx, throat)
咽，喉
25 tongue
舌
26 lower lip
下唇
27 upper jaw (maxilla)
上颚（颌）
28-37 tooth
牙齿
28 periodontal membrane (periodontium, pericementum)
齿根膜，齿骨膜，齿周膜，齿根骨膜
29 cement (dental cementum, crusta petrosa)
白垩质（牙齿的白垩质）

30 enamel
珐琅质
31 dentine (dentin)
齿质
32 dental pulp (tooth pulp, pulp)
齿髓
33 nerves and blood vessels
神经和血管
34 incisor
门齿
35 molar tooth (molar)
白齿
36 root (fang)
齿根
37 crown
齿冠
38-51 eye
眼，目，视官
38 eyebrow (supercilium)
眉，眉毛
39 upper eyelid (upper palpebra)
上眼睑
40 lower eyelid (lower palpebra)
下眼睑
41 eyelash (cilium)
睫毛
42 iris
虹膜
43 pupil
瞳孔
44 eye muscles (ocular muscles)
眼肌
45 eyeball
眼球
46 vitreous body
玻璃体
47 cornea
眼角膜
48 lens
晶状体
49 retina
视网膜
50 blind spot
盲点
51 optic nerve
视神经
52-63 foot
脚，足
52 big toe (great toe, first toe, hallux, digitus I)
大脚趾（第一趾，大拇趾）
53 second toe (digitus II)
第二趾
54 third toe (digitus III)
第三趾
55 fourth toe (digitus IV)
第四趾
56 little toe (digitus minimus, digitus V)
小脚趾（第五趾）
57 toenail
趾甲（脚趾甲）
58 ball of the foot
脚的球状体
59 lateral malleolus (external malleolus, outer malleolus, malleolus fibulae)
外（侧）踝
60 medial malleolus (internal malleolus, inner malleolus, malleolus tibulae, malleolus medialis)
内踝

61 instep (medial longitudinal arch, dorsum of the foot, dorsum pedis)
足背（足の背部）
62 sole of the foot
足底，脚底，蹠
63 heel
足跟，踵
64-83 hand
手
64 thumb (pollex, digitus I)
大拇指（拇指，第一指）
65 index finger (forefinger, second finger, digitus II)
食指（第二指）
66 middle finger (third finger, digitus medius, digitus III)
中指（第三指）
67 ring finger (fourth finger, digitus anularis, digitus IV)
环指，无名指（第四指）
68 little finger (fifth finger, digitus minimus, digitus V)
小指（第五指，小拇指）
69 radial side of the hand
手的桡骨侧
70 ulnar side of the hand
手的尺骨侧
71 palm of the hand (palma manus)
手掌
72-74 lines of the hand
掌纹，手纹
72 life line (line of life)
生命线
73 head line (line of the head)
智慧线
74 heart line (line of the heart)
感情线
75 ball of the thumb (thenar eminence)
拇指球
76 wrist (carpus)
腕
77 phalanx (phalange)
指骨
78 finger pad
指垫
79 fingertip
指尖
80 fingernail (nail)
指甲
81 lunule (lunula) of the nail
指甲弧影（小月斑）
82 knuckle
手关节
83 back of the hand (dorsum of the hand, dorsum manus)
手背

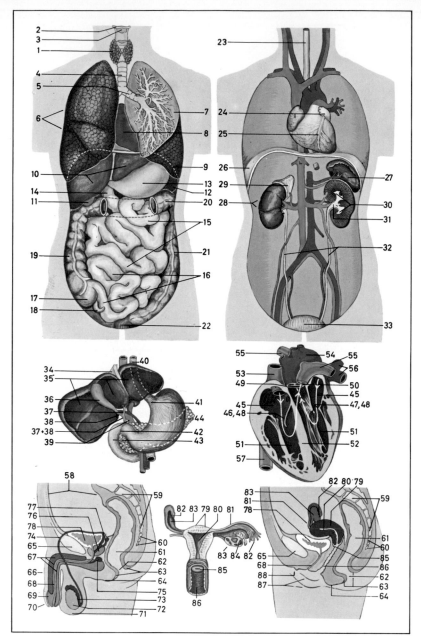

1-57 internal organs [front view]
内部器官，内脏[前视图]

1 thyroid gland
甲状腺

2-3 larynx
喉（头）

2 hyoid bone (hyoid)
舌骨

3 thyroid cartilage
甲状软骨

4 trachea (windpipe)
气管

5 bronchus
支气管

6 - 7 lung
肺

6 right lung
右肺

7 upper pulmonary lobe (upper lobe of the lung) [section]
上肺叶（肺的上叶）[剖面图]

8 heart
心脏

9 diaphragm
横隔膜

10 liver
肝（脏）

11 gall bladder
胆囊

12 spleen
脾

13 stomach
胃

14-22 intestines (bowel)
肠

14-16 small intestine (intestinum tenue)
小肠

14 duodenum
十二指肠

15 jejunum
空肠

16 ileum
迴肠

17-22 large intestine (intestinum crassum)
大肠

17 caecum (cecum)
盲肠

18 appendix (vermiform appendix)
阑尾

19 ascending colon
升结肠

20 transverse colon
横结肠

21 descending colon
降结肠

22 rectum
直肠

23 oesophagus (esophagus, gullet)
食道

24-25 heart
心脏

24 auricle
心房

25 anterior longitudinal cardiac sulcus
前纵心沟

26 diaphragm
隔膜

27 spleen
脾脏

28 right kidney
右肾

29 suprarenal gland
肾上腺

30-31 left kidney [longitudinal section]
左肾[纵剖面图]

30 calyx (renal calyx)
肾萼（肾盏）

31 renal pelvis
肾盂

32 ureter
输尿管

33 bladder
膀胱

34-35 liver [from behind]
肝脏[后视图]

34 falciform ligament of the liver
肝的镰状韧带

35 lobe of the liver
肝叶

36 gall bladder
胆囊

37-38 common bile duct
总胆管

37 hepatic duct (common hepatic duct)
肝管（总肝管）

38 cystic duct
胆囊管

39 portal vein (hepatic portal vein)
门静脉（肝门静脉）

40 oesophagus (esophagus, gullet)
食道

41-42 stomach
胃

41 cardiac orifice
贲门孔

42 pylorus
幽门

43 duodenum
十二指肠

44 pancreas
胰脏

45-57 heart [longitudinal section]
心脏[纵剖面图]

45 atrium
心房

46-47 valves of the heart
心瓣

46 tricuspid valve (right atrioventricular valve)
三尖瓣（右心房瓣）

47 bicuspid valve (mitral valve, left atrioventricular valve)
二尖瓣（左心房瓣）

48 cusp
瓣尖

49 aortic valve
大动脉瓣

50 pulmonary valve
肺动脉瓣

51 ventricle
心室

52 ventricular septum (interventricular septum)
心室隔膜

53 superior vena cava
上大静脉

54 aorta
大动脉

55 pulmonary artery
肺动脉

56 pulmonary vein
肺静脉

57 inferior vena cava
下大静脉

58 peritoneum
腹膜

59 sacrum
荐骨

60 coccyx (coccygeal vertebra)
尾骨（尾椎）

61 rectum
直肠

62 anus
肛门

63 anal sphincter
肛门括约肌

64 perineum
会阴

65 pubic symphisis (symphisis pubis)
耻缝，耻骨联合

66-77 male sex organs [longitudinal section]
男性生殖器[纵剖面图]

66 penis
阴茎

67 corpus cavernosum and spongiosum of the penis (erectile tissue of the penis)
阴茎海绵体（阴茎的勃起组织）

68 urethra
尿道

69 glans penis
阴茎头，龟头

70 prepuce (foreskin)
包皮

71 scrotum
阴囊

72 right testicle (testis)
右睾丸

73 epididymis
副睾

74 spermatic duct (vas deferens)
输精管

75 Cowper's gland (bulbourethral gland)
考伯氏腺，尿道球腺

76 prostate (prostate gland)
摄护腺，前列腺

77 seminal vesicle
贮精囊

78 bladder
膀胱

79-88 female sex organs [longitudinal section]
女性生殖器[纵剖面图]

79 uterus (matrix, womb)
子宫

80 cavity of the uterus
子宫腔

81 fallopian tube (uterine tube, oviduct)
输卵管

82 fimbria (fimbriated extremity)
输卵管繖

83 ovary
卵巢

84 follicle with ovum (egg)
带卵子的滤泡

85 os uteri externum
子宫外口

86 vagina
阴道

87 lip of the pudendum (lip of the vulva)
阴唇

88 clitoris
阴蒂，阴核

1-13 emergency bandages
紧急缠带法

1 arm bandage
手臂缠带

2 triangular cloth used as a sling (an arm sling)
用作吊带的三角布（吊腕带）

3 head bandage (capeline)
头部缠带

4 first aid kit
急救包

5 first aid dressing
急救（包紮用的）药品

6 sterile gauze dressing
消毒（无菌）纱布敷料

7 adhesive plaster (sticking plaster)
绊创膏

8 wound
伤口

9 bandage
缠带

10 emergency splint for a broken limb (fractured limb)
骨折用的紧急夹板

11 fractured leg (broken leg)
骨折的腿

12 splint
夹板

13 headrest
靠头之物

14-17 measures for stanching the blood flow (tying up of, ligature of, a blood vessel)
止血法（包紮血管）

14 pressure points of the arteries
动脉压迫点

15 emergency tourniquet on the thigh
大腿紧急止血带

16 walking stick used as a screw
固定用的拐杖

17 compression bandage
压迫缠带

18-23 rescue and transport of an injured person
负伤者的救助和运送

18 Rautek grip (for rescue of victim of a car accident)
Rautek 氏握法（对车祸伤者的营救）

19 helper
救助者，营救人

20 injured person (casualty)
负伤者（受伤者）

21 chair grip
坐椅握法

22 carrying grip
运送（搬）握法

23 emergency stretcher of sticks and a jacket
棍棒和夹克做的应急担架

24-27 the positioning of an unconscious person and artificial respiration (resuscitation)
失去知觉人的安放（置）和人工呼吸

24 coma position
昏迷（厥）的姿态

25 unconscious person
失去知觉的人

26 mouth-to-mouth resuscitation (*variation*: mouth-to-nose resuscitation)
口对口人工呼吸法（另有：口对鼻人工呼吸法）

27 resuscitator (respiratory apparatus, resuscitation apparatus), a respirator (artificial breathing device)
人工呼吸器（人工呼吸装置）

28-33 methods of rescue in ice accidents
冰上意外事故的营救法

28 person who has fallen through the ice
冰上遇难者

29 rescuer
营救者

30 rope
粗绳

31 table (or similar device)
桌子[或类似物]

32 ladder
梯子

33 self-rescue
自救

34-38 rescue of a drowning person
溺水者的营救

34 method of release (release grip, release) to free rescuer from the clutch of a drowning person
救助者被溺水者紧抱时的解困法

35 drowning person
溺水者

36 lifesaver
救生员

37 chest grip, a towing grip
胸部抱拖法

38 tired swimmer grip (hip grip)
疲劳泳者的抱拖法（抱腰法）

32-74 surgery
外科手术室

32 chart of eyegrounds
眼底图表

33 doctor's bag (doctor's case)
医生的手提箱（包）

34 intercom
对讲机（内部通话装置）

35 medicine cupboard
药橱，药柜

36 swab dispenser
消毒药品定量分配器（拭子分配器）

37 inflator (Politzer bag)
吹张器（普立兹袋）

38 electrotome
电刀

39 steam sterilizer
蒸汽消毒器

40 cabinet
（存放或陈列用的）小橱

41 medicine samples
药物样品

42 baby scales
小型秤盘

43 examination couch
诊察（疗）脉（台）

44 directional lamp
定向灯

45 instrument table
器具桌（台）

46 tube holder
管架

47 tube of ointment
药膏（油膏，软膏）管

48-50 instruments for minor surgery
小手术用器具

48 mouth gag
张口器，开口器

49 Kocher's forceps
Kocher 氏钳（动脉钳）

50 scoop (curette)
短勺（刮匙，刮除器）

51 angled scissors
有角剪

52 forceps
镊子

53 olive-pointed (bulb-headed) probe
橄榄头（球头）探针

54 syringe for irrigations of the ear or bladder
耳或膀胱的冲洗注射器

55 adhesive plaster (sticking plaster)
绊创膏

56 surgical suture material
手术缝合器材

57 curved surgical needle
弯曲的手术缝针

58 sterile gauze
消毒纱布

59 needle holder
缝针托盘

60 spray for disinfecting the skin
皮肤消毒用的喷雾器

61 thread container
缝线容器

62 ophthalmoscope
检眼镜

63 freezer for cryosurgery
冷冻手术用的冷凝装置

64 dispenser for plasters and small pieces of equipment
胶布和小器具的配给架

65 disposable hypodermic needles and syringes
只用一次的皮下注射针头和注射器

66 scales, sliding weight scales
磅秤，体重计

67 weighing platform
称重台

68 sliding weight (jockey)
滑动砝码

69 height gauge (*Am.* gage)
身高测量器

70 waste bin (*Am.* trash bin)
垃圾筒

71 hot-air sterilizer
热气消毒器

72 pipette
吸管

73 percussor
听诊器

74 aural speculum (auriscope, aural syringe)
耳镜（耳镜，耳注射器）

1 consulting room
诊察室

2 general practitioner
一般医师（各科皆看的医师）

3-21 **instruments for gynecological and proctological examinations**
妇科和直肠检查的器具

3 warming the instruments up to body temperature
将器具加温至体温的温度

4 examination couch
诊察台（床）

5 colposcope
阴道镜

6 binocular eyepiece
双目镜

7 miniature camera
小型照相机

8 cold light source
冷光源

9 cable release
电缆断路器

10 bracket for the leg support
支脚的腕木托腿架

11 leg support (leg holder)
支脚架（托腿座）

12 holding forceps (sponge holder)
夹持钳（海绵钳）

13 vaginal speculum
阴道窥镜

14 lower blade of the vaginal speculum
阴道窥镜的下叶板

15 platinum loop (for smears)
白金圈（抹片用）

16 rectoscope
直肠镜

17 biopsy forceps used with the rectoscope (proctoscope)
和直肠镜联用的活组织检查钳（直肠镜）

18 insufflator for proctoscopy (rectoscopy)
直肠镜检查用的吹气器

19 proctoscope (rectal speculum)
直肠镜

20 urethroscope
尿道镜

21 guide for inserting the proctoscope
直肠镜插入时用的引导器

22 diathermy unit (short-wave therapy apparatus)
透热疗法设备（短波治疗装置）

23 radiator
辐射器

24 inhaling apparatus (inhalator)
吸入装置（吸入器）

25 basin (for sputum)
痰盂

26-31 **ergometry**
肌力试验，测力试验

26 bicycle ergometer
脚踏测力器

27 monitor (visual display of the ECG and of pulse and respiratory rates when performing work)
监视器（测试时心电图、脉搏和呼吸数的显示装置）

28 ECG (electrocardiograph)
心电图仪（心动电流描记器）

29 suction electrodes
吸引电极

30 strap-on electrodes for the limbs
肢体连接的电极

31 spirometer (for measuring respiratory functions)
呼吸计，吸量计（量呼吸功能用）

32 measuring the blood pressure
量血压

33 sphygmomanometer
血压计

34 inflatable cuff
量血压用可膨胀的臂带

35 stethoscope
听诊器

36 microwave treatment unit
微波治疗设备

37 faradization unit (application of low-frequency currents with different pulse shapes)
感应电疗装置（应用不同形式脉冲的低频电流）

38 automatic tuner
自动调谐器

39 short-wave therapy apparatus
短波治疗设备

58 URINE SEDIMENTS

40 timer
计时器

41-59 laboratory
实验室，化验室

41 medical laboratory technician
医学化验技师

42 capillary tube stand for blood sedimentation
血液沉淀用的毛细管架

43 measuring cylinder
量筒

44 automatic pipette
自动吸管

45 kidney dish
肾形盘

46 portable ECG machine for emergency use
急救用的手提心电图仪（心电描记器）

47 automatic pipetting device
自动吸管（移）装置

48 constant temperature water bath
恒温水槽

49 tap with water jet pump
喷射泵水龙头

50 staining dish (for staining blood smears, sediments and other smears)
染色皿（用于染血抹片，沉淀和其他抹片）

51 binocular research microscope
双目检查显微镜

52 pipette stand for photometry
光度测法用的吸管架

53 computer and analyser for photometry
光度测法用的电脑和分析器

54 phtotometer
光度计

55 potentiometric recorder
电位（电势）记录仪

56 transforming section
变换部件

57 laboratory apparatus (laboratory equipment)
化验器材（实验室装置）

58 urine sediment chart
尿沉淀图表

59 centrifuge
离心机

1 dentist (dental surgeon)
  牙医师
2 patient
  病人，患者
3 dentist's chair
  牙科椅子
4 dental instruments
  牙科诊疗器具
5 instrument tray
  器具盘
6 drills with different handpieces
  具不同手柄的牙钻
7 medicine case
  药箱
8 storage unit (for dental instruments)
  （牙科器具的）贮藏装置
9 assistant's unit
  牙科助手的器具柜
10 multi-purpose syringe (for cold and warm water, spray or air)
   多功能注射器（水枪）（喷冷水，热水或空气）
11 suction apparatus
   吸水装置
12 basin
   唾液盆
13 water glass, filled automatically
   自动充水的玻璃杯
14 stool
   凳子
15 washbasin
   洗脸盆，洗手盆

16 instrument cabinet
   器具柜
17 drawer for drills
   放凿子的抽屉
18 dentist's assistant
   牙医助手
19 dentist's lamp
   牙科用灯
20 ceiling light
   室内照明灯
21 X-ray apparatus for panoramic pictures
   X光全像摄影机
22 X-ray generator
   X光（射线）发生器
23 microwave treatment unit, a radiation unit
   微波医疗装置，一种辐射医疗装置
24 seat
   座位

25 denture (set of false teeth)
假牙（整组假牙）
26 bridge (dental bridge)
牙桥（齿桥）
27 prepared stump of the tooth
预备好的牙根
28 crown (*kinds*: gold crown, jacket crown)
齿冠（种类：金齿冠，甲冠）
29 porcelain tooth (porcelain pontic)
瓷牙（瓷假牙）
30 filling
填（补）料
31 post crown
合钉继续齿冠
32 facing
镶牙
33 diaphragm
隔膜
34 post
牙桩
35 carborundum disc (disk)
金钢砂盘
36 grinding wheel
磨（牙）轮
37 burs
牙钻，圆头钻
38 flame-shaped finishing bur
火焰形钻子
39 fissure burs
裂钻
40 diamond point
钻石刻刀
41 mouth mirror
口镜（口腔检查器）
42 mouth lamp
口腔灯
43 cautery
烧灼器，烙器
44 platinum-iridium electrode
铂铱电极
45 tooth scalers
清齿牙器
46 probe
探针
47 extraction forceps
拔牙钳
48 tooth-root elevator
（牙）齿根起子
49 bone chisel
骨凿
50 spatula
压舌板
51 mixer for filling material
填料搅拌器
52 synchronous timer
同步计时器
53 hypodermic syringe for injection of local anaesthetic
局部麻醉用的皮下注射器
54 hypodermic needle
皮下注射针
55 matrix holder
牙模支持器
56 impression tray
（牙齿）印模托盘
57 spirit lamp
酒精灯

1-30 intensive care unit
加护病房设备

1 - 9 control room
控制室

1 central control unit for monitoring heart rhythm (cardiac rhythm) and blood pressure
监视心律和血压的中心控制装置

2 electrocardiogram monitor (ECG monitor)
心电图监视器

3 recorder
记录器

4 recording paper
记录纸带

5 patient's card
病人卡片

6 indicator lights (with call buttons for each patient)
指示灯（附有每个病人的呼叫按钮）

7 spatula
压舌板，药匙

8 window (observation window, glass partition)
窗（观察窗，玻璃隔板）

9 blind
百叶窗

10 bed (hospital bed)
病床

11 stand for infusion apparatus
点滴（输液）装置的立架

12 infusion bottle
点滴瓶（输液瓶）

13 tube for intravenous drips
静脉注射的点滴注管

14 infusion device for water-soluble medicaments
水溶性药物的输入装置

15 sphygmomanometer
血压计

16 cuff
血压计的臂带

17 inflating bulb
充气小球

18 mercury manometer
水银测压器

19 bed monitor
床头盘视器（装置）

20 connecting lead to the central control unit
连接中心控制设备的导线

21 electrocardiogram monitor (ECG monitor)
心电图监视器

22 manometer for the oxygen supply
氧气供给用的测压计

23 wall connection for oxygen treatment
氧气治疗用的接头部分

24 mobile monitoring unit
移动式的监视装置

25 electrode lead to the short-term pacemaker
短期定调器的电极导线

26 electrodes for shock treatment
休克治疗用的电极

27 ECG recording unit
心电图记录装置

28 electrocardiogram monitor (ECG monitor)
心电图监视器

29 control switches and knobs (controls) for adjusting the monitor
调整监视器用的控制开关和旋钮

30 control buttons for the pacemaker unit
定调装置的控制按钮

31 **pacemaker** (cardiac pacemaker)
（心脏）定调器
32 mercury battery
水银电池
33 programmed impulse generator
程序脉冲发生器
34 electrode exit point
电极出口点
35 electrode
电极
36 implantation of the pacemaker
定调器的植入
37 internal cardiac pacemaker
(internal pacemaker,
pacemaker)
体内心脏定调器（体内定调器，定调器）
38 electrode inserted through the
vein
通过静脉插入电极
39 cardiac silhouette on the X-ray
X 光（射线）照射下心脏的影像
40 **pacemaker control unit**
定调器控制装置
41 electrocardiograph (ECG
recorder)
心电图记录器
42 automatic impulse meter
脉搏自动计测器
43 ECG lead to the patient
心电图仪与病人连接的导线

44 monitor unit for visual
monitoring of the pacemaker
impulses
脉搏定调器的视觉监视用的监视器（装置）
45 long-term ECG analyser
长期心电图分析仪
46 magnetic tape for recording the
ECG impulses during analysis
分析心电图脉冲时记录用的磁带
47 ECG monitor
心电监视器
48 automatic analysis on paper of
the ECG rhythm
心电图节律纸带上的自动分析
49 control knob for the ECG
amplitude
心电振幅控制旋钮
50 program selector switches for
the ECG analysis
分析心电图用的程式选择开关
51 charger for the pacemaker
batteries
定调器的电池充电器
52 battery tester
电池检查器
53 pressure gauge (Am. gage) for
the right cardiac catheter
右心导管用的压力计（血压计）
54 trace monitor
轨迹监视器
55 pressure indicator
血压指示器

56 connecting lead to the paper
recorder
连接纸带记录器的导线
57 paper recorder for pressure
traces
描述血压曲线的纸带记录器

34-54 preparation and sterilization room
准备和消毒室

34 dressing material
包扎材料

35 small sterilizer
小型消毒器

36 carriage of the operating table
手术台杆架

37 mobile instrument table
移动器具台

38 sterile cloth
消毒布

39 instrument tray
器具盘

40-53 surgical instruments
外科手术器具

40 olive-pointed (bulb-headed) probe
橄榄形（球头）探针

41 hollow probe
空心探针

42 curved scissors
弯剪刀

43 scalpel (surgical knife)
解剖刀（手术刀）

44 ligature-holding forceps
结扎线支持钳

45 sequestrum forceps
死骨镊，腐骨钳

46 jaw
钳头（口）

47 drainage tube
泄液管，导液管

48 surgeon's tourniquet
外科压脉器

49 artery forceps
动脉钳

50 blunt hook
钝钩

51 bone nippers (bone-cutting forceps)
骨钳（剪骨钳）

52 scoop (curette) for erasion (curettage)
刮除杓（刮匙）

53 obstetrical forceps
分娩钳（产科钳）

54 roll of plaster
绊创膏卷

1-35 X-ray unit
X 射线装置

1 X-ray examination table
X 射线检查台

2 support for X-ray cassettes
X 光（射线）胶片盒支架

3 height adjustment of the central beam for lateral views
侧面摄影用中心束高度调整器

4 compress for pyelography and cholecystography
肾盂和胆囊摄影用的压迫带

5 instrument basin
器具盆

6 X-ray apparatus for pyelograms
肾盂摄影用的 X 射线装置

7 X-ray tube
X 光（射线）管

8 telescopic X-ray support
伸缩的 X 射线管支架

9 central X-ray control unit
中心 X 射线控制装置

10 control panel (control desk)
控制盘

11 radiographer (X-ray technician)
放射线技师（X 射线技师）

12 window to the angiography room
血管 X 射线检查室的窗口

13 oxymeter
量氧计

14 pyelogram cassettes
肾盂摄影用胶片盒

15 contrast medium injector
造影剂注入器

16 X-ray image intensifier
X 射线萤光增倍装置

17 C-shaped frame
C 型框架

18 X-ray head with X-ray tube
带 X 射线管的 X 射线头

19 image converter with converter tube
带变换管的影像变换器

20 film camera
软片摄影机

21 foot switch
脚踏开关

22 mobile mounting
移动式托架

23 monitor
监视器

24 swivel-mounted monitor support
旋转式监视器支架

25 operating lamp
手术灯

26 angiographic examination table
血管 X 射线检查台

27 pillow
枕头

28 eight-channel recorder
八线记录器

29 recording paper
记录纸

30 catheter gauge (*Am.* gage) unit for catheterization of the heart
心导管液压计

31 six-channel monitor for pressure graphs and ECG
血压图和心电图用的六线路监视器

32 slide-in units of the pressure transducer
血压传感器的滑动装置

33 paper recorder unit with developer for photographic recording
摄影记录用的影影纸带记录器（装置）

34 recording paper
记录纸

35 timer
计时器

36-50 spirometry
肺活量测定法

36 spirograph for pulmonary
function tests
肺功能检验呼吸描记器

37 breathing tube
呼吸管

38 mouthpiece
吹口

39 soda-lime absorber
碱石灰吸收器

40 recording paper
记录纸

41 control knobs for gas supply
供气控制旋钮

42 O_2-stabilizer
氧稳定器

43 throttle valve
节流阀

44 absorber attachment
吸收装置的配件

45 oxygen cylinder
氧气筒（瓶）

46 water supply
供水

47 tube support
管子支撑装置

48 mask
面罩

49 CO_2 consumption meter
二氧化碳耗量计

50 stool for the patient
病人坐凳

1 collapsible cot 可摺叠的婴儿床	**18** layette box 婴儿全套用品箱
2 bouncing cradle 弹性摇床	**19** feeding bottle 奶瓶
3 baby bath 婴儿浴盆	**20** teat （奶瓶上的）橡皮奶咀
4 changing top 更换蓬	**21** bottle warmer 奶瓶保温器
5 baby (new-born baby) 婴儿（新生婴儿）	**22** rubber baby pants for disposable nappies (*Am.* diapers) 使用一次的尿布
6 mother 母亲	**23** vest 内衣
7 hairbrush 发刷	**24** leggings （小孩）护腿套裤
8 comb 梳子	**25** baby's jacket 婴儿上衣
9 hand towel 手巾	**26** hood 兜帽
10 toy duck 玩具鸭	**27** baby's cup 婴儿杯
11 changing unit 更换用品柜	**28** baby's plate, a stay-warm plate 婴儿盘，一种保温盘
12 teething ring 出牙环，出牙圈	**29** thermometer 温度计
13 cream jar 面霜盒	
14 box of baby powder 婴儿粉盒	
15 dummy 奶咀	
16 ball 球	
17 sleeping bag 睡袋	

30 bassinet, a wicker pram 有篷摇篮，柳条婴儿车	**46** teddy bear 玩具熊（泰迪熊）
31 set of bassinet covers 全套摇篮盖	**47** potty (baby's pot) 小孩便罐
32 canopy 摇篮罩篷	**48** carrycot 可携带的婴儿床
33 baby's high chair, a folding chair 婴儿用的高脚椅，一种摺叠椅	**49** window 透明窗
34 pram (baby-carriage) [with windows] 有透明窗的婴儿车	**50** handles 手提带子
35 folding hood 摺叠车篷	
36 window 透明窗	
37 pushchair (*Am.* stroller) 折叠式婴儿车	
38 foot-muff (*Am.* foot-bag) 暖脚袋	
39 play pen 幼儿用围栏	
40 floor of the play pen 围栏底板	
41 building blocks (building bricks) 积木	
42 small child 幼儿，婴儿	
43 bib 围兜	
44 rattle (baby's rattle) 幼儿摇摇响玩具	
45 bootees 幼儿之轻便短靴	

1-12 baby clothes
婴儿服装

1 pram suit
婴儿车装

2 hood
兜帽

3 pram jacket (matinée coat)
婴儿车短上衣

4 pompon (bobble)
绒球；毛球

5 bootees
毛线鞋

6 sleeveless vest
无袖背心

7 envelope-neck vest
无领汗衫

8 wrapover vest
罩衫

9 baby's jacket
婴儿上衣（夹克）

10 rubber baby pants
婴儿橡皮质尿兜裤

11 playsuit
游戏装

12 two-piece suit
两件式套装

13-30 infants' wear
儿童服装

13 child's sundress, a pinafore dress
女孩夏服，一种无袖的便服

14 frilled shoulder strap
有饰边肩带

15 shirred top
可伸缩的上半部

16 sun hat
遮阳帽

17 one-piece jersey suit
上下连身运动装

18 front zip
前拉链

19 catsuit (playsuit)
游戏装

20 motif (appliqué)
图案（缝饰）

21 romper
背心连裤子的衣服

22 playsuit (romper suit)
小孩的游戏装（玩耍服）

23 coverall (sleeper and strampler)
连身睡衣

24 dressing gown (bath robe)
晨衣（浴衣）

25 children's shorts
儿童短裤，吊带裤

26 braces (*Am.* suspenders)
吊带

27 children's T-shirt
儿童（短袖）圆领汗衫

28 jersey dress (knitted dress)
针织衣服

29 embroidery
刺绣

30 children's ankle socks
儿童的（只到足踝的）短袜

31-47 school children's wear
学童服

31 raincoat (loden coat)
雨衣

32 leather shorts (lederhosen)
皮短裤

33 staghorn button
鹿角钮扣

34 braces (*Am.* suspenders)
吊带

35 flap
飞兜

36 girl's dirndl
女孩紧身连衫裙

37 cross lacing
交叉系带

38 snow suit (quilted suit)
防雪装（以羽毛等填缝的服装）

39 quilt stitching (quilting)
褶缝线

40 dungarees (bib and brace)
粗棉布工作服型的童装（围兜和吊带）

41 bib skirt (bib top pinafore)
围兜裙（围兜无袖便服）

42 tights
紧身裤

43 sweater (jumper)
毛衣（上衣）

44 pile jacket
绒面夹克，软毛上衣

45 leggings
护胫套裤

46 girl's skirt
女孩裙子

47 child's jumper
短袖毛衣（衫）

48-68 teenagers' clothes
青少年服装

48 girl's overblouse (overtop)
下摆外露的女上衣

49 slacks
宽松的裤子

50 girl's skirt suit
少女裙装

51 jacket
夹克衫，短上衣

52 skirt
裙子

53 knee-length socks
长统袜

54 girl's coat
女孩外套

55 tie belt
腰带

56 girl's bag
肩袋

57 woollen (*Am.* woolen) hat
羊毛帽

58 girl's blouse
女用衬衫

59 culottes
裤裙

60 boy's trousers
男孩长裤

61 boy's shirt
男孩衬衫

62 anorak
附有风帽的御寒夹克

63 inset pockets
插（口）袋

64 hood drawstring (drawstring)
兜帽束紧带（拉绳）

65 knitted welt
针织的束紧裤口

66 parka coat (parka)
带有兜帽的皮毛外套

67 drawstring (draw cord)
束紧带，拉绳

68 patch pockets
缝贴在外的口袋

1 mink jacket
貂皮袄

2 cowl neck jumper
大围领套头衫（附有领巾之妇女上衣）

3 cowl collar
宽松的围领

4 knitted overtop
针织套头衫

5 turndown collar
翻领（摺领）

6 turn-up (turnover) sleeve
反摺袖

7 polo neck jumper
套头紧领衫

8 pinafore dress
宽罩型洋装

9 blouse with revers collars
翻领上衣（类似衬衫）

10 shirt-waister dress, a button-through dress
单排扣束腰洋装

11 belt
腰带

12 winter dress
冬季洋装

13 piping
衣服上的管状窄条饰缘，滚边

14 cuff
袖口

15 long sleeve
长袖

16 quilted waistcoat
背心型短袄

17 quilt stitching (quilting)
车缝线

18 leather trimming
皮质滚边

19 winter slacks
冬季便裤

20 striped polo jumper
条纹套头紧领衫

21 boiler suit (dungarees, bib and brace)
衫裤相连的工作装（粗棉布做的工作服，围兜和吊带）

22 patch pocket
贴袋

23 front pocket
胸前袋

24 bib
围兜

25 wrapover dress (wrap-around dress)
无袖长袍裙服

26 shirt
衬衫

27 peasant-style dress
农民式服装

28 floral braid
花边饰带

29 tunic (tunic top, tunic dress)
垂至臀部或低於臀部的宽松外衣

30 ribbed cuff
有棱线的袖口

31 quilted design
车缝纹

32 pleated shirt
百褶裙

33 two-piece knitted dress
针织的两件式套装

34 boat neck, a neckline
船形领，领口

35 turn-up
卷袖或袖口翻边

36 kimono sleeve
连肩袖

37 knitted design
针织图案

38 lumber-jacket
伐木者穿的夹克

39 cable pattern
缆纹图样

40 shirt-blouse
衬衫式上衣

41 loop fastening
环扣

42 embroidery
刺绣，绣花

43 stand-up collar
立领

44 cossack trousers
哥萨克型裤子

45 two-piece combination (shirt top and long skirt)
两件式套装（衬衫和长裙）

46 tie (bow)
束腰带（蝴蝶结）

47 decorative facing
衣领饰边

48 cuff slit
袖口开叉

49 side slit
下摆开叉

50 tabard
无袖外衣

51 inverted pleat skirt
对摺裙

52 godet
女裙开叉处所附三角布片（用以显示摺纹）

53 evening gown
晚礼服

54 pleated bell sleeve
带摺喇叭袖

55 party blouse
宴会礼衫

56 party skirt
宴会裙

57 trouser suit (slack suit)
裤装

58 suede jacket
麂皮袄

59 fur trimming
毛皮饰边

60 fur coat (kinds: Persian lamb, broadtail, mink, sable)
毛皮大衣（种类：波斯羔羊皮大衣，粗尾羊皮，貂皮，黑貂皮大衣）

61 winter coat (cloth coat)
冬季大衣

62 fur cuff (fur-trimmed cuff)
毛皮袖口（毛皮装饰袖口）

63 fur collar (fur-trimmed collar)
毛皮领（毛皮装饰领）

64 loden coat
防水大衣

65 cape
披肩

66 toggle fastenings
索环扣

67 loden skirt
防水裙

68 poncho-style coat
斗篷式大衣

69 hood
兜帽，风帽

1 skirt suit
裙装（上衣加裙子的套装）
2 jacket
短上衣，夹克衫
3 skirt
裙子
4 inset pocket
插入式口
5 decorative stitching
装饰缝线
6 dress and jacket combination
礼服和上衣的联合装
7 piping
滚边
8 pinafore dress
围裙式洋装
9 summer dress
无袖夏季洋装
10 belt
腰带
11 two-piece dress
二件式套装
12 belt buckle
腰带扣（装饰扣）
13 wrapover (wrap-around) skirt
单片裙
14 pencil silhouette
铅笔状轮廓，线条
15 shoulder buttons
肩扣
16 batwing sleeve
蝙蝠翼式袖子
17 overdress
外衣
18 kimono yoke
和服式的抵肩
19 tie belt
系腰带
20 summer coat
夏季外衣
21 detachable hood
可分开的风帽
22 summer blouse
夏季短衫
23 lapel
大翻领
24 skirt
裙子
25 front pleat
前摺
26 dirndl (dirndl dress)
紧身连衫裙，阿尔卑斯村女服装（紧胸，褶腰，大裙）
27 puffed sleeve
灯笼袖
28 dirndl necklace
领口花饰
29 dirndl blouse
短衫
30 bodice
紧身胸衣
31 dirndl apron
围裙
32 lace trimming (lace), cotton lace
花边装饰，棉质花边
33 frilled apron
（褶边）饰边围裙
34 frill
饰边，褶边
35 smock overall
工作服，罩衫
36 house frock (house dress)
家居简便洋装
37 poplin jacket
毛葛夹克（短外衣）

38 T-shirt
T 恤，无袖圆领衫
39 ladies' shorts
女士短裤
40 trouser turn-up
裤脚翻折边
41 waistband
腰带，束腰带
42 bomber jacket
轰炸机员式的夹克
43 stretch welt
松紧带镶边
44 Bermuda shorts
百慕达短裤
45 saddle stitching
鞍具式的缝线
46 frill collar
绉褶领
47 knot
装饰花结
48 culotte
裤裙
49 twin set
羊毛外衣与套头绒线衣成套者
50 cardigan
羊毛上衣
51 sweater
毛衣
52 summer (lightweight) slacks
夏季轻便裤
53 jumpsuit
跳伞装
54 turn-up
翻折边
55 zip
拉链
56 patch pocket
贴袋
57 scarf (neckerchief)
领巾，围巾
58 denim suit
斜纹粗布服，牛仔装
59 denim waistcoat
斜纹粗棉布背心，牛仔背心
60 jeans (denims)
牛仔裤
61 overblouse
下摆外露的上衣（不扣于裤内或裙内）
62 turned-up sleeve
卷袖
63 stretch belt
松紧腰带
64 halter top
露背装
65 knitted overtop
针织洋装
66 drawstring waist
束腰绳（带）
67 short-sleeved jumper
短袖运动衫
68 V-neck (vee-neck)
V 型领
69 turndown collar
翻领
70 knitted welt
针织带状镶边
71 shawl
披肩

1-15 ladies' underwear (ladies' underclothes, lingerie)
妇女内衣（贴身衣类）
1 brassière (bra)
乳罩，胸罩
2 pantie-girdle
紧身内裤
3 pantie-corselette
连胸衣的紧身短内裤
4 longline brassière (longline bra)
长线乳罩
5 stretch girdle
有伸缩性短内裤
6 suspender
吊袜带
7 vest
贴身衣，衬衣
8 pantie briefs
紧身三角裤
9 ladies' knee-high stocking
女用中统袜
10 long-legged (long leg) panties
紧身七分内裤
11 long pants
紧身长内裤
12 tights (pantie-hose)
裤袜
13 slip
连身衬裙
14 waist slip
短衬裙
15 bikini briefs
比基尼三角裤
16-21 ladies' nightwear
妇女睡衣裤
16 nightdress (nightgown, nightie)
睡衣
17 pyjamas (*Am.* pajamas)
宽松睡衣裤
18 pyjama top
睡衣
19 pyjama trousers
睡裤
20 housecoat
家居服，长便袍
21 vest and shorts set [for leisure wear and as nightwear]
背心短裤装[休闲服和当为睡衣]
22-29 men's underwear (men's underclothes)
男士内衣裤
22 string vest
网线汗衫
23 string briefs
网线三角裤
24 front panel
正面遮片
25 sleeveless vest
无袖汗衫，背心
26 briefs
男用三角裤
27 trunks
平口内裤
28 short-sleeved vest
短袖汗衫
29 long johns
长内裤
30 braces (*Am.* suspenders)
吊带
31 braces clip
吊带夹子
32-34 men's socks
男士短袜
32 knee-length sock
中统袜

33 elasticated top
松紧袜口
34 long sock
长短袜
35-37 men's nightwear
男士睡衣裤
35 dressing gown
睡袍
36 pyjamas (*Am.* pajamas)
宽松睡衣裤
37 nightshirt
长睡衫
38-47 men's shirts
男士衬衫
38 casual shirt
便衫
39 belt
腰带
40 cravat
围巾
41 tie
领带
42 knot
领结
43 dress shirt
着於礼服下的衬衫
44 frill (frill front)
（衬衫前装饰用的）绉边
45 cuff
袖口
46 cuff link
袖扣
47 bow-tie
蝴蝶领结

1-67 men's fashion
男士时装

1 single-breasted suit, a men's suit
单排扣西装，一种男士西装（服）

2 jacket
（西服的）上装

3 suit trousers
西（装）裤

4 waistcoat (vest)
背心

5 lapel
翻领

6 trouser leg with crease
有摺痕（裤线）的裤管

7 dinner dress, an evening suit
晚礼服

8 silk lapel
丝绸翻领

9 breast pocket
胸前口袋

10 dress handkerchief
外衣手绢，装饰用

11 bow-tie
蝴蝶领结

12 side pocket
侧袋

13 tailcoat (tails), evening dress
燕尾服，晚礼服

14 coat-tail
燕尾

15 white waistcoat (vest)
白色背心

16 white bow-tie
白蝴蝶领结

17 casual suit
便服

18 pocket flap
口袋盖

19 front yoke
前抵肩

20 denim suit
斜纹粗布服（牛仔服）

21 denim jacket
斜纹粗布夹克（牛仔夹克）

22 jeans (denims)
牛仔裤

23 waistband
腰带

24 beach suit
海滩装

25 shorts
短裤

26 short-sleeved jacket
短袖夹克（上衣）

27 tracksuit
运动服

28 tracksuit top with zip
有拉链的运动衫

29 tracksuit bottoms
运动裤

30 cardigan
开襟的羊毛上衣

31 knitted collar
针织领

32 men's short-sleeved pullover
(men's short-sleeved sweater)
短袖套头羊毛衫

33 short-sleeved shirt
短袖衬衫

34 shirt button
衬衫钮扣

35 turn-up
袖口卷边，滚边

36 knitted shirt
针织衬衫

37 casual shirt
便衫

38 patch pocket
贴袋

39 casual jacket
夹克式的短外衣

40 knee-breeches
（长至膝盖的）七分裤，马裤

41 knee strap
裤管束带

42 knee-length sock
中统袜

43 leather jacket
皮夹克

44 bib and brace overalls
有围兜吊带的连身工作服

45 adjustable braces (*Am.* suspenders)
可调整的吊带

46 front pocket
胸前口袋

47 trouser pocket
裤（口）袋

48 fly
拉链或钮扣洞遮盖

49 rule pocket
工具袋

50 check shirt
格子衬衫

51 men's pullover
男士套头衫

52 heavy pullover
厚套头衫

53 knitted waistcoat (vest)
针织毛背心

54 blazer
一种宽松非正式外衣（所用颜色有时系代表某一学校、会社、球队等）

55 jacket button
外衣钮扣

56 overall
宽大的罩衣

57 trenchcoat
有带的风（雨）衣

58 coat collar
衣领

59 coat belt
腰带

60 poplin coat
毛葛大衣

61 coat pocket
大衣口袋

62 fly front
钮扣遮盖正面

63 car coat
短大衣

64 coat button
大衣钮扣

65 scarf
围巾

66 cloth coat
布面大衣

67 glove
手套

1-25 men's beards and hairstyles (haircuts)
男士的胡须和发型

1 long hair worn loose
蓄着披头长发

2 allonge periwig (full-bottomed wig), a wig; *shorter and smoother*: bob wig, toupet
假发（底部尽量张开的假发）；一种较短且较平滑的假发：短辫假发，假发（络）

3 curls
卷发

4 bag wig (purse wig)
囊式假发

5 pigtail wig
辫子式假发；蓄辫假发

6 queue (pigtail)
辫子

7 bow (ribbon)
蝴蝶结（丝带）

8 handlebars (handlebar moustache, *Am.* mustache)
八字胡

9 centre (*Am.* center) parting
中分（头发的分边）

10 goatee (goatee beard), chintuft
山羊胡，下巴上的一撮胡子

11 closely-cropped head of hair (crew cut)
短发（平头）

12 whiskers
腮胡

13 Vandyke beard (stiletto beard, bodkin beard), with waxed moustache (*Am.* mustache)
髭间涂腊的范大克式髭（剑形髭，锥形须）

14 side parting
侧分

15 full beard (circular beard, round beard)
大胡子（环形胡须）

16 tile beard
瓦形胡须

17 shadow
短髭

18 head of curly hair
卷发头

19 military moustache (*Am.* mustache) (English-style moustache)
军人胡（英式髭）

20 partly bald head
局部秃头

21 bald patch
秃头部分

22 bald head
全秃头

23 stubble beard (stubble, short beard bristles)
残须（短且硬的胡子）

24 side-whiskers (sideboards, sideburns)
鬓

25 clean shave
剃光的面颊

26 Afro look (for men and women)
非洲人的发型（男女通用）

27-38 ladies' hairstyles (coiffures, women's and girls' hairstyles)
女士发型（头发式样，妇女和少女的发型）

27 ponytail
马尾巴

28 swept-back hair (swept-up hair, pinned-up hair)
头发向后紧梳成髻的发型

29 bun (chignon)
假髻

30 plaits (bunches)
编辫子

31 chaplet hairstyle (Gretchen style)
花冠式发型（Gretchen 式发型）

32 chaplet (coiled plaits)
花冠（盘绕的发辫）

33 curled hair
卷发

34 shingle (shingled hair, bobbed hair)
短发

35 pageboy style
娃娃头（西瓜皮式）

36 fringe (*Am.* bangs)
刘海

37 earphones
耳机式发型

38 earphone (coiled plait)
耳机发（盘绕的发辫）

1-21 ladies' hats and caps
女士有边帽和无边帽

1 milliner making a hat
制女帽的人

2 hood
帽兜

3 block
帽模

4 decorative pieces
帽饰

5 sombrero
墨西哥帽，宽边帽

6 mohair hat with feathers
带羽饰的毛帽

7 model hat with fancy appliqué
带花饰的模特儿帽

8 linen cap (jockey cap)
亚麻布帽（骑士帽）

9 hat made of thick candlewick yarn
粗烛芯纱所编的帽子

10 woollen (*Am.* woolen) hat (knitted hat)
毛线帽（针织帽）

11 mohair hat
毛帽（安哥拉山羊毛帽）

12 cloche with feathers
带羽毛的钟型帽

13 large men's hat made of sisal with corded ribbon
由琼麻和丝线制的仿男士帽

14 trilby-style hat with fancy ribbon
带丝饰的呢帽

15 soft felt hat
软毡（毛）帽

16 Panama hat with scarf
附有领巾的巴拿马帽

17 peaked mink cap
（有帽尖的）貂皮帽（无边）

18 mink hat
貂皮帽（有边）

19 fox hat with leather top
皮顶狐皮帽

20 mink cap
貂皮帽（无边）

21 slouch hat trimmed with flowers
有花饰的垂边软帽

22-40 men's hats and caps
男士无边和有边帽

22 trilby hat (trilby)
软呢帽

23 loden hat (Alpine hat)
粗绒布帽（阿尔卑斯山帽）

24 felt hat with tassels (Tyrolean hat, Tyrolese hat)
带穗的毡（毛）帽（提洛尔帽）

25 corduroy cap
楞条花布帽（灯心绒帽）

26 woollen (*Am.* woolen) hat
毛线帽

27 beret
贝雷帽（绒质或羊毛制的扁圆无边帽）

28 bowler hat
礼帽

29 peaked cap (yachting cap)
大盘帽（游艇帽）

30 sou'wester (southwester)
风雨天用的防水帽（后面帽缘较宽）

31 fox cap with earflaps
有耳盖的狐皮帽

32 leather cap with fur flaps
有软毛耳盖的皮帽

33 musquash cap
麝鼠皮帽

34 astrakhan cap, a real or imitation astrakhan cap
（苏俄）阿斯特拉罕羔羊皮帽，真品或仿制品

35 boater
硬草帽

36 (grey, *Am.* gray, or black) top hat made of silk taffeta; *collapsible*: crush hat (opera hat, claque)
高顶丝质礼帽；可摺叠而不致损坏的帽（歌剧帽，捧场员帽）

37 sun hat (lightweight hat) made of cloth with small patch pocket
有小贴袋的布质遮阳帽

38 wide-brimmed hat
宽边帽

39 toboggan cap (skiing cap, ski cap)
雪橇帽（滑雪帽）

40 workman's cap
工作帽

1 set of jewellery (*Am.* jewelry)
一套珠宝饰物
2 necklace
项链
3 bracelet
手镯
4 ring
戒指
5 wedding rings
结婚戒指
6 wedding ring box
结婚戒指盒
7 brooch, a pearl brooch
胸针（领针），一种珍珠胸针
8 pearl
珍珠
9 cultured pearl bracelet
人工养殖珍珠手镯
10 clasp, a white gold clasp
扣子，一种白金扣子
11 pendant earrings (drop earrings)
（垂式）耳坠
12 cultured pearl necklace
人工养殖珍珠项链
13 earrings
耳饰
14 gemstone pendant
宝石坠子
15 gemstone ring
宝石戒指
16 choker (collar, neckband)
项圈（颈圈，颈带）
17 bangle
手镯

18 diamond pin
钻石别针
19 modern-style brooches
时髦饰针
20 man's ring
男士戒指
21 cuff links
袖扣
22 tiepin
领带别针
23 diamond ring with pearl
带有珍珠的钻石戒指
24 modern-style diamond ring
时髦的钻石戒指
25 gemstone bracelet
宝石手镯
26 asymmetrical bangle
不对称的手镯（脚镯）
27 asymmetrical ring
不对称的戒指
28 ivory necklace
象牙项链
29 ivory rose
象牙玫瑰花
30 ivory brooch
象牙胸针
31 jewel box (jewel case)
珠宝盒
32 pearl necklace
珍珠项链
33 bracelet watch
手镯表
34 coral necklace
珊瑚项链

35 charms
饰物（护身符）
36 coin bracelet
钱币手镯
37 gold coin
金币
38 coin setting
硬币镶座
39 link
链子
40 signet ring
徽章戒指
41 engraving (monogram)
雕刻（字母组合的图案）
42-86 cuts and forms
各种形状的琢磨
42-71 faceted stones
多刻面石
42-43 standard round cut
标准圆形切割
44 brilliant cut
多角形切割
45 rose cut
玫瑰花式切割
46 flat table
平台形
47 table en cabochon
平台凸形宝石（照天然形状琢磨的宝
石）
48 standard cut
标准切割
49 standard antique cut
标准传统切割

50 rectangular step-cut
长方阶状切割
51 square step-cut
方形阶状切割
52 octagonal step-cut
八边形阶状切割
53 octagonal cross-cut
八边形交叉状切割
54 standard pear-shape
(pendeloque)
标准梨形
55 marquise (navette)
两头尖的卵形宝石
56 standard barrel-shape
标准桶形
57 trapezium step-cut
梯形阶状切割
58 trapezium cross-cut
梯形交叉状切割
59 rhombus step-cut
菱形阶状切割
60-61 triangular step-cut
三角形阶状切割
62 hexagonal step-cut
六边形阶状切割
63 oval hexagonal cross-cut
椭圆六边交叉状切割
64 round hexagonal step-cut
正六边形阶状切割
65 round hexagonal cross-cut
正六边交叉状切割
66 chequer-board cut
棋盘状切割

67 triangle cut
三角形切割
68-71 fancy cuts
华丽精巧的切割
72-77 ring gemstones
戒指宝石
72 oval flat table
椭圆平台型
73 rectangular flat table
长方平台形
74 octagonal flat table
八边平台形
75 barrel-shape
桶形
76 antique table en cabochon
传统平台凸圆形
77 rectangular table en cabochon
长方平台凸圆形
78-81 cabochons
平底凸圆形宝石
78 round cabochon (simple
cabochon)
简单凸圆形
79 high dome (high cabochon)
高拱圆形（高凸圆形）
80 oval cabochon
椭圆凸圆形
81 octagonal cabochon
八边凸圆形
82-86 spheres and pear-shapes
球形和梨形
82 plain sphere
无花饰球形

83 plain pear-shape
无花饰梨形
84 faceted pear-shape
多刻面梨形
85 plain drop
无花饰滴状琢磨
86 faceted briolette
三角形多刻面梨形

1-53 detached house
独立住宅

1 basementt
地下室

2 ground floor (*Am.* first floor)
底楼（[美]一楼）

3 upper floor (first floor, *Am.*
second floor)
上层楼（一楼，[美]二楼）

4 loft
阁楼

5 roof, a gable roof (saddle roof,
saddleback roof)
屋顶，山形屋顶（鞍形屋顶）

6 gutter
屋顶边沟（承霤）

7 ridge
屋脊

8 verge with bargeboards
簷缘板

9 eaves, rafter-supported eaves
屋簷，椽支撑屋簷

10 chimney
烟囱

11 gutter
屋顶边沟（承霤）

12 swan's neck (swan-neck)
鹅颈形导水管

13 rainwater pipe (downpipe, *Am.*
downspout, leader)
雨水管（排水管）

14 vertical pipe, a cast-iron pipe
垂直管，一种铸铁管

15 gable (gable end)
山形墙

16 glass wall
玻璃墙

17 base course (plinth)
墙脚

18 balcony
阳台

19 parapet
栏杆

20 flower box
花架

21 French window (French
windows) opening on to the
balcony
开向阳台的落地窗（法式窗）

22 double casement window
双扇门式玻璃窗

23 single casement window
单扇门式玻璃窗

24 window breast with window sill
有槛窗台

25 lintel (window head)
窗楣（梁）

26 reveal
窗框

27 cellar window (basement
window)
地下室窗子

28 rolling shutter
可卷的活动遮板

29 rolling shutter frame
遮板架

30 window shutter (folding shutter)
窗板（摺叠式窗板）

31 shutter catch
窗板搭扣

32 garage with tool shed
附工具棚的车库

33 espalier
树架

34 batten door (ledged door)
木板门（车棚门）

35 fanlight with mullion and
transom
有櫺的气窗，门顶气窗

36 terrace
露台

37 garden wall with coping stones
铺压顶石的花园墙

38 garden light
园灯

39 steps
台阶

40 rockery (rock garden)
石园

41 outside tap (*Am.* faucet) for the
hose
室外水（管）龙头

42 garden hose
园艺用水管

43 lawn sprinkler
草皮洒水器

44 paddling pool
戏水池

45 stepping stones
踏脚石

46 sunbathing area (lawn)
日光浴区（草地）

47 deck-chair
轻便椅，摺叠式躺椅

48 sunshade (garden parasol)
遮阳伞（花园阳伞）

49 garden chair
花园靠椅

50 garden table
花园桌

51 frame for beating carpets
拍地毯用的架子

52 garage driveway
车库车道

53 fence, a wooden fence
栅栏，木栅栏

54-57 housing estate (housing
development)
住宅区（住宅开发区）

54 house on a housing estate (on a
housing development)
住宅区的房子

55 pent roof (penthouse roof)
单斜面屋顶

56 dormer (dormer window)
屋顶窗（天窗）

57 garden
花园

58-63 terraced house 'one of a row
of terraced houses', **stepped**
台阶形的排式住宅

58 front garden
宅前花园

59 hedge
灌木树篱

60 pavement (*Am.* sidewalk,
walkway)
人行道

61 street (road)
街道（路）

62 street lamp (street light)
街灯

63 litter bin (*Am.* litter basket)
垃圾箱

64-68 house divided into two flats
(*Am.* house divided into two
apartments, duplex house)
双户公寓（住宅）

64 hip (hipped) roof
四斜面屋顶

65 front door
前门

66 front steps
前门台阶

67 canopy
雨遮

68 flower window (window for
house plants)
花窗

**69-71 pair of semi-detached houses
divided into four flats** (*Am.*
apartments.
双併四户公寓

69 balcony
阳台

70 sun lounge (*Am.* sun parlor)
日光休息室

71 awning (sun blind, sunshade)
遮阳篷

72-76 block of flats (*Am.* apartment
building, apartment house) with
access balconies
含附属阳台的公寓大楼

72 staircase
楼梯间

73 balcony
阳台

74 studio flat (*Am.* studio
apartment)
套房

75 sun roof, a sun terrace
日光屋顶

76 open space
公共露天场地

77-81 multi-storey block of flats
(*Am.* multistory apartment
building, multistory apartment
house)
多层公寓

77 flat roof
公寓屋顶

78 pent roof (shed roof, lean-to
roof)
单斜面屋顶

79 garage
车库

80 pergola
藤架

81 staircase window
楼梯间窗户

82 high-rise block of flats (*Am.*
high-rise apartment building,
high-rise apartment house)
高楼（层）公寓大厦

83 penthouse
顶楼小屋

84-86 weekend house, a timber
house
渡周末的房子，木头房子

84 horizontal boarding
横钉的木板壁

85 natural stone base course
(natural stone plinth)
天然石墙脚

86 strip windows (ribbon windows)
一个接一个成排的窗户

1-29 attic
阁楼，顶楼
1 roof cladding (roof covering)
屋顶复盖层
2 skylight
天窗
3 gangway
通路板
4 cat ladder (roof ladder)
屋顶梯子，爬梯
5 chimney
烟囱
6 roof hook
屋顶钩
7 dormer window (dormer)
阁楼窗户
8 snow guard (roof guard)
防雪板（屋顶防护装置）
9 gutter
屋顶边沟（承霤）
10 rainwater pipe (downpipe, Am.
downspout, leader)
雨水管（排水管）
11 eaves
屋檐
12 pitched roof
斜屋顶
13 trapdoor
活板门
14 hatch
天花板入口
15 ladder
梯子
16 stile
梯子竖框
17 rung
梯子脚踏横木
18 loft (attic)
阁楼
19 wooden partition
木板壁
20 lumber room door (boxroom
door)
储藏室门
21 padlock
挂锁，扣锁
22 hook [for washing line]
（晒衣绳的）挂钩
23 clothes line (washing line)
晒衣绳
24 expansion tank for boiler
锅炉的膨胀槽
25 wooden steps and balustrade
木梯及扶手栏杆
26 string (Am. stringer)
楼梯斜梁
27 step
踏板
28 handrail (guard rail)
扶手
29 baluster
栏杆柱
30 lightning conductor (lightning
rod)
避雷针
31 **chimney sweep** (Am. chimney
sweeper)
烟囱清理者
32 brush with weight
带重锤的刷子
33 shoulder iron
肩铁
34 sack for soot
煤尘收集袋
35 flue brush
（烟囱的）通烟道清洁刷

36 broom (besom)
扫帚
37 broomstick (broom handle)
扫帚柄（扫帚把手）
**38-81 hot-water heating system, full
central heating**
热水暖气系统，完全中央供暖装置
38-43 boiler room
锅炉房
38 coke-fired central heating system
烧焦炭的中央暖气系统
39 ash box door (Am. cleanout
door)
炭灰箱门（美：清灰门）
40 flueblock
暖气通气道
41 poker
火钳，拨火棒
42 rake
拨灰耙子
43 coal shovel
煤铲
**44-60 oil-fired central heating
system**
烧油中央暖气系统
44 oil tank
油槽
45 manhole
检修出入孔
46 manhole cover
检修出入孔盖
47 tank inlet
油槽入口，给油口
48 dome cover
圆盖
49 tank bottom valve
油槽底阀
50 fuel oil (heating oil)
燃料油
51 air-bleed duct
通气管
52 air vent cap
排气孔盖
53 oil level pipe
油位管，油量计管
54 oil gauge (Am. gage)
油量计
55 suction pipe
吸油管
56 return pipe
回油管
57 central heating furnace (oil
heating furnace)
中央暖气炉（烧油暖气炉）
58-60 oil burner
燃油器
58 fan
风扇，送风机
59 electric motor
电动马达
60 covered pilot light
有盖指示灯（点火用的指示灯）
61 charging door
进料门
62 inspection window
检查窗
63 water gauge (Am. gage)
水量计，水压计
64 furnace thermometer
炉内温度计
65 bleeder
排水孔
66 furnace bed
炉床（台）
67 control panel
控制板

68 hot water tank (boiler)
热水槽（锅炉）
69 overflow pipe (overflow)
溢流管
70 safety valve
安全阀
71 main distribution pipe
主配管
72 lagging
隔热层
73 valve
阀，气门
74 flow pipe
流入管
75 regulating valve
调节阀
76 radiator
散热器
77 radiator rib
散热片
78 room thermostat
室内温度调节器
79 return pipe (return)
回流管
80 return pipe [in two-pipe system]
[双管系统中的]回流管
81 smoke outlet (smoke extract)
排烟口

1 housewife
家庭主妇
2 refrigerator (fridge, *Am.* icebox)
冰箱
3 refrigerator shelf
冰箱搁板（架）
4 salad drawer
蔬菜抽屉
5 frozen food compartment
食品冷冻室
6 bottle rack (in storage door)
瓶架（在贮藏门内）
7 upright freezer
立式冷冻库
8 wall cupboard, a kitchen
cupboard
壁式碗橱，厨房碗橱
9 base unit
底层设备
10 cutlery drawer
餐具抽屉
11 working top
工作桌面
12-17 cooker unit
烹调（炊）具
12 electric cooker (*also:* gas cooker)
电炉（另有：煤气炉）
13 oven
烤箱
14 oven window
烤箱窗
15 hotplate (automatic high-speed
plate)
热板（自动高速加热板）
16 kettle (whistling kettle)
水壶（鸣笛壶）

17 cooker hood
排油烟机
18 pot holder
罐锅壶等的托垫
19 pot holder rack
托垫挂架
20 kitchen clock
厨房钟
21 timer
定时器
22 hand mixer
手搅拌器
23 whisk
（蛋，奶油的）搅拌器
24 electric coffee grinder (with
rotating blades)
电动咖啡研磨机（带旋转刀片）
25 lead
电线
26 wall socket
墙上插座
27 corner unit
角落装置
28 revolving shelf
旋转架
29 pot (cooking pot)
锅
30 jug
（有把手的）水壶
31 spice rack
调味品架
32 spice jar
调味品瓶
33-36 sink unit
流理设备
33 dish drainer
盘碟滴水架

34 tea plate
茶盘
35 sink
洗物槽
36 water tap (*Am.* faucet) (mixer
tap, *Am.* mixing faucet)
自来水龙头（混合水龙头）
37 pot plant, a foliage plant
盆景，一种观赏植物
38 coffee maker
咖啡（煮）壶
39 kitchen lamp
厨房灯
40 dishwasher (dishwashing
machine)
洗碟机
41 dish rack
盘碟架
42 dinner plate
餐盘
43 kitchen chair
厨房椅子（靠背椅）
44 kitchen table
厨房桌

1 general-purpose roll holder
with kitchen roll (paper towels)
附有厨房卷纸的通用卷纸托架

2 set of wooden spoons
木匙组

3 mixing spoon
搅拌匙

4 frying pan
平底锅

5 thermos jug
热水瓶

6 set of bowls
碗组

7 cheese dish with glass cover
附玻璃盖的乳酪盘

8 three-compartment dish
三格盘子

9 lemon squeezer
搾柠檬器

10 whistling kettle
鸣笛水壶

11 whistle
笛

12-16 pan set
锅组

12 pot (cooking pot)
烹饪锅

13 lid
锅盖

14 casserole dish
有盖烤锅

15 milk pot
牛奶罐

16 saucepan
长柄有盖的深锅

17 immersion heater
浸入式加热器

18 corkscrew [with levers]
（有操纵杆的）拔塞钻

19 juice extractor
水果、蔬菜等的液汁抽出器

20 tube clamp (tube clip)
管夹（管钳）

21 pressure cooker
压力锅（快锅）

22 pressure valve
压力阀

23 fruit preserver
水果保存器

24 removable rack
活动架

25 preserving jar
保存罐

26 rubber ring
橡皮圈

27 spring form
弹性箍

28 cake tin
饼模（盒型）

29 cake tin
饼模（盆型）

30 toaster
烤面包机

31 rack for rolls
面包卷架

32 rotisserie
烤肉箱

33 spit
烤肉叉

34 electric waffle iron
电气烤饼铁模

35 sliding-weight scales
滑动砝码秤

36 sliding weight
滑动砝码

37 scale pan
秤盘

38 food slicer
食物切片机

39 mincer (*Am.* meat chopper)
绞肉机

40 blades
绞肉机用的刀片

41 chip pan
炸马铃薯锅

42 basket
篮，筐

43 potato chipper
马铃薯切片器

44 yoghurt maker
凝态发酵乳制造器

45 mixer
搅拌器

46 blender
混合器

47 bag sealer
塑胶袋封口器

1-29 hall (entrance hall)
门厅（进门厅）
1 coat rack
衣架
2 coat hook
挂衣钩
3 coat hanger
挂衣架
4 rain cape
雨披肩（雨斗篷）
5 walking stick
手杖
6 hall mirror
门厅镜子
7 telephone
电话
8 chest of drawers for shoes, etc.
鞋柜
9 drawer
抽屉
10 seat
坐台
11 ladies' hat
妇女宽边帽
12 telescopic umbrella
折伞
13 tennis rackets (tennis racquets)
网球拍
14 umbrella stand
雨伞架
15 umbrella
雨伞
16 shoes
鞋

17 briefcase
公事包
18 fitted carpet
地毯
19 fuse box
保险丝盒
20 miniature circuit breaker
小型断路器
21 tubular steel chair
钢管靠背椅
22 stair light
楼梯灯
23 handrail
扶手
24 step
阶梯
25 front door
前门
26 door frame
门框
27 door lock
门锁
28 door handle
门把手
29 spyhole
探视孔，猫眼（门上窥视的小孔）

1 **wall units**
   各种壁橱柜
2 **side wall**
   侧壁
3 **bookshelf**
   书架
4 **row of books**
   成排的书
5 **display cabinet unit**
   摆饰橱
6 **cupboard base unit**
   橱柜底座部分
7 **cupboard unit**
   橱柜
8 **television set (TV set)**
   电视机
9 **stereo system (stereo equipment)**
   立体音响装置
10 **speaker (loudspeaker)**
   喇叭，扬声器
11 **pipe rack**
   烟斗架
12 **pipe**
   烟斗
13 **globe**
   地球仪
14 **brass kettle**
   铜壶
15 **telescope**
   望远镜
16 **mantle clock**
   有罩的钟
17 **bust**
   半身雕塑

18 **encyclopaedia [in several volumes]**
   百科全书[多卷本]
19 **room divider**
   室内分隔设计
20 **drinks cupboard**
   饮料柜（酒柜）
21-26 **upholstered suite (seating group)**
   家具组（坐椅组合）
21 **armchair**
   扶手椅
22 **arm**
   扶手
23 **seat cushion (cushion)**
   坐垫
24 **settee**
   有靠背的长椅（中型沙发）
25 **back cushion**
   背垫，靠垫
26 **[round] corner section**
   [圆形]拐角部分
27 **scatter cushion**
   小块的垫子
28 **coffee table**
   咖啡桌
29 **ashtray**
   烟灰缸
30 **tray**
   托盘
31 **whisky (whiskey) bottle**
   威士忌瓶酒
32 **sode water bottle (soda bottle)**
   汽水瓶，苏打水瓶

33-34 **dining set**
   用餐桌椅
33 **dining table**
   餐桌
34 **chair**
   椅子
35 **net curtain**
   网状帘子
36 **indoor plants (houseplants)**
   室内植物

1 wardrobe(*Am.* clothes closet)
  衣柜，衣橱
2 linen shelf
  放置衬衣床单等等的搁板
3 cane chair
  藤椅
4-13 **double bed** (*sim.*: double divan)
  双人床（类似：双人睡椅）
4 - 6 **bedstead**
  床架
4 foot of the bed
  床脚板
5 bed frame
  床架（框）
6 headboard
  床头板
7 bedspread
  床罩
8 duvet, a quilted duvet
  羽毛被；棉被
9 sheet, a linen sheet
  被单，一种以亚麻布制成的被单
10 mattress, a foam mattress with drill tick
  床垫，一种斜纹布包面的泡沫床垫
11 [wedge-shaped] bolster
  楔形垫枕
12-13 **pillow**
  枕头
12 pillowcase (pillowslip)
  枕（头）套
13 tick
  褥套

14 bookshelf [attached to the headboard]
  床头板上的书架
15 reading lamp
  阅读灯
16 electric alarm clock
  电子闹钟
17 bedside cabinet
  床头柜
18 drawer
  抽屉
19 bedroom lamp
  寝室灯
20 picture
  画
21 picture frame
  画框
22 bedside rug
  床边小地毯
23 fitted carpet
  地毯
24 dressing stool
  梳妆凳子
25 dressing table
  梳妆柜
26 perfume spray
  香水喷雾器
27 perfume bottle
  香水瓶
28 powder box
  粉盒
29 dressing-table mirror (mirror)
  梳妆台镜

1-11 dinning set
进餐家具
1 dining table
餐桌
2 table leg
桌脚
3 table top
桌面
4 place mat
餐具垫
5 place (place setting, cover)
一人分的一套（副）餐具
6 soup plate (deep plate)
汤盆（深盆）
7 dinner plate
西餐盘
8 soup tureen
有盖汤盆
9 wineglass
高脚杯，小酒杯
10 dining chair
餐椅
11 seat
（椅子的）座部
12 lamp (pendant lamp)
灯（吊灯）
13 curtains
窗帘
14 net curtain
网状窗帘
15 curtain rail
窗帘轨（窗帘横杆）
16 carpet
地毯

17 wall unit
墙壁挂橱
18 glass door
玻璃门
19 shelf
板架
20 sideboard
餐具柜
21 cutlery drawer
刀叉（餐具）抽屉
22 linen drawer
餐巾/桌巾抽屉
23 base
柜子底座，基座
24 round tray
圆托盘
25 pot plant
盆栽
26 china cabinet (display cabinet)
瓷器橱（陈列橱）
27 coffee set (coffee service)
咖啡组（整套咖啡用具）
28 coffee pot
咖啡壶
29 coffee cup
咖啡杯
30 saucer
碟
31 milk jug
牛奶壶
32 sugar bowl
（有盖和柄的）糖罐
33 dinner set(dinner service)
成套餐具

1 **dining table**
　餐桌
2 **tablecloth, a damask cloth**
　桌布，一种花缎桌布
3-12 place (place setting, cover)
　一副餐具（餐具摆设）
3 **bottom plate**
　底盘（垫盘）
4 **dinner plate**
　餐盘
5 **deep plate** (soup plate)
　深盆（汤盆）
6 **dessert plate** (dessert bowl)
　甜点盘（甜点碗）
7 **knife and fork**
　刀和叉
8 **fish knife and fork**
　吃鱼用的刀和叉
9 **serviette** (napkin, table napkin)
　餐巾
10 **serviette ring** (napkin ring)
　套餐巾的小环
11 **knife rest**
　刀叉台
12 **wineglasses**
　酒杯，玻璃酒杯
13 **place card**
　（宴会等的）席次牌
14 **soup ladle**
　汤杓
15 **soup tureen** (tureen)
　汤盆（有盖的）
16 **candelabra**
　装饰用的支状大烛台

17 **sauceboat** (gravy boat)
　船形调味汁容器
18 **sauce ladle** (gravy ladle)
　调味杓
19 **table decoration**
　餐桌装饰
20 **bread basket**
　面包篮
21 **roll**
　小圆面包
22 **slice of bread**
　面包片
23 **salad bowl**
　沙拉碗
24 **salad servers**
　整套沙拉用器
25 **vegetable dish**
　蔬菜盆
26 **meat plate** (*Am.* meat platter)
　肉盘
27 **roast meat** (roast)
　烤肉
28 **fruit dish**
　水果碟
29 **fruit bowl**
　水果盆
30 **fruit** (stewed fruit)
　水果（泡於糖水中的水果）
31 **potato dish**
　马铃薯盆
32 **serving trolley**
　服务手推车（上菜小柏车）

33 **vegetable plate** (*Am.* vegetable platter)
　蔬菜盘
34 **toast**
　吐司
35 **cheeseboard**
　乳酪板
36 **butter dish**
　奶油碟
37 **open sandwich**
　切开的三明治
38 **filling**
　三明治所夹的食品
39 **sandwich**
　三明治
40 **fruit bowl**
　水果盘
41 **almonds** (*also:* potato crisps, peanuts)
　杏仁（马铃薯片，花生）
42 **oil and vinegar bottle**
　油瓶和醋瓶
43 **ketchup** (catchup, catsup)
　蕃茄酱
44 **sideboard**
　餐具架
45 **electric hotplate**
　电热器
46 **corkscrew**
　拔塞钻
47 **crown cork bottle-opener** (crown cork opener), a bottle-opener
　开瓶器

48 liqueur decanter
盛烈性甜酒的细颈酒瓶
49 nutcrackers (nutcracker)
胡桃钳
50 knife
餐刀
51 handle
刀柄
52 tang (tongue)
刀根（舌榫）
53 ferrule
金属箍
54 blade
刀刃
55 bolster
承板
56 back
刀背
57 edge (cutting edge)
刃口，刀口
58 fork
叉子
59 handle
叉柄
60 prong (tang, tine)
叉尖
61 spoon; here: dessert spoon
匙；此指：吃甜点用汤匙
62 handle
匙柄
63 bowl
匙的凹处
64 fish knife
（吃鱼用的）刀

65 fish fork
（吃鱼用的）叉
66 dessert spoon (fruit spoon)
吃甜点用的匙（水果匙）
67 salad spoon
沙拉匙
68 salad fork
沙拉叉
69-70 carving set (serving cutlery)
切肉用的刀叉（上菜用的刀叉用具）
69 carving knife
分切刀
70 serving fork
上菜叉
71 fruit knife
水果刀
72 cheese knife
乳酪刀
73 butter knife
奶油刀
74 vegetable spoon, a serving spoon
蔬菜上菜用匙
75 potato server (serving spoon for potatoes)
马铃薯上菜用匙
76 cocktail fork
鸡尾叉（西餐头道开胃食品所用的叉）
77 asparagus server (asparagus slice)
芦笋铲
78 sardine server
沙丁鱼叉
79 lobster fork
龙虾叉

80 oyster fork
牡蛎叉
81 caviare knife
抹鱼子酱用的刀
82 white wine glass
白葡萄酒杯
83 red wine glass
红葡萄酒杯
84 sherry glass (madeira glass)
雪莉酒酒杯
85-86 champagne glasses
香槟酒酒杯
85 tapered glass
锥形杯
86 champagne glass, a crystal glass
香槟水晶杯
87 rummer
大酒杯
88 brandy glass
白兰地酒杯
89 liqueur glass
（具甜味而芳香的烈）酒杯
90 spirit glass
烈酒酒杯
91 beer glass
啤酒杯

1 wall units (shelf units)
壁橱架设置（壁架）

2 wardrobe door (*Am.* clothes closet door)
衣橱门

3 body
壁橱/架本体

4 side wall
侧墙

5 trim
(壁架的)装饰横木

6 two-door cupboard unit
双门碗柜

7 bookshelf unit (bookcase unit) [with glass door]
（有玻璃门的）书柜

8 books
书

9 display cabinet
陈列橱

10 card index boxes
索引卡箱（盒）

11 drawer
抽屉

12 decorative biscuit tin
装饰的饼乾盒

13 soft toy animal
软的玩具动物

14 television set (TV set)
电视机

15 records (discs)
唱片

16 bed unit
床、床铺

17 scatter cushion
小块软垫

18 bed unit drawer
床铺抽屉

19 bed unit shelf
床铺架

20 magazines
杂志

21 desk unit (writing unit)
书桌（写字柏）

22 desk
书桌

23 desk mat (blotter)
书桌上的衬垫（吸墨纸）

24 table lamp
柏灯

25 wastepaper basket
废纸篓

26 desk drawer
书桌抽屉

27 desk chair
椅子

28 arm
扶手，靠手

29 kitchen unit
厨房设备

30 wall cupboard
壁式碗碟柜（橱）

31 cooker hood
抽油烟机

32 electric cooker
电炉

33 refrigerator (fridge, *Am.* icebox)
冰箱

34 dining table
餐桌

35 table runner
装饰用的狭长桌布

36 oriental carpet
东方地毯

37 standard lamp
落地灯

1 **children's bed, a bunk-bed**
儿童床，（一种附梯子的）双层床
2 **storage box**
贮存箱
3 **mattress**
床垫
4 **pillow**
枕头
5 **ladder**
梯子
6 **soft toy elephant, a cuddly toy animal**
柔软玩具象，（儿童喜欢抱着睡觉的）玩具动物
7 **soft toy dog**
软质玩具狗
8 **cushion**
垫子
9 **fashion doll**
洋娃娃
10 **doll's pram**
玩具娃娃车
11 **sleeping doll**
睡觉的洋娃娃
12 **canopy**
车篷
13 **blackboard**
黑板
14 **counting beads**
算珠
15 **toy horse for rocking and pulling**
摇摆和拖拉用的玩具木马
16 **rockers**
（摇椅、摇篮下装设的）弧状底部
17 **children's book**
儿童书
18 **compendium of games**
几种游戏
19 **ludo**
一种骰子游戏
20 **chessboard**
供盘
21 **children's cupboard**
儿童用的小柜子
22 **linen drawer**
放置毛巾、床单等的抽屉
23 **drop-flap writing surface**
拆摺写字板
24 **notebook (exercise book)**
笔记本（练习簿）
25 **school books**
教科书
26 **pencil** (*also:* crayon, felt tip pen, ballpoint pen)
铅笔（另有：蜡笔，毛笔，原子笔）
27 **toy shop**
（扮家家酒用的）玩具店
28 **counter**
柜台
29 **spice rack**
（玩具）调味品架
30 **display**
陈列品
31 **assortment of sweets (*Am.* candies)**
什锦糖果
32 **bag of sweets (*Am.* candies)**
糖果袋
33 **scales**
磅秤
34 **cash register**
现金出纳机
35 **toy telephone**
玩具电话
36 **shop shelves (goods shelves)**
商品架（货物架）
37 **wooden train set**
木制火车组
38 **dump truck, a toy lorry (toy truck)**
倾卸车，一种玩具卡车
39 **tower crane**
塔式起重机玩具
40 **concrete mixer**
混凝土搅拌机玩具
41 **large soft toy dog**
大型柔软玩具狗
42 **dice cup**
骰子杯

1-20 pre-school education
学龄前（儿童）教育（托儿所教育）
1 nursery teacher
幼稚园（托儿所）教师
2 nursery child
幼稚园（托儿所）儿童
3 handicraft
（手工艺品）劳作作品
4 glue
胶水，粘胶
5 watercolour painting (*Am.* watercolor)
水彩画
6 paintbox
颜料盒
7 paintbrush
画笔
8 glass of water
玻璃水杯
9 jigsaw puzzle (puzzle)
拼图玩具
10 jigsaw puzzle piece
拼图玩具块（片）
11 coloured (*Am.* colored) pencils (wax crayons)
彩色笔（蜡笔）
12 modelling (*Am.* modeling) clay (plasticine)
制模粘土（塑像用粘土）
13 clay figures (plasticine figures)
粘土塑像
14 modelling (*Am.* modeling) board
制模板
15 chalk (blackboard chalk)
粉笔（黑板粉笔）
16 blackboard
黑板

17 counting blocks
计算块
18 felt pen (felt tip pen)
毛笔（毛尖笔）
19 shapes game
造型游戏
20 group of players
一小组游戏者
21-32 toys
玩具
21 building and filling cubes
建造和填塞用的立体方块
22 construction set
积木组件
23 children's books
儿童书
24 doll's pram, a wicker pram
娃娃车，柳条童车
25 baby doll
婴儿娃娃
26 canopy
娃娃车篷
27 building bricks (building blocks)
积木砖（积木块）
28 wooden model building
木制模型建筑物
29 wooden train set
木制火车组
30 rocking teddy bear
摇动玩具熊
31 doll's pushchair
玩具娃娃推车
32 fashion doll
流行玩具娃娃
33 child of nursery school age
幼稚园儿童

34 cloakroom
衣帽间，寄物处

1 bath
浴缸，澡盆
2 mixer tap (*Am.* mixing faucet)
for hot and cold water.
冷热水混合的水龙头
3 foam bath (bubble bath)
泡沫澡水
4 toy duck
玩具鸭
5 bath salts
浴盐
6 bath sponge (sponge)
洗澡海绵
7 bidet
净身盆
8 towel rail
毛巾架
9 terry towel
毛巾
10 toilet roll holder (*Am.* bathroom tissue holder)
卫生纸卷架
11 toilet paper (*coll.* loo paper, *Am.* bathroom tissue), a roll of crepe paper
卫生纸，一种绉纹纸卷
12 toilet (lavatory, W.C., *coll.* loo)
厕所，洗手间
13 toilet pan (toilet bowl)
抽水马桶
14 toilet lid with terry cover
铺绒布的马桶盖
15 toilet seat
马桶坐
16 cistern
水箱

17 flushing lever
冲水杆
18 pedestal mat
基座垫（脚垫）
19 tile
瓷砖
20 ventilator (extraction vent)
通风孔，换气窗（抽气孔）
21 soap dish
肥皂碟
22 soap
肥皂
23 hand towel
手巾，毛巾
24 washbasin
洗脸盆
25 overflow
溢流口（孔）
26 hot and cold water tap
冷热水龙头
27 washbasin pedestal with trap (anti-syphon trap)
装有防臭 U 型管的洗脸盆基座
28 tooth glass (tooth mug)
漱口杯
29 electric toothbrush
电动牙刷
30 detachable brush heads
可折卸的牙刷头
31 mirrored bathroom cabinet
洗手间的小镜橱
32 fluorescent lamp
日光灯
33 mirror
镜子
34 drawer
抽屉

35 powder box
粉盒
36 mouthwash
漱口药（剂）
37 electric shaver
电动刮胡刀
38 aftershave lotion
刮脸后用的化妆水
39 shower cubicle
淋浴室（间）
40 shower curtain
淋浴（间）门帘
41 adjustable shower head
可调垫的淋浴莲蓬头
42 shower nozzle
淋浴喷咀
43 shower adjustment rail
淋浴调节杆
44 shower base
淋浴间的地板
45 waste pipe (overflow)
废水管（溢流管）
46 bathroom mule
浴室拖鞋
47 bathroom scales
浴室磅秤
48 bath mat
浴室防滑垫子（踏干脚用）
49 medicine cabinet
药柜

1-20 irons
熨烫用具

1 electric ironing machine
电熨烫机

2 electric foot switch
电动脚踏开关

3 roller covering
滚筒罩

4 ironing head
熨烫头

5 sheet
被单

6 electric iron, a lightweight iron
电熨斗（轻便型熨斗）

7 sole-plate
（熨斗）底板

8 temperature selector
调温选择器

9 handle (iron handle)
熨斗手把

10 pilot light
指示灯

11 steam, spray, and dry iron
蒸汽、喷雾和干熨熨斗

12 filling inlet
注水口

13 spray nozzle for damping the washing
喷湿衣物的喷咀

14 steam hole (steam slit)
蒸汽口（孔）

15 ironing table
熨斗架

16 ironing board (ironing surface)
熨烫板

17 ironing-board cover
熨烫板罩布

18 iron well
熨斗搁架

19 aluminium (*Am.* aluminum) frame
铝架

20 sleeve board
烫袖板

21 linen bin
待洗衣物箱

22 dirty linen
脏的衣物

23-34 washing machines and driers
洗衣机和乾衣机

23 washing machine (automatic washing machine)
洗衣机（自动洗衣机）

24 washing drum
洗衣槽

25 safety latch (safety catch)
安全卡梢（安全掣子）

26 program selector control
程序选择控制器

27 front soap dispenser 'with several compartments'
正面洗涤剂分配器[有数格]

28 tumble drier
滚转乾衣机

29 drum
滚槽

30 front door with ventilation slits
设通风细缝的前门

31 work top
工作台面

32 airer
晾衣架

33 clothes line (washing line)
晒衣绳

34 extending airer
摺叠式晾衣架

35 stepladder (steps), an aluminium (*Am.* aluminum) ladder
四脚梯，一种铝制梯子

36 stile
梯子两侧的直条框

37 prop
支柱

38 tread (rung)
梯架踏板

39-43 shoe care utensils
鞋子的保养工具

39 tin of shoe polish
鞋油盒

40 shoe spray, an impregnating spray
鞋油喷雾器，一种浸润的喷雾器

41 shoe brush
鞋刷

42 brush for applying polish
鞋油刷

43 tube of shoe polish
鞋油膏

44 clothes brush
衣刷

45 carpet brush
地毯刷

46 broom
地板刷

47 bristles
刷毛

48 broom head
刷头

49 broomstick (broom handle)
地板刷杆（刷把）

50 screw thread
螺纹

51 washing-up brush
洗涤刷

52 pan (dust pan)
畚斗（畚箕）

53-86 floor and carpet cleaning
地板和地毯的清扫

53 brush
毛刷

54 bucket (pail)
水桶

55 floor cloth (cleaning rag)
擦地板布（清洗抹布）

56 scrubbing brush
清洁刷子

57 carpet sweeper
地毯清扫器

58 upright vacuum cleaner
立式吸尘器

59 changeover switch
转换开关

60 swivel head
旋转接头

61 bag-full indicator
（吸尘）袋满指示器

62 dust bag container
灰尘袋容器

63 handle
把手

64 tubular handle
管式把手

65 flex hook
电线挂钩

66 wound-up flex
缠绕好的电线

67 all-purpose nozzle
多功能吸咀（喷咀）

68 cylinder vacuum cleaner
筒式吸尘器

69 swivel coupling
旋转接头（连接器）

70 extension tube
延长管

71 floor nozzle (*sim.:* carpet beater nozzle)
地板吸尘咀（类似：地毯拍打器的吸咀）

72 suction control
吸尘控制

73 bag-full indicator
袋满指示器

74 sliding fingertip suction control
指推式吸尘开关

75 hose (suction hose)
软管（吸尘用软管）

76 combined carpet sweeper and shampooer
地毯清扫和洗涤两用的机器

77 electric lead (flex)
电线

78 plug socket
插座

79 carpet beater head (*sim.:* shampooing head, brush head)
地毯的拍打器头（类似：洗涤器头，毛刷头）

80 all-purpose vacuum cleaner (dry and wet operation)
万能真空吸尘器（干湿两用）

81 castor
脚轮

82 motor unit
马达装置

83 lid clip
盖夹

84 coarse dirt hose
粗脏物软管

85 special accessory (special attachment) for coarse dirt
粗脏物专用附件

86 dust container
灰尘容器

87 shopper (shopping trolley)
购物车（购物用的手推车）

1-35 flower garden
花园

1 pergola
绿廊，花架，蔓藤花棚，藤架

2 deck-chair
折叠式躺椅

3 lawn rake (wire-tooth rake)
草耙子（铁丝耙子）

4 garden rake
花园耙子

5 Virginia creeper (American ivy, woodbine), a climbing plant (climber, creeper)
美国藤，五叶地锦（一种生长在北美的爬山虎类植物，忍冬），攀缘植物（匍匐植物）

6 rockey (rock garden)
岩石园（岩石花园）

7 rock plants; *varieties:* stonecrop (wall pepper), houseleek, dryas, aubretia
岩生植物，种植：景天，石莲花，仙女木属，南庭荠属

8 pampas grass
蒲草

9 garden hedge
绿篱

10 blue spruce
云杉

11 hydrangeas
八仙花，绣球花

12 oak (oak tree)
橡树

13 birch (birch tree)
桦木（白桦树）

14 garden path
花园小路

15 edging
（小路）边饰

16 garden pond
花园池塘

17 flagstone (stone slab)
石板

18 water lily
睡莲

19 tuberous begonias
球根秋海棠

20 dahlias
大丽花，天竺牡丹

21 watering can (*Am.* sprinkling can)
喷水壶（洒水壶）

22 weeding hoe
除草锄

23 lupin
羽扁豆

24 marguerite (oxeye daisies, white oxeye daisies)
茼莴菊，木春菊（牛眼菊，春白菊）

25 standard rose
嫁接於树干上的玫瑰（花）

26 gerbera
非洲菊，大丁菊属，大丁草

27 iris
鸢尾属，鸢尾，蝴蝶花

28 gladioli
唐菖蒲，剑兰

29 chrysanthemums
菊花

30 poppy
罂粟花

31 blazing star
矮百合

32 snapdragon (antirrhinum)
金鱼草，龙头花，龙口花

33 lawn
草地

34 dandelion
蒲公英

35 sunflower
向日葵

1-32 allotment (fruit and
vegetable garden)
果菜园
1, 2, 16, 17, 29 dwarf fruit trees
(espaliers, espalier fruit trees)
矮干果树（树篱，篱式果树）
1 quadruple cordon, a wall
espalier
四干形（果树），一种树篱
2 vertical cordon
直立单干形（果树）
3 tool shed (garden shed)
工具棚（园内小屋）
4 water butt (water barrel)
水桶
5 climbing plant (climber, creeper,
rambler)
攀缘植物（攀缘植物，匍匐植物，蔓生
植物）
6 compost heap
堆肥
7 sunflower
向日葵
8 garden ladder (ladder)
果园梯子
9 perennial (flowering perennial)
多年生植物（开花的多年生植物）
10 garden fence (paling fence,
paling)
果菜园栅栏（木栅，园篱）
11 standard berry tree
嫁接於树干上的浆果树

12 climbing rose (rambling rose) on
the trellis arch
攀缘在拱架上的蔷薇（蔓生蔷薇）
13 bush rose (standard rose tree)
丛生性蔷薇（嫁接於树干上的蔷薇）
14 summerhouse (garden house)
凉亭（园舍）
15 Chinese lantern (paper lantern)
中国式灯笼（纸灯笼）
16 pyramind tree (pyramidal tree,
pyramid), a free-standing
espalier
角锥形树（金字塔形的树），一种独立
式树篱
17 double horizontal cordon
水平双干形（果树）
18 flower bed, a border
花坛，花床
19 berry bush (gooseberry bush,
currant bush)
浆果灌木（醋栗灌木，酸果灌木）
20 concrete edging
混凝土边饰
21 standard rose (standard rose
tree)
嫁接於树干上的蔷薇（树）
22 border with perennials
多年生植物花坛
23 garden path
果菜园小路
24 allotment holder
家庭果菜园园主

25 asparagus patch (asparagus bed)
芦笋床
26 vegetable patch (vetetable plot)
蔬菜区
27 scarecrow
稻草人
28 runner bean (*Am.* scarlet
runner), a bean plant on
poles (bean poles)
攀缘豆类（美，红花菜豆），一种攀缘
在支架上的豆类植物
29 horizontal cordon
水平单干果树
30 standard fruit tree
直立式果树
31 tree stake
树木支柱
32 hedge
缘篱

1 pelargonium (crane's bill), a
geranium
天竺葵（老鹳草），老鹳草属

2 passion flower (Passiflora), a
climbing plant (climber, creeper)
西番莲（西番莲属），攀缘植物

3 fuchsia, an anagraceous plant
倒挂金钟，吊金钟，灯笼海棠，柳叶菜科

4 nasturtium (Indian cress,
tropaeolum)
金莲花，旱金莲（印第安水芹）

5 cyclamen, a primulaceous herb
仙客来，一种樱桃科植物

6 petunia, a solanaceous herb
矮牵牛，一种茄科草本植物

7 gloxinia (Sinningia), a
gesneriaceous plant
大岩桐（大岩桐属），一种苦苣苔科植物

8 Clivia minata, an amaryllis
(narcissus)
君子兰，孤挺花（水仙属）

9 African hemp (Sparmannia), a
tiliaceous plant, a linden plant
非洲大麻（一种田麻科植物，椴科植物）

10 begonia
秋海棠

11 myrtle (common myrtle,
Myrtus)
董宝莲（桃金娘科）

12 azalea, an ericaceous plant
杜鹃花（一种石南科植物）

13 aloe, a liliaceous plant
芦荟（百合科植物）

14 globe thistle (Echinops)
球蓟（单州漏卢属）

15 stapelia (carrion flower), an
asclepiadaceous plant
萝藦（牛尾菜），一种萝藦科植物

16 Norfolk Island Pine (an
araucaria, grown as an
ornamental)
小叶南洋杉（南洋杉属，装饰植物）

17 galingale, a cyperacious plant of
the sedge family
香根莎草（莎草科植物之一种）

1 seed sowing (sowing)
   播种
2 seed pan
   种子箱
3 seed
   种子
4 label
   标签
5 pricking out (pricking off,
   transplanting)
   移植
6 seedling (seedling plant)
   幼苗（植物幼苗）
7 dibber (dibble)
   点播器（挖穴器）
8 flower pot (pot)
   花盆（花钵）
9 sheet of glass
   玻璃片
10 propagation by layering
   压枝繁殖
11 layer
   压条
12 layer with roots
   带根压条
13 forked stick used for fastening
   固定用的叉状枝
14 propagation by runners
   匍匐茎繁殖
15 parent (parent plant)
   母本，亲本（母本植物）
16 runner
   纤匍枝，匍匐茎

17 small rooted leaf cluster
   带细根的叶簇
18 setting in pots
   盆中定植
19 cutting in water
   水中插枝
20 cutting (slip, set)
   插条，插枝
21 root
   根
22 bud cutting on vine tendril
   藤本上的芽插（芽接）
23 scion bud, a bud
   接芽，芽
24 sprouting (shooting) cutting
   嫩芽（新梢）插枝
25 stem cutting (hardwood cutting)
   茎插（硬木插）
26 bud
   芽，萌芽
27 propagation by bulbils (brood
   bud bulblets)
   珠芽繁殖，小鳞茎（小鳞茎群）繁殖
28 old bulb
   老鳞茎
29 bulbil (brood bud bulblet)
   小鳞茎（小鳞茎群）
30-39 **grafting** (graftage)
   嫁接（嫁接法）
30 budding (shield budding)
   芽接（T字形芽接）
31 budding knife
   芽接用刀

32 T-cut
   T字形切口
33 support (stock, rootstock)
   砧木
34 inserted scion bud
   插入的接芽
35 raffia layer (bast layer)
   莱菲麻层（韧皮层）
36 side grafting
   腹接，侧接
37 scion (shoot)
   接穗（新梢）
38 wedge-shaped notch
   楔形切口
39 splice graft (splice grafting)
   搭接法

1-51 **market garden** (*Am.* truck garden, truck farm)
商品菜园（花园）
1 tool shed
工具棚
2 water tower (water tank)
水塔
3 market garden (*Am.* truck garden, truck farm), a tree nursery
树苗圃
4 hothouse (forcing house, warm house)
暖房（人工加速栽培室，温室）
5 glass roof
玻璃屋顶
6 matting, e.g. straw matting, reed matting
覆盖物，如：麦杆、芦苇
7 boiler room (boiler house)
锅炉房
8 heating pipe (pressure pipe)
暖气管，加温管（压力管）
9 shading panel (shutter)
遮光板，遮阳板
10-11 **ventilators (vents)**
通风口
10 ventilation window (window vent, hinged ventilator)
通风窗（铰接通风窗）
11 ridge vent
屋脊通风口
12 potting table (potting bench)
盆栽桌（盆栽枱）

13 riddle (sieve, garden sieve, upright sieve)
粗筛（筛，园艺筛，立筛）
14 garden shovel (shovel)
园艺铁锹（锹，铲）
15 heap of earth (composted earth, prepared earth, garden mould, *Am.* mold)
土堆（堆肥土，调配土，园用肥土）
16 hotbed (forcing bed, heated frame)
温床（促成栽培的温床，温框）
17 hotbed vent (frame vent)
温床通风口
18 vent prop
通风口支柱
19 sprinkler (sprinkling device)
洒水器（洒水装置）
20 gardener (nursery gardener, grower, commercial grower)
园工（苗圃园工，栽培者，商品生产者）
21 cultivator (hand cultivator, grubber)
耕耘器具，耘锄（手耘锄，除草工具）
22 plank
厚木板
23 pricked-out seedlings (pricked-off seedlings)
移植幼苗
24 forced flowers [forcing]
促成栽培的花
25 potted plants (plants in pots, pot plants)
盆栽植物

26 watering can (*Am.* sprinkling can)
洒水壶（[美]喷水壶）
27 handle
把手
28 rose
喷咀
29 water tank
水池
30 water pipe
水管

31 bale of peat
泥炭土包
32 warm house (heated greenhouse)
暖房（加温的温室）
33 cold house (unheated greenhouse)
冷房（不加温的温室）
34 wind generator
风力发电机
35 wind wheel
风轮
36 wind vane
风向标
37 shrub bed, a flower bed
灌木苗床，花坛
38 hoop edging
围
39 vegetable plot
蔬菜圃，蔬菜区
40 plastic tunnel (polythene greenhouse)
塑胶棚（聚乙烯暖房）
41 ventilation flap
通风活板
42 central path
中央通道
43 vegetable crate
蔬菜板条箱
44 tomato plant
番茄植物
45 nursery hand
苗圃工人
46 nursery hand
苗圃工人

47 tub plant
盆栽植物，桶栽植物
48 tub
木桶，木盆
49 orange tree
柑橘树
50 wire basket
铁丝篮
51 seedling box
幼苗箱

1 dibber (dibble)
点播器，穴植器
2 spade
铲，铁锹
3 lawn rake (wire-tooth rake)
草耙子（铁丝耙子）
4 rake
耙子
5 ridging hoe
作埂锄
6 trowel
（移植用的）小铲
7 combined hoe and fork
锄耙两用工具
8 sickle
镰刀
9 gardener's knife (pruning knife, billhook)
园艺刀（剪枝刀，钩刀）
10 asparagus cutter (asparagus knife)
芦笋割刀
11 tree pruner (long-handled pruner)
高枝剪（长柄剪枝刀）
12 semi-automatic spade
半自动铲
13 three-pronged cultivator
三齿耘锄，三叉耙
14 tree scraper (bark scraper)
树皮刮刀
15 lawn aerator (aerator)
草地通气器（灌气器）
16 pruning saw (saw for cutting branches)
修剪锯
17 battery-operated hedge trimmer
电动绿篱修剪机
18 motor cultivator
马达耕耘机
19 electric drill
电钻
20 gear
齿轮
21 cultivator attachment
耕耘机的附件
22 fruit picker
果实采集器
23 tree brush (bark brush)
树皮刷
24 sprayer for pest control
药剂喷雾器
25 lance
喷枪
26 hose reel (reel and carrying cart)
浇水软管卷筒（车）
27 garden hose
花园浇水管
28 motor lawn mower (motor mower)
机动刈草机
29 grassbox
草箱
30 two-stroke motor
二冲（行）程发动机
31 electric lawn mower (electric mower)
电动刈（剪）草机
32 electric lead (electric cable)
电线（电缆线）
33 cutting unit
割草部件
34 hand mower
手推刈草机
35 cutting cylinder
切割滚刀

36 blade
刀刃，刀口
37 riding mower
乘车型刈草机
38 brake lock
制动杆
39 electric starter
电起动机
40 brake pedal
制动踏板，脚煞车
41 cutting unit
切割部件
42 tip-up trailer
翻卸拖车
43 revolving sprinkler, a lawn sprinkler
旋转洒水器，一种草地洒水器
44 revolving nozzle
旋转喷嘴
45 hose connector
软管接头
46 oscillating sprinkler
振荡洒水器
47 wheelbarrow
手推车，独轮手车
48 grass shears
剪草剪刀
49 hedge shears
修篱剪刀
50 secateurs (pruning shears)
剪枝刀（修枝铗）

1-11 leguminous plants (Leguminosae)
豆科植物（豆科）

1 pea, a plant with a papilionaceous corolla
豌豆，蝶形花冠植物

2 pea flower
豌豆花

3 pinnate leaf
羽状叶

4 pea tendril, a leaf tendril
豌豆卷须，叶卷须

5 stipule
托叶

6 legume (pod), a seed vessel (pericarp, legume)
豆荚

7 pea [seed]
豌豆〔子〕

8 bean plant (bean), a climbing plant (climber, creeper); *varieties:* broad bean (runner bean, *Am.* scarlet runner), climbing bean (climber, pole bean), scarlet runner bean; *smaller:* dwarf French bean (bush bean)
豆科植物，一种攀缘植物；变种：蚕豆（扁豆类，[美]红花菜豆），攀缘豆（攀缘茎类豆），红花菜豆；株型小的：矮法国豆（矮性豆）

9 bean flower
豆科植物的花

10 twining beanstalk
缠绕豆茎

11 bean [pod with seeds]
菜豆（带有豆实的荚果）

12 tomato
番茄

13 cucumber
胡瓜，黄瓜

14 asparagus
芦笋，石刁柏

15 radish
萝蔔（做生菜用的）

16 white radish
白萝蔔

17 carrot
胡萝蔔

18 stump-rooted carrot
短粗的胡萝蔔

19 parsley
香芹，洋芫荽

20 horse-radish
辣根（十字花科）

21 leeks
韭葱（石蒜科）

22 chives
细葱，细香葱（石蒜科）

23 pumpkin (*Am.* squash); *sim.:* melon
南瓜；类似：甜瓜

24 onion
洋葱

25 onion skin
洋葱皮

26 kohlrabi
球茎甘蓝

27 celeriac
根芹菜

28-34 brassicas (leaf vegetables)
芸苔属（叶菜类）

28 chard (Swiss chard, seakale beet)
莙菜（牛皮菜，莙莛菜）

29 spinach
菠菜

30 Brussels sprouts (sprouts)
抱子甘蓝（十字花科）

31 cauliflower
花椰菜，菜花

32 cabbage (round cabbage, head of cabbage), a brassica; *cultivated races (cultivars):* green cabbage, red cabbage
甘蓝（包心菜，圆甘蓝），芸苔属的一种；栽培品种：青甘蓝，赤甘蓝

33 savoy (savoy cabbage)
皱叶甘蓝

34 kale (curly kale, kail), a winter green
羽衣甘蓝，一种冬季蔬菜

35 scorsonera (black salsify)
菊牛蒡（黑婆罗门参）

36-40 salad plants
生菜（沙拉）植物

36 lettuce (cabbage lettuce, head of lettuce)
莴苣，生菜

37 lettuce leaf
莴苣叶

38 corn salad (lamb's lettuce)
野苣（败酱科）

39 endive (endive leaves)
菊莴苣（生菜食品）

40 chicory (succory, salad chicory)
菊苣

41 globe artichoke
朝鲜蓟（花头可作蔬菜）

42 sweet pepper (Spanish paprika)
甜椒（西班牙辣椒）

1-30 soft fruit (berry bushes)
浆果（浆果灌木）

1-15 Ribes
虎耳草科醋栗属的植物

1 gooseberry bush
醋栗矮灌木

2 flowering gooseberry cane
开花的醋栗茎

3 leaf
叶子

4 flower
花

5 magpie moth larva
醋栗尺蠖幼虫

6 gooseberry flower
醋栗花

7 epigynous ovary
上位子房

8 calyx (sepals)
花萼

9 gooseberry, a berry
醋栗，一种浆果

10 currant bush
红醋栗树（灌木）

11 cluster of berries
一串浆果，一串果粒

12 currant
红醋栗

13 stalk
梗（柄）

14 flowering cane of the currant
穗醋栗状花茎

15 raceme
总状花序，串状花

16 strawberry plant; *varieties:* wild strawberry (woodland strawberry), garden strawberry, alpine strawberry
草莓植物；变种；野草莓（森林草莓），园生草莓，高山草莓

17 flowering and fruit-bearing plant
开花结果的植物

18 rhizome
根茎，根状茎

19 ternate leaf (trifoliate leaf)
三出叶（三叶轮性）

20 runner (prostrate stem)
纤匍茎（匍匐茎）

21 strawberry, a pseudocarp
草莓，一种假果

22 epicalyx
副萼

23 achene (seed)
瘦果（种子）

24 flesh (pulp)
果肉

25 raspberry bush
树莓矮灌木（覆盆子矮灌木）

26 raspberry flower
树莓花

27 flower bud (bud)
花蕾

28 fruit (raspberry), an aggregate fruit (compound fruit)
果实（树莓），一种聚合果（复果）

29 blackberry
黑莓

30 thorny tendril
刺状卷须

31-61 pomiferous plants
梨果类植物

31 pear tree; *wild:* wild pear tree
梨树；野梨树

32 flowering branch of the pear tree
开花的梨树枝

33 pear [longitudinal section]
梨[纵切面]

34 pear stalk (stalk)
梨果梗（柄）

35 flesh (pulp)
梨果肉（果肉）

36 core (carpels)
果心（心皮）

37 pear pip (seed), a fruit pip
梨的小种子，果仁

38 pear blossom
梨花

39 ovules
胚珠

40 ovary
子房

41 stigma
柱头

42 style
花柱

43 petal
花瓣

44 sepal
萼片，花萼

45 stamen (anther)
雄蕊（花药）

46 quince tree
榅桲树

47 quince leaf
榅桲树叶

48 stipule
托叶

49 apple-shaped quince [longitudinal section]
苹果形的榅桲[纵切面]

50 pear-shaped quince [longitudinal section]
梨形的榅桲[纵切面]

51 apple tree; *wild:* crab apple tree
苹果树；野苹果树；山楂子树

52 flowering branch of the apple tree
开花的苹果树枝

53 leaf
叶子

54 apple blossom
苹果花

55 withered flower
凋谢的花

56 apple [longitudinal section]
苹果[纵切面]

57 apple skin
苹果皮

58 flesh (pulp)
（苹）果肉

59 core (apple core, carpels)
果心（苹果心，心皮）

60 apple pip, a fruit pip
苹果的小种子，果仁

61 apple stalk (stalk)
苹果梗（柄）

62 codling moth (codlin moth)
苹果卷叶蛾

63 burrow (tunnel)
虫蛀洞穴

64 larva (grub, caterpillar) of a small moth
一种小蛾的幼虫（幼蛾，蠋）

65 wormhole
虫孔

1-36 drupes (drupaceous plants)
核果树（核果类植物）

1-18 cherry tree
樱桃树

1 flowering branch of the cherry tree (branch of the cherry tree in blossom)
开花的樱桃树枝

2 cherry leaf
樱桃叶

3 cherry flower (cherry blossom)
樱桃花

4 peduncle (pedicel, flower stalk)
花梗

5 cherry; *varieties:* sweet cherry (heart cherry), wild cherry (bird cherry), sour cherry, morello cherry (morello)
樱桃；种类：西洋甜樱桃（心形樱桃），野樱桃，酸樱桃，黑樱桃

6-8 cherry (cherry fruit) [cross section]
樱桃果（樱桃）[横剖面]

6 flesh (pulp)
樱桃肉

7 cherry stone
樱桃核

8 seed
种子

9 flower (blossom) [cross section]
樱桃花[横剖面]

10 stamen (anther)
雄蕊（花药）

11 corolla (petals)
花冠（花瓣）

12 sepal
萼片，花萼

13 carpel (pistil)
心皮（雌蕊叶）

14 ovule enclosed in perigynous ovary
包在子房中心内的胚珠

15 style
花柱

16 stigma
柱头

17 leaf
叶子

18 nectary (honey gland)
蜜腺

19-23 plum tree
李树，梅树

19 fruit-bearing branch
结果的树枝

20 oval, black-skinned plum
椭圆形黑皮李子

21 plum leaf
李树叶

22 bud
芽

23 plum stone
李核

24 greengage
青梅

25 mirabelle (transparent gage), a plum
黄李子（透明的李子），李属植物

26-32 peach tree
桃树

26 flowering branch (branch in blossom)
开花的桃树枝（花枝）

27 peach flower (peach blossom)
桃花

28 flower shoot
花枝

29 young leaf (sprouting leaf)
嫩叶

30 fruiting branch
结果枝

31 peach
桃子

32 peach leaf
桃树叶

33-36 apricot tree
杏树

33 flowering apricot branch (apricot branch in blossom)
开花的杏树枝

34 apricot flower (apricot blossom)
杏花

35 apricot
杏子

36 apricot leaf
杏树叶

37-51 nuts
坚果树

37-43 walnut tree
胡桃树，核桃树

37 flowering branch of the walnut tree
开花的胡桃树枝

38 female flower
雌花

39 male inflorescence (male flowers, catkins with stamens)
雄花序（雄花，雄蕊花）

40 alternate pinnate leaf
互生羽状叶

41 walnut, a drupe (stone fruit)
核桃，胡桃（核果）

42 soft shell (cupule)
软外壳（壳斗）

43 walnut, a drupe (stone fruit)
核桃，胡桃（核果）

44-51 hazel tree (hazel bush), an anemophilous shrub (a wind-pollinating shrub)
榛树（矮灌木），风媒灌木

44 flowering hazel branch
开花的榛树枝

45 male catkin
雄葇荑花序

46 female inflorescence
雌花序

47 leaf bud
叶芽

48 fruit-bearing branch
结果枝

49 hazelnut (hazel, cobnut, cob), a drupe (stone fruit)
榛实，一种核果

50 involucre (husk)
总苞（皮，苞叶）

51 hazel leaf
榛树叶

1 snowdrop (spring
snowflake)
石蒜科雪花莲 (雪片莲)

2 garden pansy (heartsease
pansy), a pansy
园三色堇 (三色堇)

3 trumpet narcissus (trumpet
daffodil, Lent lily), a narcissus
喇叭水仙，一种水仙

4 poet's narcissus (pheasant's eye,
poet's daffodil); *sim.*:
polyanthus narcissus
雉眼水仙；类似：多花水仙

5 bleeding heart (lyre flower), a
fumariaceous flower
荷包牡丹，一种紫堇科花卉

6 sweet william (bunch pink), a
carnation
美洲石竹，洋石竹

7 gillyflower (gilliflower, clove
pink, clove carnation)
紫罗兰 (香石竹，康乃馨)

8 yellow flag (yellow water flag,
yellow iris), an iris
黄菖蒲

9 tuberose
晚香玉，夜来香

10 columbine (aquilegia)
耧斗菜

11 gladiolus (sword lily)
唐菖蒲 (剑兰)

12 Madonna lily (Annunciation
lily, Lent lily), a lily
白色百合花，一种百合

13 larkspur (delphinium), a
ranunculaceous plant
飞燕草，一种毛茛科植物

14 moss pink (moss phlox), a phlox
尖叶福禄考，福禄考属

15 garden rose (China rose)
园中玫瑰 (月季花)

16 rosebud, a bud
玫瑰花苞，蓓蕾

17 double rose
重瓣玫瑰

18 rose thorn, a thorn
玫瑰花刺

19 gaillardia
天人菊

20 African marigold (tagetes)
万寿菊

21 love-lies-bleeding, an
amaranthine flower
千穗谷，苋属花

22 zinnia
百日草

23 pompon dahlia, a dahlia
绒球大丽花，大丽菊属

1 corn flower (bluebottle), a
  centaury
  矢车菊（翠蓝），矢车菊属植物
2 corn poppy (field poppy), a
  poppy
  虞美人，丽春花，舞草（罂粟科）
3 bud
  芽
4 poppy flower
  罂粟花
5 seed capsule containing poppy
  seeds
  含罂粟种子的蒴果
6 corn cockle (corn campion,
  crown-of-the-field)
  麦秆石竹
7 corn marigold (field marigold),
  a chrysanthemum
  孔雀菊（琉球金盏花），菊属
8 corn camomile (field camomile,
  camomile, chamomile)
  黄金菊
9 shepherd's purse
  荠，大荠菜（十字花科）
10 flower
  荠菜花
11 fruit (pouch-shaped pod)
  荠菜果（袋形荚果）
12 common groundsel
  壹吾属之杂草
13 dandelion
  蒲公英
14 flower head (capitulum)
  蒲公英花序（头状花序）
15 infructescence
  果实序
16 hedge mustard, a mustard
  药用大蒜芥，芥子的一种
17 stonecrop
  景天
18 wild mustard (charlock, runch)
  野芥子
19 flower
  野芥花
20 fruit, a siliqua (pod)
  野芥果，长角（荚果）
21 wild radish (jointed charlock)
  野生萝葡（有节野芥）
22 flower
  野生萝葡花
23 fruit (siliqua, pod)
  野生萝葡果（长角荚果）
24 common orache (common
  orach)
  滨藜属
25 goosefoot
  藜
26 field bindweed (wild morning
  glory), a bindweed
  旋花（牵牛花），三色旋花属植物
27 scarlet pimpernel (shepherd's
  weatherglass, poor man's
  weatherglass, eye-bright)
  琉璃繁缕，海绿（报春花科）
28 wild barley (wall barley)
  野生大麦
29 wild oat
  野生燕麦
30 common couch grass (couch,
  quack grass, quick grass, quitch
  grass, scutch grass, twitch grass,
  witchgrass); *sim.*: bearded
  couch grass, sea couch grass
  茅草；类似有：有须茅草，海茅草
31 gallant soldier
  辣子草

32 field eryngo (Watling Street
  thistle), a thistle
  野刺芹（野蓟），一种蓟
33 stinging nettle, a nettle
  刺毛荨麻，荨麻科

1 house
  房子，农舍
2 stable
  畜廄
3 house cat (cat)
  家猫
4 farmer's wife
  农妇
5 broom
  扫帚
6 farmer
  农夫
7 cowshed
  牛棚
8 pigsty (sty, *Am.* pigpen, hogpen)
  猪栏，猪圈，猪舍
9 outdoor trough
  户外饲槽
10 pig
  猪
11 above-ground silo (fodder silo)
  贮塔（饲料贮塔）
12 silo pipe (standpipe for filling
  the silo)
  饲料管（装饲料的竖管）
13 liquid manure silo
  液廄肥池（槽）

14 **outhouse**
外屋，附属的建筑物（与正屋分开，如
谷仓等）
15 **machinery shed**
机器房（棚）
16 **sliding door**
滑门，拉门
17 **door to the workshop**
至工作场的门
18 **three-way tip-cart, a transport vehicle**
三面倾卸车，一种运输车辆
19 **tipping cylinder**
倾卸气（汽）缸
20 **shafts**
车轮轴
21 **manure spreader (fertilizer spreader, manure distributor)**
堆肥撒布机（化学肥料撒布机）
22 **spreader unit (distributor unit)**
撒肥装置（排肥器）
23 **spreader cyclinder (distributor cylinder)**
撒肥缸（排肥缸）
24 **movable scraper floor**
活动刮板
25 **side planking (side board)**
侧板
26 **wire mesh front**
金属网挡板
27 **sprinkler stand**
洒水车
28 **sprinkler cart**
洒水机（立）架

29 **sprinkler, a revolving sprinkler**
洒水机，旋转式洒水机
30 **sprinkler hoses**
洒水软管
31 **farmyard**
农家的中庭
32 **watchdog**
看门狗
33 **calf**
小牛，牛犊
34 **dairy cow (milch-cow, milker)**
乳牛
35 **farmyard hedge**
场院树篱
36 **chicken (hen)**
小鸡（母鸡）
37 **cock (*Am.* rooster)**
公鸡
38 **tractor**
牵引机，曳引机
39 **tractor driver**
牵引机司机
40 **all-purpose trailer**
万用拖车
41 **[folded] pickup attachment**
[折叠式]拾取附件
42 **unloading unit**
卸载组件
43 **polythene silo, a fodder silo**
聚乙烯饲料包，饲料袋
44 **meadow**
（牧）草地
45 **grazing cattle**
放牧的牛

46 **electrified fence**
带电栅栏

1-41 work in the fields
田间工作

1 fallow (fallow field, fallow ground)
休耕地，休闲地

2 boundary stone
界石

3 boundary ridge, a balk (baulk)
界埂，田埂

4 field
田地

5 farmworker (agricultural worker, farmhand, farm labourer, *Am.* laborer)
农场工人

6 plough (*Am.* plow)
犁

7 clod
土块，泥块

8 furrow
犁沟，畦

9 stone
石头，石块

10-12 sowing
播种

10 sower
播种者

11 seedlip
播种袋

12 seed corn (seed)
谷种（种子）

13 field guard
田间守卫者

14 chemical fertilizer, (artificial fertilizer); *kinds*: potash fertilizer, phosphoric acid fertilizer, lime fertilizer, nitrogen fertilizer
化学肥料，（人工肥料）种类：钾肥，磷肥，石灰肥料，氮肥

15 cartload of manure (farmyard manure, dung)
一车肥料（农家肥，粪肥）

16 oxteam (team of oxen, *Am.* span of oxen)
二牛拉车

17 fields (farmland)
农田（耕地）

18 farm track (farm road)
农场小路

19-30 hay harvest (haymaking)
牧草的收获作业

19 rotary mower with swather (swath reaper)
旋转刈幅割草机（刈幅收割机）

20 connecting shaft (connecting rod)
连结轴（连杆）

21 power take-off (power take-off shaft
动力分导装置（动力输出轴）

22 meadow
草地

23 swath (swathe)
刈下的一行草

24 tedder (rotary tedder)
摊草机（旋转摊草机）

25 tedded hay
摊开晒的干草

26 rotary swather
旋转刈幅机

27 trailer with pickup attachment
有拾取附件的拖车

28 fence rack (rickstand), a drying rack for hay
围篱草架，晒草架

29 rickstand, a drying rack for hay
干草（立）架，晒草架

30 hay tripod
干草三脚架

31-41 grain harvest and seedbed preparation
谷物收割和苗床整地

31 combine harvester
联合收获机

32 cornfield
（小）麦田，谷物地

33 stubble field
残株田地

34 bale of straw
藁秆捆

35 straw baler (straw press), a highpressure baler
藁秆打包机，一种高压打包机

36 swath (swathe) of straw (windrow of straw)
刈幅藁秆（刈下后晒乾翻堆成草堆的干草）

37 hydraulic bale loader
液压草捆装载机

38 trailer
拖车

39 manure spreader
肥料撒布机

40 four-furrow plough (*Am.* plow)
四犁犁

41 combination seed-harrow
组合播种耙

1-33 combine harvester
(combine)
联合收获机

1 divider
分禾器,分茎器

2 grain lifter
扶茎器,扶穗器

3 cutter bar
刀具杆,割刀杆

4 pickup reel, a spring-tine reel
(拾取器的)拾取轮,有弹簧齿的拔禾轮

5 reel gearing
拾取驱动装置

6 auger
木螺钻

7 chain and slat elevator
链板式升降器

8 hydraulic cylinder for adjusting the cutting unit
调节切割组件的液压缸

9 stone catcher (stone trap)
集石器(除石器)

10 awner
除芒器,脱芒机

11 concave
(脱粒)凹板,凹面

12 threshing drum (drum)
脱谷圆筒

13 revolving beater [for freeing straw from the drum and preparing it for the shakers]
旋转式搅打机[以圆筒脱谷再送往摇动器(筛)]

14 straw shaker (strawwalker)
稻草筛(稻草摇动器)

15 fan for compressed-air winnowing
压气式簸谷送风机(风扇)

16 preparation level
预加工平面

17 louvred-type sieve
鱼鳞筛

18 sieve extension
鱼鳞筛的延长线

19 shoe sieve (reciprocating sieve)
下筛(振动筛)

20 grain auger
谷粒木螺钻

21 tailings auger
筛除物木螺钻

22 tailings outlet
筛除物排出口

23 grain tank
粮箱

24 grain tank auger
粮箱木螺钻

25 augers feeding to the grain tank unloader
粮箱卸载装置的喂送木螺钻

26 grain unloader spout
卸粮槽

27 observation ports for checking tank contents
检查箱容量观察口

28 six-cylinder diesel engine
六气缸柴油发动机

29 hydraulic pump with oil reservoir
带贮油器的液压泵

30 driving axle gearing
驱动轴齿轮驱动装置

31 driving wheel tyre (*Am.* tire)
驱动轮胎

32 rubber-tyred (*Am.* rubber-tired) wheel on the steering axle
转向轴上的橡胶轮胎

33 driver's position
驾驶员座位

34-39 self-propelled forage harvester
(self-propelled field chopper)
自走式草料收割机

34 cutting drum (chopper drum)
切削圆筒(切碎圆筒)

35 corn head
玉米收割台

36 cab (driver's cab)
驾驶室

37 swivel-mounted spout (discharge pipe)
旋转悬挂式卸载管(排泄管)

38 exhaust
排气管

39 rear-wheel steering system
后轮转向系统

40-45 rotary swather
旋转刈幅机

40 cardan shaft
方向轴

41 running wheel
行驶轮

42 double spring tine
双弹齿

43 crank
曲柄,手摇柄

44 swath rake
集草(铺条)耙

45 three-point linkage
三点连结装置

46-58 rotary tedder
旋转式摊草机

46 tractor
牵引机

47 draw bar
拉杆

48 cardan shaft
十字接头轴

49 power take-off (power take-off shaft)
功率输出轴

50 gearing (gears)
齿轮驱动,传动装置

51 frame bar
框杆

52 rotating head
旋转圆盘

53 tine bar
耙齿杆

54 double spring tine
双弹齿

55 guard rail
护轨

56 running wheel
行驶轮

57 height adjustment crank
高度调节手摇柄

58 wheel adjustment
轮调整机构

59-84 potato harvester
马铃薯收获机

59 control levers for the lifters of the digger and the hopper and for adjusting the shaft
调整挖斗、漏斗提升器,和调节轴的控制杆

60 adjustable hitch
可调系扣

61 drawbar
拉杆,牵引杆

62 drawbar support
拉杆支座

63 cardan shaft connection
十字接头轴接头

64 press roller
压榨辊子

65 gearing (gears) for the hydraulic system
液压系统的齿轮装置

66 disc (disk) coulter (*Am.* colter) (rolling coulter)
圆犁刀

67 three-bladed share
三叶犁头

68 disc (disk) coulter (*Am.* colter) drive
圆犁驱动装置

69 open-web elevator
开网式升降器

70 agitator
搅拌器,搅动器

71 multi-step reduction gearing
多级减速齿轮装置

72 feeder
进给器,进料器

73 haulm stripper (flail rotor)
茎叶摘除器,截穗机(连枷式转子)

74 rotary elevating drum
旋转提升鼓轮

75 mechanical tumbling separator
机械滚筒分离器(选别器)

76 haulm conveyor with flexible haulm strippers
有弹性的茎叶摘除器的输送带

77 haulm conveyor agitator
茎叶输送带搅动器

78 haulm conveyor drive with V-belt
茎叶输送带的三角皮带驱动装置

79 studded rubber belt for sorting vines, clods and stones
分拣藤蔓,泥块和石头用的加强橡皮带

80 trash conveyor
残屑输送器

81 sorting table
分拣台

82 rubber-disc (rubber-disk) rollers for presorting
预拣橡皮圆盘

83 discharge conveyor
卸薯输送器

84 endless-floor hopper
循环活动底板漏斗

85-96 beet harvester
甜菜收获机

85 topper
截顶器,切顶器

86 feeler
测隙片,触

87 topping knife
切甜菜顶刀

88 feeler support wheel with depth adjustment
具有耕深调节装置的测隙片支承轮

89 beet cleaner
甜菜清理装置

90 haulm elevator
茎叶升降器

91 hydraulic pump
液压泵

92 compressed-air reservoir
压缩空气(贮气)筒

93 oil tank (oil reservoir)
油箱(油槽)

94 tensioning device for the beet elevator
甜菜升降器的拉紧装置

95 beet elevator belt
甜菜升降器皮带

96 beet hopper
甜菜漏斗

1 **wheel plough** (*Am.* plow), a
  single-bottom plough [form.]
  轮式犁，一种单杆犁
2 handle
  手柄
3 plough (*Am.* plow) stilt (plough
  handle)
  犁把，犁柄
4-8 **plough** (*Am.* **plow**) **bottom**
  犁体
4 mouldboard (*Am.* moldboard)
  拨土板
5 landside
  犁侧板
6 sole (slade)
  犁底（板）
7 ploughshare (share, *Am.*
  plowshare)
  犁头
8 frog (frame)
  犁托
9 beam (plough beam, *Am.*
  plowbeam)
  犁架
10 knife coulter (*Am.* colter), a
  coulter
  犁刀
11 skim coulter (*Am.* colter)
  前犁（副犁）
12 guide-chain crossbar
  导链横杆
13 guide chain
  导链
14-19 **forecarriage**
  前车架，前轮架
14 adjustable yoke (yoke)
  可调整轭（轭）
15 land wheel
  地轮
16 furrow wheel
  （犁的）沟轮
17 hake chain
  牵引调节链
18 draught beam (drawbar)
  牵引杆（拉杆）
19 hake
  牵引调节板
20 **tractor** (general-purpose tractor)
  牵引机（通用牵引机）
21 cab frame (roll bar)
  座舱架（轧辊条）
22 seat
  座位
23 power take-off gear-change
  (gearshift)
  功率输出齿轮变速装置（变速器）
24-29 **power lift**
  动力升降装置
24 ram piston
  动力油缸活塞
25 lifting rod adjustment
  提升杆调整
26 drawbar frame
  拉杆架
27 top link
  上连杆
28 lower link
  下连杆
29 lifting rod
  提升杆
30 drawbar coupling
  拉杆联结器
31 live power take-off (live power
  take-off shaft, take-off shaft)
  有效动力输出轴

32 differential gear (differential)
  差速齿轮（差速器）
33 floating axle
  浮动轴
34 torque converter lever
  扭矩变速器杆
35 gear-change (gearshift)
  齿轮变速器（齿轮换挡）
36 multi-speed transmission
  多速变速器
37 fluid clutch (fluid drive)
  液体离合器（流体驱动）
38 power take-off gear
  功率输出齿轮
39 main clutch
  主离合器
40 power take-off gear-change
  (gearshift) with power take-off
  clutch
  配有功率输出离合器的有效功率输出齿
  轮变速装置
41 hydraulic power steering and
  reversing gears
  液压动力转向及回动
42 fuel tank
  燃料箱，燃油箱
43 float lever
  浮动杆
44 four-cylinder diesel engine
  四汽缸柴油发动机
45 oil sump and pump for the
  pressure-feed lubrication system
  压力给油润滑系统的油池和油泵
46 fresh oil tank
  新油油箱，清洁油箱
47 track rod (*Am.* tie rod)
  轮距杆（[美]系杆）
48 front axle pivot pin
  前轴支轴销
49 front axle suspension
  前轴悬架
50 front coupling (front hitch)
  前联结装置
51 radiator
  散热器，水箱（汽车）
52 fan
  风扇
53 battery
  电池组，电池
54 oil bath air cleaner (oil bath air
  filter)
  油浸式空气清洁器（滤清器）
55 **cultivator** (grubber)
  耕耘机
56 sectional frame
  分节机架
57 spring tine
  弹性锄齿，弹齿
58 share, a diamond-shaped share;
  sim.: chisel-shaped share
  锄铲，菱形锄齿；类似：凿形锄齿
59 depth wheel
  限深轮
60 depth adjustment
  深度调节器
61 coupling (hitch)
  联结装置，联结（系扣）
62 **reversible plough** (*Am.* plow), a
  mounted plough
  双向犁，翻转犁
63 depth wheel
  限深轮
64-67 **plough** (*Am.* **plow**) **bottom,** a
  general-purpose plough bottom
  犁体，一种通用犁体

64 mouldboard (*Am.* moldboard)
  拨土板
65 ploughshare (share, *Am.*
  plowshare), a pointed share
  犁头，一种尖犁头
66 sole (slade)
  犁底（板）
67 landside
  犁侧板
68 skim coulter (*Am.* colter)
  前犁（副犁）
69 disc (disk) coulter (*Am.* colter)
  (rolling coulter)
  圆盘刀
70 plough (*Am.* plow) frame
  犁架
71 beam (plough beam, *Am.*
  plowbeam)
  犁辕
72 three-point linkage
  三点连结装置
73 swivel mechanism
  旋转装置
74 **drill**
  条播机，播种机
75 seed hopper
  种子漏斗
76 drill coulter (*Am.* colter)
  条播犁刀（头）
77 delivery tube, a telescopic tube
  输送管，套筒伸缩管
78 feed mechanism
  进给装置
79 gearbox
  齿轮箱
80 drive wheel
  驱动轮
81 track indicator
  轮迹指示器
82 **disc (disk) harrow,** a
  semimounted implement
  圆盘耙片，一种半固定式农具
83 discs (disks) in X-configuration
  X 形圆盘耙片组
84 plain disc (disk)
  普通圆盘耙片
85 serrated-edge disc (disk)
  锯齿缘圆盘耙片
86 quick hitch
  快速系扣
87 **combination seed-harrow**
  组合播种耙
88 three-section spike-tooth harrow
  三组钉齿耙
89 three-section rotary harrow
  三组旋转耙
90 frame
  机架

1 draw hoe (garden hoe)
除草锄（园圃锄）
2 hoe handle
锄柄
3 three-pronged (three-tined) hay fork (fork)
三齿干草叉
4 prong (tine)
叉子（齿）
5 potato fork
马铃薯叉
6 potato hook
马铃薯手掘叉
7 four-pronged (four-tined) manure fork (fork)
四齿施肥叉
8 manure hoe
施肥锄耙
9 whetting hammer [for scythes]
磨削锤（磨镰刀用）
10 peen (pane)
锤尖头
11 whetting anvil [for scythes]
磨砺（铁）砧
12 scythe
长柄镰刀
13 scythe blade
长柄镰刀刀片
14 cutting edge
切削刃
15 heel
刀刃根部
16 snath (snathe, snead, sneath)
大镰刀柄
17 handle
柄，把手
18 scythe sheath
长柄镰刀鞘
19 whetstone (scythestone)
磨石（磨刀石）
20 potato rake
马铃薯耙
21 potato planter
马铃薯种植器
22 digging fork (fork)
挖掘用叉
23 wooden rake (rake, hayrake)
木制草耙
24 hoe (potato hoe)
锄（马铃薯锄）
25 potato basket, a wire basket
马铃薯篮，铁丝提篮
26 clover broadcaster
三叶草种子撒播机

1 oscillating spray line
摆动式喷管
2 stand (steel chair)
支架（钢座）
3 portable irrigation system
可移动式灌溉系统
4 revolving sprinkler
旋转洒水器
5 standpipe coupler
立管联结器
6 elbow with cardan joint (cardan coupling)
带十字接头的肘管
7 pipe support (trestle)
水管支座（支架）
8 pump connection
水泵连接器（接头）
9 delivery valve
输送阀
10 pressure gauge (*Am.* gage) (manometer)
压力计，压力表（液体压力计）
11 centrifugal evacuating pump
离心式抽水泵
12 basket strainer
篮式（过）滤器
13 channel
水道，沟渠
14 chassis of the p.t.o.-driven pump (power take-off-driven pump)
功率输出驱动泵的底盘
15 p.t.o.-driven (power take-off-driven) pump
动力分导装置从动泵

16 cardan shaft
十字接头轴，万向接头轴
17 tractor
牵引机，曳引机
18 long-range irrigation unit
长距离灌溉设备
19 drive connection
驱动连接器
20 turbine
涡轮
21 gearing (gears)
（齿轮）传动装置
22 adjustable support
可调节支座
23 centrifugal evacuating pump
离心式抽水泵
24 wheel
轮
25 pipe support
水管支座
26 polyester pipe
聚酯管
27 sprinkler nozzle
洒水器喷咀
28 quick-fitting pipe connection with cardan joint
带十字接头的速装管连接器
29 M-cardan
M 型万向接头
30 clamp
钳，铁箍，夹子
31 V-cardan
V 型万向接头

32 revolving sprinkler, a field sprinkler
旋转洒水器，一种田地洒水器
33 nozzle
喷咀
34 breaker
打水板
35 breaker spring
打水板弹簧
36 stopper
塞子，阻塞器
37 counterweight
重量平衡器
38 thread
螺纹

1-47 arable crops (agricultural produce, farm produce)
适於耕种的农作物（农产品）

1-37 varieties of grain (grain, cereals, farinaceous plants, bread-corn)
谷类，谷物

1 rye (*also:* corn, 'corn' often meaning the main cereal of a country or region; in Northern Germany; rye; in Southern Germany and Italy: wheat; in Sweden: barley; in Scotland: oats; in North America; maize; in China: rice)
裸麦（[corn] 通常指一个国家和地区的主要粮食作物；德国北部：黑麦；德国南部和意大利：小麦；瑞典：大麦；苏格兰：燕麦；北美：玉蜀黍；中国：稻）

2 ear of rye, a spike (head)
裸麦穗，谷穗

3 spikelet
小穗

4 ergot, a grain deformed by fungus [shown with mycelium]
麦角病，一种由真菌（有菌丝体）引起的谷物病

5 corn stem after tillering
分蘖后的谷物茎

6 culm (stalk)
秆，茎

7 node of the culm
（茎）秆节

8 leaf (grain leaf)
叶子（谷物的叶子）

9 leaf sheath (sheath)
叶鞘

10 spikelet
小穗（状花序）

11 glume
颖片

12 awn (beard, arista)
芒，谷刺（谷针，刺角芒）

13 seed (grain, kernel, farinaceous grain)
种子（颖果，含淀粉的子实）

14 embryo plant
胚芽植物

15 seed
种子

16 embryo
胚芽

17 root
根

18 root hair
根毛

19 grain leaf
谷叶

20 leaf blade (blade, lamina)
叶片（叶身）

21 leaf sheath
叶鞘

22 ligule (ligula)
叶舌，舌状片

23 wheat
小麦

24 spelt
小麦的一种

25 seed; *unripe:* green spelt, a soup vegetable
种子；未成熟的：青麦，一种汤用植物

26 barley
大麦

27 oat panicle, a panicle
燕麦圆锥花序

28 millet
黍，稷，小米

29 rice
稻

30 rice grain
稻谷

31 maize (Indian corn, *Am.* corn); *varieties:* popcorn, dent corn, flint corn (flint maize, *Am.* Yankee corn), pod corn (*Am.* cow corn, husk corn), soft corn (*Am.* flour corn, squaw corn), sweet corn
玉米；种类：爆玉米，马齿玉米，硬玉米，荚玉米，甜玉米

32 female inflorescence
雌花序

33 husk (shuck)
外壳（外皮）

34 style
花柱

35 male inflorescence (tassel)
雄花序

36 maize cob (*Am.* corn cob)
玉米穗轴

37 maize kernel (grain of maize)
玉米粒（仁）

38-45 root crops
根菜作物

38 potato plant (potato), a tuberous plant; *varieties:* round, roundoval (pear-shaped), flat-oval, long, kidney-shaped potato; *according to colour:* white (*Am.* Irish), yellow, red, purple potato
马铃薯植物，一种块茎植物；种类：圆形，圆椭圆形（梨子形），扁椭圆形，长形，肾脏形等马铃薯；以颜色区分有：白色，黄色，红色，紫红色等马铃薯

39 seed potato (seed tuber)
马铃薯种（种块）

40 potato tuber (potato, tuber)
马铃薯块茎

41 potato top (potato haulm)
马铃薯叶

42 flower
马铃薯花

43 poisonous potato berry (potato apple)
有毒的马铃薯浆果

44 sugar beet, a beet
甜菜

45 root (beet)
甜菜根

46 beet top
甜菜顶部

47 beet leaf
甜菜叶

1-28 fodder plants (forage plants) for tillage
（耕地上的）饲料植物

1 red clover (purple clover)
红三叶草（紫红三叶草）

2 white clover (Dutch clover)
白三叶草（荷兰三叶草）

3 alsike clover (alsike)
杂种三叶草

4 crimson clover
深红三叶草

5 four-leaf (four-leaved) clover
四叶苜蓿草

6 kidney vetch (lady's finger, ladyfinger)
野腰子豆

7 flower
花

8 pod
荚蓏，荚果

9 lucerne (lucern, purple medick)
紫苜蓿

10 sainfoin (cock's head, cockshead)
红豆草

11 bird's foot (bird-foot, bird's foot trefoil)
叶或花像鸟足的植物

12 corn spurrey (spurrey, spurry), a spurrey (spurry)
大爪草（石竹科）

13 common comfrey, one of the borage family (Boraginaceae)
雏菊（紫草科）

14 flower (blossom)
花

15 field bean (broad bean, tick bean, horse bean)
蚕豆，扁豆，马豆

16 pod
荚蓏，荚果

17 yellow lupin
黄色羽扇豆

18 common vetch
大巢菜，野豌豆

19 chick-pea
鹰咀豆，小藜豆

20 sunflower
向日葵

21 mangold (mangelwurzel, mangoldwurzel, field mangel)
饲料甜菜（一种饲牛用的甜菜）

22 false oat (oat-grass)
假燕麦草

23 spikelet
小穗

24 meadow fescure grass, a fescue
田边草

25 cock's foot (cocksfoot)
鸭茅草，鸡脚草

26 Italian ryegrass; *sim.:* perennial ryegrass (English ryegrass)
意大利黑麦草；类似：多年生黑麦草（英国黑麦草）

27 meadow foxtail, a paniculate grass
狐尾草，一种有圆锥花序的草

28 greater burnet saxifrage
较大的地榆虎耳草

1 **bulldog**
戏牛犬，牛头犬
2 **ear, a rose-ear**
耳朵，一种玫瑰耳
3 **muzzle**
狗的鼻和咀
4 **nose**
鼻
5 **foreleg**
前腿
6 **forepaw**
前脚爪
7 **hind leg**
后腿
8 **hind paw**
后脚爪
9 **pug (pug dog)**
哈巴狗
10 **boxer**
拳师犬
11 **withers**
肩隆（两肩骨间隆起的部分）
12 **tail, a docked tail**
尾巴（剪短的尾）
13 **collar**
（狗颈上的）项圈
14 **Great Dane**
大丹狗，丹麦狗
15 **wire-haired fox terrier**
猎狐刚毛狗（㹴）
16 **bull terrier**
牛头犬与㹴杂交所生之之犬
17 **Scottish terrier**
苏格兰㹴

18 **Bedlington terrier**
贝德林顿㹴
19 **Pekinese (Pekingese, Pekinese dog, Pekingese dog)**
小狮子狗，北京狗
20 **spitz (Pomeranian)**
丝毛狗
21 **chow (chow-chow)**
中国狗的一种，松狮狗
22 **husky**
爱斯基摩犬
23 **Afghan (Afghan hound)**
阿富汗猎狗
24 **greyhound (*Am.* grayhound), a courser**
灵堤（一种躯瘦，腿长，眼光锐利，奔跑迅速的猎犬）
25 **Alsatian (German sheepdog, *Am.* German shepherd), a police dog, watch dog, and guide dog**
一种大狼狗（德国牧羊犬），常予以训练使担任警犬任务
26 **flews (chaps)**
猎犬上唇松垂的部分
27 **Dobermann terrier**
㹴之一种（毛短而润，呈暗色，带棕色斑点）

28 dog brush
狗刷子
29 dog comb
狗梳子
30 lead (dog lead, leash); *for hunting:* leash
牵狗的绳或皮带；尤指：拴猎犬的皮带
31 muzzle
口套，口络
32 feeding bowl (dog bowl)
狗食钵（碗）
33 bone
骨头
34 Newfoundland dog
纽芬兰狗
35 schnauzer
德国种刚毛硬犬
36 poodle; *sim. and smaller:* pygmy (pigmy) poodle
贵宾狗；类似且较小的：皮格米种贵宾狗
37 St. Bernard (St. Bernard dog)
圣伯尔纳犬，雪山救人犬
38 cocker spaniel
西班牙长耳狗，一种长毛垂耳之犬
39 dachshund, a terrier
德国种腊肠狗（一种短腿小狗）
40 German pointer
德国短毛大猎犬
41 English setter
英国塞特种猎狗，一种长毛猎狗
42 trackhound
追踪猎犬

43 pointer, a trackhound
短毛大猎犬，一种追踪猎犬

1-6 equitation (high school riding, haute école)
骑术，马术（骑马特技，高超的骑术）
1 piaffe
比快步稍慢的步伐
2 walk
慢步行
3 passage
斜行
4 levade (pesade)
马后腿直立前腿上提向后收缩的一种姿势
5 capriole
腾跃
6 courbette (curvet)
腾跃（先举前二蹄，在未著地时举后两蹄）
7-25 harness
马具
7-13 bridle
马勒，辔辔
7-11 headstall (headpiece, halter)
络头
7 noseband
鼻羁
8 cheek piece (cheek strap)
颊带（面颊带）
9 browband (front band)
额带（前额带）
10 crownpiece
马两颊之辔绳
11 throatlatch (throatlash)
（马喉下之）辔带
12 curb chain
马衔链，马勒链
13 curb bit
马嚼铁，马衔铁
14 hasp (hook) of the hame (*Am.* drag hook)
马颈轭搭钮（[美]马颈轭上的牵引钩）
15 pointed collar, a collar
有尖角的马轭
16 trappings (side trappings)
马饰
17 saddle-pad
马鞍褥
18 girth
肚带，系带
19 backband
背带
20 shaft chain (pole chain)
辕杆链
21 pole
辕杆
22 trace
马车之挽辔，挽绳
23 second girth (emergency girth)
辅助肚带（应急肚带）
24 trace
挽辔，挽绳
25 reins (*Am.* lines)
辔绳
26-36 breast harness
护马具
26 blinker (*Am.* blinder, winker)
（马的）眼罩
27 breast collar ring
胸轭环
28 breast collar (Dutch collar)
胸轭（荷兰式轭）
29 fork
叉皮，叉形带
30 neck strap
马颈皮带
31 saddle-pad
马鞍褥

32 loin strap
马腰带
33 reins (rein, *Am.* line)
辔绳
34 crupper (crupper-strap)
兜过马尾下之皮带；马尾鞧
35 trace
挽鞧
36 girth (belly-band)
马肚带（马的腹带）
37-49 saddles
马鞍
37-44 stock saddle (*Am.* western saddle)
放牧马鞍（[美]西部式马鞍）
37 saddle seat
鞍座
38 pommel horn (horn)
鞍头（鞍最前端向上突起的部分）
39 cantle
鞍后的弓形部
40 flap (*Am.* fender)
鞍的护垫
41 bar
木条（鞍架的一部分）
42 stirrup leather
马镫皮带
43 stirrup (stirrup iron)
马镫（马镫铁）
44 blanket
马鞍毯
45-49 English saddle (cavalry saddle)
英国式马鞍（骑兵马鞍）
45 seat
鞍座
46 cantle
马鞍后之弓形部
47 flap
鞍的护垫
48 roll (knee roll)
鞍卷（膝卷）
49 pad
鞍褥
50-51 spurs
踢马刺，靴刺
50 box spur (screwed jack spur)
环形靴刺
51 strapped jack spur
用带搭扣螺旋顶靴刺
52 curb bit
马嚼铁，马衔铁
53 gag bit (gag)
箝口具
54 currycomb
马梳
55 horse brush (body brush, dandy brush)
马刷（马体刷，刷马之硬毛刷）

1-38 points of the horse
马的各部分

1-11 head (horse's head)
马头

1 ear
马耳（朵）

2 forelock
马的额毛，马额上的长毛

3 forehead
马额

4 eye
马眼（睛）

5 face
马脸

6 nose
马鼻子

7 nostril
（马）鼻孔

8 upper lip
上咀唇

9 mouth
马咀

10 underlip (lower lip)
下咀唇

11 lower jaw
下颌

12 crest (neck)
马颈脊（头颈）

13 mane (horse's mane)
马的鬃毛

14 crest (horse's crest)
颈脊（马的颈脊）

15 neck
颈

16 throat (*Am.* throatlatch, throatlash)
马的咽喉，喉头，颈前

17 withers
鬐甲（马两肩骨间的隆起部分）

18-27 forehand
马身的前部

18 shoulder
马的肩胛

19 breast
胸（脯）

20 elbow
肘

21 forearm
前臂（肘至腕间的部分）

22-26 forefoot
前脚，前足

22 knee (carpus, wrist)
膝（腕）

23 cannon
马胫骨

24 fetlock
（生距毛的）肢关节

25 pastern
（马足的）骹

26 hoof
马蹄

27 chestnut (castor), a callosity
蹄蝉，马前腿内部的胼胝，胼胝体

28 spur vein
靴刺静脉

29 back
马背

30 loins (lumbar region)
马腰（腰部）

31 croup (rump, crupper)
臀部（马屁股）

32 hip
髋

33-37 hind leg
后腿

33 stifle (stifle joint)
后膝关节

34 root (dock) of the tail
马尾骨肉部分（不包括尾上的毛）

35 haunch
腰臀部

36 gaskin
下大腿

37 hock
髁，后膝，飞节

38 tail
尾巴

39-44 gaits of the horse
马的步法

39 walk
慢步

40 pace
侧步伐

41 trot
小跑，快步

42 canter (hand gallop)
慢步小跑

43-44 full gallop
马飞奔步法

43 full gallop at the moment of descent on to the two forefeet
前足下落时的飞奔步法

44 full gallop at the moment when all four feet are off the ground
四足离地时的飞奔步法

1-2 cattle
家畜；牲口
1 cow, a ruminant; *m.* bull; *c.* ox;
f. cow; *y.* calf
母牛，反刍动物；公牛，阉牛；母牛；
小牛
2 horse; *m.* stallion; *c.* gelding; *f.*
mare; *y.* foal
马；未阉的雄马；阉割过的马；母马；
小马（驹）
3 donkey
驴子
4 pack saddle (carrying saddle)
驮鞍（荷鞍）
5 pack (load)
驮载物
6 tufted tail
丛毛尾巴
7 tuft
丛毛
8 mule, a cross between a male
donkey and a mare
骡（子）；公驴与母马杂交的混合种
9 pig, a cloven-hoofed animal; *m.*
boar; *f.* sow; *y.* piglet
猪，一种偶蹄家畜；公猪；母猪；小猪
（猪仔）
10 pig's snout (snout)
猪咀（猪的口鼻部）
11 pig's ear
猪耳朵
12 curly tail
卷曲的尾巴
13 sheep; *m.* ram; *c.* wether; *f.* ewe;
y. lamb
羊；绵羊；公羊；阉羊；母羊；小羊
（羔羊）

14 goat
山羊
15 goat's beard
山羊胡须
16 dog, a Leonberger; *m.* dog; *f.*
bitch; *y.* pup (puppy, whelp)
狗，一种利奥贝尔格狗；雄狗；母狗；
小狗（幼犬）
17 cat, an Angora cat (Persian cat);
m. tom (tom cat)
猫，一种安哥拉猫（波斯猫）；雄猫
18-36 small domestic animals
小家畜
18 rabbit; *m.* buck; *f.* doe
兔子；雄兔；雌兔
19-26 poultry (domestic fowl)
家禽
19-26 chicken
鸡
19 hen
母鸡
20 crop (craw)
嗉囊（鸡胃）
21 cock (*Am,* rooster); *c.* capon
公鸡（雄鸡）；阉鸡
22 cockscomb (comb, crest)
鸡冠（雄鸡冠）
23 lap
耳垂（鸡耳朵）
24 wattle (gill, dewlap)
（鸡）肉垂（鸡颈下的垂肉，喉部的垂
肉）
25 falcate (falcated) tail
镰形公鸡尾巴
26 spur
雄鸡肉距

27 guinea fowl
珠鸡
28 turkey; *m.* turkey cock
(gobbler); *f.* turkey hen
火鸡；公火鸡；雌火鸡
29 fan tail
扇形尾（巴）
30 peacock
孔雀
31 peacock's feather
孔雀的羽毛
32 eye (ocellus)
孔雀饲斑（眼状斑）
33 pigeon; *m.* cock pigeon
鸽子；雄鸽子
34 goose; *m.* gander; *y.* gosling
鹅；雄鹅；小鹅（幼鹅）
35 duck; *m.* drake; *y.* duckling
鸭；公鸭；小鸭
36 web (palmations) of webbed
foot (palmate foot)
鸭脚蹼（蹼足）

**1-27 poultry farming
(intensive poultry management)**
养鸡场（集约家禽管理）

**1-17 straw yard (strawed yard)
system**
草盖鸡场系统

1 fold unit for growing stock
(chick unit)
移动式养鸡遮棚（小鸡棚）

2 chick
小鸡

3 brooder (hover)
孵卵器，伞状育雏器

4 adjustable feeding trough
可调整饲槽

5 pullet fold unit
小母鸡棚

6 drinking trough
饮水槽

7 water pipe
水管

8 litter
垫草，垫褥

9 pullet
小母鸡

10 ventilator
通风设备

**11-17 broiler rearing (rearing of
broiler chickens)**
肉鸡的饲育

11 chicken run (*Am.* fowl run)
鸡房

12 broiler chicken (broiler)
肉鸡

13 mechanical feeder (self-feeder,
feed dispenser)
自动喂器（饲料分送器）

14 chain
链条

15 feed supply pipe
饲料供给管

16 mechanical drinking bowl
(mechanical drinker)
自动饮水钵

17 ventilator
通风设备

18 battery system (cage system)
层架式鸡笼系统

19 battery (laying battery)
、育雏笼

20 tiered cage (battery cage,
stepped cage)
层架式鸡笼

21 feeding trough
饲槽

22 egg collection by conveyor
以输送器集蛋

**23-27 mechanical feeding and
dunging** (manure removal,
droppings removal)
自动喂料和排粪

23 rapid feeding system for battery
feeding (mechanical feeder)
层架式鸡笼快速饲养（自动喂器）

24 feed hopper
漏斗饲槽

25 endless-chain conveyor (chain
feeder)
无端链运机（链式喂器）

26 water pipe (liquid feed pipe)
水管（液状饲料管）

27 dunging chain (dunging
conveyor)
排粪链（粪便输送器）

28 [cabinet type] setting and
hatching machine
〔橱式〕调节孵蛋机

29 ventilation drum [for the
setting compartment]
〔调节室的〕通风滚筒

30 hatching compartment (hatcher)
孵蛋室（孵化器）

31 metal trolley for hatching trays
孵化盘金属手推车

32 hatching tray
孵化盘

33 ventilation drum motor
通风滚筒马达

34-53 egg production
鸡蛋生产

34 egg collection system (egg
collection)
集蛋系统（集蛋）

35 multi-tier transport
多层运输装置

36 collection by pivoted fingers
有轴指耙收集器

37 drive motor
驱动马达

38 sorting machine
分类机，选别机

39 conveyor trolley
输送小车

40 fluorescent screen
萤光幕，萤光屏

41 suction apparatus (suction box)
for transporting eggs
运输蛋的吸入装置（吸入箱）

42 shelf for empty and full egg
boxes
空箱或装蛋箱架

43 egg weighers
蛋秤

44 grading
分级（产品）

45 egg box
蛋箱

46 fully automatic egg-packing
machine
全自动鸡蛋包装机

47 radioscope box
放射线照射装置

48 radioscope table
放射线照射台

49-51 feeder
�2料器

49 suction transporter
吸入运输装置

50 vacuum line
真空管路

51 supply table
供给台

52 automatic counting and grading
自动计数和分级

53 packing box dispenser
包装箱分配器

54 leg ring
足轮，脚环

55 wing tally (identification tally)
翼形计数签（识别标志）

56 bantam
矮脚鸡

57 laying hen
生蛋鸡

58 hen's egg (egg)
鸡蛋

59 eggshell, an egg integument
蛋壳，鸡蛋外壳

60 shell membrane
壳膜

61 air space
气室

62 white [of the egg] (albumen)
蛋白

63 chalaza (*Am.* treadle)
卵带

64 vitelline membrane (yolk sac)
卵黄膜（蛋黄囊）

65 blastodisc (germinal disc, cock's
tread, cock's treadle)
胚盘（鸡胎）

66 germinal vesicle
胚囊，卵核包

67 white
蛋白

68 yolk
蛋黄

1 stable
畜底（马底）

2 horse stall (stall, horse box, box)
马底（畜舍内的分隔栏，马栏，马底中供马活动部分）

3 feeding passage
饲养通道

4 pony
小马

5 bars
栏杆，栅栏

6 litter
垫草，垫褥

7 bale of straw
草捆

8 ceiling light
天窗，天花板窗

9 sheep pen
羊栏，羊圈

10 mother sheep (ewe)
母羊

11 lamb
羔羊，小羊

12 double hay rack
双棚条式乾草架

13 hay
干草

14 dairy cow shed
要把牛拴住的乳牛棚

15-16 tether
（拴牲畜用的）系链，系绳

15 chain
系链

16 rail
围栏横木

17 dairy cow (milch-cow, milker)
乳牛

18 udder
（牛的）乳房

19 teat
乳头，奶头

20 manure gutter
粪便沟

21 manure removal by sliding bars
滑板排肥

22 short standing
简便牛舍

23 milking parlour (*Am.* parlor), a
herringbone parlour
挤乳间，鱼刺形挤乳

24 working passage
工作通道

25 milker (*Am.* milkman)
挤乳人

26 teat cup cluster
全套挤乳杯

27 milk pipe
挤乳（导）管

28 air line
空气管线

29 vacuum line
真空管路

30 teat cup
挤乳杯

31 window
窗

32 pulsator
脉动泵，真空泵

33 release phase
放乳节拍

34 squeeze phase
挤压节拍

35 pigsty (*Am.* pigpen, hogpen)
猪圈，猪舍

36 pen for young pigs
小猪栏，猪仔圈

37 feeding trough
饲养槽

38 partition
隔板

39 pig, a young pig
猪，小猪，乳猪

40 farrowing and store pen
分娩围栏（猪栏）

41 sow
母猪

42 piglet (*Am.* shoat, shote) (sow
pig [for first 8 weeks])
小猪（产下八星期后的小猪）

43 farrowing rails
分娩护架

44 liquid manure channel
液体粪便沟

1-48 dairy (dairy plant)
乳品厂

1 milk reception
乳品接收设备

2 milk tanker
乳品搬运车；乳罐车

3 raw milk pump
生乳泵

4 flowmeter, an oval (elliptical) gear meter
流量表（计），一种椭圆形齿轮计量器

5 raw milk storage tank
生乳储存槽

6 gauge (*Am.* gage)
计量表

7 central control room
中央控制室，主控制室

8 chart of the dairy
乳品厂图表

9 flow chart (flow diagram)
流程图

10 storage tank gauges (*Am.* gages)
储存槽表计

11 control panel
控制板

12-48 milk processing area
牛乳加工区

12 sterilizer (homogenizer)
灭菌器

13 milk heater; *sim.*; cream heater
牛乳加热器；类似：乳油加热器

14 cream separator
油分离机

15 fresh milk tanks
鲜乳槽

16 tank for sterilized milk
灭菌乳槽

17 skim milk (skimmed milk) tank
脱脂乳槽

18 buttermilk tank
酪乳槽

19 cream tank
乳油槽

20 fresh milk filling and packing plant
鲜乳装瓶和包装设备

21 filling machine for milk cartons; *sim.*: milk tub filler
乳瓶装箱机；类似：乳盒装箱机

22 milk carton
牛乳纸箱

23 conveyor belt (conveyor)
运送带（输送器）

24 shrink-sealing machine
收缩封口机，缩封机

25 pack of twelve in shrink foil
12 瓶缩箔包装

26 ten-litre filling machine
10 公升填装机

27 heat-sealing machine
热封口机；热封机

28 plastic sheets
塑胶片

29 heat-sealed bag
热封袋

30 crate
条板箱

31 cream maturing vat
奶油熟化桶

32 butter shaping and packing machine
奶油成形包装机

33 butter churn, a creamery butter machine for continuous butter making
牛油搅动机，连续提炼牛油的乳脂机

34 butter supply pipe
牛油供给管

35 shaping machine
成形机

36 packing machine
包装机

37 branded butter in 250 g packets
250 公克包装标示的奶油

38 plant for producing curd cheese (curd cheese machine)
制凝乳酪机（凝乳酪机）

39 curd cheese pump
凝乳酪泵

40 cream supply pump
奶油供应泵

41 curds separator
凝乳分离机

42 sour milk vat
酸乳桶

43 stirrer
搅拌器

44 curd cheese packing machine
凝乳酪包装机

45 packeted curd cheese
凝乳酪包

46 bottle-capping machine (capper)
封盖机，瓶盖机

47 cheese machine
乾酪机

48 rennet vat
制凝乳

1-25 bee (honey-bee, hive-bee)
蜜蜂

1, 4, 5 castes (social classes) of bees
蜂级（蜜蜂之社会等级）

1 worker (worker bee)
工蜂

2 three simple eyes (ocelli)
三只单眼睛（单眼）

3 load of pollen on the hind leg
采粉足（蜜蜂的后足）

4 queen (queen bee)
雌蜂（蜂王）

5 drone (male bee)
雄蜂

6-9 left hind leg of a worker
工蜂的左后足

6 pollen basket
花粉篮

7 pollen comb (brush)
花粉梳（刷）

8 double claw
双爪

9 suctorial pad
吸盘

10-19 abdomen of the worker
工蜂的腹部

10-14 stinging organs
螯针器官，刺针器官

10 barb
倒刺

11 sting
螯针，针

12 sting sheath
螯针鞘，刺鞘

13 poison sac
毒囊

14 poison gland
毒腺

15-19 stomachic-intestinal canal
肠胃管，胃肠管

15 intestine
肠

16 stomach
胃

17 contractile muscle
收缩肌肉

18 honey bag (honey sac)
蜜囊

19 oesophagus (esophagus, gullet)
食物道（食道,食管）

20-24 compound eye
复眼

20 facet
（复眼中的一个）小眼

21 crystal cone
水晶体

22 light-sensitive section
感光区，光敏区

23 fibre (*Am.* fiber) of the optic nerve
视神经纤维

24 optic nerve
视神经

25 wax scale
蜜蜂蜡鳞

26-30 cell
（蜂房的）巢室

26 egg
蜂卵

27 cell with the egg in it
有卵的巢室

28 young larva
幼体,幼虫

29 larva (grub)
幼虫

30 chrysalis (pupa)
蜂蛹（蛹）

31-43 honeycomb
蜂房,蜂巢

31 brood cell
孵卵巢室,育幼巢室

32 sealed (capped) cell with chrysalis (pupa)
有蛹的密封巢室

33 sealed (capped) cell with honey (honey cell)
有蜜的密封巢室（蜂蜜室）

34 worker cells
工蜂巢室

35 storage cells, with pollen
花粉贮存室

36 drone cells
雄蜂巢室

37 queen cell
蜂王巢室

38 queen emerging from her cell
蜂王出巢（房）

39 cap (capping)
蜂罩

40 frame
蜂巢架

41 distance piece
定距片

42 [artificial] honeycomb
[人工]蜜蜂窝,蜂巢

43 septum (foundation, comb foundation)
蜂窝隔膜（巢基,蜂巢基）

44 queen's travelling (*Am.* traveling) box
蜂王移动箱

45-50 beehive, a movable-frame hive (movable-comb hive)
框架式蜂窝（移动框架式蜂窝）

45 super (honey super) with honeycombs
带蜂窝的蜂房上层活动架（蜂房架）

46 brood chamber with breeding combs
带繁殖蜂窝的育蜂室

47 queen-excluder
蜂王隔板,隔王板

48 entrance
入口,巢门

49 flight board (alighting board)
着陆板（降落板），前板

50 window
窗

51 old-fashioned bee shed
旧式的蜂棚

52 straw hive (skep), a hive
稻草蜂巢,蜂房

53 swarm (swarm cluster) of bees
蜂群

54 swarming net (bag net)
捕蜂群网（袋网）

55 hooked pole
钩杆

56 apiary (bee house)
养蜂场（养蜂房）

57 beekeeper (apiarist, *Am.* beeman)
养蜂家（养蜂者,[美]养蜂人）

58 bee veil
养蜂面罩

59 bee smoker
蜜蜂熏烟器

60 natural honeycomb
天然蜂巢（窝）

61 honey extractor (honey separator)
蜂蜜抽出器（蜂蜜分离器）

62-63 strained honey (honey)
滤过的蜂蜜

62 honey pail
蜂蜜桶

63 honey jar
蜂蜜瓶

64 honey in the comb
在蜂窝中的蜂蜜

65 wax taper
蜜蜡蕊,蜂蜡蕊

66 wax candle
蜜蜡烛,蜂蜡烛

67 beeswax
蜜蜡,蜂蜡

68 bee sting ointment
蜂刺（螯）软膏

1-21 vineyard area
葡萄园
1 vineyard using wire trellises for
training vines
用金属格子架栽培葡萄的葡萄园
2-9 vine (*Am.* grapevine)
葡萄藤
2 vine shoot
葡萄蔓
3 long shoot
长蔓
4 vine leaf
葡萄叶
5 bunch of grapes (cluster of
grapes)
一串葡萄
6 vine stem
葡萄茎
7 post (stake)
柱，支柱
8 guy (guy wire)
牵线，牵索
9 wire trellis
金属格子架
10 tub for grape gathering
葡萄采集桶
11 grape gatherer
葡萄采集（者）人
12 secateurs for pruning vines
修剪葡萄用的大剪刀
13 wine grower (viniculturist,
viticulturist)
葡萄栽培者

14 dosser carrier
背负葡萄筐的搬运夫
15 dosser (pannier)
背筐，笭筐
16 crushed grape transporter
挤葡萄的运输机
17 grape crusher
葡萄压榨器
18 hopper
漏斗
19 three-sided flap extension
三面板加长部分
20 platform
装卸台，平台
21 vineyard tractor, a narrow-track
tractor
葡萄园曳引机，一种窄轨距曳引机

1-22 wine cellar (wine vault)
葡萄酒窖（酒窖）
1 vault
拱形圆屋顶，地窖
2 wine cask
葡萄酒桶
3 wine vat, a concrete vat
（供酿造、发酵用的）大桶
4 stainless steel vat (*also*. vat made of synthetic material)
不锈钢桶（另有：合成材料制作的大桶）
5 propeller-type high-speed mixer
螺旋桨式高速混合机
6 propeller mixer
螺旋桨式混合机
7 centrifugal pump
离心泵
8 stainless steel sediment filter
不锈钢沉积物讨滤器
9 semi-automatic circular bottling machine
半自动圆形制瓶机
10 semi-automatic corking machine
半自动制（软木）塞机
11 bottle rack
酒瓶架
12 cellarer's assistant
管理酒窖的店员（伙计）
13 bottle basket
酒瓶篮
14 wine bottle
葡萄酒瓶

15 wine jug
酒壶
16 wine tasting
品嚐葡萄酒
17 head cellarman
酒窖经理
18 cellarman
酒窖店员（酒窖管理员）
19 wineglass
酒杯
20 inspection apparatus [for spotchecking samples]
检验器[抽样检验]
21 horizontal wine press
水平式葡萄酒压榨机
22 humidifier
潮化机，增湿器

1-19 fruit pests
水果害虫，果虫
1 gipsy (gypsy) moth
柿毛虫
2 batch (cluster) of eggs
卵块，一团卵
3 caterpillar
幼虫，毛虫
4 chrysalis (pupa)
蛹
5 small ermine moth, an ermine
moth
果蛾属巢蛾科
6 larva (grub)
幼虫
7 tent
巢网
8 caterpillar skeletonizing a leaf
把树叶吃剩了叶脉的毛虫
9 fruit surface eating tortrix moth
(summer fruit tortrix moth)
食心虫，属小卷叶蛾科
10 appleblossom weevil, a weevil
苹果花象鼻虫
11 punctured, withered flower
(blossom)
刺穿和凋谢了的花
12 hole for laying eggs
产卵洞，产卵孔
13 lackey moth
苹果蠹蛾
14 caterpillar
幼虫，毛虫
15 eggs
虫卵
16 winter moth, a geometrid
柿星尺蠖，属尺蠖科
17 caterpillar
幼虫，毛虫
18 cherry fruit fly, a borer
樱桃苍蝇
19 larva (grub, maggot)
幼虫，蛆

20-27 vine pests
葡萄害虫
20 downy mildew, a mildew, a
disease causing leaf drop
茸毛霉，霉病，圆星性落叶病
21 grape affected with downy
mildew
感染霉病的葡萄
22 grape-berry moth
葡萄锈壁虱，茸毛病虱
23 first-generation larva of the
grape-berry moth (*Am.* grape
worm)
葡萄锈壁虱第一代幼虫（葡萄虫）
24 second-generation larva of the
grape-berry moth (*Am.* grape
worm)
葡萄锈壁虱第二代幼虫（葡萄虫）
25 chrysalis (pupa)
虫蛹（蛹）
26 root louse, a grape phylloxera
葡萄根蚜虫
27 root gall (knotty swelling of the
root, nodosity, tuberosity)
根部虫瘿（树根上的结节）
28 brown-tail moth
枣刺虫
29 caterpillar
幼虫，毛虫
30 batch (cluster) of eggs
卵块
31 hibernation cocoon
越冬茧，冬眠茧

32 woolly apple aphid (American
blight), an aphid
苹果毛蚜虫，一种蚜虫
33 gall caused by the woolly apple
aphid
由毛蚜虫产生的虫瘿
34 woolly apple aphid colony
苹果毛蚜虫群体
35 San-José scale, a scale insect
(scale louse)
圣约瑟虫，一种介壳虫
36 larvae (grubs) [*male* elongated,
female round]
幼虫[长形雄幼虫，圆形雌幼虫]

37-55 field pests
田间害虫
37 click beetle, a snapping beetle
(*Am.* snapping bug)
磕头虫
38 wireworm, larva of the click
beetle
铁线虫，磕头虫的幼虫
39 flea beetle
跳甲虫，跳蚤
40 Hessian fly, a gall midge (gall
gnat)
麦蝇（似蚊，属瘿虫科）
41 larva (grub)
幼虫，蛆
42 turnip moth, an earth moth
芜菁蛾，土蛾
43 chrysalis (pupa)
蛹
44 cutworm, a caterpillar
糖蛾之幼虫，毛虫
45 beet carrion beetle
食腐烂甜菜的甲虫
46 larva (grub)
幼虫（蛴螬）
47 large cabbage white butterfly
菜粉蝶，菜白蝶，白蝴蝶，白粉蝶
48 caterpillar of the small cabbage
white butterfly
（菜粉蝶的幼虫为）青虫，菜虫
49 brown leaf-eating weevil, a
weevil
稻象鼻虫
50 feeding site
吃去的部分，被食部分
51 sugar beet eelworm, a nematode
(a threadworm, hairworm)
甜菜线虫，线虫类动物
52 Colorado beetle (potato beetle)
科罗拉多甲虫（薯虫）
53 mature larva (grub)
成熟的幼虫（蛴螬）
54 young larva (grub)
幼虫（蛴螬）
55 eggs
虫卵

1-14 house insects
家虫

1 lesser housefly
小家蝇

2 common housefly
普通家蝇

3 chrysalis (pupa, coarctate pupa)
蛹

4 stable fly (biting housefly)
厩蝇（叮人的家蝇）

5 trichotomous antenna
三歧触须

6 wood louse (slater, *Am.* sow bug)
土鳖，地鳖（一种小甲虫，居於朽木及湿地）

7 house cricket
家庭蟋蟀

8 wing with stridulating apparatus (stridulating mechanism)
带有鸣叫器官的羽翼

9 house spider
蜘蛛

10 spider's web
蜘蛛网

11 earwig
小蜈蚣，蠼螋

12 caudal pincers
尾螯，尾钳

13 clothes moth, a moth
蠹虫，蠹鱼子

14 silverfish (*Am.* slicker), a bristletail
蠹鱼，无翅昆虫

15-30 food pests (pests to stores)
粮食害虫（仓库害虫）

15 cheesefly
乾酪蝇

16 grain weevil (granary weevil)
谷象鼻虫

17 cockroach (black beetle)
蟑螂

18 meal beetle (meal worm beetle, flour beetle)
食粉甲虫

19 spotted bruchus
绿豆象

20 larva (grub)
幼虫（蛴螬）

21 chrysalis (pupa)
蛹

22 leather beetle (hide beetle)
龟甲虫

23 yellow meal beetle
豆象

24 chrysalis (pupa)
蛹

25 cigarette beetle (tobacco beetle)
烟草甲虫

26 maize billbug (corn weevil)
谷象

27 one of the Cryptolestes, a grain pest
谷类害虫的一种

28 Indian meal moth
玉米螟，属螟蛾科

29 Angoumois grain moth (Angoumois moth)
长毛稻螟

30 Angoumois grain moth caterpillar inside a grain kernel
在谷粒中的稻螟幼虫

31-42 parasites of man
人体内的寄生虫

31 round worm (maw worm)
蛔虫

32 female
雌蛔虫

33 head
蛔虫的头部

34 male
雄蛔虫

35 tapeworm, a flatworm
绦虫

36 head, a suctorial organ
绦虫头部，吸吮器官

37 sucker
吸盘

38 crown of hooks
钩状器官的顶部

39 bug (bed bug, *Am.* chinch)
臭虫（床虱）

40 crab louse (a human louse)
毛

41 clothes louse (body louse, a human louse)
衣虱（附在人体上的虱子）

42 flea (human flea, common flea)
跳蚤

43 tsetse fly
（热带非洲的）采采蝇（传播睡眠病）

44 malaria mosquito
疟蚊

1 cockchafer (May bug), a
  lamellicorn
  金龟子，末端有扁平触须的甲虫
2 head
  金龟子的头部
3 antenna (feeler)
  触须
4 thoracic shield (prothorax)
  前胸
5 scutellum
  盾状甲
6-8 legs
  腿（部）
6 front leg
  前腿
7 middle leg
  中腿
8 back leg
  后腿
9 abdomen
  腹（下腹）
10 elytron (wing case)
  鞘翅（翅鞘）
11 membranous wing
  翅膜（翅膀膜）
12 cockchafer grub, a larva
  金龟子蛴螬，一种幼虫
13 chrysalis (pupa)
  金龟子蛹
14 processionary moth, a nocturnal
   moth (night-flying moth)
   行军虫，夜盗虫，属夜蛾科
15 moth
  飞蛾
16 caterpillars in procession
  前进的行军虫（幼虫）
17 nun moth (black arches moth)
  毒蛾之一种（黑斑纹毒蛾）
18 moth
  舞蛾
19 eggs
  蛾卵
20 caterpillar
  幼虫，毛虫
21 chrysalis (pupa) in its cocoon
  茧内的（蛾）蛹
22 typographer beetle, a bark
   beetle
   印刷甲虫，一种在树皮下钻孔的小甲虫
23-24 galleries under the bark
   树皮下的坑道
23 egg gallery
  卵坑道
24 gallery made by larva
  幼虫挖的坑道
25 larva (grub)
  幼虫
26 beetle
  甲虫
27 pine hawkmoth, a hawkmoth
  松树天蛾，一种天蛾科的蛾
28 pine moth, a geometrid
  松树蛾，尺蠖蛾
29 male moth
  雄蛾
30 female moth
  雌蛾
31 caterpillar
  尺蠖蛾其幼虫为（尺蠖）
32 chrysalis (pupa)
  蛹
33 oak-gall wasp, a gall wasp
  五倍子黄蜂
34 oak gall (oak apple), a gall
  虫瘿

35 wasp
  黄蜂，胡蜂
36 larva (grub) in its chamber
  虫瘿中的幼虫
37 beech gall
  山毛榉虫瘿
38 spruce-gall aphid
  针纵树瘿蚜虫
39 winged aphid
  有翅蚜虫
40 pineapple gall
  凤梨状虫瘿
41 pine weevil
  松木象鼻虫
42 beetle (weevil)
  甲虫（象鼻虫）
43 green oak roller moth (green
   oak tortrix), a leaf roller
   橡树卷叶蛾科的一种
44 caterpillar
  幼虫，毛虫
45 moth
  卷叶蛾
46 pine beauty
  夜蛾的一种（食松树的害虫）
47 caterpillar
  幼虫，毛虫
48 moth
  夜蛾

1 area spraying
地区喷雾，区域喷雾
2 tractor-mounted sprayer
安装在牵引机上的喷雾器
3 spray boom
喷杆
4 fan nozzle
扇形喷雾咀
5 spray fluid tank
喷液箱
6 foam canister for blob marking
滴液划行泡沫罐
7 spring suspension
弹簧悬架
8 spray
喷洒，喷雾
9 blob marker
滴液划行器
10 foam feed pipe
泡沫供给管
11 vacuum fumigator (vacuum fumigation plant) of a tobacco factory
烟草厂的真空熏蒸消毒器（机）
12 vacuum chamber
真空室
13 bales of raw tobacco
未加工的烟叶捆
14 gas pipe
气管
15 mobile fumigation chamber for fumigating nursery saplings, vine layers, seeds, and empty sacks with hydrocyanic (prussic) acid
用氢氰酸熏蒸苗床树苗，藤压条机，种子和倒空袋的移动熏蒸器
16 gas circulation unit
气体循环装置
17 tray
托盘
18 spray gun
喷铨
19 twist grip (control grip, handle) for regulating the jet
调节喷射（注）的控制手把（柄）
20 finger guard
手指护板
21 control lever (operating lever)
控制杆（操作杆）
22 spray tube
喷管，喷雾管
23 cone nozzle
锥形喷咀
24 hand spray
手动（式）喷雾器
25 plastic container
塑胶容器
26 hand pump
手动泵
27 pendulum spray for hop growing on slopes
增加跳动斜度的摆式喷雾器
28 pistol-type nozzle
手枪式喷咀
29 spraying tube
喷雾管
30 hose connection
软管接头，软管连接（结）
31 tube for laying poisoned bait
布毒饵管，毒饵撒布管
32 fly swat
苍蝇拍

33 soil injector (carbon disulphide, *Am.* carbon disulfide, injector) for killing the vine root louse
土壤消毒器（注射二硫化碳於根部，以杀除藤根寄生虫）
34 foot lever (foot pedal, foot treadle)
踏杆（踏板），深度调整板
35 gas tube
气管
36 mousetrap
捕鼠机
37 vole and mole trap
田鼠和鼴鼠捕捉机
38 mobile orchard sprayer, a wheelbarrow sprayer (carriage sprayer)
移动式果园喷雾机，一种手推车式喷雾机
39 spray tank
药液喷雾箱
40 screw-on cover
螺旋盖
41 direct-connected motor-driven pump with petrol motor
与汽油发动机直接联结的直联式马达驱动泵
42 pressure gauge (*Am.* gage) (manometer)
压力计（压力表）
43 plunger-type knapsack sprayer
柱塞式背负喷雾机
44 spray canister with pressure chamber
具有压力室的喷雾箱
45 piston pump laver
活塞式泵杆
46 hand lance with nozzle
带喷咀的手动枪
47 semi-mounted sprayer
半悬挂式喷雾器
48 vineyard tractor
葡萄园用牵引机
49 fan
风扇
50 spray fluid tank
喷洒液箱
51 row of vines
葡萄树行
52 dressing machine (seed-dressing machine) for dry-seed dressing (seed dusting)
乾式种子消毒机
53 dedusting fan (dust removal fan) with electric motor
带有电动机的除尘风扇
54 bag filter
袋滤器
55 bagging nozzle
装袋咀
56 dedusting screen (dust removal screen)
除尘网
57 water canister [containing water for spraying]
[喷雾含水]水箱
58 spray unit
喷洒器[装置]
59 conveyor unit with mixing screw
带有混合螺旋的输送装置
60 container for disinfectant powder with dosing mechanism
有配药装置的消毒剂罐
61 castor
脚轮

62 mixing chamber
混合室

1-34 forest, a wood
森林，林地

1 ride (aisle, lane, section line)
林间车道（森林中两排树间的小径，小
路）

2 compartment (section)
林班（森林区划）

3 wood haulage way, a forest
track
集材道，林中小道

4-14 clear-felling system
皆伐作业

4 standing timber
立木

5 underwood (underbrush,
undergrowth, brushwood, *Am.*
brush)
矮林（生长在大树下的草木，灌木丛）

6 seedling nursery, a tree nursery
播种苗圃，树苗圃

7 deer fence (fence), a wire netting
fence (protective fence for
seedlings); *sim.*: rabbit fence
防鹿篱，一种金属网篱（苗圃中小树的
防护篱）；类似：防兔篱

8 guard rail
护栏

9 seedlings
播种苗，幼苗

10-11 young trees
小树，幼树

10 tree nursery after transplanting
移植苗圃（移植的树苗圃）

11 young plantation
人工幼林

12 young plantation after brashing
整枝后的人工幼林

13 clearing
皆伐

14 tree stump (stump, stub)
树桩（残干）

15-37 wood cutting (timber cutting, tree felling, *Am.* lumbering)
森林砍伐（林木砍伐，树木砍伐）

15 timber skidded to the stack (stacked timber, *Am.* yarded timber)
堆积的木材（集材）

16 stack of logs, one cubic metre (*Am.* meter) of wood
圆木堆，含有一立方公尺体积的木材

17 post (stake)
桩（支柱）

18 forest labourer (woodsman, *Am.* logger, lumberer, lumberjack, lumberman, timberjack) turning (*Am.* canting) timber
在翻转木材的林业工人（林业工，[美]伐木工）

19 bole (tree trunk, trunk, stem)
树干，树身

20 feller numbering the logs
给圆木编号的伐木工

21 steel tree calliper (caliper)
钢制测径尺（卡尺）

22 power saw (motor saw) cutting a bole
切割树干的动力锯

23 safety helmet with visor and ear pieces
带有面甲和耳罩的安全盔

24 annual rings
年轮

25 hydraulic felling wedge
液压伐木楔

26 protective clothing [orange top, green trousers]
防护衣[橙色上衣，绿色裤子]

27 felling with a power saw (motor saw)
用机力锯伐木

28 undercut (notch, throat, gullet, mouth, sink, kerf, birdsmouth)
下口，下槽

29 back cut
上口，上槽

30 sheath holding felling wedge
装伐木楔的护套（鞘）

31 log
圆木

32 free-cutting saw for removing underwood and weeds
清除矮林和杂草的易削锯（高速锯）

33 circular saw (or activated blade) attachment
圆锯附件（圆锯片）

34 power unit (motor)
动力装置（马达）

35 canister of viscous oil for the saw chain
锯链用的润滑油桶

36 petrol canister (*Am.* gasoline canister)
汽油箱

37 felling of small timber (of smallsized thinnings) (thinning)
小木材的采伐（采伐小径木）

1 axe (*Am.* ax)
斧
2 edge (cutting edge)
斧刃
3 handle (helve)
斧柄
4 felling wedge (falling wedge)
with wood insert and ring
带木塞和卡箍的伐木楔块
5 riving hammer (cleaving
hammer, splitting hammer)
劈锤
6 lifting hook
吊钩
7 cant hook
搬钩
8 barking iron (bark spud)
剥树皮用的铲（树皮铲）
9 peavy
尖头钩挺
10 slide calliper (caliper) (calliper
square)
滑动卡尺
11 billhook, a knife for lopping
钩刀，砍枝用柴刀
12 revolving die hammer (marking
hammer, marking iron, *Am.*
marker)
旋转烙印铁
13 power saw (motor saw)
机力锯
14 saw chain
锯链
15 safety brake for the saw chain,
with finger guard
带手指防护装置锯链的安全制动器
16 saw guide
锯导板
17 accelerator lock
油门销
18 snedding machine (trimming
machine, *Am.* knotting
machine, limbing machine)
修整机
19 feed rolls
进给辊子
20 flexible blade
柔性刀片
21 hydraulic arm
液压臂
22 trimming blade
修整刀片
23 debarking (barking, bark
stripping) of boles
树干剥皮
24 feed roller
进给滚子
25 cyclinder trimmer
圆筒式修木机
26 rotary cutter
镟片机，旋切刀
27 short-haul skidder
短途集材车
28 loading crane
装载起重机
29 log grips
圆木握爪
30 post
车立柱，支柱
31 Ackermann steering system
滚架式折腰转向装置
32 log dump
圆木堆
33 number (identification number)
号印（标志号印）

34 skidder
集材车
35 front blade (front plate)
前护板
36 crush-proof safety bonnet (*Am.*
safety hood)
防压碎安全盖帽
37 Ackermann steering system
滚架式折腰转向装置
38 cable winch
缆索绞车
39 cable drum
缆索圆筒
40 rear blade (rear plate)
后护板
41 boles with butt ends held off the
ground
粗端离地的树干
42 haulage of timber by road
木材的道路运输（方式）
43 tractor (tractor unit)
曳引机，牵引机
44 loading crane
装载起重机
45 hydraulic jack
液压千斤顶
46 cable winch
缆索绞车
47 post
车立柱，支柱
48 bolster plate
承梁板
49 rear bed (rear bunk)
后挂车底架

1-52 kinds of hunting
各种狩猎方式，狩猎的种类
1-8 stalking (deer stalking, *Am.*
stillhunting) in the game
preserve
在禁猎地潜随猎物
1 **huntsman** (hunter)
猎人
2 **hunting clothes**
猎人装
3 **knapsack**
背包
4 **sporting gun** (sporting rifle,
hunting rifle)
猎枪
5 **huntsman's hat**
猎帽
6 **field glasses, binoculars**
（小型的）双筒望远镜
7 **gun dog**
猎犬
8 **track** (trail, hoofprints)
踪迹（足迹，足印）
**9-12 hunting in the rutting season
and the pairing season**
在猎物的发情期和交配期狩猎
9 **hunting screen** (screen, *Am.*
blind)
狩猎隐蔽屏（[美]障蔽物）
10 **shooting stick** (shooting seat,
seat stick)
狩猎座杖
11 **blackcock, displaying**
求偶炫跃的黑色公鸡

12 **rutting stag**
发情的牡鹿
13 **hind, grazing**
吃草的红雌鹿
14-17 hunting from a raised hide
(raised stand)
从高台隐蔽处狩猎（高台）
14 **raised hide** (raised stand, high
seat)
高台隐蔽处（高台，高架）
15 **herb within range**
射程内的兽群
16 **game path** (*Am.* runway)
猎物跑道
17 **roebuck, hit in the shoulder and
killed by a finishing shot**
肩部中弹受伤而后被击毙的雄鹿
18 **phaeton**
四轮敞篷马车
19-27 types of trapping
设陷阱诱捕野兽的方式
19 **trapping of small predators**
小食肉动物的诱捕
20 **box trap** (trap for small
predators)
箱形捕捉机（小食肉动物的捕捉机）
21 **bait**
诱饵，饵
22 **marten, a small predator**
貂，一种小食肉动物
23 **ferreting** (hunting rabbits out of
their warrens)
用雪貂狩猎（将野兔从兔穴中逐出以捕
捉之）

24 **ferret**
雪貂
25 **ferreter**
捕猎者
26 **burrow** (rabbit burrow, rabbit
hole)
穴（兔穴，兔洞）
27 **net** (rabbit net) over the burrow
opening
张於穴口的网

28 feeding place for game
(winter feeding place)
放饵处（冬季放饵处），放饵场

29 poacher
（侵入他人地界）偷猎者

30 carbine, a short rifle
卡宾枪，一种短来福枪

31 boar hunt
野猪狩猎区

32 wild sow (sow, wild boar)
野猪

33 boarhound (hound, hunting
dog; *collectively*: pack, pack of
hounds)
（猎野猪的）大猎犬（尤指大丹狗，集
合称：群，一群猎犬）

34-39 beating (driving, hare
hunting)
追赶猎物

34 aiming position
瞄准姿势

35 hare, furred game, ground game
野兔，有软毛的猎物，地面上的猎物

36 retrieving
猎狗寻回猎物

37 beater
追猎者

38 bag (kill)
猎物

39 cart for carrying game
猎物搬运车

40 waterfowling (wildfowling, duck
shooting, *Am.* duck hunting)
猎水禽（猎水鸟，猎野鸭）

41 flight of wild ducks, winged
game
飞翔的野鸭，展翅飞行的猎物

42-46 falconry (hawking)
鹰猎（放鹰捕猎）

42 falconer
养猎鹰者，鹰猎者

43 reward, a piece of meat
报酬（奖赏），一块肉

44 falcon's hood
鹰的头罩

45 jess
鹰的足带

46 falcon, a hawk, a male hawk
(tiercel) swooping (stooping) on
a heron
猎鹰，猛扑苍鹭的雄鹰

47-52 shooting from a butt
由靶垛射猎

47 tree to which birds are lured
引诱鸟的树，诱鸟树

48 eagle owl, a decoy bird (decoy)
大鹃鸺，一种诱鸟

49 perch
楼木

50 decoyed bird, a crow
被诱鸟，一隻乌鸦

51 butt for shooting crows or eagle
owls
射击乌鸦或大鹃鸺的靶垛

52 gun slit
猎枪的狭缝口

1-40 sporting guns (sporting
rifles, hunting rifles)
猎枪（狩猎来福枪）
1 single-loader (single-loading
rifle)
单发猎枪（单发来福枪）
2 repeating rifle, a small-arm
(fire-arm), a repeater (magazine
rifle, magazine repeater)
连发猎枪，轻武器（火器），连发步枪
（弹匣式枪）
3, 4, 6, 13 stock
枪托
3 butt
枪托
4 cheek [on the left side]
贴腮[左侧面]
5 sling ring
吊环
6 pistol grip
握把
7 small of the butt
枪托的腰部
8 safety catch
保险锁，安全掣子
9 lock
枪机
10 trigger guard
扳机护圈
11 second set trigger (firing trigger)
待触发板机（射击板机）
12 hair trigger (set trigger)
微力板机

13 foregrip
前握把
14 butt plate
枪托底板
15 cartridge chamber
弹膛
16 receiver
接收器
17 magazine
（连发枪之）弹匣，弹夹
18 magazine spring
弹匣弹簧
19 ammunition (cartridge)
弹药（枪弹）
20 chamber
弹膛
21 firing pin (striker)
撞针
22 bolt handle (bolt lever)
枪栓柄
23 triple-barrelled (triple-barreled)
rifle, a self-cocking gun
三管步枪，自动步枪
24 reversing catch (*in various guns:*
safety catch)
反向锁扣（在各种枪中：保险锁）
25 sliding safety catch
滑动保险锁
26 rifle barrel (rifled barrel)
来福枪管
27 smooth-bore barrel
滑膛枪管
28 chasing
枪身活板架

29 telescopic sight (riflescope,
telescope sight)
望远镜瞄准器（步枪上的望远镜瞄准
器）
30 graticule adjuster screws
标线片调整具螺丝
31-32 graticule (sight graticule)
标线片（瞄准器的标线片）
31 various graticule systems
复合标线片系统
32 cross wires (*Am.* cross hairs)
十字瞄准线
33 over-and-under shotgun
重叠式双管猎枪，上下二连管猎枪
34 rifled gun barrel
来福枪管
35 barrel casing
枪管壳
36 rifling
膛线
37 rifling calibre (*Am.* caliber)
膛线的尺寸（口径）
38 bore axis
枪膛轴
39 land
阳膛线
40 calibre (bore diameter, *Am.*
caliber)
枪膛口径（枪膛直径，[美]口径）

41-48 hunting equipment
狩猎装备

41 double-edged hunting knife
双刃猎刀

42 [single-edged] hunting knife
[单刃]猎刀

43-47 calls for luring game (for calling game)
引诱猎物的号（哨）

43 roe call
小雌鹿号

44 hare call
兔号

45 quail call
鹌笛

46 stag call
雄鹿号

47 partridge call
鹧鸪（松鸡）哨

48 bow trap (bow gin), a jaw trap
弓框捕捉器

49 small-shot cartridge
散弹药筒

50 cardboard case
硬纸板弹壳

51 small-shot charge
散弹

52 felt wad
填弹塞

53 smokeless powder (*different kind:* black powder)
无烟火药（不同种类的：黑色火药）

54 cartridge
枪弹

55 full-jacketed cartridge
完整枪弹

56 soft-lead core
（弹头）软铅芯

57 powder charge
（一发子弹装的）火药

58 detonator cap
起爆管

59 percussion cap
雷管

60 hunting horn
狩猎号

61-64 rifle cleaning kit
步枪的擦拭用具

61 cleaning rod
（枪枝的）通条

62 cleaning brush
枪刷，擦膛刷

63 cleaning tow
除尘粗麻屑

64 pull-through (*Am.* pull-thru)
枪膛清扫绳

65 sights
瞄准器

66 notch (sighting notch)
V 字形照门

67 back sight leaf
表尺

68 sight scale division
表尺刻度

69 back sight slide
表尺游标

70 notch [to hold the spring]
表尺沟（安装弹簧用）

71 front sight (foresight)
前瞄准器

72 bead
准星，山形准星

73 ballistics
弹道学

74 azimuth
方位，方位角

75 angle of departure
发射角

76 angle of elevation
仰角

77 apex (zenith)
顶点

78 angle of descent
（降）落角

79 ballistic curve
弹道曲线

1-27 red deer
（欧洲及亚洲产的）赤鹿

1 hind (red deer), a young hind or a dam; *collectively*: anterless deer, (*y*.) calf
雌性马鹿（赤鹿），一种小母鹿，总称：小雌性马鹿

2 tongue
舌

3 neck
颈

4 rutting stag
发情期的牡赤鹿

5-11 antlers
鹿角

5 burr (rose)
鹿角根部隆起部分，枝角轮

6 brow antler (brow tine, brow point, brow snag)
额角角

7 bez antler (bay antler, bay, bez tine)
鹿角的叉枝

8 royal antler (royal, tray)
鹿角从下往上数的第三枝

9 surroyal antlers (surroyals)
鹿角最上面的叉枝（又称冕角）

10 point (tine)
鹿角突出的尖端或叉齿

11 beam (main trunk)
鹿角主干，角干

12 head
头

13 mouth
嘴

14 larmier (tear bag)
鹿的泪腺（泪囊）

15 eye
眼睛

16 ear
耳朵

17 shoulder
肩部

18 loin
腰部

19 scut (tail)
鹿的短尾（尾巴）

20 rump
臀部

21 leg (haunch)
腰腿部（动物的腰腿）

22 hind leg
后腿

23 dew claw
伪蹄，悬蹄

24 hoof
蹄

25 foreleg
前腿

26 flank
腰窝（肋骨与臀部间之部分）

27 collar (rutting mane)
颈鬃（发情鬃）

28-39 roe (roe deer)
鹿

28 roebuck (buck)
牡鹿，雄鹿

29-31 antlers (horns)
鹿角

29 burr (rose)
鹿角根部隆起部分，枝角轮

30 beam with pearls
鹿角的主干，角干

31 point (tine)
鹿角突出的尖端或叉齿

32 ear
耳朵

33 eye
眼睛

34 doe (female roe), a female fawn or a barren doe
雌鹿，未满一岁的小母鹿

35 loin
腰部

36 rump
臀部

37 leg (haunch)
腰腿部

38 shoulder
肩部

39 fawn, (*m*.) young buck, (*f*.) young doe
未满一岁的幼鹿，小雄鹿，小雌鹿

40-41 fallow deer
（欧洲产淡黄色带白斑的）梅花鹿

40 fallow buck, a buck with palmate (palmated) antlers, (*f*.) doe
淡黄带白斑的雄鹿，一种具有掌状角的雄鹿，雌鹿

41 palm
掌状物

42 red fox, (*m*.) dog, (*f*.) vixen, (*y*.) cub
赤狐，雄狐，雌狐，幼狐

43 eyes
眼（复）

44 ear
耳朵

45 muzzle (mouth)
狐、狗等的口（口鼻部）

46 pads (paws)
肉趾（足掌）

47 brush (tail)
狐尾（尾巴）

48 badger, (*f*.) sow
獾，雌獾

49 tail
尾巴

50 paws
脚爪

51 wild boar, (*m*.) boar, (*f*.) wild sow (sow), (*y*.) young boar
野猪，野公猪，野母猪，小野猪

52 bristles
鬃毛

53 snout
猪鼻（口鼻部）

54 tusk
长牙，獠牙

55 shield
防护厚皮（肩胛上的厚皮）

56 hide
野猪皮，兽皮

57 dew claw
悬蹄，伪蹄

58 tail
尾巴

59 hare, (*m*.) buck, (*f*.) doe
野兔，公兔，母兔

60 eye
眼睛

61 ear
耳朵

62 scut (tail)
兔的短尾巴

63 hind leg
后腿

64 foreleg
前腿

65 rabbit
家兔，兔子

66 blackcock
黑色雄松鸡

67 tail
尾羽

68 falcate (falcated) feathers
镰状尾羽

69 hazel grouse (hazel hen)
黄棕色松鸡

70 partridge
鹧鸪

71 horseshoe (horseshoe marking)
马蹄形斑纹

72 wood grouse (capercaillie)
雷鸟，雷鸡

73 beard
髯毛

74 axillary marking
腋斑

75 tail (fan)
扇形尾羽

76 wing (pinion)
鸟翼（翮）

77 common pheasant, a pheasant, (*m*.) cock pheasant (pheasant cock), (*f*.) hen pheasant (pheasant hen)
雉鸡或环颈雉，雄雉，雌雉

78 plumicorn (feathered ear, ear tuft, ear, horn)
耳羽（角状耳羽）

79 wing
翅膀，翼

80 tail
尾羽

81 leg
腿

82 spur
肉距

83 snipe
鹬，沙锥鸟

84 bill (beak)
鸟喙

1-19 fish farming (fish culture, pisciculture)
鱼类养殖

1 cage in running water
流水中的网箱

2 hand net (landing net)
袋网，手网

3 semi-oval barrel for transporting fish
运送鱼用的半椭圆形桶

4 vat
大桶

5 trellis in the overflow
溢流中的拦鱼栅（格子栅）

6 trout pond; *sim.*: carp pond, a fry pond, fattening pond, or cleansing pond
鳟鱼池，类似；鲤鱼池，一种鱼苗池，育肥池，清洗池

7 water inlet (water supply pipe)
给水口（给水管）

8 water outlet (outlet pipe)
排水口（排水管）

9 monk
净化池

10 screen
滤网

11-19 hatchery
鱼卵孵化所

11 stripping the spawning pike (seed pike)
挤梭子鱼卵

12 fish spawn (spawn, roe, fish eggs)
鱼卵

13 female fish (spawner, seed fish)
雌鱼（产卵期之鱼）

14 trout breeding (trout rearing)
鳟鱼孵化（鳟鱼养殖）

15 Californian incubator
加利福尼亚孵化器

16 trout fry
鳟鱼苗

17 hatching jar for pike
梭子鱼孵化瓶

18 long incubation tank
长形孵化槽

19 Brandstetter egg-counting board
布兰德斯特计卵板

20-94 angling
钓鱼

20-31 coarse fishing
垂钓

20 line shooting
放钓线

21 coils
线卷

22 cloth (rag) or paper
布片或纸片

23 rod rest
钓竿扶架

24 bait tin
饵罐

25 fish basket (creel)
鱼篓（柳条鱼篮）

26 fishing for carp from a boat
船上钓鲤

27 rowing boat (fishing boat)
划艇渔船（渔船）

28 keep net
活鱼笼

29 drop net
落下网

30 pole (punt pole, quant pole)
篙（撑船篙）

31 casting net
撒网

32 two-handed side cast with fixed-spool reel
具有固定轴的两手操作的侧撒网

33 initial position
起始位置

34 point of release
释放点

35 path of the rod tip
钓竿端轨迹

36 trajectory of the baited weight
诱饵重量的轨迹

37-94 fishing tackle
钓具

37 fishing pliers
捕鱼钳

38 filleting knife
切鱼（片）刀

39 fish knife
（食）鱼刀

40 disgorger (hook disgorger)
取饵钩

41 bait needle
饵针

42 gag
张口器，撑口器

43-48 floats
浮标

43 sliding cork float
滑动软木浮标

44 plastic float
塑胶浮标

45 quill float
羽茎浮子，翎管浮标

46 polystyrene float
聚苯乙烯浮标

47 oval bubble float
卵形（椭圆形）气泡浮标

48 lead-weighted sliding float
滑动铅锤浮标

49-58 rods
钓竿，钓鱼竿

49 solid glass rod
实心玻璃钓竿

50 cork handle (cork butt)
软木把

51 spring-steel ring
弹性钢环

52 top ring (end ring)
顶环（端环）

53 telescopic rod
套筒式鱼竿

54 rod section
鱼竿节，钓竿节

55 bound handle (bound butt)
有包紮的手把

56 ring
鱼竿环，钓竿环

57 carbon-fibre rod; *sim.*: hollow glass rod
碳纤维竿；类似有：空心玻璃钓竿

58 all-round ring (butt ring for long cast), a steel bridge ring
鱼竿引线环（放长线的托环），一种桥式钢环

59-64 reels
（卷绕线的）线轴，卷筒

59 multiplying reel (multiplier reel)
多股线轴

60 line guide
钓线导轮

61 fixed-spool reel (stationary-drum reel)
卷线固定轴

62 bale arm
控制柄

63 fishing line
钓丝（线）

64 controlling the cast with the index finger
用食指控制抛线

65-76 baits
鱼饵

65 fly
假蝇

66 artificial nymph
蛹形拟饵

67 artificial earthworm
蚯蚓拟饵

68 artificial grasshopper
蚱蜢拟饵

69 single-jointed plug (single-jointed wobbler)
单节拟饵

70 double-jointed plug (double-jointed wobbler)
双节拟饵

71 round wobbler
圆形拟饵

72 wiggler
孑子鱼饵

73 spoon bait (spoon)
匙形诱饵

74 spinner
旋转匙形诱饵

75 spinner with concealed hook
带隐钩旋转匙形诱饵

76 long spinner
长旋转匙形诱饵

77 swivel
转镮

78 cast (leader)
接钩绳（引线）

79-87 hooks
鱼钩，钓钩

79 fish hook
鱼钩

80 point of the hook with barb
带倒刺的鱼钩尖

81 bend of the hook
钩的弯头

82 spade (eye)
钩柄（钩眼）

83 open double hook
双钩

84 limerick
鱼钩

85 closed treble hook (triangle)
三头钩（三角钩）

86 carp hook
鲤鱼钩

87 eel hook
鳗鱼钩

88-92 leads (lead weights)
铅锤

88 oval lead (oval sinker)
椭圆形铅锤

89 lead shot
铅球

90 pear-shaped lead
梨形铅锤

91 plummet
铅锤

92 sea lead
海上铅锤

93 fish ladder (fish pass, fish way)
鱼梯（鱼道）

94 stake net
张网

1-23 deep-sea fishing
远洋渔业
1-10 drift net fishing
漂网渔业，流网渔业
1 herring lugger (fishing lugger, lugger)
捕鲱帆船（帆船）
2-10 herring drift net
鲱流网，鲱漂网
2 buoy
浮标，浮筒
3 buoy rope
浮标索（绳）
4 float line
浮标绳（索）
5 seizing
绑紧用的细绳
6 wooden float
木质浮标
7 headline
顶绳，浮标绳
8 net
（鱼）网
9 footrope
底绳
10 sinkers (weights)
沉子（铅锤）
11-23 trawl fishing (trawling)
拖网渔业
11 factory ship, a trawler
加工船，拖网船
12 warp (trawl warp)
拖网索
13 otter boards
开网口板，拖网板
14 net sonar cable
鱼网声纳电缆

15 wire warp
金属拖网索
16 wing
袖网
17 net sonar device
鱼网声纳装置
18 footrope
底绳
19 spherical floats
球状浮标
20 belly
网腹
21 1,800 kg iron weight
1,800 公斤重的铁锤
22 cod end (cod)
端部囊网（网囊）
23 cod line for closing the cod end
闭合囊网之囊网束绳
24-29 inshore fishing
近海渔业
24 fishing boat
捕鱼小船，渔船
25 ring net cast in a circle
环状网
26 cable for closing the ring net
闭合网口用之缆索
27 closing gear
闭合齿轮装置
28-29 long-line fishing (long-lining)
延绳钓
28 long line
多钩长线
29 suspended fishing tackle
悬浮钓具

1-34 windmill
风车,风力磨坊

1 windmill vane (windmill sail, windmill arm)
风车叶片(风车翼板,风车臂)

2 stock (middling, back, radius)
翼帆主轴(中间支撑臂,翼支板,翼背板)

3 frame
骨架

4 shutter
风门片

5 wind shaft (sail axle)
翼帆轴(翼板轴)

6 sail top
翼帆(帆)顶

7 brake wheel
制动轮

8 brake
制动器

9 wooden cog
木齿

10 pivot bearing (step bearing)
枢轴轴承(止推轴承)

11 wallower
灯型轮

12 mill spindle
磨石心轴

13 hopper
漏斗

14 shoe (trough, spout)
进料槽

15 miller
磨坊工人

16 millstone
石磨盘

17 furrow (flute)
沟槽(凹槽)

18 master furrow
主槽

19 eye
石磨孔,磨盘孔

20 hurst (millstone casing)
磨石壳

21 set of stones (millstones)
磨石组

22 runner (upper millstone)
上层磨石

23 bed stone (lower stone, bedder)
下层磨石

24 wooden shovel
木制铲

25 bevel gear (bevel gearing)
斜齿轮

26 bolter (sifter)
筛(筛子)

27 wooden tub (wooden tun)
大木桶

28 flour
面粉

29 smock windmill (Dutch windmill)
转帽式风车(荷兰风车)

30 rotating (revolving) windmill cap
风车转帽

31 post windmill (German windmill)
支柱式风车(德国风车)

32 tailpole (pole)
后支柱(支撑)

33 base
基柱,支承

34 post
支柱

35-44 watermill
水车,水力磨坊

35 overshot mill wheel (high-breast mill wheel), a mill wheel (waterwheel)
上射式水车(胸射水车),一种水车轮(水车)

36 bucket (cavity)
水斗(戽斗)

37 middleshot mill wheel (breast mill wheel)
中射式水车(胸射水车)

38 curved vane
弧形叶片

39 undershot mill wheel
下射式水车

40 flat vane
平承叶片

41 headrace (discharge flume)
引水渠(放水沟)

42 mill weir
水车用的堰

43 overfall (water overfall)
溢水门

44 millstream (millrace, *Am.* raceway)
(水车)出水道,导水路

1-41 preparation of malt (malting)
麦芽制造的设备

1 malting tower (maltings)
麦芽制造塔

2 barley hopper
大麦漏斗

3 washing floor with compressed-air washing unit
有压缩空气洗涤装置的洗涤层

4 outflow condenser
外流凝结器

5 water-collecting tank
集水箱

6 condenser for the steep liquor
浸液用的凝结器

7 coolant-collecting plant
冷却剂收集装置

8 steeping floor (steeping tank, dressing floor)
浸渍层（浸渍槽，清选层）

9 cold water tank
冷水箱

10 hot water tank
热水箱

11 pump room
水泵房

12 pneumatic plant
压缩空气场

13 hydraulic plant
液压装置

14 ventilation shaft (air inlet and outlet)
通风管道（进气口和出气口）

15 exhaust fan
排风机

16-18 kilning floors
烘干机层

16 drying floor
干燥层

17 burner ventilator
燃烧送风机

18 curing floor
加工处理层

19 outlet from the kiln
干燥气的出口管

20 finished malt collecting hopper
成品麦芽收集漏斗

21 transformer station
变电所

22 cooling compressors
冷冻压缩机

23 green malt (germinated barley)
绿麦芽（发芽的大麦）

24 turner (plough)
翻拌器

25 central control room with flow diagram
有流程图的中央控制室

26 screw conveyor
螺旋运送机

27 washing floor
洗涤层

28 steeping floor
浸渍层

29 drying kiln
干燥器

30 curing kiln
加工处理器

31 barley silo
大麦储仓

32 weighing apparatus
衡量器

33 barley elevator
大麦升降机

34 three-way chute (three-way tippler)
三通滑槽（三通倾卸装置）

35 malt elevator
麦芽升降机

36 cleaning machine
滤选机（清选机）

37 malt silo
麦芽储仓

38 corn removal by suction
抽除麦粒

39 sacker
装袋器

40 dust extractor
灰尘抽出器

41 barley reception
大麦的接收

42-53 mashing process in the mashhouse
酿酒厂的酿酒过程

42 premasher (converter) for mixing grist and water
混合麦芽和水的转化器

43 mash tub (mash tun) for mashing the malt
麦芽浆槽（桶）

44 mash copper (mash tun, *Am.* mash kettle) for boiling the mash
麦芽浆煮槽锅（桶，壶）

45 dome of the tun
槽顶

46 propeller (paddle)
螺旋桨

47 sliding door
滑门，拉门

48 water (liquor) supply pipe
供（液体）水管

49 brewer (master brewer, masher)
啤酒酿造者

50 lauter tun for settling the draff (grains) and filtering off the wort
沉淀残泽和过滤麦芽汁用的过滤槽

51 lauter battery for testing the wort for quality
麦芽汁品质检查用的过滤器具

52 hop boiler (wort boiler) for boiling the wort
煮沸麦芽汁用的锅炉

53 ladle-type thermometer (scoop thermometer)
长柄勺式温度计

1-31 brewery (brewhouse)
啤酒厂

1 - 5 wort cooling and break removal (trub removal)
麦芽汁的冷却和沉淀物的除去

1 control desk (control panel)
控制台（操纵台）

2 whirlpool separator for removing the hot break (hot trub)
除去高温沉淀物所用的漩涡分离器

3 measuring vessel for the kieselguhr
板状矽藻土计量器

4 kieselguhr filter
硅藻土过滤器

5 wort cooler
麦芽汁冷却器

6 pure culture plant for yeast (yeast propagation plant)
酵母纯粹培养设备（酵母繁殖室）

7 fermenting cellar
发酵室

8 fermentation vessel (fermenter)
发酵槽

9 fermentation thermometer (mash thermometer)
发酵温度计（醪温度计）

10 mash
麦芽汁

11 refrigeration system
冷却系统

12 lager cellar
贮酒室

13 manhole to the storage tank
贮酒槽的人孔

14 broaching tap
龙头

15 beer filter
啤酒过滤器

16 barrel store
酒桶仓库

17 beer barrel, an aluminium (*Am.* aluminum) barrel
啤酒桶，铝桶

18 bottle-washing plant
洗瓶机

19 bottle-washing machine (bottle washer)
洗瓶机

20 control panel
控制盘

21 cleaned bottles
已清洗过的瓶子

22 bottling
装瓶

23 forklift truck (fork truck, forklift)
堆高机

24 stack of beer crates
啤酒箱堆

25 beer can
罐装啤酒

26 beer bottle, a Eurobottle with bottled beer; *kinds of beer:* light beer (lager, light ale, pale ale or bitter), dark beer (brown ale, mild), Pilsener beer, Munich beer, malt beer, strong beer (bock beer), porter, ale, stout, Salvator beer, wheat beer, small beer
瓶装啤酒，一种欧式瓶装啤酒；啤酒种类：淡味啤酒（储藏啤酒，淡麦酒，弱麦酒或苦味啤酒），深色啤酒（棕色啤酒，口味温和啤酒），皮耳森啤酒，慕尼克啤酒，麦芽啤酒，烈性啤酒（烈性黑啤酒），黑啤酒，淡啤酒，烈啤酒，萨尔瓦多啤酒，小麦啤酒，小啤酒

27 crown cork (crown cork closure)
皇冠形瓶盖

28 disposable pack (carry-home pack)
简便包装（便於携带的包装）

29 non-returnable bottle (single-trip bottle)
不回收的瓶子（单程瓶）

30 beer glass
啤酒杯

31 head
泡沫

1 slaughterman (*Am.* slaughterer, killer)
　屠夫
2 animal for slaughter, an ox
　要屠宰的动物，牛
3 captive-bolt pistol (pneumatic gun), a stunning device
　屠牛枪（空气枪），一种击昏的器械
4 bolt
　枪栓
5 cartridges
　弹药，子弹
6 release lever (trigger)
　释放杆（板机）
7 electric stunner
　电击昏器
8 electrode
　电极
9 lead
　电线
10 hand guard (insulation)
　手护挡（绝缘体）
11 pig (*Am.* hog) for slaughter
　要屠宰的猪
12 knife case
　刀箱
13 flaying knife
　剥皮刀
14 sticking knife (sticker)
　刺戳刀（尖刀）
15 butcher's knife (butcher knife)
　屠宰刀
16 steel
　磨刀用的钢棒
17 splitter
　劈刀
18 cleaver (butcher's cleaver, meat axe (*Am.* meat ax))
　切肉刀（屠夫的切肉刀，切肉斧）
19 bone saw (butcher's saw)
　骨锯（屠夫锯）
20 meat saw for sawing meat into cuts
　将肉锯成块的肉锯
21–24 cold store (cold room)
　冷冻库（冷藏室）
21 gambrel (gambrel stick)
　马脚状的铁钩（挂肉刺钩）
22 quarter of beef
　包括整条腿的大块牛肉
23 side of pork
　猪体的侧面
24 meat inspector's stamp
　食肉检查员的戳记

left : meat side .左：肉侧边：
right : bone side .右：骨侧边

1-13 *animal* : calf; *meat* : veal
动物：小牛；肉：小牛肉
1 leg with hind knuckle
后腿肉[有后关节，（后肘）的腿肉]
2 flank
（肋腹肉，腰窝肉）软肋肉
3 loin and rib
腰肉和肋肉
4 breast (breast of veal)
胸肉（小牛的胸肉）
5 shoulder with fore knuckle
[有前关节（前肘）的腿肉]前腿肉
6 neck with scray (scrag end)
颈肉
7 best end of loin (of loin of veal)
最好的牛腰肉
8 fore knuckle
前肘（关节）
9 shoulder
肩膀肉
10 hind knuckle
后肘（关节）
11 roasting round (oyster round)
腿肉（适於烤制的圆而厚的牛肉）
12 cutlet for frying or braising
用於煎或火炖煮的肉片
13 undercut (fillet)
腰部下侧嫩肉（里脊）

14-37 *animal* : ox; *meat* : beef
动物：牛；肉：牛肉
14 round with rump and shank
包括臀部和小腿的圆而厚的牛肉
15-16 flank
（肋腹肉）软肋肉
15 thick flank
（厚肋腹肉）厚软肋肉
16 thin flank
（薄肋腹肉）薄软肋肉

17 sirloin
上部腰肉
18 prime rib (fore ribs, prime fore rib)
主肋骨（前肋骨，主前肋骨）
19 middle rib and chuck
中肋骨和颈与肩部的肉
20 neck
颈肉
21 flat rib
扁平肋骨
22 leg of mutton piece (bladebone) with shin
有牛胫的（肩胛骨）腿肉
23 brisket (brisket of beef)
胸肉（牛胸肉）
24 fillet (fillet of beef)
牛腰条肉（里脊肉）
25 hind brisket
后胸肉
26 middle brisket
中胸肉
27 breastbone
胸骨
28 shin
（肩胛骨肉）牛的前腿肉
29 leg of mutton piece
有肩胛骨的前腿肉
30 bladebone [meat side]
肩胛骨
31 part of top rib
上肋骨的一部分
32 bladebone [bone side]
肩胛骨（骨侧面）
33 shank
牛小腿肉
34 silverside
最上端牛腿肉
35 rump
臀部肉

36 thick flank
厚软肋肉（厚肋腹肉）
37 top side
顶边肉
38-54 *animal* : pig; *meat* : pork
动物：猪；肉：猪肉
38 leg with knuckle and trotter
有肘（关节）和蹄的猪腿
39 ventral part of the belly
腹的下部位
40 back fat
背部肥肉
41 belly
腹肉
42 bladebone with knuckle and trotter
有肘（关节）和蹄的肩胛骨肉
43 head (pig's head)
头（猪头）
44 fillet (fillet of port)
腰条肉（猪里脊）
45 leaf fat (pork flare)
腰子附近的（脂肪层）肥肉
46 loin (port loin)
腰肉
47 spare rib
排骨肉，带肉的猪肋骨
48 trotter
猪脚（蹄）
49 knuckle
（关节）肘肉
50 butt
肩肉
51 fore end (ham)
大腿前端肉
52 round end for boiling
可用来炖煮的臀部肉
53 fat end
脂肪部分
54 gammon steak
大腿肉

1-30 butcher's shop
　肉店
1 - 4 meat
　食用肉
1 ham on the bone
　火腿
2 flitch of bacon
　醃熏的猪肋肉
3 smoked meat
　熏肉
4 piece of loin (piece of sirloin)
　一块腰肉（一块牛腰肉）
5 lard
　猪油
6-11 sausages
　腊肠，香肠
6 price label
　价格牌
7 mortadella
　煮熟的烟熏香肠
8 scalded sausage; *kinds:* Vienna
　sausage (Wiener), Frankfurter
　sausage (Frankfurter)
　熟的香肠；种类：维也纳香肠，法兰克
　福香肠
9 collared pork (*Am.* headcheese)
　猪肉卷 [美]肉冻）
10 ring of Lyoner sausage
　里昂香肠圈
11 pork sausages; *also:* beef
　sausages
　猪肉香肠，牛肉香肠
12 cold shelves
　冷冻架

13 meat salad (diced meat salad)
　凉拌肉食（方块凉拌肉食）
14 cold meats (*Am.* cold cuts)
　各种冻肉
15 pâté
　小馅饼
16 mince (mincemeat, minced meat)
　碎肉
17 knuckle of pork
　猪肘子
18 basket for special offers
　特价品盘
19 price list for special offers
　特价品的价格表
20 special offer
　特价品
21 freezer
　冷藏柜
22 pre-packed joints
　预先包装的肉块
23 deep-frozen ready-to-eat meal
　低温冷冻的现成餐食
24 chicken
　鸡肉
25 canned food
　罐头食品
26 can
　罐头
27 canned vegetables
　蔬菜罐头
28 canned fish
　鱼罐头

29 salad cream
　沙拉酱
30 soft drinks
　不含酒精的饮料（清凉饮料）

31-59 manufacture of sausages
香肠的制造

31-37 butcher's knives
各种屠刀

31 slicer
切片刀

32 knife blade
刀身

33 saw teeth
锯齿

34 knife handle
刀柄

35 carver (carving knife)
切肉刀

36 boning knife
去骨刀

37 butcher's knife (butcher knife)
屠刀

38 butcher (master butcher)
屠夫，肉贩

39 butcher's apron
屠夫的围裙

40 meat-mixing tough
绞肉槽

41 sausage meat
香肠肉

42 scraper
刮刀

43 skimmer
网杓

44 sausage fork
香肠叉

45 scalding colander
烫滤器

46 waste bin (Am. trash bin)
废物箱，垃圾箱

47 cooker, for cooking with steam or hot air
蒸柜，蒸笼

48 smoke house
烟熏室

49 sausage filler (sausage stuffer)
灌腊肠（香肠）机

50 feed pipe (supply pipe)
输料管

51 containers for vegetables
蔬菜容器

52 mincing machine for sausage meat
香肠肉的绞肉机

53 mincing machine (meat mincer, mincer, Am. meat grinder)
绞肉机

54 plates (steel plates)
盘（钢盘）

55 meathook (butcher's hook)
挂肉钩

56 bone saw
骨锯

57 chopping board
砧板

58 butcher, cutting meat
切肉的屠夫

59 piece of meat
一块肉

1-54 baker's shop
面包店

1 shop assistant (*Am.* salesgirl, saleslady)
店员（女售货员）

2 bread (loaf of bread, loaf)
面包（一条面包）

3 crumb
面包心

4 crust (bread crust)
面包皮

5 crust (*Am.* heel)
面包端头

6-12 kinds of bread (breads)
面包的种类

6 round loaf, a wheat and rye bread
圆面包，一种小麦和裸麦做的面包

7 small round loaf
小圆块面包

8 long loaf (bloomer), a wheat and rye bread
长面包（灯笼形面包），一种小麦和裸麦做的面包

9 white loaf
白面包

10 pan loaf, a wholemeal rye bread
全麦面包，一种全麦做的面包

11 yeast bread (*Am.* stollen)
发酵包

12 French loaf (baguette, French stick)
法国面包（长条形面包，法国棒式面包）

13-16 rolls
小圆面包

13 brown roll
全麦小圆面包

14 white roll
白小圆面包

15 finger roll
细长的面包卷

16 rye-bread roll
裸麦小圆面包

17-47 cakes (confectionery)
各种点心（饼干）

17 cream roll
奶油卷

18 vol-au-vent, a puff pastry (*Am.* puff paste)
馅饼，一种压叠成层的和面

19 Swiss roll (*Am.* jelly roll)
瑞士卷（果酱卷）

20 tartlet
小型的果子馅饼

21 slice of cream cake
多层奶油饼（西点）

22-24 flans (*Am.* pies) and gateaux (torten)
派和糕饼

22 fruit flan (*kinds:* strawberry flan, cherry flan, gooseberry flan, peach flan, rhubarb flan)
水果派（种类：草霉派、樱桃派、醋果派、桃子派、大黄派）

23 cheesecake
乳酪蛋糕

24 cream cake (*Am.* cream pie) (*kinds:* butter-cream cake, Black Forest gateau)
奶油蛋糕（奶油派）（种类：奶油蛋糕，黑森林蛋糕）

25 cake plate
蛋糕盘

26 meringue
由蛋白和砂糖制成的糕饼

27 cream puff
泡芙（奶油松饼）

28 whipped cream
发泡奶油饼

29 doughnut (*Am.* bismarck)
甜甜圈

30 Danish pastry
丹麦糕饼

31 saltstick (saltzstange) (*also:* caraway roll, caraway stick)
盐条（香菜卷，香菜条）

32 croissant (crescent roll, *Am.* crescent)
牛角面包

33 ring cake (gugelhupf)
环形蛋糕（圆形大蛋糕）

34 slab cake with chocolate icing
巧克力糖衣蛋糕

35 streusel cakes
核桃酥饼

36 marshmallow
绵绵糖

37 coconut macaroon
蛋白杏仁饼乾

38 pastry whirl
蜗形饼

39 iced bun
圆形糖衣面包

40 sweet bread
甜面包

41 plaited bun (plait)
辫形圆面包

42 Frankfurter garland cake
花环腊肠饼

43 slices (*kinds:* streusel slices, sugared slices, plum slices)
千层派（种类：碎粒饼，糖衣饼，葡萄乾饼）

44 pretzel
咸脆饼

45 wafer(*Am.* waffle)
薄饼（威化饼）；鸡蛋饼

46 tree cake (baumkuchen)
树形蛋糕

47 flan case
装派的盒子

48-50 wrapped bread
包装好的面包

48 wholemeal bread (*also:* wheatgerm bread)
全麦面包（麦芽面包）

49 pumpernickel (wholemeal rye bread)
粗制裸麦面包（全裸麦面包）

50 crispbread
脆面包

51 gingerbread (*Am.* lebkuchen)
姜味面包

52 flour (*kinds:* wheat flour, rye flour)
面粉（种类：小麦粉，裸麦粉）

53 yeast (baker's yeast)
酵母（发酵粉）

54 rusks (French toast)
干面包（法式吐司）

55 74 bakery (bakehouse)
面包房

55 kneading machine (dough mixer)
揉面机（揉混机）

56-57 bread unit
面包设备

56 divider
分割机

57 moulder (*Am.* molder)
压模机

58 premixer
预混合机

59 dough mixer
揉混机，揉面机

60 workbench
工作台

61 roll unit
滚压设备

62 workbench
工作台

63 divider and rounder (rounding machine)
分划器和划圆机

64 crescent-forming machine
新月成型机

65 freezers
冷冻库

66 oven [for baking with fat]
烤箱[带油烘烤]

67-70 confectionery unit
制果糕的设备

67 cooling table
冷却台

68 sink
洗涤槽

69 boiler
锅炉

70 whipping unit [with beater]
搅打装置[带搅打器]

71 reel over (oven)
迴转炉（烤炉）

72 fermentation room
发酵室

73 fermentation trolley
（发酵室用）手推车

74 flour silo
面粉筒仓

1-87 grocer's shop (grocer's, delicatessen shop, *Am.* grocery store, delicatessen store), a retail shop (*Am.* retail store)
杂货店（熟食品商店），一种零售商店
1 window display
橱窗陈列
2 poster (advertisement)
海报（广告）
3 cold shelves
冷藏箱
4 sausages
香肠，腊肠
5 cheese
乳酪
6 roasting chicken (broiler)
烤鸡
7 poulard, a fattened hen
阉母鸡，一种肥母鸡
8-11 baking ingredients
烘烤配料
8 raisins; *sim.:* sultanas
葡萄干，无子葡萄干
9 currants
小粒无子葡萄干
10 candied lemon peel
柠檬果皮蜜饯
11 candied orange peel
橘皮蜜饯
12 computing scale, a rapid scale
计量磅秤，一种快速磅秤
13 shop assistant (*Am.* salesclerk)
店员（售货员）
14 goods shelves (shelves)
货架，商品架
15-20 canned food
罐头食品

15 canned milk
罐装牛奶
16 canned fruit (cans of fruit)
水果罐头
17 canned vegetables
蔬菜罐头
18 fruit juice
果汁
19 sardines in oil, a can of fish
油浸沙丁鱼，一种鱼罐头
20 canned meat (cans of meat)
肉罐头
21 margarine
人造牛油
22 butter
牛油
23 coconut oil, a vegetable oil
椰子油，一种植物油
24 oil; *kinds:* salad oil, olive oil, sunflower oil, wheatgerm oil, ground-nut oil
油；种类：沙拉油，橄榄油，葵花子油，麦芽油，花生油
25 vinegar
醋
26 stock cube
浓缩的汤料块
27 bouillon cube
浓缩的肉汤块
28 mustard
芥茉
29 gherkin (pickled gherkin)
小黄瓜（醃渍小黄瓜）
30 soup seasoning
汤的调味料

31 shop assistant (*Am.* salesgirl, saleslady)
女店员（女售货员）
32-34 pastas
面食
32 spaghetti
细通心面（意大利面食）
33 macaroni
通心粉，通心面
34 noodles
面条
35-39 cereal products
谷物制品
35 pearl barley
[小粒，球状的]精白麦
36 semolina
粗粒小麦
37 rolled oats (porridge oats, oats)
燕麦（燕麦片）
38 rice
米
39 sago
西谷米
40 salt
食盐
41 grocer (*Am.* groceryman), a shopkeeper (tradesman, retailer, *Am.* storekeeper)
食品杂货商，店主（商人，零售商）
42 capers
醃渍续随子花蕾
43 customer
顾客
44 receipt (sales check)
收据
45 shopping bag
购物袋

1-96 supermarket, a self-service food store
超级市场，自助式食品店

1 shopping trolley
购物手推车

2 customer
顾客

3 shopping bag
购物袋

4 entrance to the sales area
商场入口

5 barrier
栅栏

6 sign (notice) banning dogs
禁止狗进入的标示

7 dogs tied by their leads
被绳索栓住的狗

8 basket
篮，筐

9 **bread and cake counter** (bread counter, cake counter)
面包和糕饼柜台

10 display counter for bread and cakes
面包和糕饼的陈列柜台

11 kinds of bread (breads)
各式面包

12 rolls
小圆面包

13 croissants (crescent rolls, *Am.* crescents)
新月形面包，牛角面包

14 round loaf
圆块面包

15 gateau
嘉陀（一种浓味糕饼）

16 pretzel 'made with yeast dough'
脆饼'由发酵的面团做的'

17 shop assistant (*Am.* salesgirl, saleslady)
店员，（[美]女售货员）

18 customer
顾客

19 sign listing goods
商品告示牌

20 fruit flan
水果馅饼

21 slab cake
长方块蛋糕

22 ring cake
环形蛋糕

23 **cosmetics gondola,** a gondola (sales shelves)
化妆品陈列架，设于商场中央之陈列架（售货架）

24 canopy
篷子

25 hosiery shelf
袜类、内衣等货品架

26 stockings (nylons)
（尼龙）长袜

27-35 **toiletries** (cosmetics)
化妆品

27 jar of cream (*kinds:* moisturising cream, day cream, night-care cream, hand cream)
瓶装面霜（种类：润肤膏，白日用面霜，夜晚保养用面霜，手部保养霜）

28 packet of cotton wool
脱脂棉包

29 talcum powder
爽身粉

30 packet of cotton wool balls
脱脂棉球包

31 toothpaste
牙膏

32 nail varnish (nail polish)
指甲油

33 shaving cream
刮胡霜

34 bath salts
浴盐

35 sanitry articles
卫生用品（保健用品）

36-37 **pet foods**
宠物食品

36 complete dog food
营养完全的狗食物

37 packet of dog biscuits
狗饼干包

38 bag of cat litter
猫窝袋

39 **cheese counter**
乳酪柜台

40 whole cheese
全脂乳酪

41 Swiss cheese (Emmental cheese) with holes
瑞士乳酪，多孔的乳酪

42 Edam cheese, a round cheese
依顿乾酪，一种圆的乳酪

43 gondola for dairy products
乳制品陈列架

44 long-life milk; *also:* pasteurized milk, homogenized milk
保久乳；亦称：杀过菌的牛乳，均质牛乳

45 plastic milk bag
塑胶袋装牛乳

46 cream 奶油	**62** **gondola for baking ingredients and cereal products** 烘烤配料和和谷类品的陈列架
47 butter 牛油	**63** wheat flour 小麦粉
48 margarine 人造牛油	**64** sugar loaf 甜面包
49 box of cheeses 盒装乳酪	**65** packet of noodles 小包面条
50 box of eggs 盒装鸡蛋	**66** salad oil 沙拉油
51 **fresh meat counter** (meat counter) 新鲜肉柜台（肉柜台）	**67** packet of spice 调味包
52 ham on the bone 火腿	**68-70 tea, coffee, etc.** 茶、咖啡等
53 meat (meat products) 食用肉（各种肉类）	**68** coffee 咖啡
54 sausages 香肠	**69** packet of tea 小包茶叶
55 ring of pork sausage 香肠圈（猪肉做的）	**70** instant coffee 即溶咖啡
56 ring of blood sausage 香肠圈（猪肉和血做的）	**71** **drinks gondola** 饮料陈列架
57 freezer 冷藏室	**72** soft drinks 不含酒精成份之饮料
58-61 frozen food 冷冻食品	**73** can of beer (canned beer) 罐装啤酒
58 poulard 阉母鸡	**74** bottle of fruit juice (bottled fruit juice) 瓶装果汁
59 turkey leg (drumstick) 火鸡腿	**75** can of fruit juice (canned fruit juice) 罐装果汁
60 boiling fowl 煮熟的禽肉	**76** bottle of wine 瓶装葡萄酒
61 frozen vegetables 冷藏蔬菜	**77** bottle of Chianti 瓶装红葡萄酒

78 bottle of champagne
瓶装香槟酒

79 emergency exit
紧急出口，安全门

80 **fruit and vegetable counter**
水果和蔬菜柜台

81 vegetable basket
菜篮

82 tomatoes
蕃茄

83 cucumbers
黄瓜

84 cauliflower
花菜

85 pineapple
凤梨

86 apples
苹果

87 pears
梨子

88 scales for weighing fruit
称水果的秤

89 grapes (bunches of grapes)
葡萄（葡萄串）

90 bananas
香蕉

91 can
罐头

92 **checkout**
付款台

93 cash register
现金出纳机，收银机

94 cashier
出纳员

95 chain
链条

1-68 shoemaker's workshop
(bootmaker's workshop)
（皮）鞋匠的工作室
1 finished (repaired) shoes
做好的（修好的）鞋子
2 auto-soling machine
自动装（配）鞋底机
3 finishing machine
完工机（完成最后一道手续的机器）
4 heel trimmer
鞋根修整机
5 sole trimmer
鞋底修整机
6 scouring wheel
研磨轮
7 naum keag
浮石研磨机
8 drive unit (drive wheel)
驱动装置（驱动轮）
9 iron
切削压铁
10 buffing wheel
擦光轮
11 polishing brush
擦光刷
12 horsehair brush
马毛刷
13 extractor grid
抽出器的格栅
14 automatic sole press
自动鞋底压型机
15 press attachment
压型机附件

16 pad
缓冲垫，衬垫
17 press bar
压杆
18 stretching machine
伸张（展）机
19 width adjustment
宽度调整
20 length adjustment
长度调整
21 stitching machine
缝合机，缝纫机
22 power regulator (power control)
动力调整器（动力控制）
23 foot
机脚
24 handwheel
手轮，操纵（作）轮
25 arm
腕木，托架，支撑臂
26 sole stitcher (sole-stitching
machine)
鞋底缝纫（合）机
27 foot bar lever
脚踏杆
28 feed adjustment (feed setting)
进给调整器（进给装置）
29 bobbin (cotton bobbin)
线轴团（棉线轴）
30 thread guide (yarn guide)
导线杆
31 sole leather
鞋底皮革

32 [wooden] last
（木制）鞋型
33 workbench
工作台
34 last
鞋楦（制鞋用的型）
35 dye spray
染色喷雾器
36 shelves for materials
材料架

37 shoemaker's hammer
鞋匠的铁锤（榔头）
38 shoemaker's pliers (welt pincers)
鞋匠的钳子（镶边钳）
39 sole-leather shears
鞋底皮革剪
40 small pincers (nippers)
小铁钳
41 large pincers (nippers)
大铁钳
42 upper-leather shears
靴皮剪
43 scissors
剪刀
44 revolving punch (rotary punch)
旋转打孔器（钳）
45 punch
打孔器
46 punch with handle
有把手（柄）的打孔器
47 nail puller
拔钉钳
48 welt cutter
皮革切断器（切削刀）
49 shoemaker's rasp
鞋锉
50 cobbler's knife (shoemaker's knife)
（补）鞋匠刀
51 skiving knife (skife knife, paring knife)
切皮革的刀（薄片刀，削皮刀）
52 toecap remover
鞋尖拆卸钳

53 eyelet, hook, and press-stud setter
穿带孔，鞋扣和压钮定位器
54 stand with iron lasts
带鞋楦的立架
55 width-setting tree
宽度调整鞋楦
56 nail grip
起钉抓手
57 boot
靴子
58 toecap
鞋尖
59 counter
鞋面后跟部分
60 vamp
靴面
61 quarter
鞋帮的后侧部分
62 hook
鞋扣
63 eyelet
穿带孔
64 lace (shoelace, bootlace)
鞋带
65 tongue
鞋舌
66 sole
鞋底
67 heel
鞋跟
68 shank (waist)
鞋底（鞋跟上不著地的部分）

1 winter boot
冬季长统靴

2 PVC sole (plastic sole)
聚氯乙烯鞋底（塑胶鞋底）

3 high-pile lining
长绒毛衬里

4 nylon
尼龙

5 men's boot
男长统靴

6 inside zip
内侧拉链

7 men's high leg boot
男式高统靴

8 platform sole (platform)
平台鞋底

9 Western boot (cowboy boot)
牛仔靴

10 pony-skin boot
连毛小马皮长统靴

11 cemented sole
胶合鞋底

12 ladies' boot
女式靴子

13 men's high leg boot
男式高统靴

14 seamless PVC waterproof
wellington boot
无缝聚氯乙烯防水的威灵顿式靴子

15 natural-colour (Am. natural-
color) sole
自然色鞋底，本色鞋底

16 toecap
鞋头，鞋尖

17 tricot lining (knitwear lining)
斜纹毛织品衬里（针织品衬里）

18 hiking boot
健行靴

19 grip sole
防滑鞋底

20 padded collar
衬垫鞋口

21 tie fastening (lace fastening)
鞋带

22 open-toe mule
露趾无后跟女式拖鞋

23 terry upper
厚绒布鞋帮

24 polo outsole
外鞋底

25 mule
无后跟女式拖鞋

26 corduroy upper
灯心绒鞋帮

27 evening sandal (sandal court
shoe)
高跟凉鞋

28 high heel (stiletto heel)
高跟（女子高跟鞋的细鞋跟）

29 court shoe (Am. pump)
（没鞋扣或鞋带的）女轻便高跟鞋

30 moccasin
鹿皮鞋

31 shoe, a tie shoe (laced shoe,
Oxford shoe, Am. Oxford)
牛津鞋（绑带鞋，一种便鞋）

32 tongue
鞋舌

33 high-heeled shoe (shoe with
raisedheel)
高跟鞋

34 casual
便鞋

35 trainer (training shoe)
教练鞋，运动鞋

36 tennis shoe
网球鞋

37 counter (stiffening)
主跟

38 natural-colour (Am. natural-
color) rubber sole
自然色（本色）橡皮鞋底

39 heavy-duty boot (Am. stogy,
stogie)
工作鞋（粗而坚牢的靴）

40 toecap
鞋尖

41 slipper
轻便套鞋

42 woollen (Am. woolen) slip sock
毛织软袜

43 knit stitch (knit)
编织缝线

44 clog
木底鞋，木屐

45 wooden sole
木鞋底

46 soft-leather upper
软皮鞋帮

47 sabot
粗革面的木底鞋

48 toe post sandal
夹趾凉鞋

49 ladies' sandal
女式凉鞋

50 surgical footbed (sock)
足床

51 sandal
凉鞋

52 shoe buckle (buckle)
鞋扣

53 sling-back court shoe (Am. sling
pump)
后空半跟女鞋

54 fabric court shoe
轻便的平底半高跟布鞋

55 wedge heel
楔形后跟

56 baby's first walking boot
婴儿学步鞋

1 backstitch seam
   回针针迹线缝缝
2 chain stitch
   链缝，链式针（线）迹
3 ornamental stitch
   饰缝，花式线迹
4 stem stitch
   茎干缝，梗形线迹
5 cross stitch
   十字缝，十字形针迹
6 buttonhole stitch (button stitch)
   细孔缝，锁眼针迹
7 fishbone stitch
   鱼骨缝，鱼骨形针迹
8 overcast stitch
   缝边缝法，包边针迹
9 herringbone stitch (Russian
   stitch, Russian cross stitch)
   人字形交叉缝（俄罗斯十字线迹）
10 satin stitch (flat stitch)
   缎子缝法，绸纹刺绣针迹
11 eyelet embroidery (broderie
   anglaise)
   饰孔刺绣，穿孔刺绣
12 stiletto
   打孔器（锥）
13 French knot (French dot,
   knotted knot, twisted knot
   stitich)
   法式结（法国结点，打结针迹，编织的
   结缝）
14 hem stitch work
   抽丝后做成花边装饰的刺绣（垂缝刺
   绣）

15 tulle work (tulle lace)
   网状薄纱刺绣，六角网眼花边刺绣
16 tulle background (net
   background)
   网状纱底，网布素底（网眼底）
17 darning stitch
   补缀缝，织补针迹
18 pillow lace (bobbin lace, bone
   lace); kinds: Valenciennes,
   Brussels lace
   梭结花边，枕式花边（种类：瓦朗西
   花边，布鲁塞尔花边）
19 tatting
   梭织（结）花边
20 tatting shuttle (shuttle)
   梭织的绕线轮（梭）
21 knotted work (macrame)
   打结花边（丝结的饰缘，流苏花边）
22 filet (netting)
   方眼花边网（结网）
23 netting loop
   结网圈（环），编网网圈
24 netting thread
   结网线，编网丝
25 mesh pin (mesh gauge)
   网眼饰针（网眼规）
26 netting needle
   结网针
27 open work
   透孔织物
28 gimping (hairpin work)
   嵌心绣法（发绣）
29 gimping needle (hairpin)
   发针

30 needlepoint lace (point lace,
   needlepoint); kinds: reticella
   lace, Venetian lace, Alençon
   lace; sim. with metal thread:
   filigree work
   针织花边；种类：针绣挖花花边，威尼
   斯式花边，阿朗松式花边，类似：以金
   属丝织的，金银丝花边细工
31 braid embroidery (braid work)
   编结刺绣（彩饰）（编结织品）

1-27 dressmaker's workroom
裁缝工作室

1 dressmaker
裁缝师

2 tape measure (measuring tape),
a metre (*Am.* meter) tape
measure
卷尺，一种公制的卷尺

3 cutting shears
裁剪刀

4 cutting table
裁剪布

5 model dress
衣服的式样

6 dressmaker's model
(dressmaker's dummy, dress
form)
服装模特儿（裁缝师的模型，服装模
型）

7 model coat
模型女式外套，式样大衣

8 sewing machine
缝纫机

9 drive motor
驱动马达

10 drive belt
驱动带

11 treadle
踏板

12 sewing machine cotton (sewing
machine thread) [on boobin]
缝纫机线（线筒）

13 cutting template
裁剪样板（模板）

14 seam binding
滚边材料

15 button box
钮扣盒

16 remnant
碎布，布头

17 movable clothes rack
可移动的衣架

18 hand-iron press
手工熨斗

19 presser (ironer)
熨衣工

20 steam iron
（喷）蒸汽电熨斗

21 water feed pipe
供水管，自来水管

22 water container
水箱，存水桶

23 adjustable-tilt ironing surface
可调整倾斜的熨烫台

24 lift device for the iron
熨斗的升降装置

25 steam extractor
蒸汽排出器

26 foot switch controlling steam
extraction
控制蒸汽排出器的脚踏开关

27 pressed non-woven woollen
(*Am.* woolen) fabric
熨烫的无纺毛织物

1-32 tailor's workroom
裁缝师工作室

1 triple mirror
三面镜

2 lengths of material
各种衣料

3 suiting
衣料，西服料

4 fashion journal (fashion
magazine)
时装杂志

5 ashtray
烟灰缸

6 fashion catalogue
时装目录

7 workbench
工作台

8 wall shelves (wall shelf unit)
壁架

9 cotton reel
棉线卷筒

10 small reels of sewing silk
小卷的缝纫丝线

11 hand shears
手工裁剪刀

12 combined electric and treadle
sewing machine
电动和脚踏两用的缝纫机

13 treadle
（脚）踏板

14 dress guard
扩衣板

15 band wheel
皮带轮

16 bobbin thread
筒子线

17 sewing machine table
缝纫机台面

18 sewing machine drawer
缝纫机抽屉

19 seam binding
滚边材料

20 pincushion
针垫

21 marking out
划线

22 tailor
裁缝

23 shaping pad
样垫

24 tailor's chalk (French chalk)
裁缝划笔（滑石）

25 workpiece
工作件

26 steam press (steam pressing
unit)
蒸汽熨烫装置

27 swivel arm
旋转臂

28 pressing cushion (pressing pad)
烫平垫

29 iron
熨斗

30 hand-ironing pad
手工熨烫垫

31 clothes brush
衣刷

32 pressing cloth
熨烫布

1-39 ladies' hairdressing salon and beauty salon (*Am.* beauty parlor, beauty shop)
女子理发厅和美容院

1-16 hairdresser's tools
理发工具

1 bowl containing bleach
装漂白剂的碗

2 detangling brush
梳理缠结的发刷

3 bleach tube
管装漂白剂

4 curler [used in dyeing]
染发用的卷发夹子

5 curling tongs (curling iron)
烫发钳

6 comb (back comb, side comb)
发梳（后梳，边梳）

7 haircutting scissors
理发剪

8 thinning scissors (*Am.* thinning shears)
削发剪

9 thinning razor
削发剃刀

10 hairbrush
发刷，毛刷

11 hair clip
发夹

12 roller
卷发器

13 curl brush
卷发刷

14 curl clip
卷发夹

15 dressing comb
润饰梳

16 stiff-bristle brush
（硬）钢毛刷

17 adjustable hairdresser's chair
可调整的理容椅

18 footrest
搁脚板

19 dressing table
梳妆台

20 salon mirror (mirror)
理发厅镜子

21 electric clippers
电动理发推子

22 warm-air comb
热吹风梳

23 hand mirror (hand glass)
手镜

24 hair spray (hair-fixing spray)
发喷雾器

25 drier, a swivel-mounted drier
干燥器，装于旋臂上的干燥器

26 swivel arm of the drier
干燥器的旋臂

27 round base
圆型底座

28 shampoo unit
洗发设备

29 shampoo basin
洗发盆

30 hand spray (shampoo spray)
手持喷雾器（洗发喷雾器）

31 service tray
工具托盘

32 shampoo bottle
瓶装洗发精

33 hair drier (hand hair drier, hand-held hair drier)
吹风机（手持吹风机）

34 cape (gown)
披肩

35 hairdresser
理容师

36 perfume bottle
香水瓶

37 bottle of toilet water
瓶装花露水

38 wig
假发

39 wig block
陈列假发的木头架

1-42 men's salon (men's
hairdressing salon, barber's
shop, *Am.* barbershop)
男士理发厅，男士理发店
1 hairdresser (barber)
理发师
2 overalls (hairdresser's overalls)
罩衣工作服（理发师工作服）
3 hairstyle (haircut)
发型（理发）
4 cape (gown)
肩巾，披肩
5 paper towel
纸毛巾
6 salon mirror (mirror)
理发厅镜子
7 hand mirror (hand glass)
手镜
8 light
（电）灯
9 toilet water
化妆水
10 hair tonic
洗发剂
11 shampoo unit
洗发设备
12 shampoo basin
洗发盆
13 hand spray (shampoo spray)
手持喷雾器（洗发喷雾器）
14 mixer tap (*Am.* mixing faucet)
（冷热水的）混合龙头
15 sockets, e.g. for hair drier
插座；例如吹风机用的插座

16 adjustable hairdresser s chair
(barber's chair)
可调整的理发椅
17 height-adjuster bar (height
adjuster)
高度调整杆（高度调整器）
18 armrest
靠椅扶手
19 footrest
搁脚板
20 shampoo
洗发精
21 perfume spray
香水喷雾器
22 hair drier (hand hair drier,
hand-held hair drier)
吹风机（手持吹风机）
23 setting lotion in a spray can
喷罐装的做发化妆水（洗发精）
24 hand towels for drying hair
擦乾头发用的毛巾
25 towels for face compresses
敷脸用的毛巾
26 crimping iron
烫发钳
27 neck brush
颈刷
28 dressing comb
润饰梳
29 warm-air comb
热风梳
30 warm-air brush
热风刷

31 curling tongs (hair curler,
curling iron)
卷发钳
32 electric clippers
电动理发推子
33 thinning scissors (*Am.* thinning
shears)
削发剪
34 haircutting scissors; *sim.:* styling
scissors
理发剪，类似有，各类发型的剪刀
35 scissor-blade
剪刀刃部
36 pivot
枢轴
37 handle
手柄
38 open razor (straight razor)
开式剃刀（直柄剃刀）
39 razor handle
剃刀柄
40 edge (cutting edge, razor's edge,
razor's cutting edge)
刀刃（剃刀刀刃）
41 thinning razor
削发剃刀
42 diploma
执照，营业许可证

1 cigar box
雪茄烟盒
2 cigar; *kinds:* **Havana cigar (Havana), Brazilian cigar, Sumatra cigar**
雪茄；种类：哈瓦那雪茄，巴西雪茄，苏门答腊雪茄
3 cigarillo
小雪茄烟
4 cheroot
方头雪茄烟
5 wrapper
雪茄烟的外卷叶
6 binder
中卷叶
7 filler
雪茄烟烟心
8 cigar case
雪茄烟盒
9 cigar cutter
雪茄切割器
10 cigarette case
香烟盒
11 cigarette packet (*Am.* **pack)**
一包香烟
12 cigarette, a filter-tipped cigarette
香烟，有滤咀的香烟
13 cigarette tip; *kinds:* **cork tip, gold tip**
香烟滤咀；种类：软木滤咀，金箔滤咀
14 Russian cigarette
俄国香烟
15 cigarette roller
卷烟器
16 cigarette holder
香烟烟咀
17 packet of cigarette papers
一盒香烟纸

18 pigtail (twist of tobacco)
撚草烟，烟草卷
19 chewing tobacco; *a piece:* **plug (quid, chew)**
咀嚼烟草；一块的称作：嚼烟块
20 snuff box, containing snuff
鼻烟盒
21 matchbox
火柴盒
22 match
火柴
23 head (match head)
火柴头
24 striking surface
擦火柴磷面
25 packet of tobacco; *kinds:* **find cut, shag, navy plug**
一包烟草；种类：细切烟丝，板烟，口嚼烟草块
26 revenue stamp
印花
27 petrol cigarette lighter (petrol lighter)
汽油香烟打火机（汽油打火机）
28 flint
打火石
29 wick
灯心
30 gas cigarette lighter (gas lighter), a disposable lighter
瓦斯香烟打火机（瓦斯打火机），可随意使用的打火机（用完即丢的打火机）
31 flame regulator
火焰调节器
32 chibouk (chibouque)
长烟斗
33 short pipe
短烟斗

34 clay pipe (Dutch pipe)
陶制烟斗（荷兰烟斗）
35 long pipe
长管烟斗
36 pipe bowl (bowl)
烟斗的燃斗
37 bowl lid
烟斗盖
38 pipe stem (stem)
烟斗柄（杆）
39 briar pipe
石南根所制的烟斗
40 mouthpiece
烟咀
41 sand-blast finished or polished briar grain
喷沙精制或磨光的石南纹烟斗
42 hookah (narghile, narghileh), a water pipe
水烟筒，一种水烟斗
43 tobacco pouch
烟草袋
44 smoker's companion
吸烟者的用具
45 pipe scraper
烟斗刮刀
46 pipe cleaner
烟管除垢器
47 tobacco presser
烟草加压器
48 pipe cleaner
烟管除垢杆

1 wire and sheet roller
金属丝和金属板的滚轧机

2 drawbench (drawing bench)
拉丝台

3 wire (gold or silver wire)
金属丝（金丝或银丝）

4 archimedes drill (drill)
阿基米得钻（螺旋钻）

5 crossbar
横杆

6 suspended (pendant) electric
drilling machine
挂式电动钻孔机

7 spherical cutter (cherry)
球面刀具（樱桃木柄）

8 melting pot
熔罐

9 fireclay top
耐火泥顶

10 graphite crucible
石墨坩锅

11 crucible tongs
坩锅钳

12 piercing saw (jig saw)
穿孔锯（钢丝锯，细线锯）

13 piercing saw blade
穿孔锯刃

14 soldering gun
烊铨

15 thread tappepr
螺纹板牙

16 blast burner (blast lamp) for
soldering
烊接用的鼓风燃烧器（喷灯）

17 goldsmith
金匠，金饰工

18 swage block
型砧

19 punch
打孔器

20 workbench (bench)
工作台

21 bench apron
工作台围板

22 needle file
针状锉刀

23 metal shears
金属剪刀

24 wedding ring sizing machine
结婚戒指打造机

25 ring gage (Am. gage)
戒指量具

26 ring-rounding tool
戒指成圆环工具

27 ring gauge (Am. gage)
戒指量具

28 steel set-square
钢制直角规

29 leather pad
皮垫

30 box of punches
打孔器盒

31 punch
打孔器

32 magnet
磁铁，磁石

33 bench brush
工作台刷

34 engraving ball (joint vice, clamp)
雕刻球形钳（接合虎钳，钳子）

35 gold and silver balance (assay
balance), a precision balance
金、银天平（试金天平），一种精密天
平

36 soldering flux (flux)
烊接用的熔接剂

37 charcoal block
炭块

38 stick of solder
烊接棒

39 soldering borax
烊接硼砂

40 shaping hammer
成形槌

41 chasing (enchasing) hammer
雕刻（镂）槌

42 polishing and brunishing
machine
磨光和擦光机

43 dust exhauster (vacuum cleaner)
吸尘器（真空吸尘器）

44 polishing wheel
磨光轮

45 dust collector (dust catcher)
集尘器（除尘器）

46 buffing machine
擦光机

47 round file
圆锉

48 bloodstone (haematite,
hematite)
血石（赤铁矿）

49 flat file
扁锉

50 file handle
锉的手柄

51 polishing iron (burnisher)
擦光铁棒

1 watchmaker; *also:* clockmaker
钟表匠；即：修理钟表的人

2 workbench
工作台

3 armrest
扶手、搁手板

4 oiler
加油笔

5 oil stand
油台

6 set of screwdrivers
成（整）套螺丝起子

7 clockmaker's anvil
钟表匠用砧

8 broach, a reamer
拉刀，一种绞刀

9 spring pin tool
弹簧销工具

10 hand-removing tool
表拆卸工具

11 watchglass-fitting tool
钟表皿（护面玻璃）装配工具

12 workbench lamp, a multi-purpose lamp
工作灯，一种多功能（用途）灯

13 multi-purpose motor
多功能马达

14 tweezers
镊子

15 polishing machine attachments
磨光机附件

16 pin vice (pin holder)
针钳（针夹）

17 burnisher, for burnishing, polishing, and shortening of spindles
压光机，用於心轴的压光、磨光和缩短

18 dust brush
灰尘刷

19 cutter for metal watch straps
金属表带切断器

20 precision bench lathe (watchmaker's lathe)
台式精密车床（钟表匠的车床）

21 drive-belt gear
驱动带齿轮装置

22 workshop trolley for spare parts
工作室装零件的手推车

23 ultrasonic cleaner
超音波清洁器

24 rotating watch-testing machine for automatic watches
自动表的旋转测试机器

25 watch-timing machine for electronic components
电子钟表校正仪

26 testing device for waterproof watches
防水表的测试装置

27 electronic timing machine
电子校时器

28 vice (*Am.* vise)
虎钳

29 watchglass-fitting tool for armoured (*Am.* armored) glasses
钟表皿（防护玻璃）的装配工具

30 [automatic] cleaning machine for conventional cleaning
一般清洗钟表用的[自动]清洗机

31 cuckoo clock (Black Forest clock)
布谷鸣钟（黑森林钟）

32 wall clock (regulator)
墙钟挂钟（标准时钟）

33 compensation pendulum
补整摆子

34 kitchen clock
厨房钟

35 timer
定时器

1 electronic wristwatch
电子手表

2 digital readout, a light-emitting diode (LED) readout; *also:* liquid crystal readout
数字显示，一种发光二极体的显示；即液态晶体读出器

3 hour and minute button
时和分的按钮

4 date and second button
日期和秒的按钮

5 strap (watch strap)
表带

6 tuning fork principle (principle of the tuning fork watch)
音叉原理（音叉表原理）

7 power source (battery cell)
电源（电池）

8 transformer
变压器

9 tuning fork element (oscillating element)
音叉元件（摆动元件）振荡要素

10 wheel ratchet
棘轮

11 wheels
轮

12 minute hand
分针（长针）

13 hour hand
时针（短针）

14 principle of the electronic quartz watch
电子石英表的原理

15 quartz
石英

16 integrated circuit
积体电路

17 oscillation counter
振荡计数器

18 decoder
解码器

19 calendar clock (alarm clock)
日曆钟（闹钟）

20 digital display with flip-over numerals
翻转数字显示器

21 second indicator
秒指示器

22 stop button
停止按钮

23 forward and backward wind knob
调前或调后的旋钮

24 grandfather clock
有钟摆的落地大时钟

25 face
钟面

26 clock case
钟壳

27 pendulum
钟摆

28 striking weight
打点重锤，响槌

29 time weight
计时动锤

30 sundial
日晷

31 hourglass (egg timer)
沙漏，水漏（蛋形计时器）

32–43 components of an automatic watch (automatic wristwatch)
自动表的零件

32 weight (rotor)
摆块（转动体）

33 stone (jewel, jewelled bearing), a synthetic ruby
宝石（宝石轴承），一种合成红宝石

34 click
掣子

35 click wheel
掣子轮

36 clockwork (clockwork mechanism)
钟表装置（钟表机械装置）

37 bottom train plate
底部连动板，主夹板

38 spring barrel
发条匣

39 balance wheel
平衡轮，摆轮

40 escape wheel
擒纵轮

41 crown wheel
冠状轮

42 winding crown
发条钮

43 drive mechanism
驱动装置

20-47 optician's workshop
眼镜商工作室
20 workbench
工作台
21 universal centring (centering) apparatus
万能定心仪
22 centring (centering) suction holder
定心吸力托盘
23 sucker
吸盘
24 edging machine
磨边机
25 formers for the lens edging machine
镜片磨边机用的样品（型，模型）
26 inserted former
插入模型
27 rotating printer
旋转磨板
28 abrasive wheel combination
磨轮组
29 control unit
控制箱（装置）
30 machine part
机械部分
31 cooling water pipe
冷却水管
32 cleaning fluid
洗净液，洗涤液
33 focimeter (vertex refractionometer)
焦距测定器（顶点视力检测器）

34 metal-blocking device
金属压模装置
35 abrasive wheel combination and forms of edging
磨轮组和磨边用的模型
36 roughing wheel for preliminary surfacing
粗磨表面用的粗磨轮
37 fining lap for positive and negative lens surfaces
正负透镜表面的精研磨轮
38 fining lap for special and flat lenses
特殊和平面镜的精研磨轮
39 plano-concave lens with a flat surface
具一个平面的平凹透镜
40 plano-concave lens with a special surface
具特殊表面的平凹透镜
41 concave and convex lens with a special surface
具特殊表面的凹凸透镜
42 convex and concave lens with a special surface
具特殊表面的凸凹透镜
43 ophthalmic test stand
眼睛测试，验光台
44 phoropter with ophthalmometer and optometer (refractometer)
具眼膜曲率计和验光计（屈光计）的光觉计
45 trial lens case
验光镜箱

46 collimator
准直仪，准直管，平行光管
47 acuity projector
敏锐度投影器

1 laboratory and research
   microscope, *Leitz system*
   实验室和研究用显微镜，列兹系统
2 stand
   机架
3 base
   底座
4 coarse adjustment
   粗调整
5 fine adjustment
   微调整
6 illumination beam path
   (illumination path)
   照明光束路径（照明光线）
7 illumination optics
   照明光学部件
8 condenser
   聚光器
9 microscope (microscopic,
   object) stage
   显微镜台
10 mechanical stage
   机械台
11 objective turret (revolving
   nosepiece)
   物镜旋转盘（换镜旋座）
12 binocular head
   双目镜头
13 beam-splitting prisms
   分光棱镜
14 transmitted-light microscope
   with camera and polarizer, *Zeiss
   system*
   带照相机和起偏振镜的透射光显微镜，
   蔡司系统
15 stage base
   台架底座
16 aperture-stop slide
   孔径光阑滑动片
17 universal stage
   万向旋转台
18 lens panel
   镜头盘，透镜盘
19 polarizing filter
   起偏振滤光器
20 camera
   相机
21 focusing screen
   调焦屏
22 discussion tube arrangement
   检讨（分析）管装置
23 wide-field metallurgical
   microscope, a reflected-light
   microscope (microscope for
   reflected light)
   广域冶金显微镜，一种反射光显微镜
24 matt screen (ground glass
   screen, projection screen)
   无光泽屏（毛玻璃屏，投影屏）
25 large-format camera
   大型照相机
26 miniature camera
   小型照相机
27 base plate
   底座板
28 lamphouse
   灯室（箱）
29 mechanical stage
   机械台
30 objective turret (revolving
   nosepiece)
   物镜旋转塔（换镜旋座）
31 surgical microscope
   外科（手术的）显微镜
32 pillar stand
   柱座

33 field illumination
   视场（界）照明
34 photomicroscope
   显微照相机
35 miniature film cassette
   小型软片盒
36 photomicrographic camera
   attachment for large-format or
   television camera
   供大型相机和电视摄影机用的显微照相
   机附件
37 surface-finish microscope
   表面修整的显微镜
38 light section tube
   光线部分管
39 rack and pinion
   齿条和齿轮
40 zoom stereomicroscope
   变焦体视显微镜
41 zoom lens
   可变焦透镜
42 dust counter
   尘埃计
43 measurement chamber
   测量室
44 data output
   数据输出
45 analogue (*Am.* analog) output
   相似输出，模拟输出
46 measurement range selector
   测定域选择器
47 digital display (digital readout)
   数字显示（数字读出）
48 dipping refractometer for
   examining food
   检验食品用的浸渍折射计
49 microscopic photometer
   显微光度计
50 photometric light source
   光度计的光源
51 measuring device
   (photomultiplier, multiplier
   phototube)
   测量装置（光电倍加管）
52 light source for survey
   illumination
   测量照明用的光源
53 remote electronics
   遥控电子设备
54 universal wide-field microscope
   万能广域显微镜
55 adapter for camera or projector
   attachment
   照相机或投影机附件用的接合器
56 eyepiece focusing knob
   目镜调焦钮
57 filter pick-up
   滤色片插口
58 handrest
   扶手（板），搁手台
59 lamphouse for incident (vertical)
   illumination
   入射（垂直）照明灯箱
60 lamphouse connector for
   transillumination
   透视照明灯箱连接座
61 wide-field stereomicroscope
   广域体视显微镜
62 interchangeable lenses
   (objectives)
   可互换的镜头（物镜）
63 incident (vertical) illumination
   (incident top lighting)
   （垂直）入射照明（顶入射照明）

64 fully automatic microscope
   camera, a camera with
   photomicro mount adapter
   全自动显微照相机，有显微镜座架接头
   的照相机
65 film cassette
   软片盒
66 universal condenser for research
   microscope 1
   研究显微镜用的万向聚光器
67 universal-type measuring
   machine for photogrammetry
   (phototheodolite)
   照相测量用的（照相经纬仪）全能测量
   机
68 photogrammetric camera
   测量照相机
69 motor-driven level, a
   compensator level
   马达驱动杆，补整器杆
70 electro-optical
   distance-measuring
   instrument
   电光学的测距仪器
71 stereometric camera
   体视测量照相机
72 horizontal base
   水平基座
73 one-second theodolite
   一秒经纬仪

1 **2.2m reflecting telescope (reflector)**
2.2 米（公尺）反射望远镜
2 pedestal (base)
支架（底座）
3 axial-radial bearing
轴向—径向轴承
4 declination gear
倾斜齿轮（偏差转动装置）
5 declination axis
倾斜轴（偏差轴）
6 declination bearing
偏差轴承
7 front ring
前环
8 tube (body tube)
镜筒（筒身）
9 tube centre (*Am.* center) section
镜筒中心部分
10 primary mirror (main mirror)
初镜（主反射镜）
11 secondary mirror (deviation mirror, corrector plate)
次镜（偏向反射镜，校正板）
12 fork mounting (fork)
叉状装置（叉架）
13 cover
遮盖，复盖
14 guide bearing
导向轴承
15 main drive unit of the polar axis
极轴的主驱动装置
16-25 telescope mountings (telescope mounts)
望远镜的各种座架
16 refractor (refracting telescope) on a German-type mounting
德式座架的折射望远镜
17 declination axis
偏差轴
18 polar axis
极轴

19 counterweight (counterpoise)
平衡锤（对重，配重）
20 eyepiece
接目镜
21 knee mounting with a bent column
弯柱支架（座）
22 English-type axis mounting (axis mount)
英式轴型座架
23 English-type yoke mounting (yoke mount)
英式轭铁型座架
24 fork mounting (fork mount)
叉型座架
25 horseshoe mounting (horseshoe mount)
马蹄型座架
26 meridian circle
子午环，子午仪
27 divided circle (graduated circle)
刻度圆盘（分度圆盘）
28 reading microscope
读数显微镜
29 meridian telescope
子午线望远镜
30 electron microscope
电子显微镜
31-39 microscope tube (microscope body, body tube)
显微镜镜筒（显微镜镜身）
31 electron gun
电子枪
32 condensers
聚光器
33 specimen insertion air lock
样品插入气闸
34 control for specimen stage adjustment
样品台调整用的控制器

35 control for the objective apertures
物镜孔径控制器
36 objective lens
物镜
37 intermediate image screen
中间显像屏
38 telescope magnifier
望远镜放大镜
39 final image tube
最终（末级）显像管
40 photographic chamber for film and plate magazines
软片和感光板用的照相室

1 miniature camera
(35mm camera)
小型照相机（35 毫米照相机）
2 viewfinder eyepiece
取景器目镜
3 meter cell
曝光计电池
4 accessory shoe
附件插座板
5 flush lens
嵌入式镜头
6 rewind handle (rewind, rewind
crank)
退片杆（退片装置，退片曲柄）
7 miniature film cassette (135 film
cassette, 35 mm cassette)
小型底片壳（135 底片壳，35 毫米底片
壳）
8 film spool
片轴
9 film with leader
有片头的底片
10 cassette slit (cassette exit slot)
底片壳夹缝（底片壳出口槽）
11 cartridge-loading camera
匣式装片照相机
12 shutter release (shutter release
button)
快门放松器（快门放松器按钮）
13 flash cube contact
方形闪光灯接点
14 rectangular viewfinder
矩形取景器
15 126 cartridge (instamatic
cartridge)
126 底片（插入式）匣式底片
16 pocket camera (subminiature
camera)
袖珍照相机（超小型照相机）
17 110 cartridge (subminiature
cartridge)
110 底片（超小型底片）
18 film window
底片计数窗
19 120 rollfilm
120 底片
20 rollfilm spool
底片盘筒轴
21 backing paper
衬纸

22 twin-lens reflex camera
双镜头反射照相机
23 folding viewfinder hood
(focusing hood)
摺叠式取景窗遮光罩（聚焦遮光罩）
24 meter cell
曝光计电池
25 viewing lens
取景镜头
26 object lens
物镜
27 spool knob
片轴钮
28 distance setting (focus setting)
距离调整装置（焦点调整装置）
29 exposure meter using
needle-matching system
用指针调准方式的曝光计
30 flash contact
闪光灯接点
31 shutter release
快门放松器
32 film transport (film advance,
film wind)
底片板送装置（底片前进装置，卷片装
置）
33 flash switch
闪光灯开关
34 aperture-setting control
光圈调整装置
35 shutter speed control
快门速度控制
36 large-format hand camera (press
camera)
大型手提照相机（新闻照相机）
37 grip (handgrip)
柄（手柄）
38 cable release
快门线
39 distance-setting ring (focusing
ring)
距离调整环（调焦环）
40 rangefinder window
测距器的观测窗
41 multiple-frame viewfinder
(universal viewfinder)
多框观景窗（通用观景窗）
42 tripod
三脚架
43 tripod leg
三脚架腿

44 tubular leg
管型撑腿
45 rubber foot
橡胶（皮）脚
46 central column
中心柱
47 ball and socket head
球形座头
48 cine camera pan and tilt head
电影照相机可上下左右移动的座头
49 large-format folding camera
大型摺叠照相机
50 optical bench
光具座
51 standard adjustment
标准调整装置
52 lens standard
透镜标准
53 bellows
蛇腹（皮腔）
54 camera back
机背
55 back standard adjustment
机背标准调整装置
56 hand-held exposure meter
(exposure meter)
手提曝光计
57 calculator dial
计算刻度盘
58 scales (indicator scales) with
indicator needle (pointer)
带指针的刻度盘（指示盘）
59 range switch (high / low range
selector)
量程开关（高／低量程选择器）
60 diffuser for incident light
measurement
测量入射光线的漫射体
61 probe exposure meter for large
format cameras
大型照相机用的试探曝光计
62 meter
计量器
63 probe
探针
64 dark slide
底片盒
65 battery-portable electronic flash
(battery-portable electronic
flash unit)
电池供电手提式的电子闪光灯
66 powerpack unit (battery)
动力单元（电池）
67 flash head
闪光灯头
68 single-unit electronic flash
(flashgun)
单一光源电子闪光灯（闪光枪）
69 swivel-mounted reflector
旋转座反射镜
70 photodiode
光电二极管
71 foot
足部
72 hot-shoe contact
直接接点，直接接触闪光
73 flash cube unit
方形闪光装置
74 flash cube
方形闪光灯
75 flash bar
棒状闪光灯
76 slide projector
幻灯机
77 rotary magazine
旋转式片盒

1-105 system camera
照相机系统

1 miniature single-lens reflex camera
小型单镜头反光照相机

2 camera body
机身

3 - 8 lens, a normal lens (standard lens)
镜头,标准镜头

3 lens barrel
镜头筒

4 distance scale in metres and feet
用公尺和英呎的距离标尺

5 aperture ring (aperture-setting ring, aperture control ring)
光圈环(光圈调整环,光圈控制环)

6 front element mount with filter mount
具滤色片(接口)的镜头前镜片座

7 front element
镜头前镜片

8 focusing ring (distance-setting ring)
调焦环[远近(距离)调整环]

9 ring for the carrying strap
携带用的皮带环

10 battery chamber
电池槽

11 screw-in cover
螺丝盖

12 rewind handle (rewind, rewind crank)
迴片杆(迴片装置,迴片曲柄)

13 battery switch
电池开关

14 flash socket for F and X contact
F 和 X 接点用的闪光灯插座

15 self-time lever (setting lever for the self-timer, setting lever for the delayed-action release)
自动拍照杆(自动拍照器用的调整杆,延迟作用放松杆用的调整杆)

16 single-stroke film advance lever
单一冲程底片调节杆

17 exposure counter (frame counter)
曝光计数器(框格计数器)

18 shutter release (shutter release button)
快门放松器(快门放松器按钮)

19 shutter speed setting knob (shutter speed control)
快门速度调整钮(快门速度控制)

20 accessory shoe
附件插座

21 hot-shoe flash contact
直接闪光接点

22 viewfinder eyepiece with correcting lens
带校正透镜的观景窗目镜

23 camera back
照相机背

24 pressure plate
压板

25 take-up spool of the rapid-loading system
快速软片系统的收片盘

26 transport sprocket
输片齿轮

27 rewind release button (reversing clutch)
迴片钮(换向离合器)

28 film window
底片计数窗

29 rewind cam
迴片凸杆

30 tripod socket (tripod bush)
三角架插座

31 reflex system (mirror reflex system)
反射系统(镜面反射系统)

32 lens
镜头

33 reflex mirror
反射镜

34 film window
底片计数窗

35 path of the image beam
影像射束光程(通路)

36 path of the sample beam
样本射束光程(通路)

37 meter cell
计器电池

38 auxiliary mirror
辅助反射镜

39 focusing screen
调焦屏

40 field lens
视场透镜

41 pentaprism
五棱镜

42 eyepiece
接目镜

43-105 system of accessories
附件系统

43 interchangeable lenses
可互换镜头

44 fisheye lens (fisheye)
鱼眼镜头

45 wide-angle lens (short focal length lens)
广角镜头(短焦距镜头)

46 normal lens (standard lens)
标准镜头

47 medium focal length lens
中焦距镜头

48 telephoto lens (long focal length lens)
望远镜头(长焦距镜头)

49 long-focus lens
长焦距镜头

50 mirror lens
反射镜镜头

51 viewfinder image
观景窗探视器影像

52 signal to switch to manual control
转向手动控制的信号

53 matt collar (ground glass collar)
毛玻璃环

54 microprism collar
显微棱镜环

55 split-image rangefinder (focusing wedges)
分割影像的测距器(调焦光楔)

56 aperture scale
光圈刻度

57 exposure meter needle
曝光计指针

58-66 interchangeable focusing screens
可互换调焦屏

58 all-matt screen (ground glass screen) with microprism spot
具显微棱镜光点的全无泽屏(毛玻璃屏)

59 all-matt screen (ground glass screen) with microprism spot and split-image rangefinder
具显微棱镜和分割影像测距器的全无泽屏(毛玻璃屏)

60 all-matt screen (ground glass screen) without focusing aids
无聚焦辅助设备的全无泽屏(毛玻璃屏)

61 matt screen (ground glass screen) with reticule
具标线片的无泽屏(毛玻璃屏)

62 microprism spot for lenses with a large aperture
大光圈镜头用的显微棱镜光点

63 microprism spot for lenses with an aperture of f = 1 : 3.5 or larger
孔径 f = 1 : 3.5 或更大的镜头显微棱镜光点

64 Fresnel lens with matt collar (ground glass collar) and split-image rangefinder
具无泽环(毛玻璃环)和分割影像测距器的夫瑞奈镜头

65 all-matt screen (ground glass screen) with finely matted central spot and graduated markings
具精密无泽中心光点和刻度线的全无泽屏(毛玻璃屏)

66 matt screen (ground glass screen) with clear spot and double cross hairs
具清晰光点和双十字线(丝)的无泽屏(毛玻璃屏)

67 data recording back for exposing data about shots
记录各镜头曝光数据的装置

68 viewfinder hood (focusing hood)
观景窗(探视器)遮光罩

69 interchangeable pentaprism viewfinder
可互换的五角棱镜的观景窗(探视器)

70 pentaprism
五角棱镜

71 right-angle viewfinder
直角(垂直)观景窗(探视器)

72 correction lens
校正镜头

73 eyecup
眼罩

74 focusing telescope
聚焦望远镜

75 battery unit
电池装置

76 combined battery holder and control grip for the motor drive
马达驱动用的电池组座和控制手柄

77 rapid-sequence camera
快速照相机(连续照相机)

78 attachable motor drive
可附装的马达驱动装置

79 external (outside) power supply
外接电源

80 ten meter film back (magazine back)
十米底片盒背(片盒背)

81-98 close-up and macro equipment
特写(近距摄影)和放大用装备

81 extension tube
延伸管

82 adapter ring
接口环(圈)

83 reversing ring
换向环
84 lens in retrofocus position
谇焦点位置的镜头
85 bellows unit (extension bellows,
close-up bellows attachment)
蛇腹（皮腔）装置（延伸蛇腹，特写蛇
腹附件）
86 focusing stage
聚焦台
87 slide-copying attachment
幻灯片复制附件
88 slide-copying adapter
幻灯片复制接合器
89 micro attachment
(photomicroscope adapter)
显微附件（显微镜照相机，接合器）

90 copying stand (copy stand,
copypod)
复制台
91 spider legs
二脚架脚
92 copying stand (copy stand)
复制台
93 arm of the copying stand (copy
stand)
复制台悬臂
94 macrophoto stand
放大照相机台
95 stage plates for the macrophoto
stand
放大照相机台的台板
96 insertable disc (disk)
可插入的圆盘

97 Lieberkühn reflector
来伯古恩反射器
98 mechanical stage
机械台
99 table tripod (table-top tripod)
桌上三角架
100 rifle grip
来福式夹
101 cable release
快门线
102 double cable release
双快门线
103 camera case (ever-ready case)
照相机皮套（常备套）
104 lens case
镜头箱
105 soft-leather lens pouch
软皮镜头袋

1-60 darkroom equipment
暗房装备（设备）

1 developing tank
显影罐（冲片槽）

2 spiral (developing spiral, tank
reel)
卷盘[显影（冲片）卷盘，槽形卷轴]

3 multi-unit developing tank
多单元显影罐（冲片槽）

4 multi-unit tank spiral
多单元槽形卷盘

5 daylight-loading tank
日光下装片显影罐

6 loading chamber
装片室

7 film transport handle
底片扳动手柄

8 developing tank thermometer
显影槽温度计

9 collapsible bottle for developing
solution
装显影液可折叠的瓶子

10 chemical bottles for first
developer, stop bath, colour
developer, bleach-hardener,
stabilizer
初次显影剂，停影剂，彩色显影剂，漂
白硬化剂，稳定剂等等的化学药剂瓶

11 measuring cylinders
量筒

12 funnel
漏斗

13 tray thermometer (dish
thermometer)
托盘温度计（盘子温度计）

14 film clip
底片夹

15 wash tank (washer)
洗涤槽，冲洗槽（洗涤器）

16 water supply pipe
供水管

17 water outlet pipe
排水管

18 laboratory timer (timer)
（实验室）暗房计时器

19 automatic film agitator
底片自动搅拌器

20 developing tank
显影槽

21 darkroom lamp (safelight)
暗房灯（安全灯）

22 filter screen
滤光屏

23 film drier (drying cabinet)
底片干燥器（干燥箱）

24 exposure timer
曝光定时器

25 developing dish (developing
tray)
显影盘（显影托盘）

26 enlarger
放大机

27 baseboard
底板，台板

28 angled column
有角度的支柱

29 lamphouse (lamp housing)
放大机的光源（灯室），灯光屏蔽罩

30 negative carrier
底片夹

31 bellows
蛇腹，皮腔

32 lens
镜头

33 friction drive for fine adjustment
精密调整（细调）的磨擦驱动装置

34 height adjustment (scale
adjustment)
高度调整器（标尺调整器）

35 masking frame (easel)
遮蔽架（照片架）

36 colour (*Am.* color) analyser
析色器

37 colour (*Am.* color) analyser
lamp
析色器灯

38 probe lead
试探具（探针）导线

39 exposure time balancing knob
曝光时间调整旋钮

40 colour (*Am.* color) enlarger
彩色放大机

41 enlarger head
放大机头

42 column
支柱

43-45 **colour-mixing** (*Am.*
color-mixing) knob
色彩调整旋钮

43 magenta filter adjustment
(minus green filter adjustment)
紫红色过滤调整装置（减绿过滤调整装
置）

44 yellow filter adjustment (minus
blue filter adjustment)
黄色过滤调整装置（减蓝过滤调整装
置）

45 cyan filter adjustment (minus
red filter adjustment)
青色过滤调整装置（减红过滤调整装
置）

46 red swing filter
摆动红色过滤器

47 print tongs
晒印夹

48 processing drum
显影筒

49 squeegee
橡胶滚筒

50 range (assortment) of papers
相纸类

51 colour (*Am.* color) printing
paper, a packet of photographic
printing paper
彩色相纸，整盒相纸

52 colour (*Am.* color) chemicals
(colour processing chemicals)
彩色显像用化学药品（彩色显像处理化
学药品）

53 enlarging meter (enlarging
phototmeter)
放大机测光器（光度计）

54 adjusting knob with paper speed
scale
具相纸感光速度标尺的调整旋钮

55 probe
试探具

56 semi-automatic thermostatically
controlled developing dish
半自动恒温控制显影盆

57 rapid print drier (heated print
drier)
快速晒印干燥器

58 glazing sheet
上光板

59 pressure cloth
压布

60 automatic processor (machine
processor)
自动显影机（机械显影机）

1 **cine camera,** a Super-8 sound camera
电影摄影机，一种超八型有声摄影机

2 interchangeable zoom lens (variable focus lens, varifocal lens)
可互换变焦镜头（可变焦距镜头）

3 distance setting (focus setting) and manual focal length setting
距离（焦点）调整和手动焦距调整

4 aperture ring (aperture-setting ring, aperture control ring) for manual aperture setting
手动光圈调整用的光圈环（光圈调整环，光圈控制环）

5 handgrip with battery chamber
带电池槽的手柄

6 shutter release with cable release socket
附快门线插座的快门放松器

7 pilot tone or pulse generator socket for the sound recording equipment (with the dual film-tape system)
录音装置（具胶转磁，磁转胶双重转录系统）用的导频音和脉动发生器插座

8 sound connecting cord for microphone or external sound source (in single-system recording)
供麦克风或外部声源（单音道录音）所用的声源连接电线

9 remote control socket (remote control jack)
摇控插座（摇控插座）

10 headphone socket (*sim.:* earphone socket)
耳机插座

11 autofocus override switch
（自动聚焦装置）自动焦过载开关

12 filming speed selector
拍摄速度选择器

13 sound recording selector switch for automatic or manual operation
自动或手动操作录音选择开关

14 eyepiece with eyecup
带眼罩的接目镜

15 diopter control ring (dioptric adjustment ring)
屈光度控制环（屈光度调整环）

16 recording level control (audio level control, recording sensitivity selector)
录音水平控制（声音水平控制，录音感度选择器）

17 manual/automatic exposure control switch
手动或自动曝光控制开关

18 film speed setting
拍摄速度设定

19 power zooming arrangement
自动变焦装置

20 automatic aperture control
自动光圈控制

21 **sound track system**
（声带系统）录音道系统

22 sound camera
同步录音摄影机

23 telescopic microphone boom
伸缩的麦克风吊杆

24 microphone
麦克风

25 microphone connecting lead (microphone connecting cord)
麦克风连结导线（连结电线）

26 **mixing console** (mixing desk, mixer)
混合操作台

27 inputs from various sound sources
从不同声源的输入

28 output to camera
至摄影机的输出

29 **Super-8 sound film cartridge**
超八型有声电影片盒

30 film gate of the cartridge
片盒的片门

31 feed spool
供片轴

32 take-up spool
收片轴

33 recording head (sound head)
录音头

34 transport roller (capstan)
输片滑轮（绞盘）

35 rubber pinch roller (capstan idler)
橡皮压片滑杆（绞盘惰轮）

36 guide step (guide notch)
导阶（导槽）

37 exposure meter control step
曝光计控制阶

38 conversion filter step (colour, *Am.* color, conversion filter step)
变换滤光片引入阶（彩色变换滤光片引入阶）

39 **single-8 cassette**
单条 8 毫米卡式带

40 film gate opening
片门孔

41 unexposed film
未曝光影片

42 exposed film
已曝光影片

43 **16 mm camera**
16 毫米摄影机

44 reflex finder (through-the-lens reflex finder)
反射式观景窗（分光式反射观景窗）

45 magazine
片盒

46-49 **lens head**
镜头转座

46 lens turret (turret head)
镜头转塔（转塔头）

47 telephoto lens
远距照相镜头

48 wide-angle lens
广角镜头

49 normal lens (standard lens)
标准镜头

50 winding handle
卷片手柄

51 **compact Super-8 camera**
小型超八摄影机

52 footage counter
影片长度计数器

53 macro zoom lens
近摄变焦镜头

54 zooming lever
变焦杆

55 macro lens attachment (close-up lens)
近摄镜头附件（特写镜头）

56 macro frame (mount for small originals)
近摄架（供小尺寸原底片用的支架）

57 **underwater housing** (underwater case)
水下摄影机罩

58 direct-vision frame finder
直视观景窗（器）架

59 measuring rod
测量杆

60 stabilizing wing
稳定翼

61 grip (handgrip)
柄（手柄）

62 locking bolt
锁紧螺栓

63 control lever (operating lever)
控制杆（操作杆）

64 porthole
（观察孔）机窗

65 **synchronization start** (sync start)
同步起动摄影机

66 professional press-type camera
专业新闻型摄影机

67 cameraman
摄影师

68 camera assistant (sound assistant)
摄影助手（录音助手）

69 handclap marking sync start
同步起动拍手信号

70 **dual film-tape recording using a tape recorder**
使用录音机的胶带转磁带的双重录音

71 pulse-generating camera
脉动发生摄影机

72 pulse cable
脉动电线

73 cassette recorder
卡式录音机

74 microphone
麦克风

75 **dual film-tape reproduction**
双重录音的再生装置

76 tape cassette
卡带

77 synchronization unit
同步装置

78 cine projector
电影放映机

79 film feed spool
供片盘

80 take-up reel (take-up spool), an automatic take-up reel (take-up spool)
收片盘，自动收片盘

81 **sound projector**
有声放映机

82 sound film with magnetic stripe (sound track, track)
具磁性条纹的有声影片（录音道）

83 automatic-threading button
自动穿片按钮

84 trick button
特殊画面按钮

85 volume control
音量控制

86 reset button
重置按钮

87 fast and slow motion switch
快慢动作开关

88 forward, reverse, and still projection switch
前进、回转和静止的放映开关

89 splicer for wet splices
湿法接片用的接续机

90 hinged clamping plate
绞接夹板
91 **film viewer** (animated viewer
editor)
看片器（影片编辑机器）
92 foldaway reel arm
褶叠式片盘臂
93 rewind handle (rewinder)
回卷柄（回卷机）
94 viewing screen
银幕
95 film perforator (film marker)
影片穿孔机（影片标志器）

96 **six-turn-table film and sound
cutting table** (editing table,
cutting bench, animated sound
editor)
六转盘影片和声带的剪辑（接）台（剪
辑台，影片声音剪辑台）
97 monitor
监控器
98 control buttons (control well)
控制钮（控制插孔）
99 film turntable
影片转盘

100 first sound turntable, e.g. for
live sound
实况录音用的初次录音装置
101 second sound turntable for
post-sync sound
后同步录音用的第二次录音装置
102 film and tape synchronizing
head
影片和磁带同步头

211

1-49 **carcase** (carcass, fabric)
[house construction, carcassing]
房架（房架，结构体）[房屋构造，房架的建造]

1 basement of tamped (rammed) concrete
捣固混凝土的地下室

2 concrete base course
混凝土基层

3 cellar window (basement window)
地下室窗户

4 outside cellar steps
户外地下室阶梯

5 utility room window
公用设备室窗

6 utility room door
公用设备室门

7 ground floor (*Am.* first floor)
底层（[美]一楼）

8 brick wall
砖墙

9 lintel (window head)
楣（窗楣）

10 reveal
窗之侧壁

11 jamb
门窗框边框

12 window ledge (window sill)
窗台板（窗槛）

13 reinforced concrete lintel
混凝土过梁

14 upper floor (first floor, *Am.* second floor)
二楼

15 hollow-block wall
空心砖（壁）墙

16 concrete floor
水泥地板

17 work platform (working platform)
工作台（架）

18 bricklayer (*Am.* brickmason)
砌砖工

19 bricklayer's labourer (*Am.* laborer); *also:* builder's labourer
小工

20 mortar trough
砂浆槽

21 chimney
烟囱

22 cover (boards) for the staircase
楼梯间盖（板）

23 scaffold pole (scaffold standard)
鹰架，脚手架支柱

24 platform railing
平台栏杆

25 angle brace (angle tie) in the scaffold
鹰架的角撑（角铁条条），脚手架角撑

26 ledger
鹰架踏板横木，脚手架横木

27 putlog (putlock)
鹰架踏脚板横木（短），脚手架踏板

28 plank platform (board platform)
木板平台

29 guard board
护板

30 scaffolding joint with chain or lashing or whip or bond
以链或绳或缠或细绑於鹰架上的接合点

31 builder's hoist
（工事用）施工用吊车（吊机）

32 mixer operator
搅拌机操作人，拌和机操作工

33 concrete mixer, a gravity mixer
混凝土拌和机，一种重力拌和机

34 mixing drum
拌和鼓

35 feeder skip
供料吊斗

36 concrete aggregate [sand and gravel]
混凝土骨材[砂和砾石]

37 wheelbarrow
独轮手推车

38 hose (hosepipe)
软管，水管

39 mortar pan (mortar trough, mortar tub)
砂浆盆（槽，桶）

40 stack of bricks
砖堆

41 stacked shutter boards (lining boards)
堆积的衬板（裙板，面板）

42 ladder
梯子

43 bag of cement
水泥袋

44 site fence, a timber fence
工地围栏，一种木围栏

45 signboard (billboard)
揭示牌，告示牌

46 removable gate
可拆下的门

47 contractors' name plates
承包商名牌，营造厂名牌

48 site hut (site office)
（工地小屋）工寮（棚），工地办事处

49 building site latrine
建筑工地厕所

50-57 **bricklayer's** (*Am.* brickmason's) **tools**
砌砖工用工具

50 plumb bob (plummet)
垂球，铅锤

51 thick lead pencil
粗铅笔

52 trowel
镘刀（抹子）

53 bricklayer's (*Am.* brickmason's) hammer (brick hammer)
砖工用锤（砖锤）

54 mallet
木锤，大头锤

55 spirit level
水平器，气泡水平器

56 laying-on trowel
涂抹镘刀（抹子）

57 float
抹子

58-68 **masonry bonds**
砖石砌法

58 brick (standard brick)
砖（标准砖）

59 stretching bond
顺砌法

60 heading bond
丁砌法

61 racking (raking) back
砌砖时留齿缝（阶梯形）待砌

62 English bond
英国式砌法

63 stretching course
顺砌层

64 heading course
丁砌层

65 English cross bond (Saint Andrew's cross bond)
英国式十字砌法（圣安德鲁十字砌法）

66 chimney bond
烟囱砌法

67 first course
第一层

68 second course
第二层

69-82 **excavation**
开挖，挖方

69 profile (*Am.* batterboard) [fixed on edge at the corner]
[固定於墙的]水平标板

70 intersection of strings
水线交叉

71 plumb bob (plummet)
铅锤，垂球

72 excavation side
开挖边

73 upper edge board
上边板

74 lower edge board
下边板

75 foundation trench
基槽

76 navvy (*Am.* excavator)
挖土工人（挖土机）

77 conveyor belt (conveyor)
输送带（输送机）

78 excavated earth
挖掘的泥土

79 plank roadway
铺板路面

80 tree guard
树的保护栏

81 mechanical shovel (excavator)
机械铲，怪手（挖土机）

82 shovel bucket (bucket)
铲斗

83-91 **plastering**
涂抹灰泥

83 plasterer
泥水匠

84 mortar trough
砂浆槽

85 screen
筛

86-89 **ladder scaffold**
梯架

86 standard ladder
梯架立柱，脚手架立柱

87 boards (planks, platform)
木板（厚板，平台）

88 diagonal strut (diagonal brace)
斜撑（斜支柱）

89 railing
栏杆

90 guard netting
防护网

91 rope-pulley hoist
绳索滑轮吊车

1-89 reinforced concrete (ferroconcrete) construction
钢筋混凝土构造

1 reinforced concrete (ferro-concrete) skeleton construciton
钢筋混凝土骨架结构

2 reinforced concrete (ferroconcrete) frame
钢筋混凝土框架（构架）

3 inferior purlin
下梁（桁梁）

4 concrete purlin
混凝土梁

5 ceiling joist
天花板托梁

6 arch (flank)
拱

7 rubble concrete wall
粗（碎石）混凝土墙

8 reinforced concrete (ferroconcrete) foor
钢筋混凝土楼板

9 concreter (concretor), flattening out
抹平混凝土工

10 projecting reinforcement (Am. connection rebars)
突出的钢筋

11 column box
柱子模板

12 joist shuttering
托梁模板

13 shuttering strut
模板支撑

14 diagonal bracing
斜架（撑）

15 wedge
楔块

16 board
木板

17 sheet pile wall (sheet pile, sheet piling)
板桩墙

18 shutter boards (lining boards)
模板

19 circular saw (buzz saw)
圆锯，轮锯

20 bending table
弯曲钢筋的工作台

21 bar bender (steel bender)
钢筋工

22 hand steel shears
手动钢剪

23 reinforcing steel (reinforcement rods)
钢筋（钢筋条）

24 pumice concrete hollow block
浮石混凝土空心砖

25 partition wall, a timber wall
隔墙，一种木板墙

26 concrete aggregate [gravel and sand of vaious grades]
混凝土骨材[各种级配的砾石和砂]

27 crane track
起重机轨道

28 tipping wagon (tipping truck)
倾卸车

29 concrete mixer
混凝土搅拌机，混凝土拌和机

30 cement silo
水泥仓，水泥储仓

31 tower crane (tower slewing crane)
高塔起重机（塔式回转起重机）

32 bogie (*Am.* truck)
转向架

33 counterweight
配重，平衡铊

34 tower
塔架

35 crane to driver's cabin (crane driver's cage)
起重机驾驶室

36 jib (boom)
起重臂（吊杆，撑臂）

37 bearer cable
吊索

38 concrete bucket
混凝土输送斗，混凝土吊桶

39 sleepers (*Am.* ties)
轨枕

40 chock
楔形塞块

41 ramp
斜坡道

42 wheelbarrow
独轮手推车

43 safety rail
安全栏杆

44 site hut
工寮

45 canteen
工地福利社

46 tubular steel scaffold (scaffolding)
钢管鹰架

47 standard
支架

48 ledger tube
横管

49 tie tube
系管

50 shoe
桩尖，底座

51 diagonal brace
斜撑

52 planking (platform)
铺板（平台）

53 coupling (coupler)
管接头

54-76 formwork (shuttering) and reinforcement
模板和钢筋

54 bottom shuttering (lining)
底模板

55 side shutter of a purlin
正梁的侧模板

56 cut-in bottom
梁底板

57 cross beam
大梁，横梁

58 cramp iron (cramp, dog)
铁扒钉

59 upright member, a standard
垂直支柱

60 strap
连接板，系板

61 cross piece
横梁，横木

62 stop fillet
固定块

63 strut (brace, angle brace)
支撑（角支撑）

64 frame timber (yoke)
框架木材（轭）

65 strap
连接板，系板

66 reinforcement binding
钢筋，绑扎

67 cross strut (strut)
横撑

68 reinforcement
钢筋

69 distribution steel
分布钢筋

70 stirrup
肋筋，箍筋

71 projecting reinforcement (*Am.* connection rebars)
突出的钢筋

72 concrete (heavy concrete)
混凝土（重质混凝土）

73 column box
柱形模板

74 bolted frame timber (bolted yoke)
以螺栓固定的架材

75 nut (thumb nut)
螺帽

76 shutter board (shuttering board)
厚木板

77-89 tools
工具

77 bending iron
弯曲钢筋用的板手

78 adjustable service girder
可调整的工作架

79 adjusting screw
调整螺钉

80 round bar reinforcement
圆钢筋

81 distance piece (separator, spacer)
定位垫块

82 Torsteel
异形钢筋

83 concrete tamper
混凝土捣棒

84 mould (*Am.* mold) for concrete test cubes
混凝土立方体模子

85 concreter's tongs
混凝土工夹钳

86 sheeting support
钢管支承

87 hand shears
手剪（钢筋手剪）

88 immersion vibrator (concrete vibrator)
浸入式（混凝土）震动器

89 vibrating cylinder (vibrating head, vibrating poker)
震动棒（震动头）

1-59 carpenter's yard
木工场

1 stack of boards (planks)
木板堆

2 long timber (Am. lumber)
长圆木（原木）

3 sawing shed
锯木棚（间）

4 carpenter's workshop
木工工作场

5 workshop door
工场门

6 handcart
手推车

7 roof truss
屋架

8 tree [used for topping out ceremony], with wreath
带花环的树[用於上主梁仪式]

9 timber wall
木板墙

10 squared timber (building timber, scantlings)
方木（建筑用木材，制材）

11 drawing floor
划线工作台

12 carpenter
木工

13 safety helmet
安全帽

14 cross-cut saw, a chain saw
横断锯，一种链锯

15 chain guide
导链装置

16 saw chain
锯链

17 mortiser (chain cutter)
凿孔机（链式切割机）

18 trestle (horse)
枪架，支架（马凳）

19 beam mounted on a trestle
置於支架上的梁

20 set of carpenter's tools
一套木工工具

21 electric drill
电钻

22 dowel hole
销钉孔，木钉孔

23 mark for the dowel hole
钻孔的标记（未钻孔之前）

24 beams
梁

25 post (stile, stud, quarter)
柱（立木，短支柱，间柱）

26 corner brace
角支撑

27 brace (strut)
支撑（支柱）

28 base course (plinth)
底层（基脚，柱脚）

29 house wall (wall)
墙（墙壁）

30 window opening
窗口

31 reveal
窗之侧壁

32 jamb
门窗框边框

33 window ledge (window sill)
窗台板（窗槛）

34 cornice
飞簷

35 roundwood (round timber)
圆木

36 floorboards
楼板

37 hoisting rope
吊索

38 ceiling joist (ceiling beam, main beam)
平顶搁棚（平顶梁，主梁）

39 wall joist
墙梁

40 wall plate
承梁板

41 trimmer (trimmer joist, Am. header, header joist)
承梁（搁棚承梁，槽梁）

42 dragon beam (dragon piece)
支承脊椽梁

43 false floor (inserted floor)
假楼板

44 floor filling of breeze, loam, etc.
填煤渣，土等的楼板

45 fillet (cleat)
垫板（楔子）

46 stair well (well)
楼梯井（井）

47 chimney
烟囱

48 framed partition (framed wall)
构架（框墙），间壁（构架墙）

49 wall plate
承梁板

50 girt
围梁

51 window jamb, a jamb
窗框，边框

52 corner stile (corner strut, corner stud)
角支柱（角立木）

53 principal post
主柱

54 brace (strut) with skew notch
具斜接头的支撑（支柱）

55 nogging piece
压墙槛

56 sill rail
窗台槛

57 window lintel (window head)
窗过梁（窗楣）

58 head (head rail)
楣（框面）

59 filled-in panel (bay, pan)
砌成之嵌板（间格）

60-82 carpenter's tools
木工工具

60 hand saw
手锯

61 bucksaw
架锯

62 saw blade
锯片

63 compass saw (keyhole saw)
圆锯（开孔锯）

64 plane
铇

65 auger (gimlet)
螺旋钻（木钻）

66 screw clamp (cramp, holdfast)
螺旋夹钳（夹钳，夹住器）

67 mallet
木鎚，大头鎚

68 two-handed saw
双人用锯

69 try square
直角尺，曲尺

70 broad axe (Am. broadax)
阔斧

71 chisel
凿

72 mortise axe (mortice axe, Am. mortise ax)
榫眼斧

73 axe (Am. ax)
斧

74 carpenter's hammer
木工用锤

75 claw head (nail claw)
拔钉爪头（拔钉钳）

76 folding rule
摺尺

77 carpenter's pencil
木工用铅笔

78 iron square
铁直角尺

79 drawknife (drawshave, drawing knife)
拉刀（刮刀）

80 shaving
铇花

81 bevel
斜角规

82 mitre square (Am. miter square, miter angle)
斜榫（角）尺

83-96 building timber
建筑用木材

83 undressed timber (Am. rough lumber)
原木

84 heartwood (duramen)
心材（木心）

85 sapwood (sap, alburnum)
边材

86 bark (rind)
树皮（树木外皮）

87 baulk (balk)
梁木

88 halved timber
对分材

89 wane (waney edge)
梁木，缺边材

90 quarter baulk (balk)
四等分梁木（四分材）

91 plank (board)
板，板材

92 end-grained timber
纹端向外的木材

93 heartwood plank (heart plank)
木心板

94 unsquared (untrimmed) plank (board)
未修整板材，毛边板材

95 squared (trimmed) board
已修整板材

96 slab (offcut)
板，底板

1-26 styles and parts of roofs
屋顶型式及其各部分
1 gable roof (saddle roof, saddleback roof)
山形屋顶（鞍形屋顶）
2 ridge
屋脊
3 verge
山墙檐口
4 eaves
屋檐
5 gable
山墙
6 dormer window (dormer)
屋顶天窗（老虎窗）
7 pent roof (shed roof, lean-to roof)
单坡屋顶（棚顶，坡屋顶）
8 skylight
天窗
9 fire gable
防火山墙
10 hip (hipped) roof
四落水屋顶（四坡顶）
11 hip end
端坡，肩脊端
12 hip (arris)
屋脊，角
13 hip (hipped) dormer window
四坡屋顶天窗
14 ridge turret
屋脊小塔
15 valley (roof valley)
屋顶排水沟
16 hipped-gable roof (jerkin head roof)
四坡山墙屋顶（半山头屋顶）
17 partial-hip (partial-hipped) end
小面端坡，小肩脊端
18 mansard roof (Am. gambrel roof)
折角屋顶（复斜屋顶）
19 mansard dormer window
折角屋顶天窗
20 sawtooth roof
锯齿式屋顶
21 north light
朝北窗
22 broach roof
塔形屋顶
23 eyebrow
遮阳板
24 conical broach roof
圆锥形屋顶
25 imperial dome (imperial roof)
葱头形圆屋顶
26 weather vane
风信标

27-83 roof structures of timber
木材的屋顶结构
27 rafter roof
椽屋顶
28 rafter
椽
29 roof beam
屋架梁
30 diagonal tie (cross tie, sprocket piece, cocking piece)
斜拉杆（横木小椽）
31 arris fillet (tilting fillet)
簷垫
32 outer wall
外墙
33 beam head
梁头

34 collar beam roof (trussed-rafter roof)
桁架式椽屋顶
35 collar beam (collar)
环梁，系梁
36 rafter
椽
37 strutted collar beam roof structure
支柱式环梁屋顶结构
38 collar beams
环梁，系梁
39 purlin
桁条
40 post (stile, stud)
柱（立木，短支柱）
41 brace
支撑（斜撑）
42 unstrutted (king pin) roof structure
非支柱式（中枢）屋顶结构
43 ridge purlin
脊桁
44 inferior purlin
次桁条
45 rafter head (rafter end)
椽头
46 purlin roof with queen post and pointing sill
双柱及活闸门槛式屋顶
47 pointing sill
活闸门槛
48 ridge beam (ridge board)
脊梁（脊板）
49 simple tie
单系条
50 double tie
双系条
51 purlin
桁条
52 purlin roof structure with queen post
双柱屋架结构
53 tie beam
系梁
54 joist (ceiling joist)
栏栅（屋顶搁栅）
55 principal rafter
主椽
56 common rafter
普通椽
57 angle brace (angle tie)
角撑（角系条）
58 brace (strut)
支撑（支柱）
59 ties
系条
60 hip (hipped) roof with purlin roof structure
具桁条结构的四坡屋顶
61 jack rafter
小椽
62 hip rafter
角椽
63 jack rafter
小椽
64 valley rafter
沟椽
65 queen truss
偶杆桁架
66 main beam
主梁
67 summer (summer beam)
搁栅梁
68 queen post (truss post)
偶柱（桁架支柱）

69 brace (strut)
支撑（支柱）
70 collar beam (collar)
环梁（系梁）
71 trimmer (Am. header)
承梁（顶梁）
72 solid-web girder
实腹版梁
73 lower chord
下弦
74 upper chord
上弦
75 boarding
安装木板
76 purlin
桁条
77 supporting outer wall
支承外墙
78 roof truss
屋顶桁架
79 lower chord
下弦
80 upper chord
上弦
81 post
柱
82 brace (strut)
支撑（支柱）
83 support
支承（支座）

84-98 timber joints
木材接合
84 mortise (mortice) and tenon joint
榫眼和榫接
85 forked mortise (mortice) and tenon joint
叉形榫眼和接
86 halving (halved) joint
半缺合（对搭接）
87 simple scarf joint
单嵌接合
88 oblique scarf joint
斜嵌接合
89 dovetail halving
对分鸠尾榫
90 single skew notch
单缺口斜接头
91 double skew notch
双缺口斜接头
92 wooden nail
木钉
93 pin
梢
94 clout nail (clout)
大帽钉
95 wire nail
铁钉
96 hardwood wedges
硬木楔
97 cramp iron (timber dog, dog)
铁扒钉（木扒钉，扒钉）
98 bolt
螺栓

1 tiled roof
瓦屋顶

2 plain-tile double-lap roofing
双搭接平瓦屋顶

3 ridge tile
脊瓦

4 ridge course tile
屋脊瓦，层瓦

5 under-ridge tile
屋簷瓦

6 plain (plane) tile
平瓦

7 ventilating tile
通风瓦，换气瓦

8 ridge tile
脊瓦

9 hip tile
斜脊瓦

10 hipped end
肩脊端

11 valley (roof valley)
屋顶排水沟

12 skylight
天窗

13 chimney
烟囱

14 chimney flashing, made of sheet zinc
（薄锌板做成的）烟囱范水

15 ladder hook
梯头钩

16 snow guard bracket
挡雪板托架

17 battens (slating and tiling battens)
木条（挂瓦木条）

18 batten gauge (*Am.* gage)
木条量尺（规）

19 rafter
橡

20 tile hammer
瓦锤

21 lath axe (*Am.* ax)
板条斧

22 hod
灰泥桶

23 hod hook
桶钩

24 opening (hatch)
开口（升降口）

25 gable (gable end)
山形墙（山墙头）

26 toothed lath
齿形板条

27 soffit
挑簷底面

28 gutter
天沟

29 rainwater pipe (downpipe)
雨水管（落水管）

30 swan's neck (swan-neck)
鹅颈弯管

31 pipe clip
管夹

32 gutter bracket
天沟托架

33 tile cutter
切瓦器

34 scaffold
脚手架，施工架

35 safety wall
安全壁

36 eaves
屋簷

37 outer wall
外墙

38 exterior rendering
外墙刷底

39 frost-resistant brickwork
抗冻砖工

40 inferior purlin
下桁条

41 rafter head (rafter end)
橡头

42 eaves fascia
封簷挡板

43 double lath (tilting lath)
双层板条（斜板条）

44 insulating boards
隔热板

45-60 tiles and tile roofings
瓦和瓦屋顶

45 split-tiled roof
分开式瓦屋顶

46 plain (plane) tile
平瓦

47 ridge course
屋脊层

48 slip
滑动

49 eaves course
簷瓦层

50 plain-tiled roof
平瓦屋顶

51 nib
瓦尖

52 ridge tile
脊瓦

53 pantiled roof
波形瓦屋顶

54 pantile
波形瓦

55 pointing
勾缝

56 Spanish-tiled roof (*Am.* mission-tiled roof)
西班牙式瓦屋顶（拱形瓦屋顶）

57 under tile
下瓦

58 over tile
上瓦

59 interlocking tile
联锁瓦

60 flat interlocking tile
平联锁瓦

61-89 slate roof
石板瓦屋顶

61 roof boards (roof boarding, roof sheathing)
屋顶板（屋顶防水衬板）

62 roofing paper (sheathing paper); *also:* roofing felt (*Am.* rag felt)
屋面油纸（复盖油纸），屋面油毛毡（粗油毛毡）

63 cat ladder (roof ladder)
便梯（屋顶用梯）

64 coupling hook
联结挂钩

65 ridge hook
屋脊挂钩

66 roof trestle
屋顶栈桥

67 trestle rope
栈桥绳

68 knot
绳结

69 ladder hook
梯子挂钩

70 scaffold board
脚手板

71 slater
石板瓦工

72 nail bag
钉子袋

73 slate hammer
石板瓦工用锤

74 slate nail, a galvanized wire nail
石板瓦工用钉，镀锌铁钉

75 slater's shoe, a bast or hemp shoe
石板瓦工用鞋，韧皮或麻线鞋

76 eaves course (eaves joint)
簷瓦层（簷口接缝）

77 corner bottom slate
屋角底石板瓦

78 roof course
屋顶层

79 ridge course (ridge joint)
脊瓦层（屋脊接缝）

80 gable slate
山墙石板瓦

81 tail line
瓦的下边线

82 valley (roof valley)
屋顶排水沟

83 box gutter (trough gutter, parallel gutter)
箱形簷槽（槽，平行沟）

84 slater's iron
石板瓦工用铁件

85 slate
石板瓦

86 back
石板瓦背

87 head
石板瓦头

88 front edge
石板瓦前缘

89 tail
石板瓦尾

90-103 asphalt-impregnated paper roofing and corrugated asbestos cement roofing
柏油纸板屋顶和波形石棉水泥板屋顶

90 asphalt-impregnated paper roof
柏油纸板屋顶

91 width [parallel to the gutter]
宽度[与簷槽平行]

92 gutter
簷槽，天沟

93 ridge
屋脊

94 join
连接缝

95 width [at right angles to the gutter]
宽度[与簷槽成直角]

96 felt nail (clout nail)
毛毡钉（大头钉）

97 corrugated asbestos cement roof
波形石棉水泥板屋顶

98 corrugated sheet
波形薄板

99 ridge capping piece
屋脊盖顶片

100 lap
搭接

101 wood screw
木螺丝

102 rust-proof zinc cup
防锈锌杯

103 lead washer
橡皮垫圈（使接头与螺丝密合的垫圈）

1 basement wall, a concrete
  wall
  地下室墙壁，混凝土墙
2 footing (foundation)
  基脚（基础）
3 foundation base
  墙基
4 damp course (damp-proof
  course)
  防湿层，防潮层
5 waterproofing
  防水工作，防水层
6 rendering coat
  涂底层，底涂
7 brick paving
  砖铺面，砖铺路面
8 sand bed
  砂垫层，砂床
9 ground
  地面，粉刷底层
10 shuttering
  模板，模
11 peg
  木栓，桩，木橛，木钉
12 hardcore
  碎石层，硬底层
13 oversite concrete
  混凝土面层
14 cement screed
  水泥匀（刮）平层
15 brickwork base
  砖砌座
16 basement stairs, solid concrete
  stairs
  地下室楼梯，混凝土楼梯
17 block step
  台阶
18 curtail step (bottom step)
  楼梯最低梯级，起步（梯）级
19 top step
  楼梯最高梯级
20 nosing
  凸缘，踏步挑头
21 skirting (skirting board, *Am.*
  mopboard, washboard, scrub
  board, base)
  壁脚板（壁脚板，护壁板）
22 balustrade of metal bars
  金属楼梯栏杆（扶手）
23 ground-floor (*Am.* first-floor)
  landing
  地面层（一楼）
24 front door
  前门
25 foot scraper
  脚刮板
26 flagstone paving
  板石砌，板石铺面
27 mortar bed
  水泥砂浆层
28 concrete ceiling, a reinforced
  concrete slab
  混凝土天花，钢筋混凝土板
29 ground-floor (*Am.* first-floor)
  brick wall
  地面层（一楼）砖墙
30 ramp
  倾斜面，坡道，坡台
31 wedge-shaped step
  楔形阶
32 tread
  楼梯踏板，级宽
33 riser
  楼梯踢脚板，起步板
34–41 landing
  平台

34 landing beam
  平台梁
35 ribbed reinforced concrete floor
  钢筋混凝土层
36 rib
  肋
37 steel-bar reinforcement
  钢筋
38 subfloor (blind floor)
  底层地板
39 level layer
  水平层
40 finishing layer
  修整层
41 top layer (screed)
  顶层（刮板）
**42–44 dog-legged staircase, a
  staircase without a well**
  人型楼梯，无井楼梯
42 curtail step (bottom step)
  楼梯最低梯级，起步（梯）级
43 newel post (newel)
  栏杆柱
44 outer string (*Am.* outer stringer)
  外侧斜梁
45 wall string (*Am.* wall stringer)
  贴墙斜梁
46 staircase bolt
  楼梯螺栓
47 tread
  楼梯踏板，级宽
48 riser
  楼梯踢脚板，起步板
49 wreath piece (wreathed string)
  （扭曲）弯曲部分（斜梁）
50 balustrade
  楼梯栏杆（扶手）
51 baluster
  栏杆小柱
52–62 intermediate landing
  休息平台
52 wreath
  弯曲扶手
53 handrail (guard rail)
  扶手（护栏）
54 head post
  楼梯端柱
55 landing beam
  平台梁
56 lining board
  面板，裙板，衬板
57 fillet
  嵌条，填角，线角
58 lightweight building board
  轻纤维板
59 ceiling plaster
  天花板墁灰面
60 wall plaster
  墙壁墁灰面
61 false ceiling
  假天花板，假平顶
62 strip flooring (overlay flooring,
  parquet strip)
  细条地板（表层地板，镶木地板）
63 skirting board (*Am.* mopboard,
  washboard, scrub board, base)
  壁脚板（护壁板）
64 beading
  串珠状缘饰
65 staircase window
  楼梯窗
66 main landing beam
  主平台梁
67 fillet (cleat)
  嵌条（栓），填角

68–69 false ceiling
  假天花板
68 false floor (inserted floor)
  假楼板（嵌入楼板）
69 floor filling (plugging, pug)
  楼板填料（隔音材料，泥料）
70 laths
  板条
71 lathing
  板条
72 ceiling plaster
  天花板墁灰面
73 subfloor (blind floor)
  底层地板
74 parquet floor with
  tongued-and-grooved blocks
  具企口缝（凹凸缝）块的镶木地板
75 quarter-newelled (*Am.*
  quarter-neweled) staircase
  直角转弯楼梯
76 winding staircase (spiral
  staircase) with open newels
  (open-newel staircase)
  螺旋式楼梯
77 winding staircase (spiral
  staircase) with solid newels
  (solid-newel staircase)
  实心中柱式螺旋楼梯
78 newel (solid newel)
  楼梯栏杆柱（实心中心柱）
79 handrail
  扶手

1 glazier's workshop
玻璃匠工作房

2 frame wood samples (frame samples)
框架木样

3 frame wood
框架木

4 mitre joint (mitre, *Am.* miter joint, miter)
斜接

5 sheet glass; *kinds:* window glass, frosted glass, patterned glass, crystal plate glass, thick glass, milk glass, laminated glass (safety glass, shatterproof glass)
平板玻璃；种类：窗户玻璃、毛玻璃、压花玻璃、结晶玻璃板、厚玻璃、乳白玻璃、层压玻璃（安全玻璃、防碎玻璃）

6 cast glass; *kinds:* stained glass, ornamental glass, raw glass, bull's-eye glass, wired glass, line glass (lined glass)
压铸玻璃，种类：有色玻璃，装饰玻璃，粗玻璃，牛眼玻璃，嵌有金丝网的玻璃，有线道玻璃

7 mitring (*Am.* mitering) machine
斜接机

8 glassworker (*e.g.* building glazier, glazier, decorative glass worker)
玻璃工人（例如：建筑玻璃工，玻璃匠，装饰玻璃工）

9 glass holder
玻璃托架

10 piece of broken glass
玻璃碎片

11 lead hammer
铅锤

12 lead knife
铅刀

13 came (lead came)
有槽铅条

14 leaded light
花饰铅条窗

15 workbench
工作台

16 pane of glass
窗玻璃

17 putty
油灰

18 glazier's hammer
玻璃匠用锤

19 glass pliers
玻璃钳

20 glazier's square
玻璃匠用角尺

21 glazier's rule
玻璃匠用尺

22 glazier's beam compass
玻璃匠用长臂圆规

23 eyelet
小环

24 glazing sprig
镶玻璃用的簧片（无头钉）

25-26 glass cutters
玻璃刀

25 diamond glass cutter
钻石玻璃刀

26 steel-wheel (steel) glass cutter
钢砂轮玻璃刀

27 putty knife
油灰刀

28 pin wire
拔无头针用的金属丝

29 panel pin
无头针

30 mitre (*Am.* miter) block (mitre box) [with saw]
带锯子的斜锯架

31 mitre (*Am.* miter) shoot (mitre board)
斜接滑槽（斜接板）

1 metal shears (tinner's snips,
  Am. tinner's shears)
  金属剪（洋铁匠剪刀）
2 elbow snips (angle shears)
  弯剪，角剪
3 gib
  矫直板
4 lapping plate
  搭接板
5-7 propane soldering apparatus
  丙烷烓接装置
5 propane soldering iron, a
  hatchet iron
  丙烷烓接棒，一种斧形烙铁
6 soldering stone, a sal-ammoniac
  block
  烓接块（石），硇砂块（石）
7 soldering fluid (flux)
  烓接剂
8 beading iron for forming
  reinforcement beading
  形成加强烓道用的烓缝铁
9 angled reamer
  斜角铰刀（钻孔器）
10 workbench (bench)
  工作台
11 beam compass (trammel, *Am.*
  beam trammel)
  长臂圆规
12 electric hand die
  手持电动打孔模
13 hollow punch
  空心打孔器

14 chamfering hammer
  去角锤
15 beading swage (beading
  hammer)
  烓接铁锤
16 abrasive-wheel cutting-off
  machine
  磨轮切割机
17 plumber
  铅管工人
18 mallet
  大槌
19 mandrel
  心轴
20 socket (tinner's socket)
  插座
21 block
  铁座
22 anvil
  砧
23 stake
  小铁砧
24 circular saw (buzz saw)
  圆锯
25 flanging, swaging, and wiring
  machine
  压（摺）缘，压模，配线机
26 sheet shears (guillotine)
  薄板剪（剪板机）
27 screw-cutting machine
  (thread-cutting machine, die
  stocks)
  螺纹切割机（螺纹模夹把）

28 pipe-bending machine (bending
  machine, pipe bender)
  弯管机（弯曲机，弯管器）
29 welding transformer
  电熔接变压器
30 bending machine (rounding
  machine) for shaping funnels
  漏斗形弯曲机

1 gas fitter and plumber
瓦斯匠和铅管工

2 stepladder
摺梯，四脚梯

3 safety chain
安全链条

4 stop valve
停止阀

5 gas meter
瓦斯表

6 bracket
托座

7 service riser
立管

8 distributing pipe
分配管

9 supply pipe
供气管

10 pipe-cutting machine
切管机

11 pipe repair stand
管子修理架

12-25 gas and water appliances
瓦斯和供水设备

12-13 geyser, an instantaneous water heater
热水器，瞬间热水装置

12 gas water heater
瓦斯热水器

13 electric water heater
电热水器

14 toilet cistern
盥洗室水箱

15 float
浮球，浮筒

16 bell
钟形阀

17 flush pipe
冲洗管

18 water inlet
进水口

19 flushing lever (lever)
冲水杆

20 radiator
放热器，（热）辐射器

21 radiator rib
放热器肋

22 two-pipe system
双管（供热）系统

23 flow pipe
供水管

24 return pipe
回水管

25 gas heater
瓦斯加热炉

26-37 plumbing fixtures
卫生设备

26 trap (anti-syphon trap)
弯管（反虹吸弯管）

27 mixer tap (*Am.* mixing faucet) for washbasins
洗脸盆（冷热水混合使用）的水龙头

28 hot tap
热水龙头

29 cold tap
冷水龙头

30 extendible shower attachment
可伸长的莲蓬头附件

31 water tap (pillar tap) for washbasins
洗脸盆用之水龙头（柱式龙头）

32 spindle top
心轴顶部

33 shield
护照

34 draw-off tap (*Am.* faucet)
水龙头

35 supatap
双阀水龙头

36 swivel tap
旋转龙头

37 flushing valve
冲洗阀

38-52 fittings
零件配件

38 joint with male thread
外螺纹接头

39 reducing socket (reducing coupler)
异径管节（异径管接头）

40 elbow screw joint (elbow coupling)
肘管螺纹接头（弯管接头）

41 reducing socket (reducing coupler) with female thread
带内螺纹的异径管节（异径管接头）

42 screw joint
螺纹接头

43 coupler (socket)
管接头（管节）

44 T-joint (T-junction joint, tee)
T型接头（三通接头，T 接头）

45 elbow screw joint with female thread
带内螺纹的肘管接头

46 bend
弯管接头

47 T-joint (T-junction joint, tee) with female taper thread
锥形内螺纹 T 型接头（三通接头，T 型接头）

48 ceiling joint
平顶接头

49 reducing elbow
异径肘管

50 cross
十字接头

51 elbow joint with male thread
带外螺纹的肘管接头

52 elbow joint
肘管接头

53-57 pipe supports
管架

53 saddle clip
鞍形夹

54 spacing bracket
间隔（定位）托架

55 plug
塞栓

56 pipe clips
管夹

57 two-piece spacing clip
双层定位夹

58-86 plumber's tools, gas fitter's tools
铅管工工具，瓦斯匠工具

58 gas pliers
瓦斯钳

59 footprints
瓦斯管螺旋钳

60 combination cutting pliers
钢丝钳

61 pipe wrench
管扳钳

62 flat-nose pliers
扁咀钳，平头钳

63 nipple key
螺纹套管扳手

64 round-nose pliers
圆头钳

65 pincers
尖手钳

66 adjustable S-wrench
可调整 S 型扳手

67 screw wrench
螺旋（丝）扳手

68 shifting spanner
活动扳手（移位扳手）

69 screwdriver
螺丝起子

70 compass saw (keyhole saw)
圆锯（钥匙锯）

71 hacksaw frame
弓锯架

72 hand saw
手锯

73 soldering iron
烙铁

74 blowlamp (blowtorch) [for soldering]
扦接时用的喷灯

75 sealing tape
密封带

76 tin-lead solder
锡铅焊料

77 club hammer
手锤（大头锤）

78 hammer
榔头，锤子

79 spirit level
水平仪

80 steel-leg vice (*Am.* vise)
钢管老虎钳

81 pipe vice (*Am.* vise)
管虎钳

82 pipe-bending machine
弯管机

83 former (template)
绕线模（模板）

84 pipe cutter
切管刀

85 hand die
手动扳牙

86 screw-cutting machine (thread-cutting machine)
螺纹切削机

1 electrician (electrical fitter, wireman)
电工（电气装修工，线路检修工）
2 bell push (doorbell) for low-voltage safety current
电铃按钮（门铃）[低压安全电流]
3 house telephone with call button
带呼唤按钮的室内电话
4 [flush-mounted] rocker switch
[嵌装式]摇杆开关
5 [flush-mounted] earthed socket (wall socket, plug point, Am. wall outlet, convenience outlet, outlet)
[嵌装式]接地插座（壁上插座，插塞式插座，[美]壁上插座，便利插座，插座）
6 [surface-mounted] earthed double socket (double wall socket, double plug point, Am. double wall outlet, double convenience outlet, double outlet)
[表面安装式]接地双插座（壁上双插座，插塞式双插座，[美]壁上双插座，便利双插座，双插座）
7 switched socket (switch and socket)
开关插座（开关和插座）
8 four-socket (four-way) adapter
四插座（四路）转接器
9 earthed plug
接地插头
10 extension lead (Am. extension cord)
延长线
11 extension plug
延长线插头
12 extension socket
延长线插座
13 surface-mounted three-pole earthed socket [for three-phase circuit] with neutral conductor
（三相电路用）表面安装式有中性导体的三极接地插座
14 three-phase plug
三相插头
15 electric bell (electric buzzer)
电铃（电蜂鸣器）
16 pull-switch (cord-operated wall switch)
拉线开关（绳索操纵的墙壁开关）
17 strip of sheet metal [on which wallpaper is laid for cutting]
（裁壁纸用的）薄金属片
18 drill-cast rotary switch
定位式旋转开关
19 miniature circuit breaker (screw-in circuit breaker, fuse)
小型断路器（旋入式断路器，熔断器）
20 resetting button
重接按钮
21 set screw [for fuses and miniature circuit breakers]
[熔断器和小型断路器用的]固定螺钉
22 underfloor mounting (underfloor sockets)
装设於地板下的插座
23 hinged floor socket for power lines and communication lines
电源线和通信线用的铰链地面插座
24 sunken floor socket with hinged lid (snap lid)
带铰链盖凹入地面的插座

25 surface-mounted socket outlet (plug point) box
表面安装式插座出线盒
26 pocket torch, a torch (Am. flashlight)
袖珍手电筒
27 dry cell battery
干电池
28 contact spring
接触弹簧
29 strip of thermoplastic connectors
热塑连接器的插座板
30 steel draw-in wire (draw wire) with threading key, and ring attached
带插入键和环的钢拉线
31 electricity meter cupboard
电表厨
32 electricity meter
电表
33 miniature circuit breakers (miniature circuit breaker consumer unit)
小型断路器（小型断路器消耗装置）
34 insulating tape (Am. friction tape)
绝缘带
35 fuse holder
保险座
36 circuit breaker (fuse), a fuse cartridge with fusible element
断路器（熔断器），带易熔元件的保险丝盒
37 colour (Am. color) indicator [showing current rating]
颜色指示器[显示额定电流]
38-39 contact maker
接触装置
40 cable clip
电缆夹
41 universal test meter (multiple meter for measuring current and voltage)
多用途电表（测量电流电压的多用电表）
42 thermoplastic moisture-proof cable
热塑防潮电缆
43 copper conductor
铜导体
44 three-core cable
三心电缆
45 electric soldering iron
电烙铁
46 screwdriver
螺丝起子
47 pipe wrench
管子扳手，管钳
48 shock-resisting safety helmet
抗震安全头盔
49 tool case
工具箱
50 round-nose pliers
圆头钳
51 cutting pliers
剪钳
52 junior hacksaw
轻型弓锯
53 combination cutting pliers
老虎钳，钢丝钳
54 insulated handle
绝缘把手
55 continuity tester
电路连续性测试器

56 electric light bulb (general service lamp, filament lamp)
电灯泡（普通灯，灯丝电灯泡）
57 glass bulb (bulb)
玻璃灯泡（灯泡）
58 coiled-coil filament
绕线式灯丝
59 screw base
螺纹管座
60 lampholder
灯座
61 fluorescent tube
萤光管，日光灯管
62 bracket for fluorescent tubes
日光灯管座
63 electrician's knife
电工刀
64 wire strippers
剥线钳
65 bayonet fitting
卡口座
66 three-pin socket with switch
带开关的三脚插座
67 three-pin plug
三脚插头
68 fuse carrier with fuse wire
带保险丝的保险丝架
69 light bulb with bayonet fitting
带卡口的灯泡

1-17 preparation of surfaces
墙面的準备
1 wallpaper-stripping liquid (stripper)
壁纸剥除液
2 plaster (plaster of Paris)
熟石膏
3 filler
填料
4 glue size (size)
浆糊，胶水
5 lining paper, a backing paper
衬纸，衬背纸
6 primer
底漆
7 fluate
氟化物
8 shredded lining paper
小块衬纸
9 wallpaper-stripping machine (stripper)
壁纸剥除器
10 scraper
刮除器
11 smoother
堰刀
12 perforator
打孔器
13 sandpaper block
砂纸打磨用的木块
14 sandpaper
砂纸
15 stripping knife
剥除刀
16 masking tape
掩蔽胶带
17 strip of sheet metal [on which wallpaper is laid for cutting]
（裁壁纸用的）薄金属片
18-53 wallpapering (paper hanging)

18 wallpaper (*kinds:* wood pulp paper, wood chip paper, fabric wallhangings, synthetic wallpaper, metallic paper, natural (*e.g.* wood or cork) paper, tapestry wallpaper)
壁纸（种类：木浆纸，木屑纸，纤维纸，合成纤维壁纸，金属纸，天然（木或软木）纸，织绵壁纸）
19 length of wallpaper
壁纸的长度
20 butted paper edges
壁纸对接边
21 matching edge
叠合边
22 non-matching edge
非叠合边
23 wallpaper paste
壁纸粘剂
24 heavy-duty paste
强力粘合剂
25 pasting machine
刷胶机
26 paste [for the pasting machine]
（刷胶机用的）粘合剂
27 paste brush
刷胶用刷子
28 emulsion paste
乳状胶
29 picture rail
划线的长板条
30 beading pins
珠状钉
31 pasteboard (paperhanger's bench)
刷胶台（裱糊枱）
32 gloss finish
罩光漆
33 paperhanging kit
裱糊工具箱

34 shears (bull-nosed scissors)
剪刀（整平的剪刀）
35 filling knife
装填的铲刀
36 seam roller
压缝滚轮
37 hacking knife
割刀
38 knife (trimming knife)
修边刀
39 straightedge
直尺
40 paperhanging brush
裱糊刷
41 wallpaper-cutting board
裁壁纸板
42 cutter
裁刀
43 trimmer
修剪器
44 plastic spatula
塑胶刮板
45 chalked string
划线绳（弹粉线）
46 spreader
涂抹刀
47 paper roller
滚筒
48 flannel cloth
法兰绒布
49 dry brush
乾刷
50 ceiling paperhanger
天花板裱糊工具
51 overlap angle
折角
52 paperhanger's trestles
裱糊壁纸用的合（扶）梯
53 ceiling paper
天花板纸

1 **painting**
上漆
2 painter
油漆工
3 paintbrush
油漆刷
4 emulsion paint (emulsion)
乳胶漆
5 stepladder
四脚梯
6 can (tin) of paint
油漆罐
7-8 cans (tins) of paint
各种油漆罐
7 can (tin) with fixed handle
有固定手柄的油漆罐
8 paint kettle
油漆桶
9 drum of paint
大桶油漆
10 paint bucket
漆桶
11 paint roller
油漆滚筒
12 grill [for removing excess paint from the roller]
[从滚筒去除过量油漆用的]铁格子
13 stippling roller
点彩滚筒
14 **varnishing**
涂漆
15 oil-painted dado
涂漆的护壁
16 canister for thinner
稀释用罐
17 flat brush for larger surfaces (flat wall brush)
较大表面用的扁平刷
18 stippler
点彩刷

19 fitch
画笔
20 cutting-in brush
削角刷，切入刷
21 radiator brush (flay brush)
暖气炉刷（剥皮刷）
22 paint scraper
油漆刮刀
23 scraper
刮刀
24 putty knife
油灰刀
25 sandpaper
砂纸
26 sandpaper block
砂纸打磨块
27 floor brush
地板刷
28 **sanding and spraying**
砂打磨和喷漆
29 grinder
研磨器
30 sander
砂磨器
31 pressure pot
压力罐
32 spray gun
喷枪
33 compressor (air compressor)
压缩机（空气压缩机）
34 flow coating machine for flow coating radiators, etc.
用於流动涂层暖气机等的流动涂层机
35 hand spray
人力喷雾（漆）器
36 airless spray unit
无空气喷漆装置
37 airless spray gun
无空气喷（漆）枪

38 efflux viscometer
流出粘度计
39 seconds timer
秒表
40 **lettering and gilding**
书写和粉饰
41 lettering brush (signwriting brush, pencil)
书写刷（写广告用笔，铅笔）
42 tracing wheel
描绘轮
43 stencil knife
模板镂花刀
44 oil gold size
金油胶
45 gold leaf
金箔
46 outline drawing
轮廓描绘
47 mahlstick
腕木
48 pouncing
以印花粉印花样
49 pounce bag
印花粉袋
50 gilder's cushion
镀金工用的软垫
51 gilder's knife
镀金工用的刀子
52 sizing gold leaf
涂胶於金箔
53 filling in the letters with stipple paint
用点画漆填写文字
54 gilder's mop
涂金用的刷把

1-25 furrier's workroom
皮货制造工
1 furrier
毛皮衣制造工
2 steam spray gun
蒸汽喷枪
3 steam iron
蒸汽熨斗
4 beating machine
（敲）搅打机
5 cutting machine for letting out furskins
毛皮放长切割机
6 uncut furskin
未切割之毛皮
7 let-out strips (let-out sections)
放长皮条（放长切片）
8 fur worker
毛皮工人
9 fur-sewing machine
毛皮缝纫机
10 blower for letting out
毛皮放长用的吹风机
11-21 furskins
毛皮
11 mink skin
貂皮
12 fur side
毛面
13 leather side
皮革面
14 cut furskin
裁剪下的毛皮

15 lynx skin before letting out
放长前的山猫毛皮
16 let-out lynx skin
放长山猫毛皮
17 fur side
毛面
18 leather side
皮革面
19 let-out mink skin
放长貂皮
20 lynx fur, sewn together (sewn)
缝合的山猫毛皮
21 broadtail
宽尾毛皮
22 fur marker
毛皮标签
23 fur worker
毛皮工人
24 mink coat
貂皮大衣
25 ocelot coat
豹猫皮大衣

1-73 joiner's workshop
细木匠工作室

1-28 joiner's tools
细木匠工具

1 wood rasp
粗木锉

2 wood file
平锉

3 compass saw (keyhole saw)
圆锯（钥孔锯）

4 saw handle
锯柄

5 [square-headed] mallet
[方头]木槌

6 try square
矩尺

7-11 chisels
凿子

7 bevelled-edge chisel (chisel)
斜边凿子

8 mortise (mortice) chisel
榫眼凿

9 gouge
圆凿

10 handle
凿柄

11 framing chisel (cant chisel)
框凿（斜面凿）

12 glue pot in water bath
水槽中的胶罐

13 glue pot (glue well), an insert for joiner's glue
胶罐，放入盛胶罐的热水容器

14 handscrew
手动螺旋（丝）

15-28 planes
刨子

15 smoothing plane
光刨

16 jack plane
粗刨

17 toothing plane
齿刨

18 handle (toat)
手柄

19 wedge
木楔

20 plane iron (cutter)
刨刀

21 mouth
刨咀

22 sole
刨底

23 side
刨侧

24 stock (body)
刨身

25 rebate (rabbet) plane
槽口刨

26 router plane (old woman's tooth)
起槽刨

27 spokeshave
辐刨刀

28 compass plane
圆刨

29-37 woodworker's bench
木工台

29 foot
台脚

30 front vice (Am. vise)
前虎钳（台钳）

31 vice (Am. vise) handle
虎钳手柄

32 vice (Am. vise) screw
虎钳螺丝

33 jaw
钳口

34 bench top
台面板

35 well
工作台上的槽

36 bench stop (bench holdfast)
刨台栓（刨台反转装置）

37 tail vice (Am. vise)
刨台尾部虎钳

38 cabinet maker (joiner)
木工，木匠

39 trying plane
中级刨

40 shavings
刨花

41 wood screw
木螺丝

42 saw set
整锯齿工具

43 mitre (Am. miter) box
斜口锯箱

44 tenon saw
榫锯

45 thicknesser (thicknessing machine)
压刨床（刨成一定厚度的机械）

46 thicknessing table with rollers
带滚筒的压刨台

47 kick-back guard
逆转护板

48 chip-extractor opening
排屑口

49 chain mortising machine (chain mortiser)
链式榫眼机

50 endless mortising chain
环形榫眼链

51 clamp (work clamp)
夹板，夹子

52 knot hole moulding (Am. molding) machine
造节孔机

53 knot hole cutter
节孔刀具

54 quick-action chuck
快速夹头（卡盘）

55 hand lever
手杆

56 change-gear handle
换齿轮手柄

57 sizing and edging machine
尺度矫正，摺边机（裁割修边机）

58 main switch
主开关（电源开关）

59 circular-saw (buzz saw) blade
圆盘锯锯片

60 height (rise and fall) adjustment wheel
高度（上下）调整轮

61 V-way
V 型导轨

62 framing table
构架台

63 extension arm (arm)
延长臂

64 trimming table
修饰台

65 fence
挡板

66 fence adjustment handle
挡板调整手柄

67 clamp lever
夹紧杆

68 board-sawing machine
锯板机

69 swivel motor
旋转马达

70 board support
木板支架

71 saw carriage
锯架

72 pedal for raising the transport rollers
上升运转滚轮用的踏板

73 block board
整块胶合板

1 veneer-peeling machine
(peeling machine, peeler)
薄板剥皮机（剥皮机）

2 veneer
薄板

3 veneer-splicing machine
薄板编结机（斜切皮机）

4 nylon-thread cop
尼龙线团（圆锥形）

5 sewing mechanism
缝纫机械装置

6 dowel hole boring machine
(dowel hole borer)
定位孔搪床（定位孔搪开孔机）

7 boring motor with hollow-shaft
boring bit
具有空心轴搪刀尖块的搪孔马达

8 clamp handle
夹紧手柄

9 clamp
夹钳

10 clamping shoe
夹紧环箍

11 stop bar
停止杆

12 edge sander (edge-sanding
machine)
边缘磨边机

13 tension roller with extension
arm
其延长臂的拉力滚筒

14 sanding belt regulator
(regulating handle)
砂磨带调节器（调整手柄）

15 endless sanding belt (sand belt)
环形砂磨带

16 belt-tensioning lever
砂磨带拉力（紧）杆

17 canting table (tilting table)
倾斜台（倾斜台）

18 belt roller
砂带滚筒

19 angling fence for mitres (*Am.*
miters)
斜接用的角板

20 opening dust hood
开口防尘罩

21 rise adjustment of the table
台面升降调整装置

22 rise adjustment wheel for the
table
台面升降调整轮

23 clamping screw for the table rise
adjustment
台面升降（高度）调整装置的夹紧螺丝

24 console
托架

25 foot of the machine
机脚

26 edge-veneering machine
边缘胶合机

27 sanding wheel
砂磨轮

28 sanding dust extractor
砂磨吸尘器

29 splicing head
编结机头

30 single-belt sanding machine
(single-belt sander)
单带砂磨机

31 belt guard
砂带防护装置

32 bandwheel cover
带轮罩

33 extractor fan (exhaust fan)
抽风机（排风机）

34 frame-sanding pad
框式砂磨垫板

35 sanding table
砂磨台

36 fine adjustment
微动装置

37 fine cutter and jointer
细切断器和刨木机

38 saw carriage
锯架

39 trailing cable hanger (trailing
cable support)
拖曳缆吊架（牵索支架）

40 air extractor pipe
排气管

41 rail
护栏

42 frame-cramping
(frame-clamping) machine
框架夹紧机

43 frame stand
框架座

44 workpiece, a window frame
工件（工作件），窗框

45 compressed-air line
压缩空气管

46 pressure cylinder
压力缸

47 pressure foot
加压脚

48 frame-mounting device
框架固定装置

49 rapid-veneer press
快速胶合板压力机

50 bed
压床

51 press
压力机

52 pressure piston
压力活塞

1-34 tool cupboard (tool
cabinet) for do-it-yourself work
自己动手做用的工具橱
1 smoothing plane
光刨
2 set of fork spanners (fork
wrenches, open-end wrenches)
整组叉形扳手（叉形扳手，开口扳手）
3 hacksaw
弓锯
4 screwdriver
螺丝起子
5 cross-point screwdriver
十字螺丝起子
6 saw rasp
锯锉
7 hammer
榔头，锤子
8 wood rasp
木锉
9 roughing file
粗锉
10 small vice (*Am.* vise)
小虎钳
11 pipe wrench
管形扳手
12 multiple pliers
多功用剪钳（钢丝钳）
13 pincers
尖手钳
14 all-purpose wrench
万用扳手
15 wire stripper and cutter
剥线和剪线钳
16 electric drill
电钻
17 hacksaw
弓锯
18 plaster cup
灰泥桶
19 soldering iron
烙铁
20 tin-lead solder wire
锡铅钎丝
21 lamb's wool polishing bonnet
羔羊皮抛光圆盘
22 rubber backing disc (disk)
橡皮衬垫圆盘
23 grinding wheel
磨轮，砂轮
24 wire wheel brush
钢丝轮刷
25 sanding discs (disks)
砂磨盘
26 try square
矩尺
27 hand saw
手锯
28 universal cutter
万能刀具
29 spirit level
（酒精）水平仪
30 firmer chisel
短凿
31 centre (*Am.* center) punch
中心冲
32 nail punch
钉冲头
33 folding rule (rule)
摺（叠）尺
34 storage box for small parts
小零件的存放箱
35 tool box
工具箱

36 woodworking adhesive
木工粘著剂
37 stripping knife
铲刀
38 adhesive tape
胶带
39 storage box with compartments
for nails, screws, and plugs
具放钉子，螺丝和插头的分格存放箱
40 machinist's hammer
机匠榔头（锤）
41 collapsible workbench
(collapsible bench)
可摺叠的工作台
42 jig
夹具，夹紧装置
43 electric percussion drill (electric
hammer drill)
电动冲击钻机（电动锤打钻）
44 pistol grip
手枪式握柄
45 side grip
侧握柄
46 gearshift switch
变速开关
47 handle with depth gauge (*Am.*
gage)
带深度规的手柄
48 chuck
卡盘，夹头
49 twist bit (twist drill)
麻花钻头（麻花钻）
50-55 attachments for an electric
drill
电钻附件
50 combined circular saw (buzz
saw) and bandsaw
圆（盘）锯和带锯组合机
51 wood-turning lathe
木工车床
52 circular saw attachment
圆（盘）锯（附件）
53 orbital sanding attachment
(orbital sander)
轨道式砂磨机
54 drill stand
钻架
55 hedge-trimming attachment
(hedge trimmer)
树篱修剪机
56 soldering gun
电烙枪
57 soldering iron
烙铁
58 high-speed soldering iron
高速烙铁
59 upholstery, upholstering an
armchair
铺垫，为扶手椅铺上布套
60 fabric (material) for upholstery
布套用的布料
61 do-it-yourself enthusiast
自己动手做的热衷者

1-26 turnery (turner's workshop)
车床工厂（车床工作室）
1 wood-turning lathe (lathe)
木工车床
2 lathe bed
车床床台
3 starting resistance (starting resistor)
起动电阻（起动变阻器）
4 gearbox
齿轮箱
5 tool rest
刀架
6 chuck
卡盘，夹头
7 tailstock
车床尾座
8 centre (*Am.* center)
顶尖
9 driving plate with pin
带销的驱动盘
10 two-jaw chuck
双颚夹头
11 live centre (*Am.* center)
活动顶尖
12 fretsaw
圆锯，线锯
13 fretsaw blade
圆锯（线锯）锯片
14, 15, 24 turning tools
车削刀具

14 thread chaser, for cutting threads in wood
於木头上切螺纹用的单用螺纹钣刀
15 gouge, for rough turning
粗车削用的圆凿
16 spoon bit (shell bit)
匙头钻（壳形钻）
17 hollowing tool
掏空用的刀具
18 outside calliper (caliper)
外卡钳（卡钳）
19 turned work (turned wood)
车好的工件（旋好的木件）
20 master turner (turner)
车床工
21 [piece of] rough wood
[一段]粗木料（未加工木料）
22 drill
钻子
23 inside calliper (caliper)
内卡钳
24 parting tool
割断工具
25 glass paper (sandpaper, emery paper)
玻璃砂纸（砂纸，金刚砂纸）
26 shavings
木屑，刨花

1-40 basket making (basketry, basketwork)
编篮（篮细工）

1-4 weaves (strokes)
编织法式样

1 randing
涮旋编织

2 rib randing
棱条编织

3 oblique
斜纹编织

4 randing, a piece of wickerwork (screen work)
涮旋编织品，一件柳条编织物

5 weaver
编织工

6 stake
柳条

7 workboard; *also:* lapboard
工作板；亦称：搭膝板

8 screw block
编织用横的突出板

9 hole for holding the block
砧板定位孔

10 stand
支架

11 chip basket (spale basket)
木片条篮子（刨片条篮）

12 chip (spale)
木片条（刨片条）

13 soaking tub
浸渍盆

14 willow stakes (osier stakes)
柳条，柳枝

15 willow rods (osier rods)
细柳条，细柳枝

16 basket, a piece of wickerwork (basketwork)
筐，一件柳条编织物

17 border
筐边

18 woven side
编织面

19 round base
圆底

20 woven base
编织底

21 slath
筐底交叉肋

22-24 covering a frame
框架的外披

22 frame
框架

23 end
末梢（绳头）

24 rib
肋条

25 upsett
骨架，框架

26 grass; *kinds:* esparto grass, alfalfa grass
禾本科植物草；种类：茅草，苜蓿草

27 rush (bulrush, reed mace)
灯心草（芦苇，香蒲）

28 reed
芦苇

29 raffia (bast)
拉菲亚树的纤维（勒皮，内皮，勒皮纤维）

30 straw
麦秆，稻秆

31 bamboo cane
竹料

32 rattan (ratan) chair cane
藤条料

33 basket maker
编篮工

34 bending tool
弯曲工具

35 cutting point (bodkin)
锥子

36 rapping iron
敲铁

37 pincers
钳子

38 picking knife
刮刀

39 shave
刨刀

40 hacksaw
弓锯

1-8 hearth (forge) with blacksmith's fire
锻工炉
1 hearth (forge)
锻炉
2 shovel (slice)
煤铲
3 swab
水刷
4 raker
炉耙
5 poker
火钩
6 blast pipe (tue iron)
鼓风管（锻炉风咀）
7 chimney (cowl, hood)
烟囱（烟囱罩，烟囱帽）
8 water trough (quenching trough, bosh)
水槽（冷却槽，金属锭冷却槽）
9 power hammer
机力
10 ram (tup)
撞锤（锤头）
11-16 anvil
砧
11 anvil
铁砧
12 flat beak (beck, bick)
铁砧平面端
13 round beak (beck, bick)
铁砧圆角端
14 auxiliary table
辅助工作台

15 foot
砧脚
16 upsetting block
锻粗块
17 swage block
型铁砧，花砧
18 tool-grinding machine (tool grinder)
工具磨床
19 grinding wheel
磨轮
20 block and tackle
滑车组
21 workbench (bench)
工作台
22-39 blacksmith's tools
铁工工具
22 sledge hammer
大锤
23 blacksmith's hand hammer
锻铁锤
24 flat tongs
平口钳
25 round tongs
圆口钳
26 parts of the hammer
锤子的各部分
27 peen (pane, pein)
锤头扁顶端
28 face
锤面
29 eye
榫眼

30 haft
锤柄
31 cotter punch
扁冲头
32 hardy (hardie)
錾
33 set hammer
锻缩锤
34 sett (set, sate)
平头錾
35 flat-face hammer (flatter)
平面锤
36 round punch
圆冲头
37 angle tongs
角钳
38 blacksmith's chisel (scaling hammer, chipping hammer)
铁匠凿锤（去锈锤，凿锤）
39 moving iron (bending iron)
活动铁（弯钢材工具）

1 compressed-air system
　压缩空气系统
2 electric motor
　电动机，电马达
3 compressor
　压缩机
4 compressed-air tank
　压缩空气槽
5 compressed-air line
　压缩空气管路
6 percussion screwdriver
　冲击螺丝起子
7 pedestal grinding machine (floor
　grinding machine)
　基座式磨床
8 grinding wheel
　磨轮，砂轮
9 guard
　防护罩
10 trailer
　拖车
11 brake drum
　轫鼓，刹车鼓
12 brake shoe
　轫块，刹车块
13 brake lining
　刹车衬
14 testing kit
　试验仪器
15 pressure gauge (*Am.* gage)
　压力计（表）
16 brake-testing equipment, a
　rolling road
　刹车试验装置，滚动车道

17 pit
　坑（修车坑）
18 braking roller
　刹车（掣动）滚子
19 meter (recording meter)
　表（记录表）
20 precision lathe for brake drums
　刹车鼓的精密车床
21 lorry wheel
　载货车轮
22 boring mill
　搪床
23 power saw, a hacksaw (power
　hacksaw)
　动力锯，一种弓锯（动力弓锯）
24 vice (*Am.* vise)
　虎钳，台钳
25 saw frame
　锯框
26 coolant supply pipe
　冷却剂供应管
27 riveting machine
　铆接机
28 trailer frame (chassis) under
　construction
　建造中的拖车架（车底盘）
29 inert-gas welding equipment
　钝气熔接装置
30 rectifier
　整流器
31 control unit
　控制装置
32 CO_2 cylinder
　二氧化碳气瓶

33 anvil
　铁砧
34 hearth (forge) with
　blacksmith's fire
　锻匠炉
35 trolley for gas cylinders
　瓦斯筒用的手推车
36 vehicle under repair, a tractor
　正修理中的车辆，曳引机，牵引机

1 continuous furnace with grid hearth for annealing of round stock
圆材退火用带格子炉床的连续炉

2 discharge opening (discharge door)
排料口（排料门）

3 gas burners
燃气器

4 charging door
进料门

5 counterblow hammer
对击锻锤

6 upper ram
上撞锤

7 lower ram
下撞锤

8 ram guide
撞锤滑槽

9 hydraulic drive
液压驱动装置

10 column
（支）柱

11 short-stroke drop hammer
短冲程落锤机

12 ram (tup)
撞锤（锤头）

13 upper die block
上模块

14 lower die block
下模块

15 hydraulic drive
液压驱动装置

16 frame
构架

17 anvil
铁砧

18 forging and sizing press
锻压机

19 standard
台架，机架

20 table
工作台

21 disc (disk) clutch
圆形离合器

22 compressed-air pipe
压缩空气管

23 solenoid valve
电磁阀

24 air-lift gravity hammer (air-lift drop hammer)
气升式落锤

25 drive motor
驱动马达

26 hammer (tup)
锤（锤头）

27 foot control (foot pedal)
脚踏控制（脚踏板）

28 preshaped (blocked) workpiece
预成形（成块）工件

29 hammer guide
落锤滑槽

30 hammer cylinder
落锤汽缸

31 anvil
铁砧

32 mechanical manipulator to move the workpiece in hammer forging
锤锻时移动工件的机械操作机

33 dogs
牵转具

34 counterweight
配重

35 hydraulic forging press
液压锻压机

36 crown
液压机顶梁

37 cross head
十字头

38 upper die block
上模块

39 lower die block
下模块

40 anvil
铁砧

41 hydraulic piston
液压活塞

42 pillar guide
柱导槽，柱滑槽

43 rollover device
翻转（滚）装置

44 burden chain (chain sling)
负重链（勾环吊链）

45 crane hook
起重机钩

46 workpiece
工件

47 gas furnace (gas-fired furnace)
瓦斯炉

48 gas burner
燃气器

49 charging opening
进料口

50 chain curtain
链式栅幕

51 vertical-lift door
上升门

52 hot-air duct
热气管

53 air preheater
空气预热器

54 gas pipe
瓦斯管

55 electric door-lifting mechanism
电动门机构

56 air blast
鼓风装置

1-22 metalwork shop
(mechanic's workshop, fitter's
workshop, locksmith's
workshop)
金属加工厂（机械修理工厂，装配工作
厂，锁匠工厂）

1 metalworker (*e.g.* mechanic,
fitter, locksmith; *form. also:*
wrought-iron craftsman)
金属加工工人（如：机械修理工，装配
工，锁匠，亦包括：锻铁匠）

2 parallel-jaw vice (*Am.* vise)
平行颈虎钳

3 jaw
夹，钳口

4 screw
螺杆

5 handle
手柄

6 workpiece
工件

7 workbench (bench)
工作台

8 files (*kinds:* rough file, smooth
file, precision file)
锉刀（种类：粗锉，细锉，精（密）
锉）

9 hacksaw
弓锯

10 leg vice (*Am.* vise), a spring vice
长脚（老）虎钳，一种弹簧虎钳

11 muffle furnace, a gas-fired
furnace
烙室炉，一种瓦斯点火炉

12 gas pipe
瓦斯管

13 hand brace (hand drill)
曲柄钻（手摇钻）

14 swage block
型铁砧，花砧

15 filing machine
锉机

16 file
锉刀

17 compressed-air pipe
压缩空气管

18 grinding machine (grinder)
磨床

19 grinding wheel
磨轮，砂轮

20 guard
防护罩

21 goggles (safety glasses)
护目镜（安全眼镜）

22 safety helmet
安全帽

23 machinist's hammer
机工锤（榔头）

24 hand vice (*Am.* vise)
手虎钳

25 cape chisel (cross-cut chisel)
起槽凿（横割凿，尖咀錾）

26 flat chisel
扁凿

27 flat file
扁锉

28 file cut (cut)
锉削

29 round file (*also:* half-round file)
圆锉（另有：半圆锉）

30 tap wrench
螺丝攻扳手

31 reamer
绞刀

32 die (die and stock)
螺纹模

33-35 key
钥匙

33 stem (shank)
匙杆（匙柄）

34 bow
匙弓

35 bit
匙齿

36-43 door lock, a mortise (mortice) lock
门锁，一种榫眼锁

36 back plate
均力板，背板

37 spring bolt (latch bolt)
弹簧螺栓（弹簧锁）

38 tumbler
锁的制栓

39 bolt
螺栓

40 keyhole
钥匙孔

41 bolt guide pin
螺栓导销

42 tumbler spring
制栓弹簧

43 follower, with square hole
带方孔的从动轮（件）

44 cylinder lock (safety lock)
圆筒锁（安全锁）

45 cylinder (plug)
圆筒

46 spring
弹簧

47 pin
销

48 safety key, a flat key
安全钥匙，一种扁平钥匙

49 lift-off hinge
上提绞链

50 hook-and-ride band
有套钩和骑带的铰链

51 strap hinge
带条铰链

52 vernier calliper (caliper) gauge (*Am.* gage)
游标卡尺

53 feeler gauge (*Am.* gage)
测隙规

54 vernier depth gauge (*Am.* gage)
游标深度尺

55 vernier
游标

56 straightedge
直尺，标尺

57 square
角尺

58 breast drill
胸压钻

59 twist bit (twist drill)
麻花钻头（麻化钻）

60 screw tap (tap)
螺丝攻

61 halves of a screw die
螺模的两半

62 screwdriver
螺丝起子

63 scraper (*also:* pointed triangle scraper)
刮刀（即：尖三角刮刀）

64 centre (*Am.* center) punch
中心冲

65 round punch
圆冲头

66 flat-nose pliers
鸭嘴钳

67 detachable-jaw cut nippers
可分解的颈口剪钳

68 gas pliers
镊子

69 pincers
尖手钳

1 gas cylinder manifold
各种贮气瓶
2 acetylene cylinder
乙炔气瓶
3 oxygen cylinder
氧气瓶
4 high-pressure manometer
高压计（高压液压计）
5 pressure-reducing valve
(reducing valve, pressure
regulator)
减压阀（降压阀，调压器）
6 low-pressure manometer
低压计（低压液压计）
7 stop valve
停止阀
8 hydraulic back-pressure valve
for low-pressure installations
低压装置用的液压止回阀
9 gas hose
瓦斯管
10 oxygen hose
氧气管
11 welding torch (blowpipe)
（纤枪）熔接氧炬（吹管）
12 welding rod (filler rod)
熔接条，纤条（填充纤料）
13 welding bench
熔接台
14 grating
格栅
15 scrap box
废料盒（箱）

16 bench covering of chamotte
slabs
耐火板复盖的工作台
17 water tank
水槽
18 welding paste (flux)
熔接剂（纤剂）
19 welding torch (blowpipe) with
cutting attachment and guide
tractor
带切割附件和导向器的熔接气炬
（纤管，吹管）
20 workpiece
工件
21 oxygen cylinder
氧气瓶
22 acetylene cylinder
乙炔气瓶
23 cylinder trolley
气瓶手推车
24 welding goggles
熔接护目镜
25 chipping hammer
凿锤
26 wire brush
钢丝刷
27 torch lighter (blowpipe lighter)
气炬（纤枪）点火器，吹管点火器
28 welding torch (blowpipe)
熔接气炬（纤枪，吹管）
29 oxygen control
氧气控制钮

30 oxygen connection
氧气接头
31 gas connection (acetylene
connection)
瓦斯接头（乙炔接头）
32 gas control (acetylene control)
瓦斯控制钮（乙炔控制钮）
33 welding nozzle
熔接（纤枪）喷咀
34 cutting machine
切割机
35 circular template
圆形模板
36 universal cutting machine
万能切割机
37 tracing head
（切割机的）描跡头
38 cutting nozzle
切割喷咀

1 welding transformer
电熔接变压器
2 arc welder
电（弧）熔接工，电钎工
3 arc welding helmet
电（弧）熔接帽
4 flip-up window
可向上翻的护目镜窗
5 shoulder guard
护肩
6 protective sleeve
防护袖
7 electrode case
电熔接条盒
8 three-fingered welding glove
三指熔接（电钎）手套
9 electrode holder
电钎熔接夹把，电极夹
10 electrode
电极，电熔接条（电钎条）
11 leather apron
皮围裙
12 shin guard
护胫
13 welding table with fume
extraction equipment
具抽气装置的熔接（电钎）台
14 table top
台面
15 movable extractor duct
可移动的抽气管
16 extractor support
抽出器支架

17 chipping hammer
凿锤
18 wire brush
钢丝刷
19 welding lead
熔接导线
20 electrode holder
电熔接条夹把，电极夹
21 welding bench
熔接（电钎）工作台
22 spot welding
点熔接，点钎
23 spot welding electrode holder
点熔接电极夹
24 electrode arm
电熔接条臂，电极臂
25 power supply (lead)
电源（导线）
26 electrode-pressure cylinder
电极压圆筒
27 welding transformer
电熔接变压器
28 workpiece
工件
29 foot-operated spot welder
脚控制的点熔接（点钎）机
30 welder electrode arms
点熔接器（点钎器）的电极臂
31 foot pedal for welding pressure
adjustment
熔接（钎接）电压（压力）调节用的脚
踏板

32 five-fingered welding glove
熔接（钎接）用的五指手套
33 inert-gas torch for inert-gas
welding (gas-shielded arc
welding)
钝气熔接用的钝气气炬（气体遮蔽式的
电弧熔接）
34 inert-gas (shielding-gas) supply
钝气供给管
35 work clamp (earthing clamp)
工作夹（接地夹）
36 fillet gauge (*Am.* gage) (weld
gauge) [for measuring throat
thickness]
[测量熔接喉厚用的]内圆角规
37 micrometer
分厘卡
38 measuring arm
测量臂
39 arc welding helmet
电弧熔接头盔
40 filter lens
滤光镜
41 small turntable
小型转盘（磨削机）

[material: steel, brass, aluminium (*Am.* aluminum), plastics, etc.; in the following, steel was chosen as an example]
[材料：钢，铜，铝，塑胶等等，以下选钢材为例]

1 angle iron (angle)
角铁

2 leg (flange)
边（凸缘）

3-7 steel girders
钢梁

3 T-iron (tee-iron)
T 型铁

4 vertical leg
垂直边

5 flange
凸缘，缘板

6 H-girder (H-beam)
H 型钢梁（工字钢）

7 E-channel (channel iron)
E 型槽钢（槽铁）

8 round bar
圆杆，圆条

9 square iron (*Am.* square stock)
方铁杆

10 flat bar
扁条

11 strip steel
带钢

12 iron wire
铁丝

13-50 screws and bolts
螺丝和螺栓

13 hexagonal-head bolt
六角头螺栓

14 head
六角头

15 shank
螺柄（杆）

16 thread
螺纹

17 washer
整圈，垫圈

18 hexagonal nut
六角头螺帽

19 split pin
开尾梢

20 rounded end
圆端

21 width of head (of flats)
六角头的宽度

22 stud
螺椿

23 point (end)
螺栓头（端）

24 castle nut (castellated nut)
堡形螺帽

25 hole for the split pin
开尾梢孔

26 cross-head screw, a sheet-metal screw (self-tapping screw)
十字头螺丝，薄金属板螺丝（自攻螺丝）

27 hexagonal socket head screw
六角承窝头螺丝

28 countersunk-head bolt
埋头螺栓

29 catch
（螺栓）掣子

30 locknut (locking nut)
併紧螺帽（锁紧螺帽）

31 bolt (pin)
螺栓（梢）

32 collar-head bolt
有领螺栓

33 set collar (integral collar)
定位（固定）环

34 spring washer (washer)
弹簧垫圈

35 round nut, an adjusting nut
圆螺帽，调整螺帽

36 cheese-head screw, a slotted screw
平顶圆头螺钉，有槽螺丝

37 tapered pin
推拔销

38 screw slot (screw slit, screw groove)
螺丝槽（螺丝开缝，螺丝沟槽）

39 square-head bolt
方头螺栓

40 grooved pin, a cylindrical pin
有槽梢（销），圆柱形销

41 T-head bolt
T 形头螺栓

42 wing nut (fly nut, butterfly nut)
翼形螺帽（翼形螺帽）

43 rag bolt
棘螺栓

44 barb
倒钩

45 wood screw
木螺丝

46 countersunk head
埋头

47 wood screw thread
木螺纹

48 grub screw
无头螺钉

49 pin slot (pin slit, pin groove)
销槽（销缝，销槽）

50 round end
圆尾端

51 nail (wire nail)
钉（铁钉）

52 head
钉头

53 shank
钉杆

54 point
钉尖

55 roofing nail
大头钉

56 riveting (lap riveting)
铆接，铆（搭铆）

57-60 rivet
铆钉

57 set head (swage head, die head), a rivet head
铆头（型砧头，螺模头），一种铆钉头

58 rivet shank
铆钉柄

59 closing head
铆钉结头

60 pitch of rivets
铆钉节距

61 shaft
轴

62 chamfer (bevel)
去角面（斜面）

63 journal
轴颈

64 neck
轴承颈

65 seat
轴承座

66 keyway
键槽

67 conical seat (cone)
锥形座（锥体）

68 thread
螺纹

69 ball bearing, an antifriction bearing
滚珠轴承，一种低摩擦轴承

70 steel ball (ball)
钢滚珠（滚珠）

71 outer race
（轴承）外圈

72 inner race
（轴承）内圈

73-74 keys
键

73 sunk key (feather)
埋头键（滑键）

74 gib (gib-headed key)
嵌条（带头键）

75-76 needle roller bearing
滚针轴承

75 needle cage
滚针保持器

76 needle
滚针

77 castle nut (castellated nut)
堡形螺帽

78 split pin
开尾梢

79 casing
壳箱

80 casing cover
罩盖

81 grease nipple (lubricating nipple)
加油脂咀，黄油咀（注润滑脂的螺纹接头）

82-96 gear wheels, cog wheels
传动轮，（附）齿轮

82 stepped gear wheel
塔传动轮

83 cog (tooth)
轮齿（轮牙）

84 space between teeth
齿间（距）

85 keyway (key seat, key slot)
键槽（键座，键槽）

86 bore
内径，口径

87 herringbone gear wheel
人字传动轮

88 spokes (arms)
轮辐

89 helical gearing (helical spur wheel)
螺旋齿轮（螺旋正齿轮）

90 sprocket
链轮

91 bevel gear wheel (bevel wheel)
斜面转动轮（斜面齿轮）

92-93 spiral toothing
螺旋齿轮

92 pinion
小齿轮

93 crown wheel
冠状轮

94 epicyclic gear (planetary gear)
周转齿轮（行星齿轮）

95 internal toothing
内齿轮

96 external toothing
外齿轮

97-107 absorption dynamometer
吸收式测功器

97 shoe brake (check brake, block
   brake)
   块状钔，块状刹车
98 brake pulley
   钔滑轮，刹车滑轮
99 brake shaft (brake axle)
   钔轴（刹车轴）
100 brake block (brake shoe)
   钔块

101 pull rod
   拉杆
102 brake magnet
   掣动磁铁
103 brake weight
   掣动重量
104 band brake
   带钔

105 brake band
   钔带
106 brake lining
   刹车衬
107 adjusting screw, for even
   application of the brake
   使掣动器平稳用的调节螺丝

1-51 coal mine (colliery, pit)
煤矿（煤矿，采掘场）

1 pithead gear (headgear)
坑口井架

2 winding engine house
卷扬动力机房

3 pithead frame (head frame)
坑口井架

4 pithead building
坑口建筑物

5 processing plant
煤处理（加工）场

6 sawmill
锯木厂

7-11 coking plant
炼焦厂

7 battery of coke ovens
炼焦炉组

8 larry car (larry, charging car)
运煤车

9 coking coal tower
焦煤塔

10 coke-quenching tower
熄焦塔

11 coke-quenching car
熄焦车

12 gasometer
煤气罐（库）

13 power plant (power station)
发电厂

14 water tower
水塔

15 cooling tower
冷却塔

16 mine fan
矿井换气装置

17 depot
仓库

18 administration building (office
building, offices)
行政大楼（办公大楼，办事处）

19 tip heap (spoil heap)
矿渣堆

20 cleaning plant
清洗设备

21-51 underground workings
(underground mining)
地下作业（地下采矿）

21 ventilation shaft
通风井

22 fan drift
扇风机风道

23 cage-winding system with cages
运矿笼的升降系统

24 main shaft
主立坑道

25 skip-winding system
吊斗升降系统

26 winding inset
坑底车场装卸处

27 staple shaft
坑内小坑

28 spiral chute
螺旋溜槽（溜道）

29 gallery along seam
沿矿层的坑道

30 lateral
横坑

31 cross-cut
石门

32 tunnelling (*Am.* tunneling)
machine
（坑）隧道开掘机

33-37 longwall faces
长壁工作面

33 horizontal ploughed longwall
face
水平控煤长壁工作面（挖掘面）

34 horizontal cut longwall face
水平切割长壁工作面（挖掘面）

35 vertical pneumatic pick longwall
face
垂直气压掘起长壁工作面（挖掘面）

36 diagonal ram longwall face
对角长壁工作面

37 goaf (gob, waste)
采掘路

38 air lock
气流闸

39 transportation of men by cars
人员车辆的运输

40 belt conveying
带状运送机

41 raw coal bunker
原煤（粗煤）仓

42 charging conveyor
装煤运送机

43 transportation of supplies by
monorail car
单轨车供应品的运输

44 transportation of men by
monorail car
单轨车人员的运输

45 transportation of supplies by
mine car
煤车供料运输

46 drainage
排水设备

47 sump (sink)
水仓

48 capping
表土

49 [layer of] coal-bearing rock
含煤层

50 coal seam
煤层

51 fault
断层

1-21 oil drilling
石油钻井

1 drilling rig
钻井机械（设备）

2 substructure
井架底座（底部结构）

3 crown safety platform
杆顶安全台

4 crown blocks
杆顶滑车

5 working platform, an intermediate platform
工作平台，中间平台

6 drill pipes
钻管

7 drilling cable (drilling line)
钻油井用的钢丝绳

8 travelling (*Am.* traveling) block
游动滑车

9 hook
大钩

10 swivel
旋转龙头

11 draw works, a hoist
绞车（卷扬机，起重机）

12 engine
发动机，引擎

13 standpipe and rotary hose
竖管和（旋转）水管

14 kelly
方钻杆

15 rotary table
转盘

16 slush pump (mud pump)
废液泵（泥浆泵）

17 well
井

18 casing
套管

19 drilling pipe
钻管

20 tubing
油管

21 drilling bit; *kinds:* fishtail (blade) bit, rock (*Am.* roller) bit, core bit
钻头，种类：鱼尾钻头，岩石钻头，砂心（心型）钻头

22-27 oil (crude oil) production
石油（原油）生产

22 pumping unit (pump)
抽油装置（泵）

23 plunger
柱塞

24 tubing
油管

25 sucker rods (pumping rods)
抽油杆

26 stuffing box
填料函

27 polish (polished) rod
抛光杆

28-30 treatment of crude oil [diagram]
原油的处理[简图]

28 gas separator
气体分离器

29 gas pipe (gas outlet)
气管（排气管）

30 wet oil tank (wash tank)
湿油槽

31 water heater
热水器

32 water and brine separator
水、盐分离器

33 salt water pipe (salt water outlet)
盐水管（盐水排出管）

34 oil tank
油槽

35 trunk pipeline for oil [to the refinery or transport by tanker lorry (*Am.* tank truck), oil tanker, or pipeline]
油管干线[通到炼油厂或经油罐车油槽，管路的运输]

36-64 processing of crude oil [diagram]
原油加工流程简图

36 oil furnace (pipe still)
油炉（管式蒸馏器）

37 fractionating column (distillation column) with trays
带托盘的分馏塔（蒸馏塔）

38 top gases (tops)
塔顶气

39 light distillation products
轻蒸馏物

40 heavy distillation products
重蒸馏物

41 petroleum
石油，原油
42 gas oil component
汽油成分
43 residue
残滓，残油
44 condenser (cooler)
冷凝器（冷却器）
45 compressor
压缩机
46 desulphurizing
(desulphurization, *Am.*
desulfurizing, desulfurization)
plant
去硫装置（设备）
47 reformer (hydroformer,
platformer)
重整装置，改质装置（氢重整，铂重整）
48 catalytic cracker (cat cracker)
催化裂解装置
49 distillation column
蒸馏塔
50 de-waxing (wax separation)
脱腊（腊分离）
51 vacuum equipment
真空设备
52-64 oil products
石油产品
52 fuel gas
燃料气
53 liquefied petroleum gas (liquid
gas)
液化石油气（液化气）

54 regular grade petrol (*Am.***
gasoline)**
正规汽油，普通汽油
55 super grade petrol (*Am.***
gasoline)**
超级汽油
56 diesel oil
柴油
57 aviation fuel
航空燃料
58 light fuel oil
轻燃料油
59 heavy fuel oil
重燃料油
60 paraffin (paraffin oil, kerosene)
石腊（石腊油，煤油）
61 spindle oil
心轴油，锭子油
62 lubrication oil
润滑油
63 cylinder oil
汽缸油
64 bitumen
沥青
65-74 oil refinery
炼油厂
65 pipeline (oil pipeline)
管路（输油管）
66 distillation plants
蒸馏装置
67 lubricating oil refinery
润滑油炼油厂

68 desulphurizing
(desulphurization, *Am.*
desulfurizing, desulfurization)
plant
去硫装置（设备）
69 gas-separating plant
气体分离装置
70 catalytic cracking plant
催化裂解装置
71 catalytic reformer
催化重整装置
72 storage tank
储存槽
73 spherical tank
球面（形）槽
74 tanker terminal
油轮码头

1-39   drilling rig (oil rig)
钻探设备，钻油设备

1-37   drilling platform
钻探平台

1   power station
发电站（发电所）

2   generator exhausts
发电机排气装置

3   revolving crane (pedestal crane)
旋转起重机（托架式起重机）

4   piperack
管架

5   turbine exhausts
涡轮机排气装置

6   materials store
材料仓库

7   helicopter deck (heliport deck, heliport)
直升机降落平台，直升机场甲板

8   elevator
升降机

9   production oil and gas separator
油汽分离器

10   test oil and gas separators (test separators)
试验用油汽分离器（试验分离器）

11   emergency flare stack
紧急照明弹（闪光）装置

12   derrick
井架

13   diesel tank
柴油槽

14   office building
办公室

15   cement storage tanks
水泥储槽

16   drinking water tank
饮水槽

17   salt water tank
盐水槽

18   jet fuel tanks
喷汽燃料槽

19   lifeboats
救生艇

20   elevator shaft
升降机架

21   compressed-air reservoir
压缩储气筒（罐）

22   pumping station
泵水站

23   air compressor
空气压缩机

24   air lock
气闸

25   seawater desalination plant
海水去盐设备

26   inlet filters for diesel fuel
柴油输入过滤器

27   gas cooler
气体冷却器

28   control panel for the separators
分离器控制盘

29   toilets (lavatories)
盥洗室

30   workshop
工厂

31   pig trap [the 'pig' is used to clean the oil pipeline]
[用来清理油管的]刮管器

32   control room
控制室

33   accommodation modules (accommodation)
居住单位

34   high-pressure cementing pumps
高压水泥泵

35   lower deck
下甲板

36   middle deck
中甲板

37   top deck (main deck)
顶甲板（主甲板）

38   substructure
下部结构

39   mean sea level
海平面

1-20 blast furnace plant
鼓风炉设备

1 blast furnace, a shaft furnace
鼓风炉，一种高炉

2 furnace incline (lift) for ore and flux or coke
装入铁矿、助熔剂或焦炭的炉上斜桥

3 skip hoist
吊斗吊车

4 charging platform
加料台

5 receiving hopper
受料漏斗

6 bell
送矿钟

7 blast furnace shaft
鼓风高炉

8 smelting section
冶炼区

9 slag escape
熔渣出口

10 slag ladle
熔渣桶

11 pig iron (crude iron, iron) runout
生铁溢流管

12 pig iron (crude iron, iron) ladle
生铁桶

13 downtake
下降的排气管

14 dust catcher, a dust-collecting machine
吸尘器，一种集尘机

15 hot-blast stove
热风炉

16 external combustion chamber
外燃室

17 blast main
主送风管

18 gas pipe
瓦斯管

19 hot-blast pipe
热风管

20 tuyère
风口，风咀

21-69 steelworks
钢厂

21-30 Siemens-Martin open-hearth furnace
西门马丁平炉

21 pig iron (crude iron, iron) ladle
生铁桶

22 feed runner
受铁槽

23 stationary furnace
固定炉

24 hearth
炉床

25 charging machine
加料（进料）机

26 scrap iron charging box
废铁进料箱（斗）

27 gas pipe
气管

28 gas regenerator chamber
瓦斯（煤气）蓄热室

29 air feed pipe
空气供给管

30 air regenerator chamber
空气蓄热室

31 [bottom-pouring] steel-casting ladle with stopper
具栓（停止器）的[底浇铸模]钢铸浇桶

32 ingot mould (*Am.* mold)
铸锭模

33 steel ingot
钢锭

34-44 pig-casting machine
生铁铸造机

34 pouring end
浇注端

35 metal runner
铁制流道

36 series (strand) of moulds (*Am.* molds)
铸模的排列

37 mould (*Am.* mold)
铸模

38 catwalk
桥形通道

39 discharging chute
卸料滑槽

40 pig
生铁块

41 travelling (*Am.* traveling) crane
移动式起重机

42 top-pouring pig iron (crude iron, iron) ladle
倾注式生铁浇桶

43 pouring ladle lip
浇桶注口

44 tilting device (tipping device, *Am.* dumping device)
倾注装置（倾卸装置）

45-50 oxygen-blowing converter (L-D converter, Linz-Donawitz converter)
吹氧转炉

45 conical converter top
圆锥形转炉炉帽

46 mantle
外罩

47 solid converter bottom
转炉整体炉底

48 fireproof lining (refractory lining)
防火炉衬（耐火炉衬）

49 oxygen lance
氧吹管

50 tapping hole (tap hole)
出铁口

51-54 Siemens electric low-shaft furnace
西门子低轴电炉

51 feed
进料口

52 electrodes [arranged in a circle]
电极装置[排成圆形]

53 bustle pipe
冷却管

54 runout
流出槽

55-69 Thomas converter (basic Bessemer converter)
汤姆斯转炉（硷性柏思麦转炉）

55 charging position for molten pig iron
熔铁流入位置

56 charging position for lime
石灰装入位置

57 blow position
吹炼位置

58 discharging position
流出位置

59 tilting device (tipping device, *Am.* dumping device)
倾注（卸）设（装）置

60 crane-operated ladle
起重机操作浇桶

61 auxiliary crane hoist
辅助起重吊车

62 lime bunker
石灰斗（柜）

63 downpipe
下料管

64 tipping car (*Am.* dump truck)
倾卸车

65 scrap iron feed
废铁槽

66 control desk
控制台

67 converter chimney
转炉烟囱

68 blast main
鼓风主管

69 wind box
风箱

1-45 iron foundry
铸铁工厂

1-12 melting plant
熔化设备

1 cupola furnace (cupola), a melting furnace
熔化炉，一种熔化炉

2 blast main (blast inlet, blast pipe)
鼓风主管（鼓风入口，鼓风管）

3 tapping spout
出铁流出槽

4 spyhole
窥视孔

5 tilting-type hot-metal receiver
倾斜式熔化生铁接受器

6 mobile drum-type ladle
可移动鼓形浇桶

7 melter
熔工

8 founder (caster)
铸工

9 tap bar (tapping bar)
出铁杆（出熔液棍）

10 bott stick (*Am.* bot stick)
堵塞杆

11 molten iron
熔铁

12 slag spout
熔渣流出槽

13 casting team
浇铸班（组）

14 hand shank
手柄

15 double handle (crutch)
双手柄（叉形手柄）

16 carrying bar
搬运棒

17 skimmer rod
撇渣杆

18 closed moulding (*Am.* molding) box
闭式模箱

19 upper frame (cope)
上模箱

20 lower frame (drag)
下模箱

21 runner (runner gate, down-gate)
横流道（竖浇道）

22 riser (riser gate)
冒口（冒口进模口）

23 hand ladle
手浇桶（长柄杓）

24-29 continuous casting
连续（浇铸）铸造

24 sinking pouring floor
下沉式浇铸底板

25 solidifying pig
凝固生铁

26 solid stage
固体状态

27 liquid stage
液体状态

28 water-cooling system
水冷系统

29 mould (*Am.* mold) wall
铸型壁

30-37 moulding (*Am.* molding) **department** (moulding shop)
造模工作间（室）

30 moulder (*Am.* molder)
砂模技工

31 pneumatic rammer
气力捣锤

32 hand rammer
手捣杆

33 open moulding (*Am.* molding) box
开式模箱

34 pattern
模型

35 moulding (*Am.* molding) sand
模砂

36 core
砂心

37 core print
心型端承

38-45 cleaning shop (fettling shop)
清理场

38 steel grit or sand delivery pipe
钢砂输送管

39 rotary-table shot-blasting machine
旋转台珠击机

40 grit guard
砂粒护板

41 revolving table
回转台

42 casting
铸件

43 fettler
清理工

44 pneumatic grinder
气力磨轮

45 pneumatic chisel
气力錾

46-75 rolling mill
轧钢厂
46 soaking pit
均热坑炉
47 soaking pit crane
均热炉起重机
48 ingot
铸锭
49 ingot tipper
铸锭倾卸装置
50 blooming train (roller path)
分快滚子机组(滑子讲给路)
51 workpiece
工件
52 bloom shears
分块剪切机
53 two-high mill
二段轧机
54-55 set of rolls (set of rollers)
成套辊子
54 upper roll (upper roller)
上辊子
55 lower roll (lower roller)
下辊子
56-60 roll stand
辊子架
56 base plate
底盘
57 housing (frame)
机架
58 coupling spindle
联结轴
59 groove
轧槽
60 roll bearing
滚动轴承

61-65 adjusting equipment
调整装置
61 chock
塞子
62 main screw
主螺丝
63 gear
齿轮,转动装置
64 motor
马达,发动机
65 indicator for rough and fine adjustment
粗调和微调指示器
66-75 continuous rolling mill train for the manufacture of strip [diagram]
板条用的连续轧钢机[简图]
66-68 processing of semi-finished product
半成品的加工(处理)
66 semi-finished product
半成品
67 gas cutting installation
焰割装置
68 stack of finished steel sheets
钢板成品堆
69 continuous reheating furnaces
连续式加热炉
70 blooming train
中块辊轧机组
71 finishing train
完工机组
72 coiler
盘卷器
73 collar bearing for marketing
供贩卖的带钢卷

74 5mm shearing train
5 毫米的剪切机组
75 10mm shearing train
10 毫米的剪切机组

1 **centre** (*Am.* center) **lathe**
顶尖车床

2 headstock with gear control
(geared headstock)
带齿轮控制的主轴台

3 reduction drive lever
减速驱动杆

4 lever for normal and coarse
threads
标准螺纹和粗牙螺纹手柄

5 speed change lever
变速杆

6 leadscrew reverse-gear lever
导螺逆转齿轮杆

7 change-gear box
变换齿轮箱

8 feed gearbox (Norton tumbler
gear)
进给齿轮箱（诺顿换向齿轮）

9 levers for changing the feed and
thread pitch
变换进给和螺距用杆

10 feed gear lever (tumbler lever)
进给齿轮杆

11 switch lever for right or left
hand action of main spindle
主轴左右手动作用转换杆

12 lathe foot (footpiece)
车床脚座

13 leadscrew handwheel for
traversing of saddle
(longitudinal movement of
saddle)
鞍台横动用导螺手轮（鞍台纵向移动）

14 tumbler reverse lever
换向逆转杆

15 feed screw
进给螺旋

16 apron (saddle apron, carriage
apron)
护衬，档板（鞍台档板，滑架档板）

17 lever for longitudinal and
transverse motion
纵向横向移动的操作杆

18 drop (dropping) worm (feed
trip, feed tripping device) for
engaging feed mechanisms
接合进给机械用的下降螺杆

19 lever for engaging half nut of
leadscrew (lever for clasp nut
engagement)
接合主螺杆螺帽用的手杆（夹紧螺帽的
接合手杆）

20 lathe spindle
车床轴

21 tool post
夹刀柱

22 top slide (tool slide, tool rest)
顶滑台（刀具滑台，刀架）

23 cross slide
横滑台

24 bed slide
床身滑台

25 coolant supply pipe
冷却剂供给管

26 tailstock centre (*Am.* center)
车床尾座顶尖

27 barrel (tailstock barrel)
圆筒（尾座圆筒）

28 tailstock barrel clamp lever
尾座筒夹杆

29 tailstock
尾座

30 tailstock barrel adjusting
handwheel
尾座（架）筒调整手轮

31 lathe bed
车床床身

32 leadscrew
主螺杆

33 feed shaft
进给轴

34 reverse shaft for right and left
hand motion and engaging and
disengaging
左右手动作和离合转换轴

35 four-jaw chuck (four-jaw
independent chuck)
四爪夹头（四爪独立夹头）

36 gripping jaw
夹爪

37 three-jaw chuck (three-jaw
self-centring, self-centering,
chuck)
三爪夹头（三爪自定中心夹头）

38 **turret lathe**
转塔式车床

39 cross slide
横滑台

40 turret
转塔

41 combination toolholder
(multiple turning head)
复合刀把，组合刀具支架（多刀转塔）

42 top slide
顶滑台

43 star wheel
星形轮

44 coolant tray for collecting
coolant and swarf
收集冷却剂和切屑的冷却剂盘

45-53 **lathe tools**
车床工具

45 tool bit holder (clamp tip tool)
for adjustable cutting tips
调整截割喷咀用的刀尖块架（夹刀头的
工具）

46 adjustable cutting tip (clamp tip)
of cemented carbide or oxide
ceramic
烧结碳化物和氧化陶磁的调整截割喷咀
（刀头）

47 shapes of adjustable oxide
ceramic tips
可调氧化陶磁刀头形状

48 lathe tool with cemented carbide
cutting edge
具烧结碳化物刀刃的车床工具

49 tool shank
刀柄

50 brazed cemented carbide cutting
tip (cutting edge)
硬纤烧结碳化物刀刃

51 internal facing tool (boring tool)
for corner work
加工角内面刀具（搪孔刀具）

52 general-purpose lathe tool
一般用途的车床刀具

53 parting (parting-off) tool
割断工具

54 lathe carrier
车床牵转具

55 driving (driver) plate
驱动盘

56-72 **measuring instruments**
测定仪器，度量衡仪器

56 plug gauge (*Am.* gage)
塞规

57 'GO' gauging (*Am.* gaging)
member (end)
"通过"规件（端）

58 'NOT GO' gauging (*Am.*
gaging) member (end)
"不通过"规件（端）

59 calliper (caliper, snap) gauge
(*Am.* gage)
卡规

60 'GO' side
"通过"端

61 'NOT GO' side
"不通过"端

62 micrometer
分厘卡，测微尺

63 measuring scale
测量刻度

64 graduated thimble
刻度套管

65 frame
骨架，框架

66 spindle (screwed spindle)
轴（螺纹轴）

67 vernier calliper (caliper) gauge
(*Am.* gage)
游标卡尺

68 depth gauge (*Am.* gage)
attachment rule
深度规辅助尺

69 vernier scale
游标刻度

70 outside jaws
外爪

71 inside jaws
内爪

72 vernier depth gauge (*Am.* gage)
游标深度规

1 universal grinding machine
万能磨床
2 headstock
主轴台
3 wheelhead slide
磨轮头滑台
4 grinding wheel
磨轮
5 tailstock
车床尾座
6 grinding machine bed
磨床床身
7 grinding machine table
磨床工作台
8 two-column planing machine
(two-column planer)
双柱龙门刨床
9 drive motor, a direct current
motor
驱动马达, 一种直流电马达(电动机)
10 column
立柱
11 planer table
龙门刨床工作台
12 cross slide (rail)
横向滑台(导轨)
13 tool box
刀架, 工具架
14 hacksaw
弓锯
15 clamping device
夹紧装置
16 saw blade
锯片
17 saw frame
锯框
18 radial (radial-arm) drilling
machine
旋臂钻床
19 bed (base plate)
床身(底板)
20 block for workpiece
工件台(承座)
21 pillar
立柱
22 lifting motor
卷扬电动机
23 drill spindle
钻轴
24 arm
机臂
25 horizontal boring and milling
machine
卧式搪铣床
26 movable headstock
可移动的主轴台
27 spindle
轴
28 auxiliary table
辅助工作台
29 bed
床身
30 fixed steady
固定架
31 boring mill column
搪铣立柱
32 universal milling machine
万能铣床
33 milling machine table
铣床工作台
34 table feed drive
工作台进给驱动
35 switch lever for spindle rotation
speed
主轴转速变换杆
36 control box (control unit)
控制箱(控制装置)

37 vertical milling spindle
垂直铣轴
38 vertical drive head
垂直驱动头
39 horizontal milling spindle
横向铣轴
40 end support for steadying
horizontal spindle
稳定横向铣轴的端支座
41 machining centre (*Am.* center),
a rotary-table machine
切削机, 一种转盘(台)机器
42 rotary (circular) indexing table
旋转分度工作台
43 end mill
端面铣刀
44 machine tap
机力螺丝攻
45 shaping machine (shaper)
牛头刨床(成形机)

1 drawing board
制图板
2 drafting machine with parallel motion
平行移动的制图机
3 adjustable knob
可调整钮
4 drawing head (adjustable set square)
制图规（可调整角规）
5 drawing board adjustment
制图板调整装置
6 drawing table
制图台（桌）
7 set square (triangle)
三角板
8 triangle
三角板
9 T-square (tee-square)
丁字尺
10 rolled drawing
成卷的绘图
11 diagram
图
12 time schedule
时间进度表，工作进度表
13 paper stand
纸架
14 roll of paper
图纸卷
15 cutter
裁剪刀
16 technical drawing (drawing design)
工程制图（绘图，设计）
17 front view (front elevation)
前视图（前视图，前立面图）
18 side view (side elevation)
侧视图（侧立面图）
19 plan
平面图，俯视图
20 surface not to be machined
不加工表面
21 surface to be machined
加工表面
22 surface to be superfinished
超级工表面
23 visible edge
可见棱（边）
24 hidden edge
隐蔽棱（边）
25 dimension line
尺寸线
26 arrow head
箭头
27 section line
剖面线
28 section A-B
剖面 A-B
29 hatched surface
有剖面线的面
30 centre (Am. center) line
中心线
31 title panel (title block)
标题栏
32 technical data
工程数据
33 ruler (rule)
尺
34 triangular scale
三稜尺
35 erasing shield
擦线板
36 drawing ink cartridge
制图墨水盒

37 holders for tubular drawing pens
管式制图笔架
38 set of tubular drawing pens
整套管式制图笔
39 hygrometer
湿度计
40 cap with indication of nib size
有指示笔尖大小的插塞
41 pencil-type eraser
铅笔型橡皮擦
42 eraser
橡皮擦
43 erasing knife
刮刀（刮线小刀）
44 erasing knife blade
刮线小刀片
45 clutch-type pencil
自动铅笔
46 pencil lead (refill lead, refill, spare lead)
铅笔心（替换笔心，备用笔心）
47 glass eraser
玻璃纤维擦
48 glass fibres (Am. fibers)
玻璃纤维
49 ruling pen
鸭咀笔
50 cross joint
十字接头
51 index plate
分度板
52 compass with interchangeable attachments
可换附件的圆规
53 compass head
圆规头
54 needle point attachment
针尖附件
55 pencil point attachment
笔尖附件
56 needle
针
57 lengthening arm (extension bar)
延长臂（延长杆）
58 ruling pen attachment
鸭咀笔附件
59 pump compass (drop compass)
点圆规
60 piston
活塞
61 ruling pen attachment
鸭咀笔附件
62 pencil attachment
铅笔附件
63 drawing ink container
制图墨水容器
64 spring bow (rapid adjustment, ratchet-type) compass
弹簧圆规（快速调整，棘轮形）
65 spring ring hinge
弹簧环铰接装置
66 spring-loaded fine adjustment for arcs
装有弹簧的精调圆弧螺丝
67 right-angle needle
直角针
68 tubular ink unit
管式贮墨水装置
69 stencil lettering guide (lettering stencil)
书写导板，字规
70 circle template
圆形模板
71 ellipse template
椭圆形模板

1-28 steam-generating station,
   an electric power plant
   火力发电站，一种发电厂
1-21 boiler house
   锅炉房
1 coal conveyor
   运煤机
2 coal bunker
   煤仓
3 travelling-grate (*Am.*
   traveling-grate) stoker
   移动炉条加煤机
4 coal mill
   磨煤机
5 steam boiler, a water-tube boiler
   (radiant-type boiler)
   蒸汽锅炉，一种水管锅炉（辐射式锅
   炉）
6 burners
   燃烧器
7 water pipes
   水管
8 ash pit (clinker pit)
   煤灰池，煤灰坑（煤渣坑）
9 superheater
   过热器
10 water preheater
   水预热器
11 air preheater
   空气预热器
12 gas flue
   烟道
13 electrostatic precipitator
   静电集尘器
14 induced-draught (*Am.*
   induced-draft) fan
   抽风扇，抽风机
15 chimney (smokestack)
   烟囱
16 de-aerator
   除气流水器
17 feedwater tank
   给水槽
18 boiler feed pump
   汽锅给水泵
19 control room
   控制室
20 cable tunnel
   缆道
21 cable vault
   电缆窖
22 turbine house
   轮机房
23 steam turbine with alternator
   具交流发电机的蒸汽涡轮
24 surface condenser
   表面凝结器
25 low-pressure preheater
   低压预热器
26 high-pressure preheater
   (economizer)
   高压预热器（省煤器）
27 cooling water pipe
   冷却水管
28 control room
   控制室

1-8 control room
控制室

1-6 control console (control desk)
控制台

1 control board (control panel)
for the alternators
交流发电机的控制板

2 master switch
主（总）开关

3 signal light
号志灯光

4 feeder panel
馈电屏

5 monitoring controls for the
switching systems
开关系统的监控装置

6 controls
控制装置

7 revertive signal panel
号志回转盘

8 matrix mimic board
系统电路模拟板

9-18 transformer
变压器

9 oil conservator
储油箱

10 breather
呼吸器

11 oil gauge (*Am.* gage)
油面计

12 feed-through terminal
(feed-through insulator)
馈电端子（馈电绝缘体）

13 on-load tap changer
有载换接器

14 yoke
轭

15 primary winding (primary)
一次绕阻（一次）

16 secondary winding (secondary,
low-voltage winding)
二次绕阻（低压绕阻）

17 core
心

18 tap (tapping)
分接，分接头

19 **transformer connection**
变压器连接方式

20 star connection (star
network, Y-connection)
星接（星型网路，Y型接法）

21 delta connection (mesh
connection)
三角形接法，△接法（网形接法）

22 neutral point
中和点，中性点

23-30 steam turbine, a
turbogenerator unit
蒸汽轮机（涡轮），一种涡轮发电机装
置

23 high-pressure cylinder
高压汽缸

24 medium-pressure
cylinder
中压汽缸

25 low-pressure cylinder
低压汽缸

26 three-phase generator
(generator)
三相发电机（发电机）

27 hydrogen cooler
氢冷却器

28 leakage steam path
漏电蒸汽道

29 jet nozzle
喷射喷咀

30 turbine monitoring panel
with measuring
instruments
具测量仪表的涡轮监控盘

31 automatic voltage
regulator
自动电压调整器

32 synchro
同步器

33 **cable box**
电缆接线箱

34 conductor
导体

35 feed-through terminal
(feed-through insulator)
馈电接头（馈电绝缘体）

36 core
电缆轴心

37 casing
电缆套

38 filling compound (filler)
封填绝缘膏，填料（填料）

39 lead sheath
铅包皮

40 lead-in tube
引入管

41 cable
电缆

42 **high voltage cable,** for
three-phase current
高压三相电缆

43 conductor
导体

44 metallic paper (metallized
paper)
金属箔纸（镀金箔纸）

45 tracer (tracer element)
描踪器（描踪器元件）

46 varnished-cambric tape
漆（细葛）布带

47 lead sheath
铅包皮

48 asphalted paper
沥青纸

49 jute serving
黄麻护线

50 steel tape or steel wire armour
(*Am.* armor)
钢带或钢丝护套

51-62 air-blast circuit breaker,
a circuit breaker
气冲断路器，一种断路器

51 compressed-air tank
压缩空气罐

52 control valve (main operating
valve)
控制阀（主要操作阀）

53 compressed-air inlet
压缩空气入口

54 support insulator, a hollow
porcelain supporting insulator
支架绝缘器，一种中空的磁性支架绝缘
器

55 interrupter
断续器

56 resistor
电阻器

57 auxiliary contacts
辅助接触，副触点

58 current transformer
比流器

59 voltage transformer (potential
transformer)
比压器

60 operating mechanism housing
操作机械箱

61 arcing horn
消弧角，抬弧角

62 spark gap
火花间隙

1 **fast-breeder reactor** (fast breeder) [diagram]
快滋生反应器[简图]
2 primary circuit (primary loop, primary sodium system)
一次电路（一次环路，一次钠系统）
3 reactor
反应器
4 fuel rods (fuel pins)
燃料棒
5 primary sodium pump
一次钠泵
6 heat exchanger
热交换器
7 secondary circuit (secondary loop, secondary sodium system)
二次电路（二次环路，二次钠系统）
8 secondary sodium pump
二次钠泵
9 steam generator
蒸汽产生器
10 cooling water flow circuit
冷却水流动回路
11 steam line
蒸汽管线
12 feedwater line
给水管线
13 feed pump
给水泵
14 steam turbine
蒸汽涡轮机
15 generator
发电机
16 transmission line
输电线路
17 condenser
冷凝器，凝结器
18 cooling water
冷却水
19 **nuclear reactor,** a pressurized-water reactor (nuclear power plant, atomic power plant)
核反应器，一种压水反应器（核能发电厂，原子发电厂）
20 concrete shield (reactor building)
混凝土屏蔽（反应器建筑物）
21 steel containment (steel shell) with air extraction vent
具抽气孔的钢安全壳（钢壳）
22 reactor pressure vessel
反应器压力容器
23 control rod drive
控制棒驱动装置
24 control rods
控制棒
25 primary coolant pump
一次冷却剂泵
26 steam generator
蒸汽产生器
27 fuel-handling hoists
燃料输送吊车（起重机）
28 fuel storage
燃料仓
29 coolant flow passage
冷却剂流通管
30 feedwater line
供水管线
31 prime steam line
主蒸汽管道
32 manway
人员专用道
33 turbogenerator set
涡轮发电机组

34 turbogenerator
涡轮发电机
35 condenser
冷凝器
36 service building
服务大楼
37 exhaust gas stack
排气烟囱
38 polar crane
极性起重机
39 cooling tower, a dry cooling tower
冷却塔，一种乾冷冷塔
40 pressurized-water system
压水系统
41 reactor
反应器
42 primary circuit (primary loop)
一次电路（一次环路）
43 circulation pump (recirculation pump)
循环泵（再循环泵）
44 heat exchanger (steam generator)
热交换器（水蒸汽产生器）
45 secondary circuit (secondary loop, feedwater steam circuit)
二次电路（二次环路，给水蒸汽电路）
46 steam turbine
蒸汽涡轮机
47 generator
发电机
48 cooling system
冷却系统
49 boiling water system [diagram]
沸水系统[简图]
50 reactor
反应器
51 steam and recirculation water flow paths
蒸汽和再循环水流通道
52 steam turbine
蒸汽涡轮机
53 generator
发电机
54 circulation pump (recirculation pump)
循环泵（再循环泵）
55 coolant system (cooling with water from river)
冷却系统（以河水冷却）
56 **radioactive waste storage in salt mine**
放射性废料储放於盐矿中
57-68 geological structure of abandoned salt mine converted for disposal of radioactive waste (nuclear waste)
置放放射性废料的废盐矿之地质结构
57 Lower Keuper
下考依波
58 Upper Muschelkalk
上壳灰岩层
59 Middle Muschelkalk
中壳灰岩层
60 Lower Muschelkalk
下壳灰岩层
61 Bunter downthrow
班砂岩降侧
62 residue of leached (lixiviated) Zechstein (Upper Permian)
淋溶镁灰残留物
63 Aller rock salt
阿莱岩盐
64 Leine rock salt
莱茵岩盐

65 Stassfurt seam (potash salt seam, potash salt bed)
斯塔斯弗矿层（钾盐层，钾盐床）
66 Stassfurt salt
斯塔斯弗盐
67 grenzanhydrite
限界流体，越界流体
68 Zechstein shale
镁灰油页岩
69 shaft
矿井
70 minehead buildings
坑口建筑物
71 storage chamber
贮藏室
72 storage of medium-active waste in salt mine
盐矿中的中放射性废料的贮藏
73 511m level
511公尺的水平坑道
74 protective screen (anti-radiation screen)
保护壁（抗辐射屏）
75 lead glass window
铅玻璃窗
76 storage chamber
贮藏室
77 drum containing radioactive waste
装放射性废料的金属桶
78 television camera
电视摄影机
79 charging chamber
进料室
80 control desk (control panel)
控制盘
81 upward ventilator
向上通风装置
82 shielded container
遮蔽容器
83 490m level
490公尺的水平坑道

1 heat pump system
热泵系统

2 source water inlet
水源入口

3 cooling water heat exchanger
冷却水热交换器

4 compressor
压缩机

5 natural-gas or diesel engine
天燃气或柴油引擎

6 evaporator
蒸发器

7 pressure release valve
放压阀

8 condenser
凝结器，冷凝器

9 waste-gas heat exchanger
废气热交换器

10 flow pipe
流送管线

11 vent pipe
通气管线

12 chimney
烟囱

13 boiler
锅炉

14 fan
风扇

15 radiator
散热器

16 sink
排水槽

17-36 utilization of solar energy
太阳能的利用

17 solar (solar-heated) house
太阳能（太阳能加热的）住宅

18 solar radiation (sunlight, insolation)
太阳辐射（阳光，日晒）

19 collector
太阳能收集器

20 hot reservoir (heat reservoir)
贮热器

21 power supply
电源

22 heat pump
热泵

23 water outlet
出水口

24 air supply
供气管

25 flue
烟道，气道

26 hot water supply
热水供应

27 radiator heating
供暖辐射器

28 flat plate solar collector
平板太阳能收集器

29 blackened receiver surface with asphalted aluminium (*Am.* aluminium) foil
以沥青涂黑铝铂的接受器表面

30 steel tube
钢管

31 heat transfer fluid
传热流体

32 flat plate solar collector, containing solar cell
平板太阳能收集器，包含太阳能电池

33 glass cover
玻璃盖

34 solar cell
太阳能电池

35 air ducts
导气管

36 insulation
绝缘材料

37 tidal power plant [section]
潮汐发电装置[剖面图]

38 dam
坝，水闸

39 reversible turbine
可逆转涡轮机

40 turbine inlet for water from the sea
涡轮机海水入口

41 turbine inlet for water from the basin
涡轮机湾水入口

42 wind power plant (wind generator, aerogenerator)
风力发电厂（风力发电机，气流发电机）

43 truss tower
桁架塔

44 guy wire
牵线，拔线

45 rotor blades (propeller)
转子叶（螺旋浆）

46 generator with variable pitch for power regulation
电力调整可变节矩的发电机

1-15 coking plant 炼焦厂	**17** gas-collecting main 煤气主管	**32** crude tar tank 粗焦油槽
1 dumping of coking coal 焦煤的倾卸	**18** coal tar extraction 焦油的分离	**33** sulphuric acid (*Am.* sulfuric acid) supply 硫酸供应（入）
2 belt conveyor 带式运送机	**19** gas cooler 煤气冷却器	**34** production of sulphuric acid (*Am.* sulfuric acid) 硫酸的生产
3 service bunker 煤仓	**20** electrostatic precipitator 静电集尘器	**35** production of ammonium sulphate (*Am.* ammonium sulfate) 硫酸铵产品
4 coal tower conveyor 煤塔运送机	**21** gas extractor 煤气抽出器	**36** ammonium sulphate (*Am.* ammonium sulfate) 硫酸铵
5 coal tower 煤塔	**22** hydrogen sulphide (*Am.* hydrogen sulfide) scrubber (hydrogen sulphide wet collector) 硫化氢清洁器（硫化氢湿式收集器）	**37** recovery plant for recovering the scrubbing agents 回收洗油的回收装置
6 larry car (larry, charging car) 装煤车（运煤车）	**23** ammonia scrubber (ammonia wet collector) 氨（气）清洁器（氨气湿式收集器）	**38** waste water discharge 废水排出
7 pusher ram 推进溜板	**24** benzene (benzol) scrubber 苯清洁器	**39** phenol extraction from the gas water 从煤气水中抽取
8 battery of coke ovens 炼焦炉电池组	**25** gas holder 贮气罐	**40** crude phenol tank 粗酚槽
9 coke guide 焦煤导路	**26** gas compressor 煤气压缩机	**41** production of crude benzol (crude benzene) 粗苯产品
10 quenching car, with engine 具引擎的淬火车	**27** debenzoling by cooler and heat exchanger 冷却器和换热器脱苯	**42** crude benzol (crude benzene) tank 粗苯槽
11 quenching tower 淬火塔	**28** desulphurization (*Am.* desulfurization) of pressure gas 加压煤气的去硫	**43** scrubbing oil tank 洗涤油槽
12 coke loaking bay (coke wharf) 凉焦台	**29** gas cooling 煤气冷却	**44** low-pressure gas main 低压煤气总（主）管
13 coke side bench 放焦台	**30** gas drying 煤气乾燥	**45** high-pressure gas main 高压煤气总（主）管
14 screening of lump coal and culm 块煤和屑煤的筛分	**31** gas meter 煤气表	
15 coke loading 焦炭装载		
16-45 coke-oven gas processing 炼焦炉煤气的处理		
16 discharge (release) of gas from the coke ovens 由炼焦炉释放出的煤气		

1 sawmill
锯木厂
2 vertical frame saw (*Am.* gang mill)
立式框锯（排锯）
3 saw blades
锯条
4 feed roller
进料滚子
5 guide roller
导向滚子
6 fluting (grooving, grooves)
开槽
7 oil pressure gauge (*Am.* gage)
油压表
8 saw frame
锯框
9 feed indicator
进料指示器
10 log capacity scale
原木体积标尺
11 auxiliary carriage
辅助托车
12 carriage
送料车
13 log grips
圆木卡钩
14 remote control panel
遥控板
15 carriage motor
进料车马达
16 truck for splinters (splints)
木板输送车

17 endless log chain (*Am.* jack chain)
无端原木链（原木运输链）
18 stop plate
止板
19 log-kicker arms
推木臂
20 cross conveyor
横向运送机
21 washer (washing machine)
洗涤机，冲洗机
22 cross chain conveyor for sawn timber
锯成木材后的横向链式运送机
23 roller table
滚台
24 undercut swing saw
过切摆动圆锯，落地式摆锯
25 piling
木板堆
26 roller trestles
滚子支架
27 gantry crane
高架移动起重机
28 crane motor
起重机马达
29 pivoted log grips
枢轴原木卡钩
30 roundwood (round timber)
圆木（圆木材）
31 log dump
圆木堆
32 squared timber store
方形木材堆积场

33 sawn logs
已锯开的圆木
34 planks
厚木板
35 boards (planks)
薄木板
36 squared timber
方形木材
37 stack bearer
木材堆支座

38 automatic cross-cut chain saw
自动横割链锯
39 log grips
圆木卡钩
40 feed roller
进料滚子
41 chain-tensioning device
紧链装置
42 saw sharpening machine
锐锯机
43 grinding wheel (teeth grinder)
磨轮（锯齿磨轮）
44 feed pawl
进给掣子
45 depth adjustment for the teeth grinder
锯齿磨轮高度调整钮
46 lifter (lever) for the grinder chuck
磨床夹头升降杆（控制杆）
47 holding device for the saw blade
锯条的夹紧（固定）装置
48 horizontal bandsaw for sawing log
锯圆木用的水平带锯
49 height adjustment
高度调整装置
50 chip remover
木屑去除机
51 chip extractor
木屑抽除装置
52 carriage
车架

53 bandsaw blade
带锯条
54 automatic blocking saw
自动切块锯
55 feed channel
进料导槽
56 discharge opening
卸料口
57 twin edger (double edger)
双刃截边锯
58 breadth scale (width scale)
宽度标尺
59 kick-back guard
逆转护板
60 height scale
高度标尺
61 in-feed scale
进料标尺
62 indicator lamps
指示灯
63 feed table
进料台
64 undercut swing saw
过切摆动圆锯，落地式摆锯
65 automatic hold-down with protective hood
具保护罩的全自动压紧装置
66 foot switch
脚踏开关
67 distribution board (panelboard)
配电板（仪表板）
68 length stop
长度调整装置

1 **quarry,** an open-cast
working
采石场，露天开采
2 overburden
表土，被复岩
3 working face
开采面，已开采或正在开采的采石场
4 loose rock pile (blasted rock)
松散岩石堆（已炸开之岩石）
5 quarryman (quarrier), a quarry
worker
采石工人
6 sledge hammer
大锤
7 wedge
楔
8 block of stone
石块
9 driller
钻工
10 safety helmet
安全帽
11 hammer drill (hard-rock drill)
锤打钻（硬岩钻）
12 borehole
钻孔
13 universal excavator
万能掘凿机（挖掘机）
14 large-capacity truck
大容量的卡车
15 rock face
岩石采掘面
16 inclined hoist
倾斜起重机

17 primary crusher
初次轧碎机
18 stone-crushing plant
碎石设备
19 coarse rotary (gyratory) crusher;
sim.: fine rotary (gyratory)
crusher
旋转式粗碎石机；类似有：旋转式细碎
石机
20 hammer crusher (impact
crusher)
锤碎机（冲击轧碎机）
21 vibrating screen
振动筛
22 screenings (fine dust)
筛屑（细砂）
23 stone chippings
石屑，石片
24 crushed stone
碎石
25 shot firer
（点火）引爆工人
26 measuring rod
量杆
27 blasting cartridge
弹药包
28 fuse (blasting fuse)
信管（雷管）
29 plugging sand (stemming sand)
bucket
填塞砂桶（封口用砂）
30 dressed stone
修整过的块石

31 pick
镐
32 crowbar (pinch bar)
撬棍
33 fork
叉
34 stonemason
石匠，石工
35-38 **stonemason's tools**
石匠工具
35 stonemason's hammer
石匠用的榔头（锤子）
36 mallet
大锤
37 drove chisel (drove, boaster,
broad chisel)
粗削凿（宽凿）
38 dressing axe (*Am.* ax)
修整斧

1 clay pit
粘土坑（采掘场）

2 loam, an impure clay (raw clay)
壤土，一种不纯粘土（生粘土）

3 overburden excavator, a large-scale excavator
表土挖掘机，一种大型挖掘机

4 narrow-gauge (*Am.* narrow-gage) track system
狭（窄）轨铁道系统

5 inclined hoist
倾斜起重机

6 souring chambers
酸化室（泥料陈腐室）

7 box feeder (feeder)
箱形进料器

8 edge runner mill (edge mill, pan grinding mill)
轮碾机（轮碾机，盘式磨粉机）

9 rolling plant
压砖设备（土场）

10 double-shaft trough mixer (mixer)
双轴槽形搅拌机

11 extrusion press (brick-pressing machine)
挤压机（压砖机）

12 vacuum chamber
真空室

13 die
（压）模

14 clay column
粘土条

15 cutter (brick cutter)
切砖机

16 unfired brick (green brick)
未锻烧的砖（生坯）

17 drying shed
干燥棚

18 mechanical finger car (stacker truck)
机械操作手车（堆叠车）

19 circular kiln (brick kiln)
砖窑

20 solid brick (building brick)
硬砖（建筑用砖）

21-22 perforated bricks and hollow blocks
有孔砖和空心砖块

21 perforated brick with vertical perforations
具垂直孔的有孔砖

22 hollow clay block with horizontal perforations
具平行孔的空心粘土砖块

23 hollow clay block with vertical perforations
具垂直孔的空心粘土砖块

24 floor brick
地板砖

25 compass brick (radial brick, radiating brick)
弧形砖（扇形砖，辐射线形砖）

26 hollow flooring block
空心地板砖

27 paving brick
铺地砖

28 cellular brick [for fireplaces] (chimney brick)
格形砖[壁炉用的]（烟囱砖）

1 raw materials (limestone, clay, and marl)
原料（石灰石，粘土，泥灰）

2 hammer crusher (hammer mill)
锤碎机

3 raw material store
原料库

4 raw mill for simultaneously grinding and drying the raw materials with exhaust gas from the heat exchanger
碾磨并同时用热交换器排气来干燥原料的粗磨机

5 raw meal silos
生料（原料）粉槽

6 heat exchanger (cyclone heat exchanger)
热交换器（旋风热交换器）

7 dust collector (an electrostatic precipitator) for the heat exchanger exhaust from the raw mill
从粗磨机热交换器排出灰尘的收集器（静电集尘器）

8 rotary kiln
回转窑

9 clinker cooler
水泥熟料冷却器

10 clinker store
水泥熟料库

11 primary air blower
一次鼓风机

12 cement-grinding mill
水泥碾磨机

13 gypsum store
石膏库

14 gypsum crusher
石膏碾碎机

15 cement silo
水泥槽（水泥仓）

16 cement-packing plant
水泥包装厂（设备）

1 grinding cylinder (ball mill) for the preparation of the raw material in water
原料和水混合的磨料筒（球磨机）

2 sample sagger (saggar, seggar), with aperture for observing the firing process
具开口观察燃烧过程用的样品水泥箱

3 bottle kiln (beehive kiln) [diagram]
瓶状窑（蜂窝式窑）[简图]

4 firing mould (*Am.* mold)
燃烧模

5 tunnel kiln
坑道窑

6 Seger cone (pyrometric cone, *Am.* Orton cone) for measuring high temperatures
熔锥用以测量高温

7 de-airing pug mill (de-airing pug press), an extrusion press
真空搅拌机，一种挤制机

8 clay column
粘土条

9 thrower throwing a ball (bat) of clay
拉制粘土坯的拉坯工人

10 slug of clay
粘土块

11 turntable; *sim.*: potter's wheel
转台；类似：陶车

12 filter press
压滤机

13 filter cake
滤块

14 jiggering, with a profiling tool; *sim.*: jollying
具成形工具的旋坯；类似：镟轳

15 plaster mould (*Am.* mold) for slip casting
注浆用的石膏模

16 turntable glazing machine
转台上釉机

17 porcelain painter (china painter)
瓷器画工（陶器画工）

18 hand-painted vase
手绘花瓶

19 repairer
修理工

20 pallet (modelling, *Am.* modeling, tool)
托板（制造模形的工具）

21 shards (sherds, potsherds)
陶瓷器的碎片

1-20 sheet glass production
(flat glass production)
玻璃片的制造（平板玻璃的制造）

1 glass furnace (tank furnace) for
the Fourcault process [diagram]
富可法制玻璃熔炉[简图]

2 filling end, for feeding in the
batch (frit)
填料端，分批进料（玻璃原料）

3 melting bath
电解槽，熔化槽

4 refining bath (fining bath)
精炼槽

5 working baths (working area)
作业槽

6 burners
燃烧器

7 drawing machines
拉制机

8 Fourcault glass-drawing
machine
富可法玻璃拉制机

9 slot
沟，槽

10 glass ribbon (ribbon of glass,
sheet of glass) being drawn
upwards
将玻璃带引上（玻璃带，玻璃板带）

11 rollers (drawing rolls)
滚子（引伸滚子）

12 float glass process
浮式玻璃制造法

13 batch (frit) feeder (funnel)
玻璃原料进给装置

14 melting bath
熔化槽

15 cooling tank
冷却槽

16 float bath in a protective
inert-gas atmosphere
在惰性气体保护下的浮槽

17 molten tin
熔化的锡

18 annealing lehr
退火炉

19 automatic cutter
自动切割机

20 stacking machines
堆积机

21 IS (individual-section) machine,
a bottle-making machine
IS 机，一种制瓶机

22-37 blowing processes
吹制法
22 blow-and-blow process
吹制过程
23 introduction of the gob of molten glass
熔解玻璃原料的滴入
24 first blowing
第 次吹制
25 suction
抽吸
26 transfer from the parison mould (*Am*. mold) to the blow mould (*Am*. mold)
从玻璃瓶模转换到吹制模
27 reheating
再加热
28 blowing (suction, final shaping)
吹制（抽吸，最后成型）
29 delivery of the completed vessel
成品瓶的输送
30 press-and-blow process
压吹制法
31 introduction of the gob of molten glass
熔解玻璃原料的滴入
32 plunger
柱塞
33 pressing
挤压
34 transfer from the press mould (*Am*. mold) to the blow mould (*Am*. mold)
从挤压模转换到吹制模

35 reheating
再加热
36 blowing (suction, final shaping)
吹制（抽吸，最后成型）
37 delivery of the completed vessel
成品容器的输送
38-47 glassmaking (glassblowing, glassblowing by hand, glass forming)
玻璃制造（玻璃吹制，人工吹制玻璃，玻璃成形）
38 glassmaker (glassblower)
玻璃工人（玻璃吹制工）
39 blowing iron
吹管
40 gob
熔解的玻璃原料
41 hand-blown goblet
人工吹制（高）有脚玻璃杯
42 clappers for shaping the base (foot) of the goblet
高脚玻璃杯成形用的拍板
43 trimming tool
修饰工具
44 tongs
夹钳
45 glassmaker's chair (gaffer's chair)
玻璃工人坐椅
46 covered glasshouse pot
有盖的熔化玻璃罐
47 mould (*Am*. mold), into which the parison is blown
已成形长颈瓶的吹模

48-55 production of glass fibre (*Am*. glass fiber)
玻璃纤维的生产
48 continuous filament process
连续玻璃纤维丝的生产过程
49 glass furnace
玻璃熔炉
50 bushing containing molten glass
装熔化玻璃的套筒
51 bushing tips
套筒端
52 glass filaments
玻璃纤维丝
53 sizing
尺度矫正
54 strand (thread)
绳股
55 spool
卷线轴
56-58 glass fibre (*Am*. glass fiber) **products**
玻璃纤维产品
56 glass yarn (glass thread)
玻璃纱
57 sleeved glass yarn (glass thread)
卷筒玻璃丝（玻璃线）
58 glass wool
玻璃绒

1-13 supply of cotton
棉花的供给

1 ripe cotton boll
成熟的棉花（荚）

2 full cop (cop wound with weft yarn)
满管线纱

3 compressed cotton bale
压实的棉花包

4 jute wrapping
黄麻包装布

5 steel band
打包铁皮

6 identification mark of the bale
棉花捆包商标

7 bale opener (bale breaker)
拆包机

8 cotton-feeding brattice
给棉口

9 cotton feed
棉花供给

10 dust extraction fan
吸尘扇

11 duct to the dust-collecting chamber
通至集尘室的管道

12 drive motor
驱动马达

13 conveyor brattice
输棉口

14 **double scutcher** (machine with two scutchers)
双座打棉机

15 lap cradle
棉卷支架

16 rack head
齿条头，减磨齿杆头

17 starting handle
起动杆

18 handwheel, for raising and lowering the rack head
升降齿条头用的手轮（升降减磨齿杆头用的手轮）

19 movable lap-turner
活动的卷棉器

20 calender rollers
滚压机

21 cover for the perforated cylinders
有孔滚筒的盖子

22 dust escape flue (dust discharge flue)
排尘风道

23 drive motors (beater drive motors)
驱动马达（搅打驱动马达）

24 beater driving shaft
搅打驱动轴

25 three-blade beater (Kirschner beater)
三叶搅打机

26 grid [for impurities to drop]
格子[落尘用的]

27 pedal roller (pedal cylinder)
踏板滚子

28 control lever for the pedal roller, a pedal lever
踏板滚子的控制杆，一种脚踏杆

29 variable change-speed gear
变速齿轮箱

30 cone drum box
锥形鼓轮箱

31 stop and start levers for the hopper
棉箱的开关杆

32 wooden hopper delivery roller
木制棉箱传送滚轮

33 hopper feeder
棉箱给棉机

34 **carding machine** (card, carding engine)
梳棉机

35 card can (carding can), for receiving the coiled sliver
接受卷成长棉条的梳棉箱

36 can holder
梳棉罐支柱

37 calender rollers
滚压机

38 carded sliver (card sliver)
梳棉机棉条

39 vibrating doffer comb
振动式集棉滚筒梳

40 start-stop lever
开关杆

41 grinding-roller bearing
磨滚子承轴

42 doffer
集棉滚筒

43 cylinder
滚筒

44 flat clearer
盖板清洁辊滚子

45 flats
盖板

46 supporting pulleys for the flats
盖板支承滑轮

47 scutcher lap (carded lap)
打棉卷棉机

48 scutcher lap holder
卷棉架

49 drive motor with flat belt
具平带的驱动马达

50 main drive pulley (fast-and-loose drive pulley)
主要驱动滑轮（松紧驱动滑轮）

51 principle of the card (of the carding engine)
梳棉机（引擎）的原理

52 fluted feed roller
沟槽给棉滚轮

53 licker-in (taker-in, licker-in roller)
取棉剌滚子

54 licker-in undercasing
剌滚子漏底

55 cylinder undercasing
滚筒漏底

56 **combing machine** (comber)
精梳机

57 drive gearbox (driving gear)
驱动齿轮箱

58 laps ready for combing
精梳备用卷棉

59 calender rollers
滚压机

60 comber draw box
梳棉机的拉箱

61 counter
计数器

62 coiler top
卷轴顶部

63 principle of the comber
精梳机的原理

64 lap
卷棉

65 bottom nipper
下钳板

66 top nipper
上钳板

67 top comb
顶梳

68 combing cylinder
梳棉滚筒

69 plain part of the cylinder
滚筒的无针部分

70 needled part of the cylinder
滚筒的梳针部分

71 detaching rollers
分支滚轮

72 carded and combed sliver
精梳棉条

1 **draw frame**
併条机

2 gearbox with built-in motor
自附电动机的变速箱

3 sliver cans
棉条筒

4 broken thread detector roller
断条检测滚子

5 doubling of the slivers
棉条併合

6 stopping handle
停止把手

7 draw frame cover
併条机盖板

8 indicator lamps (signal lights)
指示灯（信号灯）

9 simple four-roller draw frame [diagram]
简易四滚子併条机[简图]

10 bottom rollers (lower rollers), fluted steel rollers
下滚轮，沟纹钢滚

11 top rollers (upper rollers) covered with synthetic
复着合成橡皮的上滚轮

12 doubled slivers before drafting
牵伸前的併合棉条

13 thin sliver after drafting
牵伸后的细棉条

14 high-draft system (high-draft draw frame) [diagram]
高速牵伸系统（高速併条机）〔简图〕

15 feeding-in of the sliver
棉条的进给

16 leather apron (composition apron)
皮圈（合成的胶圈）

17 guide bar
导杆

18 light top roller (guide roller)
轻质上滚子（导引滚子）

19 high-draft speed frame (fly frame, slubbing frame)
高速粗纺机（粗纺机，头道粗纺机）

20 sliver cans
棉条筒

21 feeding of the slivers to the drafting rollers
进给至牵伸滚轮的棉条

22 drafting rollers with top clearers
附清洁器的牵伸滚轮

23 roving bobbins
纺条筒管

24 fly frame operator (operative)
粗纺机操作工

25 flyer
整速轮，锭翼

26 frame end plate
机尾板

27 intermediate yarn-forming frame
间纺纱机

28 bobbin creel (creel)
卷线轴架

29 roving emerging from the drafting rollers
从牵伸滚轮出来的纺条（粗纱）

30 lifter rail (separating rail)
升降轨（分离轨）

31 spindle drive
锭驱动

32 stopping handle
停止把手

33 gearbox, with built-on motor
自附电动机的齿轮箱

34 **ring frame** (ring spinning frame)
钢环精纺机

35 three-phase motor
三相马达

36 motor base plate (bedplate)
电动机（马达）底座

37 lifting bolt [for motor removal]
[马达移动用的]起重螺栓

38 control gear for spindle speed
锭速度的控制齿轮

39 gearbox
齿轮箱

40 change wheels for varying the spindle speed [to change the yarn count]
改变锭速度的变换齿轮[改变纱线数]

41 full creel
满卷线轴架

42 shafts and levers for raising and lowering the ring rail
升降钢精纺机用的转轴横杆

43 spindles with separators
具隔片的锭，纺锤隔离板

44 suction box connected to the front roller underclearers
连接前下清洁滚子的吸入箱

45 **standard ring spindle**
标准环形锭子

46 spindle shaft
锭子（纺锤）羽轴（纺锤）

47 roller bearing
滚轴轴承

48 wharve (pulley)
滑轮

49 spindle catch
锭钩

50 spindle rail
锭轨

51 ring and traveller (*Am.* traveler)
环状移动器，钢领和钢圈

52 top of the ring tube (of the bobbin)
纱管（筒管）顶部

53 yarn (thread)
纱（线）

54 ring fitted into the ring rail
装入钢环轨的钢环

55 traveller (*Am.* traveler)
钢丝圈

56 yarn wound onto the bobbin
绕於筒管上的纱

57 **doubling frame**
撚线机，捻线机

58 creel, with cross-wound cheeses
装交叉卷线筒的筒管架

59 delivery rollers
输送滚轮

60 bobbins of doubled yarn
双股纱线的线轴（筒管）

1-57 processes preparatory to weaving
织布的准备过程

1 cone-winding frame
锥形导纱机

2 travelling (*Am.* traveling) blower
移动式鼓风机

3 guide rail, for the travelling (*Am.* traveling) blower
移动式鼓风机用的导轨

4 blowing assembly
鼓风机组件

5 blower aperture
鼓风机的吹口

6 superstructure for the blower rail
鼓风机导轨的上部结构

7 full-cone indicator
圆锥筒满筒指示器

8 cross-wound cone
交叉卷绕的锥形筒

9 cone creel
锥形筒架

10 grooved cylinder
有凹槽的滚筒

11 guiding slot for cross-winding the threads
交叉卷绕的线导槽

12 side frame, housing the motor
装（电动机）马达的侧架

13 tension and slub-catching device
张力和清纱装置

14 off-end framing with filter
带有过滤器的车尾机架

15 yarn package, a ring tube or mule cop
成束的纱（环管纱，锥形管纱）

16 yarn package container
成束的纱（环管纱，锥形管纱）

17 starting and stopping lever
起动停止杆

18 self-threading guide
引纱导杆

19 broken thread stop motion
断线自动停止装置

20 thread clearer
纱线清理装置

21 weighting disc (disk) for tensioning the thread
调节纱线张力的重量盘

22 warping machine
整经机

23 fan
风扇

24 cross-wound cone
交叉卷绕筒

25 creel
筒架

26 adjustable comb
可调整的梳机

27 warping machine frame
整经机架

28 yarn length recorder
纱线计长器

29 warp beam
经纱轴

30 beam flange
经轴凸缘

31 guard rail
护栏

32 driving drum (driving cylinder)
驱动鼓轮（驱动滚筒）

33 belt drive
皮带驱动

34 motor
马达

35 release for starting the driving drum
转动滚筒的自动释压踏板

36 screw for adjusting the comb setting
调整梳机装置的螺钉

37 drop pins, for stopping the machine when a thread breaks
断纱自停落针，当一支纱线折断时
自动停止装置

38 guide bar
导棒

39 drop pin rollers
落针滚轮

40 indigo dying and sizing machine
靛蓝染色和浆纱机

41 take-off stand
经轴架

42 warp beam
经纱轴

43 warp
经纱

44 wetting trough
润湿槽

45 immersion roller
浸入滚轮

46 squeeze roller (mangle)
压挤滚轮

47 dye liquor padding trough
染液浸槽

48 air oxidation passage
空气氧化通道

49 washing trough
洗涤槽

50 drying cylinders for pre-drying
预烘筒

51 tension compensator (tension equalizer)
张力补偿器（张力平衡器）

52 sizing machine
浆纱机

53 drying cylinders
烘筒

54 *for cotton:* stenter; *for wool:* tenter
用於棉织物：开幅机；用於毛织物：拉
幅机

55 beaming machine
卷轴机

56 sized warp beam
上浆经轴，织轴

57 rollers
导纱滚轮

1 **weaving machine** (automatic loom)
织布机（自动织布机）

2 pick counter (tachometer)
转速计数指示器（转速计）

3 shaft (heald shaft, heald frame) guide
转轴导件（综梁，综轴）

4 shafts (heald shafts, heald frames)
转轴（综梁，综轴）

5 rotary battery for weft replenishment
纬纱补充旋转台

6 sley (slay) cap
扣盖

7 weft pirn
纬纱纺锭

8 starting and stopping handle
开关手柄

9 shuttle box, with shuttles
织梭箱和梭子

10 reed
扣，钢扣

11 selvedge (selvage)
布的织边

12 cloth (woven fabric)
布，织成品（编织纤维）

13 temple (cloth temple)
边撑

14 electric weft feeler
电动纬线触杆

15 flywheel
飞轮

16 breast beam board
胸梁板

17 picking stick (pick stick)
投梭棒

18 electric motor
电动机（马达）

19 cloth take-up motion
织物卷紧装置

20 cloth roller (fabric roller)
卷布滚轮

21 can for empty pirns
空纺锭箱

22 lug strap, for moving the picking stick
移动投梭棒用的凸带

23 fuse box
保险丝盒

24 loom framing
织布机框架

25 metal shuttle tip
金属梭尖

26 shuttle
梭子

27 heald (heddle, wire heald, wire heddle)
综丝，综线

28 eye (eyelet, heald eyelet, heddle eyelet)
综眼，综丝眼

29 eye (shuttle eye)
梭眼

30 pirn
纺锭

31 metal contact sleeve for the weft feeler
纬线触杆的金属接触套

32 slot for the feeler
探针孔，触杆口

33 spring-clip pirn holder
纺锭固定用的弹簧夹

34 drop wire
引入线

35 weaving machine (automatic loom) [side elevation]
织布机（自动织布机）[侧视图]

36 heald shaft guiding wheels
综轴导轮

37 backrest
后扶架

38 lease rods
分纱棒

39 warp (warp thread)
经纱

40 shed
梭口，梭道

41 sley (slay)
扣座

42 race board
走梭板

43 stop rod blade for the stop motion
停机用的停止杆，停机撞头

44 bumper steel
（保险）缓冲钢板

45 bumper steel stop rod
缓冲钢板停止

46 breast beam
胸梁

47 cloth take-up roller
织物卷紧滚轮

48 warp beam
经纱梁

49 beam flange
经轴凸缘

50 crankshaft
曲轴

51 crankshaft wheel
曲轴轮

52 connector
连接器

53 sley (slay)
扣座

54 lam rods
拉综杆

55 camshaft wheel
辗轴轮

56 camshaft (tappet shaft)
辗轴（挺杆轴）

57 tappet (shedding tappet)
挺杆（挺杆盖）

58 treadle lever
踏杆

59 let-off motion
经纱放出器

60 beam motion control
织轴运动控制装置

61 rope of the warp let-off motion
经纱放出器索

62 let-off weight lever
秤杆放出器

63 control weight [for the treadle]
[踏式]控制秤杆

64 picker with leather or bakelite pad
带皮革或电木衬垫的弹棉机

65 picking stick buffer
投梭棒缓冲皮

66 picking cam
投梭盘

67 picking bowl
投梭转子

68 picking stick return spring
投梭棒回动弹簧

1-66 hosiery mill
针织工厂

1 circular knitting machine for the manufacture of tubular fabric
管形织物制造用的圆形针织机

2 yarn guide support post (thread guide support post)
导纱支柱（导线支柱）

3 yarn guide (thread guide)
导纱（导线）

4 bottle bobbin
瓶形筒管

5 yarn-tensioning device
纱线张力装置

6 yarn feeder
进纱器，导纱器

7 handwheel for rotating the machine by hand
用手旋转机器的手轮

8 needle cylinder (cylindrical needle holder)
针筒（筒形针架）

9 tubular fabric
管形织物

10 fabric drum (fabric box, fabric container)
织品筒（织品箱，织物容器）

11 needle cylinder (cylindrical needle holder) [section]
针筒（筒形针架）[断面图]

12 latch needles arranged in a circle
排成圆形的舌针

13 cam housing
凸轮箱

14 needle cams
织针凸轮

15 needle trick
针槽

16 cylinder diameter (also diameter of tubular fabric)
圆筒直径（即圆筒形织物的直径）

17 thread (yarn)
纱，线

18 Cotton's patent flat knitting machine for ladies' fully-fashioned hose
哥登氏专利的女袜平针织机

19 pattern control chain
款式控制链

20 side frame
侧架

21 knitting head
针座

22 starting rod
起动杆

23 Raschel warp-knitting machine
拉歇尔式，经纱针织机

24 warp (warp beam)
经纱（经轴）

25 yarn-distributing (yarn-dividing) beam
纱分配轴

26 beam flange
经轴凸缘

27 row of needles
针列

28 needle bar
针座

29 fabric (Raschel fabric) [curtain lace and net fabrics] on the fabric roll
卷布滚轮上的织品，（拉歇尔织品）[窗帘花边和网眼织品]

30 handwheel
手轮

31 motor drive gear
马达驱动齿轮

32 take-down weight
取下重锤

33 frame
机架

34 base plate
底座

35 hand flat (flat-bed) knitting machine
手动平针织机

36 thread (yarn)
线（纱）

37 return spring
回动弹簧

38 support for springs
弹簧支架

39 carriage
滑架（座）

40 feeder-selecting device
给纱选择装置

41 carriage handles
滑座（架）把手

42 scale for regulating size of stitches
调节织针尺寸标尺

43 course counter (tachometer)
横列计数器（转速表）

44 machine control lever
机械操纵杆

45 carriage rail
滑座轨

46 back row of needles
后排针

47 front row of needles
前排针

48 knitted fabric
已织成的针织品

49 tension bar
张力棒

50 tension weight
张力重锤

51 needle bed showing knitting action
针床上显示针（编）织的动作

52 teeth of knock-over bit
脱圈沉降片片齿

53 needles in parallel rows
平行排列的针

54 yarn guide (thread guide)
导纱导线

55 needle bed
针床

56 retaining plate for latch needles
舌针的扣板

57 guard cam
保护凸轮

58 sinker
铅锤

59 needle-raising cam
提针凸轮

60 needle butt
针粗大的部分

61 latch needle
舌针

62 loop
线圈

63 pushing the needle through the fabric
推针穿过织物

64 yarn guide (thread guide) placing yarn in the needle hook
导纱器放纱於针钩上

65 loop formation
线圈的形成（成圈）

66 casting off of loop
收针（织好了一个环），脱圈

1-65 finishing
完成，加工

1 rotary milling (fulling) machine for felting the woollen (*Am.* woolen) fabric
毛织品毡合用的邋转缩绒机

2 pressure weights
压力砝码

3 top milling roller (top fulling roller)
上铣滚轮

4 drive wheel of bottom milling roller (bottom fulling roller)
底铣滚轮的驱动轮

5 fabric guide roller
导织品滚轮

6 bottom milling roller (bottom fulling roller)
底铣滚轮

7 draft board
牵伸板

8 open-width scouring machine for finer fabrics
细织品用的扩布式精炼机

9 fabric being drawn off the machine
机器送出的织品

10 drive gearbox
驱动齿轮箱

11 water inlet pipe
进水管

12 drawing-in roller
内拉滚轮

13 scroll-opening roller
螺旋开布滚轮

14 pendulum-type hydro-extractor (centrifuge), for extracting liquors from the fabric
从织品抽除水分用的，摆子型（离心）脱水机

15 machine base
机器基座（底座）

16 casing over suspension
悬吊物的外壳

17 outer casing containing rotating cage (rotating basket)
包含旋转笼（篮）的外壳（罩）

18 hydro-extractor (centrifuge) lid
（离心）脱水机盖

19 stop-motion device (stopping device)
停止装置

20 automatic starting and braking device
自动起动机和制动装置

21 *for cotton:* stenter; *for wool:* tenter
用於棉织品：开幅机；用於毛织品：拉幅机

22 air-dry fabric
晾乾织品

23 operator's (operative's) platform
工人操作台

24 feeding of fabric by guides onto stenter (tenter) pins or clips
引导织品进给开幅机（拉幅机）

25 electric control panel
电控制盘

26 initial overfeed to produce shrink-resistant fabric when dried
开始时供料超过，当乾燥时产生防缩的织品

27 thermometer
温度计

28 drying section
干燥室

29 air outlet
空气出口

30 plaiter (fabric-plaiting device)
折叠机（织品折叠装置）

31 wire-roller fabric-raising machine for producing raised or nap surface
织品表面起毛用的钢丝滚轮起毛机

32 drive gearbox
驱动齿轮箱

33 unraised cloth
未起毛的布

34 wire-covered rollers
钢丝滚轮

35 plaiter (cuttling device)
折叠机（折叠装置）

36 raised fabric
起毛的织品

37 plaiting-down platform
折叠织品之置板

38 rotary press (calendering machine), for press finishing
旋转压平机（滚压机），压平完工用

39 fabric
织品

40 control buttons and control wheels
控制按钮和控制轮

41 heated press bowl
热压滚子

42 rotary cloth-shearing machine
邋转式剪布机

43 suction slot, for removing loose fibres (*Am.* fibers)
排除松纤维的抽吸口

44 doctor blade (cutting cylinder)
螺旋刀（剪毛圆筒）

45 protective guard
防护装置

46 rotating brush
旋转毛刷

47 curved scray entry
弧形布入口

48 treadle control
控制踏板

49 [non-shrinking] decatizing (decating) fabric-finishing machine
[织品防缩的]蒸绒机

50 perforated decatizing (decating) cylinder
多孔蒸绒滚筒

51 piece of fabric
织品

52 cranked control handle
控制曲柄

53 ten-colour (*Am.* ten-color) roller printing machine
十色滚轮印花机

54 base of the machine
机器的底座

55 drive motor
驱动马达

56 blanket [of rubber or felt]
[橡皮或毡的]衬布

57 fabric after printing (printed fabric)
印花后的织物

58 electric control panel (control unit)
电控制盘（控制装置）

59 screen printing
筛网印花

60 mobile screen frame
活动的筛网框

61 squeegee
涂染料滚轮

62 pattern stencil
图案模板

63 screen table
筛网台

64 fabric gummed down on table ready for printing
贴於工作台上准备印花的织品

65 screen printing operator (operative)
筛网印花操作工人

1-34 manufacture of
**continuous filament and staple
fibre (*Am.* fiber) viscose rayon
yarns** by means of the viscose
process
经由纤维胶过程制造的连续细丝，纤维
人造丝，和纤维胶人造丝纱

1-12 from raw material to viscose
rayon
从原料到纤维胶人造丝

1 basic material [beech and spruce
cellulose in form of sheets]
基本原料[山毛榉，赤松纤维素板]

2 mixing cellulose sheets
混和纤维素板

3 caustic soda
苛性钠，烧碱

4 steeping cellulose sheets in
caustic soda
纤维素板浸於苛性钠中

5 pressing out excess caustic soda
压出过量的苛性钠

6 shredding the cellulose sheets
将纤维素板粉碎

7 maturing (controlled oxidation)
of the alkali-cellulose crumbs
碱性纤维素碎片的成熟（控制氧化）

8 carbon disulphide (*Am.* carbon
disulfide)
二硫化碳

9 conversion of alkali-cellulose
into cellulose xanthate
把碱纤维素转化成纤维素黄酸

10 dissolving the xanthate in
caustic soda for the preparation
of the viscose spinning solution
胶纺丝溶液准备备用的黄酸溶於苛性钠中

11 vacuum ripening tanks
真空成熟槽

12 filter press
压滤机

13-27 from viscose to viscose rayon
thread
从纤维胶液至粘胶人造丝

13 metering pump
计量泵

14 multi-holed spinneret (spinning
jet)
多孔纺纱头（吐丝头）

15 coagulating (spinning) bath for
converting (coagulating) viscose
(viscous solution) into solid
filaments
由纤维胶液转变成固体人造丝的凝固槽

16 Godet wheel, a glass pulley
导丝轮，一种玻璃滑轮

17 Topham centrifugal pot (box)
for twisting the filaments into
yarn
将人造丝绕成纱所用的托普汉离心壶
（罐）

18 viscose rayon cake
纤维胶人造丝饼

19-27 processing of the cake
丝饼的处理过程

19 washing
洗涤

20 desulphurizing
(desulphurization, *Am.*
desulfurizing,
desulfurization)
去硫

21 bleaching
漂白

22 treating of cake to give filaments
softness and suppleness
使人造丝饼柔软的处理

23 hydro-extraction to remove
surplus moisture
去除过剩水分的脱水机

24 drying in heated room
於加热间烘乾

25 winding yarn from cake into
cone form
将丝饼绕成锥形丝筒

26 cone-winding machine
锥形绕线机

27 viscose rayon yarn on cone
ready for use
卷於锥形筒上可使用的纤维胶人造丝纱

28-34 from viscose spinning
solution to viscose rayon staple
fibre (*Am.* fiber)
从纤维胶纺丝液至纤维胶人造丝

28 filament tow
拖拉出来的细丝（纤维）

29 overhead spray washing plant
架空喷洗设备

30 cutting machine for cutting
filament tow to desired length
将丝切成理想长度的切割机

31 multiple drying machine for
cut-up staple fibre (*Am.* fiber)
layer (lap)
烘乾切断人造丝用的多层烘乾机

32 conveyor belt (conveyor)
输送带

33 baling press
压力打包机

34 bale of viscose rayon ready for
dispatch (despatch)
准备运送的人造丝丝包

1-62 manufacture of **polyamide** (nylon 6, perlon) **fibres** (*Am* fibers)
聚醯胺纤维（尼龙6，贝纶）的制造

1 coal [raw material for manufacture of polyamide (nylon 6, perlon) fibres (*Am.* fibers)]
煤[制造聚醯胺纤维（尼龙6，贝纶）的原料]

2 coking plant for dry coal distillation
煤干燥蒸馏用的焦化设备

3 extraction of coal tar and phenol
焦油和酚的提取

4 gradual distillation of tar
焦油的分馏

5 condenser
冷凝器

6 benzene extraction and dispatch (despatch)
苯的提取和输送

7 chlorine
氯

8 benzene chlorination
苯的氯化

9 monochlorobenzene (chlorobenzene)
一氯苯

10 caustic soda solution
苛性钠溶液

11 evaporation of chlorobenzene and caustic soda
氯苯和苛性钠的蒸发

12 autoclave
热压器

13 sodium chloride (common salt), a by-product
氯化钠（一般食盐），一种副产品

14 phenol (carbolic acid)
酚（液体石碳酸）

15 hydrogen inlet
氢气入口

16 hydrogenation of phenol to produce raw cyclohexanol
酚的氢化产生粗环己醇

17 distillation
蒸馏

18 pure cyclohexanol
纯环己醇

19 oxidation (dehydrogenation)
氧化（去氢）

20 formation of cyclohexanone (pimehinketone)
环己酮的形成

21 hydroxylamine inlet
盐酸羟胺入口

22 formation of cyclohexanoxime
环己酮的形成

23 addition of sulphuric acid (*Am.* sulfuric acid) to effect molecular rearrangement
加硫酸使分子从新排列

24 ammonia to neutralize sulphuric acid (*Am.* sulfuric acid)
加氨中和硫酸

25 formation of caprolactam oil
己醯环胺油的形成

26 ammonium sulphate (*Am.* ammonium sulfate) solution
硫酸铵溶液

27 cooling cylinder
冷却滚筒

28 caprolactam
己醯环胺

29 weighing apparatus
秤重装置

30 melting pot
熔化罐

31 pump
泵

32 filter
过滤器

33 polymerization in the autoclave
在热压器内聚合

34 cooling of the polyamide
聚醯胺的冷却

35 solidification of the polyamide
聚醯胺的固化

36 vertical lift (*Am.* elevator)
升降机

37 extractor for separating the polyamide from the remaining lactam oil
从内醯胺油中分离聚醯胺用的抽出器

38 drier
干燥机

39 dry polyamide chips
干燥的聚醯胺片

40 chip container
胶片容器

41 top of spinneret for melting the polyamide and forcing it through spinneret holes (spinning jets)
熔化聚醯胺和从喷丝孔压挤出来的喷丝头

42 spinneret holes (spinning jets)
喷丝孔

43 solidification of the polyamide filaments in the cooling tower
於冷却塔中聚醯胺丝的固化

44 collection of extruded filaments into thread form
将挤压出来的丝条集合成丝束

45 preliminary stretching (preliminary drawing)
预拉伸

46 stretching (cold-drawing) of the polyamide thread to achieve high tensile strength
聚醯胺丝线的拉伸至达到高抗拉强度

47 final stretching (final drawing)
最后拉伸

48 washing of yarn packages
丝件的洗涤

49 drying chamber
干燥室

50 rewinding
复卷筒

51 polyamide cone
聚醯胺筒

52 polyamide cone ready for dispatch (despatch)
准备运送的聚醯胺筒

53 mixer
混合器

54 polymerization under vacua
真空下的聚合（作用）

55 stretching (drawing)
拉伸

56 washing
洗涤

57 finishing of tow for spinning
纺纱用拖线的整理

58 drying of tow
拖线的干燥

59 crimping of tow
拖线的卷紧

60 cutting of tow into normal staple lengths
拖线切割成一般（标准）纤维长度

61 polyamide staple
聚醯胺纤维

62 bale of polyamide staple
聚醯胺纤维包

1-29 weaves [black squares: warp thread raised, weft thread lowered; white squares: weft thread raised, warp thread lowered]
平织组织[黑方块：经纱升起，纬纱下沉；白方块：纬纱升起，经纱下沉]

1 plain weave (tabby weave) [weave viewed from above]
平织（有波纹的织品）[从上观看织纹]

2 warp thread
经纱

3 weft thread
纬纱

4 draft (point paper design) for plain weave
平织用的编织图案

5 threading draft
穿轴图

6 denting draft (reed-threading draft)
穿扣图

7 raised warp thread
经纱升起

8 lowered warp thread
经纱下沉

9 tie-up of shafts in pairs
轴片成对的穿吊

10 treadling diagram
跳线图

11 draft for basket weave (hopsack weave, matt weave)
柳条织品图案

12 pattern repeat
重复花样

13 draft for warp rib weave
以经纱为棱织品的图案

14 section of warp rib fabric, a section through the warp
以经纱为棱织品的断面，部分断面经过经纱

15 lowered weft thread
下沉的纬纱

16 raised weft thread
上升的纬纱

17 first and second warp threads [raised]
第一和第二经纱[上升的]

18 third and fourth warp threads [lowered]
第三和第四经纱[下沉的]

19 draft for combined rib weave
混合棱平织图案

20 selvedge (selvage) thread draft (additional shafts for the selvedge)
织边穿轴图（织边附加轴）

21 draft for the fabric shafts
织品穿轴图

22 tie-up of selvedge (selvage) shafts
织边轴的穿吊

23 tie-up of fabric shafts
织品轴的穿吊

24 selvedge (selvage) in plain weave
平织的轴片

25 section through combination rib weave
经过混合棱平织的断面图

26 thread interlacing of reversible warp-faced cord
双面经线纹面交织图

27 draft (point paper design) for reversible warp-faced cord
双面经线纹面图

28 interlacing points
交织点

29 weaving draft for honeycomb weave in the fabric
蜂巢织品的平织图

30-48 basic knits
基本针织组织

30 loop, an open loop
线圈，开口线圈

31 head
圈头

32 side
圈边

33 neck
圈颈

34 head interlocking point
圈头连接点

35 neck interlocking point
圈颈连接点

36 closed loop
闭口线圈

37 mesh [with inlaid yarn]
网状组织[带镶嵌纱]

38 diagonal floating yarn (diagonal floating thread)
对角浮纱（对角浮线）

39 loop interlocking at the head
线圈在圈头交织

40 float
浮线组织

41 loose floating yarn (loose floating thread)
松散浮纱（松散浮线）

42 course
针路

43 inlaid yarn
镶嵌纱

44 tuck and miss stitch
集圈浮线组织

45 pulled-up tuck stitch
套穿集圈组织

46 staggered tuck stitch
交错集圈组织

47 2 × 2 tuck and miss stitch
2×2集圈和浮线组织

48 double pulled-up tuck stitch
双套穿集圈组织

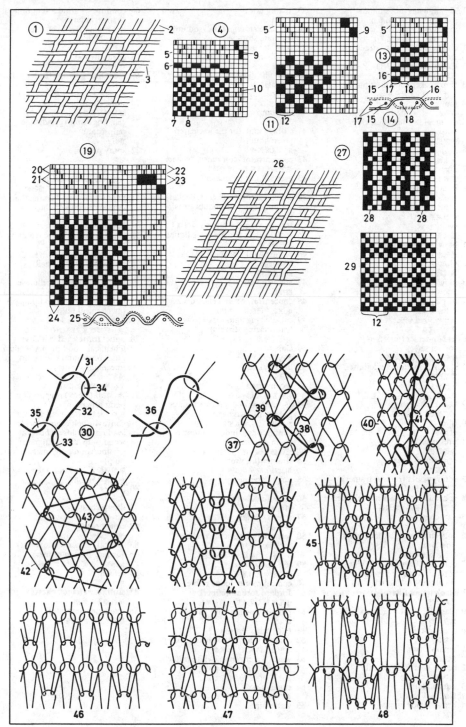

1-52 sulphate (*Am.* sulfate)
pulp mill (kraft pulp mill) [in
diagram form]
硫酸纸浆厂（牛皮纸浆厂）[图示]

1 chippers with dust extractor
带吸尘器的削片机

2 rotary screen (riffler)
回转筛

3 chip packer (chip distributor)
木片包装机（木片分配器）

4 blower
鼓风机

5 disintegrator (crusher, chip
crusher)
粉碎机（轧碎机，木片轧碎机）

6 dust-settling chamber
灰尘沉淀室（降尘室）

7 digester
蒸解釜

8 liquor preheater
溶液预热器

9 control tap
控制龙头

10 swing pipe
摆动管

11 blow tank (diffuser)
通风槽（扩散器）

12 blow valve
通风阀

13 blow pit (diffuser)
通风坑（扩散器）

14 turpentine separator
松节油分离器

15 centralized separator
集中分离器

16 jet condenser (injection
condenser)
喷射凝结器（注射凝结器）

17 storage tank for condensate
凝结液贮存槽

18 hot water tank
热水槽

19 heat exchanger
热交换器

20 filter
过滤器

21 presorter
预选别机

22 centrifugal screen
离心筛

23 rotary sorter (rotary strainer)
旋转选别机（旋转滤器）

24 concentrator (thickener, decker)
浓缩器（调稠器，增稠器）

25 vat (chest)
槽（浆槽）

26 collecting tank for backwater
(low box)
回水收集槽（低箱）

27 conical refiner (cone refiner,
Jordan, Jordan refiner)
锥形精制（浆）机（约旦精制机）

28 black liquor filter
黑液滤器

29 black liquor storage tank
黑液贮槽

30 condenser
冷凝器

31 separators
分离器

32 heater (heating element)
加热器（加热元件）

33 liquor pump
液泵

34 heavy liquor pump
浓液泵

35 mixing tank
混合槽

36 salt cake storage tank (sodium
sulphate storage tank)
盐饼贮槽（硫酸钠贮槽）

37 dissolving tank (dissolver)
溶解槽

38 steam heater
蒸汽加热器

39 electrostatic precipitator
静电集尘器

40 air pump
气泵

41 storage tank for the uncleared
green liquor
未清绿液槽

42 concentrator (thickener, decker)
浓缩器（调稠器，增稠器）

43 green liquor preheater
绿液预热器

44 concentrator (thickener, decker)
for the weak wash liquor (wash
water)
稀洗液用的浓缩器（调稠器，增稠器）

45 storage tank for the weak liquor
稀释液贮槽

46 storage tank for the cooking
liquor
蒸煮液贮槽

47 agitator (stirrer)
搅拌器

48 concentrator (thickener, decker)
浓缩器（调稠器，增稠器）

49 causticizing agitators
(causticizing stirrers)
苛化搅拌器

50 classifier
类析器

51 lime slaker
化灰器

52 reconverted lime
再转换石灰，再生石灰

53-65 groundwood mill (mechanical
pulp mill) [diagram]
磨木浆厂（机械纸浆厂）[简图]

53 continuous grinder (continuous
chain grinder)
连续磨木机（连续链式磨木机）

54 strainer (knotter)
粗滤器，滤筛（结筛）

55 pulp water pump
纸浆水泵

56 centrifugal screen
离心筛

57 screen (sorter)
筛（选别机）

58 secondary screen (secondary
sorter)
（二次）二道筛（二道选别机）

59 rejects chest
筛渣槽，废料池

60 conical refiner (cone refiner,
Jordan, Jordan refiner)
锥形精制（浆）机（约旦精制机）

61 pulp-drying machine (pulp
machine)
纸浆干燥机（纸浆机）

62 concentrator (thickener, decker)
浓缩器（调稠器，增稠器）

63 waste water pump (white water
pump, pulp water pump)
废水泵（白水泵，纸浆水泵）

64 steam pipe
蒸汽管

65 water pipe
水管

66 continuous grinder (continuous
chain grinder)
连续磨木机（连续链式磨木机）

67 feed chain
给料链

68 groundwood
磨木浆

69 reduction gear for the feed chain
drive
进料链驱动的减速齿轮

70 stone-dressing device
磨石刻石装置

71 grinding stone (grindstone,
pulpstone)
磨石

72 spray pipe
喷管

73 conical refiner (cone refiner,
Jordan, Jordan refiner)
锥形精制（浆）机（约旦精制机）

74 handwheel for adjusting the
clearance between the knives
(blades)
调整刀片间隙用的手轮

75 rotating bladed cone (rotating
bladed plug)
旋转刀片的锥部（旋转刀片插座）

76 stationary bladed shell
固定刀片壳

77 inlet for unrefined cellulose
(chemical wood pulp, chemical
pulp) or groundwood pulp
(mechanical pulp)
未精制纤维素（化学木浆）或磨木纸
浆（机械纸浆）的入口

78 outlet for refined cellulose
(chemical wood pulp, chemical
pulp) or groundwood pulp
(mechanical pulp)
精制纤维素（化学纸浆）或磨木纸浆
（机械纸浆）的出口

79-86 stuff (stock) preparation
plant [diagram]
原料、材料（存料）准备设备[简图]

79 conveyor belt (conveyor) for
loading cellulose (chemical
wood pulp, chemical pulp) or
groundwood pulp (mechanical
pulp)
装载纤维素（化学木浆）或磨木浆（机
械纸浆）的运送带

80 pulper
散浆机

81 dump chest
卸料槽

82 cone breaker
锥形轧碎机

83 conical refiner (cone refiner,
Jordan, Jordan refiner)
锥形精制（浆）机（约旦精制机）

84 refiner
精浆机

85 stuff chest (stock chest)
纸料槽（存料槽）

86 machine chest (stuff chest)
原料贮槽（纸料槽）

1 stuff chest (stock chest, machine chest), a mixing chest for stuff (stock)
原料贮槽（存料槽），原料的一种混合槽

2-10 laboratory apparatus (laboratory equipment) for analysing stuff (stock) and paper
分析原料和纸张用的实验室仪器

2 Erlenmeyer flask
锥形瓶，锥形烧瓶

3 volumetric flask
量瓶

4 measuring cylinder
量筒

5 Bunsen burner
本生灯

6 tripod
三脚架

7 petri dish
佩垂皿

8 test tube rack
试管架

9 balance for measuring basis weight
测量纸张定量的秤

10 micrometer
测微计

11 centrifugal cleaners ahead of the breastbox (headbox, stuff box) of a paper machine
造纸机网前箱的离心除渣器

12 standpipe
竖管，圆筒形水塔

13-28 paper machine (production line) [diagram]
造纸机（生产线）[简图]

13 feed-in from the machine chest (stuff chest) with sand table (sand trap, riffler) and knotter
从带砂滤器（砂阱，沉沙器）和结筛器的原料贮槽进料

14 wire (machine wire)
金属线（机械电线）

15 vacuum box (suction box)
真空箱（吸取箱）

16 suction roll
吸水滚轮

17 first wet felt
第一湿毛布（毡）

18 second wet felt
第二湿毛布（毡）

19 first press
第一压榨机

20 second press
第二压榨机

21 offset press
偏位压榨机（副压榨机）

22 drying cylinder (drier)
干燥滚筒（干燥器）

23 dry felt (drier felt)
干燥毡

24 size press
压榨机

25 cooling roll
冷却滚轮

26 calender rolls
轧光滚轮

27 machine hood
机器罩（盖）

28 delivery reel
卷取纸轴

29-35 blade coating machine (blade coater)
刮刀涂布机

29 raw paper (body paper)
粗纸（纸坯）

30 web
整卷印刷用纸

31 coater for the top side
顶面涂布器

32 infrared drier
红外线干燥器

33 heated drying cylinder
加热干燥滚筒

34 coater for the underside (wire side)
下边涂布器（网面）

35 reel of coated paper
涂布的卷筒纸

36 calender (Super-calender)
轧光机（超级轧光机）

37 hydraulic system for the press rolls
压榨滚轮的液压系统

38 calender roll
轧光滚轮

39 unwind station
退纸操作台

40 lift platform
上升台

41 rewind station(rewinder, re-reeler, reeling machine, re-reeling machine)
回卷台（回卷机，复卷筒，摇纱机，复摇纱机）

42 roll cutter
滚轮切纸机

43 control panel
控制盘

44 cutter
切纸机

45 web
整卷的印刷用纸

46-51 papermaking by hand
手工造纸

46 vatman
捞工

47 vat
纸浆槽

48 mould (*Am.* mold)
模

49 coucher (couchman)
伏工

50 post ready for pressing
为压制作准备的工作

51 felt
毡（毛布）

1 **hand-setting room**
(handcomposing room)
手工排字（排版）房
2 composing frame
排字架
3 case (typecase)
活字盘（铅字盘）
4 case cabinet (case rack)
字盘柜（字盘架）
5 hand compositor (compositor,
typesetter, maker-up)
排字工人（排字工，铅字工，手民）
6 manuscript (typescript)
原稿（打字稿）
7 sorts, types (type characters,
characters)
杂类活字符号，整套铅字（铅字，活
字）
8 rack (case) for furniture (spacing
material)
活版填料架（铅字隔条、空铅等）
9 standing type rack (standing
matter rack)
存版架
10 storage shelf (shelf for storing
formes, *Am.* forms)
保存架（印版储存架）
11 standing type (standing matter)
存版（印件）
12 galley
活版盘，铅字盘
13 composing stick (setting stick)
检字手盘
14 composing rule (setting rule)
排字量规（组字规）
15 type (type matter, matter)
铅字，活字
16 page cord
捆版绳
17 bodkin
锥子
18 tweezers
镊子
19 **Linotype line-composing (line-
casting, slug-composing, slug-
casting)machine, a
multi-magazine machine**
林诺铸版机（整行铸字机），一种万能
铸版铸字排字机
20 distributing mechanism
(distributor)
配字模装置（配字模器）
21 type magazines with matrices
(matrixes)
具有字模的活字库
22 elevator carrier for distributing
the matrices (matrixes)
配字模的升降牵转具（托架）
23 assembler
配字器
24 spacebands
齐行楔
25 casting mechanism
铸版机
26 metal feeder
金属供给装置（供铅器）
27 machine-set matter (cast lines,
slugs)
机械排字条（铸字条，铅字条）
28 matrices (matrixes) for
handsetting (sorts)
手工排字（排版）用之字模
29 Linotype matrix
整行铸排字模
30 teeth for the distributing
mechanism (distributor)
配字模装置用齿

31 face (type face, matrix)
字面（铅字面，字模）
32-45 **monotype single-unit
composing (typesetting) and
casting machine** (monotype
single-unit composition caster)
单字排字机和单字铸版机
32 monotype standard composing
(typesetting) machine
(keyboard)
标准单字排字机（键盘式）
33 paper tower
纸带架
34 paper ribbon
纸质打字机色带
35 justifying scale
整版尺（齐行标尺）
36 unit indicator
单位指示器
37 keyboard
键盘
38 compressed-air hose
压缩空气软管
39 monotype casting machine
(monotype caster)
单字铸字机
40 automatic metal feeder
自动金属供应装置（供铅器）
41 pump compression spring
(pump pressure spring)
泵压缩弹簧
42 matrix case (die case)
字模盒
43 paper tower
纸带架
44 galley with types (letters,
characters, cast single types, cast
single letters)
有活字（字母、符号、单字铸件）的铅
字盘
45 electric heater (electric heating
unit)
电热器（电热装置）
46 matrix case (die case)
字模盒
47 type matrices (matrixes) (letter
matrices)
（铅）活字字模（字母字模）
48 guide block for engaging with
the cross-slide guide
衔接横向滑件导座的导块

1-17 composition (type matter, type)
组版（铅字材料，铅字）

1 initial (initial letter)
起首字母

2 bold type (bold, boldfaced type, heavy type, boldface)
粗体铅字，黑体铅字

3 semibold type (semibold)
中黑体铅字

4 line
字行

5 space
字行间隔，行间，行距

6 ligature (double letter)
复合字（双字母）

7 italic type (italics)
斜体铅字（斜体字）

8 light face type (light face)
细体铅字

9 extra bold type (extra bold)
特黑体铅字

10 bold condensed type (bold condensed)
黑体凝缩活字

11 majuscule (capital letter, capital, upper case letter)
大写字体（大写字母）

12 minuscule (small letter, lower case letter)
小写字体（小写字母）

13 letter spacing (interspacing)
调节间隔法（中间空间），字母间隔

14 small capitals
小号大写字母

15 break
中止（段落）

16 indention
行首空白（缩进）

17 space
空铅，间隔，字间

18 type sizes [one typographic point = 0.376 mm (Didot system), 0.351 mm (Pica system)]
铅字大小（尺寸）[（欧洲制法国活字规格）一个印刷点 = 0.376 毫米（迪多点制），0.351 毫米（派卡制）（12 点大之活字规格）]

19 six-to-pica (2 points)
½ 派卡字体（英文 2 点铅字）

20 half nonpareil (four-to-pica) (3 points)
半无上字体 ⅓ 派卡（英文 3 点铅字）

21 brilliant (4 points); *sim.*: diamond (4½ points)
显明字体（英文 4 点铅字）；类似：钻石字体（英文 4½ 点铅字）

22 pearl (5 points); *sim.*: ruby (*Am.* agate) (5½ points)
珍珠字体（英文 5 点铅字）；类似：玛瑙字体（5½ 点）

23 nonpareil (6 points); *sim.*: minionette (6½ points)
无上字体（英文 6 点铅字）；类似：6½ 点字体

24 minion (7 points)
宠仆字体（英文 7 点铅字）

25 brevier (8 points)
短字体（英文 8 点铅字）

26 bourgeois (9 points)
布鲁泽依司字体（英文 9 点铅字）

27 long primer (10 points)
过高初阶字体（英文 10 点铅字）

28 pica (12 points)
派卡字体（英文 12 点铅字）

29 English (14 points)
古体英文字体（英文 14 点铅字）

30 great primer (two-line brevier, *Am.* Columbian) (16 points)
大宰相字体（两行短字体，[美]哥伦布式字体）（英文 16 点字体）

31 paragon (two-line primer) (20 points)
模范字体（两行过高初阶字体，英文 20 点字体）

32-37 typefounding (type casting)
活字（铅字）制造（铸造）

32 punch cutter
雕刻师

33 graver (burin, cutter)
雕刻刀

34 magnifying glass (magnifier)
放大镜

35 punch blank (die blank)
钢模坯体（空白之钢模）

36 finished steel punch (finished steel die)
刻好的钢模

37 punched matrix (stamped matrix, strike, drive)
冲压成之字模（钢模）

38 type (type character, character)
铅字

39 head
铅字头

40 shoulder
字肩

41 counter
字谷（字地）

42 face (type face)
字面

43 type line (bodyline)
铅字廓线（字体廓线）

44 height to paper (type height)
铅字高度

45 height of shank (height of shoulder)
字身高度（字脚至字肩高度）

46 body size (type size, point size)
铅字尺寸（铅字大小，点的大小）

47 nick
铅字缺刻

48 set (width)
铅字宽度

49 matrix-boring machine (matrix-engraving machine), a special-purpose boring machine
字模搪孔（字模雕刻机），一种特定目的之搪孔（雕刻）机器

50 stand
机架（台）

51 cutter (cutting head)
刀具（切割头）

52 cutting table
切割台

53 pantograph carriage
比例尺之滑座（轨运器）

54 V-way
V 型槽

55 pattern
字模版

56 pattern table
字模台

57 follower
从动装置

58 pantograph
缩放器

59 matrix clamp
字模夹

60 cutter spindle
刀具主轴

61 drive motor
驱动马达

Alfred **John Dodsley,** essayist and journalist, was born in Wenlock on the 5th August 1841 and died on the 4th October 1920 in Birmingham. His father was a journeyman thatcher and as a boy Dodsley was sent to work in the fields as a bird-scarer. Having taught himself to read and write fluently – for many years the only books he possessed were a Bible and a volume of Tillotson's sermons – he went to Shrewsbury to study. Living in extreme poverty he began to write for the EAST HEREFORDSHIRE GAZETTE and a collection of his essays together with some poems on country life was published in 1868 under the title *"Rural Thoughts".* Among his most popular works were *"The Diary of a Derbyshire Shepherd"* (1872), *"Rural Verses"* (1879), *"Leaves from a Country-man's Notebook"* (1893) and *"Memoirs of Nine-teenth Century Shropshire",* published posthumously. Dodsley also contributed many articles on country life to London papers and championed the cause of the agricultural worker during the depression of the 1880's. The latter years of his life were embittered by controversy raised by his protests against the unemployment caused by mechanised farming.

He was for many years president of the **Society for the Protection of the Liberties of the Farm-worker.**

· 19

⑱ 20

■ 21   N n

■ 22   N n

■ 23   N n

■ 24   N n

■ 25   N n

■ 26   N n

■ 27   N n

■ 28   N n

■ 29   N n

■ 30   N n

■ 31 N n

176 Composing Room (Phototypesetting, Photocomposition, Photosetting, Filmsetting) III

1 keyboard console (keyboard unit) for phototypesetting
照相打字之键盘操作台

2 keyboard
键盘

3 manuscript (copy)
原稿，手稿

4 keyboard operator
键盘操作者

5 tape punch (perforator)
纸带穿（打）孔机（器）

6 punched tape (punch tape)
穿孔纸带

7 filmsetter
软片卷动装置

8 punched tape (punch tape)
穿孔纸带

9 exposure control device
曝光控制装置

10 typesetting computer
照相打字组版之电脑

11 memory unit (storage unit)
记忆单位（存储单位）

12 punched tape (punch tape)
穿孔纸带（孔带）

13 punched tape (punch tape) reader
穿孔纸带阅读机

14 photo-unit (photographic unit) for computer-controlled typesetting (composition)
电脑控制排版用之照相装置

15 punchd tape (punch tape) reader
穿孔纸带阅读机

16 type matrices (matrixes) (letter matrices)
字模

17 matrix case (film matrix case)
字模盒（软片字模盒）

18 guide block
导块

19 synchronous motor
同步马达

20 type disc (disk) (matrix disc)
铅字盘（字模盘）

21 mirror assembly
反射镜组件

22 optical wedge
光楔

23 lens
透镜

24 mirror system
反射镜系统

25 film
软片（胶卷）

26 flash tubes
闪光管

27 matrix drum
字模筒

28 automatic film copier
软片自动复制机

29 central processing unit of a photocomposition system (photosetting system) for newspaper typesetting
报纸照相排版系统之资料处理机（新闻排版用照相排字机之中央处理装置）

30 punched tape (punch tape) input (input unit)
穿孔纸带输入（输入装置）

31 keyboard send-receive teleprinter (Teletype)
键盘式电传打字机

32 on-line disc (disk) storage unit
线上磁碟储存装置

33 alphanumeric (alphameric) disc (disk) store (alphanumeric disc file)
字母数字磁碟储存器（字母数字磁碟档）

34 disc (disk) stack (disc pack)
磁碟储存架

1 overhead process camera
(overhead copying camera)
吊式制版照相机（吊式复制相机）
2 focusing screen (ground glass
screen)
聚焦幕（检影玻璃板或毛玻璃板）
3 hinged screen holder
铰接聚焦托架
4 graticule
格子线
5 control console
操作控制台
6 hinged bracket-mounted control
panel
铰接的托架式控制板
7 percentage focusing charts
调焦率图表
8 vacuum film holder
真空软片吸气板
9 screen magazine
网目屏箱
10 bellows
相机之暗匣（蛇腹，暗箱）
11 standard
机架
12 register device
定位装置
13 overhead gantry
吊式门架
14 copyboard
原稿板架
15 copyholder
原稿夹框
16 lamp bracket
灯的托架
17 xenon lamp
氙气灯
18 copy (original)
原稿
19 retouching and stripping desk
修版和揭膜桌
20 illuminated screen
照明毛玻璃屏
21 height and angle adjustment
桌子高度和角度之调整器
22 copyboard
原稿板架
23 linen tester, a magnifying glass
布纹检验器，放大镜之一种
24 universal process and
reproduction camera
万能制版用之复制相机
25 camera body
相机机身
26 bellows
蛇腹，暗箱
27 lens carrier
透镜移动装置（镜头架）
28 angled mirror
角镜
29 stand
支架
30 copyboard
原稿板架
31 halogen lamp
卤素灯
32 vertical process camera, a
compact camera
立式制版照相机（简单小型式摄影机）
33 camera body
相机机身
34 focusing screen (ground glass
screen)
调焦屏（毛玻璃屏）
35 vacuum back
真空软片吸盖版

36 control panel
控制盘
37 flash lamp
闪光灯
38 mirror for right-reading images
正相镜
39 scanner (colour, *Am.* color,
correction unit)
扫描器（影色修正机）
40 base frame
基座
41 lamp compartment
灯室
42 xenon lamp housing
氙灯罩
43 feed motors
进给马达
44 transparency arm
透明臂
45 scanning drum
扫描滚筒
46 scanning head
扫描头
47 mask-scanning head
修色扫描头
48 mask drum
修色滚筒
49 recording space
记录间隔
50 daylight cassette
明室暗箱
51 colour (*Am.* color) computer
with control unit and selective
colour correction
装有控制装置与选色校色之彩色电脑
52 engraving machine
雕刻机
53 seamless engraving adjustment
无缝雕刻调整装置
54 drive clutch
驱动离合器
55 clutch flange
离合器凸缘
56 drive unit
驱动装置
57 machine bed
机座
58 equipment carrier
部件移动装置
59 bed slide
刀架滑座（板）
60 control panel
控制盘
61 bearing block
轴承座
62 tailstock
尾座
63 scanning head
扫描头
64 copy cylinder
原稿圆筒
65 centre (*Am.* center) bearing
中间轴承
66 engraving system
雕刻装置
67 printing cylinder
印刷滚筒
68 cylinder arm
圆筒臂（柄）
69 electronics (electronic) cabinet
电子设备柜（电箱）
70 computers
电脑
71 program input
程式输入

72 automatic film processor for
scanner films
软片扫描用的软片自动显影（处理）机

1-6 electrotyping plant
电铸版厂

1 cleaning tank
清洗槽

2 rectifier
整流器

3 measuring and control unit
计算与控制装置

4 electroplating tank
(electroplating bath,
electroplating vat)
电镀槽（桶）

5 anode rod (copper anodes)
阳极（铜）

6 plate rod (cathode)
阴极版

7 **hydraulic moulding (***Am.***
molding) press**
液压式制版压型机

8 pressure gauge (*Am.* gage)
(manometer)
压力计

9 apron
挡板，盖板（防止危险之金属板）

10 control panel
控制台

11 hydraulic pressure pump
（油）液压泵

12 drive motor
驱动马达

13 **curved plate casting machine**
(curved electrotype casting
machine)
弧形板铸造机（弧型电铸机）

14 motor
马达

15 control knobs
控制钮

16 pyrometer
高温计

17 mouth piece
给料口

18 core
铸造型芯（中心部分）

19 melting furnace
熔炉

20 starting lever
起动杆

21 cast curved plate (cast curved
electrotype) for rotary printing
轮转印刷用之弧型版铸造（铸造弧型电铸版）

22 fixed mould (*Am.* mold)
固定铸模（模型）

23 **etching machine**
腐蚀（制版）机

24 etching tank with etching
solution (etchant, mordant) and
filming agent (film former)
盛有腐蚀剂和成膜剂之腐蚀槽

25 paddles
搅拌桨

26 turntable
转盘

27 plate clamp
版夹

28 drive motor
驱动马达

29 control unit
控制装置

30 **twin etching machine**
双面腐蚀机

31 etching tank (etching bath)〔in
section〕
腐蚀槽（剖面图）

32 photoprinted zinc plate
照相锌版

33 paddle
搅拌桨

34 outlet cock (drain cock, *Am.*
faucet)
排水栓

35 plate rack
板架

36 control switches
控制开关

37 lid
盖子

38 **halftone photoengraving**
(halftone block, halftone plate),
a block (plate, printing plate)
半色调印相凸版

39 dot (halftone dot), a printing
element
网点，半色调印刷之要素

40 etched zinc plate
腐蚀后之锌版

41 block mount (block mounting,
plate mount, plate mounting)
凸版台（版托）

42 **line block** (line engraving, line
etching, line plate, line cut)
线条凸版（线条雕刻，线条腐蚀）

,43 non-printing, deep-etched areas
非印刷部份之深腐蚀区（无印纹区）

44 flange (bevel edge)
边缘

45 sidewall
侧壁

1 plate whirler (whirler, platecoating machine) for coating offset plates
涂布感光液用之平版烘版机

2 sliding lid
滑动盖，活动盖

3 electric heater
电热器

4 temperature gauge (*Am.* gage)
温度计

5 water connection for the spray unit
喷雾装置的给水接头

6 spray unit
喷雾装置

7 hand spray
手按喷雾器

8 plate clamps
版夹

9 zinc plate (*also*: magnesium plate, copper plate)
锌板（另有：镁板，铜板）

10 control panel
控制台

11 drive motor
驱动马达

12 brake pedal
刹车踏板

13 vacuum printing frame (vacuum frame, printing-down frame)
真空烘（晒）架

14 base of the vacuum printing frame (vacuum frame, printing-down frame)
真空烘（晒）版架之基座

15 plate glass frame
玻璃版架

16 coated offset plate
涂布感光液之平板

17 control panel
控制盘

18 exposure timer
曝光计时器

19 vacuum pump switch
真空泵开关

20 support
支架

21 point light exposure lamp, a quartz-halogen lamp
点光源，曝光灯，一种石英卤素灯

22 fan blower
吹风机

23 stripping table (make-up table) for stripping films
揭膜用之拼版台

24 crystal glass screen
水晶玻璃网

25 light box
灯光箱（光度一样时作胶卷薄膜检查之箱子）

26 straightedge rules
直尺（划直线用尺）

27 vertical plate-drying cabinet
垂直版之干燥箱

28 hygrometer
湿度计，垂直版

29 speed control
速度控制

30 brake pedal
刹车踏板

31 processing machine for presensitized plates
p.s版（预制感光板）显影机

32 burning-in oven for glueenamel plates (diazo plates)
上胶用之烘版箱（重氮基板，偶氮盐版）

33 control box (control unit)
控制箱（控制装置）

34 diazo plate
重氮基版（偶氮盐版）

1 four-colour (*Am.* four-color) rotary offset press (rotary offset machine, web-offset press)
四色平版轮转印刷机

2 roll of unprinted paper (blank paper)
未印的卷筒纸（空白纸卷）

3 reel stand (carrier for the roll of unprinted paper)
卷筒纸架（未印刷卷筒支架）

4 forwarding rolls
前进滚轮（输纸轮）

5 side margin control (margin control, side control, side lay control)
卷筒纸左右控制装置

6-13 inking units (inker units)
印版著墨装置

6, 8, 10, 12 inking units (inker units) in the upper printing unit
印刷机上部之著墨装置

6-7 perfecting unit (double unit) for yellow
黄色双面印刷装置

7, 9, 11, 13 inking units (inker units) in the lower printing unit
印刷机下部之著墨装置

8-9 perfecting unit (double unit) for cyan
青色双面印刷装置

10-11 perfecting unit (double unit) for magenta
紫红色双面印刷装置

12-13 perfecting unit (double unit) for black
黑色双面印刷装置

14 drier
干燥器

15 folder (folder unit)
折页装置

16 control desk
控制枱

17 sheet
单张，纸页

18 four-colour (*Am.* four-color) rotary offset press (rotary offset machine, web-offset press) [diagram]
四色平版轮转印刷机[简图]

19 reel stand
卷筒纸支架

20 side margin control (margin control, side control, side lay control)
左右控制装置

21 inking rollers (ink rollers, inkers)
著墨滚轮

22 ink duct (ink fountain)
油墨输送管（墨槽）

23 damping rollers (dampening rollers, dampers, dampeners)
润版滚

24 blanket cylinder
橡皮滚筒

25 plate cylinder
印版滚筒

26 route of the paper (of the web)
行纸路线

27 drier
干燥器

28 chilling rolls (cooling rollers, chill rollers)
冷却滚

29 folder (folder unit)
折页装置

30 four-colour (*Am.* four-color) sheet-fed offset machine (offset press) [diagram]
四色单张纸平版印刷机[简图]

31 sheet feeder (feeder)
（给）饀纸装置

32 feed table (feed board)
给纸桌（给纸台）

33 route of the sheets through swing-grippers to the feed drum
由输纸咬爪至给纸滚筒之给纸路线

34 feed drum
给纸滚筒

35 impression cylinder
压力滚筒

36 transfer drums (transfer cylinders)
传递滚筒

37 blanket cylinder
橡皮滚筒

38 plate cylinder
印版滚筒

39 damping unit (dampening unit)
润版（装置）单位

40 inking units (inker units)
著墨装置

41 printing unit
印刷装置

42 delivery cylinder
递纸滚筒

43 chain delivery
链式递纸装置

44 delivery pile
递纸堆

45 delivery unit (delivery mechanism)
收纸单位

46 single-colour (*Am.* single-color) offset press (offset machine)
单色平版印刷机

47 pile of paper (sheets, printing paper)
纸堆（堆纸，印刷用纸）

48 sheet feeder (feeder), an automatic pile feeder
给纸机（自动给纸机）

49 feed table (feed board)
给纸桌（给纸台）

50 inking rollers (ink rollers, inkers)
著墨滚轮

51 inking units (inker units)
著墨装置

52 damping rollers (dampening rollers, dampers, dampeners)
湿版滚

53 plate cylinder, a zinc plate
印版滚筒，一种锌版

54 blanket cylinder, a steel cylinder with rubber blanket
橡皮滚筒，一种包有橡皮布的钢滚筒

55 pile delivery unit for the printed sheets
已印刷过之单张纸的收纸装置

56 gripper bar, a chain gripper
咬纸杆，一种链式之夹纸装置

57 pile of printed paper (printed sheets)
印刷过之纸堆（印张）

58 guard for the V-belt (vee-belt) drive
V 型带转动之护板

59 single-colour (*Am.* single-color) offset press (offset machine) [diagram]
单色平版印刷机[简图]

60 inking unit (inker unit) with inking rollers (ink rollers, inkers)
具着墨滚轮之着墨装置

61 damping unit (dampening unit) with damping rollers (dampening rollers, dampers, dampeners)
具润版滚之润版装置

62 plate cylinder
印版滚筒

63 blanket cylinder
橡皮滚筒

64 impression cylinder
压力滚筒

65 delivery cylinders with grippers
具咬纸夹之递纸滚筒

66 drive wheel
驱动轮

67 feed table (feed board)
给纸台（板）

68 sheet feeder (feeder)
给纸机

69 pile of unprinted paper (blank paper, unprinted sheets, blank sheets)
未印刷纸堆（空白纸堆）

70 small sheet-fed offset press
小型单张纸平版印刷机

71 inking unit (inker unit)
著墨装置

72 suction feeder
吸式给纸机

73 pile feeder
自动堆纸机，自动续纸器

74 instrument panel (control panel) with counter, pressure gauge (*Am.* gage), air regulator, and control switch for the sheet feeder (feeder)
装有计数器，压力计，空气调节器和给纸器控制开关之仪表盘（控制盘）

75 flat-bed offset press (offset machine) ('Mailänder' proofing press, proof press)
平台平版印刷机（打样机）

76 inking unit (inker unit)
著墨装置

77 inking rollers (ink rollers, inkers)
著墨滚轮

78 bed (press bed, type bed, forme bed, *Am.* form bed)
台（印版台）

79 cylinder with rubber blanket
具橡皮布之滚筒

80 starting and stopping lever for the printing unit
印刷装置的起动杆与停止杆

81 impression-setting wheel (impression-adjusting wheel)
印刷调节轮，压力调节轮

1-65 presses (machines) for letterpress printing (letterpress printing machines)
凸版印刷机

1 two-revolution flat-bed cylinder press
二週转凸版平台印刷机

2 impression cylinder
压印滚筒

3 lever for raising or lowering the cylinder
滚筒之升降杆（手柄）

4 feed table (feed board)
给纸台（板）

5 automatic sheet feeder (feeder) [operated by vacuum and air blasts]
单张自动给纸机[利用真空与吹气操作的]

6 air pump for the feeder and delivery
给纸与收纸用之气泵

7 inking unit (inker unit) with distributing rollers (distributor rollers, distributors) and forme rollers (*Am.* form rollers)
装有散墨滚（分布滚）与触版墨滚（水滚）之著墨装置

8 ink slab (ink plate) inking unit (inker unit)
著墨装置之调墨台（板）

9 delivery pile for printed paper
已印刷好之收纸堆

10 sprayer (anti set-off apparatus, anti set-off spray) for dusting the printed sheets
印纸张喷粉用之喷粉器[防反（转）印装置，防反印喷粉]

11 interleaving device
夹入间隔纸之装备

12 foot pedal for starting and stopping the press
印刷机之起动与停止踏板

13 platen press (platen machine, platen) [in section]
平压印刷机（剖面图，俗称圆盘机）

14 paper feed and delivery (paper feeding and delivery unit)
给纸与收纸装置

15 platen
压印板

16 toggle action (toggle-joint action)
肘节（曲柄）机构

17 bed (type bed, press bed, forme bed, *Am.* form bed)
印版台

18 forme rollers (*Am.* form rollers) (forme-inking, *Am.* forminking, rollers)
触版墨滚（水滚）

19 inking unit (inker unit) for distributing the ink (printing ink)
散墨用的著墨装置

20 stop-cylinder press (stop-cylinder machine)
停週压印刷机

21 feed table (feed board)
给纸台（板）

22 feeder mechanism (feeding apparatus, feeder)
给纸机械（给纸装备，给纸机）

23 pile of unprinted paper (blank paper, unprinted sheets, blank sheets)
未印刷之纸堆，空白纸堆

24 guard for the sheet feeder (feeder)
给纸机护板

25 pile of printed paper (printed sheets)
已印好之纸堆

26 control mechanism
控制装置

27 forme rollers (*Am.* form rollers) (forme-inking, *Am.* forminking, rollers)
触版墨滚（水滚）

28 inking unit (inker unit)
著墨装置

29 [Heidelberg] platen press (platen machine, platen)
海德堡圆盘机

30 feed table (feed board) with pile of unprinted paper (blank paper, unprinted sheets, blank sheets)
具未印刷纸堆的给纸台

31 delivery table
收纸台

32 starting and stopping lever
起动杆（手柄）与停止杆

33 delivery blower
收纸吹风器

34 spray gun (sprayer)
喷枪

35 air pump for vacuum and air blasts
真空和吹气用之气泵

36 locked-up forme (*Am.* form)
装版（组版）装妥待印之活版印刷版

37 type (type matter, matter)
铅字（铅字材料）

38 chase
排版框

39 quoin
紧版楔子

40 length of furniture
活版填料之长度

41 rotary letterpress press (rotary letterpress machine, web-fed letterpress machine) for newspapers of up to 16 pages
适用於 16 页报纸之凸版轮转印刷机

42 slitters for dividing the width of the web
卷筒纸之宽度分切器

43 web
卷筒纸（滚筒纸）

44 impression cylinder
压印滚筒

45 jockey roller (compensating roller, compensator, tension roller)
操作滚轮（补偿滚轮，补偿器，张力滚轮）

46 roll of paper
卷筒纸

47 automatic brake
自动制动器

48 first printing unit
正面印刷装置（第一面印刷装置）

49 perfecting unit
双面印刷装置

50 inking unit (inker unit)
著墨装置

51 plate cylinder
印版滚筒

52 second printing unit
反面印刷装置（第二面印刷装置）

53 former
折页三角板

54 tachometer with sheet counter
具计纸量之转速器

55 folder (folder unit)
折页机

56 folded newspaper
已折叠好之报纸

57 inking unit (inker unit) for the rotary press (web-fed press) [in section]
轮转（卷筒纸）印刷机之著墨装置[剖面图]

58 web
卷筒纸

59 impression cylinder
压印滚筒

60 plate cylinder
印版滚筒

61 forme rollers (*Am.* form rollers) (forme-inking, *Am.* forminking, rollers)
触版墨滚（着墨滚）

62 distributing rollers (distributor rollers, distributors)
散墨滚（分布滚，匀墨滚）

63 lifter roller (ductor, ductor roller)
升墨滚（给水滚，给墨滚）

64 duct roller (fountain roller, ink fountain roller)
墨槽导滚（给水滚或给墨滚）

65 ink duct (ink fountain)
油墨槽，墨斗

182 Photogravure (Gravure Printing, Intaglio Printing)

1 exposure of the carbon tissue
(pigment paper)
碳素纸之曝光（颜料纸）
2 vacuum frame
真空晒版框
3 exposing lamp, a bank of
quartzhalogen lamps
曝光灯，石英卤素排灯
4 point source lamp
点光源灯
5 heat extractor
抽热器，散热器
6 carbon tissue transfer machine
(laydown machine, laying
machine)
碳素纸之转版机（过版机）凹版过版机
7 polished copper cylinder
抛光的铜滚筒
8 rubber roller for pressing on the
printed carbon tissue (pigment
paper)
压在印过碳素纸上之橡皮滚轮（颜料
纸）
9 cylinder-processing machine
滚筒式显影机（滚筒式版面冲洗机）
10 gravure cylinder coated with
carbon tissue (pigment paper)
著碳素纸之凹印滚筒
11 developing tank
显影槽
12 staging
护膜处理或分段腐蚀
13 developed cylinder
显影滚筒
14 retoucher painting out (stopping
out)
修版（局部描胶，局部涂保护剂）
15 etching machine
腐蚀机
16 etching tank with etching
solution (etchant, mordant)
装有腐蚀液（剂）之腐蚀槽
17 printed gravure cylinder
印过之凹版滚筒（已具线划之凹版滚
筒）
18 gravure etcher
凹版腐蚀工
19 calculator dial
计算器标度盘
20 timer
计时器
21 revising (correcting) the cylinder
修正滚筒架
22 etched gravure cylinder
腐蚀过之凹版滚筒
23 ledge
台板
24 multicolour (Am. multicolor)
rotogravure press
彩色轮转凹版印刷机
25 exhaust pipe for solvent fumes
溶剂气体排出管
26 reversible printing unit
反转印刷单位
27 folder (folder unit)
折页机（折页装置）
28 control desk
控制台，操纵台
29 newspaper delivery unit
报纸递（收）纸装置
30 conveyor belt (conveyor)
输纸带（输纸装置）
31 bundled stack of newspapers
捆好之报纸堆

1-35 hand bookbindery (hand
bindery)
手工书籍装订所
1 gilding the spine of the book
书背烫金
2 gold finisher (gilder), a
bookbinder
烫金工，装订工
3 fillet
饰线用之工具
4 holding press (finishing press)
烫金机（加工机）
5 gold leaf
金箔
6 gold cushion
金箔之垫板
7 gold knife
金箔之切割刀
8 sewing (stitching)
绳线订书
9 sewing frame
手工绳线装订架
10 sewing cord
订书线
11 ball of thread (sewing thread)
订书之线球
12 section (signature)
折叠目，书帖（折叠记号，印好折叠号
码待装订之纸张）
13 bookbinder's knife
装订用刀
14 gluing the spine
书背上胶

15 glue pot
胶桶
16 board cutter (guillotine)
纸板裁切机（裁断机）
17 back gauge (*Am.* gage)
后量规
18 clamp with foot pedal
脚踏式之压纸柄
19 cutting blade
切刀
20 standing press, a nipping press
固定机（加压机）
21 head piece (head beam)
顶梁
22 spindle
主轴，导杆
23 handwheel
操纵轮
24 platen
加压盘
25 bed (base)
基座
26 gilding (gold blocking) and
embossing press, a hand-lever
press; *sim.:* toggle-joint press
(toggle-lever press)
烫金压花机，手动式榫杆压力机；类
似：肘节压力机
27 heating box
加热箱
28 sliding plate
滑动板
29 embossing platen
压花板

30 toggle action (toggle-joint
action)
肘节部分
31 hand lever
手动杆
32 book sewn on gauze (mull,
scrim) (unbound book)
缝上纱布之书籍（未装订之书）
33 gauze (mull, scrim)
纱布（书背用布，平纹布，绵织品或麻
织品）
34 sewing (stitching)
线订部分（线装）
35 headband
绑带头，堵头布

1-23 bookbinding machines
书籍装订机

1 adhesive binder (perfect binder) for short runs
短版胶装机

2 manual feed station
手工给料台

3 cutoff knife and roughing station
裁刀与铣背机

4 gluing mechanism
上胶装置

5 delivery (book delivery)
收书口

6 case maker (case-making machine)
书套制作机

7 board feed hopper
给纸板装置

8 pickup sucker
吸纸器

9 glue tank
胶水槽

10 cover cylinder
书壳滚筒

11 picker head
吸纸头

12 feed table for covering materials [linen, paper, leather]
封面材料之供应台〔亚麻布，纸，皮〕

13 pressing mechanism
加压装置

14 delivery table
收书台

15 gang stitcher (gathering and wire-stitching machine, gatherer and wire stitcher)
穿线装订机（配页铁丝订书机）

16 sheet feeder (sheet-feeding station)
给纸装置

17 folder-feeding station
摺页之给纸装置

18 stitching wire feed mechanism
订书铁丝之供应装置

19 delivery table
收书台

20 rotary board cutter (rotary board-cutting machine)
轮转纸版切割机

21 feed table with cut-out section
带裁刀之给纸台

22 rotary cutter
旋转切刀

23 feed guide
给纸导规

1-35 bookbinding machines
书籍装订机械
1　guillotine (guillotine cutter,
automatic guillotine cutter)
裁纸机（自动裁纸机）
2　control panel
控制盘
3　clamp
压纸装置
4　back gauge (*Am.* gage)
后量规
5　calibrated pressure adjustment
[to clamp]
校准压力调节器"对夹具"
6　illuminated cutting scale
带照明装置之裁切标尺
7　single-hand control for the back
gauge (*Am.* gage)
后量规之单手控制器
8　combined buckle and knife
folding machine (combined
buckle and knife folder)
带扣与刀混和之摺叠机
9　feed table (feed board)
给纸台
10　fold plates
折页板
11　stop for making the buckle fold
使带扣摺叠之停止装置
12　cross fold knives
横向摺叠刀，直角摺叠用之刀
13　belt delivery for parallel-folded
signatures
平行摺叠记号之带式递送装置（纵向摺
叠）
14　third cross fold unit
三次横折装置，第三直角摺叠装置
15　delivery tray for cross-folded
signatures
直角折叠记号用之递送盘（横向摺叠）
16　sewing machine (book-sewing
machine)
绳线装订机
17　spool holder
线轴架
18　thread cop (thread spool)
圆锥型线团（线轴）
19　gauze roll holder (mull roll
holder, scrim roll holder)
纱布卷架（平纹布卷架书背用布）
20　gauze (mull, scrim)
纱布（书背用布，平纹布）
21　needle cylinder with sewing
needles
带缝纫针之针滚筒
22　sewn book
缝好纱布之书芯
23　delivery
收书之装置
24　reciprocating saddle
往复移动之骑马钉鞍座
25　sheet feeder (feeder)
给纸器
26　feed hopper
给纸装置
27　casing-in machine
装套机（上封机）
28　joint and side pasting
attachment
压槽与书脊侧上胶附件
29　blade
刮刀
30　preheater unit
预热装置

31　gluing machine for
wholesurface, stencil, edge, and
strip gluing
（上胶机）全书面，压花板，切口及书
带粘合用之上胶机
32　glue tank
胶水筒
33　glue roller
胶水滚轮
34　feed table
给书装置
35　delivery
收书台
36 book
书
37　dust jacket (dust cover,
bookjacket, wrapper), a
publisher's wrapper
书皮（书套，封套）出版社之封套（包
装纸）
38　jacket flap
书套耳页
39　blurb
印于书套耳页之广告
40-42 binding
装订
40　cover (book cover, case)
封面（书籍封面，书壳）
41　spine (backbone, back)
书背，书背
42　tailband (footband)
书背之装订线
**43-47 preliminary matter (prelims,
front matter)**
书籍正文前之附页
43　half-title
简略书名（标题）
44　half-title (bastard title, fly title)
半标题，简略书名（简略标题）
45　title page
扉页
46　full title (main title)
全书名（主标题）
47　subtitle
副标题
48　publisher's imprint (imprint)
出版社之印记
49　fly leaf (endpaper, endleaf)
衬页，糊贴页（书籍卷首或卷尾之空白
页）
50　handwritten dedication
手写题辞
51　bookplate (ex libris)
藏书者之印记，藏书签名，书本标签
52　open book
翻开之书
53　page
页
54　fold
折合处
55-58 margin
页边空白处
55　back margin (inside margin,
gutter)
书脊边空白处，订口
56　head margin (upper margin)
（页数上端）空白处上边空白
57　fore edge margin (outside
margin, fore edge)
（页数前端）空白处，前边空白
58　tail margin (foot margin, tail,
foot)
（页数下端）空白处，下边空白
59　type area
版面

60　chapter heading
章节标题
61　asterisk
星号
62　footnote
注脚，脚注
63　page number
页数
64　double-column page
双栏页
65　column
栏
66　running title (running head)
栏外标题
67　caption
标题
68　marginal note (side note)
旁注
69　signature (signatue code)
摺页符号
70　attached bookmark (attached
bookmarker)
贴付於书上之书签
71　loose bookmark (loose
bookmarker)
活书签

1-54 carriages (vehicles, conveyances, horse-drawn vehicles)
马车（车辆，马车）

1-3, 26-39, 45, 51-54 carriages and coaches (coach wagons)
马车及轿式大马车

1 berlin
有篷的四轮马车

2 waggonette (*larger*: brake, break)
（有相等两排纵座的）四轮游览马车
（较大的：四轮大马车）

3 coupé; *sim.*: brougham
双座轿式四轮马车

4 front wheel
前轮

5 coach body
车身

6 dashboard (splashboard)
挡泥板

7 footboard
踏脚板

8 coach box (box, coachman's seat, driver's seat)
车夫座位

9 lamp (lantern)
车灯

10 window
车窗

11 door (coach door)
车门

12 door handle (handle)
车门把手

13 footboard (carriage step, coach step, step, footpiece)
踏脚板（上下车踏板）

14 fixed top
固定车顶（车篷）

15 spring
弹簧

16 brake (brake block)
刹车（刹车块）

17 back wheel (rear wheel)
后轮

18 dogcart, a one-horse carriage
单马双轮小马车

19 shafts (thills, poles)
车杠，车辕（马车的杠和辕，马车的辕杆）

20 lackey (lacquey, footman)
男仆跟班（侍者，随从）

21 livery
（男仆所穿的）制服

22 braided (gallooned) collar
镶边衣领

23 braided (gallooned) coat
镶边外套

24 braided (gallooned) sleeve
镶边袖口

25 top hat
大礼帽，高顶帽

26 hackney carriage (hackney coach, cab, growler, *Am.* hack)
出租马车，二马四轮马车

27 stableman (groom)
马夫

28 coach horse (carriage horse, cab horse, thill horse, thiller)
拉马车的马

29 hansom cab (hansom), a cabriolet, a one-horse chaise (one-horse carriage)
一马二轮双座有盖小马车（车夫座位为车篷后方）

30 shafts (thills, poles)
车杠，车辕

31 reins (rein, *Am.* line)
缰绳

32 coachman (driver) with inverness
著长披肩的车夫

33 covered char-a-banc (brake, break), a pleasure vehicle
有车篷的长形游览马车

34 gig (chaise)
单马二轮马车

35 barouche
一种四轮大马车

36 landau, a two-horse carriage; *sim.*: landaulet, landaulette
四轮有顶篷的马车；类似：小型之landau马车（二人乘坐之四轮马车）

37 omnibus (horse-drawn omnibus)
公共马车（马拉交通车）

38 phaeton
轻快的四轮敞篷马车

39 Continental stagecoach (mailcoach, diligence); *also*: road coach
欧式公共马车（邮政马车，公共马车）

40 mailcoach driver
邮政马车夫

41 posthorn
马车喇叭

42 hood
可摺叠车篷

43 post horses (relay horses, relays)
驿马

44 tilbury
双轮轻便马车（供二人乘坐）

45 troika (Russian three-horse carriage)
三头马车，三马并拉的马车（俄国三马马车）

46 leader
先导马

47 wheeler (wheelhorse, pole horse)
后马，辕马

48 English buggy
英式二轮单座马车

49 American buggy
美式四轮单座马车

50 tandem
两马前后纵驾的两轮马车

51 vis-a-vis
有面对面座位的马车

52 collapsible hood (collapsible top)
可摺叠的车篷

53 mailcoach (English stagecoach)
邮政马车（英国公共马车）

54 covered (closed) chaise
箱式四轮轻便马车

1 **bicycle** (cycle, *coll.* bike, *Am.* wheel), a gent's bicycle, a touring bicycle (touring cycle, roadster)
脚踏车，自行车
2 **handlebar** (handlebars), a touring cycle handlebar
车把（手），旅行自行车车把
3 **handlebar grip** (handgrip, grip)
车把（手）握套
4 **bicycle bell**
车铃
5 **hand brake** (front brake), a rim brake
手刹车（前刹车），轮缘刹车
6 **lamp bracket**
灯架
7 **headlamp** (bicycle lamp)
前灯（脚踏车灯）
8 **dynamo**
磨电机
9 **pulley**
磨电机滑轮
10-12 **front forks**
前叉
10 **handlebar stem**
车把（轴）主干
11 **steering head**
转向头
12 **fork blades** (fork ends)
前叉脚（叉端头）
13 **front mudguard** (*Am.* front fender)
前档泥板
14-20 **bicycle frame**
车架
14 **steering tube** (fork column)
转向管（前叉立柱）
15 **head badge**
车头标记
16 **crossbar** (top tube)
车架横杆
17 **down tube**
下管

18 **seat tube**
座管
19 **seat stays**
座垫支柱管，立叉
20 **chain stays**
链条支柱管，平叉
21 **child's seat** (child carrier seat)
小孩的座位
22 **bicycle saddle**
鞍座
23 **saddle springs**
鞍座弹簧
24 **seat pillar**
鞍座支柱
25 **saddle bag** (tool bag)
鞍座袋（工具袋）
26-32 **wheel** (front wheel)
前轮
26 **hub**
轮毂
27 **spoke**
轮辐（辐条）
28 **rim** (wheel rim)
胎环，钢圈
29 **spoke nipple** (spoke flange, spoke end)
轮辐螺纹接管（轮辐凸缘，轮辐端）
30 **tyres** (*Am.* tires) (tyre, pneumatic tyre, high-pressure tyre); *inside:* tube (inner tube), *outside:* tyre (outer case, cover)
轮胎（打气轮胎，高压轮胎）；内：内胎；外：外胎
31 **valve** a tube valve with valve tube or a patent valve with ball
气门，带气门管的管阀或带浮球的特制气门阀
32 **valve sealing cap**
气门封帽
33 **bicycle speedometer** with milometer
带计转器自行车速率计
34 **kick stand** (prop stand)
偏支车架（支柱架）

35-42 **bicycle drive** (chain drive)
自行车转动装置（链条转动装置）
35-39 **chain transmission**
链条转动
35 **chain wheel**
链轮
36 **chain,** a roller chain
链条，滚轮链条
37 **chain guard**
链罩（盖）
38 **sprocket wheel** (sprocket)
链轮
39 **wing nut** (fly nut, butterfly nut)
翼形螺帽
40 **pedal**
踏板
41 **crank**
（踏板）曲柄
42 **bottom bracket bearing**
底托架轴承，中轴
43 **rear mudguard** (*Am.* rear fender)
后挡泥板
44 **luggage carrier** (carrier)
（载）带物架
45 **reflector**
反光镜
46 **rear light** (rear lamp)
后灯
47 **footrest**
搁脚板
48 **bicycle pump**
自行车气筒
49 **bicycle lock,** a wheel lock
车锁
50 **patent key**
专用钥匙
51 **cycle serial number** (factory number, frame number)
自行车号码（工厂号码，车架号码）

52 front hub (front hub assembly)
  前毂（前毂配件组合）
53 wheel nut
  车轮螺帽
54 locknut (locking nut)
  併紧螺帽
55 washer (slotted cone adjusting washer)
  垫圈（有槽锥形调整垫圈）
56 ball bearing
  球轴承
57 dust cap
  防尘盖
58 cone (adjusting cone)
  锥形螺母（可调锥形螺母）
59 centre (*Am.* center) hub
  中心毂
60 spindle
  心轴
61 axle
  车轴，轮轴
62 clip covering lubrication hole (lubricator)
  夹片盖式注油孔（润滑器）
63 free-wheel hub with back-pedal brake (with coaster brake)
  脚刹车飞轮（自动轮）毂
64 safety nut
  安全螺帽
65 lubricator
  润滑器
66 brake arm
  刹车臂
67 brake arm cone
  刹车臂锥形螺帽
68 bearing cup with ball bearings in ball race
  球珠座圈中带滚珠轴承的轴承杯
69 hub shell (hub body, hub barrel)
  毂外壳（套筒）
70 brake casing
  刹车（壳）鞘
71 brake cone
  刹车锥体

72 driver
  驱动轮
73 driving barrel
  转动筒
74 sprocket
  链轮
75 thread head
  螺纹端部（头）
76 axle
  车轴、轮轴
77 bracket
  托架
78 bicycle pedal (pedal, reflector pedal)
  自行车踏板（踏板，反光镜踏板）
79 cup
  脚蹬碗
80 spindle
  心轴
81 axle
  轴
82 dust cap
  防尘盖
83 pedal frame
  踏板架
84 rubber stud
  橡皮固定螺丝
85 rubber block (rubber tread)
  橡皮块（橡皮踏板）
86 glass reflector
  玻璃反射镜

1 folding bicycle
可摺自行车
2 hinge (*also*: locking lever)
铰接（亦称：锁杆）
3 adjustable handlebar
(handlebars)
可调整把手
4 adjustable saddle
可调整鞍座
5 stabilizers
稳定轮
6 motor-assisted bicycle
马达助动的自行车，摩托车
7 air-cooled two-stroke engine
气冷式二冲程发动机（引擎）
8 telescopic forks
可伸缩的筒式前叉
9 tubular frame
圆管车架
10 fuel tank (petrol tank, *Am.*
gasoline tank)
燃料槽（油槽）油箱
11 semi-rise handlebars
半升式车把
12 two-speed gear-change
(gearshift)
二速换档（齿轮变速器）
13 high-back polo saddle
高背马球型鞍座
14 swinging-arm rear fork
摆动后叉
15 upswept exhaust
上斜排气管
16 heat shield
遮热板
17 drive chain
传动链
18 crash bar (roll bar)
护杆（滚条）
19 speedometer (*coll.* speedo)
速率计（里程表）
20 battery-powered moped, an
electrically-powered vehicle
电池动力的摩拖车电动车的一种
21 swivel saddle
活动鞍座
22 battery compartment
蓄电池箱
23 wire basket
金属丝货篮
24 touring moped (moped)
旅行摩托车
25 pedal crank (pedal drive, starter
pedal)
踏板曲柄（脚蹬驱动，起动踏板）
26 single-cylinder two-stroke
engine
单缸二冲程发动机（引擎）
27 spark-plug cap
火星塞盖
28 fuel tank (petrol tank, *Am.*
gasoline tank)
燃料箱，油箱
29 moped headlamp (front lamp)
摩托车前灯
30-35 handlebar fittings
车把配件
30 twist grip throttle control
(throttle twist grip)
握转油门控制
31 twist grip (gear-change,
gearshift)
换档握把（变换齿轮）
32 clutch lever
离合器握柄

33 hand brake lever
手刹车握柄
34 speedometer (*coll.* speedo)
速率器
35 rear-view mirror (mirror)
后视镜
36 front wheel drum brake (drum
brake)
前轮鼓式刹车
37 Bowden cables (brake
cables)
包登式刹车索
38 stop and tail light unit
刹车灯和尾灯装置
39 light motorcycle with kickstarter
带脚蹬起动器的轻型摩托车
40 housing for instruments with
speedometer and electronic rev
counter (revolution counter)
带速率器和电子转速计（转速表）的仪
表盘
41 telescopic shock absorber
伸缩式避震器
42 twin seat
双人座
43 kickstarter
脚蹬起动器
44 pillion footrest, a footrest
后座搁脚板
45 handlebar (handlebars)
车把
46 chain guard
护链装置
47 motor scooter (scooter)
小轮摩托车（速克达）
48 removable side panel
可拆侧板
49 tubular frame
管制车架
50 metal fairings
金属整流罩（减阻物）
51 prop stand (stand)
支车架
52 foot brake
脚刹车
53 horn (hooter)
喇叭
54 hook for handbag or briefcase
手提包或公文包的挂钩
55 foot gear-change control (foot
gearshift control)
脚换档控制
56 high-riser; *sim.*: Chopper
高把自行车
57 high-rise handlebar (handlebars)
高把自行车的把手
58 imitation motorcycle fork
模仿摩托车前叉
59 banana saddle
香蕉型鞍座
60 chrome bracket
镀铬托架

1 lightweight motorcycle (light motorcycle) [50 cc]
轻型摩托车[50 cc]

2 fuel tank (petrol tank, *Am.* gasoline tank)
油箱

3 air-stroke single-cyclinder four-stroke engine (with overhead camshaft)
气冷式单缸四冲程引擎（带顶上凸轮轴）

4 carburettor (*Am.* carbouretor)
汽化器（化油器）

5 intake pipe
进气管

6 five-speed gearbox
五速齿轮箱

7 swinging-arm rear fork
摆动后叉

8 number plate (*Am.* license plate)
牌照

9 stop and tail light (rear light)
停车尾灯

10 headlight (headlamp)
前灯

11 front drum brake
前鼓轮刹车

12 brake cable (brake line), a Bowden cable
刹车线，包登式刹车线

13 rear drum brake
后鼓轮刹车

14 racing-style twin seat
赛车型双人座

15 upswept exhaust
上斜排气管

16 scrambling motorcycle (cross-country motorcycle) [125 cc], a light motorcycle
越野摩托车[125 cc]，轻型摩托车的一种

17 lightweight cradle frame
轻型炮架型车架

18 number disc (disk)
号码盘

19 solo seat
单人座

20 cooling robs
散热片，冷却肋

21 motorcycle stand
摩托车支架

22 motorcycle shain
摩托车链条

23 telescopic shock absorber
伸缩避震器

24 spokes
轮辐

25 rim (wheel rim)
（轮网，轮圈）钢圈

26 motorcycle tyre (*Am.* tire)
摩托车轮胎

27 tyre (*Am.* tire) tread
轮胎面，轮箍面

28 gear-change lever (gearshift lever)
齿轮变换杆

29 twist grip throttle control (throttle twist grip)
握转油门控制

30 rear-view mirror (mirror)
后视镜

31-58 heavy (heavyweight, large-capacity) motorcycles
重型摩托车

31 heavyweight motorcycle with water-cooled engine
具水冷式引擎的重型摩托车

32 front disc (disk) brake
前轮圆盘制动器

33 disc (disk) brake calliper (caliper)
圆盘制动卡

34 floating axle
浮动车轴

35 water cooler
水冷却器

36 oil tank
油箱

37 indicator (indicator light, turn indicator light)
指示器（指示灯，转向指示灯）

38 kickstarter
脚蹬起动器

39 water-cooled engine
水冷式引擎

40 speedometer
速率计

41 rev counter (revolution counter)
转速表

42 rear indicator (indicator light)
后方向灯（指示灯）

43 heavy (heavyweight, high-performance) machine with fairing [1 000 cc]
带流线形外壳的重型摩托车[1 000 cc]

44 integrated streamlining, an integrated fairing
流线型车罩，整体减阻罩

45 indicator (indicator light, turn indicator light)
指示器（指示灯，转向指示灯）

46 anti-mist windscreen (*Am.* windshield)
防雾挡风玻璃

47 horizontally-opposed twin engine with cardan transmission
带方向转动装置的水平对置式双缸引擎

48 light alloy wheel
轻合金车轮

49 four-cyclinder machine [400 cc]
四缸摩托车[400 cc]

50 air-cooled four-cyclinder four-stroke engine
气冷式四缸四冲程引擎

51 four-pipe megaphone exhaust pipe
四管喇叭筒式排气管

52 electric starter button
电动发动器按钮，起动器电钮

53 sidecar machine
带侧边车的摩托车

54 sidecar body
边车车身

55 sidecar crash bar
边车防护杆

56 sidelight (*Am.* sidemarker lamp)
边灯（侧面车种表示灯）

57 sidecar wheel
边车轮

58 sidecar windscreen (*Am.* windshield)
边车挡风玻璃

1 eight-cylinder V (vee)
fuelinjection spark-ignition
engine (Otto-cycle engine)
八缸 V 型燃料喷射火花点火引擎（奥图
循环引擎）

2 cross-section of spark-ignition
engine (Otto-cycle internal
combustion engine)
火花点火引擎的剖面图（奥图循环内燃
机）

3 sectional view of five-cylinder
in-line diesel engine
五汽缸单排柴油引擎剖面图

4 cross-section of diesel engine
柴油发动机的剖面图

5 two-rotor Wankel engine
(rotary engine)
二转子汪克引擎（旋缸发动机）

6 single-cylinder two-stroke
internal combustion engine
单缸二冲程内燃机

7 fan
（冷却）风扇

8 fan clutch for viscous drive
粘性驱动用的风扇离合器

9 ignition distributor (distributor)
with vacuum timing control
真空定时控制的点火分配器

10 double roller chain
双滚轮链

11 camshaft bearing
凸轮轴轴承

12 air-bleed duct
空气分供导管

13 oil pipe for camshaft lubrication
凸轮轴润滑油管

14 camshaft, an overhead camshaft
凸轮轴，一种顶上凸轮轴

15 venturi throat
文氏喉管

16 intake silencer (absorption
silencer, Am. absorption
muffler)
吸气消音器

17 fuel pressure regulator
燃料压力调节器

18 inlet manifold
进气歧管

19 cylinder crankcase
汽缸曲轴箱

20 flywheel
飞轮

21 connecting rod (piston rod)
连杆（活塞管）

22 cover of crankshaft bearing
曲轴轴承盖

23 crankshaft
曲轴

24 oil bleeder screw (oil drain plug)
放油栓（排油塞）

25 roller chain of oil pump drive
油泵驱动的滚轮链

26 vibration damper
减震器，消震器

27 distributor shaft for the ignition
distributor (distributor)
点火分配器用的分配器轴

28 oil filler neck
加油管嘴，油填注颈

29 diaphragm spring
膜片弹簧

30 control linkage
操作用的连杆组

31 fuel supply pipe (Am. fuel line)
燃料（油）供给管

32 fuel injector (injection nozzle)
燃料喷射器（喷油咀）

33 rocker arm
摇臂

34 rocker arm mounting
摇臂支座

35 spark plug (sparking plug) with
suppressor
带抑制器的火星塞

36 exhaust manifold
排气歧管

37 piston with piston rings and oil
scraper ring
带活塞环和刮油环的活塞

38 engine mounting
引擎支座

39 dog flange (dog)
牵转具凸轮

40 crankcase
曲轴箱

41 oil sump (sump)
油池

42 oil pump
油泵

43 oil filter
滤油器

44 starter motor (starting motor)
起动马达

45 cylinder head
缸盖（头）

46 exhaust valve
排气阀

47 dipstick
量油尺

48 cylinder head gasket
缸头垫片

49 double bushing chain
双轴套链

50 warm-up regulator
温车运转调整器

51 tapered needle for idling
adjustment
空转调整用的锥形针

52 fuel pressure pipe (fuel pressure
line)
燃料压力管

53 fuel leak line (drip fuel line)
漏油管（滴油管）

54 injection nozzle (spray nozzle)
喷（油）咀

55 heater plug
加热器塞

56 thrust washer
止推垫圈

57 intermediate gear shaft for the
injection pump drive
喷油泵驱动用的中间齿轮轴

58 injection timer unit
喷油定时装置

59 vacuum pump (low-pressure
regulator)
真空泵（低压调整器）

60 cam for vacuum pump
真空泵用凸轮

61 water pump (coolant pump)
水泵（冷却泵）

62 cooling water thermostat
冷水恒温器

63 thermo time switch
温度定时开关

64 fuel hand pump
手动燃（油）料泵

65 injection pump
喷油泵

66 glow plug
预热塞

67 oil pressur limiting valve
油压限制阀

68 rotor
转子

69 seal
封垫

70 torque converter
扭矩变速器

71 single-plate clutch
单片离合器

72 multi-speed gearing (multi-step
gearing)
多速齿轮转动装置（多级齿轮转动装
置）

73 port liners in the exhaust
manifold for emission control
控制排气量的排气歧管口衬垫

74 disc (disk) brake
圆盘刹车器

75 differential gear (differential)
差速齿轮

76 generator
发电机

77 foot gear-change control (foot
gearshift control)
换档控制踏板

78 dry multi-plate clutch
乾式多片离合器

79 cross-draught (Am. cross-draft)
carburettor (Am. carburetor)
交叉通气式的汽化器（化油器）

80 cooling ribs
冷却肋，散热片

**1-56 motor car (car, *Am.*
automobile, auto), a passenger
vehicle**
小轿车，一种客车
1 monocoque body (unitary body)
单壳车体（单位车体）
**2 chassis, the understructure of
the body**
底盘，车身底架
3 front wing (*Am.* front fender)
前翼（前挡板）
4 car door
车门
5 door handle
车门把手
6 door lock
车门锁
7 boot lid (*Am.* trunk lid)
行李箱盖
8 bonnet (*Am.* hood)
引擎盖（发动机盖）
9 radiator
散热器（水箱）
10 cooling water pipe
冷却水管
11 radiator grill
散热器护栅，水箱饰篦
12 badging
标记
**13 rubber-covered front bumper
(*Am.* front fender)**
用塑胶橡皮包住的前保险杆[前挡板]
14 car wheel, a disc (disk) wheel
车轮，圆盘式车轮
15 car tyre (*Am.* automobile tire)
车胎
16 rim (wheel rim)
轮辋，钢圈
17-18 disc (disk) brake
制动盘（盘式刹车）
17 brake disc (disk) (braking disc)
制动盘，刹车盘
18 calliper (caliper)
刹车夹

**19 front indicator light (front turn
indicator light)**
前指示灯（前转向指示灯）
**20 headlight (headlamp) with main
beam (high beam), dipped beam
(low beam), sidelight (side
lamp, *Am.* sidemarker lamp)**
有强光，弱光，边灯的前灯（大灯）
**21 windscreen (*Am.* windshield), a
panoramic windscreen**
挡风玻璃，一种广角挡风玻璃
22 crank-operated car window
摇把（曲轴）操纵的车窗
23 quarter light (quarter vent)
三角窗（边窗）
24 boot(*Am.* trunk)
行李箱
25 spare wheel
备用车轮
26 damper (shock absorber)
减震器
27 trailing arm
从动臂
28 coil spring
螺旋弹簧
29 silencer (*Am.* muffler)
消音器
30 automatic ventilation system
自动通风系统
31 rear seats
后座
32 rear window
后窗
**33 adjustable headrest (head
restraint)**
可调式座椅头枕
34 driver's seat, a reclining seat
驾驶员座位，倾斜式座位
35 reclining backrest
倾斜靠背
36 passenger seat
乘客座位
37 steering wheel
方向盘

**38 centre (*Am.* center) console
containing speedometer (*coll.*
speedo), revolution counter
(rev counter, tachometer), clock,
fuel gauge (*Am.* gage), water
temperature gauge, oil
temperature gauge**
中心仪表台，包括：速率表（里程
表），转速表，钟，油量表，水温表，
油温表
39 inside rear-view mirror
车内后视镜
40 left-hand wing mirror
左侧翼后视镜
**41 windscreen wiper (*Am.*
windshield wiper)**
挡风玻璃的雨刷
42 defroster vents
除霜器通气孔
43 carpeting
车垫
44 clutch pedal (*coll.* clutch)
离合器踏板
45 brake pedal (*coll.* brake)
刹车踏板
**46 accelerator pedal (*coll.*
accelerator)**
油门踏板
47 inlet vent
进气口，通风口
48 blower fan
风机
49 brake fluid reservoir
刹车油贮存器
50 battery
蓄电瓶
51 exhaust pipe
排气管
**52 front running gear with front
wheel drive**
以前轮驱动的前行齿轮
53 engine mounting
引擎架

54 intake silencer (*Am.* intake muffler)
进气消音器
55 air filter (air cleaner)
空气滤清器
56 right-hand wing mirror
右侧后视镜
57-90 dashboard (fascia panel)
仪表板
57 controlled-collapse steering column
可伸缩转向柱
58 steering wheel spoke
方向盘轮辐
59 indicator and dimming switch
转向指示灯和前灯减光开关
60 wiper/washer switch and horn
雨刷/冲洗器开关和喇叭按钮
61 side window blower
侧窗送风装置
62 sidelight, headlight, and parking light switch
侧灯、大灯和停车灯开关
63 fog lamp warning light
雾灯警示灯
64 fog headlamp and rear lamp switch
前雾灯和后雾灯开关
65 fuel gauge (*Am.* gage)
燃油表，油量表
66 water temperature gauge (*Am.* gage)
水温表
67 warning light for rear fog lamp
后雾灯警示灯号
68 hazard flasher switch
事故或危险闪光灯开关
69 main beam warning light
远光灯警示灯
70 electric rev counter (revolution counter)
电动转速表
71 fuel warning light
油量警示灯

72 warning light for the hand brake and dual-circuit brake system
手刹车和双迴路刹车系统警示灯
73 oil pressure warning light
油压警示灯
74 speedometer (*coll.* speedo) with trip mileage recorder
带行驶里程记录的速率表
75 starter and steering look
起动器和转向角限制器
76 warning lights for turn indicators and hazard flashers
转向指示灯和危险闪光灯的警示灯号
77 switch for the courtesy light and reset button for the trip mileage recorder
(车门打开后即自动开灯的)车箱灯开关和里程纪录器归零按钮
78 ammeter
电流表
79 electric clock
电钟
80 warning light for heated rear window
后窗加温警示灯
81 switch for the leg space ventilation
下部通风开关
82 rear window heating switch
后窗加温并关
83 ventilation switch
通风开关
84 temperature regulator
温度调节器
85 fresh-air inlet and control
新鲜空气入口及控制
86 fresh-air regulator
新鲜空气调节器
87 warm-air regulator
暖气调节器
88 cigar lighter
香烟点火器

89 glove compartment (glove box) lcok
工具箱锁
90 car radio
汽车收音机
91 gear lever (gearshift lever, floor-type gear-change)
变速杆(排档杆，落地式变速杆)
92 leather gaiter
防尘皮套
93 hand brake lever
手刹车杆
94 accelerator pedal
油门踏板
95 brake pedal
刹车踏板
96 clutch pedal
离合器踏板

1-15 carburettor (*Am.* carburetor), a down-draught (*Am.* downdraft) carburettor
化油器，一种下吸式化油器

1 idling jet (slow-running jet)
空转喷咀（低速运转喷咀）

2 idling air jet (idle air bleed)
空转空气喷咀（空转空气分供，排放装置）

3 air correction jet
空气调节喷咀

4 compensating airstream
补偿气流

5 main airstream
主气流

6 choke flap
阻气（挡风）板

7 plunger
柱塞

8 venturi
文氏管，喉管，窄颈管

9 throttle valve (butterfly valve)
节流阀（蝶形节流阀）

10 emulsion tube
乳化管

11 idle mixture adjustment screw
空转调整螺丝

12 main jet
主喷咀

13 fuel inlet (*Am.* gasoline inlet) (inlet manifold)
进油孔（进油歧管）

14 float chamber
浮筒室

15 float
浮筒

16-27 pressure-feed lubricating system
压力输送润滑系统

16 oil pump
油泵

17 oil sump
油池，油槽

18 sump filter
油池池过滤器

19 oil cooler
油冷却器

20 oil filter
油过滤器

21 main oil gallery (drilled gallery)
主油道

22 crankshaft drilling (crankshaft tributary, crankshaft bleed)
曲轴道（曲轴支管）

23 crankshaft bearing (main bearing)
曲轴轴承（主轴承）

24 camshaft bearing
凸轮轴轴承

25 connecting-rod bearing
连杆轴承

26 gudgeon pin (piston pin)
活塞销

27 bleed
泄放口，排放口

28-47 four-speed synchromesh gearbox
四速同步啮合齿轮箱

28 clutch pedal
离合器踏板

29 crankshaft
曲轴

30 drive shaft (propeller shaft)
驱动轴（驱动轴螺旋浆轴）

31 starting gear ring
起动齿轮圈

32 sliding sleeve for 3rd and 4th gear
三、四档的滑动套筒

33 synchronizing cone
同步驱动锥轮

34 helical gear wheel for 3rd gear
三档的螺旋齿轮

35 sliding sleeve for 1st and 2nd gear
一、二档的滑动套筒

36 helical gear wheel for 1st gear
一档的螺旋齿轮

37 lay shaft
副轴

38 speedometer drive
速计器驱动齿轮

39 helical gear wheel for speedometer drive
速率计驱动齿轮的螺旋齿轮

40 main shaft
主轴

41 gearshift rods
换档杆

42 selector fork for 1st and 2nd gear
一、二档的换档叉

43 helical gear wheel for 2nd gear
二档的螺旋齿轮

44 selector head with reverse gear
带倒车齿轮的（选择）换档器头

45 selector fork for 3rd and 4th gear
三、四档的换档叉

46 gear lever (gearshift lever)
变速杆（变速杆，换档杆）

47 gear-change pattern (gearshift pattern, shift pattern)
档位

48-55 disc (disk) brake [assembly]
盘式刹车（制动器）[组件]

48 brake disc (disk) (braking disc)
刹车盘

49 calliper (caliper), a fixed calliper with friction pads
刹车夹，具摩擦垫的固定刹车夹

50 servo cylinder (servo unit)
倍力汽缸（倍力装置）

51 brake shoes
刹车片

52 brake lining
刹车衬

53 outlet to brake line
通向刹车系统出口

54 wheel cylinder
刹车分泵

55 return spring
复位弹簧

56-59 steering gear (worm-and-nut steering gear)
转向齿轮（螺杆螺帽式转向齿轮）

56 steering column
转向机柱

57 worm gear sector
螺杆扇形齿轮

58 steering drop arm
转向垂臂

59 worm
螺杆

60-64 water-controlled heater
水控加热器

60 air intake
进气口

61 heat exchanger (heater box)
热交换器（加热器箱）

62 blower fan
风扇

63 flap valve
舌阀

64 defroster vent
除霜通气孔

65-71 live axle (rigid axle)
动轴（固定轴）

65 propeller shaft
驱动轴

66 trailing arm
前置定位臂

67 rubber bush
橡皮衬套

68 coil spring
螺旋弹簧

69 damper (shock absorber)
减震器

70 Panhard rod
横杆

71 stabilizer bar
稳定杆

72-84 MacPherson strut unit
烛式悬架装置

72 body-fixing plate
车体固定板

73 upper bearing
上轴承

74 suspension spring
悬吊弹簧

75 piston rod
活塞杆

76 suspension damper
悬吊减震器

77 rim (wheel rim)
轮缘，钢圈

78 stub axle
转（向）轴

79 steering arm
转向臂

80 track-rod ball-joint
横杆球关节

81 trailing link arm
前置定位斜臂

82 bump rubber (rubber bonding)
缓冲橡胶块（橡胶连接）

83 lower bearing
下轴承

84 lower suspension arm
下悬吊臂

1-36 car models (*Am.* **automobile models)** 小轿车型式

1 eight-cylinder limousine with three rows of three-abreast seating 三列三座八汽缸的大轿车（豪华轿车）

2 driver's door 司机门

3 rear door 后车门

4 four-door saloon car (*Am.* four-door sedan) 四门轿车

5 front door 前车门

6 rear door 后车门

7 front seat headrest (front seat head restraint) 前座头枕

8 rear seat headrest (rear seat head restraint) 后座头枕

9 convertible 摺篷车

10 convertible (collapsible) hood (top) 可摺叠车顶（篷）

11 bucket seat 箕形座（座板可翻起之座位）

12 buggy (dune buggy) 汽车，小客车（砂土车）

13 roll bar 安全铁杆（架），翻车保护杆

14 fibre glass body 玻璃纤维车身

15 estate car (shooting brake, estate, *Am.* station wagon) 实用车，客货两用轿车（旅行车）

16 tailgate 车尾闸板

17 boot space (luggage compartment) 行李箱

18 three-door hatchback 带后舱口的三门轿车

19 small three-door car 小型三门轿车

20 rear door (tailgate) 后车门（车尾闸板）

21 sill 梁（车体底框的梁）

22 folding back seat 摺叠靠背座椅

23 boot (luggage compartment, *Am.* trunk) 行李箱

24 sliding roof (sunroof, steel sunroof) 滑顶

25 two-door saloon car (*Am.* two-door sedan) 二门轿车

26 roadster (hard-top), a two-seater 双座跑车（金属顶盖）

27 hard top 金属顶盖

28 sporting coupé, a two-plus-two coupé (two-seater with removable back seats) 赛车，一种"二加二"座小客车（两个座位可折成靠背座椅）

29 fastback (liftback) 长坡度的车顶，可掀起的车顶

30 spoiler rim 扰流板边缘

31 integral headrest (integral head restraint) 整体头枕

32 GT car (gran turismo car) GT 小轿车

33 integral bumper (*Am.* integral fender) 整体式保险杆

34 rear spoiler 后扰流板

35 back 车后部

36 front spoiler 前扰流板

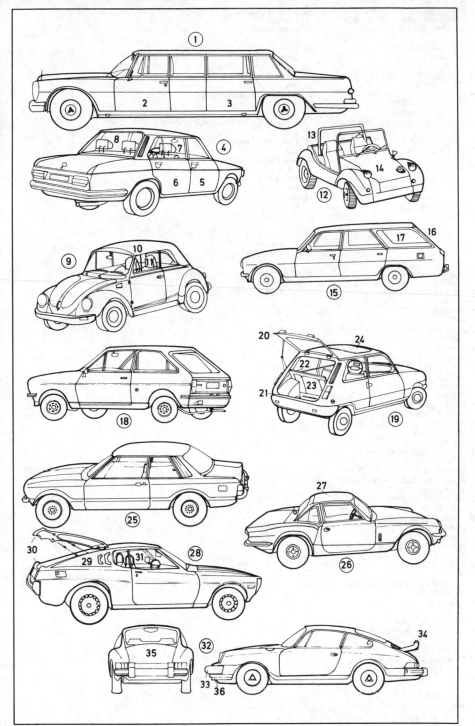

1 light cross-country lorry
(light truck, pickup truck) with
all-wheel drive (four-wheel
drive)
（全）四轮驱动的轻型越野卡车

2 cab (driver's cab)
驾驶座

3 loading platform (body)
载货台（装载台）

4 spare tyre (*Am.* spare tire), a
cross-country tyre
备用轮胎，越野轮胎

5 light lorry (light truck, pickup
truck)
轻型货车（轻型卡车轻便卡车）

6 platform truck
平台卡车

7 medium van
中型有盖卡车

8 sliding side door [for loading
and unloading]
〔装卸货物用的〕滑动侧门

9 minibus
小型公车

10 folding top (sliding roof)
摺叠式车顶（滑顶）

11 rear door
后车门

12 hinged side door
铰链侧门

13 luggage compartment
行李箱

14 passenger seat
乘客座位

15 cab (driver's cab)
驾驶座

16 air inlet
进气口

17 motor coach (coach, bus)
长途客车

18 luggage locker
行李锁柜

19 hand luggage (suitcase, case)
手提行李（皮箱）

20 heavy lorry (heavy truck, heavy
motor truck)
重型卡车

21 tractive unit (tractor, towing
vehicle)
牵引装置（拖车）

22 trailer (drawbar trailer)
拖车（拉杆拖车）

23 swop platform (body)
交换（易）台

24 three-way tipper (three-way
dump truck)
三向倾卸卡车

25 tipping body (dump body)
倾卸车体

26 hydraulic cylinder
液压汽缸

27 supported container platform
支承货柜平台

28 articulated vehicle, a vehicle
tanker
连结车，一种油罐车辆

29 tractive unit (tractor, towing
vehicle)
牵引装置（拖车）

30-33 semi-trailer (skeletal)
半拖车（骨架）

30 tank
油罐

31 turntable
转盘

32 undercarriage
车盘底盘

33 spare wheel
备用车轮

34 midi bus [for short-route town
operations]
中型公车〔短距离市内运输用〕

35 outward-opening doors
向外开的门

36 double-deck bus (double-
decker bus)
双层公共汽车

37 lower deck (lower saloon)
下层

38 upper deck (upper saloon)
上层

39 boarding platform
上车台

40 trolley bus
电车（无轨电车）

41 current collector
集电器

42 trolley (trolley shoe)
触轮

43 overhead wires
架空电线

44 trolley bus trailer
无轨电车拖车

45 pneumatically sprung rubber
connection
气动弹力橡胶连结部分

1-55 agent's garage
(distributor's garage, *Am.*
specialty shop)
代理商修车厂

1-23 diagnostic test bay
诊断试车台，测试场

1 computer
电脑

2 main computer plug
主机插头

3 computer harness (computer cable)
电脑电线

4 switch from automatic to manual
从自动到手动开关

5 slot for program cards
程式卡片插入孔

6 print-out machine (printer)
列表机

7 condition report (data print-out)
条件报告（打出数据）

8 master selector (hand control)
主选择开关（手控）

9 light read-out [green: OK; red: not OK]
灯光显示〔绿：正确，红：错误〕

10 rack for program cards
程式卡片架

11 mains button
电源按钮，主按钮

12 switch for fast readout
快速显示开关

13 firing sequence insert
启动程序输入

14 shelf for used cards
用过的卡片架

15 cable boom
电线吊架

16 oil temperature sensor
油温感应器

17 test equipment for wheel and steering alignment
车轮和转向调整试验设备

18 right-hand optic plate
右边镜片

19 actuating transistors
致动电晶体设备

20 projector switch
聚光灯开关

21 check light for wheel alignment, a row of photocells
车轮定位检查灯，一排光电池

22 check light for steering alignment, a row of photocells
转向调整检查灯，一排光电池

23 power screwdriver
电动螺丝起子

24 beam setter
光束调节器

25 hydraulic lift
液压提升装置

26 adjustable arm of hydraulic lift
液压提升装置的调整臂

27 hydraulic lift pad
液压提升装置台

28 excavation
坑道

29 pressure gauge (*Am.* gage)
压力计

30 grease gun
注油枪

31 odds-and-ends box
零星物品箱

32 wall chart [of spare parts]
〔组零件〕一览表

33 automatic computer test
电脑自动检查

34 motor car (car, *Am.* automobile, auto), a passenger vehicle
小汽车，客车

35 engine compartment
发动机（引擎）箱

36 bonnet (*Am.* hood)
发动机（引擎）罩

37 bonnet support (*Am.* hood support)
发动机（引擎）罩支柱

38 computer harness (computer cable)
电脑电线

39 main computer socket; *also:* multi-outlet socket
主机插座；多出口插座

40 oil temperature sensor
油温感应器

41 wheel mirror for visual wheel and steering alignment
目视车轮定位转向对准用的车轮镜

42 tool trolley
工具推车

43 tools
工具

44 impact wrench
冲击扳手

45 torque wrench
扭矩扳手

46 body hammer (roughing-out hammer)
车身用锤（粗车锤）

47 vehicle under repair, a minibus
修理中心的汽车，小型巴士

48 car location number
车位号码

49 rear engine
后发动机（引擎）

50 tailgate
车尾闸板

51 exhaust system
排气系统

52 exhaust repair
排气系统修理

53 motor car mechanic (motor vehicle mechanic, *Am.* automotive mechanic)
汽车修理工人

54 air hose
充气软管

55 intercom
内部通话装置

1-29 service station (petrol station, filling station, *Am.* gasoline station, gas station), a selfservice station
加油站，一种自助加油站

1 petrol (*Am.* gasoline) pump (blending pump) for regular and premium grade petrol (*Am.* gasoline (*sim.*: for derv)
用於普通和高級汽油的油泵（混合泵）

2 hose (petrol pump, *Am.* gasoline pump, hose)
软管（油泵的软管）

3 nozzle
喷咀

4 cash readout
现金数目显示（器）

5 volume read-out
容量显示（器）

6 price display
价格显示

7 indicator light
指示灯

8 driver using self-service petrol pump (*Am.* gasoline pump)
使用自助油泵的驾驶人

9 fire extinguisher
灭火器

10 paper-towel dispenser
擦手纸分配器

11 paper towel
擦手纸

12 litter receptacle
废物箱，垃圾箱

13 two-stroke blending pump
二冲程混合泵

14 meter
量器

15 engine oil
机油

16 oil can
油壶

17 tyre pressure gauge (*Am.* tire pressure gage)
轮胎压力计

18 air hose
空气软管

19 static air tank
固定贮气槽（罐）

20 pressure gauge (*Am.* gage) (manometer)
压力计

21 air filler neck
充气咀

22 repair bay (repair shop)
修理间

23 car-wash hose, a hose (hosepipe)
洗车软管

24 accessory shop
附属修理间

25 petrol can (*Am.* gasoline can)
油罐

26 rain cape
雨篷

27 car tyres (*Am.* automobile tires)
汽车轮胎

28 car accessories
汽车附件

29 cash desk (console)
付款台

1 twelve-axle articulated railcar
  for interurban rail service
  都市间铁路的十二车轴有轨电车
2 current collector
  集电器
3 head of the railcar
  有轨电车车头
4 rear of the railcar
  有轨电车车尾
5 carriage A containing the motor
  装有电动机（马达）的第一节车厢
6 carriage B (*also:* carriages C and
  D)
  第二节车厢（同样：第三及第四节车
  厢）
7 carriage E containing the motor
  装有电动机（马达）的第五节车厢
8 rear controller
  后部操纵器
9 bogie
  转向架
10 carrying bogie
  支承转向架
11 wheel guard
  护轮板
12 bumper (*Am.* fender)
  保险槓，缓冲器
13 six-axle articulated railcar
  ([Mannheim] type) for tram
  (*Am.* streetcar, trolley) and
  urban rail services
  市内有轨电车和铁路的六轴有轨电车
  （曼阿型，西德南部城市）
14 entrance and exit door, a double
  folding door
  上下车门，双折层车门
15 step
  车梯
16 ticket-cancelling machine
  轧票机
17 single seat
  一人座位
18 standing room portion
  立位部分
19 double seat
  双人座位
20 route (number) and destination
  sign
  行车路线（号码）和终点站标志
21 route sign (number sign)
  路线标志（号码标志）
22 indicator (indicator light)
  指示器（指示灯）
23 pantograph (current collector)
  缩放机（集电器）
24 carbon or aluminium (*Am.*
  aluminum) alloy trolley shoes
  碳素或铝合金的触轮滑块
25 driver's position
  驾驶室
26 microphone
  麦克风
27 controller
  控制器，操纵器
28 radio equipment (radio
  communication set)
  无线电装置（无线电通信装置）
29 dashboard
  仪表（板）盘
30 dashboard lighting
  仪表盘照明
31 speedometer
  速率计
32 buttons controlling doors,
  windscreen wipers, internal and
  external lighting
  车门，风挡雨刷，内外照明的控制按钮
33 ticket counter with change
  machine
  具零钱兑换机的售票计算器
34 radio antenna
  无线电天线
35 tram stop (*Am.* streetcar stop,
  trolley stop)
  有轨电车停靠站
36 tram stop sign (*Am.* streetcar
  stop sign, trolley stop sign)
  有轨电车停靠标志
37 electric change points
  电动转辙机（道岔）
38 points signal (switch signal)
  转辙信号
39 points change indicator
  转辙指示器
40 trolley wire contact point
  架空线接触点
41 trolley wire (overhead contact
  wire)
  架空线（架空接触线）
42 overhead cross wire
  架空交叉线
43 electric (*also:* electrohydraulic,
  electromechanical) points
  mechanism
  电动（亦称：电动液压，电动机械）转
  辙机构

1-5 road layers
路层

1 anti-frost layer
不冻层

2 bituminous sub-base course
沥青底基层

3 base course
基层

4 binder course
结合层

5 bituminous surface
沥青路面

6 kerb (curb)
路缘，镶边石

7 kerbstone (curbstone)
缘石

8 paving (pavement)
铺砌层

9 pavement (*Am.* sidewalk, walkway)
人行道（人行道，走道）

10 gutter
排水沟

11 pedestrian crosssing (zebra crossing, *Am.* crosswalk)
人行道（斑马线）

12 street corner
街角

13 street
街道

14 electricity cables
电缆

15 telephone cables
电话电缆

16 telephone cable pipeline
电话电缆管线

17 cable manhole with cover (with manhole cover)
带人孔盖的电缆人孔

18 lamp post with lamp
路灯柱和路灯

19 electricity cables for technical installations
设备用电缆

20 subscribers' (*Am.* customers') telephone lines
用户电话线

21 gas main
总气管，瓦斯总管

22 water main
总水管

23 drain
下水道

24 drain cover
下水道盖

25 drain pipe
下水道管

26 waste pipe
废水管

27 combined sewer
总下水道

28 district heating main
区域供热总管

29 underground tunnel
地下隧道

1 **refuse collection vehicle (*Am.* garbage truck)**
垃圾车

2 **dustbin-tipping device (*Am.* garbage can dumping device), a dust-free emptying system**
垃圾桶倾倒装置，垃圾清除装置

3 **dustbin (*Am.* garbage can, trash can)**
垃圾箱

4 **refuse container (*Am.* garbage container)**
垃圾容器

5 **road sweeper (*Am.* street sweeper)**
清道夫

6 **broom**
扫帚

7 **fluorescent armband**
萤光臂章

8 **cap with fluorescent band**
具萤光带的帽子

9 **road sweeper's (*Am.* street sweeper's) barrow**
清道夫手推车

10 **controlled tip (*Am.* sanitary landfill, sanitary fill)**
有管理的垃圾场

11 **screen**
遮蔽物

12 **weigh office**
过磅处

13 **fence**
栅栏

14 **embankment**
堤防

15 **access ramp**
入口坡道（倾斜路面）

16 **bulldozer**
推土机

17 **refuse (*Am.* garbage)**
垃圾

18 **bulldozer for dumping and compacting**
倾倒和压缩用的推土机

19 **pump shaft**
泵井

20 **waste water pump**
废水泵

21 **porous cover**
多孔复盖层

22 **compacted and decomposed refuse**
已压缩和分解腐烂的垃圾

23 **gravel filter layer**
碎石（砂砾）过滤层

24 **morainic filter layer**
碛石层

25 **drainage layer**
排水层

26 **drain pipe**
排水管

27 **water tank**
水槽

28 **refuse (*Am.* garbage) incineration unit**
垃圾焚烧装置

29 **furnace**
焚烧炉

30 **oil-firing system**
燃油装置

31 **separation plant**
分离用的设备

32 **extraction fan**
排气风扇

33 **low-pressure fan for the grate**
炉篦的低压风扇

34 **continuous feed grate**
连续供料炉篦

35 **fan for the oil-firing system**
燃油装置所用的风扇

36 **conveyor for separately incinerated material**
分离焚烧的材料运送装置

37 **coal feed conveyor**
供煤运送装置

38 **truck for carrying fuller's earth**
运送漂土的手推车

39 **mechanical sweeper**
清扫机

40 **circular broom**
圆扫帚

41 **road sweeping lorry (street-cleaning lorry, street cleaner)**
路面清扫车

42 **cylinder broom**
圆筒扫帚

43 **suction port**
吸尘口

44 **feeder broom**
进给扫帚

45 **air flow**
空气流

46 **fan**
鼓风机

47 **dust collector**
集尘器

1-54 road-building machinery
筑路机械

1 shovel (power shovel, excavator)
挖土机

2 machine housing
机器外壳

3 caterpillar mounting (*Am.* caterpillar tractor)
履带式装置（履带牵引机）

4 digging bucket arm (dipper stick)
挖斗臂（挖斗操纵杆）

5 digging bucket (bucket)
挖斗

6 digging bucket (bucket) teeth
挖斗齿

7 tipper (dump truck), a heavy lorry (*Am.* truck)
倾卸卡车（倾卸卡车），一种重型卡车

8 tipping body (*Am.* dump body)
倾卸车体

9 reinforcing rib
加强肋

10 extended front
延长端

11 cab (driver's cab)
驾驶室

12 bulk material
散装材料

13 concrete scraper, an aggregate scraper
混凝土铲运机，砂石铲运机

14 skip hoist
吊斗吊车

15 mixing drum (mixer drum), a mixing machine
混合筒（混合机）

16 caterpillar hauling scraper
履带牵引式铲运机

17 scraper blade
铲刮板

18 levelling (*Am.* leveling) blade (smoothing blade)
整平刮板

19 grader (motor grader)
平土机（马达平土机）

20 scarifier (ripper, road ripper, rooter)
松土机、翻掘机

21 grader levelling (*Am.* leveling) blade (grader ploughshare, *Am.* plowshare)
平土机整平刮板，平土机犁头

22 blade-slewing gear (slew turntable)
刮刀转动齿轮，转动盘

23 light railway (narrow-gauge, *Am.* narrow-gage, railway)
轻便铁路（窄轨铁路）

24 light railway (narrow-gauge, *Am.* narrow-gage) diesel locomotive
轻便铁路（窄轨铁路）柴油火车

25 trailer wagon (wagon truck, skip)
拖（货）车（货车，拖斗）

26 tamper (rammer); *heavier*: frog
捣紧机（撞锤，捣具）；较重型的：蛙形捣机

27 guide rods
导向杆

28 bulldozer
推土机

29 bulldozer blade
推土机刮板

30 pushing frame
推进架

31 road-metal spreading machine (macadam spreader, stone spreader)
碎石撒播机（碎石撒播机，石头撒播机）

32 tamping beam
捣紧梁

33 sole-plate
底板

34 side stop
侧挡板

35 side of storage bin
贮料仓侧板

36 three-wheeled roller, a road roller
三轮压路机，一种碾路机

37 roller
滚轮，碾轮

38 all-weather roof
全天候顶篷

39 mobile diesel-powered air compressor
移动式柴油引擎空气压缩机

40 oxygen cylinder
氧气筒

41 self-propelled gritter
（自动）自走式复砂机

42 spreading flap
复砂活板

43 surface finisher
整面机

44 side stop
侧挡板

45 bin
料仓，料斗

46 tar-spraying machine (bituminous distributor) with tar and bitumen heater
自带柏油和加热器的柏油喷洒车

47 tar storage tank
柏油贮槽

48 fully automatic asphalt drying and mixing plant
全自动柏油混合和乾燥装置

49 bucket elevator (elevating conveyor)
箕斗升运机（上升运送机）

50 asphalt-mixing drum (asphalt mixer drum)
柏油混合筒

51 filler hoist
填料器

52 filler opening
填料口

53 binder injector
粘结料注入器

54 mixed asphalt outlet
混合沥青出口

55 typical cross-section of a bituminous road
柏油路的典型横断面

56 grass verge
草皮路边缘

57 crossfall
横向坡度（斜度）

58 asphalt surface (bituminous layer, bituminous coating)
柏油路面（沥青复盖层）

59 base (base course)
基层（路基）

60 gravel sub-base course (hardcore sub-base course, Telford base), an anti-frost layer
碎石底基层，一种防冻层

61 sub-drainage
地下排水道

62 perforated cement pipe
多孔水泥管

63 drainage ditch
排水沟

64 soil covering
土壤复盖

**1-24 concrete road
construction** (highway
construction)
混凝土路的铺筑（公路的铺筑）

1 subgrade grader
路基整平机

2 tamping beam (consolidating
beam)
捣实梁

3 levelling (*Am.* leveling) beam
整平梁

4 roller guides for the levelling
(*Am.* leveling) beam
整平梁的滚轮导槽

5 concrete spreader
混凝土撒播机

6 concrete spreader box
混凝土撒播机箱

7 cable guides
缆绳导轮

8 control levers
控制杆，操纵杆

9 handwheel for emptying the
boxes
混凝土箱的倾倒手轮

10 concrete-vibrating compactor
混凝土振动压实机

11 gearing (gears)
齿轮装置

12 control levers (operating levers)
控制杆（操纵杆）

13 axle drive shaft to vibrators
(tampers) of vibrating beam
驱动振动梁振动器的驱动轴

14 screeding board (screeding
beam)
匀泥板（整平梁）

15 road form
路型

16 joint cutter
切缝机

17 joint-cutting blade
切缝刀片

18 crank for propelling machine
推进机器的曲柄

19 concrete-mixing plant, a
stationary central mixing plant,
an automatic batching and
mixing plant
混凝土搅拌装置，固定式中央搅拌装
置，自动配料搅拌装置

20 collecting bin
集料箱

21 bucket elevator
箕斗升运机

22 cement store
水泥贮筒

23 concrete mixer
混凝土搅拌器

24 concrete pump hopper
混凝土泵漏斗

1-38 line (track)
线路（轨道）
1 rail
铁轨
2 rail head
铁轨头部
3 web (rail web)
轨腹
4 rail foot (rail bottom)
轨底（铁轨底部）
5 sole-plate (base plate)
底板
6 cushion
减震垫
7 coach screw (coach bolt)
螺钉（螺栓）
8 lock washers (spring washers)
锁紧垫圈（弹簧垫圈）
9 rail clip (clip)
轨条扣件
10 T-head bolt
T 型螺栓
11 rail joint (joint)
轨条接头
12 fishplate
鱼尾板
13 fishbolt
鱼尾板螺栓
14 coupled sleeper (*Am.* coupled tie, coupled crosstie)
联结枕木（轨枕）
15 coupling bolt
联结螺栓
16 manually-operated points (switch)
人工操作（纵）转辙器（道岔）
17 switch stand
转换器
18 weight
转换器舱附重

19 points signal (switch signal, points signal lamp, switch signal lamp)
转辙号志（转辙器号志灯）
20 pull rod
拉杆
21 switch blade (switch tongue)
转辙器上可移动的短轨条（岔尖）
22 slide chair
滑轨座
23 check rail (guard rail)
护轨
24 frog
撤叉
25 wing rail
翼轨
26 closure rail
导轨
27 remote-controlled points (switch)
遥控转辙器
28 point lock (switch lock)
转辙器闸
29 stretcher bar
转辙棒
30 point wire
转辙器拉线
31 turnbuckle
松紧螺旋扣
32 channel
槽钢
33 electrically illuminated points signal (switch signal)
转辙器照明号志
34 trough
电缆槽
35 points motor with protective casing
带护罩的转辙电动机（马达）

36 steel sleeper (*Am.* steel tie, steel crosstie)
钢枕
37 concrete sleeper (*Am.* concrete tie, concrete crosstie)
混凝土轨枕
38 coupled sleeper (*Am.* coupled tie, coupled crosstie)
联结式轨枕
39-50 level crossings (*Am.* grade crossings)
平交道
39 protected level crossing (*Am.* protected grade crossing)
有护栏（遮断器）的平交道口
40 barrier (gate)
栅栏
41 warning cross (*Am.* crossbuck)
警示十字标志
42 crossing keeper (*Am.* gateman)
平交道口看守员
43 crossing keeper's box (*Am.* gateman's box)
平交道口看守房
44 linesman (*Am.* trackwalker)
轨道巡视员
45 half-barrier crossing
半栅栏平交道口
46 warning light
警示灯
47 intercom controlled crossing; *sim.:* telephone controlled crossing
内部控制平交道口
48 intercom system
内部通讯联络系统
49 unprotected level crossing (*Am.* unprotected grade crossing)
无护栏（遮断器）的平交道口
50 warning light
警示灯

1-6 stop signals (main signals)
停止信号灯（主号志机）

1 stop signal (main signal), a
semaphore signal in 'stop'
position
停车信号灯（主号志机），臂形号志在
停车位置

2 signal arm (semaphore arm)
信号臂（臂形号志）

3 electric stop signal (colour light,
Am. color light, signal) at 'stop'
显示停止信号的电动色灯停止信号

4 signal position: 'proceed at low
speed'
信号位置："慢行"（减速信号）

5 signal position: 'proceed'
信号位置："行进"

6 substitute signal
代用信号灯

7-24 distant signals
远处信号

7 semaphore signal at 'be
prepared to stop at next signal'
"准备於下一个信号机处停车"的臂形
信号灯

8 supplementary semaphore arm
辅助臂形号志臂

9 colour light (*Am.* color light)
distant signal at 'be prepared to
stop at next signal'
"准备於下一个信号灯处停车"的远方色
灯信号

10 signal position: 'be prepared to
proceed at low speed'
信号位置："准备慢行"（准备减速）

11 signal position: 'proceed main
signal ahead'
信号位置："在主号志前继续行进"

12 semaphore signal with indicator
plate showing a reduction in
braking distance of more than
5%
带显示不大於5%刹车距离显示板的臂
形号志

13 triangle (triangle sign)
三角号志

14 colour light (*Am.* color light)
distant signal with indicator
light for showing reduced
braking distance
带显示减少的刹车距离指示灯的远方色
灯

15 supplementary white light
辅助白灯

16 distant signal indicating 'be
prepared to stop at next signal'
(yellow light)
指示"准备於下一个信号停车"的远方
信号灯（黄色灯）

17 second distant signal (distant
signal with supplementary light,
without indicator plate)
第二个远方信号灯（带辅助灯无指示板
的远方信号灯）

18 distant signal with speed
indicator
带速度指示器的远方信号灯

19 distant speed indicator
远方速度指示器

20 distant signal with route
indicator
带进路指示器的远方信号灯

21 route indicator
进路指示器

22 distant signal without
supplementary arm in position:
'be prepared to stop at next
signal'
不带辅助臂"准备於下一个信号停车"
的远方信号灯

23 distant signal without
supplementary arm in 'be
prepared to proceed' position
不带辅助臂"准备继续行进"的远方信
号灯

24 distant signal identification plate
远方信号灯的识别板

**25-44 supplementary
signals**
辅助信号

25 stop board for indicating the
stopping point at a control
point
指示停止於指定点的停止板

26-29 approach signs
接近标志

26 approach sign 100 m from
distant signal
距离远方信号灯 100 米的接近标志

27 approach sign 175 m from
distant signal
距离远方信号灯 175 米的接近标志

28 approach sign 250 m from
distant signal
距离远方信号灯 250 米的接近标志

29 approach sign at a distance of
5% less than the braking
distance on the section
区间距离减少至5%制动（刹车）距离时
的接近标志

30 chequered sign indicating stop
signals (main signals) not
positioned immediately to the
right of or over the line (track)
指示停止信号（主号志机）的方格号
志，並未表示立即停止於右边位置或超
越位置

31-32 stop boards to indicate the
stopping point of the front of
the train
指示火车前方停止点的停止板

33 stop board (be prepared to stop)
停止板（准备停车）

34-35 snow plough (*Am.*
snowplow) signs
雪犁号志

34 'raise snow-plough (*Am.*
snowplow)' sign
雪犁升起号志

35 'lower snow-plough (*Am.*
snowplow)' sign
雪犁放下号志

36-44 speed restriction signs
限速号志

36-38 speed restriction sign
[maximum speed 3 × 10 = 30
kph]
限速号志〔最高时速 30 公里〕

36 sign for day running
白天行车号志

37 speed code number
速度标号

38 illuminated sign for night
running
夜间行车用的照明号志

39 commencement of temporary
speed restriction
暂时限速的起点

40 termination of temporary speed
restriction
暂时限速的终点

41 speed restriction sign for a
section with a permanent speed
restriction [maximum speed 5
× 10 = 50 kph]
区间长时限速的限速号志〔最高时速 50
公里〕

42 commencement of permanent
speed restriction
长时限速的起点

43 speed restriction warning sign
[only on main lines]
〔只於干线上的〕限速警示标志

44 speed restriction sign [only on
main lines]
〔只於干线上的〕限速号志

45-52 points signals (switch signals)
转辙器信号

45-48 single points (single
switches)
单转辙器

45 route straight ahead (main line)
直行进路（干线）

46 [right] branch
〔右〕支线

47 [left] branch
〔左〕支线

48 branch [seen from the frog]
支线〔由辙叉可见该标志〕

49-52 double crossover
交叉渡线

49 route straight ahead from left to
right
由左而右的直行进路

50 route straight ahead from right
to left
由右而左的直行进路

51 turnout to the left from the left
由左转左的号志

52 turnout to the right from the
right
由右转右的号志

53 manually-operated signal box
(*Am.* signal tower, switch tower)
手操作的号志箱

54 lever mechanism
握杆机构

55 points lever (switch lever)
[blue], a lock lever
转辙杆〔蓝色〕，一种锁阀

56 signal lever [red]
信号杆〔红色〕

57 catch
轮档

58 route lever
进路握杆

59 block instruments
闭塞器

60 block section panel
闭塞区间盘

61 electrically-operated signal box
(*Am.* signal tower, switch tower)
电动操作信号箱

62 points (switch) and signal knobs
转辙器和信号钮

63 lock indicator panel
锁闭指示盘

64 track and signal indicator
轨道和信号指示器

65 track diagram control layout
带线路图的控制台

66 track diagram control panel
(domino panel)
带线路图的控制盘

67 push buttons
按钮

68 routes
路线

69 intercom system
内部通讯系统

1 parcels office
包裹处理室

2 parcels
包裹

3 basket [with lock]
[带锁的]篮子

4 luggage counter
行李过磅处

5 platform scale with dial
具刻度盘的磅秤

6 suitcase (case)
手提箱

7 luggage sticker
行李标签

8 luggage receipt
行李收据

9 luggage clerk
行李（办事）员

10 poster (advertisement)
海报公告（广告）

11 station post box (*Am.* station mailbox)
车站内的邮筒

12 notice board indicating train delays
列车误点通知栏

13 station restaurant
车站餐厅

14 waiting room
候车室

15 map of the town (street map)
市区地图[街道地图]

16 timetable (*Am.* schedule)
时间表

17 hotel porter
旅馆搬运工，门僮

18 arrivals and departures board (timetable)
列车到站与开车时间（刻）表（板）

19 arrival timetable (*Am.* arrival schedule)
到站时间表

20 departure timetable (*Am.* departure schedule)
开车时间表

TO THE TRAINS

CHANGE

TICKETS

21 left luggage lockers
行李寄存柜
22 change machine
零钱兑换机
23 tunnel to the platforms
通向站台的地下道
24 passengers
旅客
25 steps to the platforms
通向站台的阶梯
26 station bookstall (*Am.* station bookstand)
车站书报摊
27 left luggage office (left luggage)
行李寄存处
28 travel centre (*Am.* center); *also:* accommodation bureau
旅游中心；即：订位处
29 information office (*Am.* information bureau)
询问处
30 station clock
车站时钟
31 bank branch with foreign exchange counter
有办外汇业务的银行分行
32 indicator board showing exchange rates
显示汇率的指示板
33 railway map (*Am.* railroad map)
铁路交通（路线）图
34 ticket office
售票处

35 ticket counter
售票柜台
36 ticket (railway ticket, *Am.* railroad ticket)
车票（火车票）
37 revolving tray
转盘
38 grill
窗口
39 ticket clerk (*Am.* ticket agent)
售票员
40 ticket-printing machine (ticket-stamping machine)
车票日期印刷机
41 hand-operated ticket printer
手操作车票印刷机
42 pocket timetable (*Am.* pocket train schedule)
火车时刻简表
43 luggage rest
行李台
44 first aid station
急救站
45 Travellers' (*Am.* Travelers') Aid
旅客救护处
46 telephone box (telephone booth, telephone kiosk, call box)
公用电话亭
47 cigarettes and tobacco kiosk
售烟亭
48 flower stand
花台
49 railway information clerk
铁路询问服务员

50 official timetable (official railway guide, *Am.* train schedule)
公务时刻表（公务铁路手册，火车行车时刻表，公家印制）

1 platform
月台

2 steps to the platform
通向月台的台阶（月台台阶）

3 bridge to the platforms
月台天桥

4 platform number
月台号码

5 platform roofing
月台顶篷

6 passengers
旅客

7-12 **luggage**
行李

7 suitcase (case)
手提箱

8 luggage label
行李标签

9 hotel sticker
旅馆标签

10 travelling (*Am.* traveling) bag
旅行袋

11 hat box
帽形盒

12 umbrella, a walking-stick umbrella
雨伞，一种手杖雨伞

13 main building; *also*: offices
办公室

14 platform
月台

15 crossing
路口

16 news trolley
售报手推车

17 news vendor (*Am.* news dealer)
售报小贩

18 reading matter for the journey
旅行读物

19 edge of the platform
月台边

20 railway policeman (*Am.* railroad policeman)
铁路警察

21 destination board
终点站牌

22 destination indicator
终点站指示牌

23 departure time indicator
开车时间指示牌

24 delay indicator
误点指示牌

25 suburban train, a railcar
郊区列车

26 special compartment
专用车

27 platform loudspeaker
月台扩音器

28 station sign
站牌

29 electric trolley (electric truck)
电动推车（电动卡车）

30 loading foreman
搬货工头（领班）

31 porter (*Am.* redcap)
搬运工

32 barrow
手推车

33 drinking fountain
饮水器

34 electric Trans-Europe Express; *also*: Intercity train
贯通欧洲的高速电气火车，亦称市际列车

35 electric locomotive, an express locomotive
电气火车头

36 collector bow (sliding bow)
弓形集电器

37 secretarial compartment
秘书厢

38 destination board
终点站牌

39 wheel tapper
检修员

40 wheel-tapping hammer
检车锤

41 station foreman
车站领班

42 signal
信号牌

43 red cap
搬运工人

44 inspector
检查员

45 pocket timetable (*Am.* pocket train schedule)
袖珍时刻表（袖珍列车时刻表）

46 platform clock
月台钟
47 starting signal
开动信号
48 platform lighting
月台照明设备
49 refreshment kiosk
食品售货亭
50 beer bottle
瓶装啤酒
51 newspaper
报纸
52 parting kiss
吻别
53 embrace
拥抱
54 platform seat
月台座椅
55 litter bin (*Am*. litter basket)
垃圾桶
56 platform post box (*Am*.
platform mailbox)
月台邮筒
57 platform telephone
月台公用电话
58 trolley wire (overhead contact
wire)
电车线（架空接触电线）
59-61 track
轨谱
59 rail
铁轨

60 sleeper (*Am*. tie, crosstie)
轨枕
61 ballast (bed)
道碴，道床

1 ramp (vehicle ramp); *sim.*:
livestock ramp
斜坡（车辆坡道）；类似：家畜车坡道

2 electric truck
电动卡车

3 trailer
拖车

4 part loads (*Am.* package freight,
less-than-carload freight); *in
general traffic:* general goods in
general consignments (in mixed
consignments)
散装货（包装货物，未满一车的货
物）；在一般运输中有：一般托运的
（各种混装托运的）一般货物

5 crate
条板箱

6 goods van (*Am.* freight car)
货车车厢

7 goods shed (*Am.* freight house)
货车车棚

8 loading strip
装载条板

9 loading dock
装载台

10 bale of peat
泥炭包

11 bale of linen (of linen cloth)
麻布捆

12 fastening (cord)
扣接绳

13 wicker bottle (wickered bottle,
demijohn)
带有柳条篓的坛子

14 trolley
手推车

15 goods lorry (*Am.* freight truck)
货运卡车

16 forklift truck (fork truck,
forklift)
叉式起重机

17 loading siding
装载线

18 bulky goods
大批货物

19 small railway-owned (*Am.*
railroad-owned) container
铁路专用小型装载箱

20 showman's caravan (*sim.:* circus
caravan)
供演艺团体用的大篷车

21 flat wagon (*Am.* flat freight car)
平板货车

22 loading gauge (*Am.* gage)
货物装载规

23 bale of straw
稻草捆

24 flat wagon (*Am.* flatcar) with
side stakes
带侧柱的平板货车

25 fleet of lorries (*Am.* trucks)
运货车队

26-39 **goods shed** (*Am.* freight
house)
货仓

26 goods office (forwarding office,
Am. freight office)
货物装载处

27 part-load goods (*Am.* package
freight)
散装货物

28 forwarding agent (*Am.* freight
agent, shipper)
运输业者，运输行

29 loading foreman
装载领班

30 consignment note (waybill)
货运单（运货单）

31 weighing machine
磅秤

32 pallet
拖板

33 porter
搬运工

34 electric cart (electric truck)
电动卡车

35 trailer
拖车

36 loading supervisor
装载督察

37 goods shed door (*Am.* freight
house door)
货仓门

38 rail (slide rail)
滑轨

39 roller
滚轮

40 weighbridge office
地磅房

41 weighbridge
地磅，秤桥

42 marshalling yard (*Am.*
classification yard, switch yard)
调车场

43 shunting engine (shunting
locomotive, shunter, *Am.* switch
engine, switcher)
调车机车

44 marshalling yard signal box
(*Am.* classification yard switch
tower)
调车场信号箱

45 yardmaster
调车场长

46 hump
调车场

47 sorting siding (classification
siding, classification track)
分类线（编组线）

48 rail brake (retarder)
铁轨制动器（减速器）

49 slipper brake (slipper)
制动器，制动滑块

50 storage siding (siding)
存车线

51 buffer (buffers, *Am.* bumper)
缓冲器

52 wagon load (*Am.* carload)
满载的货车

53 warehouse
仓库

54 container station
货柜场

55 gantry crane
高架起重机

56 lifting gear (hoisting gear)
升降装置

57 container
货柜

58 container wagon (*Am.* container
car)
货柜车

59 semi-trailer
半拖车

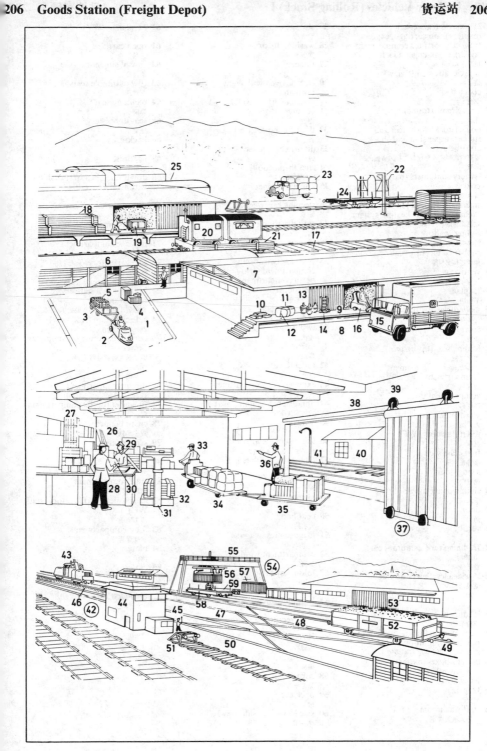

1-21 express train coach
(express train carriage, express train car, corridor compartment coach), a passenger coach
快车车厢，一种客车

1 side elevation (side view)
侧面图

2 coach body
车身

3 underframe (frame)
底架

4 bogie (truck) with steel and rubber suspension and shock absorbers
带有钢质和橡胶悬挂装置和减震器的转向架

5 battery containers (battery boxes)
蓄电池箱

6 steam and electric heat exchanger for the heating system
供暖系统的蒸汽和电热交换器

7 sliding window
滑移式窗户

8 rubber connecting seal
橡胶连接密封圈

9 ventilator
气窗，通风口

10-21 plan
平面图

10 second-class section
二等车剖面图

11 corridor
走廊

12 folding seat (tip-up seat)
摺叠座椅

13 passenger compartment (compartment)
旅客包房车厢

14 compartment door
隔间门

15 washroom
盥洗室

16 toilet (lavatory, WC)
厕所

17 first-class section
头等车剖面

18 swing door
迴旋门

19 sliding connecting door
滑式拉门

20 door
门

21 vestibule
车间过道

22-32 dining car (restaurant car, diner)
餐车

22-25 side elevation (side view)
侧视图

22 door
车门

23 loading door
装货车

24 current collector for supplying power during stops
停车时给电用之集电器（装置）

25 battery boxes (battery containers)
蓄电池箱

26-32 plan
平面图

26 staff washroom
工作人员盥洗室

27 storage cupboard
贮藏柜

28 washing-up area
洗餐具间

29 kitchen
厨房

30 electric oven with eight hotplates
具八热板的电炉（八灶式餐用电炉）

31 counter
柜台

32 dining compartment
餐室

33 dining car kitchen
餐车厨房

34 chef (head cook)
厨师领班

35 kitchen cabinet
厨房柜子

36 sleeping car (sleeper)
卧车

37 side elevation (side view)
侧视图

38-42 plan
平面图

38 two-seat twin-berth compartment (two-seat two-berth compartment, Am. bedroom)
双座双铺室

39 folding doors
摺叠车门

40 washstand
盥洗台

41 office
值班室

42 toilet (lavatory, WC)
厕所

43 express train compartment
快车车厢隔间

44 upholstered reclining seat
软垫靠背座椅

45 armrest
扶手

46 ashtray in the armrest
在扶手上的烟灰盒

47 adjustable headrest
可调整的枕靠

48 antimacassar
椅套

49 mirror
镜子

50 coat hook
大衣钩

51 luggage rack
行李架

52 compartment window
车窗

53 fold-away table (pull-down table)
可摺叠茶几

54 heating regulator
暖气调节器

55 litter receptacle
废物箱

56 curtain
窗帘

57 footrest
搁脚台

58 corner seat
角落座位

59 open car
敞车

60 side elevation (side view)
侧视图

61-72 plan
平面图

61 open carriage
连通车厢

62 row of single seats
单排座

63 row of double seats
双排座

64 reclining seat
靠椅

65 seat upholstery
座垫

66 backrest
靠背

67 headrest
头靠（枕）

68 down-filled headrest cushion with nylon cover
带尼龙套下凹头枕

69 armrest with ashtray
有烟灰盒的扶手

70 cloakroom
行李寄放处

71 luggage compartment
行李间

72 toilet (lavatory, WC)
厕所

73 buffet car (quick-service buffet car), a self-service restaurant car
自助餐车厢，一种自助餐车

74 side elevation (side view)
侧视图

75 current collector for supplying power
给电源用的集电器（装置）

76 plan
平面图

77 dining compartment
餐室

78-79 buffet (buffet compartment)
餐饮部

78 customer area
顾客购物区

79 serving area
服务区

80 kitchen
厨房

81 staff compartment
值班室

82 staff toilet (staff lavatory, staff WC)
员工厕所

83 food compartments
食物保管室

84 plates
盘子

85 cutlery
餐具

86 till (cash register)
柜台的收银抽屉

1-30 local train service
区间（普通）列车服务

1-12 local train (short-distance train)
区间列车（短程列车）

1 single-engine diesel locomotive
单（引擎）发动机柴油火车头

2 engine driver (*Am.* engineer)
司机

3 four-axled coach (four-axled car) for short-distance routes, a passenger coach (passenger car)
短程的四轴客车，客车

4 bogie (truck) [with disc (disk) brakes]
转向架（车架）〔带圆盘刹车〕

5 underframe (frame)
底架

6 coach body with metal panelling (*Am.* paneling)
带金属镶板的车

7 double folding doors
双摺门

8 compartment window
车窗

9 open carriage
中央通路式的客车

10 entrance
入口

11 connecting corridor
连接通道

12 rubber connecting seal
橡胶连结密封圈

13 light railcar, a short-distance railcar, a diesel railcar
轻便轨道列车，短程轨道列车，柴油轨道列车

14 cab (driver's cab, *Am.* engineer's cab)
驾驶室

15 luggage compartment
行李间

16 connecting hoses and coupling
连接软管和连接器

17 coupling link
连接器连杆

18 tensioning device (coupling screw with tensioning lever)
拉力装置（具拉杆的连接螺钉）

19 unlinked coupling
未连接的连接器

20 heating coupling hose (steam coupling hose)
供暖连接器软管（蒸气连接器软管）

21 coupling hose (connecting hose) for the compressed-air braking system
压缩空气制动系统连接软管

22 second-class section
二等客车的区划

23 central gangway
中央通路

24 compartment
隔间

25 upholstered seat
软垫座位

26 armrest
扶手

27 luggage rack
行李架

28 hat and light luggage rack
帽和轻型行李架

29 ashtray
烟灰缸

30 passenger
旅客，乘客

1-22 Trans-Europe Express
贯穿欧洲的快车

1 German Federal Railway
trainset, a diesel trainset or gas
turbine trainset
德意志联邦铁路列车，一种柴油列车或
燃气轮机列车

2 driving unit
驱动装置

3 drive wheel unit
驱动轮装置

4 main engine
主发动机（引擎）

5 diesel generator unit
柴油发电机装置

6 cab (driver's cab, *Am.* engineer's
cab)
驾驶室

7 second coach
二等车

8 gas turbine driving unit
[diagram]
燃气轮机驱动装置〔简图〕

9 gas turbine
燃气轮机

10 turbine transmission
轮机传动装置

11 air intake
进气管

12 exhaust with silencers (*Am.*
mufflers)
带消音器的排气管

13 dynastarter
电力起动器

14 Voith transmission
付特（液体）传动装置

15 heat exchanger for the
transmission oil
传动装置油的热交换器

16 gas turbine controller
燃气轮机控制器

17 gas turbine fuel tank
燃气轮机燃料槽

18 oil-to-air cooling unit for
transmission and turbine
传动装置和气轮机用的"油—汽"冷却
装置

19 auxiliary diesel engine
辅助柴油发动机（引擎）

20 fuel tank
燃料箱

21 cooling unit
冷却装置

22 exhaust with silencers (*Am*
mufflers)
带消音器的排气装置

23 **Société Nationale des Chemins
de Fer Français (SNCF)**
experimental trainset with
six-cylinder underfloor diesel
engine and twin-shaft gas
turbine
法国国营铁路公司，具有六缸底架柴油
发动机（引擎）和双轴燃气轮机的
SNCF 试验列车

24 turbine unit with silencers (*Am.*
mufflers)
带消音器的轮机装置

25 secretarial compartment
秘书室

26 typing compartment
打字室

27 secretary
秘书

28 typewriter
打字机

29 travelling (*Am.* traveling)
salesman
旅行的推销员，做商业旅行的商人

30 dictating machine
录音机

31 microphone
扩音器，麦克风

1-69　steam locomotives
蒸汽（火车头）机车

2-37　locomotive boiler and driving gear
机车锅炉和驱动装置

2　tender platform with coupling
带连接器的煤水（补给）平台

3　safety valve for excess boiler pressure
防止锅炉过压的安全阀

4　firebox
火箱

5　drop grate
倾卸炉篦

6　ashpan with damper doors
带风门的灰盘

7　bottom door of the ashpan
灰盘底门

8　smoke tubes (flue tubes)
烟管

9　feed pump
给水泵

10　axle bearing
车轴轴承

11　connecting rod
连（接）杆

12　steam dome
汽包

13　regulator valve (regulator main valve)
调节器阀（调节器主阀）

14　sand dome
砂包

15　sand pipes (sand tubes)
砂管

16　boiler (boiler barrel)
锅炉（锅胴）

17　fire tubes or steam tubes
火管或蒸汽管

18　reversing gear (steam reversing gear)
回动机构（蒸汽回动机构）

19　sand pipes
砂管

20　feed valve
进给阀

21　steam collector
集汽器

22　chimney (smokestack, smoke outlet and waste steam exhaust)
烟囱（烟和废汽排出口）

23　feedwater preheater (feedwater heater, economizer)
给水预热器（给水加热器，节热器）

24　spark arrester
防止火花器

25　blast pipe
排气管

26　smokebox door
烟箱门

27　cross head
十字头

28　mud drum
清泥器

29　top feedwater tray
顶部给水盘

30　combination lever
组合杆

31　steam chest
蒸汽室

32　cylinder
汽缸

33　piston rod with stuffing box (packing box)
带填料函的活塞杆

34　guard iron (rail guard, *Am.* pilot, cowcatcher)
排障器

35　carrying axle (running axle, dead axle)
从轮轴（导轮轴，静车轴）

36　coupled axle
连动轴

37　driving axle
驱动轴

38　express locomotive with tender
带煤水车的高速机车

39-63 cab (driver's cab, *Am.* engineer's cab)
驾驶室，司机室

39 fireman's seat
司炉的位置

40 drop grate lever
倾卸炉箅杆

41 line steam injector
管路蒸汽喷射器

42 automatic lubricant pump (automatic lubricator)
自动润滑泵（自动润滑器）

43 preheater pressure gauge (*Am.* gage)
预热器压力计

44 carriage heating pressure gauge (*Am.* gage)
车厢加热压力计

45 water gauge (*Am.* gage)
水位计

46 light
顶灯

47 boiler pressure gauge (*Am.* gage)
锅炉压力计

48 distant-reading temperature gauge (*Am.* gage)
遥测温度计

49 cab (driver's cab, *Am.* engineer's cab)
驾驶室

50 brake pressure gauge (*Am.* gage)
制动压力计

51 whistle valve handle
（汽）笛阀手柄

52 diver's timetable (*Am.* engineer's schedule)
驾驶时刻表

53 driver's brake valve (*Am.* engineer's brake valve)
驾驶制动阀

54 speed recorder (tachograph)
速率记录器（转速记录仪）

55 sanding valve
撒砂阀

56 reversing wheel
倒车手轮

57 emergency brake valve
紧急制动阀（刹车阀）

58 release valve
放汽阀

59 driver's seat (*Am.* engineer's seat)
（司机）驾驶的位置

60 firehole shield
炉口盖（罩）

61 firehole door
炉门

62 vertical boiler
立式锅炉

63 firedoor handle handgrip
炉门握把

64 articulated locomotive (Garratt locomotive)
活节火车头

65 tank locomotive
带水柜的火车头

66 water tank
水箱（柜）

67 fuel tender
燃料补给车

68 steam storage locomotive (fireless locomotive)
蒸汽储压火车头（贮汽火车头）

69 condensing locomotive (locomotive with condensing tender)
凝结式火车头（带凝结补给的火车头）

1 electric locomotive
电力机车

2 current collector
集电器

3 main switch
总开关

4 high-tension transformer
高压变压器

5 roof cable
篷顶电缆

6 traction motor
牵引马达

7 inductive train control system
感应列车系统

8 main air reservoir
主贮气器

9 whistle
汽笛

10-18 plan of locomotive
机车平面图

10 transformer with tap changer
带分接头变换器的变压器

11 oil cooler with blower
带鼓风机的油冷却器

12 oil-circulating pump
油循环泵

13 tap changer driving mechanism
分接头变换器的驱动机构

14 air compressor
空气压缩机

15 traction motor blower
牵引马达鼓风机

16 terminal box
端子箱

17 capacitors for auxiliary motors
辅助马达用的电容器

18 commutator cover
整流器盖（罩）

19 cab (driver's cab, *Am.* engineer's cab)
司机室

20 controller handwheel
驾驶盘

21 dead man's handle
事故刹车手柄装置

22 driver's brake valve (*Am.* engineer's brake valve)
驾驶制动阀

23 ancillary brake valve (auxiliary brake valve)
辅助制动阀

24 pressure gauge (*Am.* gage)
压力计

25 bypass switch for the dead man's handle
事故刹车手柄的旁通开关

26 tractive effort indicator
牵引力指示器

27 train heating voltage indicator
列车供暖电压指示器

28 contact wire voltage indicator (overhead wire voltage indicator)
接触线电压指示器（架空线电压指示器）

29 high-tension voltage indicator
高电压指示器

30 on/off switch for the current collector
集电器开关

31 main switch
主开关

32 sander switch (sander control)
撒砂器开关

33 anti-skid brake switch
防滑制动开关

34 visual display for the ancillary systems
补助系统用的可见显示

35 speedometer
速率计

36 running step indicator
连续行程指示器

37 clock
时钟

38 controls for the inductive train control system
感应列车系统用的控制器

39 cab heating switch
驾驶室供暖开关

40 whistle lever
汽笛杆

41 contact wire maintenance vehicle (overhead wire maintenance vehicle), a diesel railcar
接触线维修车（架空线维修车），一种柴油轨道车

42 work platform (working platform)
工作台

43 ladder
梯子

44-54 mechanical equipment of the contact wire maintenance vehicle
接触线维修车的机械设备

44 air compressor
空气压缩机

45 blower oil pump
鼓风机油泵

46 generator
发电机

47 diesel engine
柴油发动机（引擎）

48 injection pump
喷射泵

49 silencer (*Am.* muffler)
消音器

50 change-speed gear
变速齿轮，变换齿轮

51 cardan shaft
万向轴

52 wheel flange lubricator
轮凸缘润滑器

53 reversing gear
回动机构

54 torque converter bearing
扭矩变速器轴承

55 accumulator railcar (battery railcar)
蓄电池轨道车

56 battery box (battery container)
电池箱

57 cab (driver's cab, *Am.* engineer's cab)
驾驶室

58 second-class seating arrangement
二等座位配置

59 toilet (lavatory, WC)
厕所

60 fast electric multiple-unit train
高速电动多机牵引列车

61 front railcar
前端轨道车

62 driving trailer car
拖车车厢

1-84 diesel locomotives
柴油火车头

1 diesel-hydraulic locomotive, a mainline locomotive (diesel locomotive) for medium passenger and goods service (freight service)
柴油液动火车头，一种客货服务用的干线火车头

2 bogie (truck)
转向架

3 wheel and axle set
轮轴组

4 main fuel tank
主燃料槽（主油箱）

5 cab (driver's cab, *Am.* engineer's cab) of a diesel locomotive
柴油火车头驾驶室

6 main air pressure gauge (*Am.* gage)
主气压计

7 brake cylinder pressure gauge (*Am.* gage)
制动（刹车）汽缸压力计

8 main air reservoir pressure gauge (*Am.* gage)
主贮气器压力计

9 speedometer
速率计

10 auxiliary brake
辅助制动

11 driver's brake valve (*Am.* engineer's brake valve)
驾驶制动器（刹车）阀

12 controller handwheel
驾驶盘

13 dead man's handle
事故（刹车）手柄

14 inductive train control system
感应列车系统

15 signal lights
信号灯

16 clock
时钟

17 voltage meter for the train heating system
供暖系统用的电压计

18 current meter for the train heating system
供暖系统的电流表

19 engine oil temperature gauge (*Am.* gage)
发动机（引擎）油温计

20 transmission oil temperature gauge (*Am.* gage)
传动油温计

21 cooling water temperature gauge (*Am.* gage)
冷却水温计

22 revolution counter (rev counter, tachometer)
转速表

23 radio telephone
无线电话

24 diesel-hydraulic locomotive [plan and elevation]
柴油液压火车头[平面图和侧视图]

25 diesel engine
柴油发动机（引擎）

26 cooling unit
冷却装置

27 fluid transmission
液压传动装置

28 wheel and axle drive
轮轴传动机构

29 cardan shaft
方向轴

30 starter motor
起动电动机（马达）

31 instrument panel
工具盘

32 driver's control desk (*Am.* engineer's control desk)
司机驾驶台

33 hand brake
手刹车

34 air compressor with electric motor
具电动机的空气压缩机

35 equipment locker
工具柜

36 heat exchanger for transmission oil
传动油的热交换器

37 engine room ventilator
引擎室的通风口

38 magnet for the inductive train control system
感应列车控制系统的磁石

39 train heating generator
列车供暖发生器

40 casing of the train heating system transformer
列车供暖系统变压器罩

41 preheater
预热器

42 exhaust silencer (*Am.* exhaust muffler)
消音排气

43 auxiliary heat exchanger for the transmission oil
传动油用的辅助热交换器

44 hydraulic brake
液压制动器

45 tool box
工具箱

46 starter battery
起动蓄电池

47 diesel-hydraulic locomotive for light and medium shunting service
调车用中小型柴油液压机车

48 exhaust silencer (*Am.* exhaust muffler)
消音排气管

49 bell and whistle
车钟和汽笛

50 yard radio
调车场用无线电

51-67 elevation of locomotive
机车正视图

51 diesel engine with supercharged turbine
带增压轮机的柴油引擎

52 fluid transmission
流体传送装置

53 output gear box
输出齿轮箱

54 radiator
散热器

55 heat exchanger for the engine lubricating oil
引擎润滑油热交换器

56 fuel tank
燃料槽

57 main air reservoir
主贮气器

58 air compressor
空气压缩机

59 sand boxes
砂箱

60 reserve fuel tank
储备燃料槽

61 auxiliary air reservoir
辅助贮气器

62 hydrostatic fan drive
液压扇驱动装置

63 seat with clothes compartment
带衣柜的座位

64 hand brake wheel
手刹车轮

65 cooling water
冷却水

66 ballast
压载物

67 engine and transmission control wheel
引擎和传动控制轮

68 small diesel locomotive for shunting service
调车用小型柴油机车

69 exhaust casing
排气罩

70 horn
汽笛

71 main air reservoir
主贮气器

72 air compressor
空气压缩机

73 eight-cylinder diesel engine
八缸柴油引擎

74 Voith transmission with reversing gear
具回动机构的付特液体传动装置

75 heating oil tank (fuel oil tank)
供热油槽（燃料油槽）

76 sand box
砂箱

77 cooling unit
冷却装置

78 header tank for the cooling water
冷却水用的集水箱

79 oil bath air cleaner (oil bath air filter)
油池式空气清洁器

80 hand brake wheel
手刹车轮

81 control wheel
操纵轮

82 coupling
连接器

83 cardan shaft
万向轴

84 louvred shutter
散热百叶窗

1 diesel-hydraulic locomotive
   柴油液动火车头
2 cab (driver's cab, *Am.* engineer's
   cab)
   驾驶室
3 wheel and axle set
   轮轴组
4 aerial for the yard radio
   车场无线电天线
5 standard flat wagon (*Am.*
   standard flatcar)
   标准平板车
6 hinged steel stanchion
   (stanchion)
   铰接钢柱
7 buffers
   缓冲器，减震器
8 standard open goods wagon
   (*Am.* standard open freight car)
   标准敞篷货车
9 revolving side doors
   旋转式侧门
10 hinged front
   铰接端部
11 standard flat wagon (*Am.*
   standard flatcar) with bogies
   带转向架的标准平板车
12 sole bar reinforcement
   底条加强材
13 bogie (truck)
   转向架
14 covered goods van (covered
   goods wagon, *Am.* boxcar)
   有篷货车

15 sliding door
   滑门，拉门
16 ventilation flap
   通风舌门
17 snow blower (rotary snow
   plough, *Am.* snowplow), a
   track-clearing vehicle
   扫雪机（旋转雪犁），一种轨式清扫机
18 wagon (*Am.* car) with
   pneumatic discharge
   气动卸货车
19 filler hole
   填料口
20 compressed-air supply
   压缩空气供给装置
21 discharge connection valve
   放气（连接）阀
22 goods van (*Am.* boxcar) with
   sliding roof
   滑顶有盖货车
23 roof opening
   车顶开口
24 bogie open self-discharge wagon
   (*Am.* bogie open self-discharge
   freight car)
   带转向架的自卸敞篷车
25 discharge flap (discharge door)
   卸货活板（卸货门）

26 bogie wagon with swivelling
    (*Am.* swiveling) roof
    旋转车顶的转向架车
27 swivelling (*Am.* swiveling) roof
    旋转车顶
28 large-capacity wagon (*Am.*
    large-capacity car) for small
    livestock
    装载小牲畜的大容量货车
29 sidewall with ventilation flaps
    (slatted wall)
    具通风舌门的侧壁（板条壁）
30 ventilation flap
    通风舌门
31 tank wagon (*Am.* tank car)
    液罐车
32 track inspection railcar
    轨道检查车
33 open special wagons (*Am.* open
    special freight cars)
    特殊无盖货车
34 lorry (*Am.* truck) with trailer
    带拖车的货车
35 two-tier car carrier (double-deck
    car carrier)
    装小汽车的双层运载车
36 hinged upper deck
    铰接上层
37 tipper wagon (*Am.* dump car)
    with skips
    带吊斗的倾卸车
38 skip
    吊斗

39 general-purpose refrigerator
    wagon (refrigerator van, *Am.*
    refrigerator car)
    通用冷藏车
40 interchangeable bodies for flat
    wagons (*Am.* flatcars)
    可在平板车上装拆的车体

1-14 mountain railways (*Am.* mountain railroads)
登山铁路

1 adhesion railcar
粘着力轨道车

2 drive
驱动装置

3 emergency brake
紧急刹车（制动器）

4-5 rack mountain railway (rack-and-pinion railway, cog railway, *Am.* cog railroad, rack railroad)
齿条登山铁路（齿条与齿轮铁路，镶齿铁路，齿轨铁路）

4 electric rack railway locomotive (*Am.* electric rack railroad locomotive)
齿轨铁路电动机车

5 rack railway coach (rack railway trailer, *Am.* rack railroad car)
齿轨铁路客车（齿轨铁路拖车）

6 tunnel
隧道

7-11 rack railways (rack-and-pinion railways, *Am.* rack railroads) [systems]
齿轨铁路系统

7 running wheel (carrying wheel)
转动轮（运送轮）

8 driving pinion
驱动小齿轮

9 rack [with teeth machined on top edge]
齿形轨条〔顶部有齿牙〕

10 rail
轨

11 rack [with teeth on both outer edges]
齿形轨条[两侧有齿牙]

12 funicular railway (funicular, cable railway)
缆索铁道

13 funicular railway car
登山缆车，电缆车

14 haulage cable
拖索

15-38 cableways (ropeways, cable suspension lines)
缆道（索道，缆索悬挂线）

15-24 single-cable ropeways (single-cable suspension lines), endless ropeways
单缆索道，无端（循环）索道

15 drag lift
牵引缆车

16-18 chair lift
有座架缆车

16 lift chair, a single chair
缆车座，单人座

17 double lift chair, a two-seater chair
缆车双座，双人座

18 double chair (two-seater chair) with coupling
带连接器的双人座

19 gondola cableway, an endless cableway
有边车缆道，一种（循环）无端缆道

20 gondola (cabin)
有边车（座舱）

21 endless cable, a suspension (supporting) and haulage cable
（循环）无端索，一种悬吊牵引索（缆）

22 U-rail
U 型轨道

23 single-pylon support
单柱支架

24 gantry support
门型支架

25 double-cable ropeway (double-cable suspension line), a suspension line with balancing cabins
双缆索道，一种有平衡舱的架空索道

26 haulage cable
牵引缆

27 suspension cable (supporting cable)
悬吊缆索（支撑索）

28 cabin
座舱

29 intermediate support
中间支架

30 cableway (ropeway, suspension line), a double-cable ropeway (double-cable suspension line)
缆道（索道，悬吊索），一种双缆悬吊线（双缆悬吊线）

31 pylon
支撑铁塔
32 haulage cable roller
牵引缆索滚轮
33 cable guide rail (suspension cable bearing)
缆索导轨 (悬吊缆索轴承)
34 skip, a tipping bucket (*Am.* dumping bucket)
吊斗，一种倾卸斗
35 stop
止挡
36 pulley cradle
滑轮托架
37 haulage cable
牵引缆索
38 suspension cable (supporting cable)
悬吊缆索 (支撑缆索)
39 **valley station** (lower station)
山谷站 (下端站)
40 tension weight shaft
拉紧重锤升降井
41 tension weight for the suspension cable (supporting cable)
悬吊缆索 (吊索) 拉紧重锤
42 tension weight for the haulage cable
牵引缆索拉紧重锤
43 tension cable pulley
拉紧缆索滑轮
44 suspension cable (supporting cable)
悬吊缆索
45 haulage cable
牵引缆索
46 balance cable (lower cable)
平衡缆索
47 auxiliary cable (emergency cable)
辅助缆索 (应急缆索)
48 auxiliary-cable tensioning mechanism (emergency-cable tensioning mechanism)
辅助缆索拉紧装置 (紧急缆索拉紧装置)
49 haulage cable rollers
牵引缆索滚轮
50 spring buffer (*Am.* spring bumper)
弹簧缓冲器
51 valley station platform (lower station platform)
山谷月台
52 cabin (cableway gondola, ropeway gondola, suspension line gondola), a large-capacity cabin
吊舱 (缆道吊舱)，一种大容量吊舱
53 pulley cradle
滑轮托架
54 suspension gear
悬吊装置
55 stabilizer
稳定器
56 guide rail
导轨
57 **top station** (upper station)
山顶站 (上端站)
58 suspension cable guide (supporting cable guide)
悬吊缆索导轨

59 suspension cable anchorage (supporting cable anchorage)
悬吊缆索停泊点 (架空索锚固点)
60 haulage cable rollers
牵引缆索滚轮
61 haulage cable guide wheel
牵引缆索导轮
62 haulage cable driving pulley
牵引缆索驱动滑轮
63 main drive
主驱动装置
64 standby drive
备用驱动装置
65 control room
控制室
66 **cabin pulley cradle**
吊舱滑轮托架
67 main pulley cradle
主滑轮托架
68 double cradle
双托架
69 two-wheel cradle
双轮托架
70 running wheels
转动轮
71 suspension cable brake (supporting cable brake), an emergency brake in case of haulage cable failure
悬吊缆索制动器 (刹车)，一种牵引缆索失效时的紧急制动器 (刹车)
72 suspension gear bolt
悬吊齿轮
73 haulage cable sleeve
牵引缆索套管
74 balance cable sleeve (lower cable sleeve)
平衡缆索套管
75 derailment guard
防止脱轨装置
76 **cable supports** (ropeway supports, suspension line supports, intermediate supports)
缆索支承架
77 pylon, a framework support
铁塔，构架的支座
78 tubular steel pylon, a tubular steel support
钢管铁塔，一种钢管式支架
79 suspension cable guide rail (supporting cable guide rail, support guide rail)
悬吊缆索导轨 (支承导轨)
80 support truss, a frame for work on the cable
支承构架，於缆索上工作的构架
81 base of the support
支架的基部

1 cross-section of a bridge
桥梁横断面
2 orthotropic roadway
(orthotropic deck)
钢桥面车道（钢面钣）
3 truss (bracing)
桁架（支撑）
4 diagonal brace (diagonal strut)
斜支撑（斜支柱）
5 hollow tubular section
空心管型断面
6 deck slab
桥面板
7 solid-web girder bridge (beam
bridge)
实腹梁桥（梁桥）
8 road surface
路面
9 top flange
上翼缘
10 bottom flange
下翼缘
11 fixed bearing
固定支承
12 movable bearing
活动支承
13 clear span
净跨径
14 span
跨径
15 rope bridge (primitive
suspension bridge)
悬索桥（早期的吊桥）
16 carrying rope
主索
17 suspension rope
吊索
18 woven deck (woven decking)
织网桥面
19 stone arch bridge, a solid bridge
石拱桥，一种实心桥
20 arch
拱
21 pier
桥墩
22 statue
雕饰物
23 trussed arch bridge
桁架式拱桥
24 truss element
桁架构件
25 trussed arch
桁架式拱
26 arch span
拱跨
27 abutment (end pier)
桥台（岸墩）
28 spandrel-braced arch bridge
空腹拱桥
29 abutment (abutment pier)
桥台（桥墩）
30 bridge strut
桥撑
31 crown
拱顶
32 covered bridge of the Middle
Ages (the *Ponte Vecchio* in
Florence)
中世纪的有盖桥（佛罗伦斯的庞特维奇
奥）
33 goldsmiths' shops
金饰店
34 steel lattice bridge
钢格子桥

35 counterbrace (crossbrace,
diagonal member)
反杆撑（对角构件）
36 vertical member
垂直桁材
37 truss joint
桁架节点
38 portal frame
桥门架
39 suspension bridge
吊桥
40 suspension cable
主索
41 suspender (hanger)
吊索（吊杆）
42 tower
桥塔
43 suspension cable anchorage
主索锚座
44 tied beam [with roadway]
连车道（路面）的系梁
45 abutment
桥台
46 cable-stayed bridge
斜索桥（斜张桥）
47 inclined tension cable
斜拉索
48 inclined cable anchorage
斜索锚座
49 reinforced concrete bridge
钢筋混凝土桥
50 reinforced concrete arch
钢筋混凝土拱
51 inclined cable system (multiple
cable system)
（倾）斜（缆）索系统
52 flat bridge, a plate girder bridge
平桥，一种饭梁桥
53 stiffener
加劲杆
54 pier
桥墩
55 bridge bearing
桥梁支承
56 cutwater
分水角
57 straits bridge, a bridge built of
precast elements
狭桥，一种预铸件构造的桥
58 precast construction unit
预铸构件
59 viaduct
高架桥
60 valley bottom
谷底
61 reinforced concrete pier
钢筋混凝土桥墩
62 scaffolding
工作架
63 lattice swing bridge
格子旋桥
64 turntable
转盘
65 pivot pier
旋轴桥墩
66 pivoting half (pivoting section,
pivoting span, movable half) of
bridge
桥的半迴旋部分（迴旋部分，迴旋跨径
可移动之半部分）
67 flat swing bridge
平旋桥
68 middle section
中间部分

69 pivot
旋轴
70 parapet (handrailing)
栏杆

1 **cable ferry** (*also: chain ferry*), a passenger ferry
缆索渡船（链索渡船），一种旅客渡船

2 ferry rope (ferry cable)
渡船用缆索

3 river branch (river arm)
支流

4 river island (river islet)
河中岛

5 collapsed section of riverbank, flood damage
河岸塌陷部分，洪水冲损处

6 **motor ferry**
电动渡船

7 ferry landing stage (motorboat landing stage)
渡船码头

8 pile foundations
桩基础

9 current (flow, course)
水流

10 **flying ferry** (river ferry), a car ferry
高速渡船，一种汽车渡船

11 ferry boat
渡船

12 buoy (float)
浮标

13 anchorage
停泊处，抛锚处

14 harbour (*Am.* harbor) for laying up river craft
停泊河船的碇泊场

15 **ferry boat** (punt)
渡船

16 pole (punt pole, quant pole)
撑篙

17 ferryman
渡船夫

18 blind river branch (blind river arm)
盲支流

19 groyne (*Am.* groin)
丁坝

20 groyne (*Am.* groin) head
丁坝头

21 fairway (navigable part of river)
航道（河中可通航部分）

22 **train of barges**
牵引式驳船

23 river tug
河中拖船

24 tow rope (tow line, towing hawser)
拖缆，拖绳

25 barge (freight barge, cargo barge, lighter)
驳船（运货驳船）

26 bargeman (bargee, lighterman)
驳船夫

27 **towing** (hauling, haulage)
牵引

28 towing mast
牵引桅

29 towing engine
牵引发动机（引擎）

30 towing track; *form.*: tow path (towing path)
拖船道（牵道）

31 river after river training
疏浚后的河川

32 **dike** (dyke, main dike, flood wall, winter dike)
堤（主堤，洪水壁，冬季堤）

33 drainage ditch
排水沟（明沟）

34 dike (dyke) drainage sluice
堤排水闸

35 wing wall
翼墙

36 outfall
排水口

37 drain (infiltration drain)
排水沟（暗沟）

38 berm (berme)
护坡道

39 top of dike (dyke)
堤顶

40 dike (dyke) batter (dike slope)
堤防斜坡

41 flood bed (inundation area)
洪水河床（汜滥区）

42 flood containment area
蓄洪区

43 current meter
流速计

44 kilometre (*Am.* kilometer) sign
里程标

45 dikereeve's (dykereeve's) house (dikereeve's cottage); *also:* ferryman's house (cottage)
堤防管理人住屋；亦称：渡船夫住屋

46 dikereeve (dykereeve)
堤防管理人

47 dike (dyke) ramp
堤防坡道

48 summer dike (dyke)
夏季堤

49 levee (embankment)
堤防（河堤）

50 sandbags
砂袋

51-55 **bank protection** (bank stabilization, revetment)
护岸（岸坡稳定，护坡）

51 riprap
抛石，堆石

52 alluvial deposit (sand deposit)
冲积层（砂沉积）

53 fascine (bundle of wooden sticks)
沉梢（梢捆，束柴）

54 wicker fences
编枝栅栏

55 stone pitching
石砌护坡

56 **floating dredging machine** (dredger), a multi-bucket ladder dredge
挖泥船（挖泥机），一种多斗梯式挖泥船

57 bucket elevator chain
挖斗升降机链

58 dredging bucket
挖泥斗

59 **suction dredger** (hydraulic dredger) with trailing suction pipe or barge sucker
吸泥机（吸扬式挖泥船）

60 centrifugal pump
离心抽水机，离心泵

61 back scouring valve
后部冲刷阀

62 suction pump, a jet pump with scouring nozzles
抽水泵，带冲刷喷咀的喷射泵

1-14 quay wall
岸壁，码头
1 road surface
路面
2 body of wall
墙体
3 steel sleeper
钢轨枕
4 steel pile
钢桩
5 sheet pile wall (sheet pile bulkhead, sheetpiling)
板桩墙（板桩隔壁，钢板桩）
6 box pile
箱形桩
7 backfilling (filling)
回填，回填土
8 ladder
梯子
9 fender (fender pile)
护舷木（护舷桩）
10 recessed bollard
凹状系柱
11 double bollard
双系船柱
12 bollard
系船柱
13 cross-shaped bollard (cross-shaped mooring bitt)
十字型系船柱
14 double cross-shaped bollard (double cross-shaped mooring bitt)
双十字型系船柱

15-28 canal
运河

15-16 canal entrance
运河入口
15 mole
防波堤，突堤
16 breakwater
防波堤
17-25 staircase of locks
阶梯式船闸
17 lower level
下游水位
18 lock gate, a sliding gate
船闸门，滑动闸门
19 mitre (*Am.* miter) gate
人字闸门
20 lock (lock chamber)
船闸室
21 power house
发电厂
22 warping capstan (hauling capstan), a capstan
卷绞盘（牵引绞盘），一种绞盘
23 warp
拖船索
24 offices (e.g. canal administration, river police, customs)
办公处（例如：运河管理处，河上警察局，海关）
25 upper level (head)
上游水位
26 lock approach
船闸引道
27 lay-by
河道中停泊驳船处
28 bank slope
岸坡

29-38 boat lift (*Am.* boat elevator)
船之升降
29 lower pound (lower reaach)
下游区间，下游通行河道（下游河段）
30 canal bed
运河河床
31 pound lock gate, a vertical gate
河道闸门，一种垂直闸门
32 lock gate
船闸门
33 boat tank (caisson)
船槽
34 float
浮筒
35 float shaft
浮筒升降井
36 lifting spindle
提升转轴
37 upper pound (upper reach)
上游区间，上游通行河道（上游河段）
38 vertical gate
垂直闸门

39-46 pumping plant and reservoir
抽水站和水库

39 forebay
前池

40 surge tank
平压塔（取水室，水室）

41 pressure pipeline
压力管道

42 valve house (valve control house)
阀室（阀控制室）

43 turbine house (pumping station)
涡轮机室（抽水站）

44 discharge structure (outlet structure)
出水构造物

45 control station
控制室

46 transformer station
变电站

47-52 axial-flow pump (propeller pump)
轴流式抽水机（推进抽水机）

47 drive motor
传动马达

48 gear
（齿轮）传动装置

49 drive shaft
传动主轴

50 pressure pipe
压力管，压送管

51 suction head
吸水头

52 impeller wheel
动叶轮

53-56 sluice valve (sluice gate)
泄水阀（泄水闸门）

53 crank drive
曲柄传动装置

54 valve housing
阀室

55 sliding valve (sliding gate)
滑动阀（滑动闸门）

56 discharge opening
排水口

57-64 dam (barrage)
坝（堰）

57 reservoir (storage reservoir, impounding reservoir, impounded reservoir)
水库（蓄水库）

58 masonry dam
砌工坝

59 crest of dam
坝顶

60 spillway (overflow spillway)
溢洪道

61 stilling basin (stilling box, stilling pool)
静水池

62 scouring tunnel (outlet tunnel, waste water outlet)
冲刷隧道（排水道，废水排水道）

63 valve house (valve control house)
阀室（阀控制室）

64 power station
发电厂

65-72 rolling dam (weir), a barrage; *other system:* shutter weir
滚坝（堰），一种拦水坝（堰）；另一种型式是：楯堰

65 roller, a barrier
滚轴，一种栅栏

66 roller top
滚轴顶部

67 flange
[滚轴]凸缘

68 submersible roller
过水滚轴

69 rack track
齿形轨

70 recess
轨槽，凹槽

71 hoisting gear cabin
起重传动装置室

72 service bridge (walkway)
工作桥（人行道）

73-80 sluice dam
泄水坝

73 hoisting gear bridge
起重传动装置（升降装置）

74 hoisting gear (winding gear)
吊扬齿轮（卷扬机构）

75 guide groove
导槽

76 counterweight (counterpoise)
泄水平衡锤（平衡重）

77 sluice gate (floodgate)
泄水闸门（防洪闸门）

78 reinforcing rib
加强肋

79 dam sill (weir sill)
坝槛（堰槛）

80 wing wall
翼墙

1-6 Germanic rowing boat
[ca. AD 400], the Nydam
boat
德国划船（西元 400 年），一种"奈德
姆"划船
1 stern post
艉柱
2 steersman
舵手
3 oarsman
划桨手
4 stem post (stem)
艏柱
5 oar, for rowing
划船桨
6 rudder (steering oar), a side
rudder, for steering
舵（橹），控制方向的侧舵
7 **dugout,** a hollowed-out tree
trunk
独木舟，一种挖空的树干
8 paddle
桨
9-12 trireme, a Roman warship
有三层桨座的战船，罗马战船
9 ram
船首撞角
10 forecastle (fo'c'sle)
艏楼
11 grapple (grapnel, grappling
iron), for fastening the enemy
ship alongside
爪钩，钩杆（用以钩住並排敌船）
12 three banks (tiers) of oars
三排（层）桨
13-17 Viking ship (longship,
dragon ship) [Norse]
维京海盗船（中古时代北欧单帆多桨长
船，龙船）
13 helm (tiller)
舵柄
14 awning crutch with carved
horses' heads
带雕刻马头的船篷支架
15 awning
船篷
16 dragon figurehead
龙形船头
17 shield
盾
18-26 cog (Hansa cog, Hansa ship)
小船，附属於大船的供应船（汉瑟船）
18 anchor cable (anchor rope,
anchor hawser)
锚缆，锚索
19 forecastle (fo'c'sle)
艏楼
20 bowsprit
艏斜桅
21 furled (brailed-up) square sail
卷起的横帆
22 town banner (city banner)
城市旗帜
23 aftercastle (sterncastle)
艉楼
24 rudder, a stem rudder
舵，一种艏舵
25 elliptical stern (round stern)
椭圆舳（圆舳）
26 wooden fender
木碰垫
27-43 caravel (carvel) ['Santa
Maria' 1492]
轻快帆船〔圣玛琍亚号 1492 年〕

27 admiral's cabin
船长室
28 spanker boom
后纵帆杆
29 mizzen (mizen, mutton spanker,
lateen spanker), a lateen sail
后帆，大三角帆
30 lateen yard
三角帆桁
31 mizzen (mizen) mast
后帆桅
32 lashing
捆索系索
33 mainsail (main course), a square
sail
主帆（主桅主帆）、横帆的一种
34 bonnet, a removable strip of
canvas
小帆，可拆卸的帆布片
35 bowline
艏缆（张帆索）
36 bunt line (martinet)
帆脚索（纹帆索）
37 main yard
主帆桁
38 main topsail
中桅主帆
39 main topsail yard
中桅主帆桁
40 mainmast
主桅
41 foresail (fore course)
前帆
42 foremast
前桅
43 spritsail
斜杠帆
44-50 galley [15th to 18th
century], a slave galley
两排桨的帆船〔15 - 18 世纪〕，一种奴
隶船
44 lantern
灯笼，信号灯
45 cabin
船舱
46 central gangway
中间过道
47 slave driver with whip
持鞭子的奴隶监督
48 galley slaves
划船的奴隶
49 covered platform in the forepart
of the ship
船首隐蔽平台
50 gun
火炮
51-60 ship of the line (line-of-battle
ship) [18th to 19th century],
a three-decker
战舰〔18 - 19 世纪〕，三层甲板船
51 jib boom
艏帆斜桅
52 fore topgallant sail
前上桅帆
53 main topgallant sail
主上桅帆
54 mizzen (mizen) topgallant sail
后上桅帆
55-57 gilded stern
镀金船尾
55 upper stern
船尾上部
56 stern gallery
船尾了望台

57 quarter gallery, a projecting
balcony with ornamental
portholes
船侧尾了望台，一种具有装饰舷窗的突
出望台（露台）
58 lower stern
船尾下部
59 gunports for broadside fire
舷侧炮火用炮门
60 gunport shutter
炮门挡板

1-72 rigging (rig, tackle) and sails of a bark (barque)
多桅帆船的帆缆（船具，滑车辘轳）

1-9 masts
桅

1 bowsprit with jib boom
带帽桅的斜桅的帽斜桅

2-4 foremast
前桅

2 lower foremast
下前桅

3 fore topmast
前中桅

4 fore topgallant mast
前上桅

5-7 mainmast
主桅

5 lower mainmast
下主桅

6 main topmast
主中桅

7 main topgallant mast
主上桅

8-9 mizzen (mizen) mast
后桅

8 lower mizzen (lower mizen)
下后桅

9 mizzen (mizen) topmast
后中桅

10-19 standing rigging
静索

10 stay
牵索，支索

11 topmast stay
中桅支索

12 topgallant stay
上桅支索

13 royal stay
顶桅支索

14 jib stay
帽帆支索

15 bobstay
首斜桅支索

16 shrouds
桅牵索

17 fore topmast rigging (main topmast rigging, mizzen (mizen) topmast rigging)
前中桅索具（主中桅索具，后中桅索具）

18 fore topgallant rigging (main topgallant rigging)
前上帆桅索具（主上桅帆索具）

19 backstays
后支索

20-31 fore-and-aft sails
船首及船尾帆

20 fore topmast staysail
前中桅支索帆

21 inner jib
内帽帆

22 outer jib
外帽帆

23 flying jib
帽三角帆

24 main topmast staysail
主中桅支索帆

25 main topgallant staysail
主上桅支索帆

26 main royal staysail
主顶桅支索帆

27 mizzen (mizen) staysail
后桅支索帆

28 mizzen (mizen) topmast staysail
后中桅支索帆

29 mizzen (mizen) topgallant staysail
后上桅支索帆

30 mizzen (mizen, spanker, driver)
后帆（后纵帆）

31 gaff topsail
纵帆斜桁顶帆

32-45 spars
帆、桅、桁

32 foreyard
前桅桁

33 lower fore topsail yard
前中桅下帆桁

34 upper fore topsail yard
前中桅上帆桁

35 lower fore topgallant yard
前上桅下帆桁

36 upper fore topgallant yard
前上桅上帆桁

37 fore royal yard
前顶桅帆桁

38 main yard
主桅桁

39 lower main topsail yard
主中桅下帆桁

40 upper main topsail yard
主中桅上帆桁

41 lower main topgallant yard
主上桅低帆桁

42 upper main topgallant yard
主上桅上帆桁

43 main royal yard
主顶桅帆桁

44 spanker boom
后纵帆杠（杆）

45 spanker gaff
后纵帆斜桁

46 footrope
根缆

47 lifts
吊索（帆桁吊索）

48 spanker boom topping lift
后纵杠杆（杆）端吊索

49 spanker peak halyard
后纵帆杠（杆）顶吊索

50 foretop
前桅楼

51 fore topmast crosstrees
前中桅桅顶横杆

52 maintop
主桅楼

53 main topmast crosstrees
主中桅桅顶横杆

54 mizzen (mizen) top
后桅楼

55-56 square sails
横帆，方帆

55 foresail (fore course)
前帆（前桅帆）

56 lower fore topsail
前中桅下帆

57 upper fore topsail
前中桅上帆

58 lower fore topgallant sail
前上桅下帆

59 upper fore topgallant sail
前上桅上帆

60 fore royal
前顶帆

61 mainsail (main course)
主帆（主桅帆）

62 lower main topsail
主中桅下帆

63 upper main topsail
主中桅上帆

64 lower main topgallant sail
主上桅下帆

65 upper main topgallant sail
主上桅上帆

66 main royal sail
主顶帆

67-71 running rigging
转动（活动）索具

67 braces
操桅索

68 sheets
帆脚索

69 spanker sheet
后纵帆帆脚索

70 spanker vangs
后纵帆杆支索

71 bunt line
绞帆索

72 reef
卷帆部分，缩帆索，卷帆索

1-5 sail shapes
帆的类型
1 gaffsail (*small:* trysail, spencer)
斜帆（前桅之纵帆，斜桁帆）
2 jib
船首三角帆
3 lateen sail
大三角帆
4 lugsail
斜桁用横帆
5 spritsail
斜杠帆
6-8 single-masted sailing boats
(*Am.* sailboats)
单桅帆船
6 tjalk
荷兰单桅帆船（小船）
7 leeboard
下风板
8 cutter
独桅快艇（小艇）
9-10 mizzen (mizen) masted
sailing boats (*Am.* sailboats)
后桅帆船
9 ketch-rigged sailing barge
双桅帆驳船
10 yawl
小帆船
11-17 two-masted sailing boats
(*Am.* sailboats)
双桅帆船
11-13 topsail schooner
顶帆船
11 mainsail
主帆
12 boom foresail
前桅帆桁
13 square foresail
前桅横帆
14 brigantine
双桅帆船
15 half-rigged mast with fore-and-
aft sails
半边带纵帆的桅
16 full-rigged mast with square sails
全部为横帆的桅
17 brig
双桅帆船
18-27 three-masted sailing vessels
(three-masters)
三桅帆船
18 three-masted schooner
三桅纵帆船
19 three-masted topsail schooner
三桅顶帆船
20 bark (barque) schooner
多桅帆船
21-23 bark (barque) [cf. illustration
of rigging and sails in plate 219]
多桅帆船〔看图 219，帆具及帆的说明〕
21 foremast
前桅
22 mainmast
主桅
23 mizzen (mizen) mast
后桅
24-27 full-rigged ship
全帆帆船
24 mizzen (mizen) mast
后桅
25 crossjack yard (crojack yard)
后桅下桁横帆
26 crossjack (crojack)
后桅横帆

27 ports
舷窗
28-31 four-masted sailing ships
(four-masters)
四桅帆船
28 four-masted schooner
四桅纵帆船
29 four-masted bark (barque)
四桅帆船
30 mizzen (mizen) mast
后桅
31 four-masted full-rigged ship
四桅全帆帆船
32-34 five-masted bark (barque)
五桅帆船
32 skysail
顶帆上的小方帆
33 middle mast
中桅
34 mizzen (mizen) mast
后桅
35-37 development of sailing ships
over 400 years
四百年间帆船的发展
35 five-masted full-rigged ship
'Preussen' 1902-10
五桅全帆帆船"普鲁士号"（1902-1910
年）
36 English clipper ship 'Spindrift'
1867
英国快速帆船"浪花号"（1867年）
37 caravel (carvel) 'Santa Maria'
1492
多桅小帆船"圣玛琍亚号"（1492年）

1 **ULCC** (ultra large crude carrier) of the [all-aft' type
机型超大型油轮

2 foremast
前桅

3 catwalk with the pipes
有管的窄道

4 fire gun (fire nozzle)
灭火枪，灭火喷咀

5 deck crane
甲板起重机

6 deckhouse with the bridge
甲板房舱和船桥（楼）

7 aft signal (signalling) and radar mast
船尾信号和雷达桅

8 funnel
烟囱

9 **nuclear research ship** 'Otto Hahn', a bulk carrier
"奥托汉"核能研究轮，一种散装货轮

10 aft superstructure (engine room)
舳上层建筑（机舱）

11 cargo hatchway for bulk goods (bulk cargoes)
散装货物舱口

12 bridge
楼（船桥）

13 forecastle (fo'c'sle)
艏楼

14 stem
船首

15 **seaside pleasure boat**
海滨游艇

16 dummy funnel
假烟囱

17 exhaust mast
排气桅

18 **rescue cruiser**
救难巡洋舰

19 helicopter platform (working deck)
直升机平台（工作甲板）

20 rescue helicopter
救难直升机

21 **all-container ship**
全货柜轮

22 containers stowed on deck
装置於甲板上的货柜

23 **cargo ship**
货船

24-29 cargo gear (cargo-handling gear)
货物装卸装置

24 bipod mast
双脚桅

25 jumbo derrick boom (heavy-lift derrick boom)
重型吊杆（起重杆）

26 derrick boom (cargo boom)
吊杆，起重杆

27 tackle
滑轮组

28 block
滑车

29 thrust bearing
推力轴承

30 bow doors
艏门

31 stern loading door
船尾装货门

32 **offshore drilling rig supply vessel**
海上钻探补给船

33 compact superstructure
紧凑的上层建筑

34 loading deck (working deck)
载货甲板（工作甲板）

35 **liquefied-gas tanker**
液化气运输船

36 spherical tank
球型罐

37 navigational television receiver mast
航海电视接收机桅

38 vent mast
通气（风）管桅

39 deckhouse
甲板房舱

40 funnel
烟囱

41 ventilator
通风机

42 transom stern (transom)
船尾梁

43 rudder blade (rudder)
舵叶（面）

44 ship's propeller (ship's screw)
船的推进器（船的螺桨）

45 bulbous bow
球形

46 steam trawler
蒸汽拖网渔船

47 **lightship** (light vessel)
灯塔船

48 lantern (characteristic light)
信号灯

49 smack
（设有养鱼槽的）渔帆船

50 **ice breaker**
破冰船

51 steaming light mast
蒸汽灯桅

52 helicopter hangar
直升机库

53 stern towing point, for gripping the bow of ships in tow
船尾拖曳点，扣住船首以拖行

54 **roll-on-roll-off (ro-ro) trailer ferry**
（开上开下）拖车渡轮

55 stern port (stern opening) with ramp
带坡道的舳门

56 heavy vehicle lifts (*Am.* heavy vehicle elevators)
重型车辆升降机

57 **multi-purpose freighter**
多用途货船

58 ventilator-type samson (sampson) post (ventilator-type king post)
通风管式吊杆柱（通风管式king柱）

59 derrick boom (cargo boom, cargo gear, cargo-handling gear)
吊杆，起重杆（货物装卸装置）

60 derrick mast
吊杆桅

61 deck crane
甲板起重机

62 jumbo derrick boom (heavy-lift derrick boom)
重型吊杆

63 cargo hatchway
货舱口

64 **semisubmersible drilling vessel**
半潜式钻探船

65 floating vessel with machinery
带轮机的浮船

66 drilling platform
钻探平台

67 derrick
钻塔

68 **cattleship** (cattle vessel)
家畜（运输）船

69 superstructure for transporting livestock
运输家畜的上层建筑

70 fresh water tanks
新鲜（淡）水槽

71 fuel tank
燃料槽

72 dung tank
粪便槽

73 fodder tanks
饲料（草料）槽

74 **train ferry** [cross section]
火车渡轮

75 funnel
烟窗

76 exhaust pipes
排气管

77 mast
桅

78 ship's lifeboat hanging at the davit
吊於吊架上的救生艇

79 car deck
汽车甲板

80 main deck (train deck)
主甲板（火车甲板）

81 main engines
主发动机（引擎）

82 **passenger liner** (liner, ocean liner)
定期客轮（定期越洋轮）

83 stem
船首

84 funnel with lattice casing
带格子套的烟窗

85 flag dressing (rainbow dressing, string of flags extending over mastheads, e.g., on the maiden voyage)
彩旗装饰（遍布於各桅顶间的彩旗串，如：首次航行）

86 **trawler, a factory ship**
拖网渔船，一种工厂船

87 gallows
绞架，滑车架台

88 stern ramp
船尾倾斜台

89 **container ship**
货柜船

90 loading bridge (loading platform)
装卸桥（装卸平台）

91 sea ladder (jacob's ladder, rope ladder)
海上用梯（绳梯，软梯）

92 **barge and push tug assembly**
驳船和推拖船组合体

93 push tug
顶推拖船

94 tug-pushed dumb barge (tug-pushed lighter)
拖船推进的无动力驳船

95 pilot boat
引水船

96 **combined cargo and passenger liner**
定期客货轮

97 passengers disembarking by boat
经由小船上岸的旅客

98 accommodation ladder
舷梯

99 coaster (coasting vessel)
沿海船，近海船

100 customs or police launch
海关或水警汽艇

101-128 excursion steamer (pleasure steamer)
旅游汽船

101-106 lifeboat launching gear
救生艇下水装置

101 davit
吊架

102 wire rope span
顶跨钢索

103 lifeline
救生索

104 tackle
滑车组

105 block
滑车

106 fall
吊索

107 ship's lifeboat (ship's boat) covered with tarpaulin
复盖防水布罩的船载救生艇

108 stem
船首

109 passenger
旅客

110 steward
服务员

111 deck-chair
甲板座椅

112 deck hand
甲板人员

113 deck bucket
甲板水桶

114 boatswain (bo's'n, bo'sun, bosun)
水手长

115 tunic
短上衣

116 awning
（甲板上的）遮篷

117 stanchion
支柱

118 ridge rope (jackstay)
遮篷索

119 lashing
系索，绑索

120 bulwark
舷墙

121 guard rail
导轨

122 handrail (top rail)
扶手栏杆

123 companion ladder (companionway)
升降梯（口）

124 lifebelt (lifebuoy)
救生带（救生圈）

125 lifebuoy light (lifebelt light, signal light)
救生圈灯（救生带灯，信号灯）

126 officer of the watch (watchkeeper)
值班人员

127 reefer (Am. pea jacket)
双排扣厚呢上衣

128 binoculars
双眼望远镜

1-43 shipyard (shipbuilding yard, dockyard, *Am.* navy yard)
造船厂

1 administrative offices
管理办公室

2 ship-drawing office
船舶制图室（绘图室）

3-4 shipbuilding sheds
造船工场

3 mould (*Am.* mold) loft
放样间

4 erection shop
建造工场

5-9 fitting-out quay
装配码头

5 quay
码头

6 tripod crane
三脚架起重机

7 hammer-headed crane
锤型起重机

8 engineering workshop
轮机工作间

9 boiler shop
锅炉工场

10 repair quay
修理码头

11-26 slipways (slips, building berths, building slips, stocks)
船台（造船台）

11-18 cable crane berth, a slipway (building berth)
缆索起重机，一种船台（造船台）

11 slipway portal
船台门架

12 bridge support
桥支架

13 crane cable
起重机缆索

14 crab (jenny)
活动吊车（悬链导车）

15 cross piece
横梁

16 crane driver's cabin (crane driver's cage)
起重机驾驶室

17 slipway floor
船台底板

18 staging, a scaffold
搭架，一种台架

19-21 frame slipway
构架式船台

19 slipway frame
船台构架

20 overhead travelling (*Am.* traveling) crane (gantry crane)
高架式移动起重机

21 slewing crab
转动起重机

22 keel in position
放於定位上的龙骨

23 luffing jib crane, a slipway crane
悬臂式起重机，一种船台起重机

24 crane rails (crane track)
吊车轨道，起重机轨道

25 gantry crane
高架移动起重机

26 gantry (bridge)
门式起重机机架

27 trestles (supports)
架柱（支柱）

28 crab (jenny)
活动吊车，悬铸导车

29 hull frames in position
於定位的船体构架

30 ship under construction
建造中的船

31-33 dry dock
乾[船]坞

31 dock floor (dock bottom)
船坞底板

32 dock gates (caisson)
坞门

33 pumping station (power house)
泵室（动力室）

34-43 floating dock (pontoon dock)
浮坞（浮箱，驳船坞）

34 dock crane (dockside crane), a jib crane
船坞起重机，悬臂式起重机

35 fender pile
碰垫桩，护舷桩

36-43 working of docks
船坞的作业

36 dock basin
船渠

37-38 dock structure
船坞结构

37 side tank (side wall)
侧舱（侧壁）

38 bottom tank (bottom pontoon)
底舱（下浮箱）

39 keel block
龙骨墩

40 bilge block (bilge shore, side support)
舭部坞墩（舭部墩柱，边墩柱）

41-43 docking a ship
进坞的船隻

41 flooded floating dock
浸水浮坞，注水式浮坞
42 tug towing the ship
拖曳船
43 emptied (pumped-out) dock
放空水的船坞
44-61 structural parts of the ship
船的结构（构造）部分
44-56 longitudinal structure
纵向结构
44-49 shell (shell plating, skin)
船壳（船壳板，船表壳）
44 sheer strake
舷侧厚板列
45 side strake
舷板列
46 bilge stake
舭板列
47 bilge keel
舭龙骨
48 bottom plating
船底外板
49 flat plate keel (keel plate)
平板龙骨（龙骨板）
50 stringer (side stringer)
纵材，舷缘板（侧纵材）
51 tank margin plate
舷缘板
52 longitudinal side girder
侧纵梁
53 centre (*Am.* center) plate girder
(centre girder, kelson, keelson,
vertical keel)
中心板纵梁（中心纵梁，内龙骨，垂直
龙骨）

54 tank top plating (tank top, inner
bottom plating)
重底顶板，柜舱顶板（舱顶，内舱底
板）
55 centre (*Am.* center) strake
中心板列
56 deck plating
钢甲板
57 deck beam
甲板梁
58 frame (rib)
肋骨架
59 floor plate
底板
60 cellular double bottom
格子[二]重底
61 hold pillar (pillar)
舱柱
62, 63 dunnage
垫材
62 side battens (side ceiling, spar
ceiling)
舱侧条（舱侧垫材，间距垫材）
63 ceiling (floor ceiling)
舱底内板，垫材（船底垫材）
64-65 hatchway
舱口，货舱口
64 hatch coaming
舱口缘围
65 hatch cover (hatchboard)
舱口盖板
66-72 stern
船尾
66 guard rail
护栏

67 bulwark
舷墙
68 rudder stock
舵杆
69-70 Oertz rudder
欧兹舵（流线型舵）
69 rudder blade (rudder)
舵面
70-71 stern frame
船尾架
70 rudder post
舵柱
71 propeller post (screw post)
推进器柱（螺桨柱）
72 ship's propeller (ship's screw)
推进器，螺旋桨
73 draught (draft) marks
吃水桥
74-79 bow
船首
74 stem, a bulbous stem (bulbous
bow)
船首，球型艏（柱）
75 hawse
锚链
76 hawse pipe
锚链管
77 anchor cable (chain cable)
锚缆（链索）
78 stockless anchor (patent anchor)
山字锚，无杆锚
79 stocked anchor
普通锚，有杆锚

1-71 combined cargo and passenger ship [of the older type]
老式的客货轮
1 funnel
烟窗
2 funnel marking
烟窗标记
3 siren (fog horn)
汽笛（雾笛）
4-11 compass platform (compass bridge, compass flat, monkey bridge)
罗（盘）经台（甲板）
4 antenna lead-in (antenna downlead)
天线引入线（天线下引线）
5 radio direction finder (RDF) antenna (direction finder antenna, rotatable loop antenna, aural null loop antenna)
无线电测向天线（测向仪天线，可旋转的环型天线，消声环型天线）
6 magnetic compass (mariner's compass)
磁罗经（盘）（船用罗经）
7 morse lamp (signalling, *Am.* signaling, lamp)
信号灯
8 radar antenna (radar scanner)
雷达天线
9 code flag signal
信号旗信号
10 code flag halyards
信号旗的升降绳（索）

11 triatic stay (signal stay)
水平撑杆（信号撑杆）
12-18 bridge deck (bridge)
驾驶台甲板
12 radio room
无线电室（报务室）
13 captain's cabin
船长室
14 navigating bridge
驾驶台
15 starboard sidelight [green; port sidelight red]
右舷灯〔绿；左舷灯红〕
16 wing of bridge
桥翼，船桥的舷翼
17 shelter (weather cloth, dodger)
遮蔽物（挡雨布，防雨布）
18 wheelhouse
舵轮室，驾驶室
19-21 boat deck
小艇甲板
19 ship's lifeboat
救生艇
20 davit
吊柱，吊架
21 officer's cabin
高级船员室
22-27 promenade deck
散步甲板
22 sun deck (lido deck)
阳光甲板（游泳池甲板）
23 swimming pool
游泳池
24 companion ladder (companionway)
升降梯，升降口

25 library (ship's library)
图书馆
26 lounge
休息室
27 promenade
散步甲板
28-30 A-deck
A 甲板
28 semi-enclosed deck space
半封（围）闭式甲板空间
29 double-berth cabin, a cabin
双铺房舱
30 de luxe cabin
豪华舱（头等舱）
31 ensign staff
船尾旗杆
32-42 B-deck (main deck)
B 甲板（主甲板）
32 after deck
后甲板
33 poop
艉楼
34 deckhouse
甲板室
35 samson (sampson) post (king post)
吊杆柱

36 derrick boom (cargo boom)
吊杆（起重杆）
37 crosstrees (spreader)
桅顶横杆
38 crow's nest
桅杆了望台
39 topmast
中桅
40 forward steaming light
船首航行灯
41 ventilator lead
通风器导管
42 galley (caboose, cookroom, ship's kitchen)
厨房
43 ship's pantry
配膳室
44 dining room
餐厅
45 purser's office
事务长室
46 single-berth cabin
单人舱
47 foredeck
前甲板
48 forecastle (fo'c'sle)
船首楼
49–51 ground tackle
锚具
49 windlass
锚机
50 anchor cable (chain cable)
锚缆（链索）
51 compressor (chain compressor)
压缩机（链式压缩机）
52 anchor
锚

53 jackstaff
船首旗杆
54 jack
船首旗
55 after holds
后舱
56 cold storage room (insulated hold)
冷藏室〔隔（绝）热舱〕
57 store room
储藏室
58 wake
航迹
59 shell bossing (shaft bossing)
轴包架（艉轴毂）
60 tail shaft (tail end shaft)
艉轴
61 shaft strut (strut, spectacle frame, propeller strut, propeller bracket)
艉轴支架（支架，双环架，推进器，推进器拖架）
62 three-blade ship's propeller (ship's screw)
船用三叶螺旋桨
63 rudder blade (rudder)
舵面
64 stuffing box
填料函
65 propeller shaft
螺旋桨轴
66 shaft alley (shaft tunnel)
轴道
67 thrust block
推力轴承
68–74 diesel-electric drive
柴油机电力推进（驱动）

68 electric engine room
电动机（引擎）房
69 electric motor
电动机
70 auxiliary engine room
辅机房
71 auxiliary engines
辅机
72 main engine room
主机房
73 main engine, a diesel engine
主机，一种柴油发动机
74 generator
发电机
75 forward holds
前舱
76 tween deck
中甲板
77 cargo
货物
78 ballast tank (deep tank) for water ballast
水压载的压载舱（深舱）
79 fresh water tank
淡水舱
80 fuel tank
燃料舱
81 bow wave
船首波

1 **sextant**
六分仪

2 graduated arc
刻度弧

3 index bar (index arm)
指示棒

4 decimal micrometer
十进位测微器

5 vernier
游标

6 index mirror
指示镜

7 horizon glass (horizon mirror)
水平镜

8 telescope
望远镜

9 grip (handgrip)
手柄

10-13 **radar equipment** (radar apparatus)
雷达设备

10 radar pedestal
雷达基座

11 revolving radar reflector
旋转式雷达反射器

12 radar display unit (radar screen)
雷达显示装置（雷达屏幕）

13 radar image (radar picture)
雷达图像

14-38 **wheelhouse**
舵轮室，驾驶室

14 steering and control position
操舵和控制室（位置）

15 ship's wheel for controlling the rudder mechanism
控制舵机的舵轮

16 helmsman (*Am.* wheelsman)
舵手

17 rudder angle indicator
舵角指示器

18 automatic pilot (autopilot)
自航器

19 control lever for the variable-pitch propeller (reversible propeller, feathering propeller, feathering screw)
变距螺桨的控制杆（可逆向的螺旋桨，顺流螺桨）

20 propeller pitch indicator
螺旋桨螺距指示器

21 main engine revolution indicator
主（发动）机转速指示器

22 ship's speedometer (log)
速率计

23 control switch for bow thruster (bow-manoeuvring, *Am.* maneuvering, propeller)
艏操纵向推进器控制开关（艏操纵，推进器）

24 echo recorder (depth recorder, echograph)
回音记录器（深度记录器）

25 engine telegraph (engine order telegraph)
车钟（车令钟）

26 controls for the antirolling system (for the stabilizers)
抗摇系统的控制装置

27 local-battery telephone
自给电池电话

28 shipping traffic radio telephone
航运交通无线电话

29 navigation light indicator panel (running light indicator panel)
航海灯指示盘

30 microphone for ship's address system
船行位置呼叫系统用的传声器

31 gyro compass (gyroscopic compass), a compass repeater
迴转罗盘，一种罗盘重发器

32 control button for the ship's siren (ship's fog horn)
（雾）汽笛的控制按钮

33 main engine overload indicator
主机超载指示器

34 detector indicator unit for fixing the ship's position
固定船位置的探测显（指）示装置

35 rough focusing indicator
粗聚胶指示器

36 fine focusing indicator
微聚胶指示器

37 navigating officer
驾驶员

38 captain
船长

39 **Decca navigation system**
迪凯导航系统

40 master station
主台

41 slave station
副台

42 null hyperbola
零值双曲线

43 hyperbolic position line 1
双曲线的位置线 1

44 hyperbolic position line 2
双曲线的位置线 2

45 position (fix, ship fix)
船位（定位）

46-53 **compasses**
罗盘

46 liquid compass (fluid compass, spirit compass, wet compass), a magnetic compass
液体罗盘，一种磁罗盘

47 compass card
罗盘面（卡）

48 lubber's line (lubber's mark, lubber's point)
艏向刻线

49 compass bowl
罗盘碗

50 gimbal ring
平衡环

51-53 gyro compass (gyroscopic compass, gyro compass unit)
迴转罗盘

51 master compass (master gyro compass)
主罗盘

52 compass repeater (gyro repeater)
罗盘重发器

53 compass repeater with pelorus
带哑罗盘的罗盘重发器

54 **patent log** (screw log, mechanical log, towing log, taffrail log, speedometer)
测程仪（螺旋测程器，机械测程器，曳航测程器，船尾栏杆测程计，速率计）

55 rotator
转子，转轮

56 governor
调速器

57 log clock
测程指示表

58-67 **leads**
测铅，测深锤

58 hand lead
手投深锤

59 lead (lead sinker)
测铅

60 leadline
测铅线

61-67 echo sounder (echo sounding machine)
回音测深机

61 sound transmitter
声音发送机

62 sound wave (sound impulse)
音波

63 echo (sound echo, echo signal)
回音（回音信号）

64 echo receiver (hydrophone)
回音接收机（水中听音器）

65 echograph (echo sounding machine recorder)
回音记录器（回音测深机记录器）

66 depth scale
深度标尺

67 echogram (depth recording, depth reading)
深度记录图

68-108 sea marks (floating navigational marks) for buoyage and lighting systems
航标（航海浮标），浮标和灯光系统

68-83 fairway marks (channel marks)
航道标示

68 light and whistle buoy
灯光和鸣笛浮标

69 light (warning light)
灯光（警示灯）

70 whistle
笛

71 buoy
浮标

72 mooring chain
系船链（系泊链）

73 sinker (mooring sinker)
吊锤，系泊水砣

74 light and bell buoy
灯光和钟浮标

75 bell
钟

76 conical buoy
锥形浮标

77 can buoy
罐型浮标

78 topmark
顶标

79 spar buoy
杆标

80 topmark buoy
顶标浮标

81 lightship (light vessel)
灯船

82 lantern mast (lantern tower)
灯塔

83 beam of light
光线；光束

84-102 fairway markings (channel markings)
航道标志

84 wreck [green buoys]
沉船（绿色浮标）

85 wreck to starboard
右舷沉船标识

86 wreck to port
左舷沉船标识

87 shoals (shallows, shallow water, *Am.* flats)
浅滩

88 middle ground to port
左舷中洲标识

89 division (bifurcation) [beginning of the middle ground; topmark: red cylinder above red ball]
航道分岔处〔航道中洲的始端，顶标：红球上红色圆筒〕

90 convergence (confluence) [end of the middle ground; topmark: red St. Antony's cross above red ball]
航道汇合标志〔中洲终端，顶标：红球上红色圣安东尼十字架〕

91 middle ground
中洲

92 main fairway (main navigable channel)
主航道

93 secondary fairway (secondary navigable channel)
副航道

94 can buoy
罐形浮标

95 port hand buoys (port hand marks) [red]
左舷侧浮标〔红色〕

96 starboard hand buoys (starboard hand marks) [black]
右舷侧浮标〔黑色〕

97 shoals (shallows, shallow water, *Am.* flats) outside the fairway
在航道外侧的浅滩

98 middle of the fairway (mid-channel)
航道中央标识

99 starboard markers (inverted broom)
右舷标识（倒扫帚形）

100 port markers [upward-pointing broom]
左舷标识〔上向扫帚形〕

101-102 range lights (leading lights)
导标

101 lower range light (lower leading light)
低导灯

102 higher range light (higher leading light)
高导灯

103 lighthouse
灯塔

104 radar antenna (radar scanner)
雷达天线

105 lantern (characteristic light)
（特别的灯）灯室

106 radio direction finder (RDF) antenna
无线电探向器天线

107 machinery and observation platform (machinery and observation deck)
机械装置和了望台

108 living quarters
住舱

1 dock area
码头区

2 free port (foreign trade zone)
自由港（对外贸易区）

3 free zone frontier (free zone enclosure)
自由区边界

4 customs barrier
海关关卡

5 customs entrance
海关入口

6 port custom house
港口海关

7 entrepôt
仓库

8 barge (dumb barge, lighter)
驳船（无动力驳船，驳船）

9 break-bulk cargo transit shed (general cargo transit shed, package cargo transit shed)
散装货物通栈（一般货物通栈，包捆货物通栈）

10 floating crane
水上起重机

11 harbour (*Am.* harbor) ferry (ferryboat)
海港渡轮

12 fender (dolphin)
护舷（系船桩）

13 bunkering boat
燃料船，油船

14 break-bulk carrier (general cargo ship)
散装货船（一般货船）

15 tug
拖船

16 floating dock (pontoon dock)
浮船坞（浮码头）

17 dry dock
乾船坞

18 coal wharf
煤码头

19 coal bunker
煤仓

20 transporter loading bridge
装卸货的桥式吊车

21 quayside railway
码头边铁路

22 weighing bunker
过磅处

23 warehouse
仓库，货栈

24 quayside crane
码头边起重机

25 launch and lighter
汽艇和驳船

26 port hospital
港口医院

27 quarantine wing
检疫所

28 Institute of Tropical Medicine
热带医学研究所

29 excursion steamer (pleasure steamer)
游览汽艇

30 jetty
突堤码头

31 passenger terminal
旅客码头

32 liner (passenger liner, ocean liner)
定期轮（定期客轮，定期远洋轮）

33 meteorological office, a weather station
气象台，气象站

34 signal mast (signalling mast)
信号桅

35 storm signal
暴风雨信号

36 port administration offices
港口管理机关

37 tide level indicator
潮汐水位指示器

38 quayside road (quayside roadway)
码头边马路

39 roll-on roll-off (ro-ro) system (roll-on roll-off operation)
水平装卸方式

40 gantry
门式起重机的门架

41 truck-to-truck system (truck-to-truck operation)
车对车装卸方式

42 foil-wrapped unit loads
金属箔包装的单位货物

43 pallets
货盘

44 forklift truck (fork truck, forklift)
堆高机

45 container ship
货柜船

46 transporter container-loading
bridge
货柜装卸桥运输机

47 container carrier truck
货柜运输卡车

48 container terminal (container
berth)
货柜码头

49 unit load
单位货物

50 cold store
冷藏库

51 conveyor belt (conveyor)
运输机皮带

52 fruit storage shed (fruit
warehouse)
水果贮藏室

53 office building
办公大楼

54 urban motorway (*Am.* freeway)
都市高速公路

55 harbour (*Am.* harbor) tunnels
海港隧道

56 fish dock
渔船码头

57 fish market
鱼市

58 auction room
拍卖室

59 fish-canning factory
鱼罐工厂

60 push tow
顶推拖船

61 tank farm
油库

62 railway siding
铁路侧线

63 landing pontoon (landing stage)
栈台，栈桥

64 quay
码头

65 breakwater (mole)
防波堤

66 pier (jetty), a quay extension
突堤码头，延伸码头

67 bulk carrier
散装货船

68 silo
散装仓库

69 silo cylinder
散装仓库圆筒

70 lift bridge
升降桥

71 industrial plant
工业性工厂（场）

72 storage tanks
贮存罐

73 tanker
油轮

1 container terminal (container berth), a modern cargo-handling berth
货柜码头（新式货物装载码头）
2 transporter container-loading bridge (loading bridge); *sim.*: transtainer crane (transtainer)
货柜装载桥运输机；类似：移动式货柜起重机
3 container
货柜车
4 truck (carrier)
载货车
5 all-container ship
全货柜船
6 containers stowed on deck
堆放于甲板上的货柜
7 truck-to-truck handling (horizontal cargo handling with pallets)
车对车搬运（具垫架的水平货物搬运）
8 forklift truck (fork truck, forklift)
堆高机
9 unitized foil-wrapped load (unit load)
单位化金属箔包装的货物
10 flat pallet, a standard pallet
平货盘，标准货盘
11 unitized break-bulk cargo
单位化散装货
12 heat sealing machine
热封口机

13 break-bulk carrier (general cargo ship)
散装货物运输船（一般普通货船）
14 cargo hatchway
货舱口
15 receiving truck on board ship
船上的接货卡车
16 multi-purpose terminal
多用途卸货码头
17 roll-on roll-off ship (ro-ro-ship)
水平装卸船
18 stern port (stern opening)
触装卸门
19 driven load, a lorry (*Am.* truck)
载货卡车
20 ro-ro depot
水平装卸的货仓
21 unitized load (unitized package)
单位化货物
22 banana-handling terminal [section]
香蕉型装卸码头〔断面图〕
23 seaward tumbler
向海的转筒
24 jib
悬臂
25 elevator bridge
升降桥
26 chain sling
勾环吊链
27 lighting station
照明站

28 shore-side tumbler for loading trains and lorries (*Am.* trucks)
列车和卡车装载用的海岸转筒
29 bulk cargo handling
散装货物的装卸
30 bulk carrier
散装货船
31 floating bulk-cargo elevator
散装浮升降机
32 suction pipes
吸管
33 receiver
接收器
34 delivery pipe
排出管
35 bulk transporter barge
散装货运驳船
36 floating pile driver
打桩机
37 pile driver frame
打桩机架
38 pile hammer
打桩锤
39 driving guide rail
驱动导轨
40 pile
桩
41 bucket dredger, a dredger
箕斗挖泥船，一种挖泥船
42 bucket chain
箕链
43 bucket ladder
箕梯

44 dredger bucket
   挖泥箕
45 chute
   滑槽
46 hopper barge
   斗式驳船
47 spoil
   挖掘出之泥土
48 floating crane
   起重机船，水上起重机
49 jib (boom)
   悬臂
50 counterweight (counterpoise)
   配重（对重）
51 adjusting spindle
   调整轴
52 crane driver's cabin (crane
   driver's cage)
   起重机驾驶室
53 crane framework
   起重机架构骨架
54 winch house
   绞车室
55 control platform
   控制，操纵台
56 turntable
   转台
57 pontoon, a pram
   平底驳船，平底船的一种
58 engine superstructure (engine
   mounting)
   发动机上的建筑物（船楼）

1 **salvaging (salving) of a ship run aground**
搁浅船的救助

2 **ship run aground (damaged vessel)**
搁浅船（受损船）

3 **sandbank;** *also:* **quicksand**
沙洲；浮沙，流沙

4 **open sea**
公海

5 **tug (salvage tug)**
拖船（救难拖船）

6-15 **towing gear**
拖曳装置

6 **towing gear for towing at sea**
海上的拖曳装置

7 **towing winch (towing machine, towing engine)**
拖曳绞车（拖曳机）

8 **tow rope (tow line, towing hawser)**
拖缆，拖索（系船索）

9 **tow rope guide**
拖索导柱

10 **cross-shaped bollard**
十字形系船柱

11 **hawse hole**
锚链孔

12 **anchor cable (chain cable)**
锚缆（链缆）

13 **towing gear for work in harbours (*Am.* harbors)**
港内作业用的拖船装置

14 **guest rope**
系船索

15 **position of the tow rope (tow line, towing hawser)**
系船索，拖缆的位置

16 **tug (salvage tug) [vertical elevation]**
拖船（救难拖船）〔立式正面图〕

17 **bow fender (pudding fender)**
船首护舷（船首碰垫）

18 **forepeak**
船首舱

19 **living quarters**
住舱

20 **Schottel propeller**
斯科特尔螺桨

21 **Kort vent**
科特通气孔

22 **engine and propeller room**
发动机和螺桨室

23 **clutch coupling**
离合联结器

24 **compass platform (compass bridge, compass flat, monkey bridge)**
罗盘台

25 **fire-fighting equipment**
（消防）防火设备

26 **stowage**
贮舱

27 **tow hook**
拖钩

28 **afterpeak**
船尾舱

29 **stern fender**
船尾护舷（碰垫）

30 **main manoeuvring (*Am.* maneuvering) keel**
主操纵龙骨

1 **rocket apparatus (rocket gun, line-throwing gun)**
救生索火箭发射器（火箭枪，抛绳枪）
2 **life rocket (rocket)**
救生火箭
3 **rocket line (whip line)**
火箭救生绳（绕绳）
4 **oilskins**
雨衣
5 **sou' wester (southwester)**
防水帽
6 **oilskin jacket**
防水夹克
7 **oilskin coat**
防水外衣
8 **inflatable life jacket**
气胀式救生衣
9 **cork life jacket (cork life preserver)**
软木救生衣
10 **stranded ship (damaged vessel)**
搁浅的船（受损的船）
11 **oil bag, for trickling oil on the water surface**
向水面上滴油用的油袋
12 **lifeline**
救生索
13 **breeches buoy**
连裤救生衣
14 **rescue cruiser**
救难巡洋舰
15 **helicopter landing deck**
直升机著陆甲板

16 **rescue helicopter**
救难直升机
17 **daughter boat**
子船
18 **inflatable boat (inflatable dinghy)**
充气艇，橡皮艇（充气小艇）
19 **life raft**
救生筏
20 **fire-fighting equipment for fires at sea**
海难失火用的防火装置
21 **hospital unit with operating cabin and exposure bath**
具手术室和御寒室的医院装置
22 **navigating bridge**
驾驶台
23 **upper tier of navigating bridge**
驾驶台的上层
24 **lower tier of navigating bridge**
驾驶台的下层
25 **messroom**
餐厅
26 **rudders and propeller (screw)**
舵和螺旋桨
27 **stowage**
贮藏舱
28 **foam can**
灭火器（泡沫灭火器）
29 **side engines**
船侧发动机
30 **shower**
浴室

31 **coxswain's cabin**
艇长室
32 **crew member's single-berth cabin**
船员单人舱
33 **bow propeller**
船首（转向）推进器

1-14 wing configurations
机翼的配置

1 high-wing monoplane (high-wing plane)
高单翼机

2 span (wing span)
翼展

3 shoulder-wing monoplane (shoulder-wing plane)
上单翼机

4 midwing monoplane (midwing plane)
中单翼机

5 low-wing monoplane (low-wing plane)
下单翼机

6 triplane
三翼机

7 upper wing
上翼

8 middle wing (central wing)
中翼

9 lower wing
下翼

10 biplane
双翼机

11 strut
支柱

12 cross bracing wires
十字形（交叉）张线

13 sesquiplane
双翼半双翼机

14 low-wing monoplane (low-wing plane) with cranked wings (inverted gull wings)
倒海鸥式下单翼机

15-22 wing shapes
机翼形状

15 elliptical wing
椭圆形翼

16 rectangular wing
长方形翼

17 tapered wing
渐缩翼

18 crescent wing
新月形翼

19 delta wing
三角翼

20 swept-back wing with semi-positive sweepback
半正后掠角的后掠翼

21 swept-back wing with positive sweepback
正后掠角的后掠翼

22 ogival wing (ogee wing)
尖拱翼（S 形机翼）

23-36 tail shapes (tail unit shapes, empennage shapes)
尾翼形状（尾部装置形状，尾部形状）

23 normal tail (normal tail unit)
（正常）一般的尾翼（一般的机尾装置）

24-25 vertical tail (vertical stabilizer and rudder)
直尾翼（垂直安定面和方向舵）

24 vertical stabilizer (vertical fin, tail fin)
垂直安定面（直尾翅，尾翅）

25 rudder
方向舵

26-27 horizontal tail
水平尾翼

26 tailplane (horizontal stabilizer)
尾面（水平安定面）

27 elevator
升降舵

28 cruciform tail (cruciform tail unit)
十字形尾翼（十字形尾翼装置）

29 T-tail (T-tail unit)
T 形尾翼（T 形尾翼装置）

30 lobe
波瓣，舵囊，整流锥

31 V-tail (vee-tail, butterfly tail)
V 形尾翼（蝴蝶形尾翼）

32 double tail unit (twin tail unit)
双尾翼

33 end plate
端板（双垂直安定面）

34 double tail unit (twin tail unit) of a twin-boom aircraft
双尾桁机的双尾翼装置

35 raised horizontal tail with double booms
双尾桁的高水平尾翼

36 triple tail unit
三尾翼装置

37 system of flaps
襟翼系统

38 extensible slat
外伸式缝翼

39 spoiler
扰流板

40 double-slotted Fowler flap
双缝阜勒氏襟翼

41 outer aileron (low-speed aileron)
外副翼（低速副翼）

42 inner spoiler (landing flap, lift dump)
内扰流板（降落襟翼）

43 inner aileron (all-speed aileron)
内副翼（全速副翼）

44 brake flap (air brake)
制动襟翼（空中制动器）

45 basic profile
基本翼形

46-48 plain flaps (simple flaps)
简单襟翼（单襟翼）

46 normal flap
一般襟翼

47 slotted flap
开缝襟翼

48 double-slotted flap
双缝襟翼

49-50 split flaps
分裂式襟翼

49 plain split flap (simple split flap)
简单分裂式襟翼

50 zap flap
查普襟翼

51 extending flap
伸展式襟翼

52 Fowler flap
阜勒氏襟翼

53 slat
缝翼

54 profiled leading-edge flap (droop flap)
翼形前缘襟翼（下垂襟翼）

55 Krüger flap
克鲁格襟翼

1-31 **cockpit** of a single-engine
(single-engined) racing and
passenger aircraft (racing and
passenger plane)
单发动机竞赛与载客双用飞机的座舱
（驾驶舱）

1 instrument panel
仪表板

2 air-speed (*Am.* airspeed)
indicator
空速表

3 artificial horizon (gyro horizon)
人工水平仪

4 altimeter
高度表

5 radio compass (automatic
direction finder)
无线电罗盘（自动定向仪）

6 magnetic compass
磁性罗盘

7 boost gauge (*Am.* gage)
增压表

8 tachometer (rev counter,
revolution counter)
转速表

9 cylinder temperature gauge (*Am.*
gage)
汽缸温度表

10 accelerometer
加速表

11 chronometer
航行表

12 turn indicator with ball
转弯指示器

13 directional gyro
定向陀螺仪

14 vertical speed indicator (rate-
of-climb indicator, variometer)
垂直速率表（升降速率指示器）

15 VOR radio direction finder
[*VOR*: very high frequency
omnidirectional range]
极高频全向导航台无线电定向仪

16 left tank fuel gauge (*Am.* gage)
左油箱油量表

17 right tank fuel gauge (*Am.* gage)
右油箱油量表

18 ammeter
安培计（电流表）

19 fuel pressure gauge (*Am.* gage)
燃油压力表

20 oil pressure gauge (*Am.* gage)
滑油压力表

21 oil temperature gauge (*Am.*
gage)
滑油温度表

22 radio and radio navigation
equipment
无线电和无线电航行（导航）设备

23 map light
地图灯

24 wheel (control column, control
stick) for operating the ailerons
and elevators
副翼和升降舵的操纵盘

25 co-pilot's wheel
副驾驶操纵盘

26 switches
开关（电门）

27 rudder pedals
方向舵踏板

28 co-pilot's rudder pedals
副驾驶方向舵踏板

29 microphone for the radio
无线电话筒（扩音器）

30 throttle lever (throttle control)
油门操纵杆

31 mixture control
混合气控制

32-66 **single-engine (single-engined)
racing and passenger aircraft
(racing and passenger plane)**
单发动机竞赛与载客两用机

32 propeller (airscrew)
螺旋桨

33 spinner
桨鼻罩

34 flat four engine
平列四缸发动机

35 cockpit
座舱（驾驶舱）

36 pilot's seat
驾驶员座椅

37 co-pilot's seat
副驾驶员座椅

38 passenger seats
旅客座椅

39 hood (canopy, cockpit hood,
cockpit canopy)
座舱盖

40 steerable nose wheel
可操纵鼻轮

41 main undercarriage unit (main
landing gear unit)
主起落架

42 step
阶座（踏脚）

43 wing
机翼

44 right navigation light (right
position light)
右航行灯（右位置灯）

45 spar
翼梁

46 rib
肋

47 stringer (longitudinal
reinforcing member)
纵桁（纵向加强桁条）

48 fuel tank
燃油箱

49 landing light
落地灯

50 left navigation light (left
position light)
左航行灯（左位置灯）

51 electrostatic conductor
静电放电导体

52 aileron
副翼

53 landing flap
降落襟翼

54 fuselage (body)
机身

55 frame (former)
构架

56 chord
翼弦

57 stringer (longitudinal
reinforcing member)
纵桁（纵向加强桁条）

58 vertical tail (vertical stabilizer
and rudder)
直尾翼（垂直安定面和方向舵）

59 vertical stabilizer (vertical fin,
tail fin)
垂直安定面（直尾翅，尾翼）

60 rudder
方向舵

61 horizontal tail
水平尾翼

62 tailplane (horizontal stabilizer)
尾面（水平安定面）

63 elevator
升降舵

64 warning light (anticollision
light)
警告灯（防撞灯）

65 dipole antenna
偶极天线（双极天线）

66 long-wire antenna (long-
conductor antenna)
长线天线（长导线天线）

67-72 **principal manoeuvres** (*Am.*
maneuvers) of the aircraft
(aeroplane, plane, *Am.* airplane)
飞机的主要动作

67 pitching
俯仰（飞机绕其横轴之角运动）

68 lateral axis
横轴

69 yawing
偏航（飞机绕其垂直轴之运动）

70 vertical axis (normal axis)
垂直轴

71 rolling
侧滚（飞机绕其纵轴之运动）

72 longitudinal axis
纵轴

1-33 types of aircraft
(aeroplanes, planes, *Am.*
airplanes)
飞机的种类

1-6 propeller-driven aircraft
(aeroplanes, planes, *Am.*
airplanes)
螺旋桨飞机

1 single-engine (single-engined)
racing and passenger aircraft
(racing and passenger plane), a
low-wing monoplane (low-wing
plane)
单发动机（引擎）竞赛与载客飞机，一
种下单翼飞机

2 single-engine (single-engined)
passenger aircraft, a high-wing
monoplane (high-wing plane)
单发动机客机，一种高单翼飞机

3 twin-engine (twin-engined)
business and passenger aircraft
(business and passenger plane)
双发动机商用与客用飞机

4 short/medium haul airliner, a
turboprop plane (turbopropeller
plane, propeller-turbine plane)
中/短程客机，一种涡轮螺旋桨飞机

5 turboprop engine
(turbopropeller engine)
涡轮发动机

6 vertical stabilizer (vertical fin,
tail fin)
垂直安定面（直尾翅，尾翼）

7-33 jet planes (jet aeroplanes, jets,
Am. jet airplanes)
喷射机

7 twin-jet business and passenger
aircraft (business and passenger
plane)
双喷射发动机之商用与客用飞机

8 fence
折流板

9 wing-tip tank (tip tank)
翼尖油箱

10 rear engine
机尾发动机

11 twin-jet short/medium haul
airliner
双喷射发动机中/短程客机

12 tri-jet medium haul airliner
三喷射发动机中程客机

13 four-jet long haul airliner
四喷射发动机长程客机

14 wide-body long haul airliner
(jumbo jet)
广体长程客机（大型喷射客机）

15 supersonic airliner
[*Concorde*]
超音速客机[协和式飞机]

16 droop nose
下垂机头

17 **twin-jet wide-body airliner** for
short/medium haul routes
(airbus)
中/短程双喷射发动机广体客机（空中巴
士）

18 radar nose (radome, radar
dome) with weather radar
antenna
气象雷达罩

19 cockpit
座舱（驾驶舱）

20 galley
厨房

21 cargo hold (hold, underfloor
hold)
货舱（下货舱）

22 passenger cabin with passenger
seats
具旅客座椅的客舱

23 retractable nose undercarriage
unit (retractable nose landing
gear unit)
收放式鼻轮（收放式前起落架）

24 nose undercarriage flap
(nose gear flap)
鼻轮舱门

25 centre (*Am.* center) passenger
door
中央客舱门

26 engine pod with engine (turbojet
engine, jet turbine engine, jet
engine, jet turbine)
发动机短舱与喷气发动机

27 electrostatic conductors
静电放电导体

28 retractable main undercarriage
unit (retractable main landing
gear unit)
收放式主起落架

29 side window
客舱玻璃窗

30 rear passenger door
后客舱门

31 toilet (lavatory, WC)
盥洗室（厕所）

32 pressure bulkhead
压力隔框

33 auxiliary engine (auxiliary gas
turbine) for the generator unit
辅助发电机

1 **flying boat,** a seaplane
飞船，一种水上飞机

2 hull
船身

3 stub wing (sea wing)
短翼（水翼——水上安定面之俗称）

4 tail bracing wires
尾翼张线

5 floatplane (float seaplane), a seaplane
水上飞机

6 float
浮筒

7 vertical stabilizer (vertical fin, tail fin)
垂直安定面（直尾翅，尾翼）

8 **amphibian** (amphibian flying boat)
水陆两用机（水陆两用飞船）

9 hull
船身

10 retractable undercarriage (retractable landing gear)
收放式起落架

11-25 **helicopters**
直升机

11 light multirole helicopter
轻型多用途直升机

12-13 main rotor
主转子（主旋翼）

12 rotary wing (rotor blade)
旋翼（旋翼叶片，转子叶）

13 rotor head
旋翼桨毂

14 tail rotor (anti-torque rotor)
尾旋翼（反扭力旋翼片）

15 landing skids
落地滑橇（落地雪橇）

16 flying crane
飞行吊挂机

17 turbine engines
涡轮发动机

18 lifting undercarriage
起重起落架

19 lifting platform
起重平台

20 reserve tank
预备燃油箱

21 transport helicopter
运输直升机

22 rotors in tandem
串连式双旋翼

23 rotor pylon
旋翼塔座（旋翼支柱）

24 turbine engine
涡轮发动机

25 tail loading gate
尾货舱门

26-32 **V/STOL aircraft** (vertical/short take-off and landing aircraft)
垂直/短矩起落飞机

26 tilt-wing aircraft, a VTOL aircraft (vertical take-off and landing aircraft)
倾斜机翼飞机，一种垂直起落飞机

27 tilt wing in vertical position
於垂直位置的倾斜机翼

28 contrarotating tail propellers
对转尾部螺旋桨

29 gyrodyne
半动力旋翼机

30 turboprop engine (turbopropeller engine)
涡轮螺旋桨发动机

31 convertiplane
变形机

32 tilting rotor in vertical position
於垂直位置的倾斜旋翼

33-60 **aircraft engines** (aero engines)
飞机的发动机

33-50 jet engines (turbojet engines, jet turbine engines, jet turbines)
喷射发动机（涡轮喷射发动机，喷射涡轮发动机，喷射涡轮机）

33 front fan-jet
前风扇式喷射发动机

34 fan
风扇

35 low-pressure compressor
低压压缩器

36 high-pressure compressor
高压压缩器

37 combustion chamber
燃烧室

38 fan-jet turbine
风扇式喷射涡轮

39 nozzle (propelling nozzle, propulsion nozzle)
排气喷口（推进喷口）

40 turbines
涡轮

41 bypass duct
分气道

42 aft fan-jet
后风扇式喷射发动机

43 fan
风扇

44 bypass duct
分气道

45 nozzle (propelling nozzle, propulsion nozzle)
排气喷口（推进喷口）

46 bypass engine
旁通式发动机

47 turbines
涡轮

48 mixer
混合器

49 nozzle (propelling nozzle, propulsion nozzle)
排气喷口（推进喷口）

50 secondary air flow (bypass air flow)
副气流（旁通气流）

51 turboprop engine (turbopropeller engine), a twin-shaft engine
涡轮螺旋桨发动机，一种双轴发动机

52 annular air intake
环状进气口

53 high-pressure turbine
高压涡轮

54 low-pressure turbine
低压涡轮

55 nozzle (propelling nozzle, propulsion nozzle)
排气喷口（推进喷口）

56 shaft
轴

57 intermediate shaft
中间轴

58 gear shaft
齿轮轴

59 reduction gear
减速齿轮

60 propeller shaft
螺旋桨轴

1 runway
跑道

2 taxiway
滑行道

3 apron
停机坪

4 apron taxiway
停机坪滑行道

5 baggage terminal
行李站

6 tunnel entrance to the baggage terminal
通向行李站的隧道入口

7 airport fire service
机场消防站

8 fire appliance building
消防设备房

9 mail and cargo terminal
邮件和货物站

10 cargo warehouse
货仓

11 assembly point
会合点，集合点

12 pier
登机走廊

13 pierhead
登机门

14 passenger loading bridge
旅客登机桥

15 departure building (terminal)
出境大楼

16 administration building
管理大楼

17 control tower (tower)
塔台

18 waiting room (lounge)
候机室

19 airport restaurant
机场餐厅

20 spectators' terrace
接送客站台

21 aircraft in loading position (nosed in)
装载中的飞机

22 service vehicles, e.g. baggage loaders, water tankers, galley loaders, toilet-cleaning vehicles, ground power units, tankers
服务车，如：行李装运车，水车，食品车，厕所清理车，地面电源车，加油车

23 aircraft tractor (aircraft tug)
飞机牵引车（飞机拖车）

24-53 airport information symbols (pictographs)
机场标识，指示符号（标识图）

24 'airport'
机场

25 'departures'
离场（出境）

26 'arrivals'
到达（入境）

27 'transit passengers'
过境旅客

28 'waiting room' ('lounge')
候机室

29 'assembly point' ('meeting point', 'rendezvous point')
集合地点（会合点、集会点）

30 'spectators' terrace'
接送旅客站台

31 'information'
询问处

32 'taxis'
计程车搭乘站

33 'car hire'
汽车出租站

34 'trains'
火车站

35 'buses'
巴士，公共汽车站

36 'entrance'
入口

37 'exit'
出口

38 'baggage retrieval'
行李提取处

39 'luggage lockers'
小件行李存放处

40 'telephone - emergency calls only'
电话 —— 专供紧急使用

41 'emergency exit'
紧急出口

42 'passport check'
护照检查处

43 'press facilities'
新闻记者接待室

44 'doctor'
医疗室

45 'chemist' (*Am.* 'druggist')
药局

46 'showers'
淋浴

47 'gentlemen's toilet' ('gentlemen')
男厕所

48 'ladies toilet' ('ladies')   50 'restaurant'   52 'duty free shop'
女厕所   餐厅   免税商店
49 'chapel'   51 'change'   53 'hairdresser'
小教堂   兑换零钱   理发店

1 **Saturn V 'Apollo' booster**
(booster rocket) [overall view]
土星五号"阿波罗"增力火箭[全貌]

2 **Saturn V 'Apollo' booster**
(booster rocket) [overall
sectional view]
土星五号"阿波罗"增力火箭[全体剖面
图]

3 **first rocket stage (S-IC)**
第一节火箭（S-IC）

4 **F-1 engines**
F-1 发动机

5 **heat shield (thermal protection
shield)**
防热板（隔热板）

6 **aerodynamic engine fairings**
空气动力发动机整流罩

7 **aerodynamic stabilizing fins**
空气动力安定尾翅

8 **stage separation retro-rockets, 8
rockets arranged in 4 pairs**
段间分离反向火箭，排成四对的八节火
箭

9 **kerosene (RP-1) tank
[capacity: 811, 000 litres]**
燃油箱（RP-1)[容量 811,000 公升]

10 **liquid oxygen (LOX, LO$_2$)
supply lines**
液态氧（LOX, LO$_2$)供给管

11 **anti-vortex system (device for
preventing the formation of
vortices in the fuel)**
反涡流（旋）系统（防止燃料形成涡流
的装置）

12 **liquid oxygen (LOX, LO$_2$)
tank [capacity: 1,315,000
litres]**
液态氧容器[容量：1,315,000 公升]

13 **anti-slosh baffles**
（燃料箱的）防止振动板

14 **compressed-helium bottles
(helium pressure bottles)**
压缩氦气瓶

15 **diffuser for gaseous oxygen**
氧气扩散器

16 **inter-tank connector (inter-
tank section)**
油箱间连接器

17 **instruments and system-
monitoring devices**
仪器和系统监视装置

18 **second rocket stage (S-II)**
第二节火箭（S-II）

19 **J-2 engines**
J-2 发动机

20 **heat shield (thermal
protection shield)**
防热板（隔热板）

21 **engine mounts and thrust
structure**
发动机架和推力结构

22 **acceleration rockets for fuel
acquisition**
获取燃料的加速火箭

23 **liquid hydrogen (LH$_2$)
suction line**
液态氢气吸取管路

24 **liquid oxygen (LOX, LO$_2$)
tank [capacity: 1,315,000
litres]**
液态氧容器[容量 1,315,000 公升]

25 **standpipe**
立管

26 **liquid hydrogen (LH$_2$) tank
[capacity: 1,020,000 litres]**
液态氢气容器（槽）[容量：1,020,000 公
升]

27 **fuel level sensor**
燃料液面感测器

28 **work platform (working
platform)**
工作台

29 **cable duct**
电缆导管

30 **manhole**
人孔，进出口

31 **S-IC/S-II inter-stage
connector (inter-stage
section)**
S-IC/S-II 节间连接器（节间接连部分）

32 **compressed-gas container (gas
pressure vessel)**
压缩气体容器

33 **third rocket stage (S-IVB)**
第三节火箭（S-IVB）

34 **J-2 engine**
J-2 发动机

35 **nozzle (thrust nozzle)**
喷口（推力喷口）

36 **S-II/S-IVB inter-stage
connector (inter-stage
section)**
S-II/S-IVB 节间连接器[节间接连部分]

37 **four second-stage (S-II)
separation retro-rockets**
四具第二节（S-II）分离反向火箭

38 **attitude control rockets**
姿态控制火箭

39 **liquid oxygen (LOX, LO$_2$)
tank [capacity: 77,200 litres]**
液态氧容器[容量：77,200 公升]

40 **fuel line duct**
燃料管道

41 **liquid hydrogen (LH$_2$) tank
[capacity: 253,000 litres]**
液态氢气容器[容量：253,000 公升]

42 **measuring probes**
探测器，测量探针（器）

43 **compressed-helium tanks
(helium pressure vessels)**
压缩氦容器

44 **tank vent**
容器通气口（孔）

45 **forward frame section**
前框架部分

46 **work platform (working
platform)**
工作台

47 **cable duct**
电缆导管

48 **acceleration rockets for fuel
acquisition**
获取燃料的加速火箭

49 **aft frame section**
后框架部分

50 **compressed-helium tanks
(helium pressure vessels)**
压缩氦容器

51 **liquid hygrogen (LH$_2$) line**
液态氢管路

52 **liquid oxygen (LOX, LO$_2$) line**
液态氧管路

53 **24-panel instrument unit**
24 块仪器装置

54 **LM hangar (lunar module
hangar)**
登月舱棚

55 **LM (lunar module)**
登月舱

56 **Apollo SM (service module),
containing supplies and
equipment**
包括供给品和设备的阿波罗配供舱

57 **SM (service module) main
engine**
配供舱主发动机

58 **fuel tank**
燃料箱

59 **nitrogen tetroxide tank**
四氧化氮容器

60 **pressurized gas delivery
system**
压缩气体输送系统

61 **oxygen tanks**
氧气箱

62 **fuel cells**
燃料电池

63 **manoeuvring (*Am.*
maneuvering) rocket assembly**
火箭操纵装置

64 **directional antenna assembly**
定向天线装置

65 **space capsule (command
section)**
太空舱（指挥舱）

66 **launch phase escape tower**
发射阶段紧急脱离塔

1-45 Space Shuttle-Orbiter
太空梭（太空轨道飞行器）

1　twin-spar (two-spar, double-spar) vertical fin
双梁垂直安定面

2　engine compartment structure
发动机舱结构

3　fin post
垂直安定面支柱，直尾翅支柱

4　fuselage attachment [of payload bay doors]
[酬载舱门]的机身附件

5　upper thrust mount
上推力架

6　lower thrust mount
下推力架

7　keel
龙骨

8　heat shield
隔热板，隔热屏

9　waist longeron
腰（中）部纵梁

10　integrally machined (integrally milled) main rib
整体加工的主肋

11　integrally stiffened light alloy skin
整体加强轻合金蒙皮

12　lattice girder
格子桁

13　payload bay insulation
酬载舱隔热层

14　payload bay door
酬载舱门

15　low-temperature surface insulation
低温表面隔热层

16　flight deck (crew compartment)
驾驶舱（乘员室）

17　captain's seat (commander's seat)
机长座椅

18　pilot's seat (co-pilot's seat)
驾驶员座椅（副驾驶员座椅）

19　forward pressure bulkhead
前部压力舱壁

20　carbon fibre reinforced nose cone
头部碳纤维加强锥体，头部整流罩

21　forward fuel tanks
前燃料箱

22　avionics consoles
航空电子（控制系统）操纵台

23　automatic flight control panel
自动飞行控制板

24　upward observaton windows
向上观测窗

25　forward observation windows
向前观测窗

26　entry hatch to payload bay
酬载舱的舱门入口

27　air lock
气锁（闸）

28　ladder to lower deck
通下舱的梯子

29　payload manipulator arm
酬载机械手臂

30　hydraulically steerable nose wheel
液压转向鼻轮

31　hydraulically operated main landing gear
液压操作主起落架

32　removable (reusable) carbon fibre reinforced leading edge [of wing]
[机翼的]可更换（可再度使用）的碳纤维加强前缘

33　movable elevon sections
可动升降副翼部分

34　heat-resistant elevon structure
耐热升降副翼结构

35　main liquid hydrogen (LH$_2$) supply
液态氢气主要供给管路（器）

36　main liquid-fuelled rocket engine
主液态燃料火箭发动机

37　nozzle (thrust nozzle)
喷口（推力喷口）

38　coolant feed line
冷却剂供给管路

39　engine control system
发动机控制系统

40　heat shield
隔热板

41　high-pressure liquid hydrogen (LH$_2$) pump
高压液态氢气泵

42　high-pressure liquid oxygen (LOX, LO$_2$) pump
高压液态氧气泵

43　thrust vector control system
推力航向控制系统

44　electromechanically controlled orbital manoeuvring (Am. maneuvering) main engine
机电控制的轨道飞行主发动机

45　nozzle fuel tanks (thrust nozzle fuel tanks)
燃料箱喷咀（燃料箱推力喷咀）

46　**jettisonable liquid hydrogen and liquid oxygen tank (fuel tank)**
可抛弃的液态氢氧气燃料箱

47　integrally stiffened annular rib (annular frame)
整体加强的环状肋（环状框架）

48　hemispherical end rib (end frame)
半球型端肋（端框架）

49　aft attachment to Orbiter
轨道飞行器的后连接件

50　liquid hydrogen (LH$_2$) line
液态氢气管路

51　liquid oxygen (LOX, LO$_2$) line
液态氧气管路

52　manhole
进入口，人孔，进出口

53　surge baffle system (slosh baffle system)
防止冲激系统

54　pressure line to liquid hydrogen tank
液态氢气箱压力管路

55　electrical system bus
电力系统汇电板

56　liquid oxygen (LOX, LO$_2$) line
液态氧气管路

57　pressure line to liquid oxygen tank
液态氧气箱压力管路

58　**recoverable solid-fuel rocket** (solid rocket booster)
可回收固体燃料火箭（固体燃料火箭增力器）

59　auxiliary parachute bay
辅助降落伞舱

60　compartment housing the recovery parachutes and the forward separation rocket motors
回收降落伞和前分离火箭推进器舱

61　cable duct
电缆导管

62　aft separation rocket motors
后分离火箭推进器

63　aft skirt
后部侧缘

64　swivel nozzle (swivelling, Am. swiveling, nozzle)
旋转喷口（旋转喷气口）

65　**Spacelab** (space laboratory, space station)
太空实验室

66　multi-purpose laboratory (orbital workshop)
多目的实验室（轨道工作室）

67　astronaut
太空人

68　gimbal-mounted telescope
平衡环架望远镜（装於在平衡环上的望远镜）

69　measuring instrument platform
测量仪器平台

70　spaceflight module
太空飞行舱

71　crew entry tunnel
（乘员）太空人进舱通道

1-30 main hall
营业大厅

1 parcels counter
包裹柜台

2 parcels scales
包裹秤

3 parcel
包裹

4 stick-on address label with parcel registration slip
贴有包裹挂号条的地址标签

5 glue pot
粘胶筒

6 small parcel
小件包裹

7 franking machine (*Am.* postage meter) for parcel registration cards
包裹挂号卡用的邮资打印机（邮资计）

8 telephone box (telephone booth, telephone kiosk, call box)
电话间（亭）

9 coin-box telephone (pay phone, public telephone)
投币式电话（收费电话，公用电话）

10 telephone directory rack
电话号码簿架

11 directory holder
住址姓名簿架

12 telephone directory (telephone book)
电话（号码）簿

13 post office boxes
邮政信箱设备

14 post office box
邮政信箱

15 stamp counter
售邮票柜台

16 counter clerk (counter officer)
邮局柜台职员

17 company messenger
公司收发员

18 record of posting book
邮件记录簿

19 counter stamp machine
柜台（售）邮票机

20 stamp book
邮票夹

21 sheet of stamps
邮票

22 security drawer
保险柜

23 change rack
换币分类架

24 letter scales
邮件秤

25 paying-in (*Am.* deposit), post office savings, and pensions counter
存款，邮政储金和发放退休金柜台

26 accounting machine
记帐用会计机〔报表（帐目）计算机〕

27 franking machine for money orders and paying-in slips (*Am.* deposit slips)
汇票和解款单的盖印机

28 change machine (*Am.* changemaker)
零钱兑换机

29 receipt stamp
受理日戳

30 hatch
受理口，窗口

31-44 letter-sorting installation
邮件分类装置

31 letter feed
邮件的给送

32 stacked letter containers
装信用容器

33 feed conveyor
给信传送机

34 intermediate stacker
堆置信件盘

35 coding station
标码台

36 pre-distributor channel
邮件预分器通道

37 process control computer
过程控制电脑

38 distributing machine
分信机

39 video coding station
视频标码台

40 screen
屏，幕

41 address display
（收件人）地址显示

42 address
地址

43 post code (postal code, *Am.* zip code)
邮递区号

44 keyboard
键盘

45 handstamp
手戳

46 roller stamp
滚轮式邮戳

47 franking machine
打印机

48 feed mechanism
给送装置

49 delivery mechanism
排出装置

50-55 postal collection and delivery
邮件的收集与投递

50 postbox (*Am.* mailbox)
邮筒

51 collection bag
邮件袋

52 post office van (mail van)
邮车

53 postman (*Am.* mail carrier, letter carrier, mailman)
邮差

54 delivery pouch (postman's bag, mailbag)
投递邮袋

55 letter-rate item
信件投递登记条

56-60 postmarks
邮戳

56 postmark advertisement
广告邮戳

57 date stamp postmark
邮票日期戳

58 charge postmark
邮资戳

59 special postmark
专用邮戳

60 roller postmark
滚轮式邮戳

61 stamp (postage stamp)
邮票

62 perforations
邮票齿孔

1 **telephone box** (telephone booth, telephone kiosk, call box), a public telephone
电话间（亭）, 公用电话

2 telephone user (*with own telephone:* telephone subscriber, telephone customer)
电话使用人（拥有电话的用户）

3 coin-box telephone (pay phone, public telephone) for local and long-distance calls (trunk calls)
投币式市内与长途电话（收费电话, 公用电话）

4 emergency telephone
紧急电话

5 telephone directory (telephone book)
电话（号码）簿

6-26 **telephone instruments** (telephones)
电话

6 standard table telephone
标准台式（桌上型）电话

7 telephone receiver (handset)
电话（听筒）收话器（电话听筒）

8 earpiece
耳机（听筒）

9 mouthpiece (microphone)
送话器（话筒）

10 dial (push-button keyboard)
拨号盘（按钮键盘）

11 finger plate (dial finger plate, dial wind-up plate)
指孔盘（手指拨盘, 拨号盘的回转盘）

12 finger stop (dial finger stop)
止拨档

13 cradle (handset cradle, cradle switch)
托架（听筒托架, 托架开关）

14 receiver cord (handset cord)
听筒软索（线）

15 telephone casing (telephone cover)
电话机壳

16 subscriber's (customer's) private meter
用户私人用表

17 switchboard (exchange) for a system of extensions
分机系统交换台, 内线电话用交换台

18 push button for connecting main exchange lines
连结主交换线用按钮

19 push buttons for calling extensions
分机按钮, 内线电话按钮

20 push-button telephone
按钮式电话

21 earthing button for the extensions
分机接地按钮, 内线电话接地按钮

22-26 switchboard with extensions
分机（内线）电话和交换台

22 exchange
交换台

23 switchboard operator's set
交换台接线生操作台

24 main exchange line
主交换线

25 switching box (automatic switching system, automatic connecting system, switching centre, *Am.* center)
转换箱（自动转换系统, 自动连接系统, 转换中心）

26 extension
内线连接线

27-41 **telephone exchange**
电话交换台

27 fault repair service
故障修理服务台

28 maintenance technician
维修技师

29 testing board (testing desk)
实验台

30 telegraphy
电信

31 teleprinter (teletypewriter)
印刷电信机（打字电报机, 印刷电信机）

32 paper tape
纸带

33 directory enquiries
查号台

34 information position (operator's position)
询问台

35 operator
接线生

36 microfilm reader
缩影软件放映装置

37 microfilm file
缩影软件档案

38 microfilm card with telephone numbers
带电话号码的缩影软片卡

39 date indicator display
日期指示器显示

40 testing and control station
试验与控制站

41 switching centre (*Am.* center) for telephone, telex, and data transmission services
电话, 电报和数据转换中心

42 **selector,** a motor uniselector made of noble metals; *sim.:* electronic selector
选择器, 一种由贵金属制造的电动单向选择器, 类似：电子选择器

43 contact arc (bank)
接触弧

44 contact arm (wiper)
接触臂（滑臂）

45 contact field
接触区域

46 contact arm tag
接触臂金属头

47 electromagnet
电磁

48 selector motor
选择器电动机

49 restoring spring (resetting spring)
复原簧片

50 **communication links**
通信系统

51-52 satellite radio link
人造卫星无线电通讯

51 earth station with directional antenna
带定向天线的地面站（电台）

52 communications satellite with directional antenna
带定向天线的通讯人造卫星

53 coastal station
海岸站（电台）

54-55 intercontinental radio link
洲际无线电通讯

54 short-wave station
短波站（电台）

55 ionosphere
游离层

56 submarine cable (deep-sea cable)
海底电缆（深海电缆）

57 underwater amplifier
水中增幅器

58 **data transmission** (data services)
数据输送, 数据服务中心

59 input/output device for data carriers
数据载波的输入输出装置

60 data processor
资料处理器

61 teleprinter
电传印字机

62-64 data carriers
数据载体

62 punched tape (punch tape)
穿孔纸带

63 magnetic tape
磁带

64 punched card (punch card)
穿孔卡片

65 telex link
电报装置

66 teleprinter (page printer)
电传印字机（页印机）

67 dialling (*Am.* dialing) unit
拨号装置

68 telex tape (punched tape, punch tape) for transmitting the text at maximum speed
以最快速度发送电文的电报穿孔纸带

69 telex message
电报通信

70 keyboard
键盘

1-6 central recording channel of a radio station
广播电台中央录音频道

1 monitoring and control panel
监控板

2 data display terminal (video data terminal, video monitor) for visual display of computer-controlled programmes (*Am.* programs)
计算机（电脑）控制节目顺序直视显示用的数据显示终端机

3 amplifier and mains power unit
扩大器和电源装置

4 magnetic sound recording and playback deck for $\frac{1}{4}''$ magnetic tape
使用 $\frac{1}{4}$ 时磁带的磁带录音和放音机座置

5 magnetic tape, a $\frac{1}{4}''$ tape
磁带，一种 $\frac{1}{4}$ 时磁带

6 film spool holder
磁带轴架

7-15 radio switching centre (*Am.* center) control room
（无线电）收音机广播交换中心控制室

7 monitoring and control panel
监控板

8 talkback speaker
回讲扬声器（喇叭）

9 local-battery telephone
自给电池电话

10 talkback microphone
回讲微音器（麦克风）

11 data display terminal (video data terminal)
数据显示终端机

12 teleprinter
电传印字机

13 input keyboard for computer data
电脑数据输入键盘

14 telephone switchboard panel
电话交换机盘

15 monitoring speaker (control speaker)
监听扬声器（控制扬声器）

16-26 broadcasting centre (*Am.* center)
广播中心

16 recording room
录音室（间）

17 production control room (control room)
制作控制室（控制室）

18 studio
广播室（播音室）

19 sound engineer (sound control engineer)
音响工程师（音响控制工程师）

20 sound control desk (sound control console)
调音台（声音控制台）

21 newsreader (newscaster)
新闻播报（广播）员

22 duty presentation officer
值班传讲员

23 telephone for phoned reports
电话报导用的电话

24 record turntable
录音盘（转盘）

25 recording room mixing console (mixing desk, mixer)
录音室调音台（混音机座，混音器）

26 sound technician (sound mixer, sound recordist)
音响技师（调音员，录音员）

27-53 television post-sync studio
电视后同步配音室

27 sound production control room (sound control room)
音声制作（调整）控制室

28 dubbing studio (dubbing theatre, *Am.* theater)
配音室

29 studio table
配音台

30 visual signal
指示信号

31 electronic stopclock
电子码表

32 projection screen
投影屏

33 monitor
监视器

34 studio microphone
配音室微音器（麦克风）

35 sound effects box
音效箱

36 microphone socket panel
微音器（麦克风）插座板

37 recording speaker (recording loudspeaker)
录音扬声器

38 control room window (studio window)
控制室窗（配音室窗）

39 producer's talkback microphone
制作人回讲微音器（麦克风）

40 local-battery telephone
自给电池电话

41 sound control desk (sound control console)
（音响控制台）调音台

42 group selector switch
组合选择开关

43 visual display
显示盘

44 limiter display (clipper display)
限幅显示表

45 control modules
控制组件

46 pre-listening buttons
预听按钮

47 slide control
滑动控制器（调节器）

48 universal equalizer (universal corrector)
万能均衡装置（万能校正器）

49 input selector switch
输入选择器开关

50 pre-listening speaker
预听扬声器

51 tone generator
发音器

52 talkback speaker
对讲扬声器

53 talkback microphone
回讲微音器

54-59 pre-mixing room for transferring and mixing 16 mm, 17.5 mm, 35 mm perforated magnetic film
转录和混合16毫米，17.5毫米，35毫米有孔磁带的预混室

54 sound control desk (sound control console)
调音台（声音控制台）

55 compact magnetic tape recording and playback equipment
小型磁带录放音装置

56 single playback deck
单放音机座

57 central drive unit
中央驱动装置

58 single recording and playback deck
单录放音机座

59 rewind bench
倒转柏

60-65 final picture quality checking room
最后图像品质检查室

60 preview monitor
预检监控器

61 programme (*Am.* program) monitor
播出节目的监控器

62 stopclock
码表

63 vision mixer (vision-mixing console, vision-mixing desk)
图像混录台（图像混合机座）

64 talkback system (talkback equipment)
回讲系统（回讲装置）

65 camera monitor (picture monitor)
摄影监控器（图像监控器）

1-15 **outside broadcast (OB)**
vehicle (television OB van; *also:*
sound OB van, radio OB van)
转播车（电视转播车，录音转播车，广
播、收音（机）广播车）

1 **rear equipment section of the OB**
vehicle
转播车后面装备部分

2 camera cable
摄像机电缆

3 cable connection panel
电缆连接板

4 television (TV) reception aerial
(receiving aerial) for Channel I
I 频道的电视接收天线

5 television (TV) reception aerial
(receiving aerial) for Channel II
II 频道的电视接收天线

6 **interior equipment (on-board**
equipment) of the OB vehicle
转播车内部设备

7 sound production control room
(sound control room)
调音室（声音制作控制室）（声音控制
室）

8 sound control desk (sound
control console)
调音枱（声音控制台）

9 monitoring loudspeaker
监控扬声器

10 vision control room (video
control room)
影像控制室

11 video controller (vision
controller)
影像控制员

12 camera monitor (picture
monitor)
摄影机监控器（图象监控器）

13 on-board telephone
(intercommunication telephone)
转播车电话（内部连络电话）

14 microphone cable
微音器电缆，麦克风电缆

15 air-conditioning equipment
空调装置

1 colour (*Am.* color) television (TV) receiver (colour television set) of modular design
   按标准组件设计的彩色电视接收机
2 television cabinet
   电视机壳
3 television tube (picture tube)
   映像管（影像管）
4 IF (intermediate frequency) amplifier module
   中频增幅组件
5 colour (*Am.* color) decoder module
   彩色解码组件
6 VHF and UHF tuner
   特高频和超高频调谐器
7 horizontal synchronizing module
   水平同步组件
8 vertical deflection module
   垂直偏转组件
9 horizontal linearity control module
   水平线性控制组件
10 horizontal deflection module
   水平偏转组件
11 control module
   控制组件
12 convergence module
   聚焦组件
13 colour (*Am.* color) output stage module
   彩色信号输出级组件

14 sound module
   音响组件
15 colour (*Am.* color) picture tube
   彩色映像管
16 electron beams
   电子束
17 shadow mask with elongated holes
   长孔遮蔽屏
18 strip of fluorescent (luminescent, phosphorescent) material
   （发光的，发磷光的）萤光材料片
19 coating (film) of fluorescent material
   萤光材料涂层
20 inner magnetic screen (screening)
   内磁网屏
21 vacuum
   真空
22 temperature-compensated shadow mask mount
   温度补偿的遮蔽屏架
23 centring (centering) ring for the deflection system
   偏转系统的中心环
24 electron gun assembly
   电子枪组件
25 rapid heat-up cathode
   急速加热阴极
26 **television (TV) camera**
   电视摄影机
27 camera head
   摄影机头

28 camera monitor
   摄影机监控器
29 control arm (control lever)
   控制杆（操纵杆）
30 focusing adjustment
   聚焦调整装置
31 control panel
   控制盘
32 contrast control
   对比度调节装置
33 brightness control
   亮度调节装置
34 zoom lens
   可变焦镜头
35 beam-splitting prism (beam splitter)
   分光棱镜，分光镜
36 pickup unit (colour, *Am.* color, pickup tube)
   拾像装置（彩色摄像管）

1 radio cassette recorder
卡式收录音机

2 carrying handle
手提把手

3 push buttons for the cassette
recorder unit
卡式录音机录音按钮

4 station selector buttons (station
preset buttons)
选台按钮

5 built-in microphone
自附微音器，传声器（麦克风）

6 cassette compartment
卡带室

7 tuning dial
调谐标度盘

8 slide control [for volume or
tone]
〔音量或音调〕滑动控制器

9 tuning knob (tuning control,
tuner)
调谐旋钮（调谐控制，调谐器）

10 compact cassette
小型卡带

11 cassette box (cassette holder,
cassette cabinet)
卡带盒

12 cassette tape
卡式磁带

13-48 stero system (also:
quadraphonic system) made up
of Hi-Fi components
由高传真构件组成的（立体）身历声音
响系统（即：四声道系统）

13-14 stereo speakers
（立体）身历声扬声器（喇叭）

14 speaker (loudspeaker), a three-
way speaker with crossover
(crossover network)
扬声器（喇叭），一种具交越网路的三
路扬声器

15 tweeter
高音扬声器（喇叭）

16 mid-range speaker
中音（程）扬声器（喇叭）

17 woofer
低音扬声器（喇叭）

18 record player (automatic record
changer, auto changer)
唱机（盘），（自动换唱机）

19 record player housing (record
player base)
唱机（盘）外壳（唱机底座）

20 turntable
转盘

21 tone arm
唱臂

22 counterbalance (counterweight)
配重，配重

23 gimbal suspension
平衡架方向接头

24 stylus pressure control (stylus
force control)
针压调节（控制）

25 anti-skate control
防滑调节（控制）

26 magnetic cartridge with (conical
or elliptical) stylus, a diamond
带（圆锥形或椭圆形）唱针的一种金钢
石材料做的磁质唱头

27 tone arm lock
唱臂锁

28 tone arm lift
唱臂架

29 speed selector (speed changer)
转速选择器（转速变换器）

30 starter switch
起动开关

31 treble control
高音（域）控制

32 dust cover
防尘盖

33 stereo cassette deck
（立体）身历声卡式放音（走带）装
置

34 cassette compartment
卡带室

35-36 recording level meters
(volume unit meters, VU meters)
录音水平表（音量计）

35 left-channel recording level
meter
左声道录音水平表

36 right-channel recording level
meter
右声道录音水平表

37 tuner
调谐器

38 VHF (FM) station selector
buttons
特高频（调谐）电台选择器按钮

39 tuning meter
调谐指示表

40 amplifier; *tuner and amplifier
together:* receiver (control unit)
放大器（扩大器），调谐器和放大器共
同构成：接收机（控制装置）

41 volume control
音量控制

42 four-channel balance control
(level control)
四声道平衡控制（水平控制）

43 treble and bass tuning
高音和低音调节钮

44 input selector
输入选择器

45 four-channel demodulator for CD
4 records
CD4录音带四声道解调器

46 quadra/stereo converter
四声道/立体身历声转换器

47 cassette box (cassette holder,
cassette cabinet)
卡带匣，卡带座

48 record storage slots (record
storage compartments)
唱片储放槽

49 microphone
微音器，麦克风

50 microphone screen
微音器（麦克风）筛

51 microphone base (microphone
stand)
微音器（麦克风）座

**52 three-in-one stereo component
system** (automatic record
changer, cassette deck, and
stereo receiver)
三机一体（立体）身历声组合系统：自
动换片装置（唱机，唱盘），卡式录音
座，和（立体）身历声收音机

53 tone arm balance
唱臂平衡器

54 tuning meters
调谐指示表

55 indicator light for automatic
FeO/CrO$_2$ tape switch-over
氧化铁/二氧化铬带自动换指示灯

56 open-reel-type recorder, a
two of four-track unit
开式卷盘磁带录音机，盘式录音机，一
种二或四轨录音装置

57 tape reel (open tape reel)
磁带卷盘（开式磁带卷盘）

58 open-reel tape (recording
tape, $\frac{1}{4}$ tape)
开式卷盘磁带（$\frac{1}{4}$时录音带）

59 sound head housing with
erasing head (erase head),
recording head, and
reproducing head (*or:*
combined head)
具消音磁头，录音磁头和放音磁头（或
录放音磁头）的录音头盒

60 tape deflector roller and end
switch (limit switch)
录音带转向滚轮和终端开关

61 recording level meter (VU
meter)
录音水平表（音量表）

62 tape speed selector
转速选择器

63 on/off switch
开关按钮

64 tape counter
走带计数器

65 stereo microphone sockets
(stereo microphone jacks)
身历声微音器（麦克风）插座

66 headphones (headset)
耳机

67 padded headband (padded
headpiece)
加垫头带（加垫式双弓式耳机）

68 membrane
振动片（膜）

69 earcups (earphones)
耳机

70 headphone cable plug, a
standard multi-pin plug
耳机电线插头，标准多针插头

71 headphone cable (headphone
cord)
耳机电线（耳机软线）

1 group instruction using a
teaching machine
采用教学机的集体教学

2 instructor's desk with central
control unit
具中央控制装置的教师讲台

3 master control panel with
individual diplays and cross
total counters
具个别显示与交叉总计数器的主控板

4 student input device (student
response device) in the hand of a
student
在学生手中的输入装置（学生反应（应
答）装置）

5 study step counter (progress
counter)
学习进度计数器

6 overhead projector
架空式投影器

7 apparatus for producing audio
visual learning programmes
(*Am.* programs)
制作视听学习课程（程序）的装置（器
具）

8-10 frame coding device
制作编码装置

8 film viewer
纸带检查装置

9 memory unit (storage unit)
储存单元、记忆单元（装置）

10 film perforator
纸带穿孔机

11-14 audio coding equipment
(sound coding equipment)
声音编码装置

11 coding keyboard
编码键盘

12 two-track tape recorder
双轨（磁带）录音机

13 four-track tape recorder
四轨（磁带）录音机

14 recording level meter
录音水平指示表（音量计）

15 PIP (programmed individual
presentation) system
按程序分别显示系统

16 AV (audio-visual) projector for
programmed instruction
程序教学用的视听投影器

17 audio cassette
录音带

18 video cassette
录影带

19 data terminal
数据（资料）终端设备

20 telephone connection with the
central data collection station
与中央数据（资料）收集站连线的电话

21 **video telephone**
电视电话

22 conference circuit (conference
hook-up, conference connection)
会议週路（会议连线）

23 camera tube switch (switch for
transmitting speaker's picture)
摄像管开关（传播讲话人图像的开关）

24 talk button (talk key, speaking
key)
通话按钮

25 touch-tone buttons (touch-tone
pad)
触模式按钮（选号盘）

26 video telephone screen
电视电话幕

27 infrared transmission of
television sound
电视声音的红外线传播

28 television receiver (television set,
TV set)
电视机

29 infrared sound transmitter
红外线声音发射机

30 cordless battery-powered
infrared sound headphones
(headset)
不用电以电池供电的红外线声音接收
耳机（红外线耳机）

31 **microfilming system**
[diagram]
影片微缩系统〔简图〕

32 magnetic tape station (data
storage unit)
磁带架（资料（数据）储存单元）

33 buffer storage
缓冲储存器

34 adapter unit
适应器装置

35 digital control
数位控置

36 camera control
摄像机控制

37 character storage
字元储存器

38 analogue (*Am.* analog) control
类比控制

39 correction (adjustment) of
picture tube geometry
显（收）像管形状的修正（调整）

40 cathode ray tube (CRT)
阴极射线管

41 optical system
光学装置

42 slide (transparency) of a form
for mixing-in images of forms
混合影像形式的幻灯片

43 flash lamp
闪光灯

44 universal film cassettes
普通影片箱

45-84 **demonstration and teaching
equipment**
示范和教学设备

45 demonstration model of a four-
stroke engine
四冲程发动机（引擎）的示范模型

46 piston
活塞

47 cylinder head
汽缸罩

48 spark plug (sparking plug)
火星塞

49 contact breaker
接触断续（遮断）器断路器

50 crankshaft with balance weights
(counterbalance weights)
(counterbalanced crankshaft)
带（法码）配重的曲轴（配重）（配衡
曲轴）

51 crankcase
曲轴箱

52 inlet valve
进气阀

53 exhaust valve
排气阀

54 coolant bores (cooling water
bores)
冷却剂孔（冷却水孔）

55 demonstration model of a two-
stroke engine
二冲程（引擎）发动机示范模型

56 deflector piston
转向（变流）活塞

57 transfer port
送气口

58 exhaust port
排气口

59 crankcase scavenging
曲轴箱的驱气

60 cooling ribs
冷却肋，散热片

61-67 models of molecules
分子模型

61 ethylene molecule
乙烯分子

62 hydrogen atom
氢原子

63 carbon atom
碳原子

64 formaldehyde atom
甲醛原子

65 oxygen molecule
氧分子

66 benzene ring
苯环

67 water molecule
水（的）分子

68-72 electronic circuits made up of
modular elements
由基准（本）元件组成的电子线路（电
路）

68 logic element (logic module), an
integrated circuit
逻辑元件，积体电路的一种

69 plugboard for electronic
elements (electronic modules)
电子元件的插盘

70 linking (link-up, joining,
connection) of modules
组件的连结（接）

71 magnetic contact
磁性接触

72 assembly (construction) of a
circuit, using magnetic modules
使用磁性组件的电路构造

73 multiple meter for measuring
current, voltage and resistance
测量电流，电压和电阻的多功能表

74 measurement range selector
量程（测定距离选择器）

75 measurement scale
(measurement dial)
测量刻度盘

76 indicator needle (pointer)
指针

77 current/voltage meter
电流/电压表

78 adjusting screw
调整螺丝

79 optical bench
光具座

80 triangular rail
三角轨

81 laser (teaching laser, instruction
laser)
雷射机（教学雷射机）

82 diaphragm
遮光板（光阑）

83 lens system
透镜系统

84 target (screen)
靶，目标（屏幕）

1-4 AV (audio-visual) camera with recorder
录音摄影机

1 camera
摄影机

2 lens
镜头

3 built-in microphone
内装麦克风，机内（内藏式）麦克风

4 portable video (videotape) recorder (for $\frac{1}{4}''$ open-reel magnetic tape)
轻便录影带式录影机($\frac{1}{4}$时开放盘式磁带适用）

5-36 VCR (video cassette recorder) system
卡式录影机系统

5 VCR cassette (for $\frac{1}{2}''$ magnetic tape)
（$\frac{1}{2}$时磁带用的）卡式录影带

6 domestic television receiver (*also:* monitor)
家用电视机（亦可用作：监视器）

7 video cassette recorder
卡式录影机

8 cassette compartment
卡带室

9 tape counter
卡带的走带计数器

10 centring (centering) control
中心（调节）控制

11 sound (audio) recording level control
录音音量控制

12 recording level indicator
录音音量指示器

13 control buttons (operating keys)
控制按钮（操作键）

14 tape threading indicator light
插入影带的指示灯

15 changeover switch for selecting audio or video recording level display
选择录音或录影水平显示的转换开关

16 on/off switch
电源开关

17 station selector buttons (station preset buttons)
选台按钮

18 built-in timer switch
内装定时器开关，机内（内藏式）定时器开关

19 VCR (video cassette recorder) head drum
卡式录影机磁鼓

20 erasing head (erase head)
消音（影）磁头

21 stationary guide (guide pin)
固定导梢（导梢）

22 tape guide
卷带导轨，磁带导轨

23 capstan
主导轴

24 audio sync head
同步录音磁头

25 pinch roller
压带轮

26 video head
视频磁头

27 grooves in the wall of the head drum to promote air cushion formation
在磁鼓上促进气垫形成的沟纹

28 VCR (video cassette recorder) track format
卡式录影机的磁轨格式

29 tape feed
供带（方向）

30 direction of video head movement
视频磁头运动的方向

31 video track, a slant track
视频磁轨，一种倾斜磁轨

32 sound track (audio track)
音轨（声频轨踪）

33 sync track
同步磁轨

34 sync head
同步磁头

35 sound head (audio head)
录音磁头

36 video head
录影磁头

37-45 TED (television disc) system
影碟（电视影碟）（系统）

37 video disc player
影碟机

38 disc slot with inserted video disc
插入影碟的碟片槽

39 programme (*Am.* program) selector
节目（次序）选择器

40 programme (*Am.* program) scale (programme dial)
节目刻度盘

41 operating key ([play])
操作键（"播放"）

42 key for repeating a scene (scene-repeat key, [select])
影像重播键

43 stop key
停止键

44 video disc
影碟

45 video disc jacket
影碟护套

46-60 VLP (video long play) video disc system
长时间播放的影碟系统

46 video disc player
影碟机

47 cover projection (*below it:* scanning zone)
投影区（其下是：扫描区）

48 operating keys
操作键

49 slow motion control
慢动作控制

50 optical system [diagram]
光学系统[简图]

51 VLP video disc
长时间播放的影碟

52 lens
镜头

53 laser beam
雷射光束

54 rotating mirror
旋转反射镜

55 semi-reflecting mirror
半反射镜

56 photodiode
光电二极体

57 helium-neon laser
氦氖雷射机

58 video signals on the surface of the video disc
影碟表面上的影像（视频）信号

59 signal track
信号轨踪

60 individual signal element ([pit])
单个信号元（记录的最小单位）

1 disc (disk) store (magnetic
   disc store)
   磁碟储存（记忆）装置
2 magnetic tape
   磁带
3 console operator (chief operator)
   控制台操作员（主操作员）
4 console typewriter
   控制台打字机
5 intercom (intercom system)
   内部通话系统、对讲机
6 central processor with main
   memory and arithmetic unit
   具主记忆和算术单元的中央处理装置
7 operation and error indicators
   操作及错误指示器
8 floppy disc (disk) reader
   软式磁碟读取机（阅读机）
9 magnetic tape unit
   磁带装置
10 magnetic tape reel
   磁带卷盘
11 operating indicators
   操作指示器
12 punched card (punch card)
   reader and punch
   穿孔卡片的读取机和打孔机
13 card stacker
   叠卡器
14 operator
   操作员
15 operating instructions
   操作说明，作业程序

1-36 executive's office
经理室
1 swivel chair
旋转桌
2 desk
办公桌
3 writing surface (desk top)
桌面
4 desk drawer
办公桌抽屉
5 cupboard (storage area) with door
有门的小柜（储藏柜）
6 desk mat (blotter)
桌垫（吸墨垫）
7 business letter
商业信件
8 appointments diary
约会（定）记事册
9 desk set
桌上文具（笔墨用具）
10 intercom (office intercom)
办公室互通电话，内部通话设备
11 desk lamp
桌灯
12 pocket calculator (electronic calculator)
袖珍型计算机（电子计算机）
13 telephone, an executive-secretary system
电话，经理秘书的连络装置（内线）
14 dial; *also:* push-button keyboard
拨号盘，即按钮式键盘

15 call buttons
通话按钮
16 receiver (telephone receiver)
听筒（电话听筒）
17 dictating machine
口述录音机
18 position indicator
位置（表）指示器
19 control buttons (operating keys)
控制按钮（操作键）
20 cabinet
柜子
21 visitor's chair
访客座椅
22 safe
保险箱
23 bolts (locking mechanism)
螺栓（闭锁装置）
24 armour (*Am.* armor) plating
防护金属板
25 confidential documents
机密文件
26 patent
专利证明
27 petty cash
小额现金
28 picture
画
29 bar (drinks cabinet)
酒柜
30 bar set
酒柜中成套用具
31-36 conference grouping
会议用设备

31 conference table
会议桌
32 pocket-sized dictating machine (micro cassette recorder)
袖珍型口述录音机（微型卡式录音机）
33 ashtray
烟灰缸
34 corner table
墙角桌
35 table lamp
枱灯
36 two-seater sofa 'part of the conference grouping'
双座沙发〔会议整组设备的一部分〕

1-44 office equipment (office supplies, office materials)
办公室用品

1, 2 paper clips
廻纹针

3 punch
打孔器

4 stapler (stapling machine)
订书机

5 anvil
铁砧

6 spring-loaded magazine
弹簧槽

7 type-cleaning brush for typewriters
打字机铅字清洁刷

8 type cleaner (type-cleaning kit)
铅字清洁器（整套清洁铅字用具）

9 fluid container (fluid reservoir)
液体容器

10 cleaning brush
清洁刷

11 felt tip pen
毡尖笔

12 correcting paper 'for typing errors'
〔打错字所用的〕修正纸

13 correcting fluid 'for typing errors'
〔打错字所用的〕修正液

14 electronic pocket calculator
袖珍型电子计算机

15 eight-digit fluorescent display
八位数字萤光显示

16 on/off switch
开关

17 function keys
作用键

18 number keys
数字键

19 decimal key
小数点键

20 [equals] key
等号键

21 instruction keys (command keys)
指令键（命令键）

22 memory keys
（记忆）储存键

23 percent key (percentage key)
百分比键

24 π-key (pi-key) for mensuration of circles
测量圆周用的"π"键

25 pencil sharpener
削铅笔器

26 typewriter rubber
打字员用的橡皮

27 adhesive tape dispenser
胶带分配器

28 adhesive tape holder (roller-type adhesive tape dispenser)
胶带架（卷式胶带分配器）

29 roll of adhesive tape
胶带卷

30 tear-off edge
撕割胶带用的刀片

31 moistener
濡湿器

32 desk diary
桌历式日记簿

33 date sheet (calendar sheet)
日历纸

34 memo sheet
备忘纸

35 ruler
直尺

36 centimetre and millimetre (*Am.* centimeter and millimeter) graduations
厘米和毫米的刻度（公分和公釐）

37 file (document file)
文件夹，档案夹

38 spine label (spine tag)
背脊标签

39 finger hole
指孔

40 arch board file
弓形纸板文件夹

41 arch unit
弓形座

42 release lever (locking lever, release/lock lever)
释放杆（止动杆，释放/止动杆）

43 compressor
压紧器

44 bank statement (statement of account)
银行定期的财务报表

1-48 open plan office
敞开式设计办公室

1 partition wall (partition screen)
隔墙，隔板

2 filing drawer with suspension
file system
具悬挂文件系统的抽屉

3 suspension file
悬挂文件夹

4 file tab
文件标签

5 file (document file)
文件夹（档案夹）

6 filing clerk
（档案）文件处理员

7 clerical assistant
助理办事员

8 note for the files
文件（档案）记录

9 telephone
电话

10 filing shelves
文件架

11 clerical assistant's desk
助理办事员桌

12 office cupboard
办公室柜子

13 plant stand (planter)
植物架（播种器）

14 indoor plants (houseplants)
室内植物

15 programmer
程式设计师

16 data display terminal (visual
display unit)
数据（资料）显示终端机（可见显示装
置）

17 customer service representative
顾客服务代表

18 customer
顾客

19 computer-generated design
(computer-generated art)
电脑描绘的设计图样

20 sound-absorbing partition
隔音板

21 typist
打字员

22 typewriter
打字机

23 filing drawer
文件抽屉

24 customer card index
顾客卡片索引

25 office chair, a swivel chair
办公室椅，旋转椅

26 typing desk
打字桌

27 card index box
卡片索引盒

28 multi-purpose shelving
多功能（用途）架

29 proprietor
经营者

30 business letter
商业书信

31 proprietor's secretary
经营者秘书

32 shorthand pad (*Am.* steno pad)
速记簿

33 audio typist
声音打字员

34 dictating machine
（口述）录音机

35 earphone
耳机

36 statistics chart
统计图表

37 pedestal containing a cupboard
or drawers
包含小柜子或抽屉的桌架

38 sliding-door cupboard
滑动门小柜子

39 office furniture arranged in an
angular configuration
配置成角型结构的办公家具

40 wall-mounted shelf
悬挂於壁上的架子

41 letter tray
信件盘

42 wall calendar
壁上挂历

43 data centre (*Am.* center)
数据（资料）中心

44 calling up information on the
data display terminal (visual
display unit)
於数据显示终端机（可见显示装置）查
出资料

45 waste paper basket
废纸篓

46 sales statistics
销售统计表

47 EDP print-out, a continuous
fan-fold sheet
电子资料处理，打印输出，一种连续折
扇式纸（数据记录纸）

48 connecting element
连接元件

1 **electric typewriter,** a golf ball
   typewriter
   电动打字机，一种高尔夫球型打字机
2-6 keyboard
   字键
2 space bar
   间隔棒
3 shift key
   换字型键
4 line space and carrier return key
   换行和托架返回键
5 shift lock
   换字型键锁
6 margin release key
   限宽键
7 tabulator key
   定位键
8 tabulator clear key
   定位的去除键
9 on/off switch
   电源开关
10 striking force control
   (impression control)
   打印力控制（印痕控制）
11 ribbon selector
   色带选择器
12 margin scale
   限宽尺（规）
13 left margin stop
   左限停止器
14 right margin stop
   右限停止器
15 golf ball (spherical typing
   element) bearing the types
   带字母的球型打字头（球型打字元件）
16 ribbon cassette
   色带盒
17 paper bail with rollers
   将纸压於筒上的夹紧籁
18 platen
   （打字机的）滚筒
19 typing opening (typing window)
   打字孔（打字窗）
20 paper release lever
   松纸杆
21 carrier return lever
   托架返回杆
22 platen knob
   滚筒转钮
23 line space adjuster
   行距调整器
24 variable platen action lever
   可变滚筒操作杆
25 push-in platen action lever
   可变进纸卷轴
26 erasing table
   擦拭台
27 transparent cover
   透明盖
28 exchange golf ball (exchange
   typing element)
   替换的球型字头（替换的打字元件）
29 type
   铅字
30 golf ball cap (cap of typing
   element)
   球帽（打字元件帽）
31 teeth
   齿
32 **web-fed automatic copier**
   卷式自动影印机
33 magazine for paper roll
   纸卷（筒）箱
34 paper size selection (format
   selection)
   纸的尺寸选择钮（格式选择）

35 print quantity selection
   影印数量选择钮
36 contrast control
   浓淡（对比）控制
37 main switch (on/off switch)
   （电源开关）总开关
38 start print button
   起动影印钮
39 document glass
   影印用搁置原件的玻璃
40 transfer blanket
   影印纸转动毯带
41 toner roll
   影印粉筒
42 exposure system
   曝光装置
43 print delivery (copy delivery)
   影印纸出口搁板
44 **letter-folding machine**
   信件折叠机
45 paper feed
   供纸装置
46 folding mechanism
   折叠装置
47 receiving tray
   接收盘
48 **small offset press**
   小型凸版印刷机
49 paper feed
   供纸装置
50 lever for inking the plate
   cylinder
   着墨於印版滚筒的手柄
51-52 inking unit (inker unit)
   着墨装置
51 distributing roller (distributor)
   散墨滚子
52 ink roller (inking roller, fountain
   roller)
   墨滚子
53 pressure adjustment
   调压
54 sheet delivery (receiving table)
   印刷纸出口搁板
55 printing speed adjustment
   印刷速度调整
56 jogger for aligning the piles of
   sheets
   将整叠纸整行的齐纸机
57 pile of paper (pile of sheets)
   纸叠
58 folding machine
   折叠机
59 gathering machine (collating
   machine, assembling machine)
   for short runs
   少量纸的集页机（集页机）
60 gathering station (collating
   station, assembling station)
   集页装置
61 adhesive binder (perfect binder)
   for hot adhesives
   热接著剂用的接著胶合机
62 **magnetic tape dictating machine**
   磁带录音机
63 headphones (headset,
   earphones)
   耳机
64 on/off switch
   电源开关
65 microphone cradle
   微音机（麦克风）插孔（台）
66 foot control socket
   脚控制插座
67 telephone adapter socket
   电话接头插座

68 headphone socket (earphone
   socket, headset socket)
   耳机插座
69 microphone socket
   微音机（麦克风）插座
70 built-in loudspeaker
   自附扩音器、内藏式扩音器（喇叭）
71 indicator lamp (indicator light)
   指示灯
72 cassette compartment
   卡带室
73 forward wind, rewind, and stop
   buttons
   向前快转，倒带（快转），和停止按
   钮
74 time scale with indexing marks
   具刻度的时标
75 time scale stop
   时标止动器

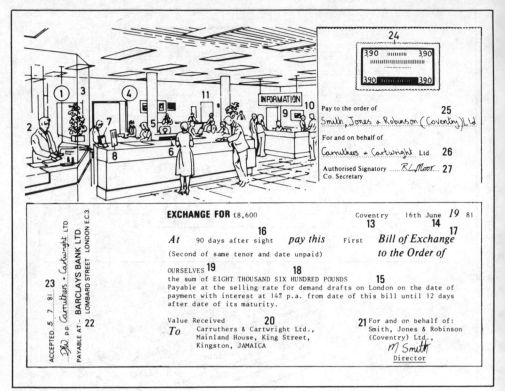

1-11 **main hall**
主厅
1 cashier's desk (cashier's counter)
出纳柜台
2 teller (cashier)
出纳员
3 bullet-proof glass
防弹玻璃
4 service counters (service and advice for savings accounts, private and company accounts, personal loans)
服务柜（储蓄，私人和公司存款，个人贷款的服务和咨询）
5 bank clerk
银行职员
6 customer
顾客
7 brochures
小册子
8 stock list (price list, list of quotations)
股票行情表（价格表，行情表）
9 information counter
询问柜
10 foreign exchange counter
外汇兑换台
11 entrance to strong room
保险库入口
12 **bill of exchange** (bill); *here:* a draft, an acceptance (a bank acceptance)
汇票；此指支票，银行承兑票据

13 place of issue
开票地点
14 date of issue
开票日期
15 place of payment
付款地点
16 date of maturity (due date)
到期日期
17 bill clause (draft clause)
支票条款
18 value
金额
19 payee (remittee)
受款人（领款人）
20 drawee (payer)
付款人
21 drawer
开票人
22 domicilation (paying agent)
付款地点
23 acceptance
承兑
24 stamp
印花
25 endorsement (indorsement, transfer entry)
背书（转让）
26 endorsee (indorsee)
被背书人
27 endorser (indorser)
背书人

1-10 stock exchange (exchange for the sale of securities, stocks, and bonds)
（股票）证券交易所（有价证券交易所，公债，证券）

1 exchange hall (exchange floor)
交易大厅

2 market for securities
证券市场

3 broker's post
（股票）经纪人位置

4 sworn stockbroker (exchange broker, stockbroker, *Am.* specialist), an inside broker
正式经纪人，场内经纪人

5 kerbstone broker (kerbstoner, curbstone broker, curbstoner, outside broker), a commercial broker dealing in unlisted securities
场外经纪人，经营未挂牌证券的商业经纪人

6 member of the stock exchange (stockjobber, *Am.* floor trader, room trader)
（股票）证券交易所的成员（股票经纪人，交易所商人）

7 stock exchange agent (boardman), a bank employee
证券交易所代理人，银行雇员

8 quotation board
行情板

9 stock exchange attendat (waiter)
（股票）证券交易所服务员

10 telephone box (telephone booth, telephone kiosk, call box)
电话间（电话亭，公用电话亭）

11-19 securities; *kinds:* share (*Am.* stock), fixed-income security, annuity, bond, debenture bond, municipal bond (corporation stock), industrial bond, convertible bond
证券；种类：股票，固定收入证券，年金，公债，公司债券，市政债券（公司债券），工业债券，可兑换债券

11 share certificate (*Am.* stock certificate); *here:* bearer share (share warrant)
股票（股份）有保证书，此指无记名股票

12 par (par value, nominal par, face par) of the share
（股票）证券面值

13 serial number
编号

14 page number of entry in bank's share register (bank's stock ledger)
银行股票登记簿的登记页码

15 signature of the chairman of the board of governors
总裁签名

16 signature of the chairman of the board of directors
董事长签名

17 sheet of coupons (coupon sheet, dividend coupon sheet)
息票（股利券）

18 dividend warrnat (dividend coupon)
股息支付证明（股息单）

19 talon
股息单交换券

1-28 coins (coin, coinage, metal money, specie, *Am.* hard money; *kinds:* gold, silver, nickel, copper, or aluminium, *Am.* aluminum, coins)
硬币（金属货币，种类：金币、银币、镍币、铜币、铝币）

1 Athens: nugget-shaped tetradrachm (tetradrachmon, tetradrachma)
雅典：金块形四德拉克马〔德拉克马为现在希腊货币单位〕

2 the owl (emblem of the city of Athens)
猫头鹰（雅典市的象征）

3 aureus of Constantine the Great
君士坦丁大帝金币

4 bracteate of Emperor Frederick Barbarossa
腓特烈一世（神圣罗马帝国）金币

5 Louis XIV louis-d'or
路易十四法国金币

6 Prussia: 1 reichstaler (speciestaler) of Frederick the Great
普鲁斯：腓特烈大帝的一种银币

7 Federal Republic of Germany: 5 Deutschmarks (DM); 1 DM = 100 pfennigs
德意志联邦共和国：5德国马克；1德国马克=100芬尼（辅币）

8 obverse
（货币的）正面

9 reverse (subordinate side)
背面

10 mint mark (mintage, exergue)
（表示造币厂的）刻印

11 legend (inscription on the edge of a coin)
刻字（硬币边缘上的铭刻）

12 device (type), a provincial coat of arms
图案（象征的图案），地方性的徽章

13 Austria: 25 schillings; 1 sch = 100 groschen
奥地利币：25先令；1先令=100格罗申（德国的古银币）

14 provincial coats of arms
地方性的徽章

15 Switzerland: 5 franc; 1 franc = 100 centimes
瑞士币：5法郎；1法郎=100生丁

16 France: 1 franc = 100 centimes
法国：1法郎；1法郎=100生丁

17 Belgium: 100 francs
比利时：100法郎

18 Luxembourg (Luxemburg): 1 franc
卢森堡：1法郎

19 Netherlands: 2½ guilders; 1 guilder (florin, gulden) = 100 cents
荷兰：2½基尔德；1基尔德=100分

20 Italy: 10 lire (*sg.* lira)
意大利：10里拉（单数lira，复数lire）

21 Vatican City: 10lire (*sg.* lira)
梵蒂冈市：10里拉

22 Spain: 1 prseta = 100 centimos
西班牙：1银币=100生丁

23 Portugal: 1 escudo = 100 centavos
葡萄牙：1埃斯库多=100分

24 Denmark: 1 krone = 100 òre
丹麦：1克郎=100欧耳

25 Sweden: 1 krona = 100 òre
瑞典：1克郎=100欧耳

26 Norway: 1 krone = 100 òre
挪威：1克郎=100欧耳

27 Czechoslovakea: 1 koruna = 100 heller
捷克：1克鲁那=100海勒

28 Yugoslavia: 1 kinar = 100 paras
南斯拉夫：1第那尔=100巴拉

29-39 banknotes (*Am.* bills) (paras money, notes, treasury notes)
钞票（纸币）

29 Federal Republic of Germany: 20 DM
德意志联邦共和国：20德国马克

30 bank of issue (bank of circulation)
发行银行

31 watermark 'a portrait'
水印〔头像〕

32 denomination
面额

33 USA: 1 dollar ($1) = 100 cents
美国：1美元=100分

34 facsimile signatures
署名的复印

35 impressed stamp
库印

36 serial number
连续号码

37 United Kingdom of Great Britain and Northern Ireland: 1 pound sterling (£1) = 100 new pence (100p.); *sg.* new penny (new p.)
大不列颠和北爱尔兰联合王国：1英磅=100新便士

38 guilloched pattern
绳纹饰图案

39 Greece: 1,000 drachmas (drachmae); 1 drachma = 100 lepta (*sg.* lepton)
希腊：1,000德拉克马=100雷普顿

40-44 striking of coins (coinage, mintage)
造币铸币

40-41 coining dies (minting dies)
银币印模

40 upper die
上印模

41 lower die
下印模

42 collar
套环

43 coin disc (disk) (flan, planchet, blank)
未加工的钱币

44 coining press (minting press)
铸币冲压机

1-3 flag of the United Nations
联合国旗杆

1 flagpole (flagstaff) with truck
顶上具木冠的旗杆

2 halyard (halliard, haulyard)
升降索

3 bunting
旗布

4 flag of the Council of Europe
欧洲会议旗

5 Olympic flag
奥运会旗

6 flag at half-mast (*Am.* at half-staff) 'as a token of mourning'
下半旗（哀弔的表征）

7-11 flag
旗

7 flagpole (flagstaff)
旗杆

8 ornamental stud
饰钉

9 streamer
饰带

10 pointed tip of the flagpole
旗杆尖顶

11 bunting
旗布

12 banner (gonfalon)
旗帜（旌旗）

13 cavalry standard (flag of the cavalry)
骑兵旗（骑兵的军旗）

14 standard of the German Federal President 'ensign of head of state'
德意志联邦总统〔国家元首旗〕

15-21 national flags
国旗

15 the Union Jack (Great Britain)
英国国旗

16 the Tricolour (*Am.* Tricolor) (France)
三色旗（法国国旗）

17 the Danebrog (Dannebrog) (Denmark)
丹麦国旗

18 the Stars and Stripes (Star-Spangled Banner) (USA)
星条旗（美国国旗）

19 the Crescent (Turkey)
新月旗（土耳其国旗）

20 the Rising Sun (Japan)
太阳旗（日本国旗）

21 the Hammer and Sickle (USSR)
锤子与镰刀旗（苏联国旗）

22-34 signal flags, a hoist
信号旗，一种国际信号旗

22-28 letter flags
字母旗

22 letter A, a burgee (swallow-tailed flag)
字母 A，船的三角旗（燕尾旗）

23 G, pilot flag
G，领港员（领水人）旗

24 H ([pilot on board])
H（领港员在船上）

25 L ([you should stop, I have something important to communicate])
L（停船，有要事传送）

26 P, the Blue Peter ([about to set sail])
P，开航旗（即将出航）

27 W ([I require medical assistance])
W（要求医药支援）

28 Z, an oblong pennant (oblong pendant)
Z，长方形（矩形）旗

29 code pennant (code pendant), used in the International Signals Code
用於国际信号码语的信号三角旗

30-32 substitute flags (repeaters), triangular flags (pennants, pendants)
代用旗，三角旗

30-34 numeral pennants (numeral pendants)
数字旗（数字三角旗）

33 number 1
数字 1

34 number 0
数字 0

35-38 customs flags
海关旗

35 customs boat pennant (customs boat pendant)
海关船三角旗

36 [ship cleared through customs]
已清关的船上用旗

37 customs signal flag
海关信号旗

38 powder flag '[inflammable (flammable) cargo]'
易爆危险品旗〔'易燃物'〕

1-36 heraldry (blazonry)
纹章
1, 11, 30-36 crests
顶饰
1-6 coat-of-arms (achievement of arms, hatchment, achievement)
纹章
1 crest
顶饰（头饰）
2 wreath of the colours (Am. colors)
绶带花圈
3 mantle (mantling)
斗篷
4, 7-9 helmets (helms)
头盔
4 tilting helmet (jousting helmet)
骑马比枪用的头盔
5 shield
盾
6 bend sinister wavy
（盾左边的）波纹
7 pot-helmet (pot-helm, heaume)
帽形头盔
8 barred helmet (grilled helmet)
格形头盔（栅式头盔）
9 helmet affronty with visor open
露面头盔
10-13 marital achievement (marshalled, Am. marshaled, coat-of-arms)
结婚纹章
10 arms of the baron (of the husband)
丈夫的纹章
11-23 arms of the family of the femme (of the wife)
妻子的纹章
11 demi-man; also: demi-woman
男子半身象，女子半身象
12 crest coronet
冠状头饰

13 fleur-de-lis
百合花型的纹章
14 mantling
斗篷
15 bull
公牛
16 unicorn
独角兽
17-23 blazon
纹章解说
17 inescutcheon (heart-shield)
中央饰有纹章的盾
18-23 quarterings one to six
盾面纵横六等分
18, 20, 22, dexter, right
盾章右半边
18-19 chief
盾的上部
19, 21, 23 sinister, left
盾章左半边
22-23 base
盾的底部
24-29 tinctures
色调色彩
24-25 metals
金属
24 or (gold) 'yellow'
金色（黄色）
25 argent (silver) 'white'
银色（白色）
26 sable
黑色
27 gules
红色
28 azure
天蓝色
29 vert
绿色
30 ostrich feathers (treble plume)
鸵鸟羽毛（三重羽饰）

31 truncheon
权杖
32 demi-goat
半身山羊
33 tournament pennons
比赛燕尾旗
34 buffalo horns
水牛角
35 harpy
〔希腊神话〕上半身为女人下半身似鸟的怪物
36 plume of peacock's feathers
孔雀羽毛饰
37-46 crowns and coronets
王冠与冠饰
37 tiara (papal tiara)
三重冠（罗马教皇（宗）的三重冠）
38 Imperial Crown 'German, until 1806'
〔德国至1806年〕王冠
39 ducal coronet (duke's coronet)
公爵冠
40 prince's coronet
王子，（小国）君主的小王冠
41 elector's coronet
〔神圣罗马帝国有权选举皇帝的〕诸侯冠
42 English Royal Crown
英国皇家王冠
43-45 coronets of rank
显贵的冠饰
43 baronet's coronet
贵族的冠冕
44 baron's coronet (baronial coronet)
男爵的冠冕
45 count's coronet
伯爵的冠冕
46 mauerkrone (mural crown) of a city crest
城市纹章的壁冠

1-98 army weaponry
陆军武器

1-39 **hand weapons**
手持武器（轻武器）

1 Pl pistol
Pl 型手枪

2 barrel
枪管

3 front sight (foresight)
准星

4 hammer
撞针

5 trigger
板机

6 pistol grip
枪柄

7 magazine holder
弹匣仓

8 MP2 machine
MP2 型机关枪

9 shoulder rest (butt)
肩托（枪托）

10 casing (mechanism casing)
（装填）机匣盖

11 barrel clamp (barrel-clamping nut)
枪管夹（枪管夹紧螺帽）

12 cocking lever (cocking handle)
枪的板机柄

13 palm rest
下护木

14 safety catch
保险（安全掣子）

15 magazine
弹匣

16 G3-A3 self-loading rifle
G3-A3 型自动步枪

17 barrel
枪管

18 flash hider (flash eliminator)
枪口闪光掩盖器

19 palm rest
下护木

20 trigger mechanism
板机

21 magazine
弹匣

22 notch (sighting notch, rearsight)
瞄准具（瞄准槽，表尺座）

23 front sight block (foresight block) with front sight (foresight)
准星座与准星

24 rifle butt (butt)
步枪托

25 44mm anti-tank rocket launcher
44 毫米（反坦克）火箭筒

26 rocket (projectile)
火箭弹（弹）

27 buffer
缓冲器

28 telescopic sight (telescope sight)
望远瞄准器

29 firing mechanism
击发装置

30 cheek rest
颊板托

31 shoulder rest (butt)
肩托（枪托）

32 MG3 machine gun (Spandau)
MG3 型机关枪

33 barrel casing
枪管护盖

34 gas regulator
气体调节器

35 belt-changing flap
弹带变换盖

36 rearsight
瞄准器表尺座（照门）

37 front sight block (foresight block) with front sight (foresight)
准星座与准星

38 pistol grip
手枪枪柄

39 shoulder rest (butt)
肩托（枪托）

40-95 **heavy weapons**
重型武器

40 120mm AM 50 mortar
120 毫米 AM50 型迫击炮

41 barrel
炮管

42 bipod
双脚架

43 gun carriage
炮托架

44 buffer (buffer ring)
缓冲器（缓冲环）

45 sight (sighting mechanism)
瞄准器（瞄准器装置）

46 base plate
底板（盘）

47 striker pad
缓冲垫

48 traversing handle
横动（转向）把手

49-74 artillery weapons mounted on self-propelled gun carriages
装在自动推进炮车上的火炮

49 175mm SFM 107 cannon
175 毫米 SFM107 大炮

50 drive wheel
驱动轮

51 elevating piston
升降活塞

52 buffer (buffer recuperator)
缓冲器（缓冲复热器）

53 hydraulic system
液压系统

54 breech ring
炮尾环

55 spade
炮车尾部

56 spade piston
炮车尾部活塞

57 155mm M 109 G self-propelled gun
155 毫米 M109G 型自动推进炮

58 muzzle
炮口

59 fume extractor
排烟器

60 barrel cradle
炮管摇架

61 barrel recuperator
炮管复进机

62 barrel clamp
炮管夹

63 light anti-aircraft (AA) machine gun
轻型高射机枪

64 Honest John M 386 rocket launcher
诚实约翰 M386 型火箭炮

65 rocket with warhead
装有弹头的火箭

66 launching ramp
倾斜发射装置

67 elevating gear
俯仰传动机构

68 jack
千斤顶，起重器

69 cable winch
缆索绞车

70 110 SF rocket launcher
110SF 型火箭炮

71 disposable rocket tubes
蜂巢式火箭发射管

72 tube bins
管仓

73 turntable
转台

74 fire control system
射击控制系统

75 2.5 tonne construction vehicle
2.5 吨工程车

76 lifting arms (lifting device)
起重臂（起重装置）

77 shovel
铲斗

78 counterweight (counterpoise)
配重

79-95 **armoured (***Am.*** armored) vehicles**
装甲车辆

79 M 113 armoured (*Am.* armored) ambulance
M113 型装甲救护车

80 Leopard 1 A 3 tank
豹式 1A3 型坦克

81 protection device
防护装置

82 infrared laser rangefinder
红外线雷射测距器

83 smoke canisters (smoke dispensers)
放烟罐（烟雾施放器）

84 armoured (*Am.* armored) turret
装甲炮塔

85 skirt
坦克防护板

86 road wheel
负重轮，稳定轮

87 track
履带

88 anti-tank tank
反战车坦克

89 fume extractor
排烟器

90 protection device
防护装置

91 armoured (*Am.* armored)
装甲输送车

92 cannon
大炮

93 armoured (*Am.* armored) recovery vehicle
装甲修护车

94 levelling (*Am.* leveling) and support shovel
平置和支撑用铲

95 jib
伸重，起重的铁臂

96 25 tonne all-purpose vehicle
25 吨通用车辆

97 drop windscreen (*Am.* drop windshield)
落地式挡风玻璃

98 canvas cover
帆布篷

1 *McDonnell-Douglas F-4F Phantom II* **intercepteor and fighter-bomber**
麦克唐纳—道格拉斯 F-4F 幽灵II式拦截轰炸战斗机

2 squadron marking
飞行中队标志

3 aircraft cannon
机关炮

4 wing tank (underwing tank)
机翼油箱（机翼下部油箱）

5 air intake
进气管

6 boundary layer control flap
边界层控制襟翼

7 in-flight refuelling (*Am.* refueling) probe (flight refuelling probe, air refuelling probe)
空中加油管

8 *Panavia 2000 Tornado* **multirole combat aircraft** (MRCA)
帕纳维亚 2000 旋风式万能战斗机

9 swing wing
摇翼

10 radar nose (radome, radar dome)
雷达锥，雷达罩

11 pitot-static tube (pitot tube)
动静压管

12 brake flap (air brake)
减速板（空中制动器）

13 afterburner exhaust nozzles of the engines
发动机后燃器排气喷嘴

14 *C160 Transall* **medium-range transport aircraft**
C160 "协同"中程运输机

15 undercarriage housing (landing gear housing)
起落架舱

16 propeller-turbine engine (turboprop engine)
涡轮螺旋桨发动机

17 antenna
天线

18 *Bell UH-ID Iroquois* **light transport and rescue helicopter**
（贝尔公司生产的）UH-ID 印第安式轻型运输和救难直升机

19 main rotor
主转子（旋翼）

20 tail rotor
尾转子（旋翼）

21 landing skids
著陆橇（落地雪橇）

22 stabilizing fins (stabilizing surfaces, stabilizers)
安定板

23 tail skid
尾橇

24 *Dornier DO28 D-2 Skyservant* **transport and communications aircraft**
（西德多尼尔公司生产的）D028 D-2 空中仆人式运输通讯机

25 engine pod
发动机（舱）箱

26 main undercarriage unit (main landing gear unit)
主起落架装置

27 tail wheel
尾轮

28 sword antenna
刀状天线

29 *F-104 G Starfighter* **fighter-bomber**
F-104G 星式战斗机轰炸机

30 wing-tip tank (tip tank)
翼尖油箱

31-32 T-tail (T-tail unit)
T 型尾翼（T 型尾翼装置）

31 tailplane (horizontal stabilizer, stabilizer)
水平尾翼（水平安定板）

32 vertical stabilizer (vertical fin, tail fin)
垂直（尾翼）安定板

1-41 *Dornier-Dassault-Breguet Alpha Jet* Franco-German jet trainer
（法国达索布雷盖航空公司和西德多尼尔公司共同生产的）阿尔发式喷射教练机

1 pitot-static tube (pitot tube)
动静压管

2 oxygen tank
氧气瓶，氧气槽

3 forward-retracting nose wheel
向前收之鼻轮

4 cockpit canopy (cockpit hood)
座舱罩

5 canopy jack
座舱盖启闭操作唧筒

6 pilot's seat (student pilot's seat), an ejector seat (ejection seat)
驾驶员弹射座椅（学员弹射座椅）

7 observer's seat (instructor's seat), an ejector seat (ejection seat)
观察员弹射座椅（教官弹射座椅）

8 control column (control stick)
驾驶（操纵）杆

9 thrust lever
推力杆

10 rudder pedals with brakes
方向舵与刹车踏板

11 front avionics bay
前电子舱

12 air intake to the engine
发动机（引擎）进气口

13 boundary layer control flap
边界层控制襟翼

14 air intake duct
进气道

15 turbine engine
涡轮发动机（引擎）

16 reservoir for the hydraulic system
液压系统油箱

17 battery housing
电瓶舱（电瓶装置舱）

18 rear avionics bay
后电子舱

19 baggage compartment
行李舱

20 triple-spar tail construction
三梁尾翼结构

21 horizontal tail
水平尾翼

22 servo-actuating mechanism for the elevator
升降舵的辅力致动机构

23 servo-actuating mechanism for the rudder
方向舵的辅力致动机构

24 brake chute housing (drag chute housing)
减速伞舱（阻力伞舱）

25 VHF (very high frequency) antenna (UHF antenna)
特高频天线（超高频天线）

26 VOR (very high frequency omnidirectional range) antenna
特高频全向天线

27 twin-spar wing construction
双梁机翼结构

28 former with integral spars
整体翼梁框架

29 integral wing tanks
机翼整体油箱

30 centre-section (*Am.* center-section) fuel tank
中翼油槽

31 fuselage tanks
机身油箱

32 gravity fuelling (*Am.* fueling) point
重力加油口

33 pressure fuelling (*Am.* fueling) point
压力加油口

34 inner wing suspension
机翼内侧支架

35 outer wing suspension
机翼外侧支架

36 navigation lights (position lights)
航行灯（方位灯）

37 landing lights
著陆灯

38 landing flap
降落襟翼

39 aileron actuator
副翼致动器

40 forward-retracting main undercarriage unit (main landing gear unit)
向前收之主起落架装置

41 undercarriage hydraulic cylinder (landing gear hydraulic cylinder)
起落架液压唧筒（著陆架液压唧筒）

1-63 light battleships
轻型战舰

1 destroyer
驱逐舰

2 hull of flush-deck vessel
平甲板船型的船身

3 bow (stem)
船首

4 flagstaff (jackstaff)
旗杆（船艏旗杆）

5 anchor, a stockless anchor
(patent anchor)
锚，无挡锚

6 anchor capstan (windlass)
起锚绞盘

7 breakwater (*Am.* manger board)
防波板

8 chine strake
舷缘侧板

9 main deck
主甲板

10-28 superstructures
上层建筑，船楼建筑

10 superstructure deck
船楼甲板

11 life rafts
救生筏

12 cutter (ship's boat)
小艇

13 davit (boat-launching crane)
吊柱吊架

14 bridge (bridge superstructure)
舰（船桥）

15 side navigation light (side
running light)
侧航行灯

16 antenna
天线

17 radio direction finder (RDF)
frame
无线电测向架

18 lattice mast
格子桅

19 forward funnel
前烟窗

20 aft funnel
后烟窗

21 cowl
烟窗帽

22 aft superstructure (poop)
舰部上层建筑（船楼建筑，舰楼）

23 capstan
绞盘

24 companion ladder
(companionway, companion
hatch)
升降梯（升降口，升降舱口）

25 ensign staff
舰旗杆

26 stern, a transom stern
舰，船尾肋骨

27 waterline
水线

28 searchlight
探照灯

29-37 armament
武器

29 100mm gun turret
100 毫米炮塔

30 four-barrel anti-submarine
rocket launcher (missile
launcher)
四管反潜艇火箭发射器

31 40mm twin anti-aircraft (AA)
gun
40 厘米双高射炮

32 MM 38 anti-aircraft (AA)
rocket launcher (missile
launcher) in launching container
在发射舱的MM38 型对空火箭发射器
（飞弹发射器）

33 anti-submarine torpedo tube
反潜艇鱼雷射管

34 depth-charge thrower
深水炸弹发射装置（投弹器）

35 weapon system radar
武器系统雷达

36 radar antenna (radar scanner)
雷达天线

37 optical rangefinder
光学测距器

38 destroyer
驱逐舰

39 bower anchor
艏锚

40 propeller guard
螺旋桨护板

41 tripod lattice mast
三角网格桅杆

42 pole mast
杆桅

43 ventilator openings (ventilator
grill)
通风机口

44 exhaust pipe
排气管

45 ship's boat
救生艇

46 antenna
天线

47 radar-controlled 127mm
all-purpose gun in turret
炮塔上雷达控制 127 毫米多目的（用
途）炮

48 127mm all-purpose gun
127 毫米多目的（用途）炮

49 launcher for Tartar missiles
鞑靼飞弹发射器

50 anti-submarine rocket (ASROC)
launcher (missile launcher)
反潜艇火箭发射器

51 fire control radar antennas
射击控制雷达天线

52 radome (radar dome)
（雷达）天线罩

53 frigate
（反潜艇）小型驱逐舰

54 hawse pipe
锚链筒

55 steaming light
航海（行）桅灯

56 navigation light (running light)
航海（行）灯

57 air extractor duct
排气管

58 funnel
烟窗

59 cowl
烟窗帽

60 whip antenna (fishpole antenna)
鞭状（钓杆状）天线

61 cutter
小艇

62 stern light
艏灯

63 propeller guard boss
螺旋桨护板毂

64-91 fighting ships
战舰

64 submarine
潜水艇

65 flooded foredeck
浸水前甲板

66 pressure hull
压力船壳

67 turret
塔，枪塔

68 retractable instruments
可伸缩的仪器

69 E-boat (torpedo boat)
E 型快艇（鱼雷快艇）

70 76mm all-purpose gun with
turret
76 毫米多目的（用途）炮（塔）

71 missile-launching housing
飞弹发射器外壳

72 deckhouse
甲板室（房舱）

73 40mm anti-aircraft (AA) gun
40 毫米高射砲

74 propeller guard moulding (*Am.*
molding)
螺旋桨护板缘饰

75 143 class E-boat (143 class
torpedo boat)
143 级 E 型快艇（143 级鱼雷快艇）

76 breakwater (*Am.* manger board)
防波板

77 radome (radar dome)
（雷达）天线罩

78 torpedo tube
鱼雷射管

79 exhaust escape flue
排气（烟）管道

80 mine hunter
扫雷艇

81 reinforced rubbing strake
加强防擦板

82 inflatable boat (inflatable
dinghy)
充气艇（充气小艇）

83 davit
吊柱，吊架

84 minesweeper
扫雷艇，扫雷艇

85 cable winch
钢缆绞车

86 towing winch (towing machine,
towing engine)
拖缆绞车

87 mine-sweeping gear (paravanes)
扫雷装置（水雷扫除器）

88 crane (davit)
起重装置（吊杆）

89 landing craft
登陆艇

90 bow ramp
船头斜台（登陆舌门）

91 stern ramp
船尾斜台（登陆舌门）

92-97 auxiliaries
辅助舰

92 tender
补给舰（船）

93 servicing craft
驳运船

94 minelayer
布雷艇

95 training ship
教练船

96 deep-sea salvage tug
深海救难船

97 fuel tanker (replenishing ship)
油船（补给船）

1 **nuclear-powered aircraft carrier** [*Nimitz ICVN 68*] (USA)
"尼米兹 ICVN68"核子动力航空母舰

2-11 body plan
船体正面图

2 flight deck
飞行甲板

3 island (bridge)
司令塔（舰桥）

4 aircraft lift (*Am.* aircraft elevator)
飞行升降机

5 eight-barrel anti-aircraft (AA) rocket launcher (missile launcher)
八管高射火箭发射器（导弹发射器）

6 pole mast (antenna mast)
杆桅（天线桅）

7 antenna
天线

8 radar antenna (radar scanner)
雷达天线

9 fully enclosed bow
全闭式船首

10 deck crane
甲板起重机

11 transom stern
方形船尾

12-20 deck plan
甲板平面图

12 angle deck (flight deck)
斜角甲板（飞行甲板）

13 aircraft lift (*Am.* aircraft elevator)
飞机升降机

14 twin launching catapult
双飞机弹射装置

15 hinged (movable) baffle board
铰链阻板（活动阻板）

16 arrester wire
拦阻索

17 emergency crash barrier
紧急栏机网

18 safety net
安全网

19 caisson (cofferdam)
沉箱（堰舱）

20 eight-barrel anti-aircraft (AA) rocket launcher (missile launcher)
八管高射火箭发射器（导弹发射器）

21 [*Kara*] *class* **rocket cruiser** (missile cruiser) (USSR)
"卡拉"级火箭巡洋舰（导弹巡洋舰）（苏俄）

22 hull of flush-deck vessel
平甲板船隻的船身

23 sheer
舷弧

24 twelve-barrel underwater salvo rocket launcher (missile launcher)
十二管水中齐发火箭发射器

25 twin anti-aircraft (AA) rocket launcher (missile launcher)
双高射火箭发射器

26 launching housing for 4 short-range rockets (missiles)
四枚短程火箭（导弹）发射装置架

27 baffle board
阻板

28 bridge
舰桥

29 radar antenna (radar scanner)
雷达天线

30 twin 76mm anti-aircraft (AA) gun turret
双 76 毫米高射炮塔

31 turret
塔（炮塔）

32 funnel
烟窗

33 twin anti-aircraft (AA) rocket launcher (missile launcher)
双高射火箭发射器

34 automatic anti-aircraft (AA) gun
自动高射炮

35 ship's boat
救生艇

36 underwater 5-torpedo housing
五部鱼雷发射架

37 underwater 6-salvo rocket launcher (missile launcher)
六管水中齐发火箭发射器

38 helicopter hangar
直升机库

39 helicopter landing platform
直升机著陆平台

40 variable depth sonar (VDS)
可变深度声纳

41 [*California*] class **rocket cruiser** (missile cruiser) (USA)
"加里佛尼亚"级火箭巡洋舰（导弹巡洋舰）（美国）

42 hull
船身

43 forward turret
前桅塔

44 aft turret
后桅塔

45 forward superstructure
船首上层建筑

46 landing craft
登陆艇

47 antenna
天线

48 radar antenna (radar scanner)
雷达天线

49 radome (radar dome)
（雷达）天线罩

50 surface-to-air rocket launcher (missile launcher)
对空火箭发射器

51 underwater rocket launcher (missile launcher)
水中火箭发射器

52 127mm gun with turret
127 毫米炮塔

53 helicopter landing platform
直升机著陆平台

54 **nuclear-powered fleet submarine**
核子动力潜艇

55-74 middle section 'diagram'
中间部分〔简图〕

55 pressure hull
耐压船壳

56 auxiliary engine room
辅机舱

57 rotary turbine pump
旋转滑轮泵

58 steam turbine generator
蒸汽涡轮发电机

59 propeller shaft
螺旋桨轴

60 thrust block
推力轴承

61 reduction gear
减速齿轮（装置）

62 high and low pressure turbine
高低压涡轮

63 high-pressure steam pipe for the secondary water circuit (auxiliary water circuit)
二次（辅助）水廻路高压蒸汽管

64 condenser
凝结器

65 primary water circuit
一次水廻路

66 heat exchanger
热交换器

67 nuclear reactor casing (atomic pile casing)
核反应器防护罩（原子堆防护罩）

68 reactor core
反应炉）核心

69 control rods
控制杆

70 lead screen
铅屏（遮蔽屏）

71 turret
塔（炮塔）

72 snorkel (schnorkel)
换气装置

73 air inlet
进气口

74 retractable instruments
可伸缩的仪器

75 **patrol submarine** with conventional (diesel-electric) drive
常规驱动（柴油电动）巡逻潜艇

76 pressure hull
耐压船壳

77 flooded foredeck
浸水前甲板

78 outer flap (outer doors) 'for torpedoes'
外闸门〔发射鱼雷用〕

79 torpedo tube
鱼雷发射器

80 bow bilge
艋

81 anchor
锚

82 anchor winch
起锚绞车

83 battery
蓄电池，电瓶

84 living quarters with folding bunks
具折叠床的居住舱

85 commanding officer's cabin
艇长舱，指挥舱

86 main hatchway
主舱口

87 flagstaff
旗杆

88-91 retractable instruments
可伸缩仪器

88 attack periscope
攻击潜望镜

89 antenna
天线

90 snorkel (schnorkel)
换气装置

91 radar antenna (radar scanner)
雷达天线

92 exhaust outlet
排气口

93 heat space (hot-pipe space)
暖气（管）室

94 diesel generators
柴油发电机

95 aft diving plane and vertical rudder
舳水平舵和垂直舵

96 forward vertical rudder
艏垂直舵

1-85 primary school
小学

1-45 classroom
教室

1 arrangement of desks in a horseshoe
成马蹄形（U型）排列的课桌

2 double desk
双人课桌

3 pupils (children) in a group (sitting in a group)
分组坐的小学生（小孩）

4 exercise book
练习簿

5 pencil
铅笔

6 wax crayon
蜡笔

7 school bag
手提式书包

8 handle
提手

9 school satchel (satchel)
背式书包

10 front pocket
书包正面小口袋

11 strap (shoulder strap)
背带（肩带）

12 pen and pencil case
钢笔和铅笔盒

13 zip
拉链

14 fountain pen (pen)
签字笔（钢笔）

15 loose-leaf file (ring file)
活页纸夹

16 reader
读物，读本

17 spelling book
拼字教科书

18 notebook (exercise book)
笔记簿（练习簿）

19 felt tip pen
毛笔，毡尖笔

20 pupil raising her hand
学生举手

21 teacher
老师

22 teacher's desk
讲台

23 register
点名簿

24 pen and pencil tray
钢笔和铅笔盘

25 desk mat (blotter)
桌垫（吸墨纸）

26 window painting with finger paints (finger painting)
指绘的窗户画

27 pupils' (children's) paintings (watercolours)
儿童画（水彩画）

28 cross
十字架

29 three-part blackboard
三块板组成的黑板

30 bracket for holding charts
挂图用的托架

31 chalk ledge
粉笔（壁）架

32 chalk
粉笔

33 blackboard drawing
黑板画

34 diagram
图解，示范图

35 reversible side blackboard
正反两面皆可使用的黑板

36 projection screen
放映幕

37 triangle
三角板

38 protractor
分度器

39 divisions
分度

40 blackboard compass
黑板用圆规，两脚规

41 sponge tray
海绵托盘

42 blackboard sponge (sponge)
海绵黑板擦

43 classroom cupboard
教室小柜

44 map (wall map)
地图（挂图）

45 brick wall
砖墙

46-85 craft room
工艺室

46 workbench
工作枱

47 vice (*Am.* vise)
虎钳

48 vice (*Am.* vise) bar
虎钳把手

49 scissors
剪刀

50-52 working with glue (sticking paper, cardboard, etc.)
粘胶工作（贴纸，硬纸板等）

50 surface to be glued
表面涂布粘胶，粘贴面

51 tube of glue
一管粘胶

52 tube cap
管帽

53 fretsaw
圆锯，线锯

54 fretsaw blade (saw blade)
锯片（叶）

55 wood rasp (rasp)
木锉

56 piece of wood held in the vice (*Am.* vise)
虎钳夹住的木块

57 glue pot
粘胶罐

58 stool
凳子

59 brush
刷子

60 pan (dust pan)
盘（灰尘盘）

61 broken china
破碎的瓷器

62 enamelling (*Am.* enameling)
上瓷釉

63 electric enamelling (*Am.* enameling) stove
电磁炉

64 unworked copper
未加功的铜器

65 enamel powder
釉粉

66 hair sieve
细筛

67-80 pupils' (children's) work
学生（儿童）作品

67 clay models (models)
粘土（泥塑）模型

68 window decoration of coloured (*Am.* colored) glass
彩色玻璃的窗饰

69 glass mosaic picture (glass mosaic)
玻璃镶嵌画

70 mobile
活动玩具

71 paper kite (kite)
纸风筝

72 wooden construction
木制品

73 polyhedron
多面体

74 hand puppets
玩偶

75 clay masks
粘土（陶）制面具

76 cast candles (wax candles)
蜡烛

77 wood carving
木雕

78 clay jug
陶罐

79 geometrical shapes made of clay
陶制几何模型

80 wooden toys
木制玩具

81 materials
材料，原料

82 stock of wood
木头

83 inks for wood cuts
版画（木刻）用的油墨

84 paintbrushes
画笔

85 bag of plaster of Paris
熟石膏袋

1-45 grammar school; *also:*
upper band of a comprehensive
school (*Am.* alternative school)
初级中学；高级综合中学
1-13 chemistry
化学
1 chemistry lab (chemistry
laboratory) with tiered rows of
seats
一排排阶梯座位的化学实验室
2 chemistry teacher
化学教员（教师）
3 demonstration bench (teacher's
bench)
实验台（教师实验台）
4 water pipe
水管
5 tiled working surface
铺瓷砖的台面
6 sink
水槽（洗涤槽）
7 television monitor, a screen for
educational programmes (*Am.*
programs)
教学用电视机（监控器）
8 overhead projector
投影器
9 projector top for skins
放幻灯片的投影器上部
10 projection lens with right-angle
mirror
带直角反射镜的投影镜头
11 pupils' (*Am.* students') bench
with experimental apparatus
具实验设备的学生实验台
12 electrical point (socket)
电插座
13 projection table
投影台
14-34 biology preparation room
(biology prep room)
生物学准备室
14 skeleton
骨骼，骨架
15 casts of skulls
头颅模型
16 calvarium of Pithecanthropus
Erectus
爪哇直立猿人（头）颅顶化石
17 skull of Steinheim man
斯坦罕姆人的头颅骨
18 calvarium of Peking man (of
Sinanthropus)
北京人（北京猿人）的（头）颅顶化石
19 skull of Neanderthal man,. a
skull of primitive man
尼安德塔人头颅化石（原始人的头
颅）
20 Australopithecine skull (skull of
Australopthecus)
更新世界灵长类动物头颅（已绝种灵长类
头骨）
21 skull of present-day man
现代人头颅
22 dissecting bench
解剖台
23 chemical bottles
化学药瓶
24 gas tap
煤气（瓦斯）栓
25 petri dish
细菌培养皿（碟）
26 measuring cylinder
量筒
27 work folder (teaching material)
工作纸夹（教材）

28 textbook
教科书课本
29 bacteriological cultures
细菌的培养
30 incubator
细菌培养室
31 test tube rack
试管架
32 washing bottle
洗涤瓶
33 water tank
水箱
34 sink
水槽（洗涤槽）
35 language laboratory
语言教室
36 blackboard
黑板
37 console
控制台
38 headphones (headset)
耳机
39 microphone
微音器（麦克风）
40 earcups
耳机套
41 padded headband (padded
headpiece)
加垫头带
42 programme (*Am.* program)
recorder, a cassette recorder
教学用录音机，一种卡式录音机
43 pupil's (*Am.* student's) volume
control
学生用的音量控制
44 master volume control
教师用的音量控制
45 control buttons (operating keys)
控制钮（操作键）

1-25 university (college)
大学（学院）
1 lecture
讲演，讲课
2 lecture room (lecture theatre, *Am.* theater)
教室，讲堂
3 university lecturer (lecturer, *Am.* assistant professor)
大学教师（讲师，[美]助教）
4 lectern
讲台
5 lecture notes
讲义，讲稿
6 demonstrator
示范者
7 assistant
助教，助手
8 diagram
挂图，图表
9 student
学生（男）
10 student
学生（女）
11-25 university library
大学图书馆
11 stack (book stack) with the stock of books
书库的藏书
12 bookshelf, a steel shelf
书架，钢制书架
13 reading room
阅览室

14 member of the reading room staff, a librarian
阅览室工作人员，图书馆管理员
15 periodicals rack with periodicals
期刊架
16 newspaper shelf
报纸架
17 reference library with reference books (handbooks, encyclopedias, dictionaries)
备有参考书（手册，百科全书，辞典）的参考书图书馆
18 lending library and catalogue (*Am.* catalog) room
借书图书馆及目录室
19 librarian
图书馆管理员
20 issue desk
发书台
21 main catalogue (*Am.* catalog)
总目录（索引）
22 card catalogue (*Am.* catalog)
卡片目录（索引）
23 card catalogue (*Am.* catalog) drawer
卡片目录（索引）抽屉
24 library user
借书人
25 borrower's ticket (library ticket)
借书证

1-15 election meeting, a public
   meeting
   （选举）政见发表会，一种公开的集
   会
1-2 committee
   委员会
1 chairman
   主席
2 committee member
   委员会委员
3 committee table
   委员席（桌）
4 bell
   铃
5 election speaker (speaker)
   政见发表人（演说者）
6 rostrum
   演讲台
7 microphone
   微（扩）音器，麦克风
8 meeting (audience)
   听众
9 man distributing leaflets
   散发传单者
10 stewards
   会场服务人员
11 armband (armlet)
   臂章
12 banner
   （宣传用）横幕
13 placard
   标语牌
14 proclamation
   宣言，布告

15 heckler
   诘问者
16-30 election
   选举
16 polling station (polling place)
   投票处
17 election officer
   选举事务员
18 electoral register
   选举人名册
19 polling card with registration
   number (polling number)
   有登记编号的投票卡片
20 ballot paper with the names of
   the parties and candidates
   具有党派名称和候选人姓名的选票
21 ballot envelope
   选票信封
22 voter
   投票人
23 polling booth
   投票间（亭）
24 elector (qualified voter)
   有选举权者
25 election regulations
   选举规则
26 clerk
   事务员，办事员
27 clerk with the duplicate list
   拿名册副本的办事员
28 election supervisor
   选举督察

29 ballot box
   （投）票箱
30 slot
   投票口

1-33 police duties
警务

1 police helicopter (traffic helicopter) for controlling (*Am.* controling) traffic from the air
从空中指挥交通的警察直升机

2 cockpit
驾驶舱

3 rotor (main rotor)
转子（主转子，主旋翼）

4 tail rotor
尾转子（旋翼）

5 police dog and handler
警犬和训练师

6 police dog
警犬

7 uniform
制服

8 uniform cap, a peaked cap with cockade
制服帽，有帽章的大盘帽

9 traffic control by a mobile traffic patrol
使用交通巡逻车指挥交通

10 patrol car
巡逻车

11 blue light
蓝灯

12 loud hailer (loudspeaker)
扩音器，扬声器

13 patrolman (police patrolman)
巡逻警察

14 police signalling (*Am.* signaling) disc (disk)
警察信号牌

15 riot duty
镇暴任务

16 special armoured (*Am.* armored) car
特别装甲车

17 barricade
路障

18 policeman (police officer) in riot gear
穿镇暴服的警察

19 truncheon (baton)
警棍（警棒）

20 riot shield
镇暴用盾牌

21 protective helmet (helmet)
护盔（头盔）

22 service pistol
警用手枪

23 pistol grip
手枪握把

24 quick-draw holster
快速拔枪枪套

25 magazine
弹匣

26 police identification disc (disk)
警察识别证

27 police badge
警徽

28 fingerprint identification (dactyloscopy)
指纹证明（指纹）

29 fingerprint
指纹

30 illuminated screen
照明透视屏

31 search
搜查

32 suspect
嫌疑犯

33 detective (plainclothes policeman)
刑事，侦探（便衣警察）

34 English policeman
英国警察

35 helmet
头盔

36 pocket book
袖珍型记事簿

37 policewoman
女警

38 police van
警车

1-26 café, *sim.:* espresso bar, tea room 咖啡店，类似：浓咖啡店，茶馆	**16** lemonade glass 柠檬水玻璃杯
1 counter (cake counter) 柜台（西点柜台）	**17** chess players playing a game of chess 下棋者
2 coffee urn 咖啡壶	**18** coffee set 整套咖啡器具
3 tray for the money 钱盘	**19** cup of coffee 一杯咖啡
4 gateau 糕饼，蛋糕	**20** small sugar bowl 小糖罐
5 meringue with whipped cream 加奶油的糕饼（蛋白与砂糖制成的）	**21** cream jug (*Am.* creamer) 奶油罐
6 trainee pastry cook 面包点心学徒	**22-24** café customers 咖啡店顾客
7 counter assistant 柜台女店员	**22** gentleman 男士
8 newspaper shelves (newspaper rack) 报纸架	**23** lady 女士
9 wall lamp 壁灯	**24** man reading a newspaper 看报的男人
10 corner seat, an upholstered seat 角落座位，铺布（皮）面的座位	**25** newspaper 报纸
11 café table 咖啡桌	**26** newspaper holder 报纸夹
12 marble top 大理石桌面	
13 waitress 女服务生，女侍者	
14 tray 托盘	
15 bottle of lemonade 瓶装柠檬水	

1-29 restaurant
餐厅

1-11 bar (counter)
柜台

1 beer pump (beerpull)
啤酒泵（生啤酒出酒把手）

2 drip tray
滴盘

3 beer glass
啤酒杯

4 froth (head)
啤酒泡沫

5 spherical ashtray for cigarette and cigar ash
球形烟灰缸

6 beer glass (beer mug)
啤酒玻璃杯（啤酒杯）

7 beer warmer
啤酒加温器

8 bartender (barman, *Am.* barkeeper, barkeep)
酒保

9 shelf for glasses
玻璃杯搁架

10 shelf for bottles
瓶子搁架

11 stack of plates
一叠盘子

12 coat stand
挂衣架

13 hat peg
挂帽钉

14 coat hook
挂衣钩

15 wall ventilator
壁式通风机（换气装置）

16 bottle
瓶

17 complete meal
一盘料理

18 waitress
女侍者，女服务员

19 tray
托盘

20 lottery ticket seller
（奖券）彩票贩卖者

21 menu (menu card)
菜单（菜单卡）

22 cruet stand
调味瓶架

23 toothpick holder
牙签筒

24 matchbox holder
火柴盒立架

25 customer
顾客

26 beer mat
啤酒杯衬垫

27 meal of the day
当日餐点

28 flower seller (flower girl)
卖花人，卖花女

29 flower basket
花篮

30-44 wine restaurant (wine bar)
酒廊（酒吧）

30 wine waiter, a head waiter
酒廊服务员，领班

31 wine list
酒名单

32 wine carafe
玻璃酒瓶

33 wineglass
酒杯

34 tiled stove
瓷砖炉灶

35 stove tile
炉灶瓷砖

36 stove bench
炉灶台

37 wooden panelling (*Am.* paneling)
木制镶板

38 corner seat
角落位置

39 corner table
角落餐桌

40 regular customer
老顾客，常客

41 cutlery chest
刀叉餐具柜

42 wine cooler
酒冷却器

43 bottle of wine
酒瓶

44 ice cubes (ice, lumps of ice)
小冰块

45-78 self-service restaurant
自助餐厅

45 stack of trays
整叠盘子

46 drinking straws (straws)
饮料吸管

47 serviettes (napkins)
餐巾

48 cutlery holders
刀叉托架

49 cool shelf
冷藏架

50 slice of honeydew melon
哈蜜瓜片，西瓜片

51 plate of salad
凉拌食品，沙拉盘

52 plate of cheeses
乳酪盘

53 fish dish
鱼碟

54 filled roll
卷形小面包

55 meat dish with trimmings
带配菜的肉碟

56 half chicken
半鸡

57 basket of fruit
水果篮

58 fruit juice
果汁

59 drinks shelf
饮料架

60 bottle of milk
瓶装牛奶

61 bottle of mineral water
瓶装矿泉水

62 vegetarian meal (diet meal)
蔬菜餐（节食餐）

63 tray
托盘

64 tray counter
放盘的柜台

65 food price list
食品价格（目）表

66 serving hatch
服务窗口

67 hot meal
热食

68 beer pump (beerpull)
啤酒泵（生啤酒出酒把手）

69 cash desk
收款柜台

70 cashier
收款员（出纳）

71 proprietor
老板，经营者

72 rail
栏杆

73 dining area
用餐区

74 table
餐桌

75 open sandwich
只有一片的三明治（馅等置於面包上）

76 ice-cream sundae
冰淇淋圣代

77 salt cellar and pepper pot
盐罐和胡椒瓶

78 table decoration (flower arrangement)
桌饰（花瓶、插花）

1-26 vestibule (foyer, reception
hall)
大厅，招待厅
1 doorman (commisionaire)
看门人（门警）
2 letter rack with pigeon holes
分小格的信件架
3 key rack
钥匙架
4 globe lamp, a frosted glass globe
球形灯，毛玻璃球形灯
5 indicator board (drop board)
指示牌（吊号牌）
6 indicator light
指示灯
7 chief receptionist
接待主管
8 register (hotel register)
登记簿
9 room key
房间钥匙
10 number tag (number tab)
showing room number
显示房间号码的号码牌
11 hotel bill
旅馆账单
12 block of registration forms
登记表格本
13 passport
护照
14 hotel guest
旅客

15 lightweight suitcase, a light
suitcase for air travel
航空旅行用的轻便手提箱
16 wall desk
壁台
17 porter (*Am.* baggage man)
搬行李工人，行李员
18-26 lobby (hotel lobby)
大厅（旅馆、饭店大厅）
18 page (pageboy, *Am.* bell boy)
侍者
19 hotel manager
旅馆经理
20 dining room (hotel restaurant)
餐厅（旅馆餐厅）
21 chandelier
树枝形吊灯
22 fireside
壁炉边
23 fireplace
壁炉
24 mantelpiece (mantelshelf)
壁炉架
25 fire (open fire)
炉火
26 armchair
扶手椅子

27-38 **hotel room,** a double room
　with bath
　旅馆房门，具浴室的双人房
27 double door
　双重门
28 service bell panel
　服务铃按钮板
29 wardrobe trunk
　衣柜
30 clothes compartment
　吊衣柜
31 linen compartment
　亚麻类衣柜
32 double washbasin
　双洗脸盆
33 room waiter
　房间服务员
34 room telephone
　房间电话
35 velour (velours) carpet
　丝绒地毯
36 flower stand
　花架
37 flower arrangement
　插花
38 double bed
　双人床
39 **banquet room**
　宴客室
40-43 private party
　私人宴会
40 speaker proposing a toast
　敬酒的讲话人

41 42's neighbour (*Am.* neighbor)
　42 的邻座
42 43's partner
　43 的同伴
43 42's partner
　42 的同伴
44-46 **thé dansant** (tea dance) in the
　foyer
　在旅馆大厅的舞会（茶舞）
44 bar trio
　酒吧三重奏
45 violinist
　小提琴手
46 couple dancing (dancing couple)
　双人舞（一对舞伴）
47 waiter
　服务员，侍者
48 napkin
　餐巾
49 cigar and cigarette boy
　卖香烟和雪茄的小孩
50 cigarette tray
　香烟托盘
51 **hotel bar**
　旅馆酒吧
52 foot rail
　脚踏栏杆
53 bar stool
　吧台凳
54 bar
　吧台
55 bar customer
　酒吧顾客

56 cocktail glass (*Am.* highball
　glass)
　鸡尾酒杯
57 whisky (whiskey) glass
　威士忌酒杯
58 champagne cork
　香槟酒的软木塞
59 champagne bucket (champagne
　cooler)
　香槟酒水桶（香槟酒冷却器）
60 measuring beaker (measure)
　量杯（量度器）
61 cocktail shaker
　鸡尾酒摇动器
62 bartender (barman, *Am.*
　barkeeper, barkeep)
　酒保
63 barmaid
　酒吧女侍
64 shelf for bottles
　酒瓶架
65 shelf for glasses
　酒杯架
66 mirrored panel
　有镜子的镶板
67 ice bucket
　冰桶

1 **parking meter**
停车计时收费表
2 **map of the town (street map)**
市镇地图（街道图）
3 **illuminated board**
照明地图板
4 **key**
按键
5 **litter bin (*Am.* litter basket)**
垃圾箱
6 **street lamp (street light)**
路灯
7 **street sign showing the name of the street**
街名标示牌
8 **drain**
排水沟
9 **clothes shop (fashion house)**
服装（时装）店
10 **shop window**
橱窗
11 **window display (shop window display)**
橱窗陈列品
12 **window decoration (shop window decoration)**
橱窗摆饰
13 **entrance**
入口
14 **window**
窗
15 **window box**
窗台

16 **neon sign**
霓虹灯广告牌
17 **tailor's workroom**
裁缝师工作室
18 **pedestrian**
行人
19 **shopping bag**
购物袋
20 **road sweeper (*Am.* street sweeper)**
清道夫
21 **broom**
扫帚
22 **rubbish (litter)**
垃圾（废物）
23 **tramlines (*Am.* streetcar tracks)**
电车路（轨道）
24 **pedestrian crossing (zebra crossing, *Am.* crosswalk)**
（斑马线）行人穿越道
25 **tram stop (*Am.* streetcar stop, trolley stop)**
电车店
26 **tram stop sign (*Am.* streetcar stop sign, trolley stop sign)**
电车站牌
27 **tram timetable (*Am.* streetcar schedule)**
电车时刻表
28 **ticket machine**
售票机
29 **[pedestrian crossing] sign**
（行人穿越道）路牌

30 **traffic policeman on traffic duty (point duty)**
执行交通勤务的交通警察
31 **traffic control cuff**
交通指挥袖套
32 **white cap**
白色大盘帽
33 **hand signal**
手势
34 **motorcyclist**
摩托车骑士
35 **motorcycle**
摩托车
36 **pillion passenger (pillion rider)**
坐於摩托车后座者
37 **bookshop**
书店
38 **hat shop (hatter's shop); *for ladies' hats:* milliner's shop**
帽店，女帽制造商
39 **shop sign**
商店招牌
40 **insurance company office**
保险公司办公室

41 department store
百货公司

42 shop front
商店前面

43 advertisement
广告

44 flags
旗帜

45 illuminated letters
灯光装饰字母

46 tram (*Am.* streetcar, trolley)
电车

47 furniture lorry (*Am.* furniture truck)
家具搬运车

48 flyover
路桥，天桥

49 suspended street lamp
悬吊路灯

50 stop line
停车线

51 pedestrian crossing (*Am.* crosswalk)
人行穿越道

52 traffic lights
红绿灯（交通信号灯）

53 traffic light post
红绿灯柱（交通信号灯柱）

54 set of lights
整组红绿灯

55 pedestrian lights
行人穿越灯

56 telephone box (telephone booth, telephone kiosk, call box)
公用电话亭

57 cinema advertisement (film poster)
电影广告（影片海报）

58 pedestrian precinct (paved zone)
徒步区

59 street café
（街旁）露天咖啡店

60 group seated (sitting) at a table
坐於桌边喝咖啡的人

61 sunshade
遮阳伞

62 steps to the public lavatories (public conveniences)
通向公共厕所的阶梯

63 taxi rank (taxi stand)
计程车停车处

64 taxi (taxicab, cab)
计程车

65 taxi sign
计程车标帜

66 traffic sign showing [taxi rank] ([taxi stand])
显示计程车停放处的交通标帜

67 taxi telephone
计程车电话

68 post office
邮局

69 cigarette machine
香烟贩卖机

70 advertising pillar
广告柱子，广告张贴处

71 poster (advertisement)
海报（广告）

72 white line
白线

73 lane arrow for turning left
左转的行驶箭头

74 lane arrow for going straight ahead
直行的行驶箭头

75 news vendor (*Am.* news dealer)
卖报人

1-66 drinking water supply
饮水供应

1 water table (groundwater level)
地下水面（地下水位）

2 water-bearing stratum (aquifer, aquafer)
含水层

3 groundwater stream (underground stream)
地下水流

4 collector well for raw water
生水集水井

5 suction pipe
抽水管

6 pump strainer (with foot valve)
（装有底阀的）泵滤网

7 bucket pump with motor
带马达的斗式泵

8 vacuum pump with motor
带马达的真空泵

9 rapid-filter plant
快速过滤设备（滤池）

10 filter gravel (filter bed)
过滤砂砾

11 filter bottom, a grid
滤床，格栅的一种

12 filtered water outlet
过滤水出口

13 purified water tank
净水槽

14 suction pipe with pump strainer and foot valve
具泵滤网和底阀的抽水管

15 main pump with motor
带马达的主泵

16 delivery pipe
输水管，供水管

17 compressed-air vessel (air vessel, air receiver)
压缩空气容器（贮气器，存气箱）

18 water tower
水塔

19 riser pipe (riser)
升管（升流管）

20 overflow pipe
溢水管

21 outlet
出水口

22 distribution main
主配水管

23 excess water conduit
废水渠

<table>
<tr><td>

4-39 tapping a spring
抽取泉水

24 chamber
闸室

25 chamber wall
闸室墙壁

26 manhole
人孔，检修孔

27 ventilator
通气孔

28 step irons
直爬梯

29 filling (backing)
充填物

30 outlet control valve
出口控制阀

31 outlet valve
出口阀

32 strainer
滤网

33 overflow pipe (overflow)
溢水管

34 bottom outlet
底部出水口

35 earthenware pipes
陶（器）管

**36 impervious stratum
(impermeable stratum)**
不透水层

37 rough rubble
粗积石

**38 water-bearing statum (aquifer,
aquafer)**
含水层

</td><td>

39 loam seal (clay seal)
壤土封层（粘土封层）

40-52 individual water supply
单独供水

40 well
水井

41 suction pipe
抽水管

42 water table (groundwater level)
地下水面（水位）

43 pump strainer with foot valve
具底阀的泵滤网

44 centrifugal pump
离心泵

45 motor
马达

46 motor safety switch
马达安全开关

47 manostat, a switching device
恒定流量装置，一种开关装置

48 stop valve
停止阀

49 delivery pipe
输水管，供水管

**50 compressed-air vessel (air vessel,
air receiver)**
压缩空气容器（贮气器，存气箱）

51 manhole
人孔

52 delivery pipe
输水管，供水管

53 water meter, a rotary meter
水表，旋转式水表

</td><td>

54 water inlet
入水口

55 counter gear assembly
计数装置

56 cover with glass lid
玻璃罩盖

57 water outlet
出水口

58 water-meter dial
水表数字盘

59 counters
计数器

**60 driven well (tube well, drive
well)**
辘轳井（管井，打桩井）

61 pile shoe
桩头

62 filter
过滤器

63 water table (groundwater level)
地下水面（位）

64 well casing
井筒

65 well head
井口

66 hand pump
手摇泵

</td></tr>
</table>

1-46 fire service drill
(extinguishing, climbing, ladder,
and rescue work)
消防演习（灭火，攀登，爬梯和救护
工作）

1-3 fire station
消防站

1 engine and appliance room
（救火车）消防车和消防装备（器具）
置放室

2 firemen's quarters
消防人员住处（宿舍）

3 drill tower
演习塔

4 fire alarm (fire alarm siren, fire
siren)
火灾警报器

5 fire engine
消防车

6 blue light (warning light), a
flashing light (*Am.* flashlight)
蓝灯（警报灯），闪光信号灯

7 horn (hooter)
警报器，警笛

8 motor pump, a centrifugal pump
马达泵，一种离心泵

9 motor turntable ladder (*Am.*
aerial ladder)
马达旋转云梯

10 ladder, a steel ladder (automatic
extending ladder)
钢梯（自动伸展梯）

11 ladder mechanism
云梯机械装置

12 jack
起重装置

13 ladder operator
云梯操作人员

14 extension ladder
伸展梯

15 ceiling hook (*Am.* preventer)
吊钩（防护钩）

16 hook ladder (*Am.* pompier
ladder)
钩梯

17 holding squad
营救班（拉开救助布的救火人员）

18 jumping sheet (sheet)
救助布（失火时用以接住跳楼者所用的
布）

19 ambulance car (ambulance)
救护车

20 resuscitator (resuscitation
equipment), oxygen apparatus
人工呼吸器，输氧装置

21 ambulance attendant
(ambulance man)
救护人员

22 armband (armlet, brassard)
臂章（臂饰，臂章）

23 stretcher
担架

24 unconscious man
失去知觉者

25 pit hydrant
地下消防栓

26 standpipe (riser, vertical pipe)
立管（升管，垂直管）

27 hydrant key
消防栓龙头（开关）

28 hose reel (*Am.* hose cart, hose
wagon, hose truck, hose
carriage)
软管卷轴（软管手推车，软管拖车，软
管手推车，软管托架）

29 hose coupling
软管连接头

30 soft suction hose
吸水软管

31 delivery hose
输水软管

32 dividing breeching
软管分接头

33 branch
水管管口

34 branchmen
水管操作人

35 surface hydrant (fire plug)
地面消防栓

36 officer in charge
消防队长

37 fireman (*Am.* firefighter)
消防队员

38 helmet (fireman's helmet, *Am.*
fire hat) with neck guard (neck
flap)
具护颈的护盔

39 breathing apparatus
呼吸保护器（装置）

40 face mask
面具
41 walkie-talkie set
无线电（通）话机
42 hand lamp
手提灯
43 small axe (*Am.* ax, pompier hatchet)
消防斧
44 hook belt
钩带
45 beltline
环状救生腰带
46 protective clothing of asbestos (asbestos suit) or of metallic fabric
石棉防火衣或金属纤维防火衣
47 breakdown lorry (*Am.* crane truck, wrecking crane)
抢救车（起重车）
48 lifting crane
起重机
49 load hook (draw hook, *Am.* drag hook)
吊钩
50 support roll
支承卷轴
51 water tender
给水车
52 portable pump
轻便泵
53 hose layer
消防器具搬运车

54 flaked lengths of hose
软管卷
55 cable drum
缆索卷筒
56 winch
绞车（盘）
57 face mask filter
防毒面具过滤器
58 active carbon (activated carbon, activated charcoal)
活性碳（活性炭）
59 dust filter
滤尘器
60 air inlet
进气口
61 portable fire extinguisher
轻便灭火器
62 trigger valve
触发阀
63 large mobile extinguisher (wheeled fire extinguisher)
大型移动式灭火器
64 foam-making branch (*Am.* foam gun)
泡沫喷射器
65 fireboat
消防艇
66 monitor (water cannon)
回转喷水管（水炮）
67 suction hose
吸水软管

1 cashier
  收款员，出纳员
2 electric cash register (till)
  电动收银机
3 number keys
  数目键
4 cancellation button
  消除按钮
5 cash drawer (till)
  现金抽屉
6 compartments (money
  compartments) for coins and
  notes (Am. bills)
  放纸币和硬币的分格抽屉
7 receipt (sales check)
  收据
8 cash total
  应付金额
9 adding mechanism
  加算器
10 goods
  商品货物
11 glass-roofed well
  玻璃屋顶天井
12 men's wear department
  男装部
13 showcase (display case, indoor
  display window)
  阵列柜
14 wrapping counter
  包装柜柏
15 tray for purchases
  售出物品放置盘

16 customer
  顾客
17 hosiery department
  袜类部
18 shop assistant (Am. salesgirl,
  saleslady)
  店员，女店员
19 price card
  价目表
20 glove stand
  手套架
21 duffle coat, a three-quarter
  length coat
  连风帽的粗呢大衣，中长（¾）大衣
22 escalator
  扶手梯（电梯）
23 fluorescent light
  (fluroescent lamp)
  日光灯
24 office (e.g. customer
  accounts office,
  travel agency,
  manager's office)
  办公室（例如：顾客事务室，旅行社，
  经理办公室）
25 poster (advertisement)
  海报（广告）
26 theatre (Am. theater) and
  concert booking office (advance
  booking office)
  剧院和音乐会订位（售票）处（预先售
  票处）
27 shelves
  商品架

28 ladies' wear department
  女装部
29 ready-made dress (ready-to-wear
  dress, coll. off-the-peg dress)
  女装成衣
30 dust cover
  防尘套
31 clothes rack
  衣架
32 changing booth (fitting booth)
  试衣室
33 shop walker (Am. floorwalker,
  floor manager)
  商场巡视员（楼层巡视员，楼层经理）
34 dummy
  人像模型
35 seat (chair)
  座椅（靠椅）
36 fashion journal (fashion
  magazine)
  时装杂志
37 tailor marking a hemline
  正在量裙下摆（底缘）的裁缝（师）
38 measuring tape (tape measure)
  皮尺，量尺
39 tailor's chalk (French chalk)
  裁缝用粉笔（滑石）
40 hemline marker
  下摆（底缘）划线器
41 loose-fitting coat
  宽松的外套
42 sales counter
  售货（柜）台

43 warm-air curtain
保温帘

44 doorman (commissionaire)
看门人

45 lift (*Am.* elevator)
电梯（升降电梯）

46 lift cage (lift car, *Am* elevator car)
电梯室（升降室）

47 lift operator (*Am.* elevator operator)
电梯操作人

48 controls (lift controls, *Am.* elevator controls)
按钮（电梯按钮）

49 floor indicator
楼层指示器

50 sliding door
滑动门，拉门

51 lift shaft (*Am.* elevator shaft)
电梯升降井

52 bearer cable
吊缆

53 control cable
操纵缆

54 guide rail
导轨

55 customer
顾客

56 hosiery
内衣

57 linen goods (table linen and bed linen)
亚麻制品（桌布，床单）

58 fabric department
纺织品部

59 roll of fabric (roll of material, roll of cloth)
布匹

60 head of department (department manager)
部门经理

61 sales counter
售货（柜）台

62 jewellery (*Am.* jewelry) department
珠宝部

63 assistant (*Am.* salesgirl, saleslady), selling new lines (new products)
卖新产品的（女）店员

64 special counter (extra counter)
特价品柜台

65 placard advertising special offers
特价品广告标语

66 curtain department
窗帘部

67 display on top of the shelves
商品架上的商品陈列

1-40 formal garden (French Baroque garden), palace gardens
正规式公园（法国巴洛克式公园），宫殿式公园

1 grotto (cavern)
洞室（洞窟）

2 stone statue, a river nymph
石像（河中仙女）

3 orangery (orangerie)
栽培橘树的温室

4 boscage (boskage)
密集的灌木

5 maze (labyrinth of paths and hedges)
迷宫（以小径和（树篱）障碍物所构成的迷宫）

6 open-air theatre (*Am.* theater)
露天剧场

7 Baroque palace
巴洛克式宫殿

8 fountains
喷泉

9 cascade (broken artificial waterfall, artificial falls)
人造小瀑布

10 statue, a monument
雕像，纪念碑的一种

11 pedestal (base of statue)
雕像底座

12 globe-shaped tree
球形树

13 conical tree
锥形树

14 ornamental shrub
装饰用灌木

15 wall fountain
壁泉

16 park bench
公园长椅

17 pergola (bower, arbour, *Am.* arbor)
藤架（树荫，凉亭）

18 gravel path (gravel walk)
碎石路

19 pyramid tree (pyramidal tree)
尖型树

20 cupid (cherub, amoretto, amorino)
爱神丘彼特

21 fountain
喷水池

22 fountain
喷泉

23 overflow basin
溢流池

24 basin
水池

25 kerb (curb)
镶边石

26 man out for a walk
散步者

27 tourist guide
导游

28 group of tourists
游客群

29 park by-laws (bye-laws)
游园须知

30 park keeper
公园管理人

31 garden gates, wrought iron gates
公园大门，锻铁门

32 park entrance
公园入口

33 park railings
公园栏杆

34 railing (bar)
栏杆

35 stone vase
石瓶

36 lawn
草坪

37 border, a trimmed (clipped) hedge
道路两旁修整的树篱

38 park path
公园小道

39 parterre
花坛（草坪）

40 birch (birch tree)
白桦（树）

41-72 **landscaped park** (jardin anglais)
风景式公园（英国式公园）
41 flower bed
花床
42 park bench (garden seat)
公园长椅
43 litter bin (*Am.* litter basket)
垃圾箱
44 play area
游玩区
45 stream
小河
46 jetty
码头
47 bridge
小桥
48 park chair
公园靠椅
49 animal enclosure
动物围栏
50 pond
小池
51-54 waterfowl
水禽，水鸟
51 wild duck with young
带小鸭的野鸭
52 goose
鹅
53 flamingo
红鹤
54 swan
天鹅

55 island
小岛
56 water lily
睡莲
57 open-air café
露天咖啡座
58 sunshade
遮阳伞
59 tree
树
60 treetop (crown)
树梢
61 group of trees
树林
62 fountain
喷泉
63 weeping willow
垂柳
64 modern sculpture
现代雕刻
65 hothouse
温室，暖房
66 park gardener
园丁
67 broom
扫帚
68 minigolf course
迷你高尔夫球场
69 minigolf player
打迷你高尔夫球的人
70 minigolf hole
迷你高尔夫球洞

71 mother with pram (baby carriage)
推婴儿车的母亲
72 courting couple (young couple)
情侣

473

1 table tennis
桌球

2 table
球桌

3 table tennis net
桌球网

4 table tennis racket (raquet) (table tennis bat)
桌球球拍

5 table tennis ball
桌球（乒乓球）

6 badminton game (shuttlecock game)
羽毛球

7 shuttlecock
羽毛球

8 maypole swing
五月柱秋千，伞式秋千

9 child's bicycle
儿童自行车

10 football (soccer)
足球

11 goal (goalposts)
球门

12 football
足球

13 goal scorer
射门得分人员

14 goalkeeper
守门员

15 skipping (*Am.* jumping rope)
跳绳

16 skipping rope (*Am.* skip rope, jump rope, jumping rope)
跳绳用绳

17 climbing tower
攀登塔

18 rubber tyre (*Am.* tire) swing
橡胶轮胎秋千

19 lorry tyre (*Am.* truck tire)
卡车轮胎

20 bouncing ball
大皮球

21 adventure playground
探险游戏场

22 log ladder
木梯

23 lookout platform
了望台

24 slide
溜滑梯

25 litter bin (*Am.* litter basket)
垃圾桶（箱）

26 teddy bear
玩具熊

27 wooden train set
木制火车列车

28 paddling pool
浅戏水池

29 sailing boat (yacht, *Am.* sailboat)
帆船

30 toy duck
玩具鸭

31 pram (baby carriage)
婴儿车

32 high bar (bar)
单槓

33 go-cart (soap box)
儿童玩具车

34 starter's flag
发号者旗

35 seesaw
跷跷板

36 robot
机器人

37 flying model aeroplanes (*Am.* airplanes)
　飞行中的模型飞机
38 model aeroplane (*Am.* airplane)
　模型飞机
39 double swing
　双座秋千
40 swing seat
　秋千座位
41 flying kites
　放风筝
42 kite
　风筝
43 tail of the kite
　风筝尾巴
44 kite string
　风筝线
45 revolving drum
　旋转鼓轮
46 spider's web
　蜘蛛网架
47 climbing frame
　攀登架
48 climbing rope
　爬绳用绳
49 rope ladder
　绳梯
50 climbing net
　攀登网
51 skateboard
　滑板
52 up-and-down slide
　起伏滑梯

53 rubber tyre (*Am.* tire) cable car
　橡胶轮胎缆索车
54 rubber tyre (*Am.* tire)
　橡胶轮胎
55 tractor, a pedal car
　牵引机，跳板车的一种
56 den
　搭栏槛
57 presawn boards
　预锯木板
58 seat (bench)
　座位（长椅）
59 Indian hut
　印第安小屋
60 climbing roof
　供攀登的屋顶
61 flagpole (flagstaff)
　旗杆
62 toy lorry (*Am.* toy truck)
　玩具卡车
63 walking doll
　能行走的玩具娃娃
64 sandpit (*Am.* sandbox)
　沙坑
65 toy excavator (toy digger)
　玩具挖土机
66 sandhill
　沙丘

1-21 spa gardens
温泉公园
1-7 salina (salt works)
制盐场
1 thorn house (graduation house)
枝条架（架条制盐装置）
2 thorns (brushwood)
枝条（柴枝）
3 brine channels
盐水槽
4 brine pipe from the pumping station
通泵站的盐水管
5 salt works attendant
制盐场管理人
6-7 inhalational therapy
吸入治疗（疗法）
6 open-air inhalatorium (outdoor inhalatorium)
露天（户外）吸入治疗处
7 patient inhaling (taking an inhalation)
接受吸入疗法的病人
8 hydropathic (pump room) with kursaal (casino)
具娱乐场的水疗院（饮矿泉处）
9 colonnade
柱廊
10 spa promenade
温泉散步场
11 avenue leading to the mineral spring
通往矿泉的道路

12-14 rest cure
休息疗法
12 sunbathing area (lawn)
日光浴区（草坪）
13 deck-chair
躺椅
14 sun canopy
遮阳篷
15 pump room
饮矿泉处
16 rack for glasses
玻璃杯架
17 tap
龙头，栓
18 patient taking the waters
饮矿泉的病人
19 bandstand
音乐台
20 spa orchestra giving a concert
温泉管弦乐队演奏
21 conductor
乐队指挥

1-33 roulette, a game of chance (gambling game)
轮盘赌，一种靠运气的赌博

1 gaming room in a casino (gambling casino)
娱乐场（赌场）中的赌室

2 cash desk
出纳柜，售筹码处

3 tourneur (dealer)
庄家

4 croupier
赌桌收付赌注者

5 rake
集拢赌金（注）的耙子

6 head croupier
赌桌收付赌注领班

7 hall manager
赌场经理

8 roulette table (gaming table, gambling table)
轮盘赌赌桌

9 roulette layout
轮盘赌赌表

10 roulette wheel
轮盘赌转轮

11 bank
庄家的赌本

12 chip (check, plaque)
筹码

13 stake
赌注

14 membership card
会员卡

15 roulette player
轮盘赌赌客

16 private detective (house detective)
私人保镖

17 roulette layout
轮盘赌赌表

18 zero (nought, O)
零

19 passe (high) [numbers 19 to 36]
高〔19 至 36 各数〕

20 pair (even numbers)
双（偶数）

21 noir (black)
黑

22 manque (low) [numbers 1 to 18]
低〔1 至 18 各数〕

23 impair [odd numbers]
单〔奇数〕

24 rouge (red)
红

25 douze premier (first dozen) [numbers 1 to 12]
第一打〔1 至 12 各数〕

26 douze milieu (second dozen) [numbers 13 to 24]
第二打〔13 至 24 各数〕

27 douze dernier (third dozen) [numbers 25 to 36]
第三打〔25 至 36 各数〕

28 roulette wheel (roulette)
轮盘赌转轮

29 roulette bowl
轮盘赌托盘

30 fret (separator)
格子

31 revolving disc (disk) showing numbers 0 to 36
显示 0 至 36 各数的转盘

32 spin
转子

33 roulette ball
轮盘赌球

1-16 chess, a game involving combinations of moves, a positional game
西洋棋，一种靠移动棋子的游戏，一种对阵游戏

1 chessboard (board) with the men (chessmen) in position
棋盘和置于原位的棋子

2 white square (chessboard square)
白方格（白色棋盘方格）

3 black square
黑方格

4 white chessmen (white pieces) [white = W]
白棋（子）

5 black chessmen (black pieces) [black = B]
黑棋（子）

6 letters and numbers for designating chess squares in the notation of chess moves and chess problems
标示记录走棋位置的棋盘格字母和数字

7 individual chessmen (individual pieces)
单一棋子

8 king
王

9 queen
皇后，女王

10 bishop
主教

11 knight
武士，骑士

12 rook (castle)
城堡

13 pawn
卒，兵

14 moves of the individual pieces
单一棋子的移动

15 mate (checkmate), a mate by knight
将军，被骑士将军

16 chess clock, a double clock for chess matches (chess championships)
棋钟，棋赛用的双钟

17-19 draughts (*Am.* checkers)
西洋跳棋

17 draughtboard (*Am.* checkerboard)
西洋跳棋盘

18 white draughtsman (*Am.* checker, checkerman); *also:* piece for backgammon and nine men's morris
白色跳棋子；西洋双六棋和九子棋

19 black draughtsman (*Am.* checker, checkerman)
黑色跳棋子

20 salta
索尔特棋

21 salta piece
索尔特棋棋子

22 backgammon board
西洋双六棋盘

23-25 nine men's morris
九子棋

23 nine men's morris board
九子棋盘

24 mill
连珠

25 double mill
双连珠

26-28 halma
跳棋

26 halma board
跳棋板（盘）

27 yard (camp, corner)
阵地（棋盘四角）

28 halma pieces (halma men) of various colours (*Am.* colors)
不同颜色的棋子

29 dice (dicing)
骰子游戏

30 dice cup
骰子筒

31 dice
骰子

32 spots (pips)
骰子上的点

33 dominoes
骨牌游戏

34 domino (tile)
西洋骨牌

35 double
对子

36 playing cards
纸牌游戏

37 playing card (card)
纸牌、扑克牌

38-45 suits
一组牌

38 clubs
黑梅花

39 spades
黑桃

40 hearts
红心

41 diamonds
红方块

42-45 German suits
德式纸牌

42 acorns
栎子（黑梅花）

43 leaves
叶子（黑桃）

44 hearts
红心

45 bells (hawkbells)
铃（红方块）

1-19 billiards
撞球，弹子
1 billiard ball, an ivory or plastic ball
撞球（弹子），一种象牙或塑胶制的球
2-6 billiard strokes (forms of striking)
弹子打法
2 plain stroke (hitting the cue ball dead centre, *Am.* center)
定杆（打击母球中心）
3 top stroke [promotes extra forward rotation]
推杆〔使球猛烈向前转动〕
4 screw-back [imparts a direct recoil or backward motion]
拉杆〔使球卷回或向后转动〕
5 side (running side, *Am.* English)
侧旋打法
6 check side
返向侧旋打法
7-19 billiard room (*Am.* billiard parlor, billiard saloon, poolroom)
弹子房（撞球场）
7 billiards (English billiards); *sim.:* pool, carom (carrom) billiards
英式撞球；类似：落袋式撞球，母球连撞二球得分式撞球
8 billiard player
撞球者
9 billiard cue (cue)
球杆
10 leather cue tip
球杆皮头
11 white cue ball
白色母球

12 red object ball
红色目标球
13 white spot ball (white dot ball)
有黑点标记的白球
14 billiard table
球桌，撞球桌
15 table bed with green cloth (billiard cloth, green baize covering)
铺绿柏布的柏面
16 cushions (rubber cushions, cushioned ledge)
球桌四边的橡皮衬垫
17 billiard clock, a timer
记时钟
18 billiard marker
记分牌（板）
19 cue rack
球杆架

1-59 camp site (camping site, *Am.* campground)
营地
1 reception (office)
接待处（办公室）
2 camp site attendant
营地工作人员
3 folding trailer (collapsible caravan, collapsible trailer)
可折叠拖车（可摺叠篷车、拖车）
4 hammock
吊床
5-6 washing and toilet facilities
洗涤和卫生设备
5 toilets and washrooms (*Am.* lavatories)
盥洗室
6 washbasins and sinks
洗脸盆和洗涤槽
7 bungalow (chalet)
平房（斜顶木屋）
8-11 scout camp
童军营地
8 bell tent
钟形帐篷
9 pennon
三角旗
10 camp fire
营火
11 boy scout (scout)
童子军
12 sailing boat (yacht, *Am.* sailboat)
帆船（轻型快艇）
13 landing stage (jetty)
浮码头（栈桥）

14 inflatable boat (inflatable dinghy)
充气船（充气橡皮艇）
15 outbroad motor (outboard)
船尾马达
16 trimaran
三船体并列的船
17 thwart (oarsman's bench)
小艇座板（划手座板）
18 rowlock (oarlock)
桨架
19 oar
桨
20 boat trailer (boat carriage)
运船拖车
21 ridge tent
屋脊形帐篷
22 flysheet
帐篷顶
23 guy line (guy)
支索，牵索
24 tent peg (peg)
帐篷桩（钉）
25 mallet
木槌
26 groundsheet ring
地面防潮布扣环
27 bell end
帐篷一边的钟状部分（堆放行李）
28 erected awning
直立遮篷
29 storm lantern, a paraffin lamp
风灯，一种蜡（煤）油灯
30 sleeping bag
睡袋
31 air mattress (inflatable air-bed)
充气垫（床）

32 water carrier (drinking water carrier)
饮用水容器
33 double-burner gas cooker for propane gas or butane gas
双火炉头（丙烷或丁烷）瓦斯炉
34 propane or butane gas bottle
丙烷或丁烷瓦斯罐
35 pressure cooker
压力锅，快锅
36 frame tent
框架帐篷
37 awning
遮篷
38 tent pole
帐篷杆（支柱）
39 wheelarch doorway
圆拱出入口
40 mesh ventilator
网状通气口
41 transparent window
透明玻璃
42 pitch number
帐篷号码
43 folding camp chair
折叠椅
44 folding camp table
折叠桌
45 camping tableware
露营用桌上餐具
46 camper
露营者
47 charcoal grill (barbecue)
炭火烤架
48 charcoal
炭，木炭

49 bellows
送风器
50 roof rack
车顶行李架
51 roof lashing
车顶捆绳
52 caravan (*Am.* trailer)
拖车
53 box for gas bottle
装瓦斯罐的箱子
54 jockey wheel
导轮
55 drawbar coupling
拉杆连结器
56 roof ventilator
车顶通风口
57 caravan awning
拖车遮篷
58 inflatable igloo tent
充气圆顶帐篷
59 camp bed (*Am.* camp cot)
行军床

1-6 surf riding (surfing)
冲浪运动
1 plan view of surfboard
冲浪板平面图
2 section of surfboard
冲浪板剖面图
3 skeg (stabilizing fin)
龙骨之后部（稳定鳍）
4 big wave riding
大浪冲浪运动
5 surfboarder (surfer)
冲浪者
6 breaker
碎浪
7-27 skin diving (underwater swimming)
潜水（水下游泳）
7 skin diver (underwater swimmer)
潜水人
8-22 underwater swimming set
潜水游泳器具
8 knife
小刀
9 neoprene wetsuit
合成橡胶制潜水衣
10 diving mask (face mask, mask), a pressure-equalizing mask
潜水面具（罩），一种均压面罩
11 snorkel (schnorkel)
（换气用）通气管
12 harness of diving apparatus
潜水器具背带
13 compressed-air pressure gauge (*Am.* gage)
压缩空气压力计

14 weight belt
负重腰带
15 depth gauge (*Am.* gage)
深度计
16 waterproof watch for checking duration of dive
潜水计时防水表
17 decometer for measuring stages of ascent
上升时测定用卡计
18 fin (flipper)
蛙鞋
19 diving apparatus (*also:* aqualung, scuba), with two cylinders (bottles)
具两个氧气筒的潜水器具（亦称：水肺）
20 two-tube demand regulator
双筒定（需用）量调节器
21 compressed-air cylinder (compressed-air bottle)
压缩空气筒（压缩空气瓶）
22 on/off valve
开关阀
23 underwater photography
水下摄影
24 underwater camera
水下相机
25 underwater flashlight
水下闪光灯
26 exhaust bubbles
呼出的气泡
27 inflatable boat (inflatable dinghy)
充气船（橡皮艇）

1 lifesaver (lifeguard)
救生员

2 lifeline
救生绳

3 lifebelt (lifebuoy)
救生圈

4 storm signal
暴风信号

5 time ball
报时球

6 warning sign
警告牌

7 tide table, a notice board showing times of low tide and high tide
潮汐表, 公布高低潮时间的布告板

8 board showing water and air temperature
气温和水温布告板

9 bathing platform
海水浴场跳板

10 pennon staff
三角旗杆

11 pennon
三角旗

12 paddle boat (peddle boat)
明轮船（水上自行车）

13 surf riding (surfing) behind motorboat
汽艇拖拉的冲浪运动

14 surfboarder (surfer)
冲浪者

15 surfboard
冲浪板

16 water ski
滑水

17 inflatable beach mattress
海滩充气垫

18 beach ball
海滩游戏用皮球

19-23 beachwear
海滩装

19 beach suit
海滩套装

20 beach hat
海滩帽

21 beach jacket
海滩夹克

22 beach trousers
海滩裤

23 beach shoe (bathing shoe)
海滩鞋

24 beach bag
海滩袋

25 bathing gown (bathing wrap)
海滩袍

26 bikini (ladies' two-piece bathing suit)
比基尼泳装（女士二件式泳装）

27 bikini bottom
比基尼装下部

28 bikini top
比基尼装上部

29 bathing cap (swimming cap)
泳帽

30 bather
游泳者

31 deck tennis (quoits)
掷套环游戏

32 rubber ring (quoit)
套环

33 inflatable rubber animal
充气的浮水（橡皮）动物

34 beach attendant
浴场服务人员

35 sandcastle
沙堡

36 roofed wicker beach chair
有顶篷的沙滩椅

37 underwater swimmmer
潜水泳者

38 diving goggles
潜水镜

39 snorkel (schnorkel)
通气管

40 hand harpoon (fish spear, fish lance)
鱼叉（鱼矛）

41 fin (flipper) for diving (for underwater swimming)
潜泳者用的蛙鞋

42 bathing suit (swimsuit)
泳装（泳衣）

43 bathing trunks (swimming trunks)
泳裤

44 bathing cap (swimming cap)
泳帽

45 beach tent, a ridge tent
沙滩帐篷, 脊形帐篷

46 lifeguard station
救生站

1-9 swimming pool with
artificial waves, an indoor pool
人工波浪游泳池，室内游泳池的一种
1 artificial waves
人工波浪
2 beach area
岸区
3 edge of the pool
泳池边
4 swimming pool attendant (pool
attendant, swimming bath
attendant)
泳池服务人员
5 sun bed
日光浴床位
6 lifebelt
救生圈
7 water wings
翼形浮袋
8 bathing cap
泳帽
9 channel to outdoor mineral bath
通向户外矿泉浴池的水道
10 solarium
日光浴室
11 sunbathing area
日光浴场
12 sun bather
日光浴者
13 sun ray lamp
太阳光线灯
14 bathing towel
浴巾
15 nudist sunbathing area
天体日光浴区
16 nudist (naturist)
天体浴者
17 screen (fence)
围墙
18 sauna (mixed sauna)
蒸汽浴（混浴蒸汽浴室）〔三温暖〕
浴室）
19 wood panelling (*Am.* paneling)
木嵌板
20 tiered benches
台阶式长凳
21 sauna stove
蒸汽浴炉
22 stones
石块
23 hygrometer
湿度计
24 thermometer
温度计
25 towel
毛巾
26 water tub for moistening the
stone in the stove
沾湿炉中石块用的水桶
27 birch rods (birches) for beating
the skin
拍打皮肤用的桦枝条
28 cooling room for cooling off
(cooling down) after the sauna
蒸汽浴后降温用的降温浴室
29 lukewarm shower
微温淋浴设备
30 cold bath
冷水浴池
31 hot whirlpool (underwater
massage bath)
热水涡流浴室（水中按摩浴室）
32 step into the bath
入浴池的台阶
33 massage bath
按摩浴池

34 jet blower
喷射鼓风机
35 hot whirlpool [diagram]
热水涡流浴池〔简图〕
36 section of the bath
浴池剖面图
37 step
台阶
38 circular seat
环形座位
39 water extractor
抽水机（装置）
40 water jet pipe
喷水管
41 air jet pipe
喷气管

1-32 swimming pool, an open-air swimming pool
游泳池，露天游泳池

1 changing cubicle
小更衣室

2 shower (shower bath)
淋浴

3 changing room
更衣室

4 sunbathing area
日光浴场

5-10 diving boards (diving apparatus)
跳板（跳水设备）

5 diver (highboard diver)
跳水者

6 diving platform
跳台

7 ten-metre (*Am.* ten-meter) platform
十公尺高跳台

8 five-metre (*Am.* five-meter) platform
五公尺高跳台

9 three-metre (*Am.* three-meter) springboard (diving board)
三公尺高跳台，弹性跳板

10 one-metre (*Am.* one-meter) springboard
一公尺高跳台，弹性跳板

11 diving pool
跳水池

12 straight header
（直体）头先入水的跳水动作

13 feet-first jump
脚先入水的跳水动作

14 tuck jump (haunch jump)
抱膝跳水

15 swimming pool attendant (pool attendant, swimming bath attendant)
游泳池服务人员

16-20 swimming instruction
游泳指导

16 swimming instructor (swimming teacher)
游泳教练

17 learner-swimmer
学习游泳者

18 float; *sim.:* water wings
浮袋；类似翼形浮袋

19 swimming belt (cork jacket)
救生带（软木救生衣）

20 land drill
陆上游泳练习

21 non-swimmers' pool
浅水池

22 footbath
洗脚池

23 swimmers' pool
深水泳池

24-32 freestyle relay race
自由式接力赛

24 timekeeper (lane timekeeper)
计时员

25 placing judge
终点裁判员

26 turning judge
转身裁判员

27 starting block (starting place)
出发台（点）

28 competitor touching the finishing line
比赛人员触池壁

29 starting dive (racing dive)
出发跳水

30 starter
发令员

31 swimming lane
泳道

32 rope with cork floats
有软木浮栓的绳索

33-39 swimming strokes
游泳姿式

33 breaststroke
蛙式

34 butterfly stroke
蝶式

35 dolphin butterfly stroke
海豚泳

36 side stroke
侧泳

37 crawl stroke (crawl); *sim.:* trudgen stroke (trudgen, double overarm stroke)
自由式；类似：爬泳

38 underwater swimming
潜泳

39 treading water
踩水

40-45 diving (acrobatic diving, fancy diving, competitive diving, highboard diving)
跳水（特技跳水，花式跳水，竞技跳水，高台跳水）

40 standing take-off pike dive
立定起跳梳式跳水

41 one-half twist isander (reverse dive)
半转体旋式跳水

42 backward somersault (double backward somersault)
（两次）后空翻跳水

43 running take-off twist dive
跑步起跳转体跳水

44 screw dive
螺旋式跳水

45 armstand dive (handstand dive)
倒立跳水

46-50 water polo
水球

46 goal
球门

47 goalkeeper
守门员

48 water polo ball
水球

49 back
后卫

50 forward
前锋

1-18 taking up positions for the regatta
就赛舟位置

1 punt, a pleasure boat
平底船，一种游船

2 motorboat
汽艇（快艇）

3 Canadian canoe
加拿大式独木舟

4 kayak (Alaskan canoe, slalom canoe), a canoe
皮船（阿拉斯加式皮船，回旋划艇），一种独木舟

5 tandem kayak
双座（前后两座）皮船

6 outboard motorboat (outboard speedboat, outboard)
汽艇（快速汽艇）

7 outboard motor (outboard)
船外（尾）马达

8 cockpit
座舱

9-16 racing boats (sportsboats)
赛船

9-15 shells (rowing boats, *Am.* rowboats)
轻型划（赛）船（划艇）

9 coxless four, a carvel-built boat
无舵手四人划艇，一种平贴船板的船

10 eight (eight-oared racing shell)
八人赛船

11 cox
舵手

12 stroke, an oarsman
桨手

13 bow ([number one])
船首桨手

14 oar
桨

15 coxless pair
无舵手双人赛船

16 single sculler (single skuller, racing sculler, racing skuller, skiff)
单人赛船

17 scull (skull)
桨

18 coxed single, a clinker-built single
有舵手的小船，船壳板重叠的小船

19 jetty (landing stage, mooring)
码头（浮架码头，停泊处）

20 rowing coach
划船教练

21 megaphone
扩音器

22 quayside steps
码头边台阶

23 clubhouse (club)
会员俱乐部

24 boathouse
船库

25 club's flag
俱乐部旗

26-33 four-oared gig, a touring boat
四桨小船，一种游艇

26 oar
桨

27 cox's seat
舵手位置

28 thwart (seat)
座板

29 rowlock (oarlock)
桨架

30 gunwale (gunnel)
舷的上缘

31 rising
船侧纵板

32 keel
龙骨

33 skin (shell, outer skin) [clinker-built]
船的外壳〔重叠搭造的〕

34 single-bladed paddle (paddle)
单叶桨

35-38 oar (scull, skull)
桨

35 grip
桨柄

36 leather sheath
皮护套

37 shaft (neck)
桨颈

38 blade
桨叶

39 double-bladed paddle (double-ended paddle)
双叶桨

40 drip ring
挡水环
41-50 sliding seat
滑动座位
41 rowlock (oarlock)
桨架
42 outrigger
舷外支架
43 saxboard
防波（浪）板
44 sliding seat
滑动座位
45 runner
滑座轨道
46 strut
斜撑支架
47 stretcher
脚蹬
48 skin (shell, outer skin)
船壳
49 frame (rib)
肋材
50 kelson (keelson)
内龙骨
51-53 rudder (steering rudder)
舵
51 yoke
横舵柄
52 lines (steering lines)
绳（操舵绳）
53 blade (rudder blade, rudder)
舵（舵叶）

54-66 folding boats (foldboats, canoes)
摺叠式船（独木舟）
54 one-man kayak
单人皮船
55 canoeist
划独木舟的人
56 spraydeck
防水舱面
57 deck
舱面
58 rubber-covered canvas hull
包橡皮的帆布船壳
59 cockpit coaming (coaming)
座舱栏板
60 channel for rafts alongside weir
筏横靠堰的水道
61 two-seater folding kayak, a touring kayak
双座摺叠式皮船，一种游艇
62 sail of folding kayak
摺叠式皮船的帆
63 leeboard
下风板
64 bag for the rods
杆袋
65 rucksack
背包
66 boat trailer (boat carriage)
运船拖车
67 frame of folding kayak
摺叠式皮船框架
68-70 kayaks
各式皮船

68 Eskimo kayak
爱斯基摩皮船
69 wild-water racing kayak
急流赛艇
70 touring kayak
游玩用皮船

1-9 windsurfing
风力冲浪
1 windsurfer
风力冲浪者
2 sail
帆
3 transparent window (window)
透明窗
4 mast
桅
5 surfboard
冲浪板
6 universal joint (movable
bearing) for adjusting the angle
of the mast and for steering
调整桅杆角度和操纵方向的万向接头
7 boom
帆桁
8 retractable centreboard (Am.
centerboard)
伸缩垂板龙骨
9 rudder
舵
**10-48 yacht (sailing boat, Am.
sailboat)**
帆船
10 foredeck
前甲板
11 mast
桅杆
12 trapeze
吊架
13 crosstress (spreader)
桅顶横桁
14 hound
桅肩
15 forestay
前桅支索
16 jib (Genoa jib)
三角帆（热内瓦三角帆）
17 jib downhaul
三角帆降帆索
18 side stay (shroud)
桅杆横支索
19 lanyard (bottlescrew)
小索（短索）
20 foot of the mast
桅杆脚
21 kicking strap (vang)
斜桁支索
22 jam cleat
防松系缆栓
23 foresheet (jib sheet)
前桅帆脚索（三角帆脚索）
24 centreboard (Am. centerboard)
case
垂板龙骨框架
25 bitt
系桩
26 centreboard (Am. centerboard)
垂板龙骨
27 traveller (Am. traveler)
活动铁环
28 mainsheet
主帆脚索
29 fairlead
导索器
30 toestraps (hiking straps)
脚趾带
31 tiller extension (hiking stick)
舵柄分杆
32 tiller
舵柄
33 rudderhead (rudder stock)
舵头

34 rudder blade (rudder)
舵面
35 transom
舵板
36 drain plug
排水塞（栓）
37 gooseneck
鹅颈圈
38 window
窗
39 boom
帆桁
40 foot
帆下缘
41 clew
帆下角铁圈（帆耳）
42 luff (leading edge)
纵帆前缘
43 leech pocket (batten cleat,
batten pocket)
帆后缘袋（条板袋）
44 batten
条板
45 leech (trailing edge)
帆后缘
46 mainsail
主帆
47 headboard
顶板
48 racing flag (burgee)
竞赛旗（燕尾旗，三角旗）
49-65 yacht classes
帆船级别
49 Flying Dutchman
飞行荷兰人级，FD 级
50 O-Joller
O 级小艇
51 Finn dinghy (Finn)
芬兰级
52 pirate
海盗级
53 12.00 m² sharpie
12.00 m² 帆船
54 tempest
暴风雨级
55 star
星级
56 soling
索林级
57 dragon
龙级
58 5.5-metre (Am. 5.5-meter) class
5.5 公尺级
59 6-metre (Am. 6-meter) R-class
6 公尺 R 级
60 30.00 m² cruising yacht
(coastal cruiser)
30.00 m² 巡航快艇
61 30.00 m² dinghy cruiser
30.00 m² 巡航小艇
62 25.00 m² one-design keelboat
25.00 m² 统一龙骨船
63 KR-class
KR 级
64 catamaran
双体船
65 twin hull
双体船壳，双体船身

1-13 points of sailing and wind directions
航行方位和风向

1 sailing downwind
顺风航行

2 mainsail
主帆

3 jib
三角帆

4 ballooning sails
满帆

5 centre (*Am.* center) line
中心线

6 wind direction
风向

7 yacht tacking
帆船迎风转向

8 sail, shivering
飘动的帆

9 luffing
转向逆风行驶

10 sailing close-hauled
逆风行驶

11 sailing with wind abeam
侧风行驶

12 sailing with free wind
顺风行驶

13 quartering wind (quarter wind)
船尾风

14-24 regatta course
帆船赛程

14 starting and finishing buoy
起点和终点浮标

15 committee boat
（赛船）委员会船

16 triangular course (regatta course)
三角航线（赛船航程）

17 buoy (mark) to be rounded
船回转浮标（标识）

18 buoy to be passed
通过浮标（标识）

19 first leg
第一段赛程

20 second leg
第二段赛程

21 third leg
第三段赛程

22 windward leg
迎风（逆风）赛程

23 downwind leg
顺风赛程

24 reachng leg
侧风赛程

25-28 tacking
迎风（逆风）转向航行

25 tack
迎风（逆风）转向

26 gybing (jibing)
移帆改向

27 going about
迎风（逆风）转向

28 loss of distance during the gybe (jibe)
移帆改向距离的损失

29-41 types of yacht hull
帆船船身类型

29-34 cruiser keelboat
巡航用龙骨船

29 stern
船尾

30 spoon bow
匙形船首

31 waterline
吃水线

32 keel (ballast keel)
龙骨（压舱龙骨）

33 ballast
压舱物

34 rudder
舵

35 racing keelboat
比赛龙骨船

36 lead keel
铅质龙骨

37-41 keel-centreboard (*Am.* centerboard) yawl
垂板龙骨小帆船

37 retractable rudder
可伸缩的舵

38 cockpit
座舱

39 cabin superstructure (cabin)
舱的上部（建筑）结构

40 straight stem
直船首

41 retractable centreboard (*Am.* centerboard)
可伸缩的垂板龙骨

42-49 types of yacht stern
帆船尾的类型

42 yacht stern
帆船船尾

43 square stern
方形艉

44 canoe stern
独木舟形艉

45 cruiser stern
游艇船尾

46 name plate
船名牌

47 deadwood
船尾鳍

48 transom stern
肋板船尾

49 transom
艉梁

50-57 timber planking
船身（体）外板

50-52 clinker planking (clench planking)
重叠的船身外板

50 outside strake
外列板

51 frame (rib)
船肋骨

52 clenched nail (riveted nail)
钉牢的钉（铆死的钉）

53 carvel planking
平接船身外板

54 close-seamed construction
密缝结构

55 stringer
纵材，承梁纵材

56 diagonal carvel planking
斜行平接船身外板

57 inner planking
内层板

1-5 motorboats (powerboats, sportsboats)
汽艇（动力艇，赛艇）

1 inflatable sportsboats with outboard motor (outboard inflatable)
装有船尾（外）马达的充气赛艇

2 z-drive motorboat (outdrive motorboat)
Z 型驱动汽艇

3 cabin cruiser
舱式游艇

4 motor cruiser
马达游艇

5 30-metre (*Am.* 30-meter) ocean-going cruiser
30 公尺远洋游艇

6 association flag
协会会旗

7 name of craft (*or:* registration number)
船名（或：船舶登记号码）

8 club membership and port of registry (*Am.* home port)
（俱乐部）协会会籍和船籍港标识

9 association flag on the starboard crosstrees
挂於右舷桅顶横杆的协会会旗

10-14 navigation lights of sportsboats in coastal and inshore waters
赛艇在沿海和近海水域的航行灯

10 white top light
白色顶灯

11 green starboard sidelight
绿色右舷灯

12 red port sidelight
红色左舷灯

13 green and red bow light (combined lantern)
绿色和红色船首灯（红绿二色信号灯）

14 white stern light
白色船尾灯

15-18 anchors
锚

15 stocked anchor (Admiralty anchor), a bower anchor
有杆锚（海军锚），一种锚锚

16-18 lightweight anchor
轻量（载）锚

16 CQR anchor (plough, *Am.* plow, anchor)
CQR 锚（犁形锚）

17 stockless anchor (patent anchor)
无杆锚

18 Danforth anchor
丹佛斯式锚

19 life raft
救生筏

20 life jacket
救生衣（夹克）

21-44 powerboat racing
动力艇比赛

21 catamaran with outboard motor
装有船尾（外）马达的双体船

22 hydroplane
水上快艇

23 racing outboard motor
竞赛用船尾（外）马达

24 tiller
舵柄

25 fuel pipe
燃料管

26 transom
舵梁

27 buoyancy tube
浮筒

28 start and finish
出发点和终点

29 start
出发

30 starting and finishing line
起点和终点线

31 buoy to be rounded
供赛艇绕过的浮标

32-37 displacement boats
排水型船

32-34 round-bilge boat
圆底船

32 view of hull bottom
船身（体）底部图

33 section of fore ship
船首剖面图

34 section of aft ship
船尾剖面图

35-37 V-bottom boat (vee-bottom boat)
V 型底船

35 view of hull bottom
船身（体）底部图

36 section of fore ship
船首剖面图

37 section of aft ship
船尾剖面图

38-44 planing boats (surface skimmers, skimmers)
滑航（行）船，（水面滑行快艇）

38-41 stepped hydroplane (stepped skimmer)
加速水面滑行快艇

38 side view
侧面图

39 view of hull bottom
船身底面图

40 section of fore ship
船首剖面图

41 section of aft ship
船尾剖面图

42 three-point hydroplane
三点水上快艇

43 fin
鳍板

44 float
浮筒

45-62 water skiing
滑水

45 water skier
滑水者

46 deep-water start
深水起滑

47 tow line (towing line)
拖缆

48 handle
手把

49-55 water-ski signalling (code of hand signals from skier to boat driver)
滑水信号（滑水者与汽艇驾驶间的手势信号）

49 signal for [faster]
"加速"信号

50 signal for [slower] ([slow down])
"减速"信号

51 signal for [speed OK]
"速度 OK"信号

52 signal for [turn]
"转弯"信号

53 signal for [stop]
"停止"信号

54 signal for [cut motor]
"熄火"信号

55 signal for [return to jetty] ([back to dock])
"返回码头"信号

56-62 types of water ski
滑水板类型

56 trick ski (figure ski), a monoski
特技滑水板，一种单型滑板

57-58 rubber binding
橡皮固定装置

57 front foot binding
前足固定装置

58 heel flap
后脚绞链板

59 strap support for second foot
后足套戴支座

60 slalom ski
弯道滑水

61 skeg (fixed fin, fin)
导流尾鳍（固定鳍板）

62 jump ski
跳跃滑水板

63 hovercraft (air-cushion vehicle)
气垫船

64 propeller
推进器

65 rudder
舵

66 skirt enclosing air cushion
边缘封闭的气垫

1 aeroplane (*Am.* airplane) tow launch (aerotowing)
  飞机曳航
2 tug (towing plane)
  拖机曳航飞机
3 towed glider (towed sailplane)
  拖曳滑翔机
4 tow rope
  拖曳索
5 winched launch
  绞车牵引起飞
6 motor winch
  机动绞车
7 cable parachute
  引索伞
8 motorized glider (powered glider)
  动力滑翔机
9 high-performance glider (high-performance sailplane)
  高性能滑翔机
10 T-tail (T-tail unit)
  T 型尾翼
11 wind sock (wind cone)
  风向袋
12 control tower (tower)
  管制塔台
13 glider field
  滑翔机场
14 hangar
  机库，棚厂
15 runway for aeroplanes (*Am.* airplanes)
  飞机跑道
16 wave soaring
  波状滑翔
17 lee waves (waves, wave system)
  背风波（波，波系）
18 rotor
  旋转
19 lenticular clouds (lenticulars)
  透镜状云，凸状云
20 thermal soaring
  上升暖气流滑翔
21 thermal
  上升暖气流
22 cumulus cloud (heap cloud, cumulus, woolpack cloud)
  积云（卷毛云）
23 storm-front soaring
  风暴锋面滑翔
24 storm front
  风暴锋面
25 frontal upcurrent
  锋面上升气流
26 cumulonimbus cloud (cumulonimbus)
  积雨云
27 slope soaring
  倾斜滑翔
28 hill upcurrent (orographic lift)
  小丘上升气流（地形上升）
29 multispar wing
  复梁翼
30 main spar, a box spar
  主梁，箱形梁
31 connector fitting
  连接件
32 anchor rib
  锚状肋
33 diagonal spar
  对角斜梁
34 leading edge
  机翼前缘
35 main rib
  主肋

36 nose rib (false rib)
  前缘肋（假肋）
37 trailing edge
  机翼后缘
38 brake flap (spoiler)
  扰流板（阻流板）
39 torsional clamp
  扭曲压板
40 covering (skin)
  蒙皮
41 aileron
  副翼
42 wing tip
  翼梢
43 hang gliding
  滑翔翼运动
44 hang glider
  滑翔翼
45 hang glider pilot
  滑翔翼驾驶者
46 control frame
  操纵架

1-9 aerobatics, aerobatic manoeuvres (*Am* maneuvers)
特技飞行
1 loop
觔斗
2 horizontal eight
水平（横）"8"字
3 rolling circle
侧滚圆周
4 stall turn (hammer head)
失速转弯（锤头式失速）
5 tail slide (whip stall)
尾滑（急坠失速）
6 vertical flick spin
直垂上升旋冲
7 spin
旋冲
8 horizontal slow roll
水平慢滚
9 inverted flight (negative flight)
倒飞
10 **cockpit**
驾驶舱，座舱
11 instrument panel
仪表板
12 compass
罗盘
13 radio and navigation equipment
无线电导航设备
14 control column (control stick)
操纵杆，驾驶杆
15 throttle lever (throttle control)
油门杆（油门控制）
16 mixture control
混合比操纵
17 radio equipment
无线电装置
18 **two-seater plane for racing and aerobatics**
比赛和特技飞行的双座飞机
19 cabin
机舱，座舱
20 antenna
天线
21 vertical stabilizer (vertical fin, tail fin)
垂直安定面（直尾翅，尾翅）
22 rudder
方向舵
23 tailplane (horizontal stabilizer)
尾面（水平安定面）
24 elevator
升降舵
25 trim tab (trimming tab)
配平片，调整片
26 fuselage (body)
机身
27 wing
机翼
28 aileron
副翼
29 landing flap
降落襟翼
30 trim tab (trimming tab)
配平片，调整片
31 navigation light (position light) [red]
航行灯（方位灯）〔红〕
32 landing light
降落灯
33 main undercarriage unit (main landing gear unit)
主起落架（主起落传动装置）
34 nose wheel
前轮，鼻轮

35 engine
引擎，发动机
36 propeller (airscrew)
螺旋桨
37-62 **parachuting**
跳伞
37 parachute
降落伞
38 canopy
伞身，伞衣
39 pilot chute
导伞
40 suspension lines
吊索（绳）
41 steering line
操纵线
42 riser
吊带
43 harness
背带，伞带
44 pack
降落伞包
45 system of slots of the sports parachute
运动降落伞的伞衣缝片方式
46 turn slots
转向翼缝
47 apex
伞顶
48 skirt
伞缘
49 stabilizing panel
安定面
50-51 **style jump**
跳伞姿势
50 back loop
后觔斗后翻
51 spiral
盘旋
52-54 **ground signals**
地面信号
52 signal for [permission to jump] ([conditions are safe]) (target cross)
"允许跳伞"信号，（安全信号）（十字标）
53 signal for [parachuting suspended-repeat flight]
"暂停跳伞，重飞"信号
54 signal for [parachuting suspended-aircraft must land]
"暂停跳伞，飞机降落"信号
55 accuracy jump
定点跳伞
56 target cross
十字标
57 inner circle [radius 25 m]
内圈〔半径 25 公尺〕
58 middle circle [radius 50 m]
中圈〔半径 50 公尺〕
59 outer circle [radius 100 m]
外圈〔半径 100 公尺〕
60-62 **free-fall positions**
自由降落姿势
60 full spread position
四肢伸展姿势
61 frog position
蛙式姿势
62 T position
T 型姿势
63-84 **ballooning**
驾驶气球
63 gas balloon
气球
64 gondola (ballon basket)
吊篮

65 ballast (sandbags)
压载物，配重（沙袋）
66 mooring line
系留索（绳）
67 hoop
篮圈
68 flight instruments (instruments)
飞行装置
69 trail rope
拖绳
70 mouth (neck)
气咀
71 neck line
气咀绳
72 emergency rip panel
紧急裂幅
73 emergency ripping line
紧急裂幅绳
74 network (net)
网
75 rip panel
裂幅
76 ripping line
裂幅绳
77 valve
气阀，气门
78 valve line
气门绳
79 hot-air balloon
热空气气球
80 burner platform
燃烧器台
81 mouth
气球咀
82 vent
排气口
83 rip panel
裂幅
84 balloon take-off
气球起飞
85-91 **flying model aeroplanes** (*Am.* airplanes)
模型飞机
85 radio-controlled model flight
无线电控制模型机飞行
86 remote-controlled free flight model
飞行模型机
87 remote control radio
遥控无线电
88 antenna (transmitting antenna)
天线（发射天线）
89 control line model
线操纵模型机
90 mono-line control system
单线操纵系统
91 flying kennel, a K9-class model
K9 级模型机棚

1-7 dressage
驯马

1 arena (dressage arena)
驯马场

2 rail
围栏

3 school horse
所驯的马

4 dark coat (black coat)
黑色外衣

5 white breeches
白色马裤

6 top hat
大礼帽

7 gait (*also:* shcool figure)
步法（亦称：驯马步法）

8-14 show jumping
障碍跳越竞技

8 obstacle (fence), an almost-fixed obstacle; *sim.:* gate, gate and rails, palisade, oxer, mound, wall
障碍物（栏栅），一种近於固定的障碍物；类似：栅门，栏，木栅，牛栏，土堤，墙

9 jumper
跳越障碍的马

10 jumping saddle
跳越障碍用的马鞍

11 girth
鞍带

12 snaffle
轻勒（小型马衔）

13 red coat (hunting pink, pink; *also:* dark coat)
红外衣（粉红猎装；深色外衣）

14 hunting cap (riding cap)
猎帽（骑手帽）

15 bandage
护腿

16-19 three-day event
三日竞技（赛）

16 endurance competition
耐力比赛（竞赛）

17 cross-country
越野赛跑道

18 helmet (*also:* hard hat, hard hunting cap)
护盔（护帽，打猎护帽）

19 course markings
赛马跑道标志

20-22 steeplechase
越野障碍赛

20 water jump, a fixed obstacle
水濠障碍，一种固定障碍物

21 jump
障碍跳越

22 riding switch
马鞭

23-40 harness racing (harness horse racing)
轻型马车（赛）

23 harness racing track (track)
轻型马车赛跑道

24 sulky
单座双轮马车

25 spoke wheel (spoked wheel) with plastic wheel disc (disk)
带塑料轮盘的有辐轮子

26 driver in trotting silks
穿竞技用骑士服的骑士

27 rein
缰绳

28 trotter
快步马

29 pieblad horse
黑的斑纹的马，杂色的马

30 shadow roll
遮眼环，遮眼革

31 elbow boot
护肘

32 rubber boot
橡皮护腿

33 number
号码

34 glass-covered grandstand with totalizator windows (tote windows) inside
内有赛马赌金计算器的玻璃遮蔽看台

35 totalizator (tote)
赛马赌金计算器

36 number
号码

37 odds (price, starting price, price offered)
差额（定价，开价，出价）

38 winners' table
赢家一览表，获胜者名单

39 winner's price
赢家金额

40 time indicator
报时器

41-49 hunt, a drag hunt; *sim.:* fox hunt, paper chase (paper hunt, hare-and-hounds)
狩猎，一种臭踪狩猎；类似猎狐，撒纸追纵游戏

41 field
参加比赛者

42 hunting pink
粉红猎装

43 whipper-in (whip)
猎犬管理人

44 hunting horn
狩猎号

45 Master (Master of foxhounds, MFH)
狩猎筹划者（指辉者）

46 pack of hounds (pack)
猎犬群

47 staghound
猎犬

48 drag
模拟臭迹

49 scented trail (artificial scent)
臭迹（人工臭迹）

50 horse racing (racing)
赛马，跑马

51 field (racehorses)
参加比赛的马

52 favourite (*Am.* favorite)
最被看好的马

53 outsider
无胜算的马

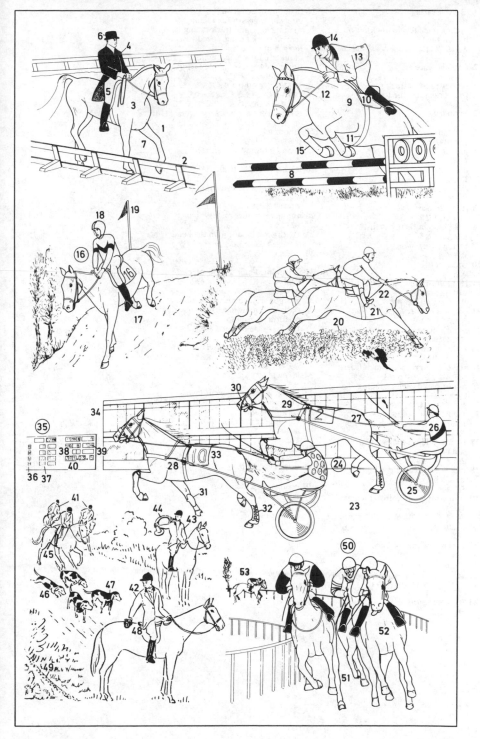

1-23 cycle racing
自行车竞赛

1 cycling track (cycle track); *here:* indoor track
赛车场；（跑道）此指室内车场（跑道）

2-7 six-day race
六日赛

2 six-day racer, a track racer (track rider) on the track
六日赛选手，跑道上的自行车选手

3 crash hat
防护帽

4 stewards
竞赛管理人员；干事

5 judge
裁判

6 lap scorer
计圈员

7 rider's box (racer's box)
选手席

8-10 road race
公路自行车竞赛

8 road racer, a racing cyclist
公路自行车选手，自行车竞赛人员

9 racing jersey
竞赛运动衫

10 water bottle
水壶

11-15 motor-paced racing (long-distance racing)
摩托车领先赛（长距离赛）

11 pacer, a motorcyclist
领先者，摩托车手

12 pacer's motorcycle
领先者骑的摩托车

13 roller, a safety device
滚筒，一种安全装置

14 stayer (motor-paced track rider)
长距离赛选手（摩托车领先赛场选手）

15 motor-paced cycle, a racing cycle
摩托车领先赛车，一种赛车

16 racing cycle (racing bicycle) for road racing (road race bicycle)
公路赛赛自行车

17 racing saddle, an unsprung saddle
赛车车垫，无弹簧车垫

18 racing handlebars (racing handlebar)
自行车把手（赛车）

19 tubular tyre (*Am.* tire) (racing tyre)
管状车胎（比赛用车胎）

20 chain
链条

21 toe clip (racing toe clip)
踏脚套

22 strap
皮带

23 spare tubula tyre (*Am.* tire)
备用管状车胎

24-38 motorsports
摩托车运动

24-28 motorcycle racing; *disciplines:* grasstrack racing, road racing, sand track racing, cement track racing, speedway [on ash or shale tracks], mountain racing, ice racing (ice speedway), scramble racing, trial, moto cross
摩托车赛；竞赛项目：草地场竞赛，公路赛，沙质跑道竞赛，水泥跑道竞赛，赛车跑道赛〔在灰质或页岩跑道〕，登山赛，冰上赛（冰上赛车跑道），爬行赛，选拔赛，越野赛

24 sand track
沙质跑道（赛车场）

25 racing motorcyc!ist (rider)
竞赛选手

26 leather overalls (leathers)
皮衣

27 racing motorcycle, a solo machine
单人用竞赛摩托车

28 number (number plate)
号码（牌）

29 sidecar combination on the bend
转弯时边车的配合动作

30 sidecar
边车

31 streamlined racing motorcycle [500 cc.]
流线型比赛用摩托车〔500 cc〕

32 gymkhana, a competition of skill; *here:* motorcyclist performing a jump
竞赛，一种竞技比赛；此指赛车手表演障碍跳越

33 cross-country race, a test in performance
越野赛，特技试验

34-38 racing cars
赛车

34 Formula One racing car (a mono posto)
I 型赛车（单人车）

35 rear spoiler (aerofoil, *Am.* airfoil)
后扰流板

36 Formula Two racing car
II 型赛车

37 Super-Vee racing car
超级 V 型赛车

38 prototype, a racing car
标准赛车

1-16 football pitch
足球场
1 field (park)
球场
2 centre (*Am.* center) circle
中圈
3 half-way line
中线
4 penalty area
罚球区
5 goal area
球门区
6 penalty spot
罚球点
7 goal line (by-line)
球门线，端线
8 corner flag
角旗
9 touch line
边线
10 goalkeeper
守门员
11 spare man
后卫
12 inside defender
内后卫
13 outside defender
边后卫
14 midfield players
中锋
15 inside forward (striker)
前锋
16 outside forward (winger)
侧翼（边锋）
17 football
足球
18 valve
气门
19 goalkeeper's gloves
守门员手套
20 foam rubber padding
泡沫垫料
21 football boot
足球鞋
22 leather lining
皮衬里
23 counter
鞋帮后跟部硬皮
24 foam rubber tongue
泡沫胶鞋舌
25 bands
条纹，条饰
26 shaft
鞋身（帮）
27 insole
鞋内底（软垫）
28 screw-in stud
鞋底针柱
29 groove
槽沟
30 nylon sole
尼龙鞋底
31 inner sole
内衬底
32 lace (bootlace)
鞋带
33 football pad with ankle guard
带护踝的足球垫
34 shin guard
护胫

goal
球门
crossbar
球门横木
post (goalpost)
球门柱
goal kick
球门球
save with the fists
以拳救球
penalty (penalty kick)
罚球
corner (corner kick)
角球
offside
越位
free kick
自由球
wall
人墙
bicycle kick (overhead bicycle kick)
倒钩球
header
头球
pass (passing the ball)
传球
receiving the ball (taking a pass)
接球
short pass (one-two)
短传
foul (infringement)
犯规

51 obstruction
阻挡
52 dribble
带球
53 throw-in
掷界外球
54 substitute
替换球员
55 coach
教练
56 shirt (jersey)
球衫（运动衫）
57 shorts
短裤
58 sock (football sock)
袜（足球袜）
59 linesman
边线裁判员
60 linesman's flag
边线裁判员旗
61 sending-off
罚出场
62 referee
裁判员
63 red card; *also:* yellow card
红牌（表示罚出场），黄牌（表示警告）
64 centre (*Am.* center) flag
中线旗

1 **handball** (indoor handball)
手球（室内手球）
2 **handball player, a field player**
手球员，场上球员
3 attacker, making a jump throw
进攻球员，跳起掷球
4 defender
防守球员
5 penalty line
罚球线
6 **hockey**
曲棍球
7 goal
球门
8 goalkeeper
守门员
9 pad (shin pad, knee pad)
护垫（护胫，护膝）
10 kicker
球鞋
11 face guard
（守门员）面罩
12 glove
手套
13 hockey stick
曲棍球杆
14 hockey ball
曲棍球
15 hockey player
曲棍球员
16 striking circle
击球圈
17 sideline
边线
18 corner
角
19 **rugby** (rugby football)
橄榄球
20 scrum (scrummage)
并列争球
21 rugby ball
橄榄球
22 **American football** (*Am.* football)
美式足球
23 football player (player) carrying the ball
带球的橄榄球员
24 helmet
护盔
25 face guard
面罩
26 padded jersey
衬软垫的运动衫
27 ball (pigskin)
球（橄榄球）
28 **basketball**
篮球
29 basketball
篮球
30 backboard
篮板
31 basket posts
篮架柱
32 basket
篮
33 basket ring
篮圈
34 target rectangle
方形篮板标区
35 basketball player shooting
投篮球员
36 end line
端线
37 restricted area
禁区，三秒钟区

38 free-throw line
罚球线
39 substitute
替补球员
40-69 baseball
棒球
40-58 field (park)
棒球场
40 spectator barrier
观众栅栏
41 outfielder
外野手
42 short stop
游击手
43 second base
二垒
44 baseman
守垒员
45 runner
跑垒员
46 first base
一垒
47 third base
三垒
48 foul line (base line)
垒线
49 pitcher's mound
投手区，投手板前隆起的土墩
50 pitcher
投手
51 batter's position
打击手位置（击球员）
52 batter
打击手（击球员）
53 home base (home plate)
本垒
54 catcher
捕手
55 umpire
裁判
56 coach's box
跑垒员指导区
57 coach
跑垒指导员
58 batting order
打击顺序
59-60 baseball gloves (baseball mitts)
棒球手套（棒球合指手套）
59 fielder's glove (fielder's mitt)
垒手及野手手套
60 catcher's glove (catcher's mitt)
捕手手套
61 baseball
棒球
62 bat
球棒
63 batter at bat
打击手击球
64 catcher
捕手
65 umpire
裁判
66 runner
跑垒员
67 base plate
垒包（垫，板）
68 pitcher
投手
69 pitcher's mound
投手板
70-76 cricket
板球
70 wicket with bails
具横木的三柱门

71 back crease (bowling crease)
底线（投球界限线）
72 crease (batting crease)
击球限界线
73 wicket keeper of the fielding sid
防守方三柱门守门员
74 batsman
打击手（击球员）
75 bat (cricket bat)
球棒（板球棒）
76 fielder (bowler)
野手（投手）
77-82 croquet
槌球
77 winning peg
起（终）点桩（杆）
78 hoop
柱门
79 corner peg
角桩
80 croquet player
槌球员
81 croquet mallet
槌球的长柄木槌
82 croquet ball
槌球

1-42 tennis
网球

1 tennis court
网球场

2-3 doubles sideline (sideline for doubles matches); *kinds of doubles:* men's doubles, women's doubles, mixed doubles
双打边线；双打种类：男子双打，女子双打，混合双打

3-10 base line
端线底线

4-5 singles sideline (sideline for singles matches); *kinds of singles:* men's singles, women's singles
单打边线；单打种类：男子单打，女子单打

6-7 service line
发球线

8-9 centre (*Am.* center) line
中线

11 centre (*Am.* center) mark
中点标识

12 service court
发球区

13 net (tennis net)
网（网球网）

14 net strap
网中心布带

15 net post
网柱

16 tennis player
网球手

17 smash
高压球

18 opponent
对手

19 umpire
裁判

20 umpire's chair
裁判椅

21 umpire's microphone
裁判用扩音器（微音器）（麦克风）

22 ball boy
球童

23 net-cord judge
网绳裁判

24 foot-fault judge
发球裁判

25 centre (*Am.* center) line judge
中线裁判

26 base line judge
端线，底线裁判

27 service line judge
发球线裁判

28 tennis ball
网球

29 tennis racket (tennis racquet, racket, racquet)
网球拍

30 racket handle (racquet handle)
球拍把手

31 strings (striking surface)
拍面网（击球面）

32 press (racket press, racquet press)
球拍夹

33 tightening screw
夹紧螺丝

34 scoreboard
记分牌（板）

35 results of sets
各场比赛成绩（结果）

36 player's name
球员姓名

37 number of sets
场数

38 state of play
比赛状况（比数，成绩）

39 backhand stroke
反手击球

40 forehand stroke
正手击球

41 volley (forehand volley at normal height)
截击（正手截击正常高度的球）

42 service
发球

43-44 badminton
羽毛球

43 badminton racket (badminton racquet)
羽毛球拍

44 shuttle (shuttlecock)
羽毛球

45-55 table tennis
桌球

45 table tennis racket (racquet) (table tennis bat)
桌球拍

46 racket (racquet) handle (bat handle)
球拍柄

47 blade covering
拍身贴面

48 table tennis ball
桌球，乒乓球

49 table tennis players; *here:* mixed doubles
桌球员此指：混合双打

50 receiver
接球员

51 server
发球员

52 table tennis table
乒乓球桌，桌球球桌

53 table tennis net
桌球网

54 centre (*Am.* center) line
中线

55 sideline
边线

56-71 volleyball
排球

56-57 correct placing of the hands
手的正确姿势

58 volleyball
排球

59 serving the volleyball
发球

60 blocker
栏网球员

61 service area
发球区

62 server
发球员

63 front-line player
前排球员

64 attack area
攻击区

65 attack line
攻击线（限制线）

66 defence (*Am.* defense) area
防守区

67 referee
主审裁判

68 umpire
副裁判

69 linesman
边线裁判

70 scoreboard
记分板

71 scorer
记分员

72-78 faustball
拳球

72 base line
底线，端线

73 tape
带，绳

74 faust ball
拳球

75 forward
前锋

76 centre (*Am.* center)
中锋

77 back
后卫

78 hammer blow
鎚击（扣击）

79-93 golf
高尔夫球

79-82 course (golf course, holes)
高尔夫球场

79 teeing ground
开球区

80 rough
生杂草的障碍区

81 bunker (*Am.* sand trap)
沙坑（沙地障碍区）

82 green (putting green)
果岭（轻打果岭）

83 golfer, driving
高尔夫球员，挥杆

84 follow-through
打球后手腕伸直的动作（完成动作）

85 golf trolley
打高尔夫球用的手推车

86 putting (holing out)
轻打区

87 hole
球洞

88 flagstick
旗杆

89 golf ball
高尔夫球

90 tee
球座

91 wood, a driver; *sim.:* brassie (brassy, brassey)
木制球杆，长打杆；类似的：镶铜球杆（第二号球杆）

92 iron
铁头高尔夫球杆

93 putter
高尔夫球轻击杆

SCORES   SETS GAMES

6·3	*BORG*	2	4
4·6			
2·6	*ASHE*	2	1
7·5			

1-33 fencing (modern fencing)
击剑（现代击剑）

1-18 foil
击剑（钝剑）

1 fencing master (fencing instructor)
剑术（击剑）教练

2 piste
击剑场

3 on guard line
预备线

4 centre (*Am.* center) line
中心线

5-6 fencers (foil fencers, foilsmen, foilists) in a bout
比赛中的（钝剑）击剑员

5 attacker (attacking fencer) in lunging position (lunging)
取刺姿的进攻者

6 defender (defending fencer), parrying
取守势的防守者

7 straight thrust, a fencing movement
直刺的击剑动作

8 parry of the tierce
第三姿势防守[格开，挡开来剑]

9 line of fencing
击剑线

10 the three fencing measures [short, medium, and long measure]
三种击剑距离[近，中，长距离]

11 foil, a thrust weapon
钝剑，一种戳刺武器

12 fencing glove
击剑手套

13 fencing mask (foil mask)
护面

14 neck flap (neck guard) on the fencing mask
附于护面上的护颈（盖）

15 metallic jacket
金属夹克

16 fencing jacket
击剑夹克

17 heelless fencing shoes
无跟击剑鞋

18 first position for fencer's salute (initial position, on guard position)
击剑者行礼时所取的第一姿势（开始姿势，预备姿势）

19-24 sabre (*Am.* saber) fencing
军刀对击

19 sabreurs (sabre fencers, *Am.* saber fencers)
军刀赛者

20 (light) sabre (*Am.* saber)
（轻）军刀

21 sabre (*Am.* saber) glove (sabre gauntlet)
军刀手套

22 sabre (*Am.* saber) mask
军刀护面

23 cut at head
劈头部

24 parry of the fifth (quinte)
第五姿势防守

25-33 épée, with electrical scoring equipment
装有电子记分装置的尖头剑术比赛

25 épéeist
尖头剑竞赛者

26 electric épée; *also:* electric foil
电动尖头剑；电动钝剑

27 épée point
剑尖

28 scoring lights
记分灯

29 spring-loaded wire spool
弹簧承载电线卷轴

30 indicator light
指示灯

31 wire
电线

32 electronic scoring equipment
电子记分装置

33 on guard position
预备姿势

34-45 fencing weapons
击剑武器

34 light sabre (*Am.* saber), a cut and thrust weapon
轻型军刀，一种劈刺武器

35 guard
护手

36 épée, a thrust weapon
尖头刀，一种刺的武器

37 French foil, a thrust weapon
法国钝剑，一种刺的武器

38 guard (coquille)
护手

39 Italian foil
意大利钝剑

40 foil pommel
剑的柄端

41 handle
剑柄

42 cross piece (quillons)
交叉柄环

43 guard (coquille)
护手

44 blade
剑身

45 button
钝头

46 engagements
剑之交叉接触

47 quarte (carte) engagement
第四姿势交叉接触

48 tierce engagement (*also:* sixte engagement)
第三姿势交叉接触（即第六姿势交叉接触）

49 circling engagement
迴圈交叉接触

50 seconde engagement (*also:* octave engagement)
第二姿势交叉接触（即第八姿势交叉接触）

51-53 target areas
有效部位

51 the whole body in épée fencing (men)
（男子）击剑的全身

52 head and upper body down to the groin in sabre (*Am.* saber) fencing (men)
（男子）军刀击剑时从头与上身至鼠蹊间的部位

53 trunk from the neck to the groin in foil fencing (ladies and men)
（女子与男子）钝剑击剑是从颈部到鼠蹊间的躯干

1 basic position (starting
position)
基本姿势（开始姿势）
2 running posture
跑步姿势
3 side straddle
侧分腿
4 straddle (forward straddle)
分腿（前分腿）
5 toe stand
以足尖站立
6 crouch
蹲
7 upright kneeling position
直体跪姿
8 kneeling position, seat on heels
跪姿（坐於足跟上）
9 squat
屈腿
10 L seat (long sitting)
L 式坐姿（直腿坐姿）
11 tailor seat (sitting tailor-style)
盘腿
12 hurdle (hurdle position)
跳栏姿势
13 V-seat
V 型姿式
14 side split
纵劈腿
15 forward split
横劈腿
16 L-support
L 型手支撑
17 V-support
V 型手支撑
18 straddle seat
分腿支撑
19 bridge
桥式
20 kneeling front support
跪俯撑
21 front support
俯撑
22 back support
后撑
23 crouch with front support
蹲撑
24 arched front support
弓撑
25 side support
侧撑
26 forearm stand (forearm balance)
前腕倒立
27 handstand
手倒立
28 headstand
头倒立（三点倒立）
29 shoulder stand (shoulder
balance)
肩倒立
30 forward horizontal stand
(arabesque)
前平衡（一脚向后伸直，一手向前，一
手向后伸的姿势）
31 rearward horizontal stand
侧平衡
32 trunk-bending sideways
体侧屈
33 trunk-bending forwards
体前屈
34 arch
体后屈
35 astride jump (butterfly)
伸腿挺身跳
36 tuck jump
缩拢跳

37 astride jump
分腿跳
38 pike
屈体跳
39 scissor jump
剪式跳
40 stag jump (stag leap)
鹿式跳（半劈腿跳）
41 running step
跑步
42 lunge
弓箭步
43 forward pace
向前走步
44 lying on back
仰卧
45 prone position
俯卧
46 lying on side
侧卧
47 holding arms downwards
两臂下垂
48 holding (extending) arms
sideways
两臂侧平举
49 holding arms raised upward
两臂上举
50 holding (extending) arms
forward
两臂前平举
51 arms held (extended) backward
两臂后平举
52 hands clasped behind the head
两手头后互握

1-11 gymnastics apparatus in men's Olympic gymnastics
男子奥运体操器械

1 long horse (horse, vaulting horse)
纵跳马（跳马）

2 parallel bars
双槓

3 bar
横槓

4 rings (stationary rings)
吊环（静止吊环）

5 pommel horse (side horse)
鞍马

6 pommel
鞍环

7 horizontal bar (high bar)
单槓（高槓）

8 bar
横槓

9 upright
柱，直柱

10 stay wires
支索

11 floor (12 m × 12 m floor area)
地板（12 米 × 12 米徒手操场地）

12-21 auxiliary apparatus and apparatus for school and club gymnastics
辅助器械和学校，俱乐部体操器械

12 springboard (Reuther board)
弹跳板（路德板）

13 landing mat
落地垫

14 bench
长体操凳

15 box
跳箱

16 small box
小跳箱

17 buck
木马

18 mattress
垫子

19 climbing rope (rope)
爬绳

20 wall bars
肋木

21 window ladder
窗形梯

22-39 positions in relation to the apparatus
与器械相关的姿势和位置

22 side, facing
正对跳箱侧面

23 side, facing away
背对跳箱侧面

24 end, facing
正对跳箱端

25 end, facing away
背对跳箱端

26 outside, facing
正对双槓外侧

27 inside, facing
正对双槓内侧

28 front support
前撑，俯撑

29 back support
后撑

30 straddle position
分腿姿势

31 seated position outside
槓上外向正坐

32 riding seat outside
槓外侧坐

33 hang
悬垂

34 reverse hang
后悬垂，吊臂悬垂

35 hang with elbows bent
屈肘悬垂，屈肘向上

36 piked reverse hang
屈体吊臂悬垂

37 straight inverted hang
直臂倒悬垂

38 straight hang
直臂支撑

39 bent hang
屈臂支撑

40-46 grasps (kinds of grasp)
握槓（各种握槓）

40 overgrasp on the horizontal bar
正握单槓

41 undergrasp on the horizontal bar
反握单槓

42 combined grasp on the horizontal bar
正反握单槓

43 cross grasp on the horizontal bar
交叉握单槓

44 rotated grasp on the horizontal bar
扭臂握单槓

45 outside grip on the parallel bars
自外握双槓

46 rotated grasp on the parallel bars
扭臂握双槓

47 leather handstrap
皮护掌

48-60 exercises
各种体操动作

48 long-fly on the horse
跳马的水平腾越

49 rise to straddle on the parallel bars
双槓向上分腿

50 crucifix on the rings
吊环上十字支撑

51 scissors (scissors movement) on the pommel horse
鞍马上的剪式动作

52 legs raising into a handstand on the floor
地板上升腿倒立

53 squat vault on the horse
跳马屈体腾越

54 double leg circle on the pommel horse
鞍马上双腿迴旋

55 hip circle backwards on the rings
吊环上向后复回环

56 lever hang on the rings
吊环上槓杆悬垂

57 rearward swing on the parallel bars
双槓上后向摆盪

58 forward kip into upper arm hang on the parallel bars
双槓上挂臂体向前

59 backward underswing on the horizontal bar
单槓上向后弧形摆

60 backward grand circle on the horizontal bar
单槓上向后大迴环

61-63 gymnastics kit
体操服

61 singlet (vest, *Am.* undershirt)
背心

62 gym trousers
体操裤

63 gym shoes
体操鞋

64 wristband
护腕

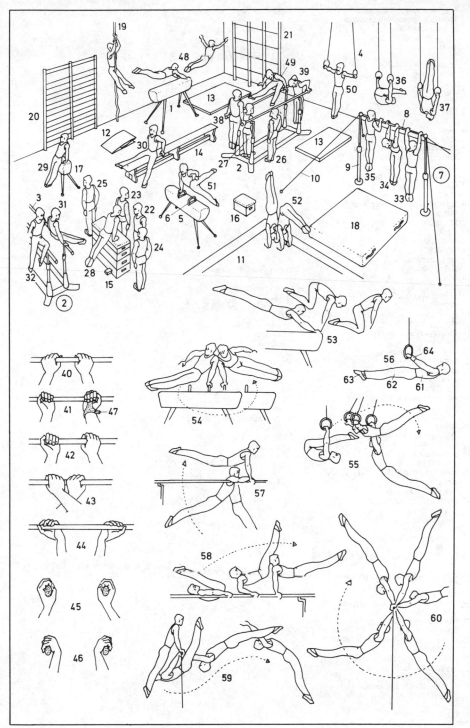

1-6 gymnastics apparatus in women's Olympic gymnastics
奥运女子体操器械
1 horse (vaulting horse)
跳马
2 beam
平衡木
3 asymmetric bars (uneven bars)
高低槓
4 bar
横槓
5 stay wires
支索
6 floor (12 m × 12 m floor area)
地板（12米 × 12米徒手操场地）
7-14 auxiliary apparatus and apparatus for school and club gymnastics
辅助器械和学校俱乐部体操器械
7 landing mat
落地垫
8 springboard (Reuther board)
弹跳板
9 small box
小跳箱
10 trampoline
弹簧跳床
11 sheet (web)
跳床面（跳床网）
12 frame
床架
13 rubber springs
橡皮弹簧
14 springboard trampoline
跳板式弹簧跳床
15-32 apparatus exercises
器械体操
15 backward somersault
后空翻
16 spotting position (standing-in position)
保护姿势
17 vertical backward somersault on the trampoline
弹簧跳床垂直后空翻
18 forward somersault on the springboard trampoline
跳板式弹簧跳床上前空翻
19 forward roll on the floor
地板上前滚翻
20 long-fly to forward roll on the floor
地板上水平腾越前滚翻
21 cartwheel on the beam
平衡木上侧翻
22 handspring on the horse
跳马上前手翻
23 backward walkover
后手翻
24 back flip (flik-flak) on the floor
地板上后手（空）翻
25 free walkover forward on the floor
地板上腾身前空翻
26 forward walkover on the floor
地板上前手翻
27 headspring on the floor
地板上头手翻
28 upstart on the asymmetric bars
高低槓腾身向上
29 free backward circle on the asymmetric bars
高低槓上腾身后回旋
30 face vault over the horse
正腾越跳马

31 flank vault over the horse
侧腾越跳马
32 back vault (rear vault) over the horse
背腾越跳马
33-50 gymnastics with hand apparatus
轻器械体操
33 hand-to-hand throw
自抛自接
34 gymnastic ball
体操球
35 high toss
上（高）抛
36 bounce
拍球
37 hand circling with two clubs
手绕双棒
38 gymnastic club
体操棒
39 swing
摆动
40 tuck jump
缩拢跳
41 bar
棒
42 skip
跳绳
43 rope (skipping rope)
绳
44 criss-cross skip
交叉跳
45 skip through the hoop
跳圈
46 gymnastic hoop
体操用藤圈
47 hand circle
单手绕圈
48 serpent
蛇舞
49 gymnastic ribbon
体操用缎（彩）带
50 spiral
螺旋舞
51-52 gymnastics kit
体操服装
51 leotard
紧身运动衣
52 gym shoes
体操鞋

1-8 running
赛跑

1-6 start
起跑

1 starting block
起跑器

2 adjustable block (pedal)
可调整起跑器（脚蹬，踏板）

3 start
起跑

4 crounch start
蹲踞式起跑

5 runner, a sprinter; *also:* middle-distance runner, long-distance runner
赛跑者，短跑选手；亦可：中距离选手，长距离（跑）选手

6 running track (track), a cinder track or synthetic track
跑道，一种煤渣（铺成的）跑道或塑胶合成跑道

7-8 hurdles (hurdle racing); *sim.:* steeplechase
跳栏比赛；类似：越野障碍赛跑

7 clearing the hurdle
跨栏

8 hurdle
栏架

9-41 jumping and vaulting
跳越运动和撑杆跳高

9-27 high jump
跳高

9 Fosbury flop (Fosbury, flop)
背浪式跳高

10 high jumper
跳高选手

11 body rotation (rotation on the body's longitudinal and latitudinal axes)
转体（沿身体纵横轴旋转）

12 shoulder landing
肩落式

13 upright
立柱

14 bar (crossbar)
横杆

15 Eastern roll
东方式（剪式）跳高

16 Western roll
西方式（滚式）跳高

17 roll
滚式跳高

18 rotation
滚式过杆

19 landing
落地

20 height scale
高度标尺

21 Eastern cut-off
剪式过杆

22 scissors (scissor jump)
剪式跳高

23 straddle (straddle jump)
腹滚式跳高

24 turn
转身，旋转

25 vertical free leg
垂直摆腿起跳

26 take-off
起跳

27 free leg
摆腿

28-36 pole vault
撑杆跳

28 pole (vaulting pole)
杆（撑杆）

29 pole vaulter (vaulter) in the pull-up phase
处於引体（力）状态下的撑杆跳选手

30 swing
旋转

31 crossing the bar
越过横杆

32 high jump apparatus (high jump equipment)
跳高设备用具

33 upright
立柱

34 bar (crossbar)
横杆

35 box
（撑杆跳）插穴

36 landing area (landing pad)
落地区（落地垫）

37-41 long jump
跳远

37 take-off
起跳

38 take-off board
起跳板

39 landing area
落地区（沙坑）

40 hitch-kick
走步式跳远

41 hang
挺身

42-47 hammer throw
掷链球

42 hammer
链球

43 hammer head
链球球体

44 handle
链球钢链

45 grip
链球手柄

46 holding the grip
握住手柄

47 glove
手套

48 shot put
推铅球

49 shot (weight)
铅球

50 O'Brien technique
背向推铅球技术

51-53 javelin throw
掷标枪

51 grip with thumb and index finger
以拇指与食指握枪

52 grip with thumb and middle finger
以拇指与中指握枪

53 horseshoe grip
马蹄式握法

54 binding
线把

1-5 weightlifting
举重

1 squat-style snatch
蹲踞式抓举

2 weightlifter
举重人

3 disc (disk) barbell
圆盘式杠铃（举重圆盘）

4 jerk with split
箭步挺举

5 maintained lift
举重持续动作

6-12 wrestling
摔角

6-9 Greco-Roman wrestling
（古希腊罗马式）古典式摔角

6 standing wrestling (wrestling in standing position)
立摔

7 wrestler
摔角选手

8 on-the-ground wrestling (*here:* the referee's position)
撑摔（此指：由裁判员位置看）

9 bridge
桥式

10-12 freestyle wrestling
自由式摔角

10 bar arm (arm bar) with grapevine
缠腿夹臂

11 double leg lock
夹双腿摔

12 wrestling mat (mat)
摔角垫

13-17 judo (*sim.:* ju-jitsu, jiu jitsu, ju-jutsu)
柔道

13 drawing the opponent off balance to the right and forward
向右前方拉对手使失去平衡

14 judoka (judoist)
柔道选手

15 coloured (*Am.* colored) belt, as a symbol of Dan grade
有色腰带，段位标志

16 referee
裁判

17 judo throw
柔道摔

18-19 karate
空手道

18 karateka
空手道选手

19 side thrust kick, a kicking technique
侧踢，一种踢腿技术

20-50 boxing (boxing match)
拳击

20-24 training apparatus (training equipment)
训练装置（设备）

20 spring-supported punch ball
弹簧（练习用）吊球

21 punch bag (*Am.* punching bag)
吊球，沙袋（包）

22 speed ball
速度球

23 suspended punch ball
悬挂式吊球

24 punch ball
吊球

25 boxer, an amateur boxer (boxes in a singlet, vest, *Am.* undershirt) or a professional boxer (boxes without singlet)
拳手，业馀拳击手（拳击时穿背心）或职业拳击手（拳击时不穿背心）

26 boxing glove
拳击手套

27 sparring partner
练拳拳伴

28 straight punch (straight blow)
直拳

29 ducking and sidestepping
闪避和侧步

30 headguard
（练习用）护盔

31 infighting; *here:* clinch
接近战，此指：揪扭，抱住对方手臂

32 uppercut
上钩拳

33 hook to the head; *here:* right hook
击向头部的钩拳，此指：右钩拳

34 punch below the belt, a foul punch (illegal punch, foul)
拳击下身，犯规的击法

35-50 boxing match (boxing contest), a title fight (title bout)
拳击比赛，一种锦标赛

35 boxing ring (ring)
拳击台

36 ropes
围绳

37 stay wire (stay rope)
支索（绳）

38 neutral corner
中立角

39 winner
优胜者

40 loser by a knockout
被击倒的失败者

41 referee
裁判

42 counting out
计秒（点数）

43 judge
台下裁判

44 second
助手

45 manager
举办人（经纪人）

46 gong
锣

47 timekeeper
计时员

48 record keeper
计分员

49 press photographer
报导摄影师

50 sports reporter (reporter)
体育记者（采访记者，实况播报员）

1-57 mountaineering
(mountain climbing, Alpinism)
登山运动

1 hut (Alpine Club hut, mountain hut, base)
小屋（登山木屋，山地小屋，基地）

2-13 climbing (rock climbing)
'rock climbing technique'
攀登（岩石攀登）〔岩石攀登技术〕

2 rock face (rock wall)
岩壁

3 fissure (vertical, horizontal, or diagonal fissure)
隙缝（垂直，水平或斜行缝隙）

4 ledge (rock ledge, grass ledge, scree ledge, snow ledge, ice ledge)
岩架（岩架，草岩架，碎石岩架，雪岩架，冰岩架）

5 mountaineer (climber, mountain climber, Alpinist)
登山者

6 anorak (high-altitude anorak, snowshirt, padded jacket)
附头巾的御寒外套（高山防风衣，雪衣，棉夹克）

7 breeches (climbing breeches)
登山裤

8 chimney
直立裂口

9 belay (spike, rock spike)
绳索套（固定）於突起岩石上（岩石尖）

10 belay
保护绳

11 rope sling (sling)
后方保护绳

12 rope
绳

13 spur
登山用鞋底钉

14-21 snow and ice climbing 'snow and ice climbing technique'
冰雪攀登〔冰雪攀登技术〕

14 ice slope (firn slope)
冰坡

15 snow and ice climber
冰雪攀登者

16 ice axe (*Am.* ax)
冰斧，冰镐

17 step (ice step)
台阶（冰台阶）

18 snow goggles
护目镜

19 hood (anorak hood)
兜帽（防风外套兜帽）

20 cornice (snow cornice)
雪簷

21 ridge (ice ridge)
山脊（冰脊）

22-27 rope (roped party)
结绳（结绳行进）

22 glacier
冰川

23 crevasse
裂隙，冰隙

24 snow bridge
雪桥

25 leader
响导，领路人

26 second man (belayer)
第二人（保护者）

27 third man (non-belayer)
第三人（非保护者）

28-30 roping down (abseiling, rapelling)
绕绳下降

28 abseil sling
绕绳下降的后方保护绳

29 sling seat
后方保护绳座

30 Dülfer seat
杜尔富座

31-37 mountaineering equipment (climbing equipment, snow and ice climbing equipment)
登山装备

31 ice axe (*Am.* ax)
冰斧

32 wrist sling
腕带

33 pick
镐尖

34 adze (*Am.* adz)
手斧（铲头）

35 karabiner hole
铁锁孔

36 short-shafted ice axe (*Am.* ax)
短柄冰斧

37 hammer axe (*Am.* ax)
鎚斧

38 general-purpose piton
多用途岩钉

39 abseil piton (ringed piton)
绕绳下降岩钉（带环岩钉）

40 ice piton (semi-tubular screw ice piton, corkscrew piton)
冰岩钉（半管状螺旋岩钉，螺旋形岩钉）

41 drive-in ice piton
打入式冰岩钉

42 mountaineering boot
登山鞋

43 corrugated sole
波形鞋底

44 climbing boot
攀登鞋

45 roughened stiff rubber upper
粗硬橡皮鞋帮

46 karabiner
铁锁

47 screwgate
螺旋保险栓

48 crampons (lightweight crampons, twelve-point crampons, ten-points crampons)
攀登用鞋底钉（轻型鞋底钉，十二齿鞋底钉，十齿鞋底钉）

49 front points
前齿

50 point guards
鞋底钉护套

51 crampon strap
鞋底钉缚带

52 crampon cable fastener
鞋底钉绳钩扣

53 safety helmet (protective helmet)
安全头盔

54 helmet lamp
头盔灯

55 snow gaiters
雪地鞋罩

56 climbing harness
登山背带

57 sit harness
坐式背带

1-72 skiing
滑雪

1 compact ski
一般雪屐（滑雪板）

2 safety binding (release binding)
安全固定装置

3 strap
带子

4 steel edge
金属刃

5 ski stick (ski pole)
雪杖

6 grip
握柄

7 loop
环

8 basket
雪杖的撑圈

9 ladies' one-piece ski suit
女式连身式滑雪服

10 skiing cap (ski cap)
滑雪帽

11 skiing goggles
滑雪用护目镜

12 cemented sole skiing boot
胶底滑雪鞋

13 crash helmet
护盔

14-30 cross-country equipment
越野赛装备

14 cross-country ski
（距离竞技）越野滑雪

15 cross-country rat trap binding
雪屐鼠夹式固定装置

16 cross-country boot
越野滑雪鞋

17 cross-country gear
越野滑雪服

18 peaked cap
遮簷帽，鸭嘴帽

19 sunglasses
太阳眼镜

20 cross-country poles made of bamboo
竹制的越野滑雪雪杖

21-24 ski-waxing equipment
滑雪涂蜡用具（器材）

21 ski wax
雪蜡

22 waxing iron (blowlamp, blowtorch)
涂蜡器（喷灯）

23 waxing cork
涂蜡栓

24 wax scraper
刮蜡器

25 downhill racing pole
下坡赛所用的雪杖

26 herringbone, for climbing a slope
人字形步登坡（分腿滑行）

27 sidestep, for climbing a slope
侧步登坡

28 ski bag
滑雪袋

29 slalom
弯道滑雪比赛

30 gate pole
旗门杆

31 racing suit
比赛服

32 downhill racing
下坡赛

33 [egg] position, the ideal downhill racing position
蛋形姿势，最理想的下坡赛姿

34 downhill ski
下坡用雪屐

35 ski jumping
飞跳姿势

36 lean forward
前倾姿势

37 number
号码

38 ski jumping ski
飞跳用雪屐

39 grooves (3 to 5 grooves)
底槽（3至5条底槽）

40 cable binding
绳索固定装置

41 ski jumping boots
飞跳滑雪鞋

42 cross-country
越野滑雪（速度滑雪）

43 cross-country stretch-suit
越野滑雪弹力服

44 course
滑道

45 course-marking flag
滑道标识旗

46 layers of a modern ski
现代雪屐（滑雪板）的层次

47 special core
特殊心板

48 laminates
积层薄板

49 stabilizing layer (stabilizer)
安定层（安定器）

50 steel edge
钢板边

51 aluminium (Am. aluminum) upper edge
铝质上板边

52 synthetic bottom (artificial bottom)
合成底

53 safety jet
安全口

54-56 parts of the binding
固定装置的部件

54 automatic heel unit
足跟部自动装置

55 toe unit
足尖部装置

56 ski stop
雪屐停止（制动）扣

57-63 ski lift
上山吊椅

57 double chair lift
双座上山吊椅

58 safety bar with footrest
带踏脚板的安全杆

59 ski lift
滑行上山

60 track
滑道

61 hook
挂钩

62 automatic cable pulley
自动拉索滑轮

63 haulage cable
拉索

64 slalom
弯道滑雪比赛

65 open gate
开口门

66 closed vertical gate
闭口垂直门

67 open vertical gate
开口垂直门

68 transversal chicane
横断双滑道

69 hairpin
U 型急转滑道

70 elbow
急转

71 corridor
回转滑道

72 Allais chicane
蛇行滑道

1-26 ice skating
溜冰

1 ice skater, a solo skater
溜冰者，单人溜

2 tracing leg
滑动腿

3 free leg
浮腿

4 pair skaters
双人溜冰者

5 death spiral
固定轴环绕

6 pivot
旋转轴

7 stag jump (stag leap)
鹿式（半劈腿跳）

8 jump-sit-spin
跳跃蹲踞旋转

9 upright spin
直立旋转

10 holding the foot
抱足

11-19 compulsory figures
固定图形

11 curve eight
"8"字形

12 change
变换形

13 three
"3"字形

14 double-three
双"3"字形

15 loop
环形

16 change-loop
变换环形

17 bracket
括弧形

18 counter
外钩手形

19 rocker
内钩手形

20-25 ice skates
溜冰鞋

20 speed skating set (speed skate)
速度（竞速）溜冰鞋，冰刀溜冰鞋

21 edge
刃

22 hollow grinding (hollow ridge, concave ridge)
凹形脊，空心脊

23 ice hockey set (ice hockey skate)
冰球鞋

24 ice skating boot
溜冰靴

25 skate guard
冰刀套

26 speed skater
速度（竞速）溜冰者

27-28 skate sailing
风帆溜冰

27 skate sailor
风帆溜冰者

28 hand sail
手帆

29-37 ice hockey
冰球（冰上曲棍球）

29 ice hockey player
冰球球员

30 ice hockey stick
冰球球杆

31 stick handle
杆柄

32 stick blade
杆刃

33 shin pad
护腿，护具

34 headgear (protective helmet)
护盔

35 puck, a vulcanized rubber disc (disk)
冰球（硬橡胶圆板）

36 goalkeeper
守门员

37 goal
球门

38-40 ice-stick shooting (Bavarian curling)
冰上击柱运动（巴伐利亚冰上溜石运动）

38 ice-stick shooter (Bavarian curler)
冰上击柱者（冰上溜石者）

39 ice stick
冰柱

40 block
石块

41-43 curling
冰上溜石（冰上掷石）

41 curler
冰上溜石者（掷石者）

42 curling stone (granite)
（溜）掷石的石块（花岗岩）

43 curling brush (curling broom, besom)
（掷）溜石帚

44-46 ice yachting (iceboating, ice sailing)
冰帆运动

44 ice yacht (iceboat)
冰上帆船

45 steering runner
方向滑橇

46 outrigged runner
舷外滑橇

1 toboggan (sledge, *Am.* sled)
平底雪橇（雪橇）
2 toboggan (sledge, *Am.* sled) with
seat of plaid straps
具方格织带座位的平底雪橇
3 junior luge toboggan (junior
luge, junior toboggan)
儿童（小型）雪橇
4 rein
雪橇绳
5 bar (strut)
杆
6 seat
座位
7 bracket
托架
8 front prop
前支柱
9 rear prop
后支柱
10 movable runner
可动滑橇
11 metal face
金属面
12 luge tobogganer
小型滑雪橇者
13 luge toboggan (luge, toboggan)
小型雪橇
14 crash helmet
护盔
15 goggles
护目镜
16 elbow pad
护肘

17 knee pad
护膝
18 Nansen sledge, a polar sledge
南森雪橇，一种极地雪橇
19-21 bobsleigh (bobsledding)
连橇
19 bobsleigh (bobsled), a two-man
bobsleigh (a boblet)
连橇，大雪橇（双人用雪橇）
20 steersman
雪橇驾驶人
21 brakeman
连橇（大雪橇）制动者
22-24 skeleton tobogganing (Cresta
tobogganing)
骨架雪橇滑雪运动
22 skeleton (skeleton toboggan)
骨架雪橇
23 skeleton rider
骨架雪橇滑雪者
24 rake, for braking and steering
用於制动或控制方向的耙齿

1 avalanche (snow avalanche, *Am.* snowslide); *kinds:* wind avalanche, ground avalanche 雪崩；种类：风崩，土崩	**12** radiator shutter and shutter opening (louvre shutter) 散热器护板和护板孔

1 avalanche (snow avalanche, *Am.* snowslide); *kinds:* wind avalanche, ground avalanche
雪崩；种类：风崩，土崩

2 avalanche wall, a deflecting wall (diverting wall); *sim.:* avalanche wedge
雪崩墙，偏向墙（使雪崩改变方向的墙）；类似：雪崩楔形墙

3 avalanche gallery
雪崩走廊

4 snowfall
下雪

5 snowdrift
雪堆

6 snow fence
防雪栅栏

7 avalanche forest 'planted as protection against avalanches'
雪崩林〔为防止雪崩而种植的〕

8 street-cleaning lorry (street cleaner)
清路车

9 snow plough (*Am.* snowplow) attachment
雪犁附件

10 snow chain (skid chain, tyre chain, *Am.* tire chain)
雪链（防滑链）

11 radiator bonnet (*Am.* radiator hood)
散热器盖

12 radiator shutter and shutter opening (louvre shutter)
散热器护板和护板孔

13 snowman
雪人

14 snowball fight
打雪杖

15 snowball
雪球

16 ski bob
骑式雪橇

17 slide
溜冰

18 boy, sliding
溜冰的男孩

19 icy surface (icy ground)
结冰的地面

20 snow-covered roof
雪复盖的屋顶

21 icicle
冰柱

22 man clearing snow
清扫积雪者

23 snow push (snow shovel)
雪铲

24 heap of snow
雪堆

25 horse-drawn sleigh (horse sleigh)
马拉雪橇

26 sleigh bells (bells, set of bells)
雪橇铃

27 foot muff (*Am.* foot bag)
脚套筒

28 earmuff
耳盖（护耳）

29 handsledge (tread sledge); *sim.:* push sledge
椅式雪橇；类似：手推雪橇

30 slush
雪水，烂泥

1-13 skittles
九柱游戏
1-11 skittle frame
小柱位置
1 front pin (front)
前柱（第一柱）
2 left front second pin (left front second)
左前第二柱
3 running three 'left'
〔左〕前柱间隙
4 right front second pin (right front second)
右前第二柱
5 running three 'right'
〔右〕前柱间隙
6 left corner pin (left corner), a corner (copper)
左角柱（警察，卒）
7 landlord
中央柱（王，主）
8 right corner pin (right corner), a corner (copper)
右角柱（警察，卒）
9 back left second pin (back left second)
左后第二柱
10 back right second pin (back right second)
右后第二柱
11 back pin (back)
后柱
12 pin
小柱
13 landlord
中央柱（王，主）
14-20 tenpin bowling
保龄球（十柱）
14 frame
保龄球各柱位置
15 bowling ball (ball with finger holes)
具指孔的保龄球
16 finger hole
指孔
17-20 deliveries
投球法
17 straight ball
直球
18 hook ball (hook)
弯球
19 curve
曲线球
20 back-up ball (back-up)
歪球
21 boules; sim.: Italian game of boccie, green bowls (bowls)
滚木球；类似意大利滚木球
22 boules player
玩滚木球者
23 jack (target jack)
靶球
24 grooved boule
刻有槽线的木球
25 group of players
一群玩滚木球者
26 rifle shooting
步枪射击
27-29 shooting position
射击姿势
27 standing position
立姿
28 kneeling position
跪姿
29 prone position
卧姿

30-33 targets
靶
30 target for 50 m events (50 m target)
50 公尺赛靶
31 circle
环
32 target for 100 m events (100 m target)
100 公尺赛靶
33 bobbing target (turning target, running-boar target)
活动靶（转动靶，跑猪靶）
34-39 ammunition
弹药
34 air rifle cartridge
空气枪子弹
35 rimfire cartridge for zimmerstutzen (indoor target rifle), a smallbore German single-shot rifle
室内短管步枪（室内靶步枪）用的底部
发火子弹，一种小口径单发枪用子弹
36 case head
弹壳
37 caseless round
弹头
38 .22 long rifle cartridge
.22 长步枪弹
39 .222 Remington cartridge
.222 雷明顿子弹
40-49 sporting rifles
运动步枪
40 air rifle
空气枪
41 optical sight
（光学）瞄准器
42 front sight (foresight)
准星
43 smallbore standard rifle
标准小口径步枪
44 international smallbore free rifle
国际小口径自动步枪
45 palm rest for standing position
立姿托座
46 butt plate with hook
带钩的枪托底板
47 butt with thumb hole
有拇指孔的枪托底板
48 smallbore rifle for bobbing target (turning target)
活动靶射击用的小口径步枪
49 telescopic sight (riflescope, telescope sight)
瞄准器（步枪瞄准器，望远镜瞄准器）
50 optical ring sight
环形瞄准器
51 optical ring and bead sight
环形瞄准器和准星
52-66 archery (target archery)
射箭运动
52 shot
射箭
53 archer
箭手
54 competition bow
比赛用的弓
55 riser
弓臂
56 point-of-aim mark
瞄准记号
57 grip (handle)
弓把
58 stabilizer
安定（防震）器
59 bow string (string)
弓弦

60 arrow
箭
61 pile (point) of the arrow
箭头
62 fletching
箭杆上所粘的羽毛
63 nock
箭扣
64 shaft
箭杆
65 cresting
箭杆上涂染的颜色
66 target
靶
67 Basque game of pelota (jai alai)
巴斯克回力球游戏
68 pelota player
回力球运动者
69 wicker basket (cesta)
柳条球拍
70-78 skeet (skeet shooting), a kind of clay pigeon shooting
飞靶射击，一种泥鸽射击运动
70 skeet over-and-under shotgun
飞靶射击用的双管枪类枪
71 muzzle with skeet choke
口径收缩的猎枪枪口
72 ready position on call
预备姿势
73 firing position
射击姿势
74 shooting range
靶场
75 high house
高抛靶房
76 low house
低抛靶房
77 target's path
靶的飞行路线
78 shooting station (shooting box)
射击位置
79 aero wheel
滚轮
80 handle
把手
81 footrest
脚凳
82 go-karting (karting)
小型车赛
83 go-kart (kart)
小型赛车
84 number plate (number)
号码牌
85 pedals
踏板
86 pneumatic tyre (Am. tire)
气胎，车胎
87 petrol tank (Am. gasoline tank)
油箱
88 frame
车架
89 steering wheel
方向盘
90 bucket seat
单人圆背摺椅
91 protective bulkhead
防护壁
92 two-stroke engine
二冲程发动机（引擎）
93 silencer (Am. muffler)
消音器，灭音器

1-48 masked ball
(masquerade, fancy-dress ball)
化装舞会
1 ballroom
舞厅
2 dance band
乐队
3 dance band musician
乐队之乐师
4 paper lantern
纸灯笼
5 festoon (string of decorations)
花采（装饰带）
6-48 disguise (fancy dress) at the masquerade
化装舞会上之化装（化装服装）
6 witch
女巫
7 mask
面具
8 fur trapper (trapper)
身穿软毛兽皮之猎人
9 Apache girl
阿帕契女郎
10 net stocking
网状丝袜
11 first prize in the tombola (raffle), a hamper
置第一奖的奖券篮
12 pierrette
（法国哑剧中）著白裤及大扣白色短衣
与戴面具之女丑角
13 half mask (domino)
半截之面具，黑色之露眼小面具

14 devil
魔鬼
15 domino
带头巾之上衣
16 hula-hula girl (Hawaii girl)
呼拉舞女郎（夏威夷女郎）
17 garland
花环
18 grass skirt (hula skirt)
草裙（呼拉舞裙）
19 pierrot
（法国哑剧中）白衣丑角，走江湖之丑
角
20 ruff
襞襟，（宽而硬呈轮状之）皱领
21 midinette
（巴黎时装店之）女店员
22 Biedermeier dress
19世纪德国式之女服
23 poke bonnet
突缘之女帽
24 décolletage with beauty spot
饰有美人痣之露胸紧身女装
25 bayadére (Hindu dancing girl)
印度舞妓
26 grandee
大公、贵族
27 Columbine
意大利喜剧中之半假面女郎
28 maharaja (maharajah)
大君（印度君候的尊称）
29 mandarin, a Chinese dignitary
中国贵族

30 exotic girl (exotic)
異国女郎
31 cowboy; sim.: gaucho (vaquero)
牛仔，类似南美之畜牧人（牧者）
32 vamp, in fancy dress
化装之妖妇
33 dandy (fop)
好打扮者著（过分讲究服饰或举止者）
34 rosette
玫瑰花饰
35 harlequin
丑角，谐角
36 gipsy (gypsy) girl
吉普赛女郎
37 cocotte (demi-monde, demi-mondaine, demi-rep)
上流社会娼妓
38 owl-glass, a fool (jester, buffoon)
小丑，（中世纪宫中之）弄臣
39 foolscap (jester's cap and bells)
丑角所带之帽（带有小铃）
40 rattle
有嘎嘎声之玩具
41 odalisque, Eastern female slave in Sultan's seraglio
女奴（土耳其宫中之东方女奴）
42 chalwar (pantaloons)
土耳其裤
43 pirate (buccaneer)
海盗
44 tattoo
纹身

45 paper hat
纸帽
46 false nose
假鼻
47 clapper (rattle)
拍版，响板（有嘎嘎声之玩具）
48 slapstick
戟板
49-54 fireworks
烟火类
49 percussion cap
雷管
50 cracker
爆竹
51 banger
鞭炮
52 jumping jack
跳娃娃（玩具）
53 cannon cracker (maroon, marroon)
大鞭炮
54 rocket
火箭炮或冲天炮
55 paper ball
纸球
56 jack-in-the-box
玩偶匣
57-70 carnival procession
狂欢节（嘉年华会）游行
57 carnival float (carnival truck)
嘉年华会游行彩车
58 King Carnival
嘉年华会国王

59 bauble (fool's sceptre, *Am.* scepter)
丑角棒
60 fool's badge
丑角所戴之徽章
61 Queen Carnival
嘉年华会皇后
62 confetti
五彩碎纸
63 giant
巨人像（讽刺性人物像）
64 beauty queen
美女皇后
65 fairy-tale figure
神话人物
66 paper streamer
彩色纸带
67 majorette
乐队队长
68 king's guard
国王之护卫
69 buffoon, a clown
小丑
70 lansquenet's drum
16-17世纪时，德国佣兵所用之军鼓

43	throwing act	59	seesaw
	抛掷表演		跷跷板
44	balancing act	60	ball
	平衡表演		球
45	support	61	camp
	支撑者，助演者		帐篷
46	pole (bamboo pole)	62	cage caravan
	杆（竹竿）		兽笼篷车
47	acrobat	63	menagerie
	特技演员		动物展览
48	equilibrist (balancer)		
	平衡倒立演员（擅保持平衡者）		
49	wild animal cage, a round cage		
	野兽笼，圆形笼子		
50	bars of the cage		
	笼子之栅栏		
51	passage (barred passage, passage for the wild animals)		
	通道（栅栏通道，野兽之通道）		
52	tamer (wild animal tamer)		
	驯兽师		
53	whip		
	鞭子		
54	fork		
	叉子，防护叉		
55	pedestal		
	台座		
56	wild animal (tiger, lion)		
	野兽（老虎，狮子）		
57	stand		
	架子		
58	hoop (jumping hoop)		
	铁圈（跳环）		

1-69 fair (annual fair)
市集（年度市集）

1 fairground
市集场所

2 children's merry-go-round, (whirligig), a roundabout (*Am.* carousel)
儿童旋转木马

3 refreshment stall (drinks stall)
小吃摊，饮食摊位

4 chairoplane
（旋转）飞椅

5 up-and-down roundabout
起伏之旋转车

6 show booth (booth)
表演棚

7 box (box office)
付款箱

8 barker
叫卖者，兜售者

9 medium
巫师

10 showman
主持人

11 try-your-strength machine
测力机

12 hawker
沿街叫卖之小贩

13 balloon
汽球

14 paper serpent
纸蛇

15 windmill
风车

16 pickpocket (thief)
扒手（小偷）

17 vendor
小贩

18 Turkish delight
橡皮糖、软糖

19 freak show
畸形人展览

20 giant
巨人

21 fat lady
胖女人

22 dwarfs (midgets)
侏儒

23 beer marquee
啤酒店棚

24 sideshow
杂耍

25-28 travelling (*Am.* traveling) artistes (travelling show people)
流动艺人

25 fire eater
吞火者

26 sword swallower
吞剑者

27 strong man
大力士

28 escapologist
脱逃术表演者

29 spectators
观众

30 ice-cream vendor (ice-cream man)
卖冰淇淋的小贩

31 ice-cream cornet
盛冰淇淋之锥形蛋卷

32 hot-dog stand
热狗摊

33 grill (*Am.* broiler)
烤架

34 hot dog
热狗

35 sausage tongs
香肠箝（夹）

36 fortune teller
占卜者、算命者

37 big wheel (Ferris wheel)
巨形大轮（大轮边缘设有座位，供人迴旋）

38 orchestrion (automatic organ)
自动风琴

scenic railway (switchback)
游乐场中，模拟之游览小火车

toboggan slide (chute)
平底雪撬之滑行场（滑行道）

swing boats
船形秋千

swing boat, turning full circle
转满圈之船形秋千

full circle
转满圈

lottery booth (tombola booth)
彩票棚，摇奖棚

wheel of fortune
幸运轮（轮盘赌具）

devil's wheel (typhoon wheel)
旋风转轮（飓风转轮）

throwing ring (quoit)
投环游戏

prizes
奖品

sandwich man on stilts
踩高跷、身前后挂广告牌的人

sandwich board (placard)
广告牌

cigarette seller, an itinerant
trader (a hawker)
售香烟者，流动小贩

tray
托盘

fruit stall
水果摊

wall of-death rider
飞车驾驶员

55 hall of mirrors
趣镜室，哈哈镜室

56 concave mirror
凹面镜

57 convex mirror
凸面镜

58 shooting gallery
射击室

59 hippodrome
马戏场，竞技场

60 junk stalls (second-hand stalls)
旧货摊

61 first aid tent (first aid post)
急救站

62 dodgems (bumper cars)
在游乐场中供游客坐的小型电动车，一
面撞别人，一面躲闪别人的游戏（碰碰
车游戏）

63 dodgem car (bumper car)
碰碰车

64-66 pottery stand
陶器摊

64 barker
叫卖者

65 market woman
女商人

66 pottery
陶器

67 visitors to the fair
市集游客

68 waxworks
蜡制品陈列馆

69 wax figure
蜡像

1 treadle sewing machine
脚踏缝纫机

2 flower vase
花瓶

3 wall mirror
壁镜

4 cylindrical stove
圆筒形火炉

5 stovepipe
火炉烟囱

6 stovepipe elbow
烟囱弯肘（头）

7 stove door
炉门

8 stove screen
火炉围屏

9 coal scuttle
煤斗（装煤之容器）

10 firewood basket
柴篮（装柴火的篓子）

11 doll
洋娃娃

12 teddy bear
玩具熊

13 barrel organ
手摇风琴

14 orchestrion
自动风琴

15 metal disc (disk)
金属圆盘

16 radio (radio set, *joc.:* [steam radio]), a superheterodyne (superhet)
收音机，超外差式接收机

17 baffle board
隔音板

18 'magic eye', a tuning indicator valve
电眼，一种调谐指示管

19 loudspeaker aperture
喇叭孔

20 station selector buttons (station preset buttons)
电台选择按钮（电台预置按钮）

21 tuning knob
调谐旋钮

22 frequency bands
波段（刻度盘）

23 crystal detector (crystal set)
晶体检波器（晶体收音机）

24 headphones (headset)
耳机

25 folding camera
折叠式照相机

26 bellows
蛇腹

27 hinged cover
铰盖

28 spring extension
弹簧

29 salesman
店员

30 box camera
盒式照相机

31 gramophone
留声机

32 record (gramophone record)
唱片（留声机唱片）

33 needle head with gramophone needle
装有唱针之唱头

34 horn
留声机之喇叭

35 gramophone box
留声机箱

36 record rack
唱片架

37 portable tape recorder
手提式盒带录音机

38 flashgun
闪光枪

39 flash bulb
闪光灯泡

40-41 electronic flash (electronic flashgun)
电子闪光灯，电子闪光枪

40 flash head
闪光灯头

41 accumulator
蓄电池

42 slide projector
幻灯片放映机

43 slide holder
幻灯片托架

44 lamphouse
灯箱

45 candlestick
烛台

46 scallop shell
扇形贝壳

538

cutlery 餐具（刀、叉、匙等）	**63** sailor's hat 水手帽
souvenir plate 纪念盘	**64** washing set 洗脸用具
drying rack for photographic plates 感光板用之乾燥台	**65** washing basin 洗脸盆
photographic plate 照相板	**66** water jug 水罐
delayed-action release 延迟（时）放松器（装置）（自拍快门 线）	**67** washstand 脸盆架
tin soldiers (*sim.:* lead soldiers) 锡制士兵（类似於铅制士兵）	**68** dolly （洗衣用）搅拌棒，捣衣杵
beer mug (stein) 啤酒杯（壶）	**69** washtub 洗衣盆
bugle 号角（喇叭）	**70** washboard 洗衣板（洗衣搓板）
second-hand books 旧书	**71** humming top 起泡陀螺
grandfather clock 大型挂钟（有钟摆的）	**72** slate 石板（瓦）
clock case 钟壳	**73** pencil box 铅笔盒
pendulum 钟摆	**74** adding machine 计算机（加算机）
time weight 钟锤	**75** paper roll 纸卷
striking weight 报时钟锤	**76** number keys 数字键
rocking chair 摇椅	**77** abacus 算盘
sailor suit 水手服	**78** inkwell, with lid 带盖的墨水池
	79 typewriter 打字机

80 [hand-operated] calculating machine (calculator)
（手摇）计算机

81 operating handle
手摇杆

82 result register (product register)
结果记录器

83 rotary counting mechanism (rotary counter)
旋转计数器（回转计算装置）

84 kitchen scales
厨房用的天平

85 waist slip (underskirt)
衬裙

86 wooden handcart
木制手车

87 wall clock
挂钟，壁钟

88 bed warmer
床用取暖器

89 milk churn
牛乳桶（牛乳搅拌器）

1-13 film studios (studio complex, *Am.* movie studios)
电影制片厂
1 lot (studio lot)
电影摄影场
2 processing laboratories (film laboratories, motion picture laboratories)
显影（冲洗）室
3 cutting rooms
剪辑（接）室
4 administration building (office building, offices)
行政大楼
5 film (motion picture) storage vault (film library, motion picture library)
影片（电影）贮藏室，影片库
6 workshop
片场
7 film set (*Am.* movie set)
布景
8 power house
发电所（厂）
9 technical and research laboratories
技术研究（实验）室
10 groups of stages
摄影棚群（各种摄影棚）
11 concrete tank for marine sequences
特殊摄影（水中摄影）用之水泥槽
12 cyclorama
圆形风景画幕

13 hill
小丘
14-60 shooting (filming)
摄影
14 music recording studio (music recording theatre, *Am.* theater)
（音乐）录音室
15 [acoustic] wall lining
（吸）隔音墙板
16 screen (projection screen)
银幕（放映幕）
17 film orchestra
影片管弦乐团
18 exterior shooting (outdoor shooting, exterior filming, outdoor filming)
室外摄影，外景摄影
19 camera with crystal-controlled drive
晶体控制驱动之摄影机
20 cameraman
摄影师
21 assistant director
助理导演
22 boom operator (boom swinger)
麦克风吊杆操作人员
23 recording engineer (sound recordist)
录音技师
24 portable sound recorder with crystal-controlled drive
手提式晶体控制驱动之录音机
25 microphone boom
麦克风吊杆

26-60 shooting (filming) in the studio (on the sound stage, on the stage, in the filming hall)
摄影棚内之拍摄（录音棚，拍摄场，录影棚）
26 production manager
制片（制作人）
27 leading lady (film actress, film star, star)
女主角（女演员，电影明星）
28 leading man (film actor, film star, star)
男主角（男演员，电影明星）
29 film extra (extra)
临时演员
30 arrangement of microphones for stereo and sound effects
录立体声音响与音效用之麦克风配置
31 studio microphone
影棚麦克风
32 microphone cable
麦克风电线
33 side flats and background
背景及侧景屏
34 clapper boy
场记
35 clapper board (clapper) with slates (boards) for the film title, shot number (scene number), and take number
写有片名，镜号（景号），和镜头号之拍板
36 make-up artist (hairstylist)
化妆师（发形设计师）

1-46 sound recording and re-recording (dubbing)
录音与混合录音（配音）

1 magnetic sound recording equipment (magnetic sound recorder)
磁性带录音设备（磁性带录音机）

2 magnetic film spool
磁性片盘

3 magnetic head support assembly
磁头组件

4 control panel
控制板（台）

5 magnetic sound recording and playback amplifier
磁性带录音与放音扩大器

6 optical sound recorder (sound recording camera, optical sound recording equipment)
光学录音机（同步录音摄影机，光学录音设备）

7 daylight film magazine
（影）软片盒

8 control and monitoring panel
监控板

9 eyepiece for visual control of optical sound recording
光学录音装置之视觉控制目镜

10 deck
盖板

11 recording amplifier and mains power unit
录音扩大器与电源

12 control desk (control console)
控制（桌）台

13 monitoring loudspeaker (control loudspeaker)
监听喇叭

14 recording level indicators
录音平衡指示器

15 monitoring instruments
监听仪器

16 jack panel
插座板

17 control panel
控制板

18 sliding control
滑动控制

19 equalizer
平衡器

20 magnetic sound deck
磁（性）带音响台`

21 mixer for magnetic film
磁性软（影）片用之配音装置

22 film projector
影片放映机

23 recording and playback equipment
录音与放音设备

24 film reel (film spool)
片夹（片盘）

25 head support assembly for the recording head, playback head, and erasing head (erase head)
录音头，放音头及消磁头之支座组件

26 film transport mechanism
放片机器（影片输送装置）

27 synchronizing filter
（声音画面）同步滤波器

28 magnetic sound amplifier
磁性扩大器

29 control panel
控制板

30 film-processing machines (film-developing machines) in the processing laboratory (film laboratory, motion picture laboratory)
影片显（冲洗）像（实验）室中之影片显（冲洗）像机

1 echo chamber
回声室

2 echo chamber loudspeaker
回声喇叭

3 echo chamber microphone
回声室麦克风

4-36 sound mixing (sound
dubbing, mixing of several
sound tracks)
电影配音（配音，数条声带之混录）

4 mixing room (dubbing room)
配音室

5 mixing console (mixing desk) for
mono or stereo sound
单声立体声之配音混录台

6 dubbing mixers (recording
engineers, sound recordists)
dubbing (mixing)
（混录人员）配音员（录音师）

7-41 synchronization (syncing,
dubbing, post-synchronization,
post-syncing)
（声画）同步（后期同步录音）

7 dubbing studio (dubbing
theatre, Am. theater)
配音室

8 dubbing director
配音导演

9 dubbing speaker (dubbing
actress)
配音员

0 boom microphone
吊式麦克风

41 microphone cable
麦克风之电线

42-46 cutting (editing)
剪辑（接）

42 cutting table (editing table,
cutting bench)
剪辑台

43 film editor (cutter)
电影剪辑人员

44 film turntable, for picture and
sound tracks
影片画面与声带用之转盘

45 projection of the picture
影片放映

46 loudspeaker
喇叭

1-23 film projection (motion picture projection)
电影放映

1 cinema (picture house, *Am.* movie theater, movie house)
电影院

2 cinema box office (*Am.* movie theater box office)
电影院售票亭

3 cinema ticket (*Am.* movie theater ticket)
电影票

4 usherette
女引座员（女的座位导引员）

5 cinemagoers (filmgoers, cinema audience, *Am.* moviegoers, movie audience)
电影观众

6 safety lighting (emergency lighting)
太平灯（出口）灯

7 emergency exit
太平门

8 stage
舞台

9 rows of seats (rows)
座位的排号

10 stage curtain (screen curtain)
舞台的布幕（银幕）

11 screen (projection screen)
银幕

12 projection room (projection booth)
放映室

13 lefthand projector
左侧放映机

14 righthand projector
右侧放映机

15 projection room window with projection window and observation port
具放映窗口与监视口之放映室窗户

16 reel drum (spool box)
片筒，片盒

17 house light dimmers (auditorium lighting control)
戏院调光器（观众席灯光控制）

18 rectifier, a selenium or mercury vapour rectifier for the projection lamps
放映灯用的一种硒或汞汽整流器

19 amplifier
扩大器

20 projectionist
放映师

21 rewind bench for rewinding the film
影片之倒片台

22 film cement (splicing cement)
影片接著剂

23 slide projector for advertisements
放广告之幻灯机

24-52 film projectors
电影放映机

24 sound projector (film projector, cinema projector, theatre projector, *Am.* movie projector)
有声电影放映机

25-38 projector mechanism
放映机器

25 fireproof reel drums (spool boxes) with circulating oil cooling system
带循环油冷却装置之防火片盒

26 feed sprocket (supply sprocket)
供片齿轮

27 take-up sprocket
卷片齿轮

28 magnetic head cluster
磁头组件

29 guide roller (guiding roller) with framing control
画面调整之导轮

30 (loop former) for smoothing out the intermittent movement; *also:* film break detector
使影片间歇转动得以平滑进行之装置（亦称：影片中断检测器）

31 film path
片路（道）

32 film reel (film spool)
影片盘

33 reel of film
影片卷轮

34 film gate (picture gate, projector gate) with cooling fan
具冷却（风扇）装置之片门（放映机片窗）

35 projection lens (projector lens)
放映机镜头

36 feed spindle
供片主轴

37 take-up spindle with friction drive
磨擦转动之收片（卷片）主轴

38 maltese cross mechanism (maltese cross movement, Geneva movement)
十字间歇供（放）片装置

39-44 lamphouse
灯箱

39 mirror arc lamp, with aspherical (non-spherical) concave mirror and blowout magnet for stabilizing the arc (*also:* high-pressure xenon arc lamp)
反射弧光灯；稳定弧光用之非球面凹镜和消磁装置（高压氙弧灯）

40 positive carbon (positive carbon rod)
阳极碳棒

41 negative carbon (negative carbon rod)
阴极碳棒

42 arc
弧光

43 carbon rod holder
碳棒夹

44 crater (carbon crater)
弧坑（碳棒发火部分），火口

45 optical sound unit [also designed for multi-channel optical stereophonic sound and for push-pull sound tracks]
光学录音装置[为多声道光学立体声和推挽声带用之设计]

46 sound optics
音声用光学装置

47 sound head
声头

48 exciter lamp in housing
带罩框之激磁灯

49 photocell in hollow drum
装纳空心圆筒之光电管

50 attachable four-track magnetic sound unit (penthouse head, magnetic sound head)
附加之四轨磁性录音装置（拾音磁头和还音磁头）

51 four-track magnetic head
四轨磁头

52 narrow-gauge (*Am.* narrow-gage) cinema projector for mobile cinema
供流动电影院用之窄规电影放映机

1-39 motion picture cameras
(film cameras)
电影摄影机

1 standard-gauge (*Am.* standard-
gage) motion picture camera
(standard-gauge, *Am.* standard-
gage, 35 mm camera)
标准规格电影摄影机（35 毫米）

2 lens (object lens, taking lens)
（透镜）镜头（物镜，摄影镜头）

3 lens hood (sunshade) with matte
box
具其毛玻璃箱之遮光罩

4 matte (mask)
遮片

5 lens hood barrel
遮光罩筒

6 viewfinder eyepiece
取景器目镜

7 eyepiece control ring
目镜控制圈

8 opening control for the
segment disc (disk) shutter
扇形快门开度装置

9 magazine housing
软片盒

10 slide bar for the lens hood
镜头罩滑杆

11 control arm (control lever)
控制杆（操纵杆）

12 pan and tilt head
全景摄影之摇动旋钮

13 wooden tripod
木制三脚架

14 degree scale
刻度盘

15 soundproof (blimped) motion
picture camera (film camera)
隔音电影摄影机

16-18 soundproof housing (blimp)
隔音罩

16 upper section of the soundproof
housing
隔音罩之上部

17 lower section of the soundproof
housing
隔音罩之下部

18 open sidewall of the soundproof
housing
隔音罩之敞开侧壁

19 camera lens
摄影机镜头

20 lightweight professional motion
picture camera
专业用轻型摄影机

21 grip (handgrip)
柄，把手（手柄）

22 zooming lever
变焦杆

23 zoom lens (variable focus lens,
varifocal lens) with infinitely
variable focus
具无限可变焦点之变焦镜头（可变焦点
镜头）

24 handgrip with shutter release
快门开关手柄

25 camera door
摄影机门

26 sound camera (newsreel camera)
for recording sound and picture
声画同步摄影机（新闻摄影机）

27 soundproof housing (blimp)
隔音罩

28 window for the frame counters
and indicator scales
画面计算器与指示器刻度窗

29 pilot tone cable (sync pulse
cable)
导（频）音电缆（同步脉电缆）

30 pilot tone generator (signal
generator, pulse generator)
导（频）音发生器（信号发生器，脉波
发生器）

31 professional narrow-gauge (*Am.*
narrow-gage) motion picture
camera, a 16 mm camera
专业窄规（窄影片）电影摄影机（16 毫
米）

32 lens turret (turret head)
镜头转座

33 housing lock
机箱锁

34 eyecup
目镜罩

35 high-speed camera, a special
narrow-gauge (*Am.* narrow-
gage) camera
高速摄影机，一种特殊窄规的摄影机

36 zooming lever
变焦杆

37 rifle grip
肩托架

38 handgrip with shutter release
快门开关手柄

39 lens hood bellows
镜头遮光罩蛇腹

1-6 the five positions (ballet positions)
五种姿势（芭蕾舞姿势）
1 first position
第一种姿势
2 second position
第二种姿势
3 third position
第三种姿势
4 fourth position [open]
第四种姿势（展开式）
5 fourth position [crossed; extended fifth position]
第四种姿势（交叉式；伸展的第五种姿势）
6 fifth position
第五种姿势
7-10 ports de bras (arm positions)
手臂姿势
7 port de bras á coté
侧臂姿势
8 port de bras en bas
手臂朝下姿势
9 port de bras en avant
手臂朝前姿势
10 port de bras en haut
手臂在上姿势
11 dégagé á la quatriéme devant
伸向前第四种姿势
12 dégagé á la quatriéme derrière
伸向后第四种姿势
13 effacé
侧身面向观众之姿势
14 sur le cou-de-pied
将动作脚放于支撑脚之舞姿
15 écarté
侧身向旁抬腿之舞姿

16 croisé
侧身面向观众之交叉舞姿
17 attitude
一脚向后举（半弯曲）之姿式
18 arabesque
一脚向后伸直，一脚以脚尖点地，一手向前，一手向后伸之姿势
19 á pointe (on full point)
脚尖点地之舞姿（全脚尖）
20 splits
两腿分开成一直线之舞姿，劈叉
21 cabriole (capriole)
跳跃中以脚碰脚之姿势
22 entrechat (entrechat quatre)
轻跳（两脚在空中交叉或相碰之姿势）
23 préparation [e.g. for a pirouette]
旋转的预备姿势
24 pirouette
旋转
25 corps de ballet
芭蕾舞团
26 ballet dancer (ballerina)
芭蕾舞者（芭蕾女舞者）
27-28 pas de trois
三人舞
27 prima ballerina
芭蕾舞女主角
28 principal male dancer (leading soloist)
芭蕾舞男主角（主要独舞演员）
29 tutu
（芭蕾舞女演员穿的）短裙
30 point shoe, a ballet shoe (ballet slipper)
足尖鞋，芭蕾舞鞋

31 ballet skirt
芭蕾舞裙

1-4 types of curtain operation
舞台布幕操作之类型

1 draw curtain (side parting)
拉幕（由两侧分开型）

2 tableau curtain (bunching up sideways)
由中间向上方两角掀起之舞台幕（向两边迤摺型）

3 combined fly and draw curtain
悬吊式舞台幕（垂直上升）

4 combined fly and draw curtain
悬吊式与拉式混合型之舞台幕

5-11 cloakroom hall (*Am.* checkroom hall)
寄物处，衣帽间大厅

5 cloakroom (*Am.* checkroom)
寄物处

6 cloakroom attendant (*Am.* checkroom attendant)
寄物处服务员

7 cloakroom ticket (*Am.* check)
寄存号牌

8 playgoer (theatregoer, *Am.* theatergoer)
戏迷

9 opera glass (opera glasses)
观剧用之眼镜

10 commissionaire
门警

11 theatre (*Am.* theater) ticket, an admission ticket
戏票，入场券

12-13 foyer (lobby, crush room)
休息室（大厅，走廊）

12 usher; *form.:* box attendant
引座员；传统称呼：包厢服务员

13 programme (*Am.* program)
节目表

14-27 auditorium and stage
观众席与舞台

14 stage
舞台

15 proscenium
前舞台

16-20 auditorium
观众席

16 gallery (balcony)
顶层楼座（包厢）

17 upper circle
第三层楼座

18 dress circle (*Am.* balcony, mezzanine)
二楼特别座，[美]楼座包厢

19 front stalls
一楼正面前排座位（特别座）

20 seat (theatre seat, *Am.* theater seat)
座位（剧场座位）

21-27 rehearsal (stage rehearsal)
排演（舞台彩排）

21 chorus
合唱团

22 singer
歌手

23 singer
歌手（女）

24 orchestra pit
管弦乐队席

25 orchestra
管弦乐队

26 conductor
指挥

27 baton (conductor's baton)
指挥棒

28-42 paint room, a workshop
布景画室（工作房）

28 stagehand (scene shifter)
舞台工作人员，布景更换人员

29 catwalk (bridge)
狭小通道

30 set piece
道具

31 reinforcing struts
加固之斜间撑架

32 built piece (built unit)
制成之道具

33 backcloth (backdrop)
天幕，背景幕

34 portable box for paint containers
颜料容器之手提盒

35 scene painter
绘景师

36 paint trolley
绘画材料之手推车

37 stage designer (set designer)
舞台设计师

38 costume designer
服装设计师

39 design for a costume
服装设计

40 sketch for a costume
服装设计草图

41 model stage
舞台模型

42 model of the set
道具模型（布景模型）

43-52 dressing room
化妆间

43 dressing room mirror
化妆间镜子

44 make-up gown
化妆用外衣

45 make-up table
化妆台

46 greasepaint stick
化妆用涂油彩棒

47 chief make-up artist (chief make-up man)
主化妆师

48 make-up artist (hairstylist)
化妆师（发形设计师）

49 wig
假发

50 props (properties)
小道具（在英国含服装在内）

51 theatrical costume
剧装

52 call light
催场灯（招呼演员准备上台之指示灯）

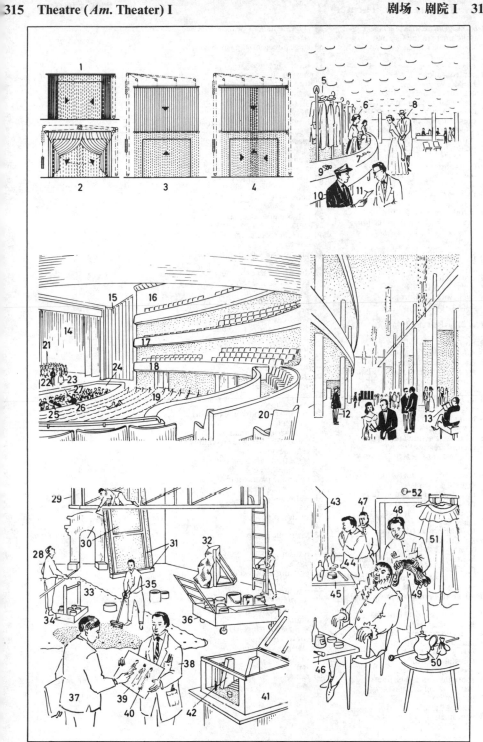

1-60 stagehouse with machinery
(machinery in the flies and
below stage)
有机械装置之舞台（舞台上空与台下之
机械装置）

1 control room
控制室

2 control console (lighting
console, lighting control
console) with preset control for
presetting lighting effects
（灯光台，灯光控制台）装有灯光效果
预置设备之灯光控制台

3 lighting plot (light plot)
灯光标示图

4 grip (gridiron)
格子顶棚（操纵垂幕之舞台天花板里之
装置）

5 fly floor (fly gallery)
悬吊长廊

6 sprinkler system for fire
prevention (for fire protection)
防火之洒水系统（防火装置）

7 fly man
舞台上方（顶棚）操纵大道具之人

8 fly lines (lines)
吊索

9 cyclorama
弧型背景画幕（大风景画幕）

10 backcloth (backdrop,
background)
背景幕

11 arch, a drop cloth
拱门吊幕

12 border
边幕（舞台上方悬挂之布景）

13 compartment (compartment-
type, compartmentalized) batten
(*Am.* border light)
隔间型边角灯光

14 stage lighting units (stage lights)
舞台灯光设置（舞台照明）

15 horizon lights (backdrop lights)
水平照明灯（背景灯）

16 adjustable acting area lights
(acting area spotlights)
可调整的舞台表演区照明灯（表演区聚
光灯）

17 scenery projectors (projectors)
布景（背景）之放映机

18 monitor (water cannon) (a piece
of safely equipment)
监控器（水枪）（一种安全装置）

19 travelling (*Am.* traveling)
lighting bridge (travelling
lighting gallery)
移动式照明灯廊（桥）

20 lighting operator (lighting man)
灯光师

21 portal spotlight (tower spotlight)
舞台口聚光灯（塔式聚光灯）

22 adjustable proscenium
可调整之舞台前部装置

23 curtain (theatrical curtain)
舞台幕（剧场台幕）

24 iron curtain (safety curtain, fire
curtain)
铁幕（安全幕，防火幕）

25 forestage (apron)
（舞台幕前部分）前舞台

26 footlight (footlights, floats)
脚灯（一舞台前端之照明设备）

27 prompt box
提词人隐藏位置

28 prompter
提词人

29 stage manager's desk
舞台监督工作桌

30 stage director (stage manager)
舞台监督

31 revolving stage
旋转舞台

32 trap opening
舞台活门之开口

33 lift (*Am.* elevator)
升降柏

34 bridge (*Am.* elevator), a rostrum
桥式升降台

35 pieces of scenery
道具

36 scene
舞台全景

37 actor
男演员

38 actress
女演员

39 extras (supers, supernumeraries)
临时演员（临时演员，小配角）

40 director (producer)
导演（制作人）

41 prompt book (prompt script)
提词本

42 director's table (producer's
table)
导演工作桌

43 assistant director (assistant
producer)
副导演（制作助理）

44 director's script (producer's
script)
导演用之剧本

45 stage carpenter
舞台木工

46 stagehand (scene shifter)
管理舞台布景之人员

47 set piece
道具

48 mirror spot (mirror spotlight)
反射聚光灯

49 automatic filter change (with
colour filters, colour mediums,
gelatines)
滤光镜自动转位装置（带有彩色滤光
片、彩色滤光板）

50 hydraulic plant room
水力装置（设备）室

51 water tank
水箱

52 suction pipe
吸水管

53 hydraulic pump
水泵

54 pressure pipe
水压管

55 pressure tank (accumulator)
水压箱（蓄水箱）

56 pressure gauge (*Am.* gage)
水压表

57 level indicator (liquid level
indicator)
水平指示器（液面指示器）

58 control lever
控制杆

59 operator
操作人员

60 rams
活塞

1 bar
  酒吧
2 barmaid
  酒吧女侍（吧枱女侍）
3 bar stool
  酒吧间凳子
4 shelf for bottles
  酒瓶架
5 shelf for glasses
  酒杯架
6 beer glass
  啤酒杯
7 wine and liqueur glasses
  葡萄酒及烈性酒酒杯
8 beer tap (tap)
  生啤酒之龙头（栓）
9 bar
  吧台
10 refrigerator (fridge, *Am.* icebox)
  冰箱（冰柜）
11 bar lamps
  酒吧间照明灯
12 indirect lighting
  间接照明
13 colour (*Am.* color) organ
  (clavilux)
  （灯光之）色彩机关
14 dancer floor lighting
  舞池照明
15 speaker (loudspeaker)
  喇叭（扬声器）
16 dance floor
  舞池

17-18 dancing couple
  一对舞伴
17 dancer
  跳舞者（女）
18 dancer
  跳舞者（男）
19 record player
  电唱机
20 microphone
  麦克风
21 tape recorder
  （磁带）盘式录音机
22-23 stereo system (stereo
  equipment)
  立体音响
22 tuner
  调谐器
23 amplifier
  扩大器
24 records (discs)
  唱片
25 disc jockey
  唱片节目主持人
26 mixing console (mixing desk,
  mixer)
  混频控制台
27 tambourine
  小手鼓（装有小铃之扁鼓）
28 mirrored wall
  镜壁
29 ceiling tiles
  天花板花砖
30 ventilators
  通风口

31 toilets (lavatories, WC)
  盥洗室（化妆室，厕所）
32 long drink
  高杯酒
33 cocktail (*Am.* highball)
  鸡尾酒

1-33 nightclub (night spot)
夜总会

1 cloakroom (*Am.* checkroom)
寄物处，衣帽间

2 cloakroom attendant (*Am.* checkroom attendant)
寄物处服务员

3 band
乐队

4 clarinet
竖笛

5 clarinettist (*Am.* clarinetist)
竖笛手

6 trumpet
小喇叭

7 trumpeter
小喇叭手

8 guitar
吉他

9 guitarist (guitar player)
吉他手

10 drums
鼓

11 drummer
鼓手

12 speaker (loudspeaker)
喇叭（扬声器）

13 bar
酒吧

14 barmaid
酒吧女侍（吧枱女侍）

15 bar
吧枱

16 bar stool
吧枱凳子

17 tape recorder
（磁带）盘式录音机

18 receiver
收音机

19 spirits
烈酒

20 cine-projector for porno films (sex films, blue movies)
色情影片用之放映机

21 box containing screen
装放映幕之箱子

22 stage
舞台

23 stage lighting
舞台灯光

24 spotlight
聚光灯

25 festoon lighting
绦灯照明设备

26 festoon lamp (lamp, light bulb)
绦灯灯泡

27-32 striptease act (striptease number)
脱衣舞表演

27 striptease artist (stripper)
脱衣舞女

28 suspender (*Am.* garter)
袜吊（袜带）

29 brassière (bra)
奶罩，（胸罩）

30 fur stole
软毛皮之长围巾

31 gloves
手套

32 stocking
长袜

33 hostess
女侍应生，女服务生

**1-33 bullfight (corrida, corrida
de toros)**
斗牛

1 mock bullfight
模拟斗牛

2 novillero
见习斗牛士

3 mock bull (dummy bull)
模拟牛

4 novice banderillero (apprentice
banderillero)
初次上场之斗牛士

5 bullring (plaza de toros)
[diagram]
斗牛场（图形）

6 main entrance
主要入口

7 boxes
包厢

8 stands
看台

9 arena (ring)
竞技场

10 bullfighters' entrance
斗牛士入场处

11 torril door
牡牛进场处

12 exit gate for killed bulls
死牛之出口

13 slaughterhouse
屠杀场

14 bull pens (corrals)
牛栏

15 paddock
围场（附有马廐之围场）

16 lancer on horseback (picador)
持矛斗牛士（骑马斗牛士）

17 lance (pike pole, javelin)
矛（标枪）

18 armoured (*Am.* armored) horse
著盔甲之马

19 leg armour (*Am.* armor)
护腿

20 picador's round hat
骑马斗牛士所戴之圆帽

21 banderillero, a torero
徒步斗牛士

22 banderillas (barbed darts)
带钩短矛

23 shirtwaist
短衬衫

24 bullfight
斗牛

25 matador (swordsman), a torero
徒步斗牛士

26 queue, a distinguishing mark of
the matador
发辫，斗牛士之明显标志

27 red cloak (capa)
斗牛士披的红色斗篷

28 fighting bull
被激怒之斗牛

29 montera [hat made of tiny
black silk chenille balls]
斗牛士所戴之黑丝绒球所制之帽

30 killing the bull (kill)
杀牛

31 matador in charity
performances [without
professional uniform]
表演之斗牛士〔未着斗牛士服装〕

32 estoque (sword)
剑

33 muleta
激怒牛用之红布

34 rodeo
牛仔竞技

35 young bull
小公牛

36 cowboy
牛仔

37 stetson (stetson hat)
宽边帽

38 scarf (necktie)
领巾

39 rodeo rider
竞技的骑士

40 lasso
套索

1-2 medieval (mediaeval) notes
中古式音符

1 plainsong notation (neumes, neums, pneumes, square notation)
无伴奏齐唱（单旋律圣歌记谱法，方形记谱法）

2 mensural notation
固定节奏记谱法

3-7 musical note (note)
音符

3 note head
符头

4 note stem (note tail)
符尾

5 hook
行钩

6 stroke
符桢

7 dot indicating augmentation of note's value
指示音符值增加的附点记号

8-11 clefs
谱号

8 treble clef (G-clef, violin clef)
高音谱号（G 谱号，小提琴谱号）

9 bass clef (F-clef)
低音谱号（F 谱号）

10 alto clef (C-clef)
中音谱号（C 谱号）

11 tenor clef
次中音谱号

12-19 note values
音值

12 breve (brevis, *Am.* double-whole note)
二全音符记号

13 semibreve (*Am.* whole note)
全音符记号

14 minim (*Am.* half note)
二分音符

15 crotchet (*Am.* quarter note)
四分音符

16 quaver (*Am.* eighth note)
八分音符

17 semiquaver (*Am.* sixteenth note)
十六分音符

18 demisemiquaver (*Am.* thirty-second note)
三十二分音符

19 hemidemisemiquaver (*Am.* sixty-fourth note)
六十四分音符

20-27 rests
休止符

20 breve rest
二全休止符

21 semibreve rest (*Am.* whole rest)
全休止符

22 minim rest (*Am.* half rest)
二分休止符

23 crotchet rest (*Am.* quarter rest)
四分休止符

24 quaver rest (*Am.* eighth rest)
八分休止符

25 semiquaver rest (*Am.* sixteenth rest)
十六分休止符

26 demisemiquaver rest (*Am.* thirty-second rest)
三十二分休止符

27 hemidemisemiquaver rest (*Am.* sixty-fourth rest)
六十四分休止符

28-42 time (time signatures, measure, *Am.* meter)
拍子（拍号）

28 two-eight time
八二拍

29 two-four time
四二拍

30 two-two time
二二拍

31 four-eight time
八四拍

32 four-four time (common time)
四四拍（普通拍子）

33 four-two time
二四拍

34 six-eight time
八六拍

35 six-four time
四六拍

36 three-eight time
八三拍

37 three-four time
四三拍

38 three-two time
二三拍

39 nine-eight time
八九拍

40 nine-four time
四九拍

41 five-four time
四五拍

42 bar (bar line, measure line)
小节线

43-44 staff (stave)
谱表（五线谱）

43 line of the staff
谱线

44 space
间（谱线之间）

45-49 scales
音阶

45 C major scale naturals: c, d, e, f, g, a, b, c
C 大音阶本位音：c, d, e, f, g, a, b, c

46 A minor scale [natural] naturals: a, b, c, d, e, f, g, a
（自然）小音阶本位音：a, b, c, d, e, f, g, a

47 A minor scale [harmonic]
和声小音阶

48 A minor scale [melodic]
旋律小音阶

49 chromatic scale
半音音阶

50-54 accidentals (inflections, key signatures)
临时记号（变音记号，调号）

50-51 signs indicating the raising of a note
升记号

50 sharp (raising the note a semitone or half-step)
升记号（升高半音记号）

51 double sharp (raising the note a tone or full-step)
重升记号（升高两个半音或一个全音记号）

52-53 signs indicating the lowering of a note
降记号

52 flat (lowering the note a semitone or half-step)
降记号（降低半音记号）

53 double flat (lowering the note a tone or full-step)
重降记号（降低两个半音或一个全音记号）

54 natural
还原记号（本位记号）

55-68 keys (major keys and the related minor keys having the same signature)
调子（大调与关系小调，符号相同）

55 C major (A minor)
C 大调（A 小调）

56 G major (E minor)
G 大调（E 小调）

57 D major (B minor)
D 大调（B 小调）

58 A major (F sharp minor)
A 大调（升 F 小调）

59 E major (C minor)
E 大调（C 小调）

60 B major (G sharp minor)
B 大调（升 G 小调）

61 F sharp major (D sharp minor)
升 F 大调（升 D 小调）

62 C major (A minor)
C 大调（A 小调）

63 F major (D minor)
F 大调（D 小调）

64 B flat major (G minor)
降 B 大调（G 小调）

65 E flat major (C minor)
降 E 大调（C 小调）

66 A flat major (F minor)
降 A 大调（F 小调）

67 D flat major (B flat minor)
降 D 大调（降 B 小调）

68 G flat major (E flat minor)
降 G 大调（降 E 小调）

1-5 chord
和弦
1-4 triad
三和弦
1 major triad
大三和弦
2 minor triad
小三和弦
3 diminished triad
减三和弦
4 augmented triad
增三和弦
5 chord of four notes, a chord of
the seventh (seventh chord,
dominant seventh chord)
由四个音叠置而成的七和弦（七和弦，
属七和弦）
6-13 intervals
音程
6 unison (unison interval)
一度（同度）音程
7 major second
大二度
8 major third
大三度
9 perfect fourth
完全四度
10 perfect fifth
完全五度
11 major sixth
大六度
12 major seventh
大七度
13 perfect octave
完全八度
14-22 ornaments (graces, grace
notes)
装饰音（装饰音，装饰音符）
14 long appoggiatura
长倚音
15 acciaccatura (short
appoggiatura)
碎音（短倚音）
16 slide
滑音
17 trill (shake) without turn
无回音之震音
18 trill (shake) with turn
有回音之震音
19 upper mordent (inverted
mordent, pralltriller)
上涟音
20 lower mordent (mordent)
下涟音
21 turn
回音
22 arpeggio
琶音
23-26 other signs in musical
notation
乐谱中其他记号
23 triplet; *corresponding groupings:*
duplet (couplet), quadruplet,
quintuplet, sextolet (sextuplet),
septolet (septuplet, septimole)
三连音；相应之连音符：二连音，四连
音，五连音，六连音，七连音
24 tie (bind)
连接线，延音线
25 pause (pause sign)
停留记号，延长记号
26 repeat mark
反复记号
27-41 expression marks (signs of
relative intensity)
表情记号（关系强度记号）

27 marcato (marcando, markiert,
attack, strong accent)
加强记号（强音）
28 presto (quick, fast)
急板（快板）
29 portato (mezzo staccato,
carried)
断奏（连续断奏，带连线的跳音）
30 tenuto (held)
持音
31 crescendo (increasing gradually
in power)
渐强（音量逐渐加强）
32 decrescendo (diminuendo,
decreasing or diminishing
gradually in power)
渐弱（音量逐渐减弱或消失）
33 legato (bound)
圆滑唱（连音）
34 staccato (detached)
断奏，断唱（断音）
35 piano (soft)
弱（柔音）
36 pianissimo (very soft)
很弱
37 pianissimo piano (as soft as
possible)
最弱（尽可能的弱）
38 forte (loud)
强
39 fortissimo (very loud)
很强
40 forte fortissimo (double
fortissimo, as loud as possible)
最强（倍强，尽可能的强）
41 forte piano (loud and
immediately soft again)
强弱（开始强，立刻弱）
42-50 divisions of the compass
音域划分
42 subcontra octave (double contra
octave)
第二列低八度
43 contra octave
中央 C 起低八度
44 great octave
大八度（五个全音二个半音）
45 small octave
小八度（五个全音一个半音）
46 one-line octave
中央 C 算起高八度
47 two-line octave
第二列高八度
48 three-line octave
第三列高八度
49 four-line octave
第四列高八度
50 five-line octave
第五列高八度

1 lur, a bronze trumpet
喇叭，青铜制喇叭

2 panpipes (Pandean pipes, syrinx)
排箫

3 aulos, a double shawm
奥鲁管（双簧吹奏乐器）

4 aulos pipe
奥鲁管的管身

5 phorbeia (peristomion, capistrum, mouth band)
双簧吹奏口缘

6 crumhorn (crummhorn, cromorne, krumbhorn, krummhorn)
克鲁姆双簧管

7 recorder (fipple flute)
英国八孔直笛（直笛同类乐器）

8 bagpipe; *sim.*: musette
风笛（类似法国之小风笛）

9 bag
风袋，风囊

10 chanter (melody pipe)
风笛之笛管

11 drone (drone pipe)
风笛之低音管

12 curved cornett (zink)
弧形短号

13 serpent
蛇形号

14 shawn (schalmeyes); *larger:* bombard (bombarde, pommer)
双簧管（中世纪用之奥博管）；较大型乐器：一种老式双簧管乐器

15 cythara (cithara); *sim. and smaller;* lyre
吉他拉琴（竖琴之一种）；同类较小乐器：里拉琴（古希腊）

16 arm
扶手

17 bridge
琴马

18 sound box (resonating chamber, resonator)
音箱（共鸣室，共鸣器）

19 plectrum, a plucking device
（弹奏弦乐器用的）拨子或弦拨

20 kit (pochette), a miniature violin
袖珍小提琴（小型小提琴）

21 cittern (cithern, cither, cister, citole), a plucked instrument; *sim.*: pandora (bandora, bandore)
西特琴，一种拨弦乐器；类似：潘朵拉琴（类似吉他之古代弦乐器）

22 sound hole
音孔

23 viol (descant viol, treble viol), a viola da gamba; *larger:* tenor viol, bass viol (viola da gamba, gamba), violone (double bass viol)
（六弦提琴，维奥尔）古提琴（高音提琴），一种置於腿上拉的提琴；较大型的：中音提琴，低音提琴，低音大提琴

24 viol bow
琴弓

25 hurdy-gurdy (vielle á roue, symphonia, arominie, organistrum)
摇弦琴

26 friction wheel
磨擦杆（轮）

27 wheel cover (wheel guard)
杆盖（轮盖）

28 keyboard (keys)
琴键

29 resonating body (resonator, sound box)
共鸣体（共鸣器，共鸣箱）

30 melody strings
旋律琴弦

31 drone strings (drones, bourdons)
低音弦

32 dulcimer
扬琴

33 rib (resonator wall)
弦乐器侧边（共鸣壁）

34 beater for the Valasian dulcimer
瓦拉辛扬琴所用之制音器

35 hammer (stick) for the Appenzell dulcimer
阿彭塞耳扬琴之琴槌

36 clavichord; *kinds:* fretted or unfretted clavichord
（击弦）（克拉维卡）古钢琴；种类：有琴格或无琴格之翼琴

37 clavichord mechanism
击弦古钢琴之内部构造（琴键）

38 key (key lever)
琴键

39 balance rail
平衡杆

40 guiding blade
导杆片

41 guiding slot
导沟（导槽）

42 resting rail
支撑杆

43 tangent
切音铜块（板）

44 string
琴弦

45 harpsichord (clavicembalo, cembalo), a wing-shaped stringed keyboard instrument; *sim.*: spinet (virginal)
（拨弦）（哈普西卡）古钢琴，一种翼形拨弦之键盘乐器；同类钢琴有：史宾奈古钢琴与维京奈古钢琴

46 upper keyboard (upper manual)
上排键盘（上排手键盘）

47 lower keyboard (lower manual)
下排键盘（下排手键盘）

48 harpsichord mechanism
拨弦古钢琴之内部构造（琴键）

49 key (key lever)
琴键（键杆）

50 jack
钢琴动力杆

51 slide (register)
滑杆（音栓）

52 tongue
琴舌

53 quill plectrum
羽管琴拨

54 damper
制音器

55 string
弦

56 portative organ, a portable organ; *larger:* positive organ (positive)
轻便之风琴；较大型同类的乐器：positive 风琴

57 pipe (flue pipe)
唇管（琴管之气孔）

58 bellows
风箱

1-62 orchestral instruments
管弦乐器

1-27 stringed instruments, bowed instruments
弦乐器，弓弦乐器

1 violin
小提琴

2 neck of the violin
琴颈

3 resonating body (violin body, sound box of the violin)
共鸣体（琴身，音箱）

4 rib (side wall)
小提琴边板（边条板）

5 violin bridge
琴马

6 F-hole, a sound hole
F 孔，一种音孔

7 tailpiece
系弦板

8 chin rest
颚托

9 strings (violin strings, fiddle strings); G-string, D-string, A-string, E-string
弦（小提琴弦）：G 弦，D 弦，A 弦，E 弦

10 mute (sordino)
弱音器

11 resin (rosin, colophony)
松脂，松香（弓弦乐器用）

12 violin bow (bow)
琴弓

13 nut (frog)
弦枕，弓根

14 stick (bow stick)
弓杆

15 hair of the violin bow (horsehair)
弓毛（马毛，通常为白色马尾）

16 violoncello (cello), a member of the da gamba violin family
大提琴，低音提琴之一种

17 scroll
（弦乐器之）漩涡状琴头

18 tuning peg (peg)
琴轸

19 pegbox
琴轸头

20 nut
弦枕

21 fingerboard
指板

22 spike (tailpin)
尾部调弦栓

23 double bass (contrabass, violone, double bass viol, *Am.* bass)
低音提琴（低音提琴，低音大提琴）

24 belly (top, soundboard)
弦乐器之面板（琴面，音板）

25 rib (side wall)
边板（边条板）

26 purfling (inlay)
镶边

27 viola
中提琴

28-38 woodwind instruments (woodwinds)
木管乐器

28 bassoon; *larger:* double bassoon (contrabassoon)
低音管，较大型之同类乐器：倍低音管

29 tube with double reed
双簧吹奏管口

30 piccolo (small flute, piccolo flute, flauto piccolo)
短笛

31 flute (German flute), a cross flute (transverse flute, side-blown flute)
长笛（德国笛），一种横笛

32 key
键

33 fingerhole
指孔

34 clarinet; *larger:* bass clarinet
单簧管（竖笛）；较大型之同类乐器：低音单簧管

35 key (brille)
键

36 mouthpiece
吹口

37 bell
喇叭口

38 oboe (hautboy); *kinds:* oboe d'amore; tenor oboes: oboe da caccia, cor anglais; heckelphone (baritone oboe)
（奥博管）双簧管，种类有：柔音管；次中音管：猎管，英国管；赫克管（上低音管）

39-48 brass instruments (brass)
铜管乐器

39 tenor horn
次中音号

40 valve
活塞（通指铜管乐器上之变音装置）

41 French horn (horn, waldhorn), a valve horn
有活塞的法国号（号，无键号）

42 bell
喇叭口

43 trumpet; *larger:* B♭ cornet; *smaller:* cornet
小号（小喇叭）；较大型之同类乐器：降 B 大调短号；较小型同类乐器：短号

44 bass tuba (tuba, bombardon); *sim.:* helicon (pellitone), contrabass tuba
士巴低音号（士巴号），本巴敦低音号；同类乐器：低音号；倍低音士巴号

45 thumb hold
拇指把位（孔）

46 trombone; *kinds:* alto trombone, tenor trombone, bass trombone
长号（伸缩喇叭）；种类：中音长号，次中音长号，低音长号

47 trombone slide (slide)
长号之伸缩管（U 型）

48 bell
喇叭口

49-59 percussion instruments
打击乐器

49 triangle
三角铁

50 cymbals
钹

51-59 membranophones
膜鸣乐器

51 side drum (snare drum)
小鼓

52 drum head (head, upper head, batter head, vellum)
鼓皮[上鼓面，敲击鼓面，犊皮（小羊皮）鼓面]

53 tensioning screw
紧鼓螺丝

54 drumstick
鼓槌（棒）

55 bass drum (Turkish drum)
大鼓（土耳其鼓）

56 stick (padded stick)
鼓槌（击鼓大槌）

57 kettledrum (timpano), a screw-tensioned drum; *sim.:* machine drum (mechanically tuned drum)
定音鼓，一种以螺丝调音之鼓；同类乐器：机械式定音鼓

58 kettledrum skin (kettledrum vellum)
定音鼓鼓面（皮）

59 tuning screw
调音螺丝

60 harp, a pedal harp
竖琴，踏板竖琴

61 strings
弦

62 pedal
踏板

1-46 popular musical instruments (folk instruments)
通俗乐器（民间乐器）

1-31 stringed instruments
弦乐器

1 lute; *large:* theorbo, chitarrone
鲁特琴；较大型的有：泰奥博琴，吉他
隆琴

2 resonating body (resonator)
共鸣体（共鸣器）

3 soundboard (belly, table)
音板（面板，琴板）

4 string fastener (string holder)
系弦板

5 sound hole (rose)
音孔（圆花饰）

6 string, a gut (catgut) string
弦，一种猫肠弦

7 neck
琴颈

8 fingerboard
指板

9 fret
琴格（指板上之格，划分音阶之用）

10 head (bent-back pegbox, swanhead pegbox, pegbox)
琴头（弓背琴轸斗，天鹅头琴轸斗，琴
轸斗）

11 tuning peg (peg, lute pin)
调音琴轸

12 guitar
吉他（琴）

13 string holder
系弦板

14 string, a gut (catgut) or nylon string
弦，猫肠弦或尼龙弦

15 resonating body (resonating chamber, resonator, sound box)
共鸣体（共鸣室，共鸣器，音箱）

16 mandolin (mandoline)
曼陀林琴

17 sleeve protector (cuff protector)
弦扣

18 neck
琴颈

19 pegdisc
琴轸

20 plectrum
琴拨，拨子

21 zither (plucked zither)
齐特琴（拨弦齐特琴）

22 pin block (wrest pin block, wrest plank)
弦栓板（调音弦栓板，调音键板）

23 tuning pin (wrest pin)
调音弦栓

24 melody strings (fretted strings, stopped strings)
旋律琴弦（有音品之琴弦，闭奏弦）

25 accompaniment strings (bass strings, unfretted strings, open strings)
伴奏琴弦（低音弦，无音品琴弦，空
弦）

26 semicircular projection of the resonating sound box (resonating body)
突出半圆形之共鸣箱（共鸣体）

27 ring plectrum
环形琴拨

28 balalaika
俄式三弦琴（类似吉他之俄国弦琴）

29 banjo
班究琴（亦名五弦琴）

30 tambourine-like body
铃鼓式琴身

31 parchment membrane
羊皮纸膜

32 ocarina, a globular flute
洋埙，一种球状之笛

33 mouthpiece
吹口

34 fingerhole
指孔

35 mouth organ (harmonica)
口琴

36 accordion; *sim.:* piano accordion, concertina, bandoneon
手风琴；同类乐器有：轻便手风琴，六
角手风琴，小六角手风琴

37 bellows
风箱（蛇腹送风器）

38 bellows strap
送风箱停止带

39 melody side (keyboard side, melody keys)
旋律键盘部分

40 keyboard (keys)
键盘

41 treble stop (treble coupler, treble register)
高音音栓［高音音键，高音音栓（整调
器）］

42 stop lever
音栓杆（变音器）

43 bass side (accompaniment side, bass studs, bass press-studs, bass buttons)
低音部分（伴奏部分，低音音键）

44 bass stop (bass coupler, bass register)
低音音栓［低音键，低音音栓（整调
器）］

45 tambourine
铃鼓

46 castanets
响板

47-78 jazz band instruments (dance band instruments)
爵士乐队乐器（舞蹈乐器乐器）

47-58 percussion instruments
打击乐器

47-54 drum kit (drum set, drums)
一套鼓器

47 bass drum
大鼓

48 small tom-tom
小印度鼓

49 large tom-tom
大印度鼓

50 high-hat cymbals (choke cymbals, Charleston cymbals, cup cymbals)
礼貌式钹（高领钹，查尔斯顿钹，杯
形钹）

51 cymbal
钹

52 cymbal stand (cymbal holder)
钹架

53 wire brush
铜丝刷

54 pedal mechanism
踏板装置

55 conga drum (conga)
康茄鼓

56 tension hoop
紧箍环

57 timbales
定音鼓

58 bongo drums (bongos)
（古巴乐器之）小鼓

59 maracas; *sim.:* shakers
响葫芦；同类乐器摇荡器

60 guiro
（拉丁美洲）打击乐器

61 xylophone; *form.:* straw fiddle; *sim.:* marimbaphone (steel marimba), tubaphone
木琴；同类乐器有：马林巴木琴，低音
木琴

62 wooden slab
木片（板）

63 resonating chamber (sound box)
共鸣室（音箱）

64 beater
槌

65 jazz trumpet
爵士小号

66 valve
活塞（变音装置）

67 finger hook
指钩

68 mute (sordino)
弱音器

69 saxophone
萨克管

70 bell
喇叭口

71 crook
变音管

72 mouthpiece
吹口

73 struck guitar (jazz guitar)
弹奏式吉他（爵士吉他）

74 hollow to facilitate fingering
便於手指弹奏之凹瓦

75 vibraphone (*Am.* vibraharp)
钟琴

76 metal frame
金属座架

77 metal bar
金属条

78 tubular metal resonator
管状金属共鸣器

1 **piano** (pianoforte, upright piano, upright, vertical piano, spinet piano, console piano), a keyboard instrument (keyed instrument); *smaller forms:* cottage piano (pianino); *earlier form:* pantaleon, celesta, with steel bars instead of strings
钢琴（直立式钢琴，小型立式古钢琴，风琴式钢琴，一种键盘乐器；较小型的形式：竖式小钢琴；早期的形式：以钢条替代弦的发音之潘塔龙琴与钢片琴）

2-18 piano action (piano mechanism)
钢琴之机械装置

2 iron frame
铁骨架

3 hammer; *collectively:* striking mechanism
琴槌；总称：击槌装置

4-5 keyboard (piano keys)
键盘（钢琴琴键）

4 white key (ivory key)
白键（象牙键）

5 black key (ebony key)
黑键（乌木键）

6 piano case
琴身板（钢琴琴箱）

7 strings (piano strings)
琴弦（钢琴琴弦）

8-9 piano pedals
钢琴踏板

8 right pedal (sustaining pedal, damper pedal; *loosely:* forte pedal, loud pedal) for raising the dampers
提起制音器之右踏板（支撑踏板，制音踏板；俗称：强音踏板）

9 left pedal (soft pedal; *loosely:* piano pedal) for reducing the striking distance of the hammers on the strings
减少琴槌在琴弦上之打击距离之左踏板（柔音踏板；俗称：弱音踏板）

10 treble strings
高音琴弦

11 treble bridge (treble belly bridge)
高音琴马

12 bass strings
低音琴弦

13 bass bridge (bass belly bridge)
低音琴马

14 hitch pin
系弦钉

15 hammer rail
琴槌杆

16 brace
支架

17 tuning pin (wrest pin, tuning peg)
调音弦钉（调音键，调音琴轸）

18 pin block (wrest pin block, wrest plank)
弦栓板（调音弦栓板，调音键板）

19 metronome
节拍机

20 tuning hammer (tuning key, wrest)
调音槌

21 tuning wedge
调音楔（正音楔）

22-39 key action (key mechanism)
琴键之机械装置

22 beam
梁

23 damper-lifting lever
制音器提杆

24 felt-covered hammer head
以毛毡包裹之琴槌头

25 hammer shank
槌柄

26 hammer rail
槌杆

27 check (back check)
校音器（后校音器）

28 check felt (back check felt)
校音器毡（后校音器毡）

29 wire stem of the check (wire stem of the back check)
校音器之铁丝杆

30 sticker (hopper, hammer jack, hammer lever)
顶杆（提高琴槌之装置）

31 button
音栓

32 action lever
连动杆

33 pilot
导杆

34 pilot wire
导杆线（铁丝）

35 tape wire
拘束带线（铁丝）

36 tape
拘束带

37 damper (damper block)
制音器（制音器块）

38 damper lifter
制音器提杆

39 damper rest rail
制音器架

40 **grand piano** (horizontal piano, grand, concert grand); *smaller:* baby grand piano, boudoir piano; *sim.:* square piano, table piano
大钢琴（平台钢琴，演奏会用钢琴）；较小型之同类乐器有：小型平台鋼琴，闺房鋼琴；其他形式：方型鋼琴，枱式钢琴

41 grand piano pedals; right pedal for raising the dampers; left pedal for softening the tone (shifting the keyboard so that only one string is struck [una corda] one)
大钢琴踏板；提起制音器用之右踏板；柔音用的左踏板（使用柔音踏板时，只有一弦受击发音，称之"乌那科达"的）

42 pedal bracket
踏板木架

43 **harmonium** (reed organ, melodium)
簧风琴

44 draw stop (stop, stop knob)
拉栓（音栓，音栓旋纽）

45 knee lever (knee swell, swell)
增音器

46 pedal (bellows pedal)
踏板（风箱踏板）

47 harmonium case
簧风琴外箱

48 harmonium keyboard (manual)
簧风琴键板

1-52 organ (church organ)
管风琴（教堂风琴）
1-5 front view of organ (organ
case) [built according to
classical principles]
管风琴正面图（琴身）[依古典原理制造]
1-3 display pipes (face pipes)
正面音管
1 Hauptwerk
主音管
2 Oberwerk
独奏音管（上部音管）
3 pedal pipes
持续音管
4 pedal tower
持续音塔
5 Rückpositiv
合奏音管
6-16 tracker action (mechanical
action); *other systems:*
pneumatic action, electric ation
连杆机械装置；其他形式：气动装置，
电动装置
6 draw stop (stop, stop knob)
拉栓
7 slider (slide)
滑杆（滑动部分）
8 key (key lever)
琴键（琴键杆）
9 sticker
木杆
10 pallet
空气调节阀

11 wind trunk
风道，送风管
12-14 wind chest, a slider wind
chest; *other types:* sliderless wind
chest (unit wind chest), spring
chest, kegellade chest (cone
chest), diaphragm chest
风腔（箱），一种滑杆风腔（箱），其
他种类：无滑杆风腔（箱）（单一装置
风箱），弹簧式风腔（箱），圆锥式风
腔（箱），膜片风腔（箱）
12 wind chest (wind chest box)
风腔（风箱）下部
13 groove
（音板）风槽
14 upper board groove
上板风槽
15 upper board
上板
16 pipe of a particular stop
特别音栓之音管
17-35 organ pipes (pipes)
风琴音管
17-22 metal reed pipe (*set of pipes:*
reed stop), a posaune stop
金属簧管（音管设备：簧音栓），一种
长号音栓
17 boot
音管套
18 shallot
声管簧管
19 tongue
簧片

20 block
塞块
21 tuning wire (tuning crook)
调音管
22 tube
共鸣管
22-30 open metal flue pipe, a
salicional
金属开口音管，一种萨尔纳唇管
23 foot
管座
24 flue pipe windway (flue pipe
duct)
开口音管，风道
25 mouth (cutup)
吹口
26 lower lip
下簧片
27 upper lip
上簧片
28 languid
簧片
29 body of the pipe (pipe)
管体
30 tuning flap (tuning tongue), a
tuning device
调音簧片（调音簧舌），一种调音装置

33 open wooden flue pipe (open wood), principal (diapason)
木制开口音管，管风琴的主要音栓（笛亚巴松音栓）
cap
音管盖
ear
管耳
tuning hole (tuning slot), with slide
滑板调音孔
stopped flue pipe
闭奏音管
stopper
闭奏栓
52 organ console (console) of an electric action organ
电子琴之操作部分
music rest (music stand)
乐谱架
crescendo roller indicator
音量渐加强之圆形指示器
voltmeter
电压计
stop tab (rocker)
音栓片
free combination stud (free combination knob)
自由组合键（旋纽）
cancel buttons for reeds, couplers etc.
簧管、联动装置用之止栓钮
manual I, for the Rückpositiv
第一键盘，伴奏键盘

43 manual II, for the Hauptwerk
第二键盘，主音管键盘
44 manual III, for the Oberwerk
第三键盘，上部音管键盘
45 manual IV, for the Schwellwerk
第四键盘，增音键盘
46 thumb pistons controlling the manual stops (free or fixed combinations) and buttons for setting the combinations
由扭指活塞控制的键盘音栓（自由或设定组合），和调节组合的按钮
47 switches for current to blower and action
电动送风开关
48 toe piston, for the coupler
脚控联动装置活塞
49 crescendo roller (general crescendo roller)
渐强音量滚轴
50 balanced swell pedal
音乐调节板
51 pedal key [natural]
踏板键（本位者）
52 pedal key [sharp or flat]
踏板键（升高者或降低音）
53 cable (transmission cable)
（输电）电缆

1-61 fabulous creatures (fabulous animals), mythical creatures
神话中之动物

1 dragon
龙

2 serpent's body
蛇身

3 claws (claw)
爪

4 bat's wing
蝙蝠翅膀

5 fork-tongued mouth
叉舌嘴

6 forked tongue
叉状舌

7 unicorn [symbol of virginity]
独角兽〔纯洁的象征〕

8 spirally twisted horn
螺旋状独角

9 Phoenix
凤凰（长生鸟）

10 flames or ashes of resurrection
复活（燃）之火焰与灰烬

11 griffin (griffon, gryphon)
鹰头狮身带翅膀怪兽

12 eagle's head
鹰头

13 griffin's claws
鹰头狮身兽之爪

14 lion's body
狮身

15 wing
翅膀

16 chimera (chimaera), a monster
狮头羊身蛇尾之吐火兽，一种怪兽

17 lion's head
狮头

18 goat's head
羊头

19 dragon's body
龙身

20 sphinx, a symbolic figure
人头狮身怪物，一种象征性的形象

21 human head
人头

22 lion's body
狮身

23 mermaid (nix, nixie, water nixie, sea maid, sea maiden, naiad, water numph, water elf, ocean nymph, sea nymph, river nymph); *sim.:* Nereids, Oceanids (sea divinities, sea deities, sea goddesses); *male:* nix (merman, seaman)
人鱼，美人鱼（水妖，女水妖，海上仙女，保护河、湖泉水之仙女）；类似：海中仙女，海中女神（海神，女海神）；雄性：水鬼，水妖（人鱼）

24 woman's trunk
女人身躯

25 fish's tail (dolphin's tail)
鱼尾（海豚尾）

26 Pegasus (favourite, *Am.* favorite, steed of the Muses, winged horse); *sim.:* hippogryph
飞马（缪司女神最喜爱之马，有翼之马）；类似：马身鹫头，长翅膀之怪物

27 horse's body
马身

28 wings
翅膀

29 Cerberus (hellhound)
冥府门狗（蛇尾，三狗头之怪物）（地狱之犬）

30 three-headed dog's body
三头之狗身

31 serpent's tail
蛇尾

32 Lernaean (Lernean) Hydra
近 Argos 市湖，沼泽之九头怪蛇

33 nine-headed serpent's body
九头蛇身

34 basilisk (cockatrice)
传说非洲沙漠之似龙与蛇之怪物

35 cock's head
鸡头

36 dragon's body
龙身

37 giant (titan)
巨人（泰坦神，太阳神）

38 rock
岩石

39 serpent's foot
蛇足

40 triton, a merman (demigod of the sea)
半人鱼之海神，雄人鱼（海中之半人半神）

41 conch shell trumpet
响螺（螺号）

42 horse's hoof
马蹄

43 fish's tail
鱼尾

44 hippocampus
马头鱼尾之怪兽

45 horse's trunk
马之躯干

46 fish's tail
鱼尾

47 sea ox, a sea monster
海牛，一种海怪

48 monster's body
海怪的躯体

49 fish's tail
鱼尾

50 seven-headed dragon of St. John's Revelation (Revelations, Apocalypse)
圣约翰启示录中之七头龙

51 wing
翅膀

52 centaur (hippocentaur), half man and half beast
人头马身之怪物，半人半兽

53 man's body with bow and arrow
拿著弓箭之人的躯体

54 horse's body
马身

55 harpy, a winged monster
鸟身人头之女妖，带翅膀之怪物

56 woman's head
女人头

57 bird's body
鸟身

58 siren, a daemon
女海妖，半人半鸟女妖

59 woman's body
女人身

60 wing
翅膀

61 bird's claw
鸟爪

1-40 prehistoric finds
史前时期之发现物

1-9 Old Stone Age (Palaeolithic, Paleolithic period) and **Mesolithic period**
旧石器时代和中石器时代

1 hand axe (*Am.* ax) (fist hatchet), a stone tool
手斧，一种石制工具

2 head of throwing spear, made of bone
由骨头所制的投掷矛头

3 bone harpoon
骨制鱼叉

4 head
斧头之头部

5 harpoon thrower, made of reindeer antler
由鹿角所制之鱼叉投掷器

6 painted pebble
彩色之小石块

7 head of a wild horse, a carving
野马头，一种雕刻品

8 Stone Age idol, an ivory statuette
石器时代之崇拜偶像，象牙彫象

9 bison, a cave painting (rock painting) [cave art, cave painting]
野牛，一幅洞穴绘画（岩石画）（洞穴艺术，洞穴画）

10-20 New Stone Age (Neolithic period)
新石器时代

10 amphora [corded ware]
双耳瓶（绳纹陶器）

11 bowl [menhir group]
体（史前时期巨石类）

12 collared flask [Funnel-Beaker culture]
带颈环之长颈瓶（古代杯斗文化）

13 vessel with spiral pattern [spiral design pottery]
带有螺旋花纹之器皿（螺旋花饰陶器）

14 bell beaker [beaker pottery]
钟形杯（杯形陶器）

15 pile dwelling (lake dwelling, lacustrine dwelling)
木桩房子（湖边桩屋，湖上桩屋）

16 dolmen (cromlech), a megalithic tomb (*coll.:* giant's tomb); *other kinds:* passage grave, gallery grave (long cist); *when covered with earth:* tumulus (barrow, mound)
都尔门（古代墓址）（环状列石），一种巨石的坟墓；其他种类：长廊墓（长箱形石坟）；用土复盖的称为：塚

17 stone cist, a contracted burail
石棺，一种简陋之葬法

18 menhir (standing stone), a monolith
纪念之巨石柱（立石），一种巨石碑

19 boat axe (*Am.* ax), a stone battle axe
船形斧，一种石制战斧

20 clay figurine (an idol)
陶土之小塑像，一种偶像

21-40 Bronze Age and **Iron Age;** *epochs:* Hallstatt period, La Téne period
青铜器时代和铁器时代；包括初期铁器时期，后期铁器时期

21 bronze spear head
青铜矛头

22 hafted bronze dagger
带柄之青铜短剑

23 socketed axe (*Am.* ax) with haft fastened to rings, a bronze axe
柄栓紧於环上之套筒斧，一种青铜斧

24 girdle clasp
带饰钩

25 necklace (lunula)
颈饰（新月形颈饰）

26 gold neck ring
金颈环

27 violin-bow fibula (safety pin)
乐弓式之扣针（安全别针）

28 serpentine fibula; *other kinds:* boat fibula, arc fibula
蛇形扣针；其他种类：船形扣针，弧形扣针

29 bulb-head pin, a bronze pin
大头别针，一种青铜别针

30 two-piece spiral fibula; *sim.:* disc (disk) fibula
双片之螺旋形扣针；类似：圆盘形扣针

31 hafted bronze knife
带柄之青铜刀

32 iron key
铁钥匙

33 ploughshare (*Am.* plowshare)
犁头

34 sheet-bronze situla, a funerary vessel
青铜水桶，一种随葬器皿

35 pitcher [chip-carved pottery]
有柄水罐（粗刻陶器）

36 miniature ritual cart (miniature ritual chariot)
小型仪式车

37 Celtic silver coin
居尔特银币

38 face urn, a cinerary urn; *other kinds:* domestic urn, embossed urn
人面形骨灰坛，骨灰坛；其他形式：家用坛，布有浮雕之坛

39 urn grave in stone chamber
石室裡的骨灰坛埋葬

40 urn with cylindrical neck
圆筒颈之骨灰坛

1 **knight's castle** (castle)
骑士（武士）城堡
2 **inner ward** (inner bailey)
内城墙（内壁）
3 draw well
汲水井
4 keep (donjon)
城楼（城堡的主楼）
5 dungeon
地牢
6 battlements (crenellation)
城垛（枪眼设备）
7 merlon
枪眼与枪眼间之凸壁
8 tower platform
塔顶平台
9 watchman
了望哨
10 ladies' apartments (bowers)
妇女的房间
11 dormer window (dormer)
老虎窗（屋顶斜面凸出之天窗）
12 balcony
阳台，骑楼
13 storehouse (magazine)
仓库（城堡之弹药库）
14 angle tower
角塔，角楼
15 curtain wall (curtains, enclosure wall)
城墙
16 bastion
稜堡
17 angle tower
角楼
18 crenel (embrasure)
枪眼（楔形之枪眼）
19 inner wall
内墙
20 battlemented parapet
城垛之胸墙
21 parapet (breastwork)
胸墙（胸壁）
22 gatehouse
门楼
23 machicolation (machicoulis)
（中世纪城堡凸出於人口的）堞眼，枪口
24 portcullis
格子吊闸（古城堡可升降之铁闸门，吊门）
25 drawbridge
吊桥
26 buttress
拱壁，扶壁
27 offices and service rooms
公务服务间
28 turret
角楼
29 chapel
小教堂
30 great hall
大厅，大会堂
31 outer ward (outer bailery)
外城墙（外壁）
32 castle gate
城门
33 moat (ditch)
城壕（壕沟）
34 approach
入口
35 watchtower (turret)
了望台（角楼）
36 palisade (pallisade, palisading)
栅栏
37 moat (ditch, fosse)
城壕（壕沟）

38-65 **knight's armour** (*Am.* armor)
骑士（武士）之甲胄（盔甲）
38 suit of armour (*Am.* armor)
整套甲胄（盔甲）
39-42 helmet
头盔
39 skull
盔顶
40 visor (vizor)
（盔之）面颊
41 beaver
（遮防下巴之）半面甲
42 throat piece
护喉
43 gorget
领甲
44 epauliére
肩甲
45 pallette (pauldron, besageur)
肩臂甲
46 breastplate (cuirass)
胸甲
47 brassard (rear brace and vambrace)
臂铠（后臂甲与前臂甲）
48 cubitiére (cubitiére, couter)
肘甲
49 tasse (tasset)
腿甲
50 gauntlet
护手
51 habergeon (haubergeon)
无袖铠甲
52 cuisse (cuish, cuissard, cuissart)
大腿甲
53 knee cap (knee piece, genouillére, poleyn)
护膝甲
54 jambeau (greave)
护胫套
55 solleret (sabaton, sabbaton)
铁靴
56 pavis (pavise, pavais)
大盾
57 buckler (round shield)
圆盾
58 boss (umbo)
（盾中心之）星标
59 iron hat
铁帽
60 morion
无面甲之头盔
61 light casque
轻便盔
62 types of mail and armour (*Am.* armor)
铠甲，甲胄之类型
63 mail (chain mail, chain armour, *Am.* armor)
锁子甲，链甲
64 scale armour (*Am.* armor)
鳞片甲
65 plate armour (*Am.* armor)
板片甲
66 **accolade** (dubbing, knighting)
骑士爵位之授礼仪式
67 liege lord, a knight
君主，武士之一种
68 esquire
后补骑士
69 cup bearer
上酒者，司酒者
70 minstrel (minnesinger, troubadour)
贵族所养之歌手，吟游诗人

71 **tournament** (tourney, joust, just, tilt)
（中世纪骑士的）马上比武
72 crusader
十字军战士
73 Knight Templar
圣堂武士
74 caparison (trappings)
装饰用马衣马饰
75 herald (marshal at tournament)
传令官（马上比赛之司令官）
76 tilting armour (*Am.* armor)
马上比武之武器，盔甲（装备）
77 tilting helmet (jousting helmet)
马上比武之头盔
78 panache (plume of feathers)
羽饰（头盔上之装饰羽毛）
79 tilting target (tilting shield)
马上比武用之小圆盾
80 lance rest
甲胄胸铠上支撑矛柄之处
81 tilting lance (lance)
马上比武用之长矛
82 vamplate
矛柄上之护手金属板
83-88 horse armour (*Am.* armor)
马之护具
83 neck guard (neck piece)
护颈甲
84 chamfron (chaffron, chafron, chamfrain, chanfron)
马头甲，马之面甲
85 poitrel
马前胸甲
86 flanchard (flancard)
马腹护甲
87 tournament saddle
马上比武用之马鞍
88 rump piece (quarter piece)
臀部甲片

1-30 Protestant church
（基督教）复原教堂

1 chancel
圣所（高坛）

2 lectern
诵经台

3 altar carpet
坛毯

4 altar (communion table, Lord's table, holy table)
圣坛（圣餐桌）

5 altar steps
圣坛台阶

6 altar cloth
圣坛台布

7 altar candle
蜡烛

8 pyx (pix)
圣饼盒

9 paten (patin, patine)
圣饼碟

10 chalice (communion cup)
圣餐杯

11 Bible (Holy Bible, Scriptures, Holy Scripture)
圣经

12 altar crucifix
耶稣受难像

13 altarpiece
圣坛后之画像

14 church window
教堂窗户

15 stained glass
彩色玻璃

16 wall candelabrum
壁上分枝烛台

17 vestry door (sacristy door)
圣器室门

18 pulpit steps
讲道坛阶梯

19 pulpit
讲道坛

20 antependium
圣坛前之装饰，帷幔

21 canopy (soundboard sounding board)
华盖，坛座罩篷（装於讲坛上使声音响亮之响板）

22 preacher (pastor, vicar, clergyman, rector) in his robes (vestments, canonicals)
身著长袍（礼服、法衣）之讲道人（牧师、助理牧师、教区长）

23 pulpit balustrade
讲道坛之栏杆

24 hymn board showing hymn numbers
有赞美诗编号之告示牌

25 gallery
边座、楼座

26 verger (sexton, sacristan)
教堂司事（教堂司事，圣器收藏室管理人）

27 aisle
通道

28 pew; collectively: pews (seating)
教堂之座席（座位）

29 churchgoer (worshippper); collectively: congregation
做礼拜者（敬拜者）集体：会众

30 hymn book
赞美诗

31-62 Roman Catholic church
罗马天主教教会

31 altar steps
圣坛台阶

32 presbytery (choir, chancel, sacrarium, sanctuary)
（教堂之）内室，牧师席，司祭席（教士或唱诗班席位，圣所，教堂之内殿）

33 altar
圣坛

34 altar candles
圣坛蜡烛

35 altar cross
圣坛十字架

36 altar cloth
台布

37 lectern
读经台

38 missal (mass book)
弥撒用书（祈祷书）

39 priest
神父

40 server
辅祭

41 sedilia
司祭席（内圣坛之南侧）

42 tabernacle
圣体柜

43 stele (stela)
刻有碑纹之石柱石碑

44 paschal candle (Easter candle)
复活节蜡烛

45 paschal candlestick (Easter candlestick)
复活节烛台

46 sanctus bell
三圣颂铃

47 processional cross
行列圣歌之十字架

48 altar decoration (foliage, flower arrangement)
圣坛装饰（植物，花之布置）

49 sanctuary lamp
教堂内殿灯（圣灯）

50 altarpiece, a picture of Christ
耶稣之画像

51 Madonna, statue of the Virgin Mary
圣母像

52 pricket
烛台

53 votive candles
还愿蜡烛

54 station of the Cross
耶稣受难像

55 offertory box
奉献箱

56 literature stand
书架

57 literature (pamphlets, tracts)
宗教书（宗教小册子）

58 verger (sexton, sacristan)
教堂司事（圣器守司，圣堂杂物员）

59 offertory bag
奉献袋

60 offering
奉献物

61 man praying
祈祷之教徒

62 prayer book
祈祷书

1 **church**
　教堂

2 steeple
　尖塔

3 weathercock
　验风器（通常状如雄鸡，亦称风信鸡）

4 weather vane (wind vane)
　风标，风信旗

5 apex
　塔尖

6 church spire (spire)
　教堂尖塔

7 church clock (tower clock)
　教堂时钟

8 belfry window
　钟楼窗户

9 electrically operated bell
　电动大钟

10 ridge cross
　屋脊上之十字架

11 church roof
　教堂屋顶

12 memorial chapel
　追思礼拜室

13 vestry (sacristy), an annexe
　(annex)
　圣器收藏室，一种加建之建筑

14 memorial tablet (memorial
　plate, wall memorial, wall stone)
　纪念碑（墙上纪念碑，墙上石碑）

15 side entrance
　侧门

16 church door (main door, portal)
　教堂大门

17 churchgoer
　做礼拜的人

18 graveyard wall (churchyard
　wall)
　墓地围墙（墓地围墙）

19 graveyard gate (churchyard
　gate, lichgate, lychgate)
　墓地大门（墓地大门，有顶盖之墓地
　门）

20 vicarage (parsonage, rectory)
　牧师住宅

21-41 **graveyard** (churchyard,
　God's acre, *Am.* burying
　ground)
　墓园（墓地）

21 mortuary
　停尸间

22 grave digger
　挖墓人

23 grave (tomb)
　坟墓

24 grave mound
　坟堆

25 cross
　十字架

26 gravestone (headstone,
　tombstone)
　墓碑（墓石）

27 family grave (family tomb)
　家族墓地

28 graveyard chapel
　墓园小教堂

29 child's grave
　童墓

30 urn grave
　骨灰瓮坟墓

31 urn
　骨灰瓮

32 soldier's grave
　军人墓

33-41 funeral (burial)
　葬礼

33 mourners
　送葬者

34 grave
　墓穴

35 coffin (*Am.* casket)
　棺木

36 spade
　铲子

37 clergyman
　牧师

38 the bereaved
　遗族

39 widow's veil, a mourning veil
　未亡人面纱，服丧面纱

40 pallbearers
　护柩者，棺侧送葬者

41 bier
　棺架

42-50 **procession** (religious
　procession)
　宗教之送葬行列仪式

42 processional crucifix
　送葬行列的耶稣受难像

43 cross bearer (crucifer)
　执十字架者

44 processional banner, a church
　banner
　送葬行列所用教堂之旗帜

45 acolyte
　辅祭

46 canopy bearer
　持幕盖者

47 priest
　神父

48 monstrance with the Blessed
　Sacrament (consecrated Host)
　盛载圣体之圣体架（神圣的圣体）

49 canopy (baldachin, baldaquin)
　幕盖（天盖，织锦）

50 nuns
　修女

51 participants in the procession
　参加送葬行列者

52-58 **monastery**
　修道院

52 cloister
　迴廊

53 monastery garden
　花园

54 monk, a Benedictine monk
　修道士，本笃会修教士

55 habit (monk's habit)
　道服（修道士之道服）

56 cowl (hood)
　（修道服上之）头巾

57 tonsure
　剃发，剃去头发之部分

58 breviary
　每日祈祷书（日课经）

59 **catacomb,** an early Christian
　underground burial place
　地下墓窖，早期基督教徒之地下埋葬所

60 niche (tomb recess, arcosolium)
　壁龛（坟墓壁龛龛）

61 stone slab
　石板

1 Christian baptism
(christening)
基督教之洗礼（施洗）
2 baptistery (baptistry)
洗礼所，洗礼堂
3 Protestant clergyman
复原派牧师
4 robes (vestments, canonicals)
礼袍，法衣
5 bands
宽领带
6 collar
衣领
7 child to be baptized (christened)
受洗之小孩
8 christening robe (christening
dress)
洗礼服
9 christening shawl
洗礼围巾
10 font
圣水器
11 font basin
洗礼盘
12 baptismal water
圣水，洗礼水
13 godparents
教父，教母
14 church wedding (wedding
ceremony, marriage ceremony)
教堂婚礼（结婚仪式）
15-16 bridal couple
新婚夫妻
15 bride
新娘
16 bridegroom (groom)
新郎
17 ring (wedding ring)
结婚戒子
18 bride's bouquet (bridal bouquet)
新娘的花束
19 bridal wreath
新娘之花冠
20 veil (bridal veil)
披纱（新娘的披纱）
21 buttonhole
钮孔，插於衣襟钮孔的花束
22 clergyman
牧师
23 witnesses [to the marriage]
婚礼之见证人
24 bridesmaid
女宾相
25 kneeler
跪垫，跪台
26 Holy Communion
圣餐
27 communicants
领受圣餐者
28 Host (wafer)
圣瓶
29 communion cup
圣餐杯
30 rosary
念珠（玫瑰经）
31 paternoster
念珠串里颂主祷文时的大珠子
32 Ave Maria; *set of 10:* decade
福哉玛丽亚，十粒珠子一串（组）
33 crucifix
耶稣受难像
34-54 liturgical vessels
(ecclesiastical vessels)
礼仪用之器皿（教会的器皿）
34 monstrance
圣体显供架

35 Host (consecrated Host, Blessed
Sacrament)
圣体（祝圣之圣体，祝圣餐）
36 lunula (lunule)
新月形圣体容器
37 rays
放射状之饰物
38 censer (thurible), for offering
incense (for incensing)
香炉，放置奉献用之香料
39 thurible chain
香炉链
40 thurible cover
香炉盖
41 thurible bowl
香炉钵
42 incense boat
香碗
43 incense spoon
香匙
44 cruet set
一组盛酒或水之壶（圣餐用）
45 water cruet
水瓶
46 wine cruet
酒瓶
47 holy water basin
圣水盒
48 ciborium containing the sacred
wafers
装圣饼之容器
49 chalice
圣餐杯
50 dish for communion wafers
装圣饼之盘子
51 paten (patin, patine)
圣体碟
52 altar bells
圣坛用铃
53 pyx (pix)
圣饼盒
54 aspergillum
洒水器
55-72 forms of Christian crosses
基督教十字架的各种类型
55 Latin cross (cross of the
Passion)
拉丁式十字架（耶稣受难十字架）
56 Greek cross
希腊式十字架
57 Russian cross
俄罗斯式十字架
58 St. Peter's crosss
圣彼得十字架
59 St. Anthony's cross (tau cross)
圣安东尼十字架（T型十字架）
60 St. Andrew's cross (saltire
cross)
圣安德鲁十字架（X型十字架）
61 Y-cross
Y型十字架
62 cross of Lorraine
洛林十字架
63 ansate cross
圆头十字架
64 patriarchal cross
大主教用之十字架
65 cardinal's cross
枢机主教用之十字架
66 Papal cross
教皇用十字架
67 Constantinian cross, a
monogram of Christ (CHR)
康斯坦丁十字架，由基督名字组合而成
之十字架

68 crosslet
小十字架（徽章式）
69 cross moline
锚形十字架
70 cross of Jerusalem
耶路撒冷十字架
71 cross botonnée (cross treflée)
三斜式十字架（各端呈叶状之十字架）
72 fivefold cross (quintuple cross)
五重式十字架

1-18 Egyptian art
埃及艺术
1 pyramid, a royal tomb
金字塔，王室坟墓
2 king's chamber
国王墓穴
3 queen's chamber
王后墓穴
4 air passage
风道，风路
5 coffin chamber
棺室
6 pyramid site
金字塔遗迹
7 funerary temple
葬礼堂
8 valley temple
谷形神殿
9 pylon, a monumental gateway
塔门，纪念碑入口
10 obelisks
方尖石塔
11 Egyptian sphinx
埃及狮身人面像
12 winged sun disc (sun disk)
带翼日轮图案
13 lotus column
莲花饰柱
14 knob-leaf capital (bud-shaped
capital)
球形瓣饰柱头（苞蕾形柱头）
15 papyrus column
纸草花饰图案之圆柱
16 bell-shaped capital
钟型柱头
17 palm column
棕榈形圆柱
18 ornamented column
饰像圆柱
19-20 Babylonian art
巴比伦艺术
19 Babylonian frieze
巴比伦屋簷下饰带
20 glazed relief tile
釉面浮雕瓷砖
21-28 art of the Persians
波斯艺术
21 tower tomb
塔形墓
22 stepped pyramid
阶形金字塔
23 double bull column
双牛饰柱
24 projecting leaves
突出之叶瓣
25 palm capital
棕榈形柱头
26 volute (scroll)
涡形装饰（花纹）
27 shaft
柱身
28 double bull capital
双牛饰柱头
29-36 art of the Assyrians
亚述艺术
29 Sargon's Palace, palace
buildings
萨尔冈王宫，宫殿建筑
30 city wall
城之外壁
31 castle wall
城堡围墙
32 temple tower (ziggurat), a
stepped (terraced) tower
神庙塔楼（亚述塔式建筑），一种阶形
（梯形）塔楼

33 outside staircase
王宫外阶梯
34 main portal
正门
35 portal relief
正门浮雕
36 portal figure
正门雕像
37 art of Asia Minor
小亚细亚艺术
38 rock tomb
石墓

1-48 Greek art
希腊艺术
1-7 the Acropolis
雅典之卫城
1 the Parthenon, a Doric temple
帕德嫩神庙，一种都利亚式神庙
2 peristyle
寺院外柱
3 pediment
（山形墙，三角墙）山形建筑正面
4 crepidoma (stereobate)
柱基（墙基，屋基）
5 statue
雕像
6 temple wall
神庙围墙
7 propylaea
神殿入口
8 Doric column
都利亚式柱
9 Ionic column
爱奥尼亚式柱
10 Corinthian column
哥林多式柱
11-14 cornice
飞簷
11 cyma
（波状花边）反曲线脚
12 corona
台口线
13 mutule
（都利亚式簷饰）外簷头
14 dentils
齿形（装）饰
15 triglyph
三竖线花纹装饰（三槽板饰）
16 metope, a frieze decoration
（都利亚建筑屋簷下的）墙面，柱间
壁，横饰带之装饰
17 regula
三槽板纹饰下之短型楞条
18 epistyle (architrave)
台轮（嵌线之最底部）
19 cyma (cymatium, kymation)
波形纹线脚反曲线脚
20-25 capital
柱头
20 abacus
圆柱冠板（顶板）
21 echinus
凸圆线脚
22 hypotrachelium (gorgerin)
柱顶凹槽（柱头房），柱颈
23 volute (scroll)
涡形饰
24 volute cushion
涡形装饰之垫层
25 acanthus
反叶饰（叶形柱头装饰）
26 column shaft
柱身
27 flutes (grooves, channels)
凹圆柱饰（圆柱上之凹槽）
28-31 base
柱基
28 [upper] torus
（上部）凸圆线脚
29 trochilus (concave moulding, *Am.* molding)
凹圆线脚
30 [lower] torus
（下部）凸圆线脚
31 plinth
基脚，柱脚
32 stylobate
柱基

33 stele (stela)
石碑
34 acroterion (acroterium, acroter)
碑顶之雕刻饰物（像墩子，吻座）
35 herm (herma, hermes)
刻有 Hermes 神像之石碑
36 caryatid; *male:* Atlas
刻有女像之柱；刻有男像之柱：称 Atlas
37 Greek vase
希腊花瓶
38-43 Greek ornamentation (Greek decoration, Greek decorative designs)
希腊装饰图案
38 bead-and-dart moulding (*Am.* molding), an ornamental band
串珠线脚，一种装饰带
39 running dog (Vitruvian scroll)
涡形条纹
40 leaf ornament
叶形饰
41 palmette
棕榈叶饰
42 egg and dart (egg and tongue, egg and anchor) cyma
蛋形与尖状之反曲线脚
43 meander
迂迴花纹（蟠螭）
44 Greek theatre (*Am.* theater)
希腊剧场
45 scene
幕
46 proscenium
（舞台前部）前台
47 orchestra
舞台前乐队席
48 thymele (altar)
舞台前之讲坛
49-52 Etruscan art
伊特拉士坎艺术
49 Etruscan temple
伊特拉士坎神庙
50 portico
门廊，柱廊
51 cella
内殿
52 entablature
柱顶线盘
53-60 Roman art
罗马艺术
53 aqueduct
输水道（桥）
54 conduit (water channel)
水道
55 centrally-planned building (centralized building)
集中式建筑
56 portico
门廊，柱廊
57 reglet
接缝嵌线
58 cupola
圆顶
59 triumphal arch
凯旋门
60 attic
阁楼
61-71 Early Christian art
早期基督教艺术
61 basilica
巴西里佳（长方形之会堂，用于法庭，集会）巴西里佳风格之教堂
62 nave
（教堂之）本堂
63 aisle
（教堂之）侧廊

64 apse
教堂东首半圆形室
65 campanile
钟楼
66 atrium
前庭（天井）
67 colonnade
柱廊
68 fountain
喷泉
69 altar
祭坛
70 clerestory (clearstory)
高窗
71 triumphal arch
凯旋式拱门
72-75 Byzantine art
拜占庭艺术
72-73 dome system
（圆顶）穹顶系统
72 main dome
主穹顶
73 semidome
半球形顶
74 pendentive
穹隅
75 eye, a lighting aperture
穹顶上之孔眼，采光孔

1-21 Romanesque art
罗马式建筑艺术
1-13 Romanesque church, a
cathedral
罗马式教堂，天主教教堂之一种
1 nave
（教堂之）本堂，中殿（廊）
2 aisle
侧廊
3 transept
翼廊
4 choir (chancel)
圣坛所
5 apse
教堂东首半圆形室
6 central tower (*Am.* center
tower)
主楼
7 pyramidal tower roof
锥形塔顶
8 arcading
连环拱
9 frieze of round arcading
圆形连环拱之壁缘
10 blind arcade (blind arcading)
暗连环拱
11 lesene, a pilaster strip
壁柱
12 circular window
圆形墙
13 side entrance
侧门
14-16 Romanesque ornamentation
(Romanesque decoration,
Romanesque decorative designs)
罗马式之装饰图案
14 chequered (*Am.* checkered)
pattern (chequered design)
棋格式图案
15 imbrication (imbricated design)
鱼鳞式图案
16 chevron design
锯齿形图案
17 Romanesque system of vaulting
罗马式之拱形系统
18 transverse arch
拱门横架
19 barrel vault (tunnel vault)
半圆（隧道）形拱顶
20 pillar
柱（撑柱）
21 cushion capital
垫形柱头
22-41 Gothic art
哥德式艺术
22 Gothic church [westwork, west
end, west facade], a cathedral
哥德式教堂〔西首建筑区；西端，西部
正面〕，天主教堂之一种
23 rose window
圆花窗
24 church door (main door, portal),
a recessed portal
教堂正门（主门），一种凹形门
25 archivolt
门饰缘
26 tympanum
三角形门楣
27-35 Gothic structural system
哥德式建筑系统
27-28 buttresses
撑墙
27 buttress
撑墙
28 flying buttress
浮拱壁

29 pinnacle
小尖塔，尖顶
30 gargoyle
（承霤口）滴水口
31-32 cross vault (groin vault)
交叉拱顶
31 ribs (cross ribs)
（交叉）拱肋
32 boss (pendant)
悬饰（浮雕）
33 triforium
拱廊（拱门与高窗间部分）
34 clustered pier (compound pier)
柱墩
35 respond (engaged pillar)
半柱（附墙柱）
36 pediment
山形建筑正面
37 finial
尖顶饰
38 crocket
卷叶花样或卷花形之浮雕
39-41 tracery window, a lancet
window
窗格花窗户，一种尖形窗
39-40 tracery
窗饰，窗格花
39 quatrefoil
四叶饰
40 cinquefoil
五叶饰
41 mullions
中框
42-54 Renaissance art
文艺复兴时期艺术
42 Renaissance church
文艺复兴时期教堂
43 projection, a projecting part of
the building
凸台建筑物之凸出部分
44 drum
鼓形柱座
45 lantern
顶塔
46 pilaster (engaged pillar)
壁柱（附墙柱）
47 Renaissance palace
文艺复兴时期之宫殿
48 cornice
飞簷
49 pedimental window
山形窗
50 pedimental window with round
gable
弧形窗
51 rustication (rustic work)
毛面砌石（粗工建筑）
52 string course
层拱，蛇腹层
53 sarcophagus
石棺
54 festoon (garland)
垂花饰

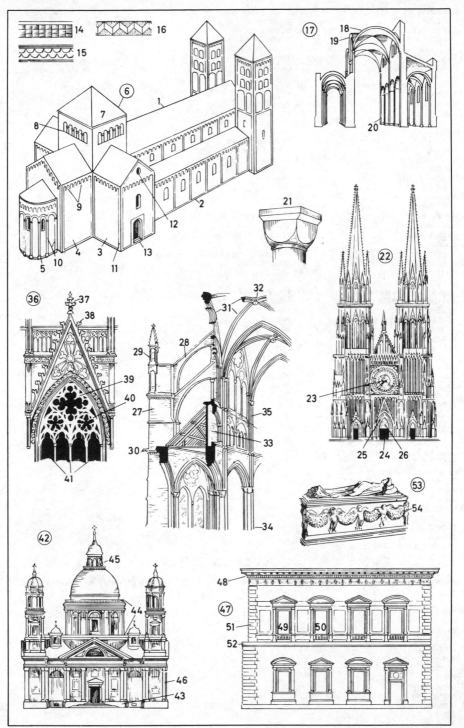

1-8 Baroque art
巴洛克艺术
1 Baroque church
巴洛克式教堂
2 bull's eye
圆窗
3 bulbous cupola
球形圆顶
4 dormer window (dormer)
老虎窗（天窗）
5 curved gable
弧形山墙
6 twin columns
双圆柱
7 cartouche
装饰镜板
8 scrollwork
涡卷装饰
9-13 Rococo art
洛可可艺术
9 Rococo wall
洛可可式墙壁
10 coving, a hollow moulding (*Am.* molding)
凹型线脚，壁带
11 framing
骨架装饰
12 ornamental moulding (*Am.* molding)
花样装饰
13 rocaille, a Rococo ornament
由贝壳或鹅卵石制的装饰，一种洛可可式的装饰
14 table in Louis Seize style (Louis Seize table)
路易十六式的桌子
15 neoclassical building (building in neoclassical style), a gateway
新古典式建筑，市门之一种
16 Empire table (table in the Empire style)
帝国式之桌子
17 Biedermeier sofa (sofa in the Biedermeier style)
彼德麦样式的沙发（19世纪前半德国家具式样之一种）
18 Art Nouveau easy chair (easy chair in the Art Nouveau style)
法国新艺术派之安乐椅
19-37 types of arch
拱门的样式
19 arch
拱门
20 abutment
支柱，墩柱
21 impost
拱门支柱
22 springer, a voussoir (wedge stone)
起拱石，一种拱石（楔石）
23 keystone
拱顶石
24 face
砌面
25 pier
方柱
26 extrados
拱背，外弧线
27 round arch
半圆拱
28 segmental arch (basket handle)
弧形拱
29 parabolic arch
抛物线拱
30 horseshoe arch
马蹄拱
31 lancet arch
尖顶拱
32 trefoil arch
三叶拱
33 shouldered arch
肩形拱
34 convex arch
凸形拱
35 tented arch
帐篷式拱
36 ogee arch (keel arch)
葱花（莲花）拱（龙骨拱）
37 Tudor arch
都铎式拱门
38-50 types of vault
拱形屋顶之样式
38 barrel vault (tunnel vault)
半圆（隧道）形拱顶
39 crown
冠状
40 side
顶侧面
41 cloister vault (cloistered vault)
迴廊拱顶
42 groin vault (groined vault)
穹窿拱顶
43 rib vault (ribbed vault)
穹棱拱顶
44 stellar vault
星状拱顶
45 net vault
网状拱顶
46 fan vault
扇状拱顶
47 trough vault
槽式拱顶
48 trough
槽
49 cavetto vault
凹形拱顶
50 cavetto
中凹处

1-6 Chinese art
中国艺术

1 pagoda (multi-storey, multistory, pagoda), a temple tower
宝塔（多层），一种庙塔

2 storey (story) roof (roof of storey)
塔顶

3 pailou (pailoo), a memorial archway
牌楼，一种纪念性的拱道（门）

4 archway
拱道

5 porcelain vase
瓷花瓶

6 incised lacquered work
漆雕艺术

7-11 Japanese art
日本艺术

7 temple
庙

8 bell tower
钟塔

9 supporting structure
支架

10 bodhisattva (boddhisattva), a Buddhist saint
菩萨，佛

11 torii, a gateway
神社前之牌坊

12-18 Islamic art
伊斯兰（回）教艺术

12 mosque
清真寺

13 minaret, a prayer tower
（回教寺院的）尖塔

14 mihrab
诵经龛

15 minbar (mimbar, pulpit)
讲经坛

16 mausoleum, a tomb
陵墓

17 stalactite vault (stalactitic vault)
钟乳饰圆顶

18 Arabian capital
阿拉伯式柱头

19-28 Indian art
印度艺术

19 dancing Siva (Shiva), an Indian god
湿婆、婆罗门教中一主神，司破坏，拯救之神

20 statue of Buddha
释迦牟尼像

21 stupa (Indian pagoda), a mound (dome), a Buddhist shrine
佛骨塔，舍利塔（印尼塔），一种圆顶土墩，佛龛

22 umbrella
伞形顶

23 stone wall (*Am.* stone fence)
石墙

24 gate
门

25 temple buildings
寺庙建筑

26 shikara (sikar, sikhara, temple tower)
锡克教庙塔

27 chaitya hall
神庙大殿厅

28 chaitya, a small stupa
佛塔，小型之佛骨塔

1-43 studio
画室

1 studio skylight
画室天窗

2 painter, an artist
画家，美术家

3 studio easel
画架

4 chalk sketch, a rough draft
以粉笔所绘素描，草图

5 crayon (piece of chalk)
蜡笔（一支粉笔）

6-19 painting materials
绘画用具

6 flat brush
平头画笔

7 camel hair brush
骆驼毛画笔

8 round brush
圆头画笔

9 priming brush
底色用画笔

10 box of paints (paintbox)
颜料盒

11 tube of oil paint
油画颜料管

12 varnish
油漆

13 thinner
稀释液

14 palette knife
调色刀

15 spatula
抹刀，油漆刀

16 charcoal pencil (charcoal, piece of charcoal)
炭笔

17 tempera (gouache)
不透明颜料（不透明水彩颜料）

18 watercolour (*Am.* watercolor)
水彩颜料

19 pastel crayon
粉腊笔

20 wedged stretcher (canvas stretcher)
张开画布的框（油画框）

21 canvas
油画布

22 piece of hardboard, with painting surface
硬质油画纸板

23 wooden board
木质板

24 fibreboard (*Am.* fiberboard)
纤维板（硬纸板）

25 painting table
颜料桌

26 folding easel
折叠式画架

27 still life group, a motif
静物组合，主题

28 palette
调色板

29 palette dipper
调色杯

30 platform
模特儿台

31 lay figure (mannequin, manikin)
人体模型

32 nude model (model, nude)
裸（人）体模特儿

33 drapery
披衣，衣饰

34 drawing easel
素描架

35 sketch pad
速写本

36 study in oils
油画习作

37 mosaic (tessellation)
镶嵌图

38 mosaic figure
镶嵌画中之人物像

39 tesserae
镶嵌物

40 fresco (mural)
壁画

41 sgraffito
将上层颜料若干处割去以显底色之对比法

42 plaster
石膏

43 cartoon
草图，底图

1 sculptor
雕刻家（师）
2 proportional dividers
比例划分器（比例规）
3 calliper (caliper)
测径器
4 plaster model, a plaster cast
石膏模特儿，石膏像之一种
5 block of stone (stone block)
石块
6 modeller (Am. modeler)
雕塑家，模型师
7 clay figure, a torso
塑像，躯干
8 roll of clay, a modelling (Am. modeling) substance
粘土卷，（造）塑型之材料
9 modelling (Am. modeling) stand
（造）塑型架
10 wooden modelling (Am modeling) tool
木制塑形工具（削刀）
11 wire modelling (Am. modeling) tool
金属丝塑形工具
12 beating wood
敲板（敲击用木板）
13 claw chisel (toothed chisel, tooth chisel)
爪形凿子（刀），齿形凿子（刀）
14 flat chisel
平口凿刀
15 point (punch)
尖凿刀

16 iron-headed hammer
铁锤
17 gouge (hollow chisel)
圆口凿刀（凹形凿刀）
18 spoon chisel
匙形凿刀
19 wood chisel, a bevelled-edge chisel
木凿刀，一种斜刃凿刀
20 V-shaped gouge
V形，圆凿刀
21 mallet
木槌
22 framework
骨架
23 baseboard
基座
24 armature support (metal rod)
塑像人体支架（金属杆）
25 armature
塑像头部支架
26 wax model
蜡像模型
27 block of wood
木块
28 wood carver (wood sculptor)
木刻家
29 sack of gypsum powder (gypsum)
石膏粉袋
30 clay box
粘土箱
31 modelling (Am. modeling) clay (clay)
造型粘土

32 statue, a sculpture
塑像，雕塑品
33 low relief (bas-relief)
浅浮雕
34 modelling (Am. modeling) board
浮雕板
35 wire frame, wire netting
金属支架，金属网
36 circular medallion (tondo)
圆形浮雕
37 mask
面具
38 plaque
饰板

1-13 wood engraving
(xylography), a relief printing
method (a letterpress printing
method)
木刻（木板印刷），一种凸版印刷法
（活版印刷法）

1 end-grain block for wood
engravings, a wooden block
木刻用的木纹板

2 wooden plank for woodcutting,
a relief image carrier
木刻用之厚木板，木刻浮雕像之托板

3 positive cut
正像雕刻（凸刻）

4 plank cut
板刻

5 burin (graver)
雕刻刀

6 U-shaped gouge
U 型圆凿

7 scorper (scauper, scalper)
平刻刀

8 scoop
铲形雕刻工具

9 V-shaped gouge
V 型圆凿

10 contour knife
轮廓刀

11 brush
刷子

12 roller (brayer)
滚筒（用手复印之滚筒）

13 pad (wiper)
打印台（海绵擦）

14-24 copperplate engraving
(chalcography), an intaglio
process; *kinds:* etching,
mezzotint, aquatint, crayon
engraving
铜板雕刻（铜板雕刻术），一种（阴
刻）凹雕，种类有：蚀刻法，网线铜板
法，铜板腐蚀法，色笔雕刻法

14 hammer
锤子

15 burin
雕刻刀

16 etching needle (engraver)
蚀刻针

17 scraper and burnisher
刮刀与磨光器

18 roulette
点线机（修板用滚网线刀）

19 rocking tool (rocker)
摇动工具

20 round-headed graver, a graver
(burin)
圆头雕刻刀

21 oilstone
油石（磨石用）

22 dabber (inking ball, ink ball)
涂料棒，散墨器

23 leather roller
皮滚筒

24 sieve
筛子

25-26 lithography (stone
lithography), a planographic
printing method
石版印刷，平版印刷法之一种

25 sponge for moistening the
lithographic stone
润湿石版用的海绵

26 lithographic crayons (greasy
chalk)
石印彩笔（蜡笔）（油性彩笔）

27-64 graphic art studio, a printing office (*Am.* printery)
印刷工艺室，印刷室

27 broadside (broadsheet, single sheet)
单面印刷

28 full-colour (*Am.* full-color) print (colour print, chromolithograph)
彩色印刷

29 platen press, a hand press
压印机（平板平压式印刷机），一种手摇印刷机

30 toggle
肘杆

31 platen
压印板

32 type forme (*Am.* form)
活版

33 feed mechanism
供结装置

34 bar (devil's tail)
手柄

35 pressman
印刷工人

36 copperplate press
铜版印刷机

37 tympan
压纸格

38 pressure regulator
压力调节器

39 star wheel
星形轮

40 cylinder
滚筒

41 bed
机台

42 felt cloth
毡布

43 proof (pull)
校样，样张

44 copperplate engraver
铜版雕刻师（工人）

45 lithographer (litho artist), grinding the stone
磨石之石版印刷师

46 grinding disc (disk)
磨盘

47 grain (granular texture)
颗粒组织

48 pulverized glass
玻璃粉（末）

49 rubber solution
橡胶溶液

50 tongs
夹具

51 etching bath for etching
蚀刻槽

52 zinc plate
锌版

53 polished copperplate
磨光之铜版

54 cross hatch
十字影线（全面直雕）

55 etching ground
铜版上所涂之防蚀剂

56 non-printing area
不印刷的部份

57 lithographic stone
平板印刷用之石头（石板石）

58 register marks
对齐号

59 printing surface (printing image carrier)
印刷面，版面（印刷图案之承载面）

60 lithographic press
石版印刷机

61 lever
操纵杆

62 scraper adjustment
刮具调节器

63 scraper
刮具

64 bed
版台

1-20 scripts of various peoples
各民族之文字

1 ancient Egyptian hieroglyphics,
a pictorial system of writing
古埃及之象形文字，一种以图形表示之
书写方式

2 Arabic
阿拉伯文字

3 Armenian
亚美尼亚文

4 Georgian
乔治亚文

5 Chinese
中文

6 Japanese
日文

7 Hebrew (Hebraic)
希伯来文

8 cuneiform script
楔形文字

9 Devanagari, script employed in
Sanskrit
梵文

10 Siamese
暹逻文，泰文

11 Tamil
坦米尔文

12 Tibetan
藏文

13 Sinaitic script
西奈文字

14 Phoenician
腓尼基文

15 Greek
希腊文

16 Roman capitals
罗马大写字母

17 uncial (uncials, uncial script)
安色尔字体

18 Carolingian (Carlovingian,
Caroline) minuscule
查里曼王朝用的小写字体

19 runes
古代北欧民族所用之文字

20 Russian
俄文

21-26 ancient writing implements
古代书写工具

21 Indian steel stylus for writing on
palm leaves
印地安人於棕榈叶上书写所用的钢针

22 ancient Egyptian reed pen
古埃及人所用之芦管笔

23 writing cane
竹笔

24 brush
毛笔

25 Roman metal pen (stylus)
罗马人所用之铁笔

26 quill (quill pen)
羽毛笔

27 Korean
韩文

図書館
图书馆 }5

新しい 6

圖書館

Τῆς παρελϑ ούσης νυχτὸ
15

IMPCAESARI·
16

ΜΙΝΙΣUΕΝΙΕ
17

addiem feſtum
18

Κожух генератора и
20

책입니다 27

21

22

23

24

25

26

1-15 types (type faces)
字体（铅字字体）

1 Gothic type (German black-letter type)
哥德体字体（德文黑体字型）

2 Schwabacher type (German black-letter type)
萧瓦巴克式字体（德文黑体字型）

3 Fraktur (German black-letter type)
法拉克特式字体（德文黑体字型）

4 Humanist (Mediaeval)
文艺复兴字体（中世纪字体）

5 Transitional
（过渡时期字体）变体字体

6 Didone
古典拉丁字体

7 Sanserif (Sanserif type, Grotesque)
无细线体之铅字（等线黑体字）

8 Egyptian
埃及文字体

9 typescript (typewriting)
打字字体

10 English hand (English handwriting, English writing)
英文手写体

11 German hand (German handwriting, German writing)
德文手写体

12 Latin script
拉丁文字体

13 shorthand (shorthand writing, stenography)
速记体（速记文字）

14 phonetics (phonetic transcription)
音标

15 Braille
点字体（盲人用）

16-29 punctuation marks (stops)
标点符号

16 full stop (period, full point)
句号（点）

17 colon
冒号

18 comma
逗号（点）

19 semicolon
分号

20 question mark (interrogation point, interrogation mark)
问号

21 exclamation mark (*Am.* exclamation point)
惊欺号

22 apostrophe
省符号（撇号）

23 dash (em rule)
破折号

24 parentheses (round brackets)
括号（圆括弧）（小括号）

25 square brackets
中括号（方括弧）

26 quotation mark (double quotatin marks, paired quotation marks, inverted commas)
引号（双引号，颠倒的逗号）

27 guillemet (French quotation mark)
引号（法文引号）

28 hyphen
连字号

29 marks of omission (ellipsis)
省略号

30-35 accents and diacritical marks (diacritics)
重音符号与读音符号

30 acute accent (acute)
重音符号

31 grave accent (grave)
抑音符号

32 circumflex accent (circumflex)
抑扬音符（转折音符）

33 cedilla [under C]
变音符（C 字下头的尾形符号）

34 diaeresis (*Am.* dieresis)[over e]
分音符号

35 tilde [over n]
n 字上头的"～"符号，鼻音符号

36 section mark
章节符号

37-70 newspaper, a national daily newspaper
报纸，全国性之日报

37 newspaper page
报纸（一页的）版面

38 front page
第一版（头版）

39 newspaper heading
报纸标题

40 contents
内容

41 price
价钱

42 date of publication
发行日期

43 place of publication
发行地点

44 headline
大字标题

45 column
专栏

46 column heading
专栏标题

47 column rule
专栏嵌线

48 leading article (leader, editorial)
社论

49 reference to related article
文章所附相关参考资料

50 brief news item
新闻摘要

51 political section
政治栏

52 page heading
版画标题

53 cartoon
漫画

54 report by newspaper's own correspondent
本报记者报导

55 news agency's sign
通讯社标记

56 advertisement (*coll.* ad)
广告，启事

57 sports section
体育栏

58 press photo
新闻照片

59 caption
照片说明

60 sports report
体育报导

61 sports news item
体育新闻

62 home and overseas news section
国内外新闻栏

63 news in brief (miscellaneous news)
简讯（各种新闻消息）

64 television programmes (*Am.* programs)
电视节目栏

65 weather report
气象报告栏

66 weather chart (weather map)
气象图

67 arts section (feuilleton)
文艺栏

68 death notice
死亡通知

69 advertisements (classified advertising)
广告栏（分类广告栏）

70 job advertisement, a vacancy (a situation offered)
职业栏（招聘广告栏）

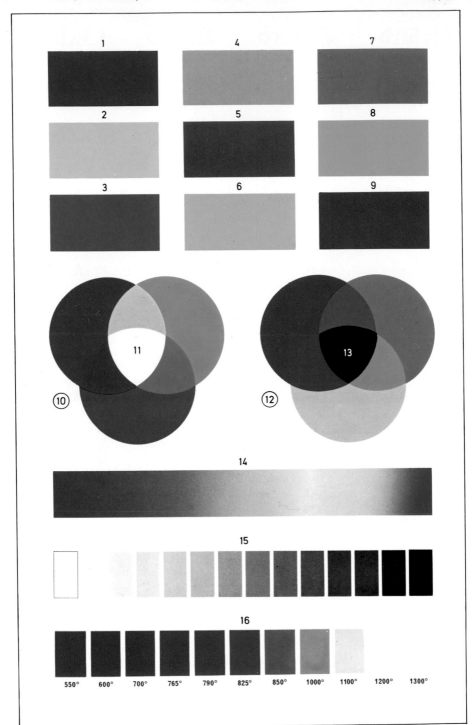

1 red
红色
2 yellow
黄色
3 blue
蓝色
4 pink
粉红色
5 brown
棕色，褐色
6 azure (sky blue)
天蓝色
7 orange
橘色，橙色
8 green
绿色
9 violet
紫色
10 additive mixture of colours (*Am.*
colors)
加色混合
11 white
白色
12 substractive mixture of colours
(*Am.* colors)
减色混合
13 black
黑色
14 solar spectrum (colours, *Am.*
colors, of the rainbow)
太阳光谱（彩虹的色彩）
15 grey (*Am.* gray) scale
灰（色标）度，灰阶
16 heat colours (*Am.* colors)
热色，高温色

1-26 arithmetic
算术
1-22 numbers
数字
1 Roman numerals
罗马数字
2 Arabic numerals
阿拉伯数字
3 abstract number, a four-figure number [8: units; 5:tens; 6: hundreds; 9: thousands]
不名数，抽象数，四位数〔8:个位；5:十位；6:佰位；9:千位〕
4 concrete number
名数
5 cardinal number (cardinal)
基数
6 ordinal number (ordinal)
序数
7 positive number [with plus sign]
（附加号之）正数
8 negative number [with minus sign]
（附减号之）负数

⑨ $a, b, c \ldots$ ⑩ $3\frac{1}{3}$ ⑪ $2, 4, 6, 8$ ⑫ $1, 3, 5, 7$

⑬ $3, 5, 7, 11$ ⑭ $3 + 2\sqrt{-1}$ ⑮ $\frac{2}{3}$ ⑯ $\frac{3}{2}$

⑰ $\dfrac{\frac{5}{6}}{\frac{3}{4}}$ ⑱ $\frac{12}{4}$ ⑲ $\frac{4}{5} + \frac{2}{7} = \frac{38}{35}$ ⑳ $0 \cdot 357$

㉑ $0 \cdot 6666 \ldots = 0 \cdot \overline{6}$ ㉒   ㉓ $3 + 2 = 5$

㉔ $3 - 2 = 1$ ㉕ $3 \cdot 2 = 6$
$3 \times 2 = 6$ ㉖ $6 \div 2 = 3$

---

9 algebraic symbols
代数符号

10 mixed number [3: whole number (integer); $\frac{1}{3}$: fraction]
带分数〔3：整数；$\frac{1}{3}$；分数〕

11 even numbers
偶数

12 odd numbers
奇数

13 prime numbers
质数

14 complex number [3: real part; $2\sqrt{-1}$: imaginary part]
复数〔3:实部，$2\sqrt{-1}$：虚部〕

5-16 vulgar fractions
普通分数

15 proper fraction [2: numerator, horizontal line; 3: denominator]
真分数〔2:分子，水平线；3：分母〕

16 improper fraction, also the reciprocal of item 15
（可约分数）假分数，也是第 15 项分数之倒数

17 compound fraction (complex fraction)
繁分数

18 improper fraction [when cancelled down produces a whole number]
可约分数（约分后等於整数）

19 fractions of different denominations [35:common denominator]
不同分母之分数（35：公分母）

20 proper decimal fraction with decimal point and decimal places [3: tenths; 5: hundredths; 7:thousandths]
（带有小数点和小数位的）真小数（3:十分位；5:百分位；7:千分位）

21 recurring decimal
循环小数

22 recurring decimal
循环小数

23-26 **fundamental arithmetical operations**
基本算数运算

23 addition (adding) [3 and 2: the terms of the sum; +: plus sign; =: equals sign; 5: the sum]
加法〔3 与 2：总和之项；+：加号〕；=：等号；5：和〕

24 subtraction (subtracting), [3. the minuend; -: minus sign; 2: the subtrahend ; 1: the remainder (difference)]
减法〔3:被减数；−：减号；2:减数；1：余（差）〕

25 multiplication (multiplying); [3:the multiplicand; × : multiplication sign; 2: the multipler; 2 and 3: factors; 6: the product]
乘法〔3:被乘数（式）×:乘号，2:乘数（式）；2与3:乘数；6：积〕

26 division (dividing); [6: the dividend; ÷ : division sign; 2: the divisor; 3: the quotient]
除法〔6：被除数；÷：除号；2：除数；3：商〕

① $3^2 = 9$ ② $\sqrt[3]{8} = 2$ ③ $\sqrt{4} = 2$

④ $3x + 2 = 12$

⑥

⑤ $4a + 6ab - 2ac = 2a(2 + 3b - c)$ $\log_{10} 3 = 0.4771$

⑦ $\dfrac{P[\pounds 1000] \times R[5\%] \times T[2\,years]}{100} = I[\pounds 100]$

1-24 arithmetic
算术
1-10 advanced arithmetical operations
高等算术运算
1 raising to a power [three squared (3^2): the power; 3: the base ; 2: the exponent (index); 9: value of the power]
乘方〔3 之平方（3^2）：乘方（幂）；3：底；2:指数；9:乘方值〕
2 evolution (extracting a root); [cube-root of 8: cube root; 8: the radical; 3: the index (degree) of the root; $\sqrt{}$: radical sign; 2: value of the root]
开方〔8 的立方根〕：立方根；8：根数；3：根指数；$\sqrt{}$ ：根号；2：根值
3 square root
平方根
4-5 algebra
代数
4 simple equation [3, 2: the coefficients; x: the unknown quantity]
简单方程式〔3, 2：系数；x：未知数〕
5 identical equation : [a, b, c: algebraic symbols]
恒等式：〔a, b, c:代数符号〕

6 logarithmic calculation (taking the logarithm, log); [log: logarithm sign; 3: number whose logarithm is required; 10: the base; 0: the characteristic; 4771: the mantissa; 0,4771: the logarithm]
对数计算；〔log:对数符号；3:真数（求对数之数）；10:底；0：（对数之）首数；4771：尾数；0.4771：对数值〕
7 simple interest formula; [P: the principal; R: rate of interest; T: time; I: Interest (profit); %: percentage sign]
简单利息公式：〔P：本金；R:利率；T：时间；I：利息；%：百分号〕

⑧
$$\frac{2 \text{ years @ £ 50}}{4 \text{ years @ £ x}}$$

⑪ $2 + 4 + 6 + 8 \ldots$

⑫ $2 + 4 + 8 + 16 + 32 \ldots$

⑬ $\dfrac{dy}{dx}$

⑨ $2 : 50 = 4 : x$

⑩ $x = £ 100$

⑭ $\displaystyle\int a x\, dx = a \int x\, dx = \frac{a x^2}{2} + C$

⑮ ∞ ⑯ $\equiv$ ⑰ $\approx$ ⑱ $\neq$ ⑲ $>$

⑳ $<$ ㉑ $\parallel$ ㉒ $\sim$ ㉓ $\angle$ ㉔ $\triangle$

8-10 rule of three (rule-of-three sum, simple proportion)
简单比例法

8 statement with the unknown quantity x
以 x 为未知量的陈述

9 equation (conditional equation)
方程式（条件方程式）

10 solution
解答

11-14 higher mathematics
高等数学

11 arithmetical series with the elements 2, 4, 6, 8
具有 2, 4, 6, 8 等元素之算术（等差）级数

12 geometrical series
几何级数（等比级数）

13-14 infinitesimal calculus
微积分（学）

13 derivative [dx, dy: the differentials; d: differential sign]
导数，微商〔dx, dy:微分；d:微分符号〕

14 integral (integration); [x: the variable; C: constant of integration; S: the integral sign; dx: the differential]
积分：〔x: 变量（数）；C:积分常数；S:积分符号；dx: 微分〕

15-24 mathematical symbols
数学符号

15 infinity
无穷（大）

16 identically equal to (the sign of identity)
恒等于（恒等符号）

17 approximately equal to
约等于，近似于

18 unequal to
不等于

19 greater than
大于

20 less than
小于

21-24 geometrical symbols
几何符号

21 parallel (sign of parallelism)
平行（平行符号）

22 similar to (sign of similarity)
相似於（相似符号）

23 angle symbol
角之符号

24 triangle symbol
三角形符号

1-58 plane geometry
(elementary geometry, Euclidian geometry)
平面几何学（初等几何学，欧几里德几何学）

1-23 point, line, angle
点，线，角
1 point [point of intersection of g_1 and g_2], the angular point of 8
点〔g_1 与 g_2 之交点〕，角 8 之顶点
2, 3 straight line g_2
直线 g_2
4 the parallel to g_2
平行于 g_2（的直线 ）
5 distance between the straight lines g_2 and g_3
直线 g_2 与 g_3 间的距离
6 perpendicular (g_4) on g_2
g_2 的垂线 (g_4)
7, 3 the arms of 8
角 8 的边
8, 13 vertically opposite angles
角 13 的对顶角
8 angle
角
9 right angle [90°]
直角〔90°〕
10, 11, 12 reflex angle
优角（大於180°，小於360°）
10 acute angle, also the alternate angle to 8
锐角，即角 8 的交错角
11 obtuse angle
钝角

12 corresponding angle to 8
角 8 的同位角
13, 9, 15 straight angle [180°]
平角〔180°〕
14 adjacent angle; *here*: supplementary angle to 13
邻角；此指：角 13 之补角
15 complementary angle to 8
角 8 之馀角
16 straight line AB
直线段 AB
17 end A
端点 A
18 end B
端点 B
19 pencil of rays
射线束
20 ray
射线
21 curved line
曲线
22 radius of curvature
曲率半径
23 centre (*Am.* center) of curvature
曲率中心
24-58 plane surfaces
平面
24 symmetrical figure
对称图形
25 axis of symmetry
对称轴
26-32 plane triangles
平面三角形

26 equilateral triangle; [A, B, C: the vertices; a, b, c: the sides; α (alpha), β (beta), γ (gamma): the interior angles; α′, β′, γ′: the exterior angles; S: the centre (*Am.* center)]
等边三角形〔A, B, C:顶点，a, b, c: 边〔α, β, γ：内角，α′, β′, γ′：外角；S：中心〕
27 isosceles triangle [a, b: the sides (legs); c: the base; h: the perpendicular, an altitude]
等腰三角形〔a, b: 边（腰股）；C:底边；h:高，顶垂线〕
28 acute-angled triangle with perpendicular bisectors of the sides
各边带中垂线的锐角三角形
29 circumcircle (circumscribed circle)
外接圆
30 obtuse-angled triangle with bisectors of the angles
带角平分线的钝三角形
31 inscribed circle
内切圆

32 right-angled triangle and the trigonometrical functions of angles; [a, b: the catheti; c: the hypotenuse; γ : the right angle;

$\dfrac{a}{c}$ = sin α (sine); $\dfrac{b}{c}$ = cos α

(cosine); $\dfrac{a}{b}$ = tan α (tangent);

$\dfrac{b}{a}$ = cot α (cotangent)]

直角三角形及角的三角形函数〔a, b:直角
边；c:（直角三角形之）斜边；γ:直角〕
$\dfrac{a}{c}$ = sin α（正弦）；$\dfrac{b}{c}$ = cos α（馀弦）；
$\dfrac{a}{b}$ = tan α（正切）；$\dfrac{b}{a}$ = cot α（馀切）〕

33-39 quadrilaterals
四边形

33-36 parallelograms
平行四边形

33 square [d: a diagonal]
正方形 [d:对角线]

34 rectangle
长方形，矩形

35 rhombus (rhomb, lozenge)
菱形

36 rhomboid
长菱形，长斜方形

37 trapezium
梯形

38 deltoid (kite)
扁方形（纸鸢形）

39 irregular quadrilateral
不规则四边形

40 polygon
多边形（多角形）

41 regular polygon
正多边形

42 circle
圆

43 centre (*Am.* center)
圆心

44 circumference (periphery)
圆周（周边）

45 diameter
直径

46 semicircle
半圆

47 radius (r)
半径 (r)

48 tangent
切线

49 point of contact (p)
切点 (p)

50 secant
割线

51 the chord AB
弦 AB

52 segment
弓形

53 arc
弧

54 sector
扇形

55 angle subtended by the arc at the centre (*Am.* center) (centre, *Am.* center, angle)
对弧圆心角

56 circumferential angle
圆周角

57 ring (annulus)
环（圆环）

58 concentric circles
同心圆

1 system of right-angled
coordinates
直角坐标系

2-3 axes of coordinates
(coordinate axes)
坐标轴

2 axis of abscissae (x-axis)
横坐标轴（x 轴）

3 axis of ordinates (y-axis)
纵坐标轴（y 轴）

4 origin of ordinates
坐标原点

5 quadrant [I-IV: 1st to 4th
quadrant]
象限〔I-IV：第一象限至第四象限〕

6 positive direction
正向

7 negative direction
负向

8 points [P_1 and P_2] in the
system of coordinates; x_1 and
y_1 [and x_2 and y_2
respectively] their
coordinates
坐标系中的点〔P_1 和 P_2〕；x_1 和 y_1〔
以及 x_2 和 y_2〕分别为其坐标

9 values of the abscissae [x_1
and x_2] (the abscissae)
横坐标值[x_1 和 x_2]（横坐标）

10 values of the ordinates [y_1
and y_2] (the ordinates)
纵坐标值[y_1 和 y_2]（纵坐标）

11-29 conic sections
圆锥曲线，二次曲线

11 curves in the system of
coordinates
坐标系中的曲线

12 plane curves [a: the gradient
(slope) of the curve; b: the
ordinates' intersection of the
curve; c: the root of the
curve]
平面曲线〔a：曲线的斜率；b：曲线与纵
轴的交点；c:曲线之根（零点））

13 inflected curves
拐曲线

14 **parabola,** a curve of the
second degree
抛物线（二次曲线之一）

15 branches of the parabola
抛物线之分支

16 vertex of the parabola
抛物线的顶点

17 axis of the parabola
抛物线的轴

18 **a curve of the third degree**
三次曲线

19 maximum of the curve
曲线的最大点（值）

20 minimum of the curve
曲线的最小点（值）

21 point of inflexion (of
inflection)
拐点，反曲点

22 **ellipse**
椭圆

23 transverse axis (major axis)
横截轴（长轴）

24 conjugate axis (minor axis)
共轭轴（短轴）

25 foci of the ellipse [F_1 and F_2]
椭圆的焦点〔F_1 and F_2〕

26 **hyperbola**
双曲线

27 foci [F_1 and F_2]
焦点〔F_1 and F_2〕

28 vertices [S_1 and S_2]
顶点〔S_1 and S_2〕

29 asymptotes [a and b]
渐近线 [a 和 b]

30-46 solids
立体图形

30 cube
立方体

31 square, a plane (plane
surface)
正方体的一个平面

32 edge
棱

33 corner
（隅角）棱角

34 quadratic prism
方形棱柱

35 base
底面

36 parallelepiped
平行六面体

37 triangular prism
三棱柱

38 cylinder, a right cylinder
圆柱，一种直圆柱

39 base, a circular plane
底面，圆形面

40 curved surface
曲面

41 sphere
球体

42 ellipsoid of revolution
廻转椭球体

43 cone
圆锥体

44 height of the cone (cone height)
圆锥的高

45 truncated cone (frustum of a
cone)
截锥（平截头圆锥体，锥台）

46 quadrilateral pyramid
四边形棱锥

1 the set A, the set {a, b, c, d,
  e, f, g}
  集合 A，集合{a, b, c, d, e, f, g}
2 elememts (members) of the set A
  集合 A 的元素（元）
3 the set B, the set {u, v, w, x, y, z}
  集合 B，集合{u, v, w, x, y, z}
4 intersection of the sets A and
  B, A ∩ B = {f, g, u}
  集合 A 和集合 B 的交集，A ∩ B = {f,
  g, u}
5-6 union of the sets A and B, A
  ∪ B = {a, b, c, d, e, f, g, u, v, w,
  x, y, z}
  集合 A 和集合 B 的联集，A ∪ B = {a,
  b, c, d, e, f, g, u, v, w, x, y, z}
7 complement of the set B, B' =
  {a, b, c, d, e}
  集合 B 的馀（补）集，B' = {a, b, c, d, e}
8 complement of the set A, A' =
  {v, w, x, y, z}
  集合 A 的馀（补）集，A' = {v, w, x, y,
  z}
9-11 mappings
  映射
9 mapping of the set M *onto* the
  set N
  由集合 M 到集合 N 上的映射
10 mapping of the set M *into* the set
  N
  由集合 M 到集合 N 内的映射
11 one-to-one mapping of the set M
  onto the set N
  由集合 M 到集合 N 上的一对一映射

1-38 laboratory apparatus
(laboratory equipment)
实验室仪器（实验室设备）
1 Scheidt globe
球形容器（施特球）
2 U-tube
U 型管
3 separating funnel
分液漏斗
4 octagonal ground-glass stopper
八角形毛玻璃栓（塞）
5 tap (*Am.* faucet)
活塞，旋塞
6 coiled condenser
盘管冷凝器
7 air lock
安全漏斗
8 wash-bottle
洗瓶
9 mortar
研体
10 pestle
研杵
11 filter funnel (Büchner funnel)
过滤漏斗（布氏漏斗）
12 filter (filter plate)
滤板
13 retort
甑（曲颈瓶）
14 water bath
水浴
15 tripod
三脚架

16 water gauge (*Am.* gage)
水位计
17 insertion rings
嵌入环
18 stirrer
搅拌器
19 manometer for measuring
positive and negative pressures
测正负压用之 U 型管
20 mirror manometer for
measuring small pressures
测微压用之反射镜压力计
21 inlet
入口（进）
22 tap (*Am.* faucet)
活塞，旋塞
23 sliding scale
滑尺
24 weighing bottle
称量瓶
25 analytical balance
分析天平
26 case
天平罩
27 sliding front panel
滑动前板
28 three-point support
三点支架
29 column (balance column)
立杜（天平立杜）
30 balance beam (beam)
天平横梁
31 rider bar
游码梁

32 rider holder
游码杆（架）
33 rider
游码
34 pointer
指针
35 scale
刻度尺
36 scale pan
秤盘
37 stop
制动器（吊耳）
38 stop knob
制动旋钮

1-63 laboratory apparatus
(laboratory equipment)
实验室仪器（实验室设备）

1 Bunsen burner
本生灯

2 gas inlet (gas inlet pipe)
瓦斯（气体）入口管

3 air regulator
空气调节器

4 Teclu burner
双层转筒燃烧器

5 pipe union
管接头

6 gas regulator
瓦斯调节器

7 stem
灯管

8 air regulator
空气调节器

9 bench torch
台式喷灯

10 casing
套管

11 oxygen inlet
氧气入口（管）

12 hydrogen inlet
氢气入口（管）

13 oxygen jet
氧气喷咀

14 tripod
三脚架

15 ring (retort ring)
铁圈（曲颈瓶环）

16 funnel
漏斗

17 pipe clay triangle
陶三角管

18 wire gauze
铁丝网

19 wire gauze with asbestos centre
(*Am.* center)
石绵芯铁丝网

20 beaker
烧杯

21 burette (for measuring the
volume of liquids)
量液体体积用的滴管（玻璃量管）

22 burette stand
滴定管架

23 burette clamp
滴定管夹

24 graduated pipette
刻度移液管，吸量管

25 pipette
移液管

26 measuring cylinder (measuring
glass)
量筒

27 measuring flask
量瓶

28 volumetric flask
容量瓶（测定体积的烧瓶）

29 evaporating dish (evaporating
basin), made of porcelain
蒸发皿（磁制品）

30 tube clamp (tube clip,
pinchcock)
螺旋夹

31 clay crucible with lid
带盖陶土坩锅

32 crucible tongs
坩锅钳

33 clamp
烧瓶夹

34 test tube
试管

35 test tube rack
试管架

36 flat-bottomed flask
平底烧瓶

37 ground glas neck
磨口瓶颈

38 long-necked round-bottomed
flask
长颈圆底烧瓶

39 Erlenmeyer flask (conical
flask)
依氏烧瓶，三角烧瓶（锥形烧瓶）

40 filter flask
吸滤瓶，抽滤瓶

41 fluted filter
波纹滤纸

42 one-way tap
单向旋塞

43 calcium chloride tube
氯化钙管（干燥管）

44 stopper with tap
制动旋塞

45 cylinder
量筒

46 distillation apparatus (distilling
apparatus)
蒸馏设备（蒸馏设备）

47 distillation flask (distilling flask)
蒸馏烧瓶

48 condenser
冷凝器

49 return tap, a two-way tap
回流旋塞，双向旋塞

50 distillation flask (distilling flask,
Claisen flask)
蒸馏烧瓶（克氏瓶）

51 desiccator
乾燥器

52 lid with fitted tube
配密接导管之盖

53 tap
旋塞

54 desiccator insert made of
porcelain
磁制乾燥器隔板

55 three-necked flask
三口烧瓶

56 connecting piece (Y-tube)
连接管（Y形管）

57 three-necked bottle
三颈瓶

58 gas-washing bottle
洗气瓶

59 gas generator (Kipp's apparatus,
Am. Kipp generator)
气体发生器（启普发生器）

60 overflow container
溢流容器

61 container for the solid
固体容器

62 acid container
酸容器

63 gas outlet
导气管

1-26 basic crystal forms and crystal combinations (structure of crystals)
晶体基本形状及晶体组合（晶体结构）

1-17 regular (cubic, tesseral, isometric) crystal system
规则晶系（立方晶系，等轴晶系）

1 tetrahedron (four-faced polyhedron) [tetrahedrite, fahlerz, fahl ore]
四面体[黝铜矿]

2 hexahedron (cube, six-faced polyhedron), a holohedron [rock salt]
六面体（立方体），全面体[岩盐]

3 centre (*Am.* center) of symmetry (crystal centre)
对称中心（晶体中心）

4 axis of symmetry (rotation axis)
对称轴（转动轴）

5 plane of symmetry
对称（平）面

6 octahedron (eight-faced polyhedron)[gold]
八面体[金矿]

7 rhombic dodecahedron [garnet]
斜方十二面体，菱形十二面体[石榴子石]

8 pentagonal dodecahedron [pyrite, iron pyrites]
五角十二面体[黄铁矿]

9 pentagon (five-sided polygon)
五边形

10 triakis-octahedron [diamond]
三八面体[金刚石]

11 icosahedron (twenty-faced polyhedron), a regular polyhedron
二十面体

12 icositetrahedron (twenty-four-faced polyhedron)[leucite]
二十四面体[白榴子石]

13 hexakis-octahedron (hexoctahedron, forty-eight-faced polyhedron) [diamond]
六八面体（四十八面体）[金刚石]

14 octahedron with cube [galena]
立方八面体[方铅矿]

15 hexagon (six-sided polygon)
六边形

16 cube with octahedron [fluorite, fluorspar]
八面立方体[氟石]

17 octagon (eight-sided polygon)
八边形

18-19 tetragonal crystal system
四方晶系

18 tetragonal dipyramid (tetragonal bipyramid)
（正）四方双锥体，（正）四方双棱锥

19 protoprism with protopyramid [zircon]
正方双锥柱体[金岩英石(风信子石)]

20-22 hexagonal crystal system
六方晶系

20 protoprism with protopyramid, deutero-pyramid and basal pinacoid [apatite]
六方双锥柱体，第二六方锥和底轴面[磷灰石]

21 hexagonal prism
六方柱体

22 hexagonal (ditrigonal) biprism with rhombohedron [calcite]
菱面六方双柱体（复三角双柱体）[方解石]

23 orthorhombic pyramid (rhombic crystal system) [sulphur, *Am.* sulfur]
斜方锥（斜方晶系）[硫黄]

24-25 monoclinic crystal system
单斜晶系

24 monoclinic prism with clinoprinacoid and hemipyramid (hemihedron) [gypsum]
带斜轴面和半棱锥面之单斜柱[石膏]

25 orthopinacoid (swallow-tail twin crystal) [gypsum]
正轴轴面（燕尾双晶体）[石膏]

26 triclinic pinacoids (triclinic crystal system) [copper sulphate, *Am.* copper sulfate]
三斜轴面（三斜晶系）[硫酸铜]

27-33 apparatus for measuring crystals (for crystallometry)
结晶测定器（用於晶粒），测量晶体的仪器

27 contact goniometer
接触测角器

28 reflecting goniometer
反射测角器

29 crystal
晶体

30 collimator
视准仪

31 observation telescope
观测望远镜

32 divided circle (graduated circle)
分度盘

33 lens for reading the angle of rotation
读旋角用之透镜

1 totem pole
图腾柱

2 totem, a carved and painted pictorial or symbolic representation
图腾，一种雕刻和绘制的图画，或象征性的图象

3 plains Indian
平原（草原）印第安人

4 mustang, a prairie horse
野马，一种草原马

5 lasso, a long throwing-rope with running noose
套索，一种带有活结的长套索抛绳

6 pipe of peace
印第安人用以表示和平和装饰的长烟管

7 wigwam (tepee, teepee)
（印第安人所居之）锥形帐篷

8 tent pole
帐篷柱

9 smoke flap
排烟口盖

10 squaw, an Indian woman
印第安女人

11 Indian chief
酋长

12 headdress, an ornamental feather headdress
头饰，一种装饰用的羽毛头饰

13 war paint
出征前在脸上所涂的花纹

14 necklace of bear claws
熊爪项练

15 scalp (cut from enemy's head), a trophy
附著头发之头皮（从敌人头上割下的），一种战利品

16 tomahawk, a battle axe (*Am.* ax)
战斧

17 leggings
绑腿，护腿

18 moccasin, a shoe of leather and bast
平底鞋，一种以皮革或韧皮制的鞋子

19 canoe of the forest Indians
森林地带印第安人所用之独木舟

20 Maya temple, a stepped pyramid
（中美）马雅人之神殿，一种阶形金字塔

21 mummy
木乃伊

22 quipa (knotted threads, knotted code of the Incas)
（古秘鲁人之）结绳文字

23 Indio (Indian of Central and South America); *here:* highland Indian
印第安人（中南美州的印第安人）；此指：高原（地）印第安人

24 poncho, a blanket with a head opening used as an armless cloak-like wrap
斗篷式披巾，南美人当作无袖斗篷外套用的中央开领口的毛毡

25 Indian of the tropical forest
热带森林区的印第安人

26 blowpipe
吹管（吹箭筒）

27 quiver
箭筒（袋）

28 dart
箭

29 dart point
箭头

30 shrunken head, a trophy
收缩的头颅，一种战利品

31 bola (bolas), a throwing and entangling device
系有（铁球）石头的绳索，一种投掷与缠牛的工具

32 leather-covered stone or metal ball
包兽皮的石头或铁球

33 pile dwelling
湖上（边）住居（房屋）

34 duk-duk dancer, a member of a duk-duk (men's secret society)
达克舞者，达克（男人秘密社团）的成员

35 outrigger canoe (canoe with outrigger)
装有舷外（浮）支架的独木舟（小船）

36 outrigger
舷外（浮）支架

37 Australian aborigine
澳洲土著（原住民）

38 loincloth of human hair
人发的腰布，缠腰带

39 boomerang, a wooden missile
回旋镖，一种木制的投掷武器

40 throwing stick (spear thrower) with spears
带矛之投掷杆（标枪）

1 Eskimo
爱斯基摩人
2 sledge dog (sled dog), a husky
拖雪橇之狗（拖小雪橇之狗），一种爱
斯基摩狗
3 dog sledge (dog sled)
狗拉的雪橇
4 igloo, a dome-shaped snow hut
爱斯基摩人所居之雪屋，一种圆顶以雪
块砌成小雪屋
5 block of snow
雪块
6 entrance tunnel
进口通道
7 blubber-oil lamp
鲸油灯
8 wooden missile
木制投掷器
9 lance
长矛
10 harpoon
（捕鲸鱼用系带绳索的）鱼叉
11 skin float
皮制浮标（浮子）
12 kayak, a light one-man canoe
爱斯基摩人用的皮舟，一种单人用的轻
便独木舟
13 skin-covered wooden or bone
frame
包兽皮的木架和骨架
14 paddle
桨
15 reindeer harness
驯鹿装具
16 reindeer
驯鹿
17 Ostyak (Ostiak)
（西伯利亚的）奥斯提亚克人
18 passenger sledge
载人雪橇
19 yurt (yurta), a dwelling tent of
the western and central Asiatic
nomads
（圆顶帐篷）蒙古包，西方和中亚游牧
民族所居住的帐篷
20 felt covering
毛毡盖
21 smoke outlet
排烟口
22 Kirghiz
吉尔吉斯人（中亚西部的住民）
23 sheepskin cap
羊皮帽
24 shaman
黄教僧人（道士）
25 decorative fringe
缘饰，穗状饰物
26 frame drum
木架（框）鼓
27 Tibetan
西藏人
28 flintlock with bayonets
带刺刀之燧发枪
29 prayer wheel
（喇嘛教之）祈祷轮，法轮
30 felt boot
毡靴
31 houseboat (sampan)
船宅（舢板）
32 junk
平底帆船
33 mat sail
蓆帆（粗布帆）
34 rickshaw (ricksha)
人力车（黄包车）

35 rickshaw coolie (cooly)
人力车夫，黄包车夫
36 Chinese lantern
中国灯笼
37 samurai
武士
38 padded armour (*Am.* armor)
带衬垫之盔甲
39 geisha
艺妓
40 kimono
和服
41 obi
（日本和服的）宽腰带
42 fan
扇子
43 coolie (cooly)
苦力，小工
44 kris (creese, crease), a Malayan
dagger
刀身成波状的短剑，马来西亚人用的短
剑
45 snake charmer
耍蛇人
46 turban
（印度男人所包的）头巾
47 flute
笛
48 dancing snake
舞蛇

1 camel caravan
骆驼商队
2 riding animal
骑乘之动物，此指骆驼
3 pack animal
载货之动物（骆驼）
4 oasis
绿州
5 grove of palm trees
棕榈树丛（林）
6 bedouin (beduin)
贝都因人（居住在阿拉伯半岛及北非之
游牧民族）
7 burnous
带有头巾的外衣
8 Masai warrior
马塞族战士（东非）
9 headdress (hairdress)
发式
10 shield
盾
11 painted ox hide
着色（彩色）的牛皮
12 long-bladed spear
长刃的矛
13 negro
黑人
14 dance drum
舞蹈用鼓
15 throwing knife
掷刀，飞刀
16 wooden mask
木制面具
17 figure of an ancestor
祖先雕像
18 slit gong
拍板（中间挖有细缝的长木块，用来敲
击传递信号用）
19 drumstick
鼓槌
20 dugout, a boat hollowed out of a
tree trunk
独木舟，由树干挖空做成的船
21 negro hut
黑人茅舍
22 negress
黑人妇女
23 lip plug (labret)
唇栓（唇饰）
24 grinding stone
磨石
25 Herero woman
赫雷娄族妇女（西南非班图族系之一
族）
26 leather cap
皮帽
27 calabash (gourd)
葫芦或葫芦所制的容器
28 beehive-shaped hut
蜂窝状的茅舍
29 bushman
南非之布希门族人
30 earplug
耳栓
31 loincloth
缠腰布
32 bow
弓
33 knobkerry (knobkerrie), a club
with round, knobbed end
圆头棒，一端为圆球状的棍棒
34 bushman woman making a fire
by twirling a stick
布希门族女人钻木取火
35 windbreak
防风林
36 Zulu in dance costume
著舞蹈服装的祖鲁人

37 dancing stick
舞棒
38 bangle
脚镯
39 ivory war horn
象牙战角
40 string of amulets and bones
一串护身符与骨头
41 pigmy
（居於非洲赤道附近的）小矮人，匹克
米族
42 magic pipe for exorcising evil
spirits
驱邪魔笛
43 fetish
物神

1 Greek woman
希腊妇女
2 peplos
披肩式外衣
3 Greek
希腊男人
4 petasus (Thessalonian hat)
低宽边帽
5 chiton, a linen gown worn as a basic garment
衬衣，当为一般衣裳穿着的亚麻长袍
6 himation, woollen (*Am.* woolen) cloak
古希腊人作长袍穿之长方布条，毛料外衣
7 Roman woman
罗马妇女
8 toupee wig (partial wig)
假发
9 stola
（古罗马妇女的）外套
10 palla, a coloured (*Am.* colored) wrap
罩袍，一种彩色披肩
11 Roman
罗马男人
12 tunica (tunic)
短袖长衣
13 toga
宽外袍
14 purple border (purple band)
紫色镶边
15 Byzantine empress
拜占庭帝国女皇

16 pearl diadem
珍珠王冠
17 jewels
珠宝
18 purple cloak
紫色斗篷
19 long tunic
长外衣
20 German princess [13th cent.]
德意志联邦公主（王妃）[13 世纪]
21 crown (diadem)
王冠
22 chinband
颔带
23 tassel
繸，缨
24 cloak cord
斗篷楞条
25 grit-up gown (grit-up surcoat, grit-up tunic)
束发长袍(束带外衣（上衣）)
26 cloak
斗篷
27 German dressed in the Spanish style [ca. 1575]
穿西班牙服饰的日尔曼人（约 1575 年）
28 wide-brimmed cap
宽边帽
29 short cloak (Spanish cloak, short cape)
短斗篷（西班牙式斗篷，短披肩）

30 padded doublet (stuffed doublet, peasecod)
衬垫（填料）紧身上衣（14-18 世纪男用上衣）（填料紧身上衣）
31 stuffed trunk-hose
填料大脚管短裤
32 lansquenet (German mercenary soldier) (ca. 1530)
德国佣兵（约 1530 年）
33 slashed doublet (paned doublet)
有叉口的紧身上衣
34 Pluderhose (loose breeches, paned trunk-hose, slops)
灯笼裤（宽松的马裤，杂色小布拼做的大管裤子）
35 woman of Basle [ca. 1525]
巴塞尔妇女（约 1525 年）
36 overgown (gown)
外长袍
37 undergown (petticoat)
衬裙
38 woman of Nuremberg [ca. 1500]
纽伦堡妇女（约 1500 年）
39 shoulder cape
披肩
40 Burgundian [15th cent.]
勃艮地人（15 世纪）
41 short doublet
短的紧身上衣
42 piked shoes (peaked shoes, copped shoes, crackowes, poulaines)
尖头鞋（14 世纪之靴或鞋）

43 pattens (clogs)
木鞋，木套鞋（木屐）

44 young nobleman [ca. 1400]
年轻的贵族（约1400年）

45 short, padded doublet (short, quilted doublet, jerkin)
填料紧身短上衣（男用无袖短皮上衣）

46 dagged sleeves (petal-scalloped sleeves)
瓣状袖

47 hose
长统袜

48 Augsburg patrician lady [ca. 1575]
（约1575年左右）奥格斯堡的贵族妇女

49 puffed sleeve
灯笼袖

50 overgown (gown, open gown, sleeveless gown)
长外衣（长外衣，无扣长外衣，无袖长外衣）

51 French lady [ca. 1600]
法国妇女（约1600年）

52 millstone ruff (cartwheel ruff, ruff)
磨盘状襞襟（车轮状襞襟，襞襟）

53 corseted waist (wasp waist)
束腰，束腹

54 gentleman [ca. 1650]
绅士（约1650年）

55 wide-brimmed felt hat (cavalier hat)
宽边毡帽（武士帽）

56 falling collar (wide-falling collar) of linen
亚麻布下翻领（落边宽领）

57 white lining
白色衬里

58 jack boots (bucket-top boots)
长统靴（翻皮长统靴）

59 lady [ca. 1650]
贵妇人（约1650年）

60 full puffed sleeves (puffed sleeves)
灯笼袖

61 gentleman [ca. 1700]
绅士（男士）（约1700年）

62 three-cornered hat
三角帽

63 dress sword
佩剑

64 lady [ca. 1700]
贵妇人（约1700年）

65 lace fontange (high headdress of lace)
（17,18世纪时）花边女帽（花边头饰）

66 lace-trimmed loose-hanging gown (loose-fitting housecoat, robe de chambre, negligée, contouche)
花边宽松长袍（家居穿著的宽松长衣，卧室内穿的宽松外袍，家常服睡袍）

67 band of embroidery
刺绣花条

68 lady [ca. 1880]
贵妇人（约1880年）

69 bustle
腰垫

70 lady [ca. 1858]
贵妇人（约1858年）

71 poke bonnet
帽子撑缘

72 crinoline
用箍扩衬著的裙子

73 gentleman of the Biedermeier period
彼德麦时期（19世纪）的德国绅士

74 high collar (choker collar)
高领

75 embroidered waistcoat (vest)
绣花面服背心（背心）

76 frock coat
（男人）大礼服

77 pigtail wig
假发辫

78 ribbon (bow)
缎带（蝴蝶结）

79 ladies in court dress [ca. 1780]
穿著朝服（宫庭服）的贵妇人（约1780年）

80 train
衣裙，拖曳的长裙

81 upswept Rococo coiffure
洛可可式向上梳的发型

82 hair decoration
发饰

83 panniered overskirt
有裙撑的外裙

1 outdoor enclosure
(enclosure)
户外围场
2 rocks
岩石
3 moat
濠沟
4 enclosing wall
围墙
5 animals on show; *here:* a pride
of lions
展示的动物，此指狮子
6 visitor to the zoo
动物园游客
7 notice
布告
8 aviary
禽舍
9 elephant enclosure
象的围场
10 animal house (e.g. carnivore
house, giraffe house, elephant
house, monkey house)
动物舍（如食肉动物舍，长颈鹿舍，象
舍，猴舍）
11 outside cage, animals' summer
quarters
户外笼，动物夏季放饲场
12 reptile enclosure
爬虫类围场
13 Nile crocodile
尼罗河鳄鱼
14 terrarium and aquarium
陆地动物饲养所和水族馆
15 glass case
玻璃柜
16 fresh-air inlet
新鲜空气入口
17 ventilator
通气口
18 underfloor heating
地下暖气设备
19 aquarium
水族馆
20 information plate
资料（说明）牌
21 flora in artificially maintained
climate
人工气候培养的植物群

1-12 unicellular (one-celled, single-celled) animals (protozoans)
单细胞动物（原生动物）

1 amoeba, a rhizopod
变形虫，根足类动物

2 cell nucleus
细胞核

3 protoplasm
原生质

4 pseudopod
伪足，虚足，假足

5 excretory vacuole (contractile vacuole, an organelle)
排泄胞（伸缩胞，一种细胞器官）

6 food vacuole
食胞

7 Actinophrys, a heliozoan
太阳虫

8 radiolarian; *here:* siliceous skeleton
放射虫类；此指，含矽质胃胳的放射虫

9 slipper animalcule, a Paramecium
草履虫

10 cilium
纤毛

11 macronucleus (meganucleus)
大核

12 micronucleus
小核

13-39 multicellular animals (metazoans)
多细胞动物（后生动物）

13 bath sponge, a porifer (sponge)
海绵，一种多孔动物(海绵动物)

14 medusa, a discomedusa (jellyfish), a coelenterate
水母，腔肠动物的一种

15 umbrella
（水母的）伞罩

16 tentacle
触手

17 red coral (precious coral), a coral animal (anthozoan, reef-building animal)
红珊瑚（珍贵珊瑚），一种珊瑚动物（花虫类动物，构成珊瑚礁的动物）

18 coral colony
珊瑚群体

19 coral polyp
珊瑚虫（水螅型）

20-26 worms (Vermes)
蠕虫，蠕虫形动物

20 leech, an annelid
水蛭，一种环节动物

21 sucker
吸盘

22 Spirographis, a bristle worm
旋（钢毛）虫，一种多毛类蠕虫

23 tube
（气）管

24 earthworm
蚯蚓

25 segment
环节

26 clitellum [accessory reproductive organ]
环带［副生殖器］

27-36 molluscs (*Am.* mollusks; *also:* testaceans and crustaceans)
软体动物（有壳类和甲壳动物）

27 edible snail, a snail
食用蜗牛，蜗牛的一种

28 creeping foot
爬行足

29 shell (snail shell)
壳（蜗牛壳）

30 stalked eye
柄眼

31 tentacle (horn, feeler)
触手（触角）

32 oyster
牡蛎

33 freshwater pearl mussel
淡水珍珠贻贝

34 mother-of-pearl (nacre)
珍珠母层

35 pearl
珍珠

36 mussel shell
贝壳

37 cuttlefish, a cephalopod
乌贼，一种头足动物

38-39 echinoderms
棘皮动物

38 starfish (sea star)
海星

39 sea urchin (sea hedgehog)
海胆（海刺蝟）

1-23 arthropods
节肢动物

1-2 crustaceans
甲壳动物

1 mitten crab, a crab
蟹的一种

2 water slater
水虱（水鼠妇）

3-23 insects
昆虫

3 dragonfly (water nymph), a homopteran (homopterous insect)
蜻蜓，同翅类动物的一种

4 water scorpion (water bug), a rhynchophore
水斧虫（水桩象），一种半翅目昆虫

5 raptorial leg
攫捕足

6 mayfly (dayfly, ephemerid)
蜉蝣

7 compound eye
复眼

8 green grasshopper (green locust, meadow grasshopper), an orthopteron (orthopterous insect)
蚱蜢（绿色蝗虫，草原蚱蜢）一种直翅目昆虫

9 larva (grub)
幼虫

10 adult insect, an imago
成虫，一种成虫

11 leaping hind leg
跳跃的后脚

12 caddis fly (spring fly, water moth), a neuropteran
飞蝼（小蛾），一种脉翅目昆虫

13 aphid (greenfly), a plant louse
蚜虫，一种树虱

14 wingless aphid
无翅蚜虫

15 winged aphid
有翅蚜虫

16-20 dipterous insects (dipterans)
双翅目昆虫

16 gnat (mosquito, midge), a culicid
蚋（蚊），蚊子的一种

17 proboscis (sucking organ)
长嘴（吮食器官）

18 bluebottle (blowfly), a fly
青蝇（绿头蝇），苍蝇的一种

19 maggot (larva)
蛆（幼虫）

20 chrysalis (pupa)
金蛹（蛹）

21-23 Hymenoptera
膜翅目

21-22 ant
蚁

21 winged female
有翅雌蚁

22 worker
工蚁

23 bumblebee (humblebee)
大黄蜂

24-39 beetles (Coleoptera)
甲虫（鞘翅目）

24 stag beetle, a lamellicorn beetle
锹螂，一种鳃角甲虫

25 mandibles
下颌

26 trophi
口器

27 antenna (feeler)
触角

28 head
头部

29-30 thorax
胸廓

29 thoracis shield (prothorax)
胸盾（前胸）

30 scutellum
小盾片，吸盘

31 tergites
背甲

32 stigma
气孔，气门

33 wing (hind wing)
翅（后翅）

34 nervure
翅脉

35 point at which the wing folds
翅摺点

36 elytron (forewing)
翅鞘（前翅）

37 ladybird (ladybug), a coccinellid
瓢虫，瓢虫科的一种

38 Ergates faber, a longicorn beetle (longicorn)
天牛，长触角的甲虫

39 dung beetle, a lamellicorn beetle
蜣螂，一种鳃角甲虫

40-47 arachnids
蜘蛛类的节肢动物

40 Euscorpius flavicandus, a scorpion
黄蝎，蝎子的一种

41 cheliped with chelicer
带螯角的螯足

42 maxillary antenna (maxillary feeler)
上颌触角

43 tail sting
尾螯针

44-46 spiders
蜘蛛

44 wood tick (dog dick), a tick
原野硬蜱，蜱的一种

45 cross spider (garden spider), an orb spinner
十字虫蜘蛛（花园蜘蛛），一种织网蜘蛛

46 spinneret
（纺织突）吐丝口

47 spider's web (web)
蛛网

48-56 Lepidoptera (butterflies and moths)
鳞翅目（蝴蝶和蛾）

48 mulberry-feeding moth (silk moth), a bombycid moth
家蚕蛾，家蚕蛾科的一种

49 eggs
卵

50 silkworm
蚕

51 cocoon
茧

52 swallowtail, a butterfly
凤蝶，蝴蝶的一种

53 antenna (feeler)
触角

54 eyespot
眼点

55 privet hawkmoth, a hawkmoth (sphinx)
水蜡树蛾（天蛾）

56 proboscis
（昆虫的）吻

1-3 flightless birds
不能飞的鸟类

1 cassowary; *sim.:* emu
食火鸡；类似：鹤鹋

2 ostrich
鸵鸟

3 clutch of ostrich eggs [12-14 eggs]
一窝鸵鸟蛋〔12-14 个〕

4 king penguin, a penguin, a flightless bird
企鹅王，企鹅的一种，不能飞的鸟类

5-10 web-footed birds
脚上有蹼的鸟类

5 white pelican, a pelican
白鹈鹕，鹈鹕的一种

6 webfoot (webbed foot)
蹼足

7 web (palmations) of webbed foot (palmate foot)
蹼足的蹼

8 lower mandible with gular pouch
具喉囊的下颌

9 northern gannet (gannet, solan goose), a gannet
北方塘鹅（塘鹅）

10 green cormorant (shag), a cormorant displaying with spread wings
绿鸬鹚（鸬鹚），一种展翅的鸬鹚

11-14 long-winged birds (seabirds)
长翅鸟（海鸟）

11 common sea swallow, a sea swallow (tern); diving for food
普通海燕，潜水觅食的普通海燕

12 fulmar
鼻暖

13 guillemot, an auk
海鸠，海雀的一种

14 black-headed gull (mire crow), a gull
黑头鸥

15-17 Anseres
雁类

15 goosander (common merganser), a sawbill
秋沙鸭（一般长咀野鸭），一种有齿突的鸟

16 mute swan, a swan
哑音天鹅，天鹅的一种

17 knob on the bill
咀上的隆突

18 common heron, a heron
一般鹭鸶

19-21 plovers
千鸟类

19 stilt (stilt bird, stilt plover)
高脚沙锥鸟

20 coot, a rail
大鹬，黑鸭

21 lapwing (green plover, peewit, pewit)
田凫

22 quail, a gallinaceous bird
鹌鹑，鹑鸡类的一种

23 turtle dove, a pigeon
斑鸠，鸽子的一种

24 swift
雨燕

25 hoopoe, a roller
戴胜鸟

26 erectile crest
勃起的肉冠

27 spotted woodpecker, a woodpecker; *related:* wryneck
斑点啄木鸟，啄木鸟的一种

28 entrance to the nest
巢的入口

29 nesting cavity
巢

30 cuckoo
杜鹃鸟

1, 3, 4, 5, 7, 9, 10 songbirds
鸣禽类

1 goldfinch, a finch
金翅，金翅属的一种鸟

2 bee eater
蜂虎

3 redstart (star finch), a thrush
红尾鸲，一种鸫类

4 bluetit, a tit (titmouse), a
resident bird (non-migratory
bird)
蓝山雀，山雀的一种，不迁徙的留鸟

5 bullfinch
红腹灰雀

6 common roller (roller)
颤声金丝雀

7 golden oriole, a migratory bird
金莺，一种迁徙鸟

8 kingfisher
翡翠鸟

9 white wagtail, a wagtail
白鹡鸰，鹡鸰鸟的一种

10 chaffinch
碛鹨（欧洲小鸣鸟）

1-20 songbirds
鸣禽类

1-3 Corvidae (corvine birds, crows)
乌鸦科（乌鸦）

1 jay (nutcracker)
樫鸟（星鸟）

2 rook, a crow
白咀鸦

3 magpie
喜鹊

4 starling (pastor, shepherd bird)
椋鸟（白头翁的一种）

5 house sparrow
麻雀

6-8 finches
雀科

6-7 buntings
颊白鸟

6 yellowhammer (yellow bunting)
黄雀

7 ortolan (ortolan bunting)
黄雀类之鸟

8 siskin (aberdevine)
金翅雀

9 great titmouse (great tit, ox eye), a titmouse (tit)
大山雀

10 golden-crested wren (goldcrest); *sim.:* firecrest, one of the Regulidae
金冠鹪鹩；类似：红胸戴菊莺

11 nuthatch
五十雀

12 wren
鹪鹩

13-17 thrushes
鸫

13 blackbird
山鸟

14 nightingale (*poet.:* philomel, philomela)
夜莺

15 robin (redbreast, robin redbreast)
知更鸟

16 song thrush (throstle, mavis)
歌鸫，画眉（善鸣的画眉鸟）

17 thrush nightingale
鸫科

18-19 larks
鹩雀，百灵鸟

18 woodlark
土百灵

19 crested lark (tufted lark)
有冠百灵鸟

20 common swallow (barn swallow, chimney swallow), a swallow
一般燕子（谷仓作巢的燕子，烟囱作巢的燕子）

1-13 diurnal birds of prey
昼行类猛禽（食肉禽）
1-4 falcons
隼科
1 merlin
穴隼〔鹰隼〕
2 peregrine falcon
游隼
3 leg feathers
腿部羽毛
4 tarsus
跗跖骨
5-9 eagles
鹰科
**5 white-tailed sea eagle (white-
tailed eagle, grey sea eagle, erne)**
白尾海鹰
6 hooked beak
钩状咀
7 claw (talon)
爪（猛禽的爪）
8 tail
尾
9 common buzzard
一般秃鹰
10-13 accipiters
鹰属
10 goshawk
苍鹰
**11 common European kite (glede,
kite)**
一般欧洲鸢
12 sparrow hawk (spar-hawk)
雀鹰

**13 marsh harrier (moor buzzard,
moor harrier, moor hawk)**
白头鹞
**14-19 owls (nocturnal birds of
prey)**
鸮鸦科（夜行性猛禽）
14 long-eared owl (horned owl)
长耳猫头鹰（枭）
15 eagle-owl (great horned owl)
鹰枭
**16 plumicorn (feathered ear, ear
tuft, ear, horn)**
耳簇（耳羽，耳簇，耳，角状羽毛）
**17 barn owl (white owl, silver owl,
yellow owl, church owl, screech
owl)**
草鸮
18 facial disc (disk)
圆形脸盘（面状羽）
19 little owl (sparrow owl)
小猫头鹰（雀枭）

1 suphur-crested cockatoo, a
parrot
有硫黄色冠的鹦鹉，鹦鹉的一种
2 blue-and-yellow macaw
蓝黄色金刚鹦鹉
3 blue bird of paradise
蓝天堂鸟
4 sappho
有羽冠的红雀鸟
5 cardinal (cardinal bird)
红鸟（红锡咀雀）
6 toucan (red-billed toucan), one
of the Piciformes
鹦鹦鸟（红咀鹦鹦），鴷形目鸟的一种
（巨咀鸟）

1-18 fishes
鱼类

1 man-eater (blue shark, requin),
a shark
食人鲨（蓝鲨，鲨鱼）

2 nose (snout)
鼻

3 gill slit (gill cleft)
鳃裂

4 mirror carp, a carp
鲤鱼，镜鲤

5 gill cover (operculum)
鳃盖

6 dorsal fin
背鳍

7 pectoral fin
胸鳍

8 pelvic fin (abdominal fin,
ventral fin)
腹鳍

9 anal fin
臀鳍

10 caudal fin (tail fin)
尾鳍

11 scale
鳞

12 catfish (sheatfish, sheathfish,
wels)
鲶鱼

13 barbel
触须

14 herring
鲱

15 brown trout, a trout
褐鳟，鳟鱼的一种

16 pike (northern pike)
梭子鱼（北方梭鱼）

17 freshwater eel (eel)
淡水鳗鱼

18 sea horse (Hippocampus,
horsefish)
海马（海马属）

19 tufted gills
鳃簇

20-26 Amphibia (amphibians)
两栖类

20-22 salamanders
蝾螈类

20 greater water newt (crested
newt), a water newt
鳃鲵，一种水蝾螈

21 dorsal crest
背冠（突）

22 fire salamander, a salamander
火蝾螈

23-26 salientians (anurans,
batrachians)
无尾两栖类

23 European toad, a toad
欧洲蟾蜍

24 tree frog (tree toad)
树蛙（树蟾蜍）

25 vocal sac (vocal pouch, croaking
sac)
声囊

26 adhesive disc (disk)
吸盘

27-41 reptiles
爬行类

27, 30-37 lizards
蜥蜴

27 sand lizard
沙蜥蜴

28 hawksbill turtle (hawksbill)
玳瑁

29 carapace (shell)
背甲

30 basilisk
一种热带美洲蜥蜴

31 desert monitor,. a monitor lizard
(monitor)
沙漠大蜥蜴

32 common iguana, an iguana
一般鬣蜥

33 chameleon, one of the
Chamaeleontidae
(Rhiptoglossa)
变色蜥蜴（变色龙），变色蜥蜴的一
种

34 prehensile foot
攀足，卷缠的足

35 prehensile tail
卷缠尾

36 wall gecko, a gecko
壁虎，守宫的一种

37 slowworm (blindworm), one of
the Anguidae
蛇蜥（盲蛇），蛇蜥科的一种

38-41 snakes
蛇类

38 ringed snake (ring snake, water
snake, grass snake), a colubrid
环纹蛇（水蛇，草蛇），无毒蛇的一种

39 collar
颈

40-41 vipers (adders)
毒蛇，蝮蛇类

40 common viper, a poisonous
(venomous) snake
一般蝮蛇，一种毒蛇

41 asp (asp viper)
（非洲）小毒蛇

1-6 butterflies
蝴蝶
1 red admiral
大西洋红蝴蝶
2 peacock butterfly
孔雀翎蝴蝶
3 orange tip (orange tip butterfly)
黄斑襟粉蝶
4 brimstone (brimstone butterfly)
鼠李粉蝶
5 Camberwell beauty (mourning cloak, mourning cloak butterfly)
黄缘酱蝴蝶，一种紫褐色大蝴蝶（属於欧洲及北美）
6 blue (lycaenid butterfly, lycaenid)
小灰蝶的统称
7-11 moths (Heterocera)
蛾（蛾亚目）
7 garden tiger
灯蛾
8 red underwing
红腹裳夜蛾
9 death's-head moth (death's-head hawkmoth), a hawkmoth (sphinx)
鬼脸天蛾，一种天蛾
10 caterpillar
蠋（一般指鳞翅目的幼虫，毛虫）
11 chrysalis (pupa)
蝶蛹

1 platypus (duck-bill, duck-mole), a monotreme (oviparous mammal)
鸭咀兽，一种单孔类卵生哺乳动物

2-3 marsupial mammals (marsupials)
有袋类哺乳动物

2 New World opossum, a didelphid
（新大陆）美洲负子袋鼠，负子袋鼠类动物

3 red kangaroo (red flyer), a kangaroo
红袋鼠，一种袋鼠类动物

4-7 insectivores (insect-eating mammals)
食虫哺乳类动物

4 mole
鼹鼠

5 hedgehog
刺猬

6 spine
刺毛

7 shrew (shrew mouse), one of the Soricidae
鼩鼱（鼩鼱鼠），鼩鼱首科的一种动物

8 nine-banded armadillo (peba)
犰狳

9 long-eared bat (flitter-mouse), a flying mammal (chiropter, chiropteran)
长耳蝙蝠，一种飞行的哺乳动物（翼手目）

10 pangolin (scaly ant-eater), a scaly mammal
鲮鲤，又名穿山甲，一种鳞甲的哺乳动物

11 two-toed sloth (unau)
二指树懒

12-19 rodents
啮齿类动物

12 guinea pig (cavy)
天竺鼠

13 porcupine
箭猪，豪猪

14 beaver
海狸

15 jerboa
跳鼠

16 hamster
大颊鼠类

17 water vole
水鼠

18 marmot
土拨鼠

19 squirrel
松鼠

20 African elephant, a proboscidean (proboscidian)
非洲象，长鼻目动物的一种

21 trunk (proboscis)
象鼻

22 tusk
象牙

23 manatee (manati, lamantin), a sirenian
海牛，一种海牛目动物

24 South African dassie (das, coney, hyrax), a procaviid
南非蹄兔，蹄兔科

25-31 ungulates
有蹄类

25-27 odd-toed ungulates
奇蹄类

25 African black rhino, a rhinoceros (nasicorn)
非洲黑犀牛，犀科的一种

26 Brazilian tapir, a tapir
巴西貘

27 zebra
斑马

28-31 even-toed ungulates
偶蹄类

28-30 ruminants
反刍动物

28 llama
骆马

29 Bactrian camel (two-humped camel)
双峰骆驼

30 guanaco
褐色骆马

31 hippopotamus
河马

1-10 ungulates, ruminants
有蹄类，反刍类

1 elk (moose)
红鹿（麋）

2 wapiti (*Am.* elk)
麋鹿

3 chamois
小羚羊

4 giraffe
长颈鹿

5 black buck, an antelope
雄鹿（一种羚羊）

6 mouflon (moufflon)
野羊

7 ibex (rock goat, bouquetin, steinbock)
原羊

8 water buffalo (Indian buffalo, water ox)
水牛（印度水牛）

9 bison
野牛

10 musk ox
麝牛

11-12 carnivores (beasts of prey)
食肉目（肉食兽）

11-13 Canidae
犬科

11 black-backed jackal (jackal)
黑背胡狼（豺类）

12 red fox
红狐

13 wolf
狼

14-17 martens
貂科

14 stone marten (beach marten)
石貂

15 sable
黑貂

16 weasel
鼬，黄鼠狼

17 sea otter, an otter
海獭

18-22 seals (pinnipeds)
海豹科（鳍脚亚目）

18 fur seal (sea bear, ursine seal)
海狗（北极熊）

19 common seal (sea calf, sea dog)
海豹（海狗）

20 walrus (morse)
海象

21 whiskers
须

22 tusk
长牙

23-29 whales
鲸类

23 bottle-nosed dolphin (bottle-nose dolphin)
槌鲸

24 common dolphin
海豚

25 sperm whale (cachalot)
抹香鲸

26 blowhole (spout hole)
鲸鱼喷水孔

27 dorsal fin
背鳍

28 flipper
鳍状肢

29 tail flukes (tail)
鲸尾裂片

1-11 carnivores (beasts of prey)
食肉目（肉食兽）

1 striped hyena, a hyena
条纹土狼，土狼的一种

2-8 felines (cats)
猫科动物

2 lion
狮子

3 mane (lion's mane)
鬃（狮子的鬃毛）

4 paw
脚爪

5 tiger
老虎

6 leopard
豹

7 cheetah (hunting leopard)
印度豹（猎豹）

8 lynx
大山猫属

9-11 bears
熊科

9 raccoon (racoon, *Am.* coon)
浣熊

10 brown bear
大黑熊（马熊）

11 polar bear (white bear)
北极熊（白熊）

12-16 primates
灵长目

12-13 monkeys
猴科动物

12 rhesus monkey (rhesus, rhesus macaque)
恒河猴

13 baboon
狒狒

14-16 anthropoids (anthropoid apes, great apes)
类人猿目（类人猿，大猿）

14 chimpanzee
黑猩猩（非洲人猿）

15 orang-utan (orang-outan)
猩猩

16 gorilla
大猩猩

1 Gigantocypris agassizi
阿氏大介虫

2 Macropharynx longicaudatus
(pelican eel)
长毛巨咽鳗（鹈鹕鳗）

3 Pentacrinus (feather star), a sea
lily, an echinoderm
五角海百合（羽星），一种海百合，棘
皮动物

4 Thaumatolampas diadema, a
cuttlefish [luminescent]
冠乌贼，一种发冷光的墨鱼

5 Atolla, a deep-sea medusa, a
coelenterate
棕色水母，一种属腔肠动物的深海水母

6 Melanocetes, a pediculate
[luminescent]
黑犀鱼属，一种发冷光的柄鳍鱼

7 Lophocalyx philippensis, a glass
sponge
菲律宾丛生海绵，玻璃海绵的一种

8 Mopsea, a sea fan [colony]
柳珊瑚，海扇群的一种

9 Hydrallmania, a hydroid polyp,
a coelenterate [colony]
螅型珊瑚虫，腔肠动物中的水螅珊瑚群

10 Malacosteus indicus, a stomiatid
[luminescent]
印度黑口鱼，发光巨口鱼，属黑口鱼的
一种

11 Brisinga endecacnemos, a sand
star (brittle star), an echinoderm
[luminescent only when
stimulated]
海盘车，棘皮动物的一种，受刺激即发
光的棘皮海星

12 Pasiphaea, a shrimp, a
crustacean
玻璃虾属，褐虾，属於甲壳动物的褐色
小虾

13 Echiostoma, a stomiatid, a fish
[luminescent]
龙口鱼，巨口亚目的发光鱼

14 Umbellula encrinus, a sea pen
(sea feather), a coelenterate
[colony, luminescent]
海伞，属腔肠动物柳珊瑚类群

15 Polycheles, a crustacean
蜘蛛蟹，一种甲壳动物

16 Lithodes, a crustacean, a crab
石蟹，一种甲壳动物

17 Archaster, a starfish (sea star),
an echinoderm
海星，一种棘皮动物

18 Oneirophanta, a sea cucumber,
an echinoderm
长须海参（海黄瓜），一种棘皮动物

19 Palaeopneustes niasicus, a sea
urchin (sea hedgehog), an
echinoderm
盘海胆（海刺蝟），一种棘皮动物

20 Chitonactis, a sea anemone
(actinia), a coelenterate
海葵，一种腔肠动物

1 tree
树
2 bole (tree trunk, trunk, stem)
树干
3 crown of tree (crown)
树冠
4 top of tree (treetop)
树顶
5 bough (limb, branch)
树枝（支干，分支）
6 twig (branch)
小枝
7 bole (tree trunk) [cross section]
树干〔横剖面〕
8 bark (rind)
树皮
9 phloem (bast sieve tissue, inner fibrous bark)
韧皮（韧皮筛管组织，内部有纤维的树皮）
10 cambium (cambium ring)
形成层（形成层圈）
11 medullary rays (vascular rays, pith rays)
髓线（维管线，射出线）
12 sapwood (sap, alburnum)
边材，白木质
13 heartwood (duramen)
心材
14 pith
木髓
15 **plant**
植物
16-18 root
根
16 primary root
主根
17 secondary root
次根
18 root hair
根毛
19-25 shoot (sprout)
芽，苗
19 leaf
叶
20 stalk
主茎，柄
21 side shoot (offshoot)
边枝（蘖枝）
22 terminal bud
顶芽
23 flower
花
24 flower bud
花蕾
25 leaf axil with axillary bud
生有腋芽的叶腋
26 **leaf**
叶
27 leaf stalk (petiole)
叶柄
28 leaf blade (blade, lamina)
叶身（叶缘）叶片
29 venation (veins, nervures, ribs)
叶脉
30 midrib (nerve)
中脉，主脉
31-38 leaf shapes
叶的形状
31 linear
线形叶
32 lanceolate
披针形叶
33 orbicular (orbiculate)
正圆形叶

34 acerose (acerous, acerate, acicular, needle-shaped)
针状形叶
35 cordate
心形叶
36 ovate
卵圆形叶
37 sagittate
箭头形叶
38 reniform
肾形叶
39-42 compound leaves
复叶
39 digitate (digitated, palmate, quinquefoliolate)
掌状叶（有五小叶的复叶）
40 pinnatifid
羽状卡裂复叶
41 abruptly pinnate
分离的羽状复叶
42 odd-pinnate
奇数羽状复叶
43-50 leaf margin shapes
叶缘形状
43 entire
全缘叶
44 serrate (serrulate, saw-toothed)
锯齿叶
45 doubly toothed
双重齿缘叶
46 crenate
圆锯齿缘叶
47 dentate
齿状叶
48 sinuate
波状叶
49 ciliate (ciliated)
有纤毛叶
50 cilium
纤毛
51 **flower**
花
52 flower stalk (flower stem, scape)
花柄（花梗，花茎）
53 receptacle (floral axis, thalamus, torus)
花托
54 ovary
子房
55 style
花柱
56 stigma
柱头
57 stamen
雄蕊
58 sepal
萼片
59 petal
花瓣
60 ovary and stamen [section]
子房和雄蕊〔剖面〕
61 ovary wall
子房壁
62 ovary cavity
子房腔
63 ovule
胚珠
64 embryo sac
胚囊
65 pollen
花粉
66 pollen tube
花粉管
67-77 inflorescences
花序

67 spike (racemose spike)
穗状花序
68 raceme (simple raceme)
总状（单总状）花序
69 panicle
圆锥花序
70 cyme
聚伞花序
71 spadix (fleshy spike)
肉穗花序
72 umbel (simple umbel)
伞形（单伞形）花序
73 capitulum
头状花序
74 composite head (discoid flower head)
复头状花序（盘状花头为花序）
75 hollow flower head
空心花头花序
76 bostryx (helicoid cyme)
螺旋聚伞花序
77 cincinnus (scorpioid cyme, curled cyme)
蝎尾状聚伞花序
78-82 roots
根
78 adventitious roots
不定根
79 tuber (tuberous root, swollen taproot)
块茎（块茎根，膨胀直根）
80 adventitious roots (aerial roots)
不定根（气生根）
81 root thorns
根剌，根塞
82 pneumatophores
呼吸根，排气组织
83-85 blade of grass
草的叶片
83 leaf sheath
叶鞘
84 ligule (ligula)
叶舌
85 leaf blade (lamina)
叶片
86 embryo (seed, germ)
胚（种子，胚芽）
87 cotyledon (seed leaf, seed lobe)
子叶
88 radicle
胚根
89 hypocotyl
胚轴
90 plumule (leaf bud)
幼芽（叶芽）
91-102 fruits
果类
91-96 dehiscent fruits
裂果
91 follicle
蓇葖果
92 legume (pod)
豆荚
93 siliqua (pod)
长角（果）
94 schizocarp
乾复裂果，离果
95 pyxidium (circumscissile seed vessel)
盖果（周裂果皮的）
96 poricidal capsule (porose capsule)
孔裂的蒴果（有孔的蒴果）
97-102 indehiscent fruits
（成熟时）不裂开的果实

97 berry
浆果

98 nut
坚果

99 drupe (stone fruit) (cherry)
核果（李属）

100 aggregate fruit (compound
fruit) (rose hip)
聚合果（复果）（蔷薇果）

101 aggregate fruit (compound
fruit) (raspberry)
聚合果（复果）（木莓）

102 pome (apple)
梨果（苹果）

1-73 deciduous trees
落叶树

1 oak (oak tree)
橡树

2 flowering branch
花枝

3 fruiting branch
果枝

4 fruit (acorn)
果实（橡实）

5 cupule (cup)
壳斗

6 female flower
雌花

7 bract
苞，苞片

8 male infloresence
雄花序

9 birch (birch tree)
桦树

10 branch with catkins, a flowering branch
带葇荑花序的枝条，花枝的一种

11 fruiting branch
果枝

12 scale (catkin scale)
鳞苞（葇荑花序鳞苞）

13 female flower
雌花

14 male flower
雄花

15 poplar
白杨

16 flowering branch
花枝

17 **flower**
花

18 fruiting branch
果枝

19 fruit
果实

20 seed
种子

21 leaf of the aspen (trembling poplar)
白杨树的叶

22 infructesence
果序列

23 leaf of the white poplar (sliver poplar, silverleaf)
银白杨树叶

24 sallow (goat willow)
阔叶柳（山羊柳）

25 branch with flower buds
带花苞（蕾）枝芽条

26 catkin with single flower
具单花的葇荑花序

27 branch with leaves
叶枝

28 fruit
果实

29 osier branch with leaves
带叶柳枝

30 alder
赤杨木

31 fruiting branch
果枝

32 branch with previous years cone
具有带前一年球果的枝条

33 beech (beech tree)
山毛榉

34 flowering branch
花枝

35 flower
花

36 fruiting branch
果枝

37 beech nut
山毛榉坚果

38 ash (ash tree)
梣树

39 flowering branch
花枝

40 flower
花

41 fruiting branch
果枝

42 mountain ash (rowan, quickbeam)
花楸

43 inflorescence
花序

44 infructescence
果序

45 fruit [longitudinal section]
果实〔纵剖面〕

46 lime (lime tree, linden, linden tree)
酸橙（酸橙树，椴椴，椴树）

47 fruiting branch
果枝

48 inflorescence
花序

49 elm (elm tree)
榆树

50 fruiting branch
果枝

51 flowering branch
花枝

52 flower
花

53 maple (maple tree)
槭树，枫树

54 flowering branch
花枝

55 flower
花

56 fruiting branch
果枝

57 maple seed with wings (winged maple seed)
有翼枫树

58 horse chestnut (horse chestnut tree, chestnut, chestnut tree, buckeye)
七叶树（栗树）

59 branch with young fruits
带幼果的枝条

60 chestnut (horse chestnut)
栗子

61 mature (ripe) fruit
成熟果子

62 flower [longitudinal section]
花〔纵剖面〕

63 hornbeam (yoke elm)
鹅耳枥属树（轭状榆树）

64 fruiting branch
果枝

65 seed
种子

66 flowering branch
花枝

67 plane (plane tree)
悬铃木属树（包括法国梧桐，美国梧桐等）

68 leaf
叶

69 infructescence and fruit
果序和果实

70 false acacia (locust tree)
假刺槐（洋槐）

71 flowering branch
花枝

72 part of the infructescence
果序部分

73 base of the leaf stalk with stipules
具有托叶的叶柄基部

1-71 coniferous trees (conifers)
针叶树

1 silver fir (European sliver fir, common silver fir)
银枞树（欧洲银枞，一般银枞）

2 fir cone, a fruit cone
枞球果，一种球果

3 cone axis
球果轴

4 female flower cone
雌花球果

5 bract scale (bract)
苞鳞（苞片）

6 male flower shoot
雄花枝

7 stamen
雄蕊

8 cone scale
果鳞

9 seed with wing (winged seed)
具翼籽（有翅种子）

10 seed [longitudinal section]
种子〔纵剖面〕

11 fir needle (needle)
籽针（针叶）

12 spruce (spruce fir)
云杉

13 spruce cone
云杉球果

14 cone scale
果鳞

15 seed
种子

16 female flower cone
雌花球果

17 male inflorescence
雄花序

18 stamen
雄蕊

19 spruce needle
云杉叶

20 pine (Scots pine)
松树（苏格兰赤松）

21 dwarf pine
矮松

22 female flower cone
雌花球果

23 short shoot with bundle of two leaves
有两叶维管束的短枝

24 male inflorescences
雄花序列

25 annual growth
一年生果枝

26 pine cone
松果

27 cone scale
果鳞

28 seed
种子

29 fruit cone of the arolla pine (Swiss stone pine)
瑞士五针松果球

30 fruit cone of the Weymouth pine (white pine)
白松果球

31 short shoot [cross section]
短枝〔横剖面〕

32 larch
落叶松

33 flowering branch
花枝

34 scale of the female flower cone
雌花球果的鳞片

35 anther
花药

36 branch with larch cones (fruit cones)
带松果的枝条

37 seed
种子

38 cone scale
果鳞

39 arbor vitae (tree of life, thuja)
侧柏（活树）金钟柏）

40 fruiting branch
果枝

41 fruit cone
果球

42 scale
鳞片

43 branch with male and female flowers
带雌花和雄花的枝条

44 male shoot
雄花枝

45 scale with pollen sacs
带粉囊的鳞片

46 female shoot
雌花枝

47 juniper (juniper tree)
杜松（杜松树）

48 female shoot [longitudinal section]
雌花枝[纵剖面]

49 male shoot
雄花枝

50 scale with pollen sacs
带粉囊的鳞片

51 fruiting branch
果枝

52 juniper berry
杜松浆果

53 fruit [cross section]
果实〔横剖面〕

54 seed
种子

55 stone pine
五针松

56 male shoot
雄花枝

57 fruit cone with seeds [longitudinal section]
带籽的果球〔纵剖面〕

58 cypress
柏树

59 fruiting branch
果枝

60 seed
种子

61 yew (yew tree)
紫杉（紫杉树）

62 male flower shoot and female flower cone
雄花枝和雌花球果

63 fruit branch
果枝

64 fruit
果实

65 ceder (cedar tree)
雪松（雪松树）

66 fruiting branch
果枝

67 fruit scale
果鳞

68 male flower shoot and female flower cone
雄花枝和雌花球果

69 mammoth tree (Wellingtonia, sequoia)
红杉（威灵顿树）

70 fruiting branch
果枝

71 seed
种子

1 forsythia
连翘
2 ovary and stamen
子房和雄蕊
3 leaf
叶
4 yellow-flowered jasmine (jasmin, jessamine)
开黄花的茉莉（素馨）
5 flower [longitudinal section] with styles, ovaries and stamens
具花柱，子房和雄蕊的花〔纵剖面〕
6 privet (common privet)
女贞，水蜡树
7 flower
花
8 infructescence
果序列
9 mock orange (sweet syringa)
山梅花
10 snowball (snowball bush, guelder rose)
雪球花
11 flower
花
12 fruits
果实
13 oleander (rosebay, rose laurel)
夹竹桃
14 flower [longitudinal section]
花〔纵剖面〕
15 red magnolia
红木兰
16 leaf
叶
17 japonica (japanese quince)
日本山茶
18 fruit
果实
19 common box (box, box tree)
锦熟黄杨（黄杨，黄杨树）
20 female flower
雌花
21 male flower
雄花
22 fruit [longitudinal section]
果实〔纵剖面〕
23 weigela (weigelia)
锦带花
24 yucca [part of the inflorescence]
丝兰花〔花序部分〕
25 leaf
叶
26 dog rose (briar rose, wild briar)
犬蔷薇（多刺蔷薇，野蔷薇）
27 fruit
果实
28 kerria
棣棠
29 fruit
果实
30 cornelian cherry
西洋山茱萸，樱（桃）树
31 flower
花
32 fruit (cornelian cherry)
果实（樱桃）
33 sweet gale (gale)
香杨梅

1 tulip tree (tulip poplar, saddle tree, whitewood)
百合木（美国鹅掌楸，白木）

2 carpels
心皮（雌蕊叶）

3 stamen
雄蕊

4 fruit
果实

5 hyssop
柳薄荷

6 flower [front view]
花〔前视图〕

7 flower
花

8 calyx with fruit
带果的花萼

9 holly
冬青属植物

10 androgynous (hermaphroditic, hermaphrodite) flower
雌雄同座花（雌雄同体花，两性花）

11 male flower
雄花

12 fruit with stones exposed
露核果

13 honeysuckle (woodbine, woodbind)
忍冬（忍冬属植物）

14 flower buds
花芽（蕾）

15 flower [cut open]
（剖开的）花

16 Virginia creeper (American ivy, woodbine)
美国地锦（美国常春藤，忍冬）

17 open flower
开放的花

18 infructescence
果序

19 fruit [longitudinal section]
果实〔纵剖面〕

20 broom
金雀花属植物

21 flower with the petals removed
除去花瓣后的花

22 immature (unripe) legume (pod)
未成熟的豆荚

23 spiraea
绣线菊属植物

24 flower [longitudinal section]
花〔纵剖面〕

25 fruit
果实

26 carpel
心皮

27 blackthorn (sloe)
黑刺李（黑刺李树）

28 leaves
（黑刺李）叶

29 fruits
果实

30 single-pistilled hawthorn (thorn, may)
单雌蕊山楂

31 fruit
果实

32 laburnum (golden chain, golden rain)
金链花

33 raceme
总状花序

34 fruits
果实

35 black elder (elder)
黑接骨木（接骨木）

36 elder flowers (cymes)
接骨木花（聚伞花序）

37 elderberries
接骨木浆果

375 Meadow Flowers and Wayside Flowers (Wild Flowers) I

1 rotundifoliate
  (rotundifolious) saxifrage
  (rotundifoliate breakstone)
  圆叶虎耳草
2 leaf
  叶
3 flower
  花
4 fruit
  果实
5 anemone (windflower)
  白头翁属（白头翁）
6 flower [longitudinal section]
  花〔纵剖面〕
7 fruit
  果实
8 buttercup (meadow buttercup,
  butterflower, goldcup, king cup,
  crowfoot)
  毛茛，金凤花（草地金凤花，毛茛）
9 basal leaf
  基生叶
10 fruit
  果实
11 lady's smock (ladysmock,
  cuckoo flower)
  布谷鸟剪秋罗（布谷鸟花）
12 basal leaf
  基生叶
13 fruit
  果实
14 harebell (hairbell, bluebell)
  吊钟柳（山小菜，蓝铃花，圆叶风铃
  草）
15 basal leaf
  基生叶
16 flower [longitudinal section]
  花〔纵剖面〕
17 fruit
  果实
18 ground ivy (ale hoof)
  连钱草
19 flower [longitudinal section]
  花〔纵剖面〕
20 flower [front view]
  花〔前视图〕
21 stonecrop
  景天
22 speedwell
  兔儿尾苗
23 flower
  花
24 fruit
  果实
25 seed
  种子
26 moneywort
  金钱草，珍珠菜
27 dehisced fruit
  裂果
28 seed
  种子
29 small scabious
  小山萝卜属植物
30 basal leaf
  基生叶
31 flower of outer series
  边花（外丛花）
32 flower of inner series
  盘花（裡丛花）
33 involucral calyx with pappus
  bristles
  带硬冠毛的总苞花萼
34 ovary with pappus
  其冠毛的子房
35 fruit
  果实
36 lesser celandine
  小白屈菜
37 fruit
  果实
38 leaf axil with bulbil
  带珠芽的叶腋
39 annual meadow grass
  一年生草地禾草
40 flower
  花
41 spikelet [side view]
  小穗状花序〔侧视图〕
42 spikelet [front view]
  小穗状花序〔前视图〕
43 caryopsis (indehiscent fruit)
  颖果（不裂果）
44 tuft of grass (clump of grass)
  一丛草
45 comfrey
  紫草科植物
46 flower [longitudinal section]
  花〔纵剖面〕
47 fruit
  果实

1 daisy (*Am.* English daisy)
雏菊

2 flower
花

3 fruit
果实

4 oxeye daisy (white oxeye daisy, marguerite)
春白菊（牛眼菊，延命菊）

5 flower
花

6 fruit
果实

7 masterwort
星芹

8 cowslip
黄花九轮草，立金花（药用樱草）

9 great mullein (Aaron's rod, shepherd's club)
大毛蕊花（麒麟草，荠菜）

10 bistort (snakeweed)
拳参

11 flower
花

12 knapweed
矢车菊

13 common mallow
一般锦葵

14 fruit
果实

15 yarrow
菊科 蓍草

16 self-heal
滁州夏枯草

17 bird's foot trefoil (bird's foot clover)
鸟足三叶草（鸟足苜蓿）

18 horsetail (equisetum) [a shoot]
木贼属的一种（木贼）[一枝]

19 flower (strobile)
花（球穗花序）

20 campion (catchfly)
剪秋罗属（捕虫草）

21 ragged robin (cuckoo flower)
仙翁花（布谷鸟剪秋罗花）

22 birth-wort
马兜铃

23 flower
花

24 crane's bill
牻牛儿苗

25 wild chicory (witloof, succory, wild endive)
野菊苣

26 common toadflax (butter-and-eggs)
柳穿鱼

27 lady's slipper (Venus's slipper, *Am.* moccasin flower)
拖鞋兰（维纳斯拖鞋兰）

28 orchis (wild orchid), an orchid
红门兰（野兰花），兰花

1 wood anemone (anemone,
   windflower)
   白头翁属（毛茛科）
2 lily of the valley
   铃兰
3 cat's foot (milkwort); *sim.:*
   sandflower (everlasting)
   猫爪（远志科植物）；类似：不凋花
4 turk's cap (turk's cap lily)
   舟形乌头（舟形乌头百合）
5 goatsbeard (goat's beard)
   假升麻
6 ramson
   熊葱
7 lungwort
   肺衣
8 corydalis
   紫堇属植物
9 orpine (livelong)
   紫景天
10 daphne
   月桂树，瑞香属植物
11 touch-me-not
   小金凤，凤仙花
12 staghorn (stag horn moss, stag's
   horn, stag's horn moss, coral
   evergreen)
   石松〔石松藓（苔）〕
13 butterwort, an insectivorous
   plant
   捕虫堇，一种食虫植物
14 sundew; *sim.:* Venus's flytrap
   茅膏菜；类似：捕蝇草
15 bearberry
   熊果
16 polypody (polypod), a fern;
   sim.: male fern, brake (bracken,
   eagle fern), royal fern (royal
   osmund, king's fern, ditch fern)
   水龙骨属植物，蕨；类似：绵马，欧洲
   蕨，王紫其
17 haircap moss (hair moss, golden
   maidenhair), a moss
   毛苔藓，苔藓的一种
18 cotton grass (cotton rush)
   画眉菅（莎草科）
19 heather (heath, ling); *sim.:* bell
   heather (cross-leaved heather)
   石南属植物；类似：钟石南（轮生叶欧
   石南）
20 rock rose (sun rose)
   岩玫瑰（半日花）
21 marsh tea
   沼生茶树
22 sweet flag (sweet calamus, sweet
   sedge)
   甜旗草（天南星科）
23 bilberry (whortleberry,
   huckleberry, blueberry); *sim.:*
   cowberry (red whortleberry),
   bog bilberry (bog whortleberry),
   crowberry (crakeberry)
   复盆子（越橘）；类似：越橘（红越
   橘），沼生复盆子（沼生越橘），岩高
   兰（红莓苔子）

1-13 alpine plants
高山植物
1 alpine rose (alpine rhododendron)
高山蔷薇花（高山杜鹃花）
2 flowering shoot
花枝
3 alpine soldanella (soldanella)
高山钟花
4 corolla opened out
展开的花冠
5 seed vessel with the style
带花柱的种囊
6 alpine wormwood
高山苦艾
7 inflorescence
花序
8 auricula
耳状根春花
9 edelweiss
火绒草
10 flower shapes
花的形状
11 fruit with pappus tuft
带冠毛簇的果实
12 part of flower head (of capitulum)
花头部分（头状花序部分）
13 stemless alpine gentian
高山无茎龙胆
14-57 aquatic plants (water plants) and marsh plants
水生植物和沼泽植物
14 white water lily
白睡莲
15 leaf
叶
16 flower
花
17 Queen Victoria water lily (Victoria regia water lily, royal water lily, Amazon water lily)
王莲属植物（大睡莲，王莲）
18 leaf
叶
19 underside of the leaf
叶的底面
20 flower
花
21 reed mace bulrush (cattail, cat's tail, cattail flag, club rush)
香蒲
22 male part of the spadix
肉穗花序的雄部分
23 male flower
雄花
24 female part
雌部
25 female flower
雌花
26 forget-me-not
忽忘草，相思草
27 flowering shoot
花枝
28 flower [section]
花[剖面图]
29 frog's bit
水鳖（马尿花）
30 watercress
水田芥
31 stalk with flowers and immature (unripe) fruits
带花和未成熟果实的花柄
32 flower
花

33 siliqua (pod) with seeds
带籽的长角（果）
34 two seeds
种子
35 duckweed (duck's meat)
浮萍（紫萍）
36 plant in flower
开花的植物
37 flower
花
38 fruit
果实
39 flowering rush
开花的灯心草
40 flower umbel
伞状花序
41 leaves
叶
42 fruit
果实
43 green alga
绿藻门
44 water plantain
泽泻属
45 leaf
叶
46 panicle
圆锥花序
47 flower
花
48 honey wrack, a brown alga
蜜海藻，一种棕色海藻
49 thallus (plant body, frond)
叶状体（植物体，叶状体）
50 holdfast
固着器
51 arrow head
慈姑属植物
52 leaf shapes
叶的形状
53 inflorescence with male flowers [above] and female flowers [below]
具雄花[上]和雌花[下]的花序
54 sea grass
浒苔属的一种植物
55 inflorescence
花序
56 Canadian waterweed (Canadian pondweed)
加拿大菲藻（加拿大角果藻）
57 flower
花

1 aconite (monkshood,
   wolfsbane, helmet flower)
   附子〔附子属植物，附子草〕

2 foxglove (Digitalis)
   毛地黄

3 meadow saffron (naked lady,
   naked boys)
   草地番红花

4 hemlock (Conium)
   毒芹（毒参）

5 black nightshade (common
   nightshade, petty morel)
   龙葵（一般龙葵，小龙葵）

6 henbane
   黑莨菪〔茄科毒草〕

7 deadly nightshade (belladonna,
   banewort, dwale), a solanaceous
   herb
   毒龙葵，一种茄科毒草

8 thorn apple (stramonium,
   stramony, *Am.* jimson weed,
   jimpson weed, Jamestown weed,
   stinkweed)
   （曼陀草，一种茄科毒草）

9 cuckoo pint (lords-and-ladies,
   wild arum, wake-robin)
   白星海芋（野海芋，延龄草）

10-13 poisonous fungi (poisonous
   mushrooms, toadstools)
   有毒真菌（毒蘑菇，毒伞菌）

10 fly agaric (fly amanita, fly
   fungus), an agaric
   蛤蟆菌，一种伞毒

11 amanita
   鬼笔鹅膏（鳞茎伞菌，有毒伞菌）

12 Satan's mushroom
   魔鬼蘑菇

13 woolly milk cap
   绵毛乳菌盖

1 camomile (chamomile, wild camomile)
春黄菊
2 arnica
山金车花
3 peppermint
胡椒薄荷
4 wormwood (absinth)
苦艾（洋艾）
5 valerian (allheal)
缬草（万灵草）
6 fennel
茴香
7 lavender
薰衣草
8 coltsfoot
款冬
9 tansy
艾菊
10 centaury
矢车菊
11 ribwort (ribwort plantain, ribgrass)
长叶车前草
12 marshmallow
药用蜀葵
13 alder buckthorn (alder dogwood)
鼠李（桤木山，茱萸）
14 castor-oil plant (Palma Christi)
蓖麻
15 opium poppy
罂粟
16 senna (cassia); *the dried leaflets:* senna leaves
山扁豆，乾小叶，番泻树叶
17 cinchona (chinchona)
金鸡纳树
18 camphor tree (champhor laurel)
樟树（樟月桂树）
19 betel palm (areca, areca palm)
槟榔树
20 betel nut (areca nut)
槟榔子

1 meadow mushroom (field mushroom)
洋蘑菇

2 mycelial threads (hyphae, mycelium) with fruiting bodies (mushrooms)
带子实体的菌丝

3 mushroom [longitudinal section]
蘑菇〔纵剖面〕

4 cap (pileus) with gills
带菌摺的菌盖

5 veil (velum)
菌幕

6 gill [section]
菌摺〔剖面〕

7 basidia [on the gill with basidiospores]
担子（在菌摺上具有担孢子）

8 germinating basidiospores (spores)
发芽的担孢子

9 truffle
块菌

10 truffle [external view]
块菌〔外观图〕

11 truffle [section]
块菌〔剖观图〕

12 interior showing asci [section]
内部显示子囊〔剖面图〕

13 two asci with the ascospores (spores)
具子囊孢子的两个子囊

14 chanterelle (chantarelle)
鸡油菌

15 Chestnut Boletus
栗色牛肝菌

16 cep (cepe, squirrel's bread, Boletus edulis)
食用牛肝菌

17 layer of tubes (hymenium)
管层（孢层）

18 stem (stipe)
茎，菌柄

19 puffball (Bovista nigrescens)
卵形马勃菌

20 devil's tobacco pouch (common puffball)
魔鬼烟袋形菌（一般马勃菌）

21 Brown Ring Boletus (Boletus luteus)
棕色环牛肝菌

22 Birch Boletus (Boletus scaber)
桦木牛肝菌（橙黄牛肝菌）

23 Russula vesca
食用伞菌

24 scaled prickle fungus
鳞状皮刺真菌

25 slender funnel fungus
细长漏斗型真菌

26 morel (Morchella esculenta)
羊肚菌（可食用的羊肚菌）

27 morel (Morchella conica)
圆锥形羊肚菌

28 honey fungus
蜜环菌

29 saffron milk cap
橘黄乳菌盖

30 parasol mushroom
高脚小伞菌

31 hedgehog fungus (yellow prickle fungus)
刺皮真菌（黄色刺皮真菌）

32 yellow coral fungus (goatsbeard, goat's beard, coral Clavaria)
黄色珊瑚真菌

33 little cluster fungus
小丛生真菌

1 coffee tree (coffee plant)
咖啡树

2 fruiting branch
果枝

3 flowering branch
花枝

4 flower
花

5 fruit with two beans
[longitudinal section]
有两颗豆的咖啡果[纵剖面]

6 coffee bean; *when processed:*
coffee
咖啡豆，加工后即成：咖啡

7 tea plant (tea tree)
茶树

8 flowering branch
花枝

9 tea leaf; *when processed:* tea
茶树叶，加工后即成：茶叶

10 fruit
茶籽

11 maté shrub (maté yerba maté,
Paraguay tea)
巴拉圭茶树

12 flowering branch with
androgynous (hermaphroditic,
hermaphrodite) flowers
具有雌雄同座花的花枝

13 male flower
雄花

14 androgynous (hermaphroditic,
hermaphrodite) flower
雌雄同座花

15 fruit
果实

16 cacao tree (cacao)
可可树

17 branch with flowers and fruits
带花和果实的可可树枝

18 flower [longitudinal section]
花[纵剖面]

19 cacao beans (cocoa beans); *when*
processed: cocoa, cocoa powder
可可豆，加工后即成：可可，可可粉

20 seed [longitudinal section]
种子[纵剖面]

21 embryo
胚

22 cinnamon tree (cinnamon)
肉桂树

23 flowering branch
花枝

24 fruit
果实

25 cinnamon bark; *when crushed:*
cinnamon
肉桂树皮，弄碎后即成：肉桂

26 clove tree
丁香树

27 flowering branch
花枝

28 flower bud; *when dried:* clove
花苞，干燥后即成：丁香

29 flower
花

30 nutmeg tree
肉荳蔻树

31 flowering branch
花枝

32 female flower [longitudinal
section]
雌花[纵剖面]

33 mature (ripe) fruit
熟果

34 nutmeg with mace, a seed with
laciniate aril
带干皮的肉荳蔻，一种具条裂假种皮的
种子

35 seed [cross section]; *when
dried:* nutmeg
种子[横剖面]，干燥后即成：荳蔻

36 pepper plant
胡椒树

37 fruiting branch
果枝

38 inflorescence
花序

39 fruit [longitudinal section]
with seed (peppercorn); *when
ground:* pepper
具有胡椒子的果实[纵剖面]，磨碎后即
成：胡椒

40 Virginia tobacco plant
维吉尼亚烟草

41 flowering shoot
花枝

42 flower
花

43 tobacco leaf; *when cured:*
tobacco
烟草叶，烤制后即成：烟叶

44 mature (ripe) fruit capsule
成熟的蒴果

45 seed
种子

46 vanilla plant
香兰

47 flowering shoot
花枝

48 vanilla pod; *when cured:* stick of
vanilla
香兰豆荚，焙制后即成：香兰棒

49 pistachio tree
阿月浑子树

50 flowering branch with female
flowers
带雌花的花枝

51 drupe (pistachio, pistachio nut)
核果（阿月浑子树核果）

52 sugar cane
甘蔗

53 plant in bloom
开花期的植物

54 panicle
圆锥花序

55 flower
花

1 rape (cole, coleseed)
油菜（油菜子）
2 basal leaf
基生菜
3 flower [longitudinal section]
花〔纵剖面〕
4 mature (ripe) siliqua (pod)
熟果荚
5 oleiferous seed
油菜籽
6 flax
亚麻
7 peduncle (pedicel, flower stalk)
花梗，花序柄（花梗，花茎）
8 seed vessel (boll)
种子囊（果荚）
9 hemp
大麻
10 fruiting female (pistillate) plant
结果的雌（雌蕊）性植物
11 female inflorescence
雌花序
12 flower
花
13 male inflorescence
雄花序
14 fruit
果实
15 seed
种子
16 cotton
棉花
17 flower
花
18 fruit
果实
19 lint [cotton wool]
皮棉[原棉]
20 silk-cotton tree (kapok tree, capoc tree, ceiba tree)
木棉树
21 fruit
果实
22 flowering branch
花枝
23 seed
种子
24 seed [longitudinal section]
种子[纵剖面]
25 jute
黄麻
26 flowering branch
花枝
27 flower
花
28 fruit
果实
29 olive tree (olive)
橄榄树
30 flowering branch
花枝
31 flower
花
32 fruit
果实
33 rubber tree (rubber plant)
橡胶树（橡胶植物）
34 fruiting branch
果枝
35 fig
无花果
36 flower
花
37 gutta-percha tree
马来树胶树

38 flowering branch
花枝
39 flower
花
40 fruit
果实
41 peanut (ground nut, monkey nut)
花生（落花生）
42 flowering shoot
花枝
43 root with fruits
带果实的根
44 nut (kernel) [longitudinal section]
坚果（果仁）[纵剖面]
45 sesame plant (simsim, benniseed)
芝麻
46 flowers and fruiting branch
花和果枝
47 flower [longitudinal section]
花[纵剖面]
48 coconut palm (coconut tree, coco palm, cocoa palm)
椰子树
49 inflorescence
花序
50 female flower
雌花
51 male flower [longitudinal section]
雄花[纵剖面]
52 fruit [longitudinal section]
果实[纵剖面]
53 coconut (cokernut)
椰子
54 oil palm
油椰（棕榈树）
55 male spadix
雄肉穗花序
56 infructescence with fruit
带果的果序
57 seed with micropyles (foramina) (foraminate seed)
带珠孔的种子（具小孔的种子）
58 sago palm
西米椰子
59 fruit
果实
60 bamboo stem (bamboo culm)
竹茎（竹竿）
61 branch with leaves
带叶的枝
62 spike
穗状花序
63 part of bamboo stem with joints
具节的一段竹茎
64 papyrus plant (paper reed, paper rush)
纸草植物（莎草科）
65 umbel
伞形花序
66 spike
穗状花序

1 date palm (date)
枣椰树

2 fruiting palm
结果的掌叶

3 palm frond
掌状叶

4 male spadix
雄肉穗花序

5 male flower
雄花

6 female spadix
雌肉穗花序

7 female flower
雌花

8 stand of fruit
果串

9 date
枣椰子

10 date kernel (seed)
枣椰子核（种子）

11 fig
无花果树

12 branch with pseudocarps
假果枝

13 fig with flowers [longitudinal section]
具花的无花果[纵剖面]

14 female flower
雌花

15 male flower
雄花

16 pomegranate
石榴树

17 flowering branch
花枝

18 flower [longitudinal section, corolla removed]
花[纵剖面，去掉花冠]

19 fruit
石榴果

20 seed [longitudinal section]
石榴籽[纵剖面]

21 seed [cross section]
种子[横剖面]

22 embryo
胚

23 lemon; sim.: tangerine (mandarin), orange, grapefruit
柠檬树；类似：柑橘树，橘子树，葡萄柚树

24 flowering branch
花枝

25 orange flower [longitudinal section]
橘花[纵剖面]

26 fruit
果实

27 orange [cross section]
橘子[横剖面]

28 banana plant (banana tree)
香蕉树

29 crown
树冠

30 herbaceous stalk with overlapping leaf sheaths
具重叠叶梢的草质柄

31 inflorescence with young fruits
具幼果的花序

32 infructescence (bunch of fruit)
果序（果枝）

33 banana
香蕉

34 banana flower
香蕉花

35 banana leaf [diagram]
香蕉叶[简图]

36 almond
杏树

37 flowering branch
花枝

38 fruiting branch
果枝

39 fruit
果实

40 drupe containing seed [almond]
含种子[杏仁]的核果

41 carob
角豆树

42 branch with female flowers
雌花枝

43 female flower
雌花

44 male flower
雄花

45 fruit
果实

46 siliqua (pod) [cross section]
长角果（荚果）[横剖面]

47 seed
种子

48 sweet chestnut (Spanish chestnut)
甜栗树（蜜栗树）

49 flowering branch
花枝

50 female inflorescence
雌花序

51 male flower
雄花序

52 cupule containing seeds (nuts, chestnuts)
含种子的壳斗

53 Brazil nut
巴西栗

54 flowering branch
花枝

55 leaf
叶

56 flower [from above]
花[俯视图]

57 flower [longitudinal section]
花[纵剖面]

58 opened capsule, containing seeds (nuts)
含种子（坚果）的开裂蒴果

59 Brazil nut [cross section]
巴西栗[横剖面]

60 nut [longitudinal section]
坚果[纵剖面]

61 pineapple plant (pineapple)
凤梨

62 pseudocarp with crown of leaves
带叶冠的假果

63 syncarp
聚合果

64 pineapple flower
凤梨花

65 flower [longitudinal section]
花[纵剖面]

Index

Ordering
In this index the entries are ordered as follows:
1. Entries consisting of single words, e.g.: 'hair'.
2. Entries consisting of noun + adjective. Within this category the adjectives are entered alphabetically, e.g. 'hair, bobbed' is followed by 'hair, closely-cropped'.
   Where adjective and noun are regarded as elements of a single lexical item, they are not inverted, e.g.: 'blue spruce', not 'spruce, blue'.
3. Entries consisting of other phrases, e.g. 'hair curler', 'ham on the bone', are alphabetized as headwords.

Where a whole phrase makes the meaning or use of a headword highly specific, the whole phrase is entered alphabetically. For example 'ham on the bone' follows 'hammock'.

References
The numbers in bold type refer to the sections in which the word may be found, and those in normal type refer to the items named in the pictures. Homonyms, and in some cases uses of the same word in different fields, are distinguished by section headings (in italics), some of which are abbreviated, to help to identify at a glance the field required. In most cases the full form referred to by the abbreviations will be obvious. Those which are not are explained in the following list:

Agr.	Agriculture/Agricultural	*Hydr. Eng.*	Hydraulic Engineering
Alp. Plants	Alpine Plants	*Impl.*	Implements
Art. Studio	Artist's Studio	*Inf. Tech.*	Information Technology
Bldg.	Building	*Intern. Combust. Eng.*	Internal Combustion Engine
Carp.	Carpenter	*Moon L.*	Moon Landing
Cement Wks.	Cement Works	*Music Not.*	Musical Notation
Cost.	Costumes	*Overh. Irrign.*	Overhead Irrigation
Cyc.	Cycle	*Platem.*	Platemaking
Decid.	Deciduous	*Plant Propagn.*	Propagation of Plants
D.I.Y.	Do-it-yourself	*Rm.*	Room
Dom. Anim.	Domestic Animals	*Sp.*	Sports
Equest.	Equestrian Sport	*Text.*	Textile[s]
Gdn.	Garden	*Veg.*	Vegetable[s]

A

Aaron's rod **376** 9
abacus **309** 77
abacus *Art* **334** 20
abattoir **94**
abdomen *Man* **16** 35-37, 36
abdomen *Bees* **77** 10-19
abdomen *Forest Pests* **82** 9
abdomen, lower ~ **16** 37
abdomen, upper ~ **16** 35
abductor hallucis **18** 49
abductor of the hallux **18** 49
aberdevine **361** 8
aborigine, Australian ~ **352** 37
abrasion platform **13** 31
abrasive wheel combination **111** 28, 35
abscissa **347** 9
abseiling **300** 28-30
abseil piton **300** 39
abseil sling **300** 28
absinth **380** 4
absorber attachment **27** 44
absorption dynamometer **143** 97-107
absorption muffler **190** 16
absorption silencer **190** 16
abutment *Bridges* **215** 27, 29, 45
abutment *Art* **336** 20
abutment pier **215** 29
acanthus **334** 25
acceleration lane **15** 16
acceleration rocket **234** 22, 48
accelerator **191** 46
accelerator lock **85** 17
accelerator pedal **191** 46, 94
accelerometer **230** 10
accent, acute ~ **342** 30

accent, circumflex ~ **342** 32
accent, grave ~ **342** 31
accent, strong ~ **321** 27
accents **342** 30-35
acceptance **250** 12, 23
access balcony **37** 72-76
access flap **6** 21, 25
accessories **115** 43-105
accessory shoe **114** 4; **115** 20
accessory shop **196** 24
access ramp **199** 15
acciaccatura **321** 15
accipiters **362** 10-13
accolade **329** 66
accommodation **146** 33
accommodation bureau **204** 28
accommodation ladder **221** 98
accomodation module **146** 33
accompaniment side **324** 43
accompaniment string **324** 25
accordion **324** 36
account, private ~ **250** 4
accounting machine **236** 26
accumulator **309** 41
accumulator *Theatre* **316** 55
accumulator railcar **211** 55
accuracy jump **288** 55
acerate **370** 34
acerose **370** 34
acerous **370** 34
acetylene connection **141** 31
acetylene control **141** 32
acetylene cylinder **141** 2, 22
achene **58** 23
achievement **254** 1-6
achievement, marital ~ **254** 10-13
achievement of arms **254** 1-6
Achilles' tendon **18** 48
acicular **370** 34

acid container **350** 62
Ackermann steering system **85** 31, 37
acolyte **331** 45
aconite **379** 1
acorn **371** 4
acorns **276** 42
acrobat **307** 47
Acropolis **334** 1-7
acroter **334** 34
acroterion **334** 34
acroterium **334** 34
acting area light **316** 16
acting area spotlight **316** 16
actinia **369** 20
Actinophrys **357** 7
action **326** 6-16
action lever **325** 32
activated blade attachment **84** 33
actor **316** 37
actress **316** 38
actuating transistor **195** 19
acuity projector **111** 47
acute **342** 30
ad **342** 56
Adam's apple **19** 13
adapter **112** 55
adapter, four-socket ~ **127** 8
adapter, four-way ~ **127** 8
adapter ring **115** 82
adapter unit **242** 34
adders **364** 40-41
adding **344** 23
adding and subtracting machine **309** 74
adding mechanism **271** 9
addition **344** 23
address **236** 42
address display **236** 41
addressing machine, transfer-type ~ **245** 7

address label **236** 4
address system, ship's ~ **224** 30
A-deck **223** 28-30
adhesion railcar **214** 1
adhesive, hot ~ **249** 61
adhesive binder *Bookbind.* **184** 1
adhesive binder *Office* **249** 61
adhesive tape dispenser **247** 27
adhesive tape dispenser, roller-type ~ **247** 28
adhesive tape holder **247** 28
adjusting cone **187** 58
adjusting equipment **148** 61-65
adjusting knob **116** 54
adjusting nut **143** 35
adjusting screw *Bldg. Site* **119** 79
adjusting screw *Mach. Parts etc.* **143** 107
adjusting screw *Inf. Tech.* **242** 78
adjusting spindle **226** 51
adjusting washer **187** 55
adjustment, circular ~ **14** 62
adjustment, coarse ~ **112** 4
adjustment, fine ~ *Optic. Instr.* **112** 5
adjustment, fine ~ *Photog.* **116** 33
adjustment, fine ~ *Joiner* **133** 36
adjustment, fine ~ *Drawing Off.* **151** 66
adjustment knob **11** 41
administration area **5** 17
administration building *Coal* **144** 18
administration building

679

camp chair, folding ~ 278 vp
camp cot 278 59
camper 278 46
camp fire 278 10
campground 278 1-59
camphor laurel 380 18
camphor tree 380 18
camping 278
camping eating utensils 278 45
camping site 278 1-59
campion 376 20
camp site 278 1-59
camp site attendant 278 2
camp table, folding ~ 278 44
camshaft 166 56; 190 11, 14
camshaft bearing 192 24
camshaft lubrication 190 13
camshaft wheel 166 55
can Butch. 96 26
can Supermkt. 99 91
can Painter 129 7
can Weaving 166 21
Canadian pondweed 378 56
Canadian waterweed 378 56
canal Map 15 57
canal Hydr. Eng. 217 15-28
canal, auditory ~ 17 34, 58
canal, stomachic-intestinal ~ 77 15-19
canal administration 217 24
canal bed 217 30
canal entrance 217 15-16
Canary Current 14 41
can buoy 224 77, 94
cancel button 326 41
cancellation button 271 4
Cancer 4 56
candelabra 45 16
candidate 263 20
candies 47 31, 32
candies Grocer 98 75-86
candle, cast ~ 260 76
candle, paschal ~ 330 44
candle, wax ~ 77 66; 260 76
candlestick 309 45
candlestick, paschal ~ 330 45
candlewick yarn 35 9
candy 98 75
cane, flowering ~ 58 14
can holder 163 36
Canidae 367 11-13
Canina 3 46
canine 19 17
Canis Major 3 14
Canis Minor 3 15
canister 84 35; 129 16
canned vegetables 98 17
cannon Horse 72 23
cannon Army 255 49, 92
cannon cracker 306 53
canoe 352 19
canoe, Alaskan ~ 283 4
canoe, Canadian ~ 283 3
canoeing 283
canoeist 283 55
canoes 283 54-66
canoe stern 285 44
canoe with outrigger 352 35
canon 13 45
canonicals Church 330 22; 332 4
canopy Infant Care etc. 28 32
canopy Dwellings 37 67
canopy Child. Rm. 47 12
canopy Kindergart. 48 26
canopy Supermkt. 99 24
canopy Aircraft 230 39
canopy Airsports 288 38
canopy Church 330 21; 331 49
canopy bearer 331 46
canopy jack 257 5
cant chisel 132 11

canteen 119 45
canter 72 42
cant hook 85 7
canting table 133 17
cantle 71 39, 46
canvas 338 21
canvas hull, rubber-covered ~ 283 58
canvas stretcher 338 20
canyon 13 45
canyon river 13 51
cap Bees 77 39
cap Drawing Off. 151 40
cap Refuse Coll. 199 8
cap Music. Instr. 326 31
cap Edib. Fungi 381 4
cap, astrakhan ~ 35 34
cap, corduroy ~ 35 25
cap, fox ~ 35 31
cap, leather ~ 35 32; 354 26
cap, linen ~ 35 8
cap, mink ~ 35 17, 20
cap, musquash ~ 35 33
cap, peaked ~ 35 17, 29; 264 8; 301 18
cap, sailor's ~ 35 28
cap, sheepskin ~ 353 23
cap, white ~ 268 32
cap, wide-brimmed ~ 355 28
capa 319 27
capacitor 211 17
cap and bells 306 39
caparison 329 74
cape 30 65; 105 34; 106 4
cape, short ~ 355 29
cape chisel 140 25
capeline 21 3
caper 98 42
capercaillie 88 72
capillary tube stand 23 42
capistrum 322 5
capital Composing Rm. 175 11
capital Art 334 20-25
capital, Arabian ~ 337 18
capital, bell-shaped ~ 333 16
capital, bud-shaped ~ 333 14
capital, Roman ~ 341 16
capital, small ~ 175 14
capitulum 61 14; 370 73; 378 12
capoc tree 383 20
cap of typing element 249 30
capon 73 21
capper 76 46
capping Bees 77 39
capping Coal 144 48
Capricorn 3 36; 4 62
capriole 71 5
caprolactam 170 28
caprolactam oil 170 25
caps, ladies' ~ 35 1-21
caps, men's ~ 35 22-40
capstan Cine Film 117 34
capstan Hydr. Eng. 217 22
capstan Audiovis. 243 23
capstan Warships 258 23
capstan idler 117 35
capsule 384 22
capsule, poricidal ~ 370 96
capsule, porose ~ 370 96
captain 224 38
caption 185 67; 342 59
car Car 191 1-56
car Garage 195 34
car Railw. 213 18
car, four-axled ~ 208 3
car, large-capacity ~ 213 28
car, open ~ 207 59
car accessory 196 28
carapace 364 29
caravan 278 52; 307 34
caravan, collapsible ~ 278 3

caravan, showman's ~ 206 20
caravan awning 278 57
caravanning 278
caravel 218 27-43; 220 37
caraway roll 97 31
caraway stick 97 31
carbide, cemented ~ 149 46
carbine 86 30
carbolic acid 170 14
carbon, active ~ 270 58
carbon, negative ~ 312 41
carbon, positive ~ 312 40
carbon atom 242 63
carbon crater 312 44
carbon disulfide 169 8
carbon disulphide 169 8
carbon disulphide injector 83 33
carbon rod, negative ~ 312 41
carbon rod, positive ~ 312 40
carbon rod holder 312 43
carbon tissue 182 1, 10
carbon tissue, printed ~ 182 8
carbon tissue transfer machine 182 6
carburetor see carburettor
carburettor 189 4; 192 1-15
carburettor, cross-draught ~ 190 79
car carrier, double-deck ~ 213 35
car carrier, two-tier ~ 213 35
carcase 118 1-49
carcass 118 1-49
carcassing 118 1-49
car coat 33 63
card Cotton Spin. 163 34, 51
card Games 276 37
card, patient's ~ 25 5
card, used ~ 195 14
cardan coupling 67 6
cardan joint 67 6, 28
cardan mount 6 36
cardan shaft 64 40, 48; 67 16; 211 51; 212 29, 83
cardan shaft connection 64 63
cardan transmission 189 47
cardboard 260 50-52
card can 163 35
card catalogue 262 22
card catalogue drawer 262 23
card deck 221 79
cardiac rhythm 25 1
cardiac sulcus, longitudinal ~ 20 25
cardigan 31 50; 33 30
cardinal Maths. 344 5
cardinal Birds 363 5
cardinal bird 363 5
card index 245 23
card index box 46 10; 248 27
carding can 163 35
carding engine 163 34, 51
carding machine 163 34
car door 191 4
card sliver 163 38
card stacker 244 13
car ferry 216 10
cargo 223 77
cargo and passenger liner 221 96
cargo and passenger ship 223 1-71
cargo barge 216 25
cargo boom 221 26, 59; 223 36
cargo gear 221 24-29, 59
cargo handling, horizontal ~ 226 7
cargo-handling berth 226 1
cargo-handling gear 221 24-29, 59
cargo hatchway 221 11, 63; 226 14

cargo hold 231 21
cargo ship 221 23
cargo warehouse 233 10
'car hire' 233 33
carload 206 52
car location number 195 48
car models 193 1-36
carnation 60 6
carnival 306
carnival float 306 57
carnival procession 306 57-70
carnival truck 306 57
carnivore house 356 10
carnivores 367 11-22; 368 1-11
carob 384 41
carom billiards 277 7
carousel 308 2
carp 89 26; 364 4
carpel 58 36, 59; 59 13; 374 2, 26
carpenter 120 12
carpenter's tools 120 60-82
carpenter's yard 120 1-59
carpet 44 16
carpet, fitted ~ 41 18; 43 23
carpet, oriental ~ 46 36
carpet, velour ~ 267 35
carpet beater head 50 79
carpet beater nozzle 50 71
carpet brush 50 45
carpet cleaning 50 53-86
carpeting 191 43
carpet sweeper 50 57
carpet sweeper and shampooer, combined ~ 50 76
carp hook 89 86
carp pond 89 6
carpus Man 17 15; 19 76
carpus Horse 72 22
car radio 191 90
carriage Hosp. 26 36
carriage Sawmill 157 12, 52
carriage Knitting 167 39
carriage Tram 197 5, 6, 7
carriage, auxiliary ~ 157 11
carriage, one-horse ~ 186 18, 29
carriage, open ~ 207 61; 208 9
carriage, three-horse ~ 186 45
carriage, two-horse ~ 186 36
carriage apron 149 16
carriage handle 167 41
carriage heating pressure gauge 210 44
carriage horse 186 28
carriage motor 157 15
carriage rail 167 45
carriages 186 1-54, 1-3,26-39,45,51-54
carriages, horse-drawn ~ 186
carriage sprayer 83 38
carriage step 186 13
carrier Bicycle 187 44
carrier Docks 226 4
carrier return lever 249 21
carrion flower 53 15
carrot 57 17
carrot, stump-rooted ~ 57 18
carrycot 28 48
carry-home pack 93 28
carrying axle 210 35
carrying bar 148 16
carrying bogie 197 10
carrying cart 56 26
carrying grip 21 22
carrying handle 241 2
carrying rope 215 16
carrying saddle 73 4
carrying strap 115 9
carrying wheel 214 7
cart 86 39

gaillardia **60** 19
gait **289** 7
gaiter, leather ~ **191** 92
gaits of the horse **72** 39-44
Galaxy **3** 35
gale **373** 33
galena **351** 14
galingale **53** 17
gall *Gdn. Pests* **80** 33
gall *Forest Pests* **82** 34
gallant soldier **61** 31
gall bladder **20** 11, 36
galleries under bark **82** 23-24
gallery *Forest Pests* **82** 24
gallery *Coal* **144** 29
gallery *Theatre* **315** 16
gallery *Church* **330** 25
gallery, drilled ~ **192** 21
gallery grave **328** 16
galley *Composing Rm.* **174** 12, 44
galley *Ship* **218** 44-50; **223** 42
galley *Aircraft* **231** 20
galley loader **233** 22
galley slave **218** 48
gall gnat **80** 40
gall midge **80** 40
gallop, full ~ **72** 43-44, 43, 44
gallows **221** 87
gall wasp **82** 33
galvanometer **11** 44
gamba **322** 23
gambling casino **275** 1
gambling game **275** 1-33
gambling table **275** 8
gambrel **94** 21
gambrel roof **121** 18
gambrel stick **94** 21
game **86** 28; **88**
game, furred ~ **86** 35
game, positional ~ **276** 1-16
game, winged ~ **86** 41
game of chance **275** 1-33
game path **86** 16
game preserve **86** 1-8
gaming room **275** 1
gaming table **275** 8
gamma radiation **1** 33, 40
gammon steak **95** 54
gander **73** 34
gang mill **157** 2
gang stitcher **184** 15
gangway **38** 3
gangway, central ~ *Railw.* **208** 23
gangway, central ~ *Ship* **218** 46
gannet **359** 9
gantry *Photomech. Reprod.* **177** 13
gantry *Shipbuild.* **222** 26
gantry *Docks* **225** 40
gantry crane **157** 27; **206** 55; **222** 20, 25
gantry support **214** 24
garage *Dwellings* **37** 32, 79
garage *Garage* **195**
garage, agent's ~ **195** 1-55
garage, distributor's ~ **195** 1-55
garage driveway **37** 52
garbage **199** 17
garbage can **199** 3
garbage can dumping device **199** 2
garbage container **199** 4
garbage disposition **199**
garbage incineration unit **199** 28
garbage truck **199** 1
garden **37** 57
garden, Baroque ~ **272**
garden, formal ~ **272** 1-

garden, front ~ **37** 58
garden chair **37** 49
gardener **55** 20
garden fence **52** 10
garden flowers **60**
garden gate **272** 31
garden hedge **51** 9
garden hoe **66** 1
garden hose **37** 42; **56** 27
garden house **52** 14
garden ladder **52** 8
garden light **37** 38
garden mould **55** 15
garden pansy **60** 2
garden parasol **37** 48
garden path **51** 14; **52** 23
garden pests **80**
garden pond **51** 16
garden rake **51** 4
garden rose **60** 15
garden seat **272** 42
garden shed **52** 3
garden shovel **55** 14
garden sieve **55** 13
garden spider **358** 45
garden strawberry **58** 16
garden table **37** 50
garden tiger **365** 7
garden tools **56**
garden wall **37** 37
gargoyle **335** 30
garland **306** 17; **335** 54
garnet **351** 7
Garratt locomotive **210** 64
garter **318** 28
gas, liquid ~ **145** 53
gas, natural ~ **12** 30
gas appliances **126** 12-25
gas bottle **278** 53
gas cap **12** 30
gas circulation unit **83** 16
gas-collecting main **156** 17
gas compressor **156** 26
gas connection **141** 31
gas control **141** 32
gas cooler *Offshore Drill.* **146** 27
gas cooler *Coking* **156** 19
gas cooling **156** 29
gas cutting installation **148** 67
gas cylinder **138** 35
gas cylinder manifold **141** 1
gas drying **156** 30
gas extractor **156** 21
gas fitter **126** 1
gas fitter's tools **126** 58-86
gas flue **152** 12
gas generator **350** 59
gas holder **156** 25
gas hose **141** 9
gas inlet **350** 2
gas inlet pipe **350** 2
gaskin **72** 36
gas lighter **107** 30
gas main **198** 21
gas main, high-pressure ~ **156** 45
gas main, low-pressure ~ **156** 44
gas meter *Plumb. etc.* **126** 5
gas meter *Coking* **156** 31
gas oil component **145** 42
gasoline can **196** 25
gasoline canister **84** 36
gasoline inlet **192** 13
gasoline pump **196** 1
gasoline pump, self-service ~ **196** 8
gasoline pump hose **196** 2
gasoline station **196** 1-29
gasoline tank **188** 10, 28; **189** 2; **305** 87
gasometer **144** 12

gas outlet *Oil, Petr.* **145** 29
gas outlet *Chem.* **350** 63
gas pipe *Pest Contr.* **83** 14
gas pipe *Forging* **139** 54
gas pipe *Metalwkr.* **140** 12
gas pipe *Oil, Petr.* **145** 29
gas pipe *Iron & Steel* **147** 18, 27
gas pliers *Plumb. etc.* **126** 58
gas pliers *Metalwkr.* **140** 68
gas pressure vessel **234** 32
gas regenerator chamber **147** 28
gas regulator **255** 34; **350** 6
gas-separating plant **145** 69
gas separator **145** 28
gas station **196** 1-29
gas supply **27** 41
gas tap **261** 24
gastrocnemius **18** 62
gas tube **83** 35
gas turbine **209** 9
gas turbine, auxiliary ~ **231** 33
gas turbine, twin-shaft ~ **209** 23
gas turbine controller **209** 16
gas turbine driving unit **209** 8
gas turbine fuel tank **209** 17
gas turbine trainset **209** 1
gas-washing bottle **350** 58
gas water **156** 39
gas welder **141**
gas welding torch **130** 14
gate **202** 40; **289** 8; **337** 24
gate, removable ~ **118** 46
gate, sliding ~ **217** 18, 55
gate, vertical ~ **217** 31, 38
gate, wrought iron ~ **272** 31
gate and rails **289** 8
gateau **99** 15; **265** 4
gateaux **97** 22-24
gatehouse **329** 22
gateman **202** 42
gate pole **301** 30
gateway **336** 15; **337** 11
gateway, monumental ~ **333** 9
gatherer and wire stitcher **184** 15
gathering and wire-stitching machine **184** 15
gathering machine **249** 59
gathering station **249** 60
gaucho **306** 31
gauge **76** 6
gauntlet **329** 50
gauze **183** 33; **185** 20
gauze, sterile ~ **22** 58
gauze, wire ~ **350** 18, 19
gauze roll holder **185** 19
G-clef **320** 8
gear *Gdn. Tools* **56** 20
gear *Iron Foundry etc.* **148** 63
gear *Road Constr.* **201** 11
gear *Hydr. Eng.* **217** 48
gear, epicyclic ~ **143** 94
gear, planetary ~ **143** 94
gearbox *Agr. Mach.* **65** 79
gearbox *Turner* **135** 4
gearbox *Cotton Spin.* **164** 2, 33, 39
gearbox, five-speed ~ **189** 6
gear-change *Agr. Mach.* **65** 35
gear-change *Motorcycles etc.* **188** 31
gear-change, floor-type ~ **191** 91
gear-change, two-speed ~ **188** 12
gear-change lever **189** 28
gear-change pattern **192** 47
gear control **149** 2
gearing *Agr. Mach.* **64** 50, 65

gearing *Overh. Irrign.* **67** 21
gearing *Road Constr.* **201** 11
gearing, helical ~ **143** 89
gearing, multi-speed ~ **190** 72
gearing, multi-step ~ **190** 72
gear lever **191** 91; **192** 46
gear meter **76** 4
gears *Agr. Mach.* **64** 50, 65
gears *Overh. Irrign.* **67** 21
gear shaft **232** 58
gear shaft, intermediate ~ **190** 57
gearshift **65** 23, 35; **188** 31
gearshift, two-speed ~ **188** 12
gearshift lever *Motorcycle* **189** 28
gearshift lever *Car* **191** 91; **192** 46
gearshift pattern **192** 47
gearshift rod **192** 41
gearshift switch **134** 46
gear wheel, helical ~ **192** 34, 36, 39, 43
gear wheel, herringbone ~ **143** 87
gear wheel, stepped ~ **143** 82
gear wheels **143** 82-96
gecko **364** 36
Geiger counter **2** 19
Geiger-Müller counter **2** 19
geisha **353** 39
gelatine **316** 49
gelding **73** 2
Gemini **3** 28; **4** 55
general cargo ship **225** 14; **226** 13
general cargo transit shed **225** 9
general practice **22** 1-74
general practitioner **23** 2
general service lamp **127** 56
generator *Nucl. Energy* **154** 15, 47, 53
generator *Energy Sources* **155** 46
generator *Intern. Combust. Eng.* **190** 76
generator *Railw.* **211** 46
generator *Ship* **223** 74
generator exhaust **146** 2
generator unit **231** 33
Geneva movement **312** 38
Genoa jib **284** 16
genouillère **329** 53
gentleman *Café* **265** 22
gentleman *Hist. Cost.* **355** 54, 61, 73
'gentlemen' **233** 47
'gentlemen's toilet' **233** 47
geodesy **14** 46-62
geography, physical ~ **11**; **12**; **13**
geology **12** 1-33
geometrical shape **260** 79
geometrid **80** 16; **82** 28
geometry **346**; **347**
geometry, elementary ~ **346** 1-58
geometry, Euclidian ~ **346** 1-58
geranium **53** 1
gerbera **51** 26
germ **370** 86
German brown trout **364** 15
German hand **342** 11
German pointer **70** 40
German sheepdog **70** 25
German shepherd **70** 25
geyser *Phys. Geog.* **11** 21
geyser *Plumb. etc.* **126** 12-13
G flat major **320** 68
gherkin, pickled ~ **98** 29
ghost train **308** 5

Z

索　引
汉语索引检字说明

1. 本索引是根据最通用的字典部首目录编排而成。

2. 检索方法：

    (1)《部首目录》共有 174 个基本部首。部首次序是按部首笔画数目排列。检索时，根据汉语词条第一个字的部首，从《部首目录》内查出该字部首的页码，然后查《检字表》。

    (2)《检字表》内，同一部首的字按笔画画数排列（部首画数不计算在内）。《中文索引》词条再按第二字或第三字分类即可找到。

3. 汉语词条后的第一个黑体数字，表示正文中的图号，紧跟的幼体阿拉伯数字，表示该图内英文词条的排序号。只需从汉语词条后的数字，便可找到相应的图和英文词条。

4. 汉语词条之前若由英文字母或阿拉伯数字起头，则均按英文字母顺序或阿拉伯数字大小排列，列入其他项内。

(一) 部首目录

一画

部首	号
一	1
丨	2
丶	3
丿	4
乙(一丁乚)	5

二画

部首	号
二	6
亠	7
冫	8
讠(言)	9
冖	10
十	11
厂	12
匚	13
匸	14
卜(卜)	15
刂	16
冂	17
八(丷)	18
人(入)	19
亻	20
勹	21
几	22
儿	23
厶	24
又	25

部首	号
廴	26
卩(㔾)	27
阝(在左)	28
阝(在右)	29
凵	30
刀(勹)	31
力	32

三画

部首	号
氵	33
忄	34
宀	35
广	36
门	37
辶	38
寸	39
扌	40
工	41
土	42
士	43
艹	44
大	45
弋	46
小(⺌)	47
口	48
囗	49
巾	50

部首	号
山	51
彳	52
彡	53
夕	54
夂	55
犭	56
饣(食)	57
彐(彐)	58
尸	59
己(巳)	60
弓	61
子(孑)	62
女	63
幺	64
纟(糸)	65
马	66
巛	67

四画

部首	号
灬	68
斗	69
文	70
方	71
火	72
心	73
户	74
礻	75

部首	号
王	76
韦	77
木	78
犬	79
歹	80
车	81
戈	82
比	83
瓦	84
止	85
支	86
日	87
曰	88
水	89
贝	90
见	91
父	92
牛(牜)	93
手	94
毛	95
气	96
攵	97
片	98
斤	99
爪(爫)	100
月	101
欠	102

部首	号
风	103
殳	104
爿	105
母	106

五画

部首	号
穴	107
立	108
疒	109
衤	110
示	111
石	112
龙	113
业	114
目	115
田	116
罒	117
皿	118
钅(金)	119
矢	120
禾	121
白	122
瓜	123
鸟	124
用	125
正	126
皮	127

一 丨 丿 乙 亠 冫 冖

(二) 检 字 表

（三）中文索引

I 部

工部

土部